Indian Ground Hill
Hampton Falls
Great Boars Head
Hampton Falls River
New Zealand Hill
Station
Titcomb Hill
Seabrook
Hampton Hbr.
NEW HAMPSHIRE
MASSACHUSETTS
Beach Hill
South Seabrook
Powwow Hill
Monday Hill
Amesbury
Whittier Hill
Salisbury Pt.
East Salisbury
BOSTON & MAINE R.R.
Newburyport Hbr.
Newburyport
Pipestave Hill
Artichoke R.
Turkey Hill
BOSTON AND MAINE RAILROAD
Indian Hill
Plum Island
Parker River
Byfield

# JOHN
# GREENLEAF
# WHITTIER

*friend of man*

# JOHN GREENLEAF WHITTIER

*friend of man*

1 9  4 9

BY JOHN A. POLLARD

HOUGHTON MIFFLIN COMPANY · BOSTON

The Riverside Press Cambridge

The Riverside Press
Cambridge · Massachusetts

Printed in the U.S.A.

THIS BOOK IS FOR

*Phyllis*

WHO HELPED GREATLY TO GET IT DONE

STRICTLY SPEAKING, WHITTIER DID NOT CARE MUCH FOR LITERATURE. HE LOVED MEN AND THINGS AND BOOKS OF BIOGRAPHY AND TRAVEL; HE LIKED TO KNOW HOW THE WORLD LOOKED AND WHAT BRAVE SPIRITS HAD WROUGHT IN IT.

Nathaniel Hawthorne, *The American Notebooks*

# Acknowledgments

WARM ACKNOWLEDGMENT is made of particular help or encouragement given, at one stage or another in the preparation of this book, by the following individuals:

Donald K. Campbell.

The late T. Franklin Currier, and Miss Margaret Currier.

Thomas E. Drake.

Angus MacDonald Frantz, M.D. (for reading and commenting on Chapter 20).

Nina Holton.

Carolyn E. Jakeman.

The late Rufus M. Jones (for reading and commenting on Chapter 27).

Norman Holmes Pearson

Henry A. Pochmann.

Pauline F. Pulsifer.

Earle O. Whittier (for reading and commenting on Chapter 1 and Appendix A).

Stanley T. Williams.

The late Carroll A. Wilson and Mrs. Wilson.

Boundless gratitude is due to staff members of the following institutions, for able and friendly help given without stint:

Amherst College Library.

Brown University Library.

Carnegie Institution of Washington, Eugenics Record Office (Dr. Milislav Demerec).

Central Offices of the Society of Friends, London.

Commonwealth of Massachusetts — Archives Division, Department of Public Health, Department of Civil Service and Registration.

Cornell University Library.

Dartmouth College, Office of Alumni Records.

Essex County, Massachusetts, Probate and Insolvency Courts.

Lowell Historical Society.

Massachusetts Medical Society.

Medical Library of Boston.

Mitchell Library, Glasgow.

National Library of Scotland.

New York Public Library.

Western Reserve University, School of Medicine.

Sincere thanks are here given to the following institutions, for permission to quote from manuscript materials:

American Antiquarian Society.

Boston Public Library.

Connecticut Historical Society

Essex Institute.

Harvard College Library.

Haverhill Historical Society.

Haverhill Public Library.

Historical Society of Pennsylvania.

Henry E. Huntington Library.

Library of Congress.

Longfellow House, Cambridge.

Massachusetts Historical Society.

Pierpont Morgan Library.

New Hampshire Historical Society.

Whittier Home Association, Amesbury.

Yale University Library.

Warm thanks are also here given, for permission generously granted by the persons or publishers indicated, to quote from specific books:

Mrs. Millicent Todd Bingham and Harper & Brothers: *Letters of Emily Dickinson*, new and enlarged edition, ed. Mabel Loomis Todd, 1931.

Charles E. Goodspeed: *Whittier as a Politician. . .*, ed. Samuel T. Pickard, 1900.

Greenleaf Whittier Pickard and Houghton Mifflin Company: Samuel T. Pickard, *Life and Letters of John Greenleaf Whittier*, one-volume revised edition, 1907.

# Contents

# Introduction

IN EIGHTEENTH-CENTURY AMERICA there were political philosophers, remarkable men, who founded the Republic and gave it its nature. In the nineteenth century there were social thinkers, remarkable men also, who refined the state and gave it its living quality. Of this company Whittier was one, a quiet, moving force among men.

The central fact of his life was his strong faith in democracy. In this form of society, he believed, truth and justice are more nearly achievable than in any other. He was himself a prime example of man in a democracy, grateful for his franchise and wise in its use, careful of the rights of fellow citizens, and active in the ageless fight to make political and religious freedom the possession of all men. Whittier preached and practiced tolerance, but was a stout exponent of principle and a strong contender for the things he believed in. And in all that he did he became the embodiment of a high ethical standard. "What," he asked, "avail great talents if they be not devoted to goodness?"

His Abolitionism sprang directly from his democratic creed. Like Jefferson and Franklin before him, and like de Tocqueville in his own day, he believed that no state which had in it slavery could have in it also truth and justice. The vent and flame of his indignation against the "peculiar institution" merely measured the strength of his conviction that it was an anomaly which had to go. In an article written in tribute to William Leggett, one of his heroes, he declared, "We are using strong language, for we feel strongly on this subject" — slavery.

He was of all Abolitionists the gentlest and yet the most firm. Probably also he was the most astute in his political judgment. He flayed Northern politicians and business interests who in any way appeased or advocated appeasing the slave power, but he commended to all Abolitionists the principle of treating "our Southern friends as intelligent and high-minded men." So he wrote in 1834, the year after he entered the Abolitionist ranks; and that was his practice always. He yet felt that in a contest of the magnitude created by the existence of chattel slavery in America the rights of people in the North, especially of labor, could not be preserved by the granting of concessions to the slave power represented in Congress. He admired Southern leaders, even Calhoun for his abilities; he excoriated Northern politicians like Everett and Webster who thought that in the way of concession to the South lay safety for the life of the Union. And he virtually parted company with the Garrison faction of Abolitionists who sought to achieve moral reform without using the weapon of political action.

Lincoln, from 1858, took his stand and made his triumphant fight for the Union on grounds that Whittier had first put forward a quarter of a century before. Invariably Whittier weighed slavery in the scale of human rights and of the life of the American nation. In his pamphlet *Justice and Expediency*, first brought out at his own expense in 1833, he stated, "Liberty and slavery cannot dwell in harmony together." He signally elaborated his convictions in an editorial article, "The Lesson of the Day," which was published on November 17, 1859, a few weeks before John Brown was executed. (As much as anything else that Whittier ever wrote in prose, this long article, given in full in Appendix E, is his political and social testament.) Lincoln said, more simply and powerfully, that "this Government cannot permanently endure half slave and half free." Whittier declared that if limited and confined, slavery would die. Lincoln came to be the firmest and most articulate advocate of the principle of its non-extension, but of not disturbing it in states where it already existed. Whittier early and forcefully championed the cause of free labor in a society of free men. In his first inaugural address Lincoln powerfully announced this principle to a world now keenly attentive to the issue being contested in America — whether or not a minority, whatever its dissatisfaction, could wreck a democratic Union of States.

Whittier's "poetic perception," his search for beauty and truth, was concerned more with the whole life of man in the world than with literary art merely.

In truth, Whittier placed a very modest estimate upon his power as a poet. Repeatedly he said that he did not consider himself truly one. Here, too, he stood for the highest standard, and he found it in Milton. For him Milton exemplified Robert Browning's belief that "a perfect bard was one who chronicled the stages of all life." Withal, beginning in the eighteen-twenties, Whittier stoutly advocated the need for a literature grounded in American life, and he was himself among the first of "local colorists." Altogether he wrote too much on native topics, some of them trivial, and he employed a method of composition so rapid as to seem at times haphazard in results. But he was and is a native singer of considerable merit, and he is still the most deeply religious poet bred in the United States. More than that, the hymns of faith and hope which his writings have yielded are the common and inspiring property of the English-speaking world. In them Whittier realized his life purpose — and undreamt rewards — from the exclusive devotion of his talents to good ends.

Whittier's house of life had few doors but many windows. He could not go abroad in the world, but he looked out upon it with penetrating and sympathetic eyes. Unusually imaginative, he had a rich talent for getting the full flavor out of his own and other people's experiences. He spoke of himself as what the Turks call "a cut-off one," but he drew vital currents to himself, and lived an alert life. Sometimes his pen seemed to be the only tendon that joined him to the society of men. Whatever its cause, and this lay probably far back in his childhood, Whittier suffered nearly all his life from an extreme and unexplained neurotic condition. This imposed geographic limitations upon him which he deplored; it did not in any way curb his sympathies or limit his broad grasp of the meaning of life. On his merits he won and held an audience, and he has it still, evidently secure for as far ahead in time as one can look.

He won it at least as much by what he was as by what he wrote. He was a plain democrat, certain that all men are one in the sight of God, and ardent in his practice of the Christian ethic of helpful concern for all. His belief in the majesty of man was as strong as Emerson's, and more active. Even more acutely than Emerson he realized that the antidote for the "abuse of formal government" is "the influence of private character, the growth of the individual . . . the appearance of the wise man." Whittier gave a lifelong and practical demonstration of Emerson's truism. He believed that God is in every man, and that opportunity for the growth of the individual is implicit in democracy, and unbounded.

That, to anyone who comes in real contact with his mind and spirit, is obviously the central meaning of his life. The vigor of it quite belies Whittier's nervous or constitutional debility, which he deplored perhaps too insistently. Actually his character was of the kind that recognizes no obstacles. In difficulty or opposition he found a test for his strength and his faith. It will be so always with intelligent people in a democracy.

As long as ours lasts, Whittier may well prove to be one of its prophets and exemplars. His tribute in 1859 to Doctor Gamaliel Bailey, late editor of the *National Era*, applies equally to himself: "He was one of those men who mould and shape the age in which they live."

Whittier knew that his life's work would be weighed. Even while he lived he was made the subject of several biographies, and he himself wrote biographical sketches of deceased friends like John G. C. Brainard (1832) and Lydia Maria Child (1882). He strove to represent them as they were. On his own account he pleaded in the poem "My Namesake":

> Let Love's and Friendship's tender debt
> Be paid by those I love in life.
> Why should the unborn critic whet
> For me his scalping-knife?

In 1886 he asked his friend William Dean Howells to write the story of his life, but Howells' willingness was overbalanced by his publishing commitments. It finally devolved upon Samuel T. Pickard, Portland (Maine) newspaper editor and husband of Whittier's niece Elizabeth, to write the biography for which, with Whittier's help, he amassed material over a period of years.

Mr. Pickard's authorized biography, brought out in 1894, is honest and workmanlike. In line with custom then prevailing he edited some matters of style and punctuation in letters from which he quoted, but he neither omitted nor underplayed information available to him which would in any important respect have changed his picture of Whittier. His chronological presentation, however, was not as sharp in outline as the more practiced Howells might have made it.

With subsequent biographers Whittier has had various fortunes. Some, notably George Rice Carpenter, have sought to be scrupulously accurate. Others have striven for a "story" or have advanced theses unsupported by facts. The legend of a blood taint descending upon him from a rascally clergyman, several generations back in his mother's family, died hard but is now officially dead past romantic revival. Legends of his vivid profanity (actually, that of a pet parrot) in his youthful days as a Boston newspaper editor, and of religious intolerance in his Haverhill home, stated without critical inquiry by a journalist and by a literary antiquarian who were silent when challenged, have somewhat distorted the picture of Whittier.

It emerges clearly enough from a careful assessment of the large amount that he wrote, and from the comments of people who knew him well. What follows is believed to be an accurate and definitive account of his life. The writing of it has many times proved Emily Dickinson's perception in what she said of biography:

> Pass to thy rendezvous of light
> Pangless except for us
> Who slowly ford the mystery
> Which thou hast leaped across.[1]

*New York, December, 1947*

[1] *Letters of Emily Dickinson*, new and enlarged edition, edited by Mabel Loomis Todd (New York, Harper & Brothers, 1931), 319.

# JOHN GREENLEAF WHITTIER

*friend of man*

# I

# A Boyhood in the Brush

No snow fell that day, December 17, 1807, in Essex County.[1] Elias Weld, the eccentric physician of its northwestern tip, could easily have called, in his familiar white-topped chaise, at the homestead of John Whittier in East Haverhill. It is pleasant and reasonable to believe that he did, for his mission would have been to deliver into the world the future fighter for freedom, John Greenleaf Whittier, who in 1866 was to make him famous as "the wise old Doctor" of *Snow-Bound*.[2] In this isolated farming region of limited culture the accident of Whittier's bond with the possessor of one of the few private libraries within reach was fortunate. Doctor Weld indeed was almost a part of the Whittier home circle as it was etched in *Snow-Bound*, and he took more than a merely professional interest in the Quaker lad. Whittier's gratitude was enduring.

One daughter, Mary, had been born to John and Abigail Whittier on September 3, 1806, and the other, Elizabeth Hussey Whittier, "our youngest and our dearest" of *Snow-Bound*, was born on December 7, 1815. Between these two came the poet and his brother, Matthew Franklin Whittier, who was born on July 18, 1812. With the parents and his father's brother Moses and his mother's sister Mercy, here was the poet's family complete.

It was an affectionate family, close-knit by the strongest bonds of religion and by gifted personalities; and the isolation of their farm made the Whittiers unusually dependent one upon another for companionship. Essex was a populous county then, as it is now,[3] but its north portion, roughly three miles wide, extending from the Merrimac River up to the New Hampshire border, and approximately twenty miles long, reaching from Haverhill eastward to the Atlantic Ocean, was sparsely settled. "Our home was somewhat lonely, half hidden in oak woods, with no house in sight," Whittier wrote in 1882, "and we had few companions of our age, and few occasions of recreation." [4] Only seven other families appear to have lived in the district of East Haverhill, and they furnished few playmates for the Whittier children.[5]

Life was genuinely real and earnest on the Whittiers' farm of 185 acres, and here Whittier was early put to work. As a farmer boy he probably arose at four o'clock in the morning, dressed by candlelight, and in winter made his morning ablutions in ice-cold water. Then, dressed in mittens, hat, and a spencer woven on his mother's loom, he joined the hired man; and thus he began the heavy work that was soon to exact a heavy penalty from his frail physique.[6] Greenleaf's brother Matthew Franklin, five years his junior but his superior in bodily strength, undertook the more arduous duties such as "breaking" the colts and steers.[7] Yet what remained for the slender Whittier to do was, if cheerfully done, still irksome to him. Though he liked cows,[8] he never relished milking the seven that fell to his care; [9] he did not like horses, but had one to tend; the care of twenty sheep was conceivably a tax upon his strength, and this also was his chore. Only in the two oxen, "Buck" and "Old Butler," did he take delight. For them he had a particular affection.[10]

Briefly, this experience of Whittier's early life parallels that of another obscure boy, born two years after him and now growing up on Knob Creek, Kentucky: Abraham Lincoln's father taught him to do yeoman's work, but never taught him to like it.

In its externals the life of the Whittier homestead was plainly similar to that of most Essex County farms of the time. Fruits and grains and doubtless vegetables were raised. Since little wheat was used, rye and Indian corn were supplied for the black bread which was a staple in rural homes. The economy of such a farm as the Whittiers' was relatively self-sustaining. Any crops in excess of domestic needs were bartered for salt, sugar, and tea, besides tools and other required articles of manufacture. To Rocks Village on the Merrimac, accordingly, the Whittiers came to trade produce for necessary household supplies. Such visits were one of Greenleaf's few means of contact with the world, in his boyhood. Later he was sometimes seen driving the team to Rocks Village with a wagonload of apples to be exchanged for salt fish, which the captains of schooners used to bring up the river to trade with families desiring a winter's supply.[11]

Whittier also had opportunities to go outside the farm on errands for his mother,[12] and so to become acquainted with the beautiful surrounding country of the lower Merrimac Valley. Of this he wrote later:

> The scenery of the lower valley of the Merrimac is not bold nor remarkably picturesque, but there is a great charm in the panorama of its soft green intervales: its white steeples rising over thick clusters of elms and maples, its neat villages on the slopes of gracefully rounded hills, dark belts of woodland, and blossoming or fruited orchards, which would almost justify the words of one who formerly sojourned on its banks, that the Merrimac is the fairest river this side of Paradise. Thoreau has immortalized it in his "Week on the Concord and Merrimack Rivers." The late Caleb Cushing, who was not by nature inclined to sentiment and enthusiasm, used to grow eloquent and poetical when he spoke of his native river. Brissot, the leader of the Girondists in the French Revolution, and Louis Philippe, who were familiar with its scenery, remembered it with pleasure. Anne Bradstreet, the wife of Governor Bradstreet, one of the earliest writers of verse in New England, sang of it at her home on its banks at Andover; and the lovely mistress of Deer Island [Harriet Prescott Spofford], who sees on one hand the rising moon lean above the low horizon of the east, and on the other the sunset reddening the track of the winding river, has made it the theme and scene of her prose and verse.[13]

Whittier also tells how,

> On all his sad or restless moods
> The patient peace of Nature stole;
> The quiet of the fields and woods
> Sank deep into his soul.[14]

What he now discovered for himself, however, could have been only a straw to what he learned from Uncle Moses. "Innocent of books" Uncle Moses was, but deeply versed in field and stream and woods, and he now opened to his nephew an abounding natural lore of a kind which no classroom could communicate. Uncle Moses was likewise rich in reminiscence, and in Greenleaf he had a rapt listener. The boy absorbed the crude literary materials with ready sympathy:

> As they worked together in the fields, or sat by the evening fireside, he enjoyed the marvelous stories of the denizens of the forest and stream,

traditions of witchcraft, and tales of strange happenings in his own times. We can imagine the moods in which these stories were received, and how they would be warmed and colored in the kindling fancy of youth. As he stood at his uncle's knee at such times, he fell into reveries from which the good man would arouse him by the sharp exclamation, "Come, boy, get out of that *stound!*" [15]

It was as a natural historian that Uncle Moses performed his greatest service for Greenleaf. By himself the boy had followed Country Brook from its origin in the New Hampshire hills down toward the Merrimac. Later, in "The Fish I Didn't Catch," he told not only of the brook's natural beauty but of its economic service to the homestead. Let him, however, go along with Uncle Moses — "a quiet, genial man, much given to hunting and fishing" — and the experience became a Homeric adventure distinctly enlarging the narrow stage upon which his life had so far moved. In fact, wrote Whittier in 1843, ". . . it was one of the great pleasures of our young life to accompany him on his expeditions to Great Hill, Brandy-brow Woods, the Pond, and, best of all, to the Country Brook." [16]

Purchase of these privileges for an afternoon by doubled exertions on the farm in the morning was not considered dear by the boy, and was, indeed, cheap. For he learned, besides natural lore, something also of practical wisdom from Uncle Moses, who was not less shrewd for being humorous.

Brandy-brow Woods lay north of the homestead, almost on the New Hampshire border, and there Whittier tracked his way, seeking the source of Country Brook. Job's Hill, named for an old Indian chief of the neighborhood, was more accessibly located just south of the homestead, and this eminence became one of the youthful Whittier's chief haunts. Here he probably first saw the other oak-crowned hilltops in the undulating countryside; and from here he must have had, as a child, his first glimpse of the sea. Great Hill, however, rising 339 feet above sea level, was the lad's peak in Darien, and from it on clear days he is said to have been able to see the expanse of ocean from Boar's Head to Cape Ann. Wider horizons lay all about him, for from this elevation, second highest in Essex County, he could see portions of more than thirty cities and towns in Massachusetts and New Hampshire. Monadnock (celebrated by Emerson) rose to a height of 3700 feet, forty miles westward in southern

New Hampshire. Wachuset lay forty-five miles southwest, near Fitchburg. Agamenticus, thirty miles northeast, stood sentinel on the coast of Maine, and at the north, in New Hampshire, the Deerfield range billowed across the horizon.[17]

Towered cities did not abound in Essex County, but there was the busy hum of men three miles from the homestead, at Haverhill, which in 1810 had a population of 2682. Beautiful country lay between the farm and the town, and was chiefly distinguished by the series of Kenoza and Saltonstall Lakes and Round Pond, which are situated just off the Amesbury-Haverhill road. Kenoza was the "Great Pond" of Whittier's youth, and it was he who in 1859 gave it its present name, an Indian word signifying pickerel.[18] Its popular hold upon him outlasted his boyhood, and appears in *The Supernaturalism of New England*, published in 1847.

> Whoever has seen Great Pond [he wrote], in the East Parish of Haverhill, has seen one of the very loveliest of the thousand little lakes or ponds of New England. With its soft slopes of greenest verdure — its white and sparkling sand-rim — its southern hem of pine and maple, mirrored, with spray and leaf, in the glassy water — its graceful hill-sentinels round about, white with the orchard-bloom of spring, or tasselled with the corn of autumn — its long sweep of blue waters, broken here and there by picturesque headlands, — it would seem a spot, of all others, where spirits of evil must shrink, rebuked and abashed, from the presence of the Beautiful. . . .[19]

Haverhill itself was now a farming and trading center, its natural beauty still unspoiled by the encroachments of industry, and still sufficient to captivate visitors. One who felt its spell, in 1789, was George Washington. During a day's visit he remarked repeatedly upon the beauty of the scenery, the pleasant location of the town, and the thrift and enterprise of its citizens. "Haverhill," he said, "is the pleasantest village I have come through"; and as he took in the then unobstructed view for miles up and down the Merrimac he exclaimed almost involuntarily, "Beautiful, beautiful!" [20]

This was Whittier's own response, early and late, to his native surroundings. It was man's sensitiveness to beauty, rather than provincial prejudice, which, implanted in Whittier, enabled him to become the regional poet for whom New England had been long waiting.

# 2

His own roots were deep in this land, where four generations of his family had lived since his great-great-grandfather, Thomas Whittier, came to Essex County from England in 1638. Early and late, John G. Whittier was proud of his descent. In a letter to the Richmond (Virginia) *Jeffersonian and Times* in 1833 he described himself as a "humble son of New England — a tiller of her rugged soil, and a companion of her unostentatious yeomanry." Time abated his pride of ancestry not a jot. Less than four years before his death he wrote:

> My ancestors since 1640 [1638] have been farmers in Essex County. I was early initiated into the mysteries of farming as it was practiced seventy years ago, and worked faithfully on the old Haverhill homestead until, at the age of thirty years, I was compelled to leave it, greatly to my regret. Ever since, if I have envied anybody, it has been the hale, strong farmer, who could till his own acres, and if he needed help could afford to hire it, because he was able to lead the work himself.[21]

Full heir to family traits as he proved to be, John Greenleaf Whittier was fitly named. His paternal grandmother was a Greenleaf of Newbury, from which line he derived some of his most strongly marked traits. The name John was given to at least one twig on the spreading family tree in every generation since Thomas Whittier set his roots down in American soil.

The meagerness of John G. Whittier's outward advantages and of his cultural background has been widely remarked. By the world's reckoning these were indeed meager. By his own account, however, Whittier was never able to be sufficiently grateful for at least two aspects of his inheritance. He was born "a very decided Yankee," [22] and he was born a Quaker: "I am a Quaker because my family before me — those whom I loved — were Quakers. And also I am one because the faith pleases me. I believe in it." [23] This is merely to say that environment and heredity worked equally in him, to an inevitable end, and to his complete contentment.

Born as he was in the fifth generation of the line descending from Thomas Whittier through his youngest son Joseph, John G. Whittier received an agrarian birthright, and one of good citizenship, sensitive social conscience, and spirituality — to which may be added plain sense. These qualities seem invariably to have inhered in his male antecedents, and to have been brought to their final flowering in Whittier by means of judicious mating. Little is known of Ruth Green, whom Thomas Whittier married, but the poet's mother, grandmother, and great-grandmother were all bred of hardy parents.

Thomas Whittier was born near Salisbury, England, about 1620,[24] the third son of Richard and Mary Rolfe (or Rolff) Whittier. The Rolfes, small landowners and farmers, were people of considerable antiquity in Wiltshire, and were staunch members of the Church of England.[25] The Whittiers, likewise members of the Church of England, were long established in Hampshire, and in Wiltshire at least as early as 1510.[26] It is therefore not certain that Thomas Whittier, as stated by John G. Whittier's authorized biographer in line with Whittier's own belief, was of Huguenot descent.[27]

It is certain that he left the spirit of formalism in religion behind him when he sailed from Southampton in the two-hundred-ton ship *Confidence*, under papers dated April 24, 1638.[28] And it is certain that nature had equipped him with a physique proper for a colonizer. Before he was twenty-one years old he weighed more than three hundred pounds and, like each of his five sons, he was more than six feet tall.[29]

Stature the Lord gave him; position the pioneer Whittier had to acquire. He was not one of the eleven men in Salisbury, where he first settled,[30] who possessed the requisite £100 for four acres of meadow land, nor £50 with which to acquire four acres of planting land. Because of his youth he appears not to have been a Prudential Man or other officer of the town. Quite the contrary, his name first appeared in the town records in January, 1645, when he was fined £2/10 for unlawfully cutting oaks on the common. This sum was to be paid to the constable at once in "pipe-staves or corn or cattle," but it was kindly abated.[31] When this fact was discovered and John G. Whittier was asked whether to omit it from his biography or not, he replied: "By no means; tell the whole story. It shows we had some enterprising ancestors, even if a bit unscrupulous." [32]

Thomas Whittier, although one of the first settlers of Salisbury, was clearly not among its favored few. Whatever grant of land he received was not in the central part of town, and did not put him in a way to prosper. Very likely his economic need and the legal contretemps of 1645 prompted his removal to Newbury, on the south side of the Merrimac, where he lived "for a short time" and where he must have married. Prospects of a more abundant life at Haverhill, roughly ten miles inland from Salisbury village and again on the north side of "the great river," attracted him there in 1647.

Here Whittier's enormous physique and muscular strength found an ample theater for operations. There were oaks to be cut, without penalty, land to be cleared of rocks, and a yeoman's tradition to be founded which was to endure to the fifth generation. A mile or two north of the Merrimac, on the bank of a small tributary then called "East Meadow Brook" and later "Country Brook," Thomas Whittier settled. Land was "plenty" and could support large families. Thomas had one. Of his ten children, all except the oldest were born here.[33] These five sons and five daughters grew up in Thomas's house of logs, situated about a half-mile southeast of the Whittier homestead which he constructed some forty years later; and in time they must have helped him to attain his local position of consequence.

By way of chattels Whittier seems to have brought to Haverhill with him from Newbury only the "best swarm of bees" which his uncle John Rolfe, whom he had accompanied from England as apprentice, willed to him. By contemporary standards this was no mean legacy.[34] In the long view it has importance merely as an emblem of the industry and thrift which Thomas bequeathed to his posterity; indeed, some members of the family have woven a device of bees into their monogram.[35]

The will to work soon brought comparative prosperity to Thomas. His sense of civic responsibility, moreover, appears to have grown equally with his property, and once he served as Constable — probably a not unimpressive incarnation of the law. In religious matters he early took a stand for liberty of conscience and freedom of worship, with the result that he was not made a freeman by the General Court until 1666 and did not acquire the right to vote until two years later.[36]

It is unlikely that Thomas Whittier had, at that time,[37] any acquaintance with the principles of the Society of Friends, although his life span ran parallel to that of George Fox, the founder, and much in his personal code would have befitted a Quaker. Chiefly there was his treatment of the Indians, in the peaceful and friendly way of William Penn, long before Penn arrived in America in 1682. At his log house on East Meadow Brook, Whittier had for nearly thirty years carried on just and fearless relations with the Indians, who frequently visited him, when in 1676 Indian raids upon the settlement were begun.[38]

"Garrison houses" were then appointed and fortified, and Thomas Whittier was one of the committee which arranged in this manner for

Haverhill's defense. That this was at best inadequate was indicated by Hannah Dustin's valorous exploit of 1697. But in the midst of Indian forays against the town, Thomas and his flock needed as protection only the respect and friendship which he had earned from the Indians in the past. Faces smeared with war-paint occasionally peered through the windows of the Whittier kitchen, but despite doors left unbarred at night, no harm befell the house.[39]

This was the house, built about 1688 — a century before ratification by neighboring New Hampshire made the Constitution the basic law of the land — which was to be home to five generations of Whittiers and which was to remain in the family's possession until 1836. Thomas selected the site for the ancestral home, three and a half miles from the center of Haverhill, with a discriminating eye. A tenacious feeling for place which became characteristic of the family shines out through John G. Whittier's description of the establishment:

> Our old homestead (the house was very old for a new country, having been built about the time that the Prince of Orange drove out James the Second) nestled under a long range of hills which stretched off to the west. It was surrounded by woods in all directions save to the southeast, where a break in the leafy wall revealed a vista of low green meadows, picturesque with wooded islands and jutting capes of upland. Through these, a small brook, noisy enough as it foamed, rippled, and laughed down its rocky falls by our garden-side, wound, silently and scarcely visible, to a still larger stream, known as the Country Brook. This brook in its turn, after doing duty at two or three saw and grist mills, the clack of which we could hear in still days across the intervening woodlands, found its way to the great river, and the river took it up and bore it down to the great sea.[40]

Thomas Whittier constructed his "cottage," like his way of life, on enduring lines. After two and a half centuries some of the original beams, survivors of the fire which destroyed the roof in 1902, remain today in serviceable condition. On his wooded acres Thomas lived out the remaining eight years of his life, and at his death on November 28, 1696, he left his family an estate appraised at £438.[41]

To his descendants he left also a pattern of life from which there was little departure for one hundred and forty years. The youngest son, Joseph, and his line down to the poet Whittier lived on and by the soil, quite aware of a God in Heaven. All except John Whittier had large families; they assiduously fulfilled the duties of good citizenship; and they manifested a scrupulous regard for the rights and welfare of their fellows. Only one basic change from Thomas's way of life may be remarked in the next three generations of the family, and this was merely nominal. Thomas clearly had respect for the Society of Friends; [42] Joseph apparently was made a convinced member of it by his marriage, in 1694, to Mary Peasley. Her grandfather, who became the leading Quaker in Haverhill, was one of the two unlicensed preachers who in 1652 raised the public issue which made Thomas Whittier his resolute defender, at the cost of delaying for fourteen years his acquisition of the rights of a "freeman." [43] Characteristically, John G. Whittier in time said of Joseph Peasley, "He was a brave confessor." [44]

Thomas Whittier was thus the poet's one "steeple-crowned progenitor" in the direct line of male descent, and even he clearly inclined more toward the Quakers' freedom of conscience in religious matters than toward dogmatic Puritanism. There is no record that any of the Whittiers suffered the harsh oppression that befell other Quakers in the Bay Colony.[45] Yet there is convincing evidence of the Whittier family's devotion to freedom, which the Quaker tie can only have strengthened.

Significantly, in its third generation in Essex County the youngest branch of the Whittier family transmuted its love of freedom into a plain willingness to fight for it. A tough bark of militancy was engrafted upon the family tree when Joseph Jr., the youngest son of Joseph and Marv Peasley Whittier, married Sarah Greenleaf on July 12, 1739.[46] During the wars of the eighteenth century some of the descendants of Joseph Whittier are said to have lost their standing as Friends by holding military titles.[47] At the same time, the Greenleafs were distinguished by various members in the learned professions and in business, and they undoubtedly brought a further increase of intellect into the Whittier line. John G. Whittier himself probably made a just estimate of the Greenleaf strain in him when he wrote:

> Without intending any disparagement of my peaceable ancestry for many generations, I have still strong suspicions that somewhat of the old Norman blood, something of the grim Berserker spirit, has been bequeathed to me. How else can I account for the intense childish eagerness with which I listened to the stories of old campaigners who sometimes fought their battles over again in my hearing? Why did I,

in my young fancy, go up with Jonathan, the son of Saul, to smite the garrisoned Philistines of Michmash, or with the fierce son of Nun against the cities of Canaan? Why was Mr. Greatheart, in Pilgrim's Progress, my favorite character? What gave such fascination to the narrative of the grand Homeric encounter between Christian and Apollyon in the valley? Why did I follow Ossian over Morven's battle-fields, exulting in the vulture-screams of the blind scald over his fallen enemies? Still later, why did the newspapers furnish me with subjects for hero-worship in the half-demented Sir Gregor McGregor, and Ypsilanti at the head of his knavish Greeks? I can account for it only on the supposition that the mischief was inherited, — an heirloom from the old sea-kings of the ninth century.[48]

Whittier's own father, John, born on November 22, 1760, was the next-to-youngest son of the eleven children born to Joseph and Sarah Greenleaf Whittier. When he was nearly forty-four years old, and part owner of the homestead, he married, on October 3, 1804, Abigail Hussey, of Somersworth, New Hampshire. This marriage also brought together Friend with Friend, sound stock with sound stock.

Whittier's mother was descended from Richard and Jane Hussey, of Dover, New Hampshire, where the name of Richard, a weaver, appeared on the tax list as early as 1690. His son Joseph became a Friend. And the Husseys had at least one additional bond with the Whittiers: they were reputable, industrious farmers, and they married consistently into old and reputable families. That they had no connection with the Christopher Hussey line of Nantucket has been clear for a half-century, and is now proved beyond further question.[49]

The legend has long existed that the poet Whittier's piercing dark eyes were derived from his connection with the Reverend Stephen Bachiler, who was of that line.[50] The legend also related Whittier to Daniel Webster and others, and ascribed to the poet some fanciful taint from Bachiler's clouded reputation. This suggestion was indeed made one of the major premises in a biography from which Whittier emerged as a philanderer and a "male coquette."[51] It is probable that Whittier's striking eyes were simply an inheritance from his mother,[52] and it is clear that she bore no relation to the Nantucket Husseys.

Whittier's father, like his forebears, industriously won his living from stubborn soil which was unsuited to farming. He was of simple tastes, and he was religious, even devout. He was a man of clear head and, under a rough exterior, of kind heart. John G. Whittier said later, "He was a man in advance of his times, remarkable for the soundness of his judgment, and freedom from popular errors of thinking." [53] Moreover, he had a sense of duty to the state, and he met his civic responsibilities scrupulously.[54] His older son described him as "a man of good natural ability, and sound judgment," [55] and so John Whittier appears to have been regarded by his fellow townsmen.[56]

A good and useful life was thus a family tradition to which John G. Whittier fell heir. Long life was another family tendency which he acquired, though he lacked the physique and the constitutional energy of the first two of his American ancestors. They and the poet's father and grandfather each averaged nearly seventy-two years in age, at death; he surpassed them all, falling only three months short of eighty-five years.

Finally, Whittier came of a branch of the family for whom, in recent generations, celibacy appears to have had some charm.[57] Of the six children, for instance, who reached maturity in his father's generation, only two besides himself married. The poet's Uncle Moses remained a bachelor at the old homestead until his death in 1824. There was also present in the household Aunt Mercy, sister of the poet's mother,

> The sweetest woman ever Fate
> Perverse denied a household mate.[58]

It was not without reason that Whittier remarked, "Matrimony was never a success in my family." [59]

Here, in brief scope, is Whittier's heritage from four generations in the Yankee tradition. From this "unostentatious yeomanry" he acquired most of the salient Yankee qualities: economy, faithfulness to duty, independence, rectitude, resourcefulness, and stability. To these Whittier added his own special quality of Yankee humor, of which there were elements in his father and in Uncle Moses, and also what has been described as the outward appearance of the Yankee: "He is usually thin and wiry, rather tall and angular, with high cheek bones and pointed chin." [60]

Whittier had good reason to consider himself "a very decided Yankee." The exact-minded Emerson knew the molding power of heredity. "Every man," he wrote, "finds room in his face for all his ancestors. Every face an *Atrium*." [61]

# II

# Mold of Home and School

All the associations with Haverhill and its area were significant, but of all the early influences upon him, Whittier's home life sank deepest into his soul. Equally with the New England landscape, a Yankee homestead and its special quality of life made a subject for a poetic eye, and it was a happy circumstance that the Whittier establishment and the family were of no ordinary sort. Home and its historic associations so deeply engaged Whittier's strong affections that the passing of a half century did not dim memories of his boyhood at the homestead. Indeed, these flowed vividly from his pen just when it had seemed dulled and his body worn out by more than thirty years of fighting in the cause of freedom.

## 1

The household that Whittier limned so clearly in 1866 in *Snow-Bound* was that of a comparatively well-to-do family of farmers. The farm was not a profitable investment, it is true, and it "was burdened with debt" to the extent of six hundred dollars; but farming on the rock-strewn soil of Massachusetts was seldom rewarding. "We had no spare money," wrote Whittier, "but with strict economy we lived comfortably and respectably." His cousin Gertrude W. Cartland, in whose Newburyport home Whittier spent the last winter of his life, testifies:

> The social privileges of the family were among the best which Haverhill and its neighborhood afforded. The father was frequently in the

public service of the town, and was intimate with such prominent men as the late Judge Minot, Colonel J. H. Duncan, a Member of Congress, Moses Wingate, State Senator, and Sheriff Bartlett, grandfather of General Bartlett, one of the most noble of the heroes of the late [Civil] war. Parson Tompkins, also, was as frequent a guest at the Whittier fireside as in the homes of his own parishioners.

Chiefly, however, as described by Harriet Minot Pitman, "Whittier's home was exceptionally charming on account of the character of its inmates." [1] The daughter of Judge Minot of Haverhill, Harriet was one of Elizabeth Whittier's best friends, and she knew the family well. She and other friends of the Whittiers agreed that the special element of the family's charm was wit. It was distinctly marked in all of the four children except Mary.

Only John Whittier, of all his family, did not qualify as "exceptionally charming." He had a sense of humor [2] but his virtues were not of a genial sort. Tall like his ancestors and of strong build, he had had in boyhood a reputation for athletic strength and quickness. Greenleaf, born when his father was forty-seven years old, characterized him in *Snow-Bound* as "a prompt, decisive man" who wasted no breath. "Last time Canada, I believe, 1799," John Whittier recorded, of his bartering trips to the north, on the back of a drawer in the old desk at the homestead. About him there was marked Yankee directness, and Greenleaf wrote later that "as he grew older he could perceive traits of his father coming out more strongly in himself." [3]

Strong sense was his mark, but John Whittier lacked something of the understanding sympathy which his children found so abundant in the two women of the household and in Uncle Moses. Yet he was a raconteur, and as such he directly fed the interests of his children. His narratives of his travels to French Canada, as reported in *Snow-Bound*, helped to offset the narrow parochialism of an isolated farm. Moreover, as a devoted Quaker he had a sound knowledge of the Bible, from which he read to the eager circle of listeners that was his family.[4]

One other distinct service John Whittier performed for his son: he was a Jeffersonian Democrat, and Greenleaf inherited his political principles. It was quite in the tradition of his family that Whittier wrote, upon assuming editorial charge of the *Haverhill Gazette* on May 7, 1836:

At a time like this, I should be unworthy of the name of a freeman, and should disgrace the memory of a republican father, and prove recreant to the principles of Democracy, which he cherished throughout his life, were I to shrink from avowing myself the friend of Universal Liberty and the advocate of Free Discussion.

In short, John Whittier was a kind and just man, devout, able, and full of the humanity, plainness, and simplicity of his ancestors. At his death in 1830 he left clothing valued at only twelve dollars, but he owned a chaise, probably the only one in the neighborhood, in which the family were conveyed to Friends' meeting at Amesbury.[5] That he governed his life by the simple economy of his class is attested by credits placed to his account by Abel Page, of Haverhill,[6] for shoe-binding at three cents a pair and shoe vamps at eighteen to twenty cents a pair, in addition to produce of the farm.[7] With a Brahmin's interest, Emerson described this phenomenon of farmers turned mechanics in winter:

Close hid in those rough guises lurk
Western magians, — here they work.
Sweat and season are their arts,
Their talismans are ploughs and carts. . . . [8]

For his father, Whittier had lasting respect, but for his mother he had an enduring love bred of a sense of even deeper obligation. He considered her "as good a woman as ever lived"; [9] and that this was not the uncritical loyalty of a son beset by a "mother-complex," as implied in an attempted Freudian interpretation of Whittier,[10] is affirmed by a competent authority, Frances C. Sparhawk:

Even in speaking the words, "My mother," his very tone changed to loving reverence. No doubt he owed much to her in the help and inspiration which great men so often owe to their mothers. Yet it was for what she embodied in herself, even more than what she was to him, that he reverenced her. She was a strong, high-souled woman, thoughtful and full of the ability and resources which the training of the Friends develops so remarkably in their women. None of the broad questions which interested her son were too great for her. On the contrary, the life of devotion to the freedom of the slave which Whittier and his sister Elizabeth lived, had been born with them and preached into their ears and laid upon their hearts from their childhood. It was not Mrs. Whittier who followed their lead for companionship with them; it was they who took up the service to which she desired and prayed to have them consecrated.[11]

Quiet strength and deep refinement vitalize the portrait of Whittier's mother which may be seen in the Amesbury home. "She was loved and honored in the neighborhood," wrote C. C. Chase, of Haverhill. He described the characteristic expression of her face as "benign." But in her full face and her well-made figure she was in contrast to her older son, who was like her, however, in being straight and tall, and dignified in bearing rather than lively.[12]

Whittier's mother was full of the kindness which lies at the root of the Friends' historic practice of helping the helpless, and she lavished it particularly upon the "Yankee gypsies."

> It was not often [Whittier wrote] that . . . my mother's prudence got the better of her charity. The regular 'old stragglers' regarded her as an unfailing friend; and the sight of her plain cap was to them an assurance of forthcoming creature-comforts.[13]

Charity of this modest sort, however, was her one indulgence, for she was a domestic manager of skill as well as taste. Besides spinning most of the woolens for the family's wearing apparel, she contrived to contribute to the family budget by the sale of yarns and wool, and by making butter and cheese of such quality as to command premium prices.[14] Higginson remarked the "exquisite Quaker neatness" of the "plain abode" at Amesbury, and how the "placid mother . . . presided with few words at the hospitable board, whose tablecloth and napkins rivaled her soul in whiteness." An "inevitable lace 'kerchief was always laid over her bodice," and, in brief, it was she who gave to Greenleaf his scrupulous neatness of person.[15]

Mercy Hussey, the poet's aunt, four years younger than her sister, lived in the Whittier home from the poet's earliest remembrance until 1846, when she died. Although she lacked something of Abigail Whittier's dignity and presence, she shared her native refinement. She "had a face which revealed a singular sweetness of temper," and was considered, with her sister, to "combine all that was sweet, lovable, and excellent in woman." She also was a pattern of Quaker neatness, and "knew how to make the pine floors shine like a looking-glass." As a celebrated maker of squash pies[16] she had perhaps an additional claim upon her nephew's affections, though clear title to them was won by her exemplary character.

Her conduct of life was in keeping with her name: she had a gift for "gentle ministrations at the bedside of the sick and suffering." [17]

The perversity of fate which denied her a household mate was a tradition in the family, and it appealed strongly to Greenleaf's imagination. The story had about it the flavor of Hoffmann or Tieck. Aunt Mercy was early betrothed. One evening, left alone at the kitchen fire of the Whittier homestead by the retirement of the rest of the family, she was somehow attracted to the window, outside which she saw her lover, mounted on horseback, approaching the house. He was known to be then absent in New York, and her astonishment at his appearance was increased when she opened the kitchen door and saw neither horse nor rider at the step upon which he should have dismounted. Only on reconstructing the incidents of her vision did Aunt Mercy notice that she had heard no beat of a horse's hoofs. Days later she received a communication which she had feared would come, written in an unknown hand and reporting the death of her fiancé on the day and precise hour of her vision. Aunt Mercy found refuge, not in marriage or seclusion, but in a life of cheerful charity.[18]

Uncle Moses, half-owner of the homestead, enjoyed the full affection of his brother's family. To the four children he stood in the relation merely of an older brother. He was a simple child of nature, a Thoreau of a sort, omitting Thoreau's Harvard education and his philosophical radicalism, and adding a vivacious humor. "He was a man for the little folks to love," wrote the neighbor C. C. Chase. ". . . I well remember the shock which the neighborhood felt when the news spread that Uncle Moses had been killed. . . . He comes to my mind as a tall, plain, sober man, far less stout and stirring than his brother John." [19]

The fecund imagination that characterized Whittier's earliest writings shines out strongly from Uncle Moses. He had still some of the belief in spirits and witchery that survived in the rural districts of New England, and he shared an interest in the subject of spiritualism both with Abigail Whittier and with her elder son. He was, moreover, an oracle to be consulted about the weather. Above all, he had extraordinary insight into the minds of children; Whittier, in "The Fish I Didn't Catch," suggests how. "I have been happy many times in my life," he wrote, "but never more intensely so than when I received that first fishing-pole from my uncle's hand, and trudged off with him through the woods and meadows." Whittier was a wiser lad when he returned home; Uncle Moses tactfully pointed this first lesson at the Brook. " 'But remember, boy,' he said, with his shrewd smile, 'never brag of catching a fish until he is on dry ground. I've seen older folks doing that in more ways than one, and so making fools of themselves. It's no use to boast of anything until it's done, nor then either, for it speaks for itself.' "[20]

With companionship of this quality and with four elders of such character for daily guides, Whittier had, in one sense, ample compensation for the want of many playmates of his own age. This is particularly true since he was not adversely affected by the steady company of elders. Rather, he matured early because of it. It is clear that under this regimen he lived, as a lad, a comparatively self-contained, austere life. He almost never knew the carefree abandon of the barefoot boy. Quaker children were early taught to walk purposefully in the sight of God. Besides, Whittier inherited from ancestors who were compelled to develop these traits in order to survive, the individuality and self-reliance which have been called the "most striking features in the character of the rural population of New England."[21]

Whittier's brother and two sisters also had their characters molded by this regimen of religion and sect. Accordingly, the household in which Whittier grew up was an unusually harmonious one, dominated by a single culture and way of life. Mary, the older sister, had the character of her father; she became a forceful woman, of masculine face and features, with Roman nose, ruddy cheeks, and raven hair.[22] She was described as temperamental in her later years, which were clouded with sorrow. In contrast, Matthew Franklin Whittier[23] — "Frank" in the family, as his brother was "Greenleaf" — had a genial and humorous character after the style of Uncle Moses', but he was in countenance and complexion quite like his sister Mary.[24]

It remained for Elizabeth, eight years younger than the poet, to comprehend nearly all the virtues of her elders and to be for Greenleaf, until her untimely death, his most satisfying companion. Like him, she inherited a sensitive, nervous temperament from her parents, and seldom knew good health; like him, she had a poetic gift, and she published her small output of verse in journals and periodicals; like him, she had an active concern for the social amelioration of mankind, and she ran the risks even of bodily injury to give force to her ideas concerning human freedom. She was a perfectionist, and as her too brief diary shows clearly, she lived her nearly fifty-two years by almost unearthly standards. Yet she was a gay and elvish companion, and if she lacked what the world calls beauty of face, she had personal charm and loveliness of a deeper and more enduring sort.

"Lizzie" had the milder, sweeter nature of her mother, but also her father's power of decision. As a child she was Greenleaf's chief delight. As a girl she responded to him with all the affection of her warm nature, and encouraged him in his social and literary pursuits. As a woman she was the chief social adornment of his home; with her ease in social intercourse, her quick affability, and her sparkling wit and fluent expression, she offset her brother's reticence among a numerous company of strangers, and she welcomed to the home the increasing numbers attracted there by his fame. Higginson, while a clergyman in Newburyport, at times sought Whittier's company, and he has left a clear picture of the Amesbury household:

> * * * and with her [Whittier's mother] was the brilliant "Lizzie," so absolutely the reverse, or complement, of her brother that they seemed between them to make one soul. She was as plain in feature as he was handsome, except that she had a pair of great, luminous dark eyes, always flashing with fun or soft with emotion, and often changing with lightning rapidity from the one expression to the other; her nose was large and aquiline, while his was almost Grecian; and she had odd motions of the head, so that her glances seemed shot at you, like sudden javelins, from each side of a prominent network. Her complexion was sallow, not rich brunette like his; and whereas he spoke seldom and with difficulty, her gay raillery was unceasing, and was enjoyed by him as much as by anybody, so that he really appeared to have transferred to her the expression of his own opinions. . . . The lively utterances thus came with double force upon the auditor, and he could not fail to go out strengthened and stimulated. . . .

Elsewhere Higginson concluded, with some plausibility:

> She was a woman never to be forgotten; and no one can truly estimate the long celibate life of the poet without bearing in mind that he had for many years at his own fireside the concentrated wit and sympathy of all womankind in this one sister.[25]

Elizabeth Whittier was, indisputably, a woman of rare gifts. She shared Greenleaf's poetic qualities and his temperament, and she had a finer aesthetic nature than his; she possessed refinements of ear and of taste in which he was deficient. It is probably a significant fact that she "was very fond of music, well nigh forbidden to Quakers in those days." Whittier, at any rate, believed that "had her health, sense of duty, and almost morbid dread of spiritual and intellectual egotism permitted, she might have taken a high place among lyrical singers." [26]

As it was, she gave willing service as her brother's closest and most confidential literary friend. It is thus easy to understand the momentarily devastating effect upon him of her death, on September 3, 1864. By only four months she had missed sharing with him one of the moments of great reward for their joint efforts — a fleeting second which Whittier captured in "Laus Deo." This poem "sang itself" to Whittier while he sat in a Friends' meeting and while bells and cannon outside in Amesbury proclaimed the passage of the Constitutional Amendment which abolished slavery in the United States.

Sadly Whittier confided, in a letter written on the day of Elizabeth's passing, "It is terrible — the great motive of life seems lost." [27]

## 2

The ancestral home in East Haverhill which this devoted family occupied until 1836 was a typical farmhouse, yet distinctive, and it now stands as a memorial to that family and to a way of American life which is long vanished.

Charmingly set in a horseshoe of high ground, the house faces southeast toward the green meadows where Fernside Brook, having tumbled over the northern shoulder of Job's Hill, soon finds its outlet in Country Brook. Sunset came early in this secluded valley, earlier than it comes today, for in Whittier's youth the surrounding hills had not lost their oaken crowns, and they shut out the afternoon sunlight earlier. In the morning alone could the slope on the left bank of Fernside Brook have the full warmth of the sun's light. Here it was that "once a garden smiled," [28] and does again; and here stood in the poet's boyhood the tall well-sweep, which has been restored.

Only to the poetic eye could the immediate setting of the house have been more than passing fair. It was in fact one of Whittier's gifts that he perceived the representative in the commonplace, and endowed it with something of universal quality. Here on the homestead was none of the sweep and variety which distinguished the view from the top of Job's Hill, but in Whittier's clear eye the simple row of butternuts, walnuts, and maples between Fernside Brook and the house was still part of that soft landscape and of God's creation. So, too, was the now vanished column of Lombardy poplars which stood at the gateway.[29]

The house in which five generations of Whittiers had their being was, then, simply representative of its type. Central heating, of a kind inadequate at best to protect an old house against New England's "hard, dull bitterness of cold," was provided by a central chimney. Family life revolved about the Whittier kitchen, where "the great throat of the chimney laughed" [30] in the largest of the five fireplaces which opened into it. With a generous hand, Thomas Whittier built his kitchen twenty-six by sixteen feet, in a house approximately thirty-six feet square, and he allowed eight feet between the jambs of the fireplace alone. The oven was on the right at the back of "the clean-winged hearth," and at the left the crane swung on its hinges, with a numerous burden of hooks, trammels, pots, and kettles to bear testimony that the family cook led a busy life.

"The old, rude-furnished room" could best be entered at the eastern end over a doorstep inlaid with a millstone which once helped to grind the family's grain, a century before the poet was born, at the gristmill on Fernside Brook. From the entrance, a glance down the length of the kitchen is a retrospect into the life of old New England. Among family heirlooms remaining is the desk which was owned by the first Joseph Whittier and upon which his great-grandson wrote his earliest verses and the last of his many poems.[31]

Because of a large underlying boulder which could not be moved when the house was constructed, the small, quaint "mother's room" at the northwest end of the kitchen was built two steps higher than the rest of the ground floor. Similarly elevated are the other two rooms in this corner of the house, the milk room in the cellar and the bedroom upstairs used by the poet and his brother, in which

> We heard the loosened clapboards tost,
> The board-nails snapping in the frost;
> And on us, through the unplastered wall,
> Felt the light sifted snow-flakes fall.[32]

On the ground floor the remaining two rooms are the parlor, at the southwest corner, and the sitting room, at the southeast end of the house. Greenleaf was born in the parlor, which was used also as a bed chamber for the numerous Friends who stopped with the Whittiers en route to Quaker meetings. Chiefly notable here are the remnants of the very small library which the poet's family owned.[33]

From the front entrance a small stairway turns narrowly against the back of the chimney up to the second floor. Here, off a large central bedroom, open the four chambers regularly used by the family. In the spacious attic above, chiefly noticeable are the stout rafters studded with pegs and nails, from which were hung braided seed-corn and medicinal herbs. Here all manner of chattels were husbanded by the thrifty Whittiers. And here Greenleaf, with livelier mentality than his antecedents appear to have possessed, early read and wrote.[34]

## 3

Whittier's memory of events in this small cosmos did not extend back beyond his sixth year, but his life might easily have ended before he began to remember it. Twice in infancy he was spared possible death, once when his sister Mary, in a rapture of childish experimentation, wrapped him — fortunately well — in a blanket and rolled him down the steep back-staircase; and again when, taken with his parents on a winter drive to Kingston, New Hampshire, near Exeter, he was nearly smothered in a superabundance of blankets. It was in fact feared that he was dead, but he was revived after long and anxious treatment in a farmhouse by the road.[35]

Otherwise, Whittier's earliest years did not abound with memorable events. His slow upward march to knowledge and wisdom seems to have begun at the age of six with the astonishing discovery that, on the day after a neighboring farm had been sold at auction, the purchaser had not removed it and left a hole in the ground where the farm had been situated.[36]

Upon this imaginative darkness, in 1814–1815 at the age of seven, Whittier was privileged to turn the dubious light of the district school. He was not yet come of "school age," but his admittance had perhaps the sanctions of authority, for both his father and his Uncle Moses were members of the district school committee that year. Greenleaf was enrolled in a class exposed to the mild rigors of learning the alphabet. It is a reasonable assumption that his careful mother had found time to give him prior tuition in "the mysteries of those weary A B C's," and a certainty that he went unprepared for what he found there. For while the district schoolhouse, on the road running north past the Whittier homestead, was undergoing repairs, instruction was given in the ell of a residence near by, where

> Through the cracked and crazy wall
> Came the cradle-rock and squall,
> And the goodman's voice, at strife
> With his shrill and tipsy wife. . . .[37]

Caterwauling of this sort created no fit atmosphere for learning, but neither did the district school system itself. The schoolhouse nearest the Whittier homestead was in 1814–1815 permitted to remain in a state of disrepair, against the day when a new building could be erected. This remained merely a pious hope until 1872 or 1873, when a new schoolhouse was built at some distance from the old site.[38]

As it was, the dilapidated old schoolhouse of "In School-Days" which Whittier depicted so clearly in 1870 conformed precisely to type. Physical conditions were uncomfortable and unhealthy, with a maximum of thirty pupils crowded into one small room. During the winter term, instruction was usually given by college students on vacation; they thus earned enough to help pay the expenses of college terms which then ran far into the summer. And what went by the name of study was dreary, often meaningless task-work.[39]

It was relieved only by a few books, a few personalities. For the reading lesson, as Whittier himself has written, the standard book was Caleb Bingham's *American Preceptor*, an anthology sprinkled through with anti-slavery sentiment. Whittier undoubtedly got real profit also from the instruction in writing, begun probably when he was nine; from the study of grammar in parsing, for which Pope's "Essay on Man" and Milton's "Paradise Lost" were fertile fields; and from the readings in John Pierpont's *American First Class Book*, in which Greenleaf probably first found, among other things, a generous representation of English romantic poetry — Byron, Campbell, Coleridge, Moore, Ossian, Scott, Southey, Thomson, and Wordsworth — besides Milton's "Lycidas" and selections from Shakespeare.[40]

It is notable that Whittier was not bred upon *The New England Primer*, which "taught millions to read and not one to sin." Early and late he was well instructed in the Bible at home, far better than he could have been taught at school, and he stood in no need of the Westminster catechism, which the pupils were required to learn from the *Primer*. Whittier possessed no copy. When the teacher ordered him to procure one, he was told by his father that he need not study the catechism, since it contained errors. To a Quaker mind the passages on the sacraments, for instance, were probably alien. Greenleaf was allowed to omit the *Primer* from his studies.[41]

Obviously, scant knowledge could be acquired and retained by the average boy or girl in twelve weeks of such studies during ten or twelve winters, since each period of study was separated from the next by forty weeks of work on the farm, for example. Moreover, the poor quality of the instructors was a bar to learning in the district schools, which were autonomous under local boards until Horace Mann became Secretary of the Massachusetts State Board of Education in 1837 and took measures to institute something resembling standards. It was Whittier's custom to say that "only two of the teachers who were employed in that district during his school days were fit for the not very exacting position they occupied." He was fortunate to encounter two. Usually the masters received only $10 or $12 a month, or at most $20 in the wealthy districts.[42] There was probably more than a humorous reason why Whittier wrote of

> The feet that, creeping slow to school,
> Went storming out to playing![43]

What quality Whittier's "ragged winter school" had was imparted to it by the service on two occasions, in 1814 and 1821, of Joshua Coffin as its teacher. He was a gift from Heaven dropped into the boy's life. Coffin had the marks of a born teacher, and even before entering Dartmouth College with the class of 1817 he had taught school. In the poem, "To My Old Schoolmaster," an outpouring of grateful remembrance in 1851, Whittier paid respect to his qualities. Coffin was affectionate, ardent, cheerful, fertile in expedient, full of historic anecdote, genial, and good-humored always. Above all, he was generations ahead of his day in making education rather the positive impression of mind and personality than the negative impression of a birchen rod.[44]

Whittier frequently erred on the side of uncritical kindness, but that Coffin undoubtedly had a gift for inspiring his pupils with a love of learning was affirmed by one other of them, Cornelius C. Felton, whom he had taught at Newbury. Felton was later (1829–60) a professor at Harvard and one of America's leading scholars of Greek, as well as president of Harvard in 1860–62.[45]

In Coffin's influence on Whittier there was a special virtue. He must have been naturally opposed to slavery, for he was one of the twelve people, including William Lloyd Garrison, who in 1832 signed the constitution of the first anti-slavery society in New England; and he had a taste for poetry. Burns and Cowper were his favorite poets, and with his preference he infected the Quaker lad.[46]

This was, it appears, wholly by accident. As master of the district school in 1821, Coffin spent numerous evenings at the Whittier home, and there by the fireside, as Whittier's mother and aunt sat knitting, he read to them from books of travel and adventure. He thus supplemented the Whittiers' library, limited in number of volumes and in its marked Quaker bias. Quite unnoticed, now, was the rapt attention of his eagerest listener, the fourteen-year-old Greenleaf. But when, one evening, Coffin brought with him a volume of Burns, and explained the Scottish dialect as he proceeded with his reading, he set the seal to a career. Whittier, who had sat entranced in his corner during the performance, at its conclusion gratefully accepted the observant Coffin's offer of the loan of the book.[47]

This was undoubtedly one of "the dews of boyhood's morning," rich literary nourishment indeed to a youth who had so far subsisted on the dry if morally excellent collection of forty books in the Whittiers' library. What welcome refreshment the book gave the lad was glowingly recalled by the man of forty-seven in his poem to Burns. Nature, the fourteen-year-old boy learned, gives to her handmaid Art "the themes of sweet discoursing," and the discerning eye can find the substance of poetry in daily life and duty. Burns taught him also that romance can be native, for, wrote Whittier:

> I matched with Scotland's heathery hills
> The sweetbrier and the clover;
> With Ayr and Doon, my native rills,
> Their wood-hymns chanting over.
>
> . . . . . .
>
> With clearer eyes I saw the worth
> Of life among the lowly;
> The Bible at his Cotter's hearth
> Had made my own more holy.[48]

As much to be thanked as Coffin, for thus putting Whittier in the way of Burns, was Doctor Elias Weld for commending to him Milton, apostle of human freedom. For Milton was at least equally Whittier's master with Burns. He not only strengthened the Quaker's inherited love of liberty but supplied specific ideas for his anti-slavery writings. Whittier's gratitude to Doctor Weld was not overdrawn in a letter addressed to him at Hallowell, Maine, and dated March 5, 1828.

> I am happy to think [wrote Whittier] that I am not entirely forgotten by those for whom I have always entertain'd the most sincere regard. I recollect perfectly well that (on one occasion in particular) after hearing thy animated praises of Milton and Thomson, I attempted to bring a few words to rhyme and measure: but whether it was poetry, or prose run mad, or as Burns says "something that was rightly neither," I cannot now ascertain. Certain I am, however, that it was in a great measure owing to thy admiration of those poets, that I ventur'd on that path which their memory has hallow'd, in pursuit of — I myself hardly know what — Time, alone, must determine.[49]

Whittier's gratitude, it may be repeated, was enduring. He corresponded with Doctor Weld for many years, and in 1863, a few months before the physician died, he inscribed "The Countess" to the man "to whose kindness I was much indebted in my boyhood. He was the one cultivated man in the neighborhood. His small but well-chosen library was placed at my disposal." [50]

What an oasis this was in the cultural desert of Whittier's boyhood is suggested by a glance at the ill-assorted contents of his family's library. Biography, for which he always had a taste, was represented by eighteen titles; ten of these were "lives" of British poets, including Milton. Five religious figures were represented, among them George Fox; and Stephen Burroughs, Benjamin Franklin, and Henry Tufts stood as curious strangers in this chaste company. The humor of their incongruous presence in his father's library was not lost upon Whittier, who reported, in a rhymed catalogue of his father's books which he composed in 1823 or 1824:

> The Life of Burroughs, too, I've read,
> As big a rogue as e'er was made;
> And Tufts, who, I will be civil,
> Was worse than an incarnate devil.[51]

Of poetry there was a minimum, and this was mainly of a fragmentary sort. For Whittier, the cream of the library was beyond question Cowper's "On the Loss of the Royal George" and Gray's "Elegy Written in a Country Churchyard," which must have been contained in the editions of the two readers available to him — the *American Preceptor* and Lindley Murray's *English Reader*. In his preface to *Child-Life in Prose* Whittier said:

> I well remember how, at a very early age, the solemn organ-roll of Gray's Elegy and the lyric sweep and pathos of Cowper's Lament for the Royal George moved and fascinated me with a sense of mystery and power felt, rather than understood. "A spirit passed before my face, but the form thereof was not discerned." Freighted with unguessed meanings, these poems spake to me, in an unknown tongue indeed, but like the wind in the pines or the waves on the beach, awakening faint echoes and responses, and vaguely prophesying of wonders yet to be revealed.[52]

Books of travel and adventure to the number of five also adorned the Whittiers' spare shelves, and very clearly confirmed the romantic strain deep in Greenleaf to which, as *Snow-Bound* records, even the tales of his father and uncle about their limited journeys had such ready appeal. Certainly Whittier had early, besides a transforming eye, a gift for mental projection into remote, far-off places. Equally he had an antiquarian and a historical flair, grounded in a reverence for old things. Only two curious volumes of forgotten lore had found their way into the Whittiers' home, but Greenleaf's early quarrying in Cornelius Agrippa's *Occult Philosophy* and Rollin's *Ancient History* was a marvel of literary economy, of which the reappearance of the protean German in the preliminary apparatus of *Snow-Bound* in 1866 served as a late and startling reminder.

It also emphasized a salient fact of Whittier's youth: even then there appeared, strongly developed, his lifelong gift for assimilating the best in his environment, however narrow. Constantly repeated readings of his family's small library, especially of the Bible, gave him a mastery of it. As a boy, he was in fact able to tell the story of the Bible from Genesis to Revelation, and he could quote the greater part of it.[53] This knowledge Whittier never lost.

Scott, too, through the family library, now got into his blood, if never thoroughly into his mind. The

> One harmless novel, mostly hid
> From younger eyes, a book forbid,

which Whittier mentioned was *The Pirate*.[54] This he read with Elizabeth under clandestine and fittingly romantic circumstances, until the burning out of their tallow dip put an end to their nocturnal vigil over it. Soon Scott peered out as a literary ghost from some of Whittier's earliest writings, but as very little more. Fundamentally, what was not moral or religious or humorous had little staying power with Whittier. "The green spots in his childish experiences" consisted rather in his literary foraging in the Bible and in *Pilgrim's Progress*, that vast arena of moral knighthood and chivalry in which his agile imagination found ready engagement.[55]

Whittier had, nevertheless, an inquiring mind, and a hunger for books of biography and travel. Lincoln he resembled in this respect also: he went miles afoot to borrow desirable books. Undoubtedly Whittier was no stranger at Doctor Weld's home in Rocks Village. The recesses of the family farmhouse also knew Whittier's probings, for he later reported having found a sermon of 1814 to read,[56] and, in the attic, a stack of Congressional Reports. These, as Whittier wrote in 1877, he read for want of other matter, and here "amid the dreary dullness of ordinary debate, I was at once attracted to the speeches of John Randolph of Roanoke." [57] Here was another token of the principles of economy in Whittier. In 1847 this enthusiasm of his boyhood poured over into the lines of "Randolph of Roanoke."

## 4

These several books, it is obvious, Whittier read avidly enough. But as a birthright Friend and a moralist, he literally made part of his being the six books in his father's library written by or about Quakers: Barclay, Baxter, Chalkley, Clarkson, Penn, and Sewel. Any one of these books singly would have schooled Whittier in the workings of practical Quakerism; taken all in all, they gave overwhelming historical sanctions to his implicit belief in the living mission of the Society of Friends.[58] Under his hand, these became literary materials almost from the day of his first scribblings. That art and morality were never separate in Whittier's mind was a predetermined fact. As a corollary, more effect than cause was his reading these six books "so much that he had steeped his mind with their thoughts. He loved their authors because they were so saintly, and yet so humbly unconscious of it." [59]

Whittier very literally *belonged* to the Society of Friends, and this was the decisive factor which gave force and direction to his life. The *Rules and Discipline of the Yearly Meeting* at Newport shaped his entire life. The Society's excellences were *his* excellences, its prejudices *his* prejudices. It was not chiefly the mystic aspect of Quakerism which held him. The intense religion in him bore not the slightest relation to theology or creed. It was the practical Quaker way of life which gripped him, the consecrated purpose to help the helpless.[60] The humanity and the simplicity of the Friends were the dominant characteristics of Whittier's own nature, and a large part of his life was nothing less than the practical application of Quaker principles to a troubled social era. Mrs. Fields wrote: "All the associations of his youth and all the canons of his education and development were grounded on the Friends' faith and doctrine. . . ." [61]

Whittier could not have been long in discovering that he belonged to a Society ennobled by oppression.[62] To suffer has always been the fate of people ahead of their times in social thinking. Whittier must have learned in "painful Sewel's ancient tome" how the Friends, believing in a God of love, suffered for their non-conformity in America under the Puritan theocracy. Sewel recorded John Endicott's treatment of the Quakers, which the poet condemned in 1880 in "The King's Missive"; the fates of Mary Dyer, William Leddra, and Cassandra Southwick, whom Whittier in season apotheosized, and a myriad Quaker facts with which his mind was stored.[63] Here, too, were stated certain historic principles of the Society: opposition to war,[64] to oaths, to religious ceremonials, and to singing in church; provision for the marriage of couples "in meeting," not by a clergyman, since the Old Testament does not stipulate that marriage is the office of a priest; belief in and practice of democratic government, and the equality of women with men in civil and religious rights. In a word, Sewel's history was a large catalogue of the Quaker precepts and prejudices to which Whittier was heir.

That the Friends had always been great champions of "causes" Whittier could have found well recounted in Thomas Clarkson's *Portraiture of Quakerism*. No Quaker, Clarkson made common cause with Friends against slavery, and developed a general interest in the Society as a group militant only against social injustice. As early as 1727 the London Yearly Meeting had testified against the importing of slaves, and in 1783 it addressed to Parliament the first petition received by that body against the slave trade. In America, Anthony Benezet (1713–84) and John Woolman (1720–72) were among the earliest workers for Abolition, and the Friends as a religious body were the earliest Abolitionists. Even before the Constitution was adopted they had freed all their slaves. William Penn, moreover, from the year 1700 had had a "concern" for the Negroes and the Indians.[65]

Briefly, Whittier received in his family's bosom and library the militant sympathy for the enslaved and the downtrodden which inevitably predisposed him to join Garrison as an Abolitionist, in 1833. We shall find him also, in season, opposing strongly with his conscience and his pen injustice to the Indians, capital punishment, imprisonment for debt, the suppression of free speech, and any other infringement by man of God-given rights.

Besides this social nature, Whittier's religion had also the quality of being lived every day of the year. In the Quaker calendar, no day outranked any other in sanctity. Precisely as appointed in the *Rules of Discipline*,[66] a home like the Whittiers' let none pass without its religious observance. The reality of the Quaker regimen did something vital for Whittier: it bred him, upon the Bible, a true child of Hebraic ethics of righteousness. As his cousin Gertrude Cartland has recorded:

> In the Whittier family the reading of the Holy Scriptures was a constant practice. On First-day afternoons especially the mother would read them with the children, endeavoring to impress their truths by familiar conversation; and to this early and habitual instruction we may attribute in great measure the full and accurate knowledge of Bible history which the poems of J. G. Whittier indicate, as well as the strong bias in favor of moral reforms which was so early manifested. It is a tradition in the family that when J. G. Whittier was very young he often sought from his father and others a solution of his doubts respecting the morality of certain acts of the patriarchs and other holy men of old; and at one time he declared that King David could not have been a member of the Society of Friends, because he was a man of war.[67]

In still another way Quakerism entered the home and subtly helped to shape Whittier's religious character. "Itinerant ministers" from both England and America, who felt the call to carry the ripest wisdom of the Society into the homes of other members, habitually in those days visited wherever the Quaker trail led. This cross-fertilization brought William Forster, of England, to the Whittier homestead about 1822 on the first of his three visits to the United States, "under impressions of religious duty," as Whittier wrote. In 1854, following Forster's death in Tennessee, the poet confessed that he had been "too weak and young to understand the serious words he said," but now,

> Low bowed in silent gratitude,
> My manhood's heart enjoys
> That reverence for the pure and good
> Which blessed the dreaming boy's.[68]

Other visiting Friends doubtless added to Forster's influence; and many of them, coming from afar, must have performed for the impressionable Whittier some slight service in bridging the gap between the world outside and his secluded home on the farm.[69]

Possibly in part because religion was in these ways an aura always about him, Whittier as a boy did not relish the eight- or nine-mile drive to First-Day (Sunday) meeting in Amesbury. Then his parents, or aunt and uncle, and as many of the children as their one-horse chaise would accommodate, went, in good weather, to this most nearly formal observance which the Friends maintain.[70] "I think I rather enjoyed staying at home and wandering in the woods, or climbing Job's Hill . . . ," wrote Whittier later. But when he did attend meeting in Amesbury, he came under the influence of a quietistic group. There was no music in the Amesbury meeting until late in his life, and little speaking ever. It was a meeting given almost wholly to silent communion with God, for —

> . . . from the silence multiplied
> By these still forms on either side,
> The world that time and sense have known
> Falls off and leaves us God alone.[71]

So Whittier learned to love solitude, and this "deep inwardness" of his religious training, enforced by his father's example of brevity, must have had some bearing upon the exceeding quiet and seeming diffidence of his later years.

# 5

This, in sum, was the intellectual and spiritual capital that Whittier banked in his youth — nature, home and family, books and the training of the district school, and Quakerism — and every part of it he transformed into inner riches. Like Wordsworth he communed with Nature. The things he saw now he saw forevermore; they "sank deep into his soul." No less did the memory of the "old stragglers" whom he later depicted in "Yankee Gypsies." Of this fraternity were Stephen Leathers, of Barrington; Jonathan Plummer, "maker of verses, pedler and poet, physician and parson, — a Yankee troubadour, — first and last minstrel of the valley of the Merrimac, encircled, to my wondering eyes, with the very nimbus of immortality"; and likewise Parson ——. Whittier caught clearly also the wandering Scottish songster who first introduced Burns to the Whittier household; "the great Indian doctor" who mistook, in his inebriety, oil for brandy; the "olive-complexioned, black-bearded Italian" who told of sunny climes and "left with us the blessing of the poor," and the entire gallery of eccentrics who constituted the floating population of rural New England in the first quarter of the nineteenth century.

It was so, in equal measure, with the life of old New England; its spirit grew now into his soul and became part of his being. A sense of the past, rising from the burying ground of his Whittier ancestors just north of the house, infected him naturally enough, and it was translated in his mind into a strong nostalgia which in his later writings turned his mind back upon olden times with perhaps too much fondness. Age never withered his spirit of memory. The village doctor might die, but life went evenly on in the village, and Whittier described it with felicitous memory:

> For the rest, all things go on as usual; the miller grinds, the blacksmith strikes and blows, the cobbler and tailor stitch and mend, old men sit in the autumn sun, old gossips stir tea and scandal, revival meetings alternate with apple-bees and huskings, — toil, pleasure, family jars, petty neighborhood quarrels, courtship and marriage, — all which make up the daily life of a country village continue as before.[72]

Of material things, in contrast, Whittier had few in his boyhood, and few even in later life when fortune came to him with both hands full. In his opinion the real things were invisible, and he regretted the lack of only two articles in his boyhood: books, and a sufficient supply of warm clothing in winter. If on summer days he preferred outdoor worship in the neighboring woods or on Job's Hill to the meeting at Amesbury, winter and rough weather merely accentuated his preference for staying at home. New England's textile industry was soundly established only about fifteen years after Whittier's birth.[73] The homespuns that he and his contemporaries wore were heavy but not warm, and blankets, flannels, and buffalo robes did not abound. But with the bulldog tenacity of their English forebears, four or five generations of New Englanders lived with English clothing in an almost Siberian climate, until the mills at Lawrence and Lowell spun a kind palliative against its rigors.[74] The meetinghouses, moreover, were seldom provided with heating systems until Whittier's youth had long passed. Inevitably he suffered, both at Amesbury meeting and en route to it. By his own account, he was so stiffened with cold, on some of the First- and Fifth-Day drives to Amesbury, that "his teeth could not chatter until he thawed out." [75]

This severe school of "toughening," if it bred a hardy race of pioneers, secured no blessings to their posterity. Whittier did not have an athletic constitution, and what nature had denied him, exposure to harsh weather and too heavy work on the farm failed to supply. He always had a slender frame, and at the age of about fifteen years he attained his full stature, five feet ten and a half inches. By the time he had become seventeen his health was permanently impaired by an injury sustained in farm work that overtaxed his physical strength.[76] The many external advantages which had been withheld from his culture might by this fact have been enlarged into a handicap beyond hope of successful survival. But Whittier's inner resources, many years in the building, gave him abundant strength to surmount it, and a residue for battle on the side of human betterment.

The remainder of the narrative of Whittier's boyhood has to do chiefly with surfaces, and is quickly told. It is a picture not richly colored with vigorous life, although there is in it, here and there, some saving tie with the legend of carefree youth. It appears that Whittier was never a swimmer, despite the enticements of an unrivaled number of natural pools near the homestead. With his Uncle Moses he probably enjoyed, however, the "contemplative man's recreation," and fished on Great Pond, otherwise Lake Kenoza.[77] Certainly Whittier discovered how sweet are plundered fruits to a boy. The boughs of a neighboring Miss Chase's cherry tree were sacred, even from the birds, and the approach of other urchins evoked a termagant wrath. But when once Whittier was caught in the tree, his kind face banished the owner's ire. "Oh, is it you, Greenleaf?" she called. "Take all the cherries you want!" On another occasion, at the age of about fourteen, Whittier had another memorable "scrape," aloft in a nut tree, and he must have come off with a harvest of abrasions and contusions, the reward of any lad who does not spend his youth in a library or a parlor.[78]

Whittier also had, evidently, his share of the frights of unenlightened childhood. Fear triumphed over his reason when, one night, he made bold to confront the ghost of Country Bridge, a structure which the hardiest native dared not risk crossing after dark. Whistling to bolster his courage, Whittier approached the fearsome place, and then turned abruptly and scampered for home with never a look behind him. But freedom of action favored him less in his encounters with a raucous but harmless gander that lived in a farmyard on a hillside midway along the road between East Haverhill and Merrimac. Whittier's father was accustomed to relieve the horse by getting out of the chaise and walking up this hill. Naturally the boy followed suit, whereupon the gander would set up his warlike commotion. The passing of seventy years did not abate Whittier's remembrance of the terrors he felt here as a boy, nor of his manfully conquering them in preference to revealing his fears to his father and running the greater risk of being laughed at.[79]

The elements which ministered to Whittier's growth in his boyhood were not, however, experiences such as these, which could have befallen any New England country lad, but rather the fundamental powers of mind and spirit. With these lasting things he zealously sought nearer acquaintance — no one more successfully in spiritual matters — but under the grave handicaps of his limited intellectual opportunities. In 1881 Whittier described this aspect of his life to a young girl in Pennsylvania who had inquired about it:

> I think at the age of which thy note inquires I found about equal satisfaction in our old rural home, with the shifting panorama of the seasons, in reading the few books within my reach, and dreaming of something wonderful and grand somewhere in the future. Neither change nor loss had then made me realize the uncertainty of all earthly

> things. I felt secure in my mother's love, and dreamed of losing nothing and gaining much. . . . I had at that time a very great thirst for knowledge and little means to gratify it. The beauty of outward nature early impressed me; and the moral and spiritual beauty of the holy lives I read of in the Bible and other good books also affected me with a sense of my own falling short and longing for a better state.

Also late in life, Whittier measured the distance he had come: "Then I wondered at my age, and if it was possible that I was the little boy on the old Haverhill farm, unknown, and knowing nobody beyond my home horizon." [80]

In sum, Whittier was twice blessed in his spiritual development by the Quakerism of his people and by his freedom from cloying urban influences. But in his mental growth he suffered from an early want of the better educational advantages which a city might have afforded, for, on the whole, he felt as his hero Milton did:

> When I was as a child, no childish play
> To me was pleasing, all my mind was set
> Serious to learn and know.[81]

It is clear that Whittier's remarkable powers of assimilation wrung the best out of the few educational resources which were available to him, and that these nowise sufficed to satisfy his thirst for knowledge. It is thus warrantable to believe that better tools in his life at this time would have made a more finished workman of him later.[82] In any event it is an absolute fact that Whittier's boyhood fitted him precisely for the station in life which he finally took to be peculiarly his own.

"I am a *man*," he wrote to Underwood in 1883, "and not a mere versemaker." [83]

# III

# First Writings

WHITTIER matured slowly as a whole man. He came early to spiritual grace but late to literary culture, and it was not until 1833 that he welded these elements into a nearly balanced character. Meanwhile, from the time of his first experiments with verse until he wrote the prose tract *Justice and Expediency* in 1833, he spent the most trying period of his life, roughly ten years, in anxious pursuit of an uncertain end. During this interlude he was a stranger to his essential being:

> . . . over restless wings of song,
> His birthright garb hung loose.[1]

He was not a complete Quaker, and was just beginning to be a man; he was a verse-maker, and not yet a poet. For a decade of imitation his half-formed intellect guided his wavering course. He got his true bearing on life only when his heart fully reasserted itself and when, like a true Quaker, he embraced a cause.

## 1

Whittier early put himself to the hard school of writing by the forcing method. Like most literary aspirants, he knew books before he had had any direct experience of life, and books were inevitably his first source of inspiration. He had delved in Doctor Weld's library before 1820, but his introduction to Burns in 1821–22 was the fillip which set him to writing.

At the age of fourteen or fifteen he scribbled on his slate, to the amusement of his schoolfellows. In turn he amused himself at the family's fireside, after chores were finished in the evening, not by doing the conventional sums on his slate but by composing rhymes. Almost the only survival of these youthful effusions shows with sufficient clarity the bent of his mind at this time:

> And must I always swing the flail,
> And help to fill the milking pail?
> I wish to go away to school;
> I do not wish to be a fool.[2]

What Whittier himself considered his first exercise in versification was written in 1823 or 1824, a rhymed list, thirty-four lines long, of the books in his father's library. Two aspects of the verse are of passing interest: it is written in rhymed octosyllabics, favorite measure of the mature Whittier, and in its way it is autobiographical, like many of his later writings. First and last, these were virtually a "song of myself," and they constituted Whittier's diary. Like his quietistic forebears, who appear to have left no written records whatever, he did not have the diarist's habit of mind. He attempted a journal only once, on his mother's suggestion and in a notebook fashioned by her out of foolscap. Greenleaf made just one entry.[3]

From his matter-of-fact father, product of three generations of Yankee yeomen, Whittier probably received scant encouragement in his literary tendencies. Greenleaf, too, would be a farmer, his father doubtless assumed. Uncle Moses would more likely have understood and sympathized with Greenleaf's literary endeavors; but Uncle Moses was killed by the fall of a tree which he was cutting down, on January 23, 1824. This was the first death in the boy's family circle, and for him it was a serious loss. However, Whittier's mother approved of his course, despite the Quakers' ban upon poetry, and his sister Mary actively abetted his versifying.[4]

This was at best tentative and awkward although, even without criticism, Whittier had progressed measurably by 1823. He had left doggerel behind and was now embarked upon his prolonged period of imitation — imitation less of word or phrase than of style and subject and atmosphere. Now and for a decade, Whittier dwelt with all too much of Byronic melancholy upon the transiency of life, counterpoised by the benediction of lasting friendship.

Inevitably bookish and derivative as the burden of his early writing was, there was yet something of his own personality and place at its core. The play of a developing talent between literary and native materials is shown clearly in a group of unpublished manuscript verses.[5] "The Martyr" told the story of the Quaker William Leddra's execution at Boston in 1659 for returning from banishment by the Puritans. To the story of Canute and the ocean, Whittier added a moral tag. "Lafayette" praised the French nobleman for having fought and bled in the American Revolution, and "Montgomery's Return" sounded a patriotic tocsin for one "who a tyrants encroachments so nobly prevented." Together these two poems looked forward to Whittier's frank admiration, in later years, of General "Chinese" Gordon — admiration tempered by regret for the means he employed. For Whittier, as a Quaker, always disapproved of war, a fact of which "The Wounded Soldier," dated June, 1824, was perhaps the earliest record.

That poem of ninety-two lines was heavily charged with sentimentalism. So, too, was "The Brothers," dated October, 1825, and written in blank verse. One of the longest poems attempted by the youthful Whittier, this was a curious composition, containing among its 166 lines hints of Milton and suggestions in theme and treatment of Wordsworth's "Michael." Twenty of the lines prefigured interestingly the vision of God in nature to which Whittier in 1876 gave choice expression in "Sunset on the Bearcamp."

Under equally obvious influence, Whittier sounded the romantics' praise of the poet in "To the Memory of Chatterton, Who Died Aged 17" — probably Whittier's own age when he wrote the poem. The twenty-four lines were extremely sentimental, but chiefly notable was the complaint, in the third stanza, which Whittier was soon to voice for himself:

> But ill thy haughty soul could bear
> To meet disdain and cold neglect
> To see those hopes which promis'd fair
> So early by misfortune check'd [.]

Still more significant was Whittier's first appreciation of Byron. This manly tribute, not too much marred by the wholly moral considerations which determined Whittier's final rejection of the apostle of freedom whom Goethe called the greatest talent of the century, was contained in an extract of a "New years Address" written on December 31, 1824. It could be wished that Whittier had left this judgment final:

One bright, bold star has fallen on thy coast
  Byron, renown'd on Albions classic page
A master spirit of the times, the boast
  The pride, the shame, the wonder of his age [.]
But peace to him, let deep oblivion shade
  The memory of his wanderings, for there was
A spirit in him which has oft display'd
  Its pure devotion to the sacred cause
Of freedom; let this serve to palliate
  His numerous errors, for the generous mind
That mourns the loss of genius mourns the fate
  Of him whose haughty form is now reclin'd
Where Pindus lifts itself.[6]

In his interest in the remote, it will be seen, Whittier was always a romantic but never a traveler. His inherited feeling for place, plus Burns' example, taught him to look for poetic subjects in life and nature close at hand. In "To Nahant," for example, Whittier delighted in the physical charm and the contemporary fame of the Essex County seashore resort, which later was much frequented by celebrated New Englanders.[7] These lines were dated August 20, 1825.

Somewhat earlier, in his first rhyming period, Whittier had written the poem "Superstition," which clearly was based upon the eery beliefs then still current in rural New England. Also at about this time Whittier penned "The Midnight Scene (A tradition from the banks of the Merrimac)," a prophecy of the *Legends of New England* which he brought together, in 1831, in his first published volume.

In the train of these and other snatches of verse — "the work of intervals, a ploughboy's lore," [8] written oftentimes by hearthlight when the day's work was done — two years brought to Whittier some increase of facility. There was wanting only an audience to encourage the eighteen-year-old boy's rhetorical efforts, and by a play of favorable circumstance it came to him through William Lloyd Garrison, who crossed his path now for the first time. Garrison was only two years older than Whittier, but he had been better favored in his early education, in relatively populous Newburyport, and he had early learned the printing trade. On March 16, 1826, he acquired the year-old *Essex Courant* and renamed it the *Newburyport Free Press.* Garrison at once gave the newspaper a humanitarian character, and won as a subscriber John Whittier.[9]

An important part of the newspaper of that day was its poetical column. Garrison promptly filled his with verse by the reigning favorites, people now mostly forgotten, who included Bernard Barton, Felicia Hemans, Letitia E. Landon, James Montgomery, John Pierpont, Lydia H. Sigourney, and Nathaniel Parker Willis. On their verse, no rich pabulum, the popular taste of the day was nourished.[10] Whittier was merely like his fellows in approving the sentimentalism which made Mrs. Hemans probably the most popular writer whose verses appeared in the American newspapers of that time. Certainly Garrison thought well of her; in the *Free Press* of May 4, 1826, he called her "this wonderful and extraordinary woman." Of this sentiment there was an echo in Whittier's reference, in the *Haverhill Gazette* of March 1, 1828, to "the gifted Felicia Hemans."

It was with such models before him in 1825–26 that Whittier practised assiduously the arts of imitation. Mary Whittier rightly believed that his outpourings were as publishable as the effusions which Garrison and other editors were currently printing as poetry. From among Greenleaf's productions she therefore selected, as most likely to be accepted, "The Exile's Departure." He had written it in 1825, but she posted it to Garrison with the date "Haverhill, June 1, 1826" and with the signature "W." [11]

Garrison was glad enough to have new talent drop free into his copy basket. In the issue of June 8 he published Whittier's poem of thirty-two lines, and he said in editorial appreciation, "If 'W.' at Haverhill, will continue to favor us with pieces, beautiful as the one inserted in our poetical department of today, we shall esteem it a favor." Whittier, who had known nothing of Mary's action, was confounded with pleasure when he saw a copy of the weekly, with his verses placed above both Byron's "To Thyrza" and an excerpt from Mrs. Hemans' work.[12]

For Whittier, of course, Garrison's request amounted to a deal. Here was Greenleaf's opportunity to be heard, and he met it better than half way. Sixteen more of his poems appeared in the columns of the *Free Press* during the remainder of 1826, nine of them in unbroken weekly succession during July and August. Whittier's first response to Garrison's invitation was "The Deity," written in 1825, which the *Free Press* published on June 22. It was based on I Kings, xix, 11–12, and was the first in the long series of poems published by the youthful Whittier on biblical themes. Garrison now gave him even stronger encouragement: "The author of the following graphic sketch (which would do credit to riper years) is a youth of only *sixteen*,[13] who, we think, bids fair to prove another *Bernard Barton*, of whose persuasion he is. His poetry bears the stamp of true poetic genius, which, if carefully cultivated, will rank him among the bards of his country." [14]

Garrison did more. Directed by the postrider, he drove, in company with a woman friend, the fourteen miles from Newburyport to the Whittiers' rural retreat. His visit was not unwelcome flattery to Greenleaf, and yet was an embarrassment. Garrison was himself just past twenty years of age, but he had polish and presence; Whittier, at their first meeting, had neither. He was burrowing for eggs under the barn when his sister Mary summoned him to meet his visitors from the city. Despite a quick — and unlucky — change of clothing, he was saved from extreme uneasiness only by Garrison's ready social tact.[15]

In person, Garrison now enlarged upon his belief expressed in the *Free Press*, that Whittier's gift deserved the discipline of a formal education. What the future reformer discovered by this visit he related later, on April 11, 1828, in the *National Philanthropist*.

> He indulged his propensity for rhyming with so much secrecy, (as his father informed us,) that it was only by removing some rubbish in the garret, where he had concealed his manuscripts, that the discovery was made. This bent of his mind was discouraged by his parents: they were in indigent circumstances, and unable to give him a suitable education, and they did not wish to inspire him with hopes which might never be fulfilled. . . . We endeavored to speak cheeringly of the prospects of their son; we dwelt upon the impolicy of warring against nature . . . — and we spoke too of fame — "Sir," replied the father with an emotion which went home to our bosom like an electric shock, "poetry will not give him *bread*." [16]

It is true that the Whittiers' financial position held no promise of a college education for Greenleaf, yet he himself wrote Garrison in 1859 that his father had not opposed his destined course — had in fact been proud of his verses. His mother, evidently, always encouraged Greenleaf.[17]

At any rate, Garrison's visit brought Whittier no immediate relief from the dull tyranny of farm work. Greenleaf nevertheless continued as before to read and write, mainly with a romantic eye for the remote or the adventurous. Likewise he shaped Quaker beliefs and history into verse. He deplored the Crusaders; they served not Christ but earthly pride. In contrast, he inscribed two paeans of praise to William Penn for his idealism and his fair dealing with the Indians. "To the Memory of David Sands" was Whittier's encomium to another Quaker messenger of peace.[18] And since most of what Whittier then wrote was a calm distillation of his reading, he praised equally the power of memory itself. In his lines —

> . . . Memory can lead
> The harass'd mind back to the scenes it lov'd
> In years departed; . . .

there was a plain forecast of *Snow-Bound*, written in 1865 out of a mind harassed by the death of Elizabeth Whittier in the previous year; and the conclusion of the poem prefigured the Chaucerian portrait-painting of Whittier's family in his New England idyll:

> Fancy can bring th' enchanting vision near,
> The sister's playful smile, the brother's laugh,
> The mother's anxious look, the father's tale
> Of other days, and all the dear delights
> Felt by youth's hopeful bosom, when the tho't
> Of evil hours, and manhood's wasting cares,
> No blight has flung upon the spring of Hope.[19]

Life itself, its meaning and end, equally engaged Whittier's early meditations. The poet Gray taught him something of the transiency of human affairs. The beliefs of the Friends settled Whittier's conviction that the world's philosophy of "getting ahead" was a sham; that position without honor was a false aim.[20] And Whittier now became convinced that life without liberty is without meaning. In "The Emerald Isle," a sonorous appreciation of Ireland's one-time greatness and a lament for her fallen state, he trumpeted a Quaker's love of freedom.[21]

For Byron's daring, dash, and grandiosity Whittier had no liking, but for his championship of liberty, the utmost admiration. When Whittier was just outgrowing his style of farmer boy, Byron, then two years in his grave, strongly influenced American literary thought. Inevitably Whittier read and seemingly reread him, and in "Byron. Written after a perusal of his works," the young Quaker balanced the "living fire" of Byron's "never-dying strain," along with his "soul-enchanting lays to beauty's power," over against the "detested vice" which soured "his tuneful numbers." Whittier ended with this characteristic tribute to Byron:

> Farewell departed minstrel,
> Where'er is freedom's clime,
> There shall thy laurels be preserv'd,
> And greener grow with time.[22]

# 2

At the end of 1826 Whittier lost one sounding board and gained another. When Garrison removed to Boston and the *Newburyport Free Press* was suspended, Whittier placed his wares on the home market. During January, 1827, the *Haverhill Gazette & Essex Patriot* published four of his poems, two of which were plagiarized in a Philadelphia magazine later that year. "Ocean" was in fact widely copied by the press of the country. Within the year, thanks to this free circulation, Whittier came to have a measure of poetical reputation.

He was known, in the first place, as a shoemaker poet. It appears that he had already determined to earn his way through Haverhill Academy, for the editor of the *Gazette*, in printing "Ocean" and "Micah" on January 13, described him as "an Apprentice to the Shoemaking business." From a hired man on the farm Whittier had learned the not uncommon winter trade of making a simple type of women's slipper which was sold at retail for twenty-five cents a pair. Of this sum the craftsman received eight cents. During the winter of 1826–27 Whittier saved enough money from his earnings to pay for a term of six months at the Academy.[23]

It was Whittier's misfortune that some well-to-do Friend did not, in accordance with a general precept of the Society, take a special interest in his education.[24] A kind fate might have sent him to the Moses Brown School, which the Quakers reopened in 1819 at Providence. Nevertheless, Whittier had good fortune of a kind in the opportune opening of Haverhill Academy in 1827.[25]

If there had remained any lingering doubt of Whittier's attending the Academy, Abijah Wyman Thayer[26] removed it by urging upon John Whittier, as Garrison had done, a classical education for the young poet. Thayer was one of the several able men who touched Greenleaf's life significantly. He became editor and publisher of the *Haverhill Gazette*[27] in February, 1827, and gratefully printed the poems which came in a flood from Whittier's pen. Thayer had indeed such an extravagantly high opinion of Greenleaf's verses that his enthusiasm must have had some weight with John Whittier. He, then in his sixty-seventh year, at length saw reason in Greenleaf's having the rudiments of a classical education. The boy's injury, two years previously, made it unlikely that he would ever be able to manage the heavy work of the farm, which had already undermined his constitution. To the Academy, then, it was agreed that Greenleaf should go, when it was opened in May.[28]

Whittier was now aflame with ambition. "Few guessed beneath his aspect grave," as he wrote, "what passions strove in chains." Fame he would have, and that quickly. He sought it by means of quantity production — and in the ripeness of years he rued this boyish rush into print. In subject and manner his youthful bagatelles were almost wholly conventional; they had in them almost no music; they were subjected to little revision, and they had almost none of the mature Whittier's felicitous touch. Hard schooling alone gave him that.

During 1827 fifty of Whittier's poems were published for the first time, in the *Haverhill Gazette*, and he achieved also the dignity of his first publication in Boston. Nathaniel Greene appropriated for the *Boston Statesman* from May to July three of "W.'s" poems which appeared in the *Gazette*. So encouraged, Whittier sent to Greene a manuscript which was published in the *Statesman* of July 19. N. P. Willis, whom Whittier seemed then to read with the most respectful attention, was co-editor of the *Recorder and Telegraph* in 1827, and on August 17 he published Whittier's poem "Loneliness." All this writing betokened a prodigious industry, which won for Whittier much untempered praise.

However slender these accomplishments were, the publicity given to Whittier in the newspaper press of the country had sent echoes of his reputation back to Haverhill, with the result that he was hailed as a prodigy when he finally entered the Academy. Here he was, after perhaps a dozen years' attendance at the district school, entering at the age of nearly twenty upon what would roughly correspond to a freshman course in a high school of today. For him the day was significant indeed, and it was no less memorable for Haverhill. Whittier for the first and last time entered the "grove of Academe," where he was to study for half of 1827 and half of 1828.

The manner of his entrance recalled the good estate of poets in ancient times, for he and Robert Dinsmoor, an aged Scottish rhymester of Windham, New Hampshire, had been appointed to march together at the head of Haverhill's academic procession, with which the dedicatory exercises were begun. Both had been requested to write poems for the occasion of April 30, 1827, and Whittier carried off his part with honor. Yet his ode, "Hail, Star of Science!" addressed to the eternal spirit in the Greek sense, was somewhat incongruously styled after the rhetorical Moore. A Haverhill man sang the aspiring three verses to the air, "Pillar of Glory." [29]

# 3

A bashful youth, made perhaps the more self-conscious by his Quaker dress, Whittier nevertheless quickly won his place, both with fellow students and with faculty. Twice previously he had come under the tutelage of able Dartmouth men, and here he met another graduate of that college, Oliver Carlton.[30] At the Academy, moreover, Whittier for the first time knew students from other localities. Sixteen of the one hundred students came from outside of Massachusetts — twelve from New Hampshire, two from Louisiana, and one each from Maine and New York — and a faint air of cosmopolitanism was imparted to the school by the seven who were enrolled from Boston.[31]

As his mother had requested, Whittier was enabled to live with the Thayers, to whose son, Professor James B. Thayer, he wrote in 1877: "I never think of thy mother without feelings of love and gratitude. She and thy father were my best friends in the hard struggle of my school-days." [32] Every Friday night Whittier walked home to spend the week end with his family. But he was not forgotten by his schoolmates, then or later. Mrs. Thayer, too, retained a clear remembrance of his schoolboy character: of his impeccable appearance, "the liveliness of his temper, his ready wit, his perfect courtesy and infallible sense of truth and justice." Whittier's character, along with his poetic reputation, made him socially sought after, and the youthful gatherings counted heavily upon his presence — especially at the teas over which young belles of school and village presided.[33]

Easily the clearest contemporary picture of Whittier during and just after his Academy days was that drawn by Harriet Minot Pitman, who wrote in part:

> . . . He was tall, slight, and very erect; a bashful youth, but *never awkward*, my mother said, who was a better judge than I of such matters.
>
> He went to school awhile at Haverhill Academy. There were pupils of all ages, from ten to twenty-five. My brother, George Minot, then about ten years old, used to say that Whittier was the best of all the big fellows, and he was in the habit of calling him "Uncle Toby." Whittier was always kind to children, and under a very grave and quiet exterior there was a real love of fun, and a keen sense of the ludicrous.

In society he was embarrassed, and his manners were, in consequence, sometimes brusque and cold. With intimate friends he talked a great deal, and in a wonderfully interesting manner; usually earnest, often analytical, and frequently playful. He had a great deal of wit. It was a family characteristic. The study of human nature was very interesting to him, and his insight was keen. He liked to draw out his young friends, and to suggest puzzling doubts and queries.

When a wrong was to be righted, or an evil to be remedied, he was readier to act than any young man I ever knew, and was very wise in his action, — shrewd, sensible, practical. The influence of his Quaker bringing-up was manifest. I think it was always his endeavor

"To render less
The sum of human wretchedness." [34]

This, I say, was his steadfast endeavor, in spite of an inborn love of teasing. He was very modest, never conceited, never egotistic.

One could never flatter him. I never tried, but I have seen people attempt it, and it was a signal failure. He did not flatter, but told very wholesome and unpalatable truths, yet in a way to spare one's self-love by admitting a doubt whether he was in earnest or in jest.

The great questions of Calvinism were subjects of which he often talked in those early days. He was exceedingly conscientious. He cared for people — quite as much for the plainest and most uncultivated, if they were original and had something in them, as for the most polished.

He was much interested in politics, and thoroughly posted. I remember, in one of his first calls at our house, being surprised at his conversation with my father [Judge Stephen Minot] upon Governor Gerry and the Gerry-mandering of the State, or the attempt to do it, of which I had until then been wholly ignorant.

He had a retentive memory and a marvellous store of information on many subjects. I once saw a little commonplace book of his, — full of quaint things, and as interesting as Southey's.

. . . . . . . . . . . . . .

I have said nothing of Whittier in his relations to women. There was never a particle of coxcombry about him. He was delicate and chivalrous, but paid few of the little attentions common in society. If a girl dropped her glove or handkerchief in his presence, she had to pick it up again, especially if she did it on purpose. * * * [35]

Whittier's eyes, if they probably were not blinded by the richness of the Academy's offerings, were yet filled with new visions. As it turned out, his choice rested not upon the Classical department but upon the English. For instruction in its several branches during each of his two periods of twenty-six weeks at the Academy he paid eight dollars, and four dollars additional for lessons in French. Likewise he gave himself practical lessons, of lasting benefit, in bookkeeping. At the end of his first six months of study he had left in his pocket precisely the twenty-five cents upon which he had calculated, after having prepared in advance an exact budget of every allowable expense. This lesson was useful to Whittier long after his school days were past. Until 1866 his income in no year was much more than five hundred dollars, but he was never seriously in debt.[36]

Scholastically, Whittier's benefits came from composing in prose, under criticism, and in wider reading. This, it appears from his current writings, was mainly in history and literature. His first "theme" was read incredulously by Carlton, but succeeding compositions convinced the twenty-six-year-old master of the ability of his nearly twenty-year-old student, and soon established a friendly and equal plane between the two.[37] This relationship seems to have typified others which Whittier now enjoyed in the village, where —

> . . . homes of wealth and beauty, wit and mirth,
> By taste refined, by eloquence and worth,
> Taught and diffused the intellect's high joy,
> And gladly welcomed e'en a rustic boy.[38]

Whittier thus had access to the few private libraries in Haverhill, and, above all, to James Gale's circulating library. Of this windfall Whittier later wrote: ". . . it was the opening of a new world of enjoyment to me. I can still remember the feeling of mingled awe and pleasure with which I gazed for the first time on his crowded bookshelves." [39]

One other profit Whittier derived from attending the Academy: an acquaintance with young ladies from outside his own family. As it happened, the males at the Academy were outnumbered three to two by the females; and to at least two of these Whittier, as a sensitive human being, was quite naturally attracted. In a letter of about 1840 he stated precisely what his cousin Mary Emerson Smith meant to him:

For myself, I owe much to the kind encouragement of female friends.

A bashful, ignorant boy, I was favored by the kindness of a lady who saw, or thought she saw, beneath the clownish exterior something which gave promise of intellect and worth. The powers of my own mind, the mysteries of my own spirit, were revealed to myself, only as they were called out by one of those dangerous relations called cousins, who, with all her boarding-school glories upon her, condescended to smile upon my rustic simplicity. She was so learned in the to me more than occult mysteries of verbs and nouns, and philosophy, and botany, and mineralogy, and French, and all that, and then she had seen something of society, and could talk (an accomplishment at that time to which I could lay no claim), that on the whole I looked upon her as a being to obtain whose good opinion no effort could be too great. I smile at this sometimes, — this feeling of my unsophisticated boyhood, — yet to a great degree it is still with me.[40]

Whittier had known his cousin before Academy days, at the Haverhill home of her grandfather, Captain Nehemiah Emerson. He, who had been an officer in Washington's army at Valley Forge and at Saratoga, married a cousin of Whittier's father. Greenleaf called her "Aunt Mary," and for a while, in his 'teens, he lived at her house while attending school. Mary Emerson Smith as a young girl passed much of her time at her grandparents' home,[41] and she was the "beautiful and happy girl" of "Memories," which Greenleaf wrote in 1841.

Differences alike of creed and of station would have prevented any stronger attachment between them than friendship, as Whittier clearly recognized.[42] Besides, he was still a minor when he left the Academy in 1828, and early marriage would have clashed both with his family's tradition and his own financial prudence. He measured clearly, however, the depth of his boyhood affection by placing "Memories" first among "Poems Subjective and Reminiscent" in his collected writings. Like any normal boy he may have been an "enraptured young noodle," but he was always a person of deep, unselfish, and lasting affections.[43] Their friendship did not end with his cousin's marriage to a Covington, Kentucky, judge. In her widowhood, late in life, Mrs. Thomas spent the summer months in New England, and she occasionally saw Whittier in the White Mountains. To the end of his days they enjoyed a friendly correspondence.[44]

Evelina Bray,[45] of Marblehead, was Whittier's other special favorite among the young ladies of the Academy, and with her also he formed an enduring friendship. She attended the Academy with Whittier only in 1828, and afterward they met seldom. Fate had set them, also, on divergent roads; the two were of different faiths, and she was, relatively, a social aristocrat. To have married any one "out of meeting" would have led to Whittier's disownment as a Friend — and that would have been intolerable to him.[46]

None the less, after Academy days Whittier maintained communication with Evelina. In the early summer of 1829, while editing the *American Manufacturer* in Boston, he attended with his mother a Quarterly Meeting of the Friends, in Salem. Before breakfast one morning he walked the two or three miles to Marblehead, and called on Evelina. She could not so early in the day receive him in the house, so they walked to the old fort, then in ruins, and sat looking out over the harbor,[47] reputed birthplace of the United States Navy. As his habit was, Whittier banked this incident in his memory. In 1874 he described the meeting in the first three stanzas of the song in "A Sea Dream." [48]

In February, 1839, Whittier posted to Evelina a book of his poems, probably a copy of the 1838 edition, and with maidenly reticence she acknowledged it on May 1, 1840.[49] About 1849 she became the wife of an English evangelist, William Downey, and a widow in 1889, three years before Whittier died. She corresponded with him occasionally, and at his suggestion she attended the reunion of his Academy classmates at Haverhill in 1885.[50]

## 4

The realization that by the world's standard he was not "eligible" was undoubtedly wormwood to a sensitive youth already well aware of his intrinsic worth; but Whittier's experience with these young ladies filled a gap, which he acknowledged, in his upbringing. If there followed now a period of brooding, Whittier, like any other youth becoming adjusted to life, was naturally destined to go through it. As late as 1832 this mood seems to have been intermittently upon him, but Whittier's religion and inner strength saved him from any danger of wasting in despair. Besides, there was work to be done, and it soon beguiled away what melancholy Whittier may honestly have felt.

His religion was unquestionably one of the stays of Whittier's life, if not the chief one. On February 3, three months before entering the Academy, he contributed a prose article, "Sacred Music," to the *Haverhill Gazette*, and stated a strictly Quaker position from which he never retreated. The subject of sacred music was in controversy in 1827, for Governor Levi Lincoln of Massachusetts had refused to sign an act incorporating the Mozart Association, which he considered merely one more useless organization.[51] In contrast, Whittier objected to sacred music almost wholly on religious grounds.

Whittier was very proud to be a Quaker, but sensitive to the world's ridicule of his "peculiar people" for their nonconformity in dress. Yet he adhered steadfastly all his life to eighteenth-century Quaker drab and cut; most New England Friends abandoned it. As Carlyle in 1833–34 specifically lauded George Fox's simplicity of dress, in *Sartor Resartus*, so Whittier in 1827 championed the typical Friend:

> Beware my good friend and revile not too rashly
> A person you know not, because of his dress;
> For, believe me, the man you have pictur'd so harshly,
> Does many a noble endowment possess.
>
> True, he has not deck'd out his humble exterior
> In those fast varying fashions, of vanity born —
> To such idle allurements his heart is superior;
> 'Tis his mind, not his person, he seeks to adorn.[52]

Often in his later work Whittier sounded this chord — in poems such as "Cassandra Southwick," "The Exiles," "The King's Missive," "The Meeting," "The Old South," and "The Quaker Alumni."

Seeds of another of Whittier's lifelong interests showed close to the surface of his 1827 output. He lyricized freedom romantically in "The Switzer's Song," based upon the bloodless revolution of 1306 which relieved Switzerland of the Austrian yoke; and he championed liberty in "Montezuma," which seared Cortez for having pretended to advance the cause of religion by his military barbarity.[53]

In addition to these inherited strains, Whittier's reading at the Academy was echoed in his contemporary verses. He read "Paradise Lost" with immediate and lasting appreciation, and took Milton's moral kingdom to be his own.[54] On the other hand, he seems to have considered Spenser's arena of moral knighthood as alien territory. In "Proem"[55] he later wrote that "I love . . . the songs of Spenser's golden days," but he seldom manifested this love. For Chaucer, unfortunately, Whittier cared little. Byron continued to fascinate and to perplex him,[56] while stimulating him to train one of the best gifts of his later writing: that of recreating distant places in his imagination. In time this talent became — almost — a compensation for his inability to travel.

Significantly, Whittier's interest in his native scene survived all the press of new enthusiasms growing out of the opportunities for wider reading which the Academy provided. With a faint promise of his future narrative skill, he told the story of a young Indian who scoffed at the tribal tradition that supernatural beings resided in the White Mountains, and lost his life in a storm conjured up by "spectral forms" which "stood above the rushing mountain flood." Whittier experimented further with native material in "The Pawnee Brave," which exhibited a marked increase in narrative skill.[57]

Beyond his reading, the social climate of the day also helped to bring Whittier's young talent to the budding stage. There were already stirring, in the nation, currents which soon eddied around Whittier and which he was later to help direct in their courses. On July 4, 1827, slavery was abolished in New York State, as it had already been regulated elsewhere.[58] Moreover, the anti-aristocratic forces which contributed to the election of Andrew Jackson as President in 1828 were already reflected in the newspapers of the day. As a Quaker and a Jeffersonian Democrat by birthright, Whittier had a natural alliance with these forces, and in two poems of 1827 he made clear his sympathy with them.[59]

Only one break occurred during 1827 in Whittier's intensive program of education and writing, and the occasion of it was his trip to Boston.[60] Harriet Beecher Stowe has described the fervor of mind with which a rural New Englander of that day made his first trip to the metropolis,[61] and into the pattern of that picture the known facts of Whittier's first visit to Boston fit well. On Whittier's part there were distinctive preparations; he was groomed by all the sartorial resources of his family. His new homespun suit of clothes was equipped with "boughten buttons," which the boyish Whittier conceived as measuring the difference between urban and rural dress. In addition, Aunt Mercy made for him, out of pasteboard, a broad-brim Quaker hat covered with drab velvet. Finally, in good Quaker style,[62] Whittier's mother gave him moral preparation for the journey by advising him strongly against attending the theater.

On the six-hour trip from Haverhill to Boston, Whittier rode in a stage-coach for probably the first time. He went to the city on the invitation of Mrs. Nathaniel Greene, who occasionally visited the Whittiers in East Haverhill. In 1827 Nathaniel Greene was postmaster of Boston and editor of the *American* (later the *Boston*) *Statesman*, forerunner of the *Boston Post* of today. He knew of the young poet's work, and during the year he published in the *Statesman* four of his poems.

Whittier slipped unnoticed into Boston, then a busy commercial city of nearly sixty thousand inhabitants. Through the confusing maze of streets he found his way alone to the Greenes' home, probably at 65 Congress Street, and there he was affectionately received. He promised to return for tea, and then, with characteristic independence, set forth to do his own exploring.

> "I wandered up and down the streets," he used to say. "Somehow it wasn't just what I expected, and the crowd was worse and worse after I got into Washington Street; and when I got tired of being jostled, it seemed to me as if the folks might get by if I waited a little while. Some of them looked at me, and so I stepped into an alleyway and waited and looked out. Sometimes there didn't seem to be so many passing, and I thought of starting, and then they'd begin again. 'Twas a terrible stream of people to me. I began to think my new clothes and the buttons were all thrown away. I stayed there a good while." (This was said with great amusement.) "I began to be homesick. I thought it made no difference at all about my having those boughten buttons." [63]

This excursion was disappointing, but at tea time Whittier had his reward. Among Mrs. Greene's guests whom he had been invited to meet there were several gay and friendly ladies who appear to have found, beneath his quaint Friend's garb, the quick wit and drollery which his handsome eyes must have betrayed. Whittier's apparent favorite among these ladies, eager to contribute to the pleasure of such an engaging youth's first visit to Boston, invited him to attend the theater that evening. She was herself the leading player of the company appearing there.

Poor Whittier's conflict of emotions may be easily imagined. Here was feminine company of the pleasantest, and it bore no marks of the wickedness imputed to stage-players by the Puritans and the Quakers. Moreover, Whittier had a natural affinity for the company of attractive women. Yet as always his Quaker scruples prevailed over his emotions of delight.

That night an uneasy spirit, aggravated by homesickness, hindered his sleep and decided him to return to Haverhill the next morning. His projected visit of one week had lasted one day. Of his encounter with the actress he spoke no word to his surprised family. Neither, in all probability, did he mention the copy of Shakespeare which he had bought.[64]

## 5

References to this book soon appeared in Whittier's writing, although from November 19, 1827, he was for twelve weeks chiefly occupied with books of another kind. Into this period was crowded his only experience of schoolteaching, an occupation which gave him no pleasure but which enabled him to attend Haverhill Academy for six months more. The committee of three men appointed to engage a master for School District Five in West Amesbury (now Merrimac) desired in him only neat handwriting. Whittier's fine eighteenth-century script won him the position, although he distrusted his general qualifications for the post.[65]

Once he had assumed the rôle of tutor, Whittier's training in mathematical subjects at the Academy did him good service, for the larger boys in the school plagued him with puzzles in "figures." He solved these, in his conscientious way, but only at the cost of sleepless nights. To this general experience he later alluded, as editor of the *New England Weekly Review*,[66] by writing of his friend Frederick A. P. Barnard's *New Treatise on Arithmetic:* "The confusion of ideas resulting from the use of technical terms before the pupil is capable of comprehending them, has been judiciously guarded against, in this treatise." Nevertheless, Whittier's patience survived twelve weeks of teaching, and in February he was paid forty-five dollars for his labors.[67]

While he was in Merrimac, Whittier lost none of his interest in Haverhill and its affairs. His concern was, in fact, so lively as to lead to the familiarity of unwonted satire, and to embarrassment. On January 5, 1828, his "New Year's Address to the Patrons of the Essex Gazette" appeared in that newspaper.[68] To the extent of thirty-five stanzas, without the benefit of a light touch, Whittier satirized the civic foibles of Haverhill. He even rallied himself for having pictured the Indians "with the glowing fancy of a poet." When a tribe of them in their birch canoes, he said, visited Haverhill in the autumn of 1827,

> I went, and saw them, all alive and real,
> And the plain truth destroy'd my *beau ideal*.

For one rollicking moment he ceased being the sweet singer of native songs, the reverent versifier of biblical tales. For his materials he went directly to life, and it taught him a practical lesson — one which he later chose to forget when he dedicated himself to the cause of abolition.

> An unlucky New Year's Address [he wrote to Doctor Weld on March 5, 1828] publish'd in the Ess. Gaz. has call'd down upon me the anathemas of some half a dozen, who *felt* that they or their follies were alluded to. I have learn'd, however, that it is an unthankful task to lash vice and prejudice. . . .

This experience, useful to Whittier, opened a second full year of intensive writing which further disciplined his mind and his hand. Nothing which he then wrote had any other value. Yet amid the ephemeral interests bred by his avid reading there were prefigurings of Whittier the reformer. On January 19, 1828, for instance, he contributed to the *Haverhill Gazette* a poem, "The Drunkard to His Bottle," which he wrote in Scottish dialect. In the Society of Friends Whittier had long heard testimonies against the use of intoxicating spirits, but in A. W. Thayer he met a militant moralist who had the means to oppose them publicly. Under his editorship the *Gazette* was reputedly the first political newspaper in the United States, and the second periodical anywhere, to advocate total abstinence from intoxicating liquors.[69]

When in 1827 the movement for temperance in Haverhill was started, there were between twenty and thirty places in the village of fewer than four thousand people where liquor was sold. It was served at funerals as well as at marriages, farmers and mechanics drank it at work, and not uncommonly it was tendered as a gift to clergymen. In courageously leading the movement for temperance in Haverhill, Thayer suffered temporary misfortune. His bearing was perhaps exemplary for young Whittier. His convictions only deepened by opposition, Thayer held resolutely to his course, and remained long enough in Haverhill to see the village become almost tinder-dry.[70]

Whittier was undoubtedly drawn by Thayer toward prohibitionism.

From the time "The Drunkard to His Bottle" appeared, Whittier's interest in the movement developed to the extent that in 1833 he was nominated a delegate from Haverhill to the convention, at Worcester, of the Massachusetts Society for the Suppression of Intemperance.[71] From that year, however, he devoted himself almost wholly to the abolition of slavery.

The year 1828 was still too early a time for Whittier to have discovered his real interests. No theme dominated his sixty-eight or more poems published that year. He was still an author in search of his literary character; and he was still seeking an education.

To both these ends Thayer sought to help him by proposing, in the *Haverhill Gazette* of January 19, 1828, the publication of "The Poems of Adrian." The required five hundred subscriptions were not forthcoming, however, and by this fact Whittier was in two ways unfortunately affected. His formal education ended by necessity with the second term of six months which he began at Haverhill Academy at the end of April 1828, and a sense of neglect in him soon made the melancholy seem real which previously he had been simulating.

On balance, it was fortunate that "Adrian's" poems did not achieve the permanency of a collected edition. Whittier was so embarrassed by his first book, *Legends of New England* (1831), that he later bought and destroyed all discoverable copies of it.[72] In February, 1828, it sufficed that his first poem to appear within the covers of a book or under his own name found a place in *Incidental Poems, Accompanied with Letters . . .*, by Robert Dinsmoor, the "Rustic Bard."[73] The composition, which was entitled "J. G. Whittier to the 'Rustic Bard,' " was published also in the *Haverhill Gazette* of February 16.

Frustrate for the moment, Whittier still felt the whip of ambition — ambition blended of desire for literary fame and for success in love — and the melancholy resulting from its fancied thwarting begot in him great confusion of mind. Melancholy now appeared, at least, to be his governing mood, occasionally offset by a note of jocular satire. Inevitably his work improved in the wrong way. In "The Confessions of a Bachelor,"[74] an effusion of 304 lines, Whittier's stanzas lost their run and form and became "the very false gallop of verses." He seems to have been deservedly censured, for in the *Gazette* of September 13, 1828, appeared "Lines, Written on Being Told There Was Too Much of Levity in My Later Writings." This piece was a marvel of self-revelation and self-defense, and resembled nothing else that Whittier ever wrote. With defiant pride he proclaimed: "I can feel a consciousness of slumbering power."

It was, of course, no discredit to him that he did not then know what he desired in life. The passing of time was the specific needed to bring order and clarity to his thinking and to his purposes. Meanwhile, his verses were a vent — a useful and necessary one — out of which he passed the mild poisons of youthful love and ambition.

His topics he found where his reading led him. Two untitled poems based respectively on passages in Job and in Mark invite notice here.[75] The first of them ("When, like the cloud before the sun") constituted one of Whittier's earliest expressions of belief in the eternal life, and the second contained one of his first references to the Inner Light. The poem ended with this significant stanza, one of the few Quaker touches in a year of frenzied writing:

> O, thou! whose power could rule the sea,
> Extend thine influence e'en to me!
> Control my will, and lay to rest
> The stormy passions of my breast;
> Check there, each wild discordant mood,
> And grant an humble quietude,
> To list, amid earth's jarring din,
> The teachings of *thy voice within.*

Most significantly of all, in his lines "Night steals upon the world,"[76] written in blank verse, Whittier rose for a moment above mere rhyming, and caught the true accent of poetry. This poem was unquestionably one of the best which he had so far written upon nature.

But logically, in this year of intensive reading, Whittier looked less to the native scene for literary materials than he did both earlier and later. During 1828 he appears to have written only one poem of merit which had a New England background, and this, "To the Merrimack," Garrison published in the *National Philanthropist* of June 6, 1828, with the remark: "We trust that this is only the commencement of a series of favors from our esteemed friend W——. Our poetical department has been lamentably deficient in original pieces, and needs to be replenished. This invitation, however, is made to *poets*, and to only such as deserve that name."

Before the year was past, Whittier began indeed to lay some claim to the title of poet; in the last three months of 1828 his grasp seemed for the first time nearly equal to his reach. It is of note that in two poems of conservative cast — "The Times" and "The Days Gone By" [77] — he began to find himself. "And yet I love the vanished past," he confessed, and so revealed again the core of his conservatism, the will to save the best in his environment, which lay at the heart of his whole life's work.

By October, too, Whittier had gained enough confidence in his work to give it in public the seal of his own name. In the *Haverhill Gazette* of October 25, 1828, "The Outlaw" was published as "By J. G. Whittier." Thenceforth, whenever Whittier's label was on his verses, it was usually represented by his name, his initials, or by "W." Earlier in the year he had continued to be "Adrian," "Donald," or "W.," but he soon called himself also "Nehemiah," "Timothy," "Ichabod," and "Micajah."

# 6

In many directions a young experimenter in verse, Whittier was possibly even more of an experimenter in prose, of which he wrote a prodigious amount during his years of literary apprenticeship. In 1828, his voluminous output of prose bore a direct and obvious relation to his reading at the Academy.

Little concerning this period, May to November, need be related. Presumably Whittier continued the studies which he had begun in the previous year. Certainly his economic habits were the same. To help pay his Academy expenses he posted the ledgers of a Haverhill merchant.[78] His abhorrence of educational debt was, indeed, a main factor in his inability to go on to college.[79] If, however, he frequently deplored the lack of books in his youth, Whittier seems never to have regretted the want of college training. He had warm respect for self-education, and in a letter written to a youth who requested financial help toward his schooling, Whittier said:

> I am sorry for the circumstance of thy condition for I have known what it is to be without money, & to live by hard labor. But, as to education, use thy leisure in *educating thyself*. Read & study a little every day, and before thee art 20 years of age, thee will find that a school is not needed. I regret that I cannot help all who ask help, as my means are limited & I have several dependent upon me. I enclose $5.00 with good wishes.[80]

As his previous habit was, Whittier during his second term at the Academy read with a catholic taste. Primarily, he was drawn to Milton even more strongly than before, and praised him heartily in an article which the *Haverhill Gazette* published on May 24, 1828. The strong early impression became permanent, for in 1866 Whittier wrote: "Milton's prose has long been my favorite reading. My whole life has felt the influence of his writings." [81] Whittier also conceived a lasting admiration for Milton as a man, and later, in "The Training," he wrote: "Blind Milton approaches nearly to my conception of a true hero." [82] By 1828 Whittier had also formed an enduring attachment to the works of Burns, whom he praised in two brief critiques in the *Gazette*. In that weekly he likewise devoted short notices to Shakespeare and others.

Meanwhile, amid all these excitements, Whittier's Quaker heart beat quietly on. On August 9 and 30, 1828, the *Gazette* published two editorials by him on war. Whittier invoked scholarship in aid of his firm, calm arguments, and he cited ancient examples of Christian testimony against the barbarity of armed conflict.

Very different was a short introductory article, breathless with awe, which in the *Gazette* of September 27 prefaced five thousand words of translation, which Whittier had read, from Johann August Apel's *Der Freischütz; or the Magic Balls*. Another strange fancy of Whittier's was reflected in an article, "Spectral Illusions," which the *Gazette* published on November 22. This prose piece manifested Whittier's wide acquaintance with the literature of the subject.

By that time Whittier had ended his studies at the Academy. In keeping with his literary thrift he commented upon the fact in an unsigned article, "Haverhill Academy," which appeared in the *American Manufacturer* of November 28. (Garrison had already procured from his former employer, the Reverend William Collier, an offer of the editorship of the *Manufacturer*.) [83]

The year 1828 was thus pivotal in Whittier's early development. During these twelve months he rose from his position as a schoolboy to the station of a steady contributor to Boston periodicals, in both verse and prose. His pedestrian pace was beginning to quicken into a running rhythm. It is true that he had not yet found his *métier*, but signs of it, moral as well as musical, were gradually appearing in his spate of verse. This served merely, in Browning's phrase, to "arrest Soul's evanescent moods." Yet it won for Whittier intermittent praise and encouragement which he needed.

Garrison, significantly, continued to keep his helpful hand and somewhat paternal eye upon the friend two years his junior. In the *National Philanthropist* of April 11 Whittier was the subject of his long editorial, "A Word for Indigent Merit." [84] Moreover, after Garrison had relinquished the editorship of that sheet on July 4 and had gone to Bennington, he continued to be interested in Whittier. This interest was reciprocal, for when Garrison started the *Journal of the Times* Whittier "wrote him a letter commending his views upon Slavery, Intemperance and War, and assuring him that he was destined to do great things." [85] Finally, in November, Garrison provided Whittier with his first editorial opportunity, in Boston.

It is important to remember that Garrison's broadening of social interests during 1828 was in the tide of humanitarian impulses then slowly swelling in the young nation. The American Peace Society, for example, was founded in 1828. Furthermore, on July 16 of that year the *Yankee*, edited by John Neal, who was of Quaker parentage, was early in the field with a forceful editorial on "Anti-Slavery Societies." Neal argued the futility of the American Colonization Society and urged New England to busy herself with constructive measures to meet the problem of slavery, if she wished longer "to be heard in the councils of the free."

Whittier, around whom incitements to social usefulness were perceptibly on the increase, was not yet quite ready to make himself heard in those councils.

# IV

# Politics Over Poetry

WHITTIER'S FIRST EDITORIAL JOB took him into the stream of life in Boston but cast him in an inappropriate rôle. Significantly, he remained in it for only seven months. As a young man full of ambition and needing experience, Whittier decided after some hesitation to join the editorial staff of the Reverend Mr. Collier. He could, as he reasoned in a long letter of November 28, 1828, to A. W. Thayer,[1] avoid a career in shoemaking or schoolteaching and the equally repugnant possibility of acquiring debts in getting a college education. Whittier was clear-headed when he wrote Thayer:

> . . . the situation of editor of the "Philanthropist" [2] is not only respectable, but it is peculiarly pleasant to one who takes so deep an interest, as I really do, in the great cause it is laboring to promote. I would enter upon my task with a heart free from misanthropy, and glowing with that feeling that wishes well to all. I would rather have the memory of a Howard, a Wilberforce, and a Clarkson than the undying fame of Byron.

Whittier accepted Collier's offer, but became editor not of the *National Philanthropist* but of the *American Manufacturer*. This was ill luck, for it made him advocate not of a social cause in which he believed but of a political philosophy which cut directly across the main path of his life's work. Son of a father who was a Jeffersonian Democrat, Whittier was miscast as an editorial exponent of "the American System" — Hamilton's aristocratic Federalism refurbished by the Whigs and made alluring to many Americans by Henry Clay, former Jeffersonian Democrat and its chief spokesman. With Whittier, hope died hard. As late as 1837 he thought that Clay really was a friend of the common man.

## 1

Protection of its young industries became one of the nation's urgent political questions in the twenty years which followed the War of 1812. The *Manufacturer*, founded in August, 1828,[3] was a symbol of New England's belated conversion to the tariff principle. By that year, however, both the cotton and the woolen manufactures were firmly secured and their "further expansion should have been left to individual enterprise." [4]

New England thus had ample safeguards for its leading two manufactures, since the "tariff of abominations" of 1828 erected the highest wall of protection known in American history up to that time. Yet the New England States felt compelled to stand their sectional ground in a struggle of exploitation, in curious alliance with the agricultural States — New York, New Jersey, Pennsylvania, Ohio, and Kentucky — which had constituted the stronghold of the protective movement up to 1828. In search of an economic panacea they had accepted the "American System," and with it Clay. Only the rise of the textile industry had committed the six New England States to the "System." [5]

Hence as editor of the *American Manufacturer* Whittier was a special pleader for the protection of his native Yankee land's interests. A Jeffersonian Democrat he was not. He shared the view prevailing in New England that the Jackson party who won the Presidential election of 1828 were mainly an unwashed mob led by an irresponsible war lord, not the determined opponents of "an engrossing political state that enlisted its sovereign powers on the side of the longest purses." [6] In 1833 Whittier referred to Jackson as "the bloodthirsty old man at the head of our government." [7] Whittier's heart was with New England; and that was all that mattered then.

His salary of nine dollars a week much less than matched his industry, but Whittier acquitted himself scrupulously of the duties of his charge. Obviously he relished the doing of plain and hard work well. Except during the period of Whittier's editorship the short-lived weekly was a clipped sheet, edited with scissors. Whittier *wrote* most of the thirty or so issues which carried his name as editor, and he also read the exchanges assiduously in the hunt for interesting material. In another sense he was married to his job; he lived in Mr. Collier's home, 30 Federal Street, very near the office, which was in Merchants Hall, located at the corner of Water and Congress Streets.[8] From there the *Manufacturer* made its appearance every Thursday morning.

In Boston at that time there were at least seven daily newspapers, and Whittier's study of them gave him the best editorial schooling which he had yet received. Nathan Hale, nephew of the famous Revolutionary spy and editor and publisher of the *Boston Daily Advertiser*, was very active in politics and public affairs. From 1817 to 1828 Joseph T. Buckingham had edited the witty and caustic *New England Galaxy*, and from 1824 to 1848 he conducted the *Boston Courier* as the leading Boston proponent of protectionism. From 1831 to 1834 he was to publish the *New England Magazine*, and in it eleven contributions from Whittier. Toward the end of 1828 Benjamin Russell had retired from newspaper work, although the politically conservative *Columbian Centinel* remained what he had made it, one of the best-informed news organs in the New England metropolis. Henry Ingraham Blake, "father of American reporting," had made the marine news of the *Palladium* first in its field. In a word, Whittier had entered a strongly competitive business not devoid of talent and ability.[9]

His start on his career attracted more notice elsewhere than in Boston. On January 3, 1829, Thayer indicated his very high opinion of Whittier's abilities by wishing him success as editor of both the *Manufacturer* and the *Philanthropist*.[10] Garrison, on January 9 in the Bennington *Journal of the Times*, feigned surprise that a poet had turned editor, but predicted that "he will unquestionably make the American Manufacturer a valuable paper." A week later, as illustration, Garrison reprinted from the January 1 issue of the *Manufacturer* Whittier's editorial on war. On January 14 the *Philadelphia Album* reported that "*F. G. Whittier*, the young poet of Haverhill, to whom we have frequently and favourably alluded, is as we anticipated elevated to the editorial ranks. . . ." Most significantly of all, George D. Prentice, who as editor of the *New England Weekly Review* in Hartford had for some time been watching Whittier, wrote on January 19:

> Mr. J. G. Whittier, well known for his beautiful poetry under the signature of "W.," has taken the editorial department of the "*American Manufacturer*," a weekly paper published in Boston. Mr. Whittier has

> received so much applause from others, that he scarce needs a good word from us — nevertheless, we will say of him, that his periodical is among the very best in New England. His articles are somewhat too highly polished for the contents of a weekly print — but he will learn carelessness soon enough we dare say.

Finally, on February 12, John Neal in the *Yankee and Boston Literary Gazette* remarked concerning the *Manufacturer* that it was one of the several American newspapers which had recently "dropped into the hands of avowed poets, who have wiped away the reproach that abides upon poetry, of disqualifying its followers for business; for to a man, they are remarkable for good common-sense, promptitude, and prose."

Whittier proved this true of himself in his first editorship, a whetstone upon which he sharpened his powers. In a time of personal journalism his conduct of the *Manufacturer* was highly personal. His own interests loomed large in its pages: some by now permanent and quite familiar to his audience, others arising from social and political events of the day. To these Whittier was extremely alert and responsive, and so he was to be always.

## 2

In the first place, some of his permanent interests stemmed from his Quaker heritage. Much that he wrote made it even clearer than before that he took his Quakerism, at this time, upon faith. Against war he spoke in his first and final issues, and repeatedly and with force. Earlier he had twice contributed editorials on war to the *Haverhill Gazette*.[11] In the *Manufacturer* he published two more, wrote a caustic editorial note on Ethan Allen, and on a fourth occasion he doubted the need for the Military Academy, at West Point.[12] In Whittier's judgment the United States was in no danger of war "so long as those, who hold the reins of government, act with that calmness and prudence which should characterize the civil officers of a christian republic." Here was thinly veiled distrust of Jackson, who was inaugurated on the previous day. Completely open, however, was Whittier's testimony against war in "The Burial of Abner," a long experiment in rime royal which he published in his last issue as editor of the *Manufacturer*, August 6, 1829.

It was also the Quaker in Whittier that scorned, in the *Manufacturer* of January 29, the legend of Puritan righteousness in New England. In a notice of John Neal's *Rachel Dyer*, Whittier mainly praised the author for speaking independently and fearlessly of "the crimes of the stern settlers of New-England. . . . There have been dark deeds done in New-England worthy only of the darkest ages of crime and bigotry." Here, unmistakably, was the germinal idea of "The King's Missive" (1881), in which Whittier was to censure Governor Endicott for his harsh treatment of Quakers in the Bay Colony.[13]

Opposing Calvinism, Whittier in sympathy was ranged on the side of the Unitarians who were now breaking its hold on the New England mind. In 1829 he could have met some of the Boston leaders of the movement, including two whom he certainly knew later — Emerson and William Ellery Channing, the acknowledged chief of the Unitarian liberals, who "breathed into theology a humane spirit." But they could only have confirmed his native liberalism. The ideas of God's beneficence and of man's excellence, for which the Unitarians gained acceptance only after stout contending, were inherent in Quakerism.

Viewed in the large, the religious controversy was only part of the growing liberal movement toward reform which was then stirring in New England — chiefly with regard to peace, slavery, temperance, and theology. Whittier was already in the spirit of the times.

In his Quaker objurgations against music he was less in tune. He would concede none of its charms. "Give us," he wrote, "the melody of mind — the music and the eloquence of thought." [14] In Haverhill Whittier's earlier opinions about music [15] had apparently passed unnoticed. Now Prentice, always something of a Puck, pricked him blithely for his prejudice. Whittier's youthful rejoinder could have been predicted: a thin-skinned defense ending with a tribute to the Quakers and a warning to Prentice that ". . . we can for his especial benefit divest ourself of quakerism in our paper, at least." [16]

With ease and humor Prentice spoke the final word in the exchange, in the *New England Weekly Review* of April 6. It is worth a glance, for it looked ahead to Whittier's engagement, fifteen months hence, to succeed Prentice as editor of the Hartford weekly.

BOSTON MANUFACTURER. — It is always a delight to us to open Mr. Whittier's paper. — The young Quaker is a fellow of such exquisite powers, and is so devoted to the great objects of human benevolence, that no one can long hold communion with him, without feeling, that he is one of the best specimens of human nature. His mind, too, is the home of poetry. Its tones of melody are flung upon the air as sweetly and with as little apparent effort, as those of the wind-harp, when its strings are swept by the dewy fingers of Twilight. And, having said this, we beg leave to *scold* the gentleman. . . .

In conclusion, friend Whittier, we would advise thee not to shake thy quill at us with too great a spirit of pugnacity. The pen is a carnal weapon, friend, and, if thee brandishes it too fiercely, the elders of thy sect may deem thee mad, and make thee exchange thy *round coat* for a *strait jacket*.

As a Quaker, Whittier was born with an interest in the improvement of society, and his concern with reforms then astir was repeatedly manifested in the columns of the *Manufacturer*. On February 18, 1829, for instance, he editorialized on "The Cause of Temperance." In the next week's issue he turned to slavery and flayed politicians "who have bowed down to the Southern Idols of their worship. . . ." When Whittier next mentioned slavery, on April 9, he warned that "the sword of vengeance" was hanging over the American people, and that it would fall unless they purged themselves speedily of the sin of human bondage. On July 23 his warning to his readers was that the "fatal catastrophe" impended. Even at this time, under the exaggeration which marred much of his editorial writing, could be discerned Whittier's honest conviction that America would pay for slavery at great cost in money and in misery.

Young Whittier also shared with other enlightened people the belief that imprisonment for debt was a legal anachronism. Against it he struck hard in the *Manufacturer* of July 16, 1829. He cited the report of the Prison Discipline Society that seventy-five thousand persons annually were imprisoned in the United States for debt, more than half of them for individual sums of less than twenty dollars. "These facts," declared Whittier, "are a disgrace to our country, — a sorrowful picture of our free institutions . . . an absurdity in our laws worthy only of the dark ages of barbarism." In 1835 he contributed a poem, "The Prisoner for Debt," to the *Boston Pearl*.

Whittier's interest in reform was developing along a clear line. Probably as a student at Haverhill Academy he had read Burke, and conceivably at that time he had noted in *Reflections on the Revolution in France* the great parliamentarian's ideal of "an honest reformer." [17] Whittier's own practice always conformed to this:

> There is something else than the mere alternative of absolute destruction, or unreformed existence. *Spartam nactus es; hanc exorna.* This is, in my opinion, a rule of profound sense, and ought never to depart from the mind of an honest reformer. I cannot conceive how any man can have brought himself to that pitch of presumption, to consider his country as nothing but *carte blanche*, upon which he may scribble whatever he pleases. A man full of warm speculative benevolence may wish his society otherwise constituted than he finds it; but a good patriot, and a true politician, always considers how he shall make the most of the existing materials of his country. A disposition to preserve, and an ability to improve, taken together, would be my standard of a statesman. Everything else is vulgar in the conception, perilous in the execution.

Burke appears, also, to have been one of Whittier's political mentors, as John Whittier had been. From the Quaker histories in his father's library, moreover, Whittier must have noticed the Friends' acute interest in strong and humane government. He was quite in character, in his first weeks as editor of the *Manufacturer*, in avowing himself a good Union man and a true democrat, with a pronouncement on "Our Constitution" and a series of three articles on "The Mechanic," "Mechanical Genius," and "Mechanics." [18] He decried the proposal of the *Richmond Enquirer* and other newspapers for a convention of States to amend the Constitution. With his habitual trust in establishment and in the wisdom of time, he declared that this troubled era was none to ". . . sit in judgment on the doings of our fathers . . . who . . . came together . . . to build up the temple of our liberties. . . ." [19]

As for politics itself, Whittier even at this early time was without illusions. In his editorial, "Political Abuses," [20] he said: "The political world is one which we have no wish to enter." He deplored "the malevolence and bitterness of party contest" and its baleful influence upon principle, integrity, and feelings of humanity. With obvious reference to John Quincy Adams, he wrote:

> The noblest and best of our citizens, — men, who are deserving only of commendation, are assailed in the most brutal manner — their private and public characters traduced, the sanctuary of their homes

violated, their motives misrepresented, and every engine of calumny put in operation against them.

But Whittier learned that politics should be every intelligent citizen's concern, and he was enmeshed in it before three years had passed. His sense of duty kept him personally interested in government all his life, and active in politics for nearly half a century.

So much for Whittier's permanent record, from the *Manufacturer*.

## 3

It would be a mistake, while spelling that out, not to emphasize that he seldom lost sight for long of the utilitarian purpose of his weekly. It was written very much in and for its day. Frequently Whittier discussed the American System. As a corollary, he took a creditably broad view of his country's resources and of its possibilities for future growth. He knew, for instance, how the opening of the Erie Canal in 1825 had stimulated the country's development, and he steadily advocated the building of the Boston & Albany Railroad,[21] as well as of other means of transportation. ("Internal improvements" were a main prop of the American System.)

As for the tariff, Whittier had much to say. In an editorial, "The System," published on March 19, 1829, he advanced merely conventional arguments for protectionism; on April 2 he praised Clay as "an unbending and consistent politician . . . one of the strongest pillars in the living temple of our republic," and on April 16 and July 2 he commended Clay further. On July 23 Whittier published a strong editorial, "The Tariff," in which he showed some knowledge of the history of protectionism in America; and one week later he sought to disprove the charge that the tariff of 1828 was creating an aristocracy in this country, although he granted that "the Tariff of 1828 might be greatly amended."

Whittier put verse, too, at the service of the System. In four rhymes entitled "Tariffiana," [22] he endeavored, on a base note, to sing its praises. He was not felicitous in speaking of the Southern and the British exponents of free trade, and his salute to President Jackson in the last of the series was not a love kiss.

Beyond any doubt, Whittier's strong opinions were grounded in his ardent hope and vision of his country's future. His editorial leader,

"American Genius," in the *Manufacturer* of March 19, 1829, was a proud utterance tinged with the jingoism of the young nation. Feelings of animosity toward England were still reflected in the newspapers of this time, and Whittier, in the *Manufacturer*, was censorious of the mother country. He scoffed at the statement of a British writer that America was fifty years behind Britain in point of mechanical genius. He cited Franklin, Fulton, and Perkins, and concluded that "it requires no gift of prophecy to foretell her [America's] destiny of glory."

In the next issue of the *Manufacturer* Whittier reinforced his arguments for protectionism with a poetic description of the bounty which Nature had lavished upon the United States. His genuine fervor made the editorial, "Our Prospects," a vastly better composition than most of his rapid outpourings. In perspective, it has value chiefly because it gives a clear view of the young Yankee striving, for the moment, to acquire a truly national vision.

As a result of his advocacy of protectionism, with its concomitant of special privilege, Whittier appeared in an anomalous light when he struck off the editorial, "Aristocracy," in the *Manufacturer* of April 9. But he was consistent now with his upbringing as a Jeffersonian Democrat, and he was in harmony with the country's masses, whose votes had put Jackson in the White House. The political revolt against aristocracy was strongest in the Northeast,[23] and Whittier, keenly alert to social currents, naturally had some comment to make upon the subject. He lamented that we did have an aristocracy of wealth, and he opposed it: "It has no foundation in justice — none in the great principles of the Republic."

Whittier even charged, in an editorial entitled "Depression of Business," [24] that "our city capitalists" (Boston merchants and shippers) were largely responsible for the current economic distress, having formed themselves into "an exclusive aristocracy," unfriendly to the rising manufactures around them.

Whittier was unequivocally on the side of people who worked and produced. His comments on aristocracy and business were closely integrated, in fact, with his genuinely felt utterances in behalf of the mechanics, most of whom, foreign-born,[25] were relegated to fixed and inferior positions in American society. Here was Whittier's idea of the genuine "American System":

If there is any situation truly enviable, it is that of the industrious mechanic, who by his own, unaided exertions, has established for himself a respectable place in society, who, commencing in poverty, has been able by his own skill and perseverance to overcome every obstacle, to vanquish every prejudice, and build up for himself a reputation, whose value is enhanced by the knowledge that it was underived from others. And let it be remembered that this situation is attainable to all, who have health, and practical knowledge of their business. Fortune will sooner or later crown their efforts with success. It is a mistaken idea that she deals about her favours, blindly and with a reckless hand. Industry and virtuous ambition are seldom exerted in vain.[26]

Two months later Whittier returned to this subject with an article "To the Young Mechanics of New England," and in four subsequent issues he elaborated upon the ideas therein expressed. On April 23 he discussed "patience and perseverance"; on April 30, the inevitability that manufacturing should become the future resource of New England, and the certainty that her mechanics, if they had knowledge reinforced by integrity, should be the most hopeful means to that laudable end. On July 9 and 16 he exhorted the mechanics of New England to set themselves high personal and moral standards. All in all, these six articles were Whittier's early testament in behalf of labor, chiefly noteworthy because, in resuming the series on April 16, he wrote that he "has been ranked among your number."

Whittier's vision of the future of his country naturally embraced the growth of a native literature, a subject at once of stern pronouncements and devout invocations during the first third of the century. But Whittier's contribution to the widespread discussion showed a characteristic and quite adult independence of mind. "The true cause of the imbecility of our poetry," he wrote in the *Manufacturer* of July 16, 1829, "is found in the dangerous encouragement which is given to the light flashes of fancy — the tinsel and drapery of poetry, without the substance." He deplored the fact that "the productions of many of our most popular poets . . . have no character of thought — no deep, engrossing interest to chain down our sympathies and work upon the sterner passions." Whittier pleaded for "a more independent mode of criticism."

# 4

He needed it himself, now, as he gave signs of realizing. None of the verse which he published in the *Manufacturer* or contributed to newspapers and magazines in Boston, Hartford, Haverhill, and Philadelphia showed striking evidence of the "manly and vigorous exertion" which he had called for on July 16. Indeed, his output of rhymes during his driven days and nights of editing had less of quality than his prose; it dripped of sentiment, in weak imitation of Byron, and much of it seemed related to his lingering fondness for his cousin, Mary Emerson Smith.

With his inbred deep affection, Whittier had a natural capacity for strong attachments, and there is convincing evidence that he held his cousin in the fervent regard of a sentimental youth. The small packet of letters which Mrs. Smith saved from their early correspondence tells all that can be reasonably said of their association: that it meant more to him than to her. Mrs. Lucia Alexander, a friend of the poet's later years, ventured to guess, "I am afraid the lady trifled a little with the honest heart." [27] Mary Emerson seems at any rate to have omitted answering Whittier's long outpouring in a letter of May 23, 1829, and it may be that in various compositions which he manufactured in the next four months he was giving a veritable case history of love hopes chilled and then dying. It is impossible to say with certainty that he was or was not. It is true that his writings of this period presumably to or about his cousin leave an impression chiefly of literary exercise and poetic convention.[28]

It remains to tell, about Whittier's first editorship, only that he received at the outset of it a journalistic hazing, which he survived in health, from Royal L. Porter, editor of the Boston *American Traveller;* that Whittier's humor emerged increasingly in his writings; and that he enjoyed the "tolerable good society" of Mrs. Sarah J. Hale and her literary club, as well as two — and only two — visits to the Boston Athenaeum.[29] Manifestly, under the weight of his editorial charge, Whittier had little time for pursuing culture in Boston — or love in Haverhill.

To his family's farm there he returned in August. In Boston he had done work of merit, but his ambition for fame was unsatisfied. Still, Prentice, whom contemporary editors considered one of the ablest of their craft, commended and encouraged him in his work, and obviously had marked him as his own successor to edit the *Review*. N. P. Willis, too, who seems to have known Whittier, noticed his work sympathetically, and in the *American Monthly Magazine*[30] ran a friendly editorial note on his retirement from the *Manufacturer*. Willis prophesied correctly, "We fear, however, that, Quaker though he be, the country will be too quiet for him after his busy Editorship. . . ."

## 5

Whittier in fact was not happy during the next five months on the farm. Pleasant reflections upon his editorial work in Boston must have been tempered by the fact that he had been the object of jealousy and detraction in the office of the Colliers. That situation, as much as the illness of Whittier's father, determined him to resign from the *Manufacturer*. "Why should you be surprised?" Whittier answered a former fellow lodger at 30 Federal Street. "You know what kind of a concern it was; you know, if I mistake not, my dissatisfaction." [31]

In the second place, Whittier's apparent resumption of shoemaking, as a financial expedient, must have contributed to his momentary unhappiness. It is hard to imagine a time when his ambitious spirit was less likely than now to sit at ease beside a shoemaker's bench on an Essex County farm. Yet he appears willy-nilly to have resumed work at "my craft" during the late summer and the autumn of 1829, evidently in the rôle of shoe-binder.[32]

Third and most important of the causes of Whittier's fleeting unhappiness was the mingled feeling of neglect and frustration which beset him now more than at any other time in his youth. He had done good work as editor of the *Manufacturer*, but had not learned that solid reputation is achieved only slowly. He had had romantic notions about his cousin, but he had not recognized woman's nature and her privilege of choosing. Whittier was feeling boxed by the world on both ears.

Something of his state of mind he had expressed in a letter of October, 1828, to John Neal:

> I have just written something for your consideration. You dislike — I believe you do, at least, — the blank verse of our modern poets. . . .

> Nevertheless, I send you a long string of it. If you don't like it, say so privately; *and I will quit poetry, and every thing else of a literary nature*, for I am sick at heart of the business. . . . Insult has maddened me. The friendless boy has been mocked at; and, years ago, he vowed to triumph over the scorners of his boyish endeavors. With the unescapable sense of wrong burning like a volcano in the recesses of his spirit, he has striven to accomplish this vow, until his heart has grown weary of the struggle. . . .[33]

The passing of a year brought not abatement but aggravation to Whittier's "sense of wrong," for after leaving the *Manufacturer* he seems to have written an even worse jeremiad to Neal. The *Yankee* editor's reply, dated Portland, Maine, September 4, 1829, was the sanative that Whittier needed.

> I hasten to reply to you [wrote Neal] . . . , that I may assure you of my good wishes and high respect. . . .
>
> The refusal to exchange, did not proceed from any want of kind feeling, nor indeed of sincere admiration for some of your poetry, and prose, but from a principle just then established.
>
> Are you not rather too sensible to what others may say of you to your disadvantage? If so — believe me when I say that I have seen some things attributed to you, of extraordinary worth, and that if you are wise you will not heed the opinion of nobody hereafter, whom you do not believe to be at the same time a man of truth and a man of talent. . . .
>
> There — I have not written so long a letter to anybody for a twelvemonth; nor ever to a correspondent. By this you will see what I think of you. Persevere, and I am sure you will have your reward in every way.[34]

Whittier did persevere; steady writing and other work were his anodynes. To the *Manufacturer* he contributed only two articles after casting loose from the Colliers,[35] but his steady rate of production — and his restless mood — was testified by the frequent appearance of his writings in other publications during the last five months of 1829.

"Silent Worship" was pure Quakerism, and the tranquil beauty of this poem also suffused "The Worship of Nature."[36] As for the worship of his cousin, Whittier clearly reduced his fervor to a cool decision to be a good loser. In advance of Browning he seemed to say, "What I aspired to be, and was not, comforts me." This, surely, is the spirit of Whittier's poem with the anagrammatic title, "To S.E.M.," which was published in the *New England Weekly Review* on September 14, 1829.

In the long view, only three other verses of this five-month period mattered. "Passages" ["Look unto heaven"] elaborated Whittier's familiar doctrine of God in Nature, and "The Minstrel-Girl" expressed badly his feeling that Nature is man's nepenthe. Finally, in "The Raven," Whittier recaptured an Ossian-like mood and pictured the raven as an embodiment of the hostile forces of Nature. This poem was published sixteen years before Poe's classic of the same title.

That is Whittier's story through his twenty-first year, one of lights and shadows and of too high hopes, but of dogged progress. If he lacked fame, which he then coveted, he wanted neither friends nor encouragement, which he also prized. In the *Philadelphia Album* of September 16 he was praised in a poem by "Henriqueta," and on October 20 the *Ladies' Miscellany* (Salem), in reprinting one of his recent verses, described Whittier as "one of the most promising young poets of the day." Finally, it remained for the observant Prentice to end 1829 most pleasantly for Whittier. In a long editorial of December 28 devoted to him, Prentice wrote, in part:

> "The culmination of that man's fame will be a proud period in the history of literature." This generous tribute to the abilities of our friend W. was contained in a letter which we recently received from one of the most distinguished men in the Country. The tribute itself was merited. Whittier is a poet and a christian, — and we find him continually presenting to his countrymen those beautiful visions of Inspiration, which can hardly fail to allure them from their idol worship. The image, to which the poets of the present day are bowing down, is not of Heaven. . . .

# 6

Whittier's old friend Thayer also remembered him, and paid him the down-to-earth compliment of offering him the editorship of the *Haverhill Gazette*.[37] This opportunity Whittier accepted, and for the next six months and a half, beginning on January 2, he produced for his native town a weekly newspaper similar to that which he had edited in Boston. In doing so he made no radical departures, in editorial policy or in contents, from the pattern which Thayer had established for the *Gazette*.

Whittier approved unreservedly of Thayer's high ethical standards, of his advocacy of temperance, and of his practice of printing one column or more of state and national news of politics, as well as news of the world culled from English journals by editors in New York and Boston. Whittier clearly announced his editorial principles in the *Gazette* of January 2, 1830. He promised political independence ("I shall obey the dictation of no political leader from personal motives"), open and firm pronouncements "whenever it is probable that my humble exertions may facilitate the progress of the reforming spirit, which is abroad in our land," and avoidance of theological discussions ("My own quiet and peculiar faith will be enjoyed in silence. . . .").

Essentially, it may be repeated, Whittier conducted the *Gazette* as he had managed the *Manufacturer*, elaborating upon what he had said before. He consistently defended the "American System" against Southern attack, and as consistently praised Clay. He published more political news than ever Thayer had. In his first issue, that of January 2, he strongly contended for temperance. As a Quaker, moreover, he pleaded for justice to the Indians, and for a generally higher social morality in the country. Above all, as a staunch Friend, he commented often upon the evil of slavery, and he reprinted a number of articles from the *Genius of Universal Emancipation* and from other anti-slavery publications. At intervals he argued against the inhumanity of war.

His zeal for philanthropy, however, did not lessen his yearning for personal fame. In the poem, "My Birth-Day," unsigned but undisguisedly his,[38] he made it clear that this remained the dominant pursuit of his life at this time. Upon this subject he had more to say on April 3. In the *Gazette* of that date his long leader, "Life," was further evidence of his baffled search, and of the Byronic gloom which continued to pervade some of his outgivings.

Not less than his own ambition, that of Henry Clay continued to be engaging to Whittier. In the *Gazette* of January 16 he discussed Clay as one of the "Presumptive Candidates" for the Presidency. About Clay's fitness he was more candid now than he could discreetly have been in the *Manufacturer*. In particular he remarked the Kentuckian's "frankness, strong feelings of friendship or dislike, and a restless ambition, whose aim has long been towards the highest office in his country." Characteristically, however, Whittier dwelt upon the "one dark stain upon his [Clay's] private history — he has been a Duellist — a deliberate contemner of the laws of God and man." Later, on June 5, Whittier defended Clay from attacks by Jackson newspapers, and he asserted, concerning a proposed visit to New England by Clay:

> The upright and independent politician; the true republican; and THE UNWAVERING FRIEND OF THE MECHANIC AND THE LABORER would be received in every town and village of New England with heartfelt demonstrations of joy. The prejudices of party would not prevent the spontaneous burst of a people's gratitude for long-continued and efficient public service.

Finally, on July 3, Whittier came out flatly in favor of Clay as a candidate for President, in the election of 1832 — a step already taken by Prentice in the *New England Weekly Review* on June 21.

Whittier's political interests, however, seldom made him blindly partisan. Nearly always he esteemed ability and character above mere loyalty to party, always men above measures. This principle, which lasted with him, he stated in an editorial entitled "Names" in the *Haverhill Gazette* of June 5, 1830. He wrote, in part:

> We are sick of this reckless and unprincipled spirit of party. It is doing a work of foul contamination among us; — it is confounding the moral distinctions of right and wrong; and it is the duty of every politician, who has the good of his country at heart, to make an honorable stand against its dangerous influence, evincing in his own example, a just and impartial discrimination in regard to men and measures.
>
> Of what consequence is it to an American citizen, whether a measure is proposed, or a speech made, by a Northern or a Southern man — by a supporter of the present Administration, or one opposed to it? Does the name of the party, or [do] the geographical divisions of the country add to, or diminish the justice of the one, or the argument and eloquence of the other? [39]

Thus in the wake of the Webster-Hayne debate Whittier reprinted [40] a sketch of Hayne from the *Washington Spectator*, and prefaced it with his own appreciative judgment of the Southern statesman. He considered

Hayne a less powerful speaker than Webster, and yet found "exalted talents" in the Carolinian, whose heart he praised equally with his head.

Yet in an editorial of March 13 entitled "Webster and Hayne," Whittier expressed towering admiration for Webster, whom evidently he had seen while working in Boston. At once, confessed Whittier, he felt that he was in the presence of an intellectual giant — "among a crowd of strangers, . . . a great man."

Meanwhile, despite politics, the humanitarian Friend was not dormant in Whittier. He plainly evinced his sect's traditional interest in the Indian question, which was again before the country in 1830. In an editorial of January 16 entitled "The Governor's Message," Whittier deplored the evident determination of President Jackson to eject the Indians from Georgia, and he scorned the representations by which Jackson sought to win the country to his purpose. On February 20, in an editorial nearly seven hundred words long, Whittier returned to the argument that the Indians' possession of their land was legally guaranteed by treaties. He regretted that "the once powerful tribes of the red men, have become a remnant," and he asserted that the Indians rightly expected justice now from the federal government.

> If then [Whittier concluded], our treaties with the red men have been made in a spirit of sincerity — and God forbid that it should prove otherwise! — the Constitution, both in letter and in spirit will be violated, by any attempt to drive out from among us the survivors of the ancient "lords of the soil." To uproot the affections which gather round the place of nativity, — to drive back into savage habits, thousands who have tasted in a measure of the blessings of civilization, — to deny the grey-haired hunter, the poor boon of a grave with his fathers, will be the consequence of carrying into effect the plan proposed for the removal of the Indians. It will cast a broad shadow upon our national character. It will place us in a disgraceful light before the eyes of other nations. The curse of slavery is enough to seal our eternal infamy; the unjust ejectment of the Indians will be a crime which man may never forget, nor eternal justice forgive.

The fundamental drives of Whittier's humanitarianism came from his religion, and its influence was seldom long absent from his writings. One consequence was his feeble talent for aesthetic criticism; his literary judgments were too often vitiated by the moral tags which he placed upon them. Nowhere was the tendency better illustrated than in two editorials on "Infidelity" which appeared in the *Gazette* on January 23 and February 6, 1830. Whittier was genuinely sincere in his conviction that unbelief was threatening the land, for on January 23 he depicted with alarm the "influence in our own highly favored country" of the doctrines of the French Encyclopedists. He considered Diderot, d'Alembert, and also Voltaire responsible for the French Revolution, "that bloody chart of untold and almost unimaginable crime." [41] The French ideas would not have been so pernicious, Whittier asserted on February 6, if they had been walled up in France; but they affected Byron and Shelley in England, and other people elsewhere. Whittier deemed Byron conspicuous "among the master spirits of Infidelity," though he believed him "haunted throughout by a secret doubt — a gnawing of conscience — an unescapable fear of the realities of religion, which he contemned." As for Shelley, "desperate and abandoned as he was," even he "could not deceive himself." Whittier's conclusion was rooted in a belief which he retained always. "There is much," he said, "in the history of this man's life to convince a rational mind of the utter worthlessness of intellectual power, and extended knowledge, when united with a depraved heart. . . ."

The *American Daily Advertiser* stoutly defended Shelley's memory against Whittier's censure, but only prompted him on February 27 to underscore his earlier opinion: that "mere Genius shall never take the precedence of Virtue, in our estimation." For good measure, Whittier in the *Gazette* of May 8, 1830, had another go at Byron, and his *apologia* in the final paragraph is significant.

> We are not insensible [Whittier wrote] to the surpassing power of Byron's genius. He was the master spirit of his time. We feel that we are not competent to set in critical judgment upon the outpourings of his lofty mind; — but we thank God for having given us a perception . . . of the pure and beautiful in nature and intellect. And, governed as we are in our remarks by this perception, we feel that we are only acting the part of our duty, in warning the young and uncontaminated against an enthusiastic reverence for the productions of Lord Byron.[42]

Even riper years did not temper in Whittier such opinions on the subject of art and morality.

By 1830 the main points of Whittier's religious position were also clearly marked out. On this subject, however, only one notable utterance appeared during his first editorship of the *Haverhill Gazette* — without title, in the issue of March 13, 1830.[43] Notably, it contained the essence of Quaker belief, as expressed in various poems by the youthful Whittier, a simple creed couched in exquisite biblical prose. Gone, for the moment, were the circumlocutions, the exaggerations, and the jargon into which the poet-at-heart slipped when he wrote journalistic prose. Whittier nearly always produced better work with his heart than with his head, and emotion, not intellect, dominated the composition of this article.

> To limit our hopes and aspirations to this life and this world [he wrote] is like remaining forever in the place of our birth, without ever lifting the veil of the visible horizon, which bent over our infancy. . . . There is religion in every thing around us; — a calm and holy religion in the unbreathing things of Nature, which men would do well to imitate. It is a meek and blessed influence, stealing in, as it were, unawares upon the heart. . . . It is the poetry of Nature.

Here, once again, was prefigured Whittier's mature conception of God in nature, which he expressed superbly in "Sunset on the Bearcamp," written in 1876.

About love, Whittier wrote little now. From January to June of 1830 he appears to have written only two love poems, and these, both signed "G." and both addressed "To Mary," were published in the *New England Weekly Review* on May 31 and June 7. His lines, however heartfelt they seemed to be, were only youth's characteristic tributes to Venus. Before Whittier was two years older, he was to learn that one young lady does not make a world.

Other and more workaday things of his world Whittier learned rather more quickly. One of lasting concern to him was the power of the press in a democracy. His first editorial on the subject, in the *Gazette* of March 20, 1830, was marred by a pontifical manner of expression, a glaring want of compression, and a too high moral tone. When, however, Whittier discussed "Editorial Independence" on May 29, he had solidly planted his feet in reality. "Editorial independence, indeed! —" he said, "we should as soon expect to find piety in his Satanic Generalship, as independence in a country Editor." He had come to realize that the loss of twenty subscribers, for expressing sentiments at variance with its readers' convictions, could embarrass a weekly periodical. "The subscribers of a country newspaper," he knew, "shackle its editor."

Whittier none the less expressed forcefully many opinions in a prodigious number of editorials for the *Gazette*. At odd times he also produced prose tales, as his habit was, none of them of high quality, and none of value except "Henry St. Clair." This appeared in the *New York Amulet and Ladies' Chronicle* on July 1, 1830, and was worth forty dollars to Whittier as winner of first prize for "the best moral tale, which shall exhibit the most deleterious consequences of vice in the most vivid colours." In depicting the certain ruin resulting from infidelity and intemperance, Whittier succeeded almost too well.[44]

Plainly, he searched in a wide arc for his literary materials. Withal, he stayed firmly on the rock where fortune had placed him. He was always a New Englander. In the *Gazette* of March 20, 1830, he stated — seldom better — "the grounds for our preference of New England":

> . . . because, it is the home of liberty and equal rights; — because the name of *slave* is not known in her borders; and because no degraded creatures of God are writhing under the oppression of her sons. We rejoice in New England, as the native home of intellect — where minds are nurtured into power, which may fitly compare with the eternal mountains of her territory, or the giant oaks which overshadow them, unbroken by the hurricanes of centuries. We love our birthplace for the manifestations of her moral power — for her free institutions, and her quiet religion. These are the monuments of her true glory, for they are unstained with blood, and unmoistened with the tears of the trodden down and oppressed. We boast of no others.

Whittier might have added that New England's historic background gave him almost untapped native material. He made account of it now in five poems — "The Unquiet Sleeper," "The Murdered Lady," "The Spectre Warriors," "The Spectre Ship of Salem," and "The Indian's Tale" [45] — which were included in his first book, *Legends of New England*, published at Hartford in 1831.

Such heavy editorial matter as he published in the *Gazette* required balance, and Whittier wisely leavened his columns with humor. He was particularly humorous about celibacy, as in the issue of June 12; and the fact that he commented repeatedly upon it, always in humor, suggests that his own singleness, which became permanent, occupied his mind at this time.

Whittier usually edited the *Gazette* at the homestead, although he seems to have enjoyed working occasionally at the office of the newspaper. An incident there which he turned to a humorous end is described in the following letter:

Gazette Office, 1st of 6th Mo, 1830

My Dear Helen Stanhope [Miss Lydia L. Dodge,
North Fields, Salem, Mass.],

Permit the Editor of the Essex Gazette to sympathize with you in your manifold misfortunes. Deaf and dumb, too! Either misfortune would seem bad enough in all conscience — but both! — it is really unsupportable to think of them.

Did the Robbers attack you, or the Witches frighten you on your return from your silent visitation?

Playfulness aside — that trick of yours was a noble one — devilishly romantic — *sui generis* — *outré*, and decidedly original. You deserve a gold medal for it.

Did you really, though, suppose that you were unsuspected? If so — you were frightfully mistaken. I *did* suspect you. At times, there was a tremour in your hand — it was the tremour of fear — was it not? Then, too, there was, occassionally, to use the word of Byron — "a laughing devil" in your eye, which had no business there.

Your friend Martha too — she was a little frightened — wasn't she? But certes, 'twas a capital affair — and it has been the means of driving off the Blues — for I have laughed hours by the town-clock when thinking of the subject. Why did you call at so many places? The whole affair was all over town in twenty four hours after.

You need not suppose by this note that I have forgiven you for your frolic — no, indeed — I shall be in Salem this Summer and shall take the liberty to return your visit. You will not find me deaf nor dumb nor blind.

John Greenleaf Whittier.[46]

Ten days after this letter was written, Whittier for the second time was saddened by loss in his family. His father died on June 11. As the elder son, Greenleaf thereupon became titular head of the family, and this he remained almost to the end of his days.

# V

# The Editor at His Post

WHITTIER now was bound more closely than before to political journalism, in the uses of which he became well schooled. John Whittier having left little material wealth to his widow and four children,[1] Greenleaf felt obliged to earn more than his salary as editor of the *Haverhill Gazette*. The opportunity came to him; but he had to go to Hartford to accept it.

Greenleaf's work with the *Gazette* had won him an increasing measure of praise, to which Prentice continued to add.[2] Whittier's several contributions to the *New England Weekly Review* during the first half of 1830, such as the poem "The Destiny" (June 4), further disposed Prentice in his favor. And the two young editors corresponded, although they never met. Quite naturally Prentice recommended his favorite as his successor when he himself went to Kentucky to write a campaign biography of Henry Clay.[3]

## 1

Whittier became editor of the *Review* on July 19, 1830, ten days after leaving the *Haverhill Gazette*. He moved into no soft berth, for Prentice,[4] five years Whittier's senior, was also a man of undoubted ability. Despite personal difficulties in Hartford, he had gained wide celebrity as editor of the *Review*. During the twenty-seven months of his management it had come to be considered one of the best weeklies published in New England. Prentice nevertheless assured readers of the *Review* that Whittier would serve them well. In his "Good Bye" of July 5, 1830, he said:

> I must now take a temporary leave of my readers for the purpose of making a tour and perhaps residing a short time in the Western States. Mr. J. G. Whittier, an old favorite with the public, will probably have charge of the Review in my absence, and I cannot do less than congratulate my readers on the prospect of their more familiar acquaintance with a gentleman of such powerful energies and such exalted purity and sweetness of character. I have made some enemies among those, whose good opinion I value, but no rational man can ever be the enemy of Mr. Whittier.

Whittier seems indeed to have made no enemies, although as editor of the leading Whig organ in Connecticut, in succession to the witty and caustic Prentice, he gave to his writings at this time an unwonted cutting edge. He and Gideon Welles, editor of the Democratic *Hartford Times* and later Secretary of the Navy in Lincoln's cabinet, fought an extended duel with their pens, governed by the ethic that political journalism was not to wound personally but merely to bruise.

Otherwise, Whittier seems to have had only pleasant relations in Hartford. Certainly he enjoyed more congenial society in this city of approximately seven thousand inhabitants than he appears to have known in Boston. Hartford in 1830, none the less, was not what it had been during the heyday of the "Hartford Wits." The city of just before Whittier's time there was described as —

> . . . a small commercial town . . . , dealing in lumber, and smelling of molasses and Old Jamaica — for it had still some trade with the West Indies. Though the semi-capital of the State . . . it was strongly impressed with a plodding, mercantile, and mechanical character. There was a high tone of general intelligence and social respectability about the place, but it had not a single institution, a single monument, that marked it as even a provincial metropolis of taste, in literature, art, or refinement.[5]

Whittier years later wrote to Charles Dudley Warner that he "knew well some of the best people in the little city." [6] This was true. Among his friends were Frederick A. P. Barnard; Isaac E. Crary[7] and Charles M. Emerson, young lawyers; Jonathan Law, who had just retired after twenty-nine years as postmaster of Hartford;[8] John Russ, Judge of Probate, city alderman, and former member of Congress; Mrs. Lydia H. Sigourney,

Doctor Eli Todd, Joseph Trumbull (banker, and later Governor of Connecticut), and Martin Welles.[9]

Whittier first lived at the old Treat Tavern, but made his home afterward with the Jonathan Laws, at 190 Main Street. Here he had access to a fine library and to the society entertained in a large house. With the Laws he seems to have enjoyed Yankee sociability to the full, and he exchanged chatty letters with them long after he had left Hartford. In a postscript to her husband's long letter of February 28, 1836, Mrs. Law assured Whittier that, despite the cold winter, "the poet's corner" had been kept warm by the stove which he used to know so well, and that if he would pay the promised visit "an empty tumbler should be filled with the beverage you were pleased to join him [Mr. Law] with some times when with us." [10]

Whittier was not a stay-at-home here, however. In Hartford he moved about in society more than his health ever again permitted. He "became a great favorite. . . . He was a sprightly conversationalist, although apt to hold his peace among strangers." His shyness, coupled with his handsome eyes and intelligent face, was fetching: certain young ladies called him "the young and gallant stranger." [11]

Withal, for Whittier the *Review* was the thing. Very late in life he recalled, "I was kept busy, very busy indeed on the Review, and chiefly for the first year avoiding the exposure of my ignorance." [12] As Collier had done, the proprietors of the *Review* and the party leaders (who were at first astonished to find a shy Quaker lad, dressed in homespuns made on a Massachusetts farm, succeeding the debonair, aggressive Prentice[13]) got more than their money's worth from Whittier. He was paid five hundred dollars a year, thirty-two dollars more than he would have received in twelve months from Collier. It was a depressed wage, and the value and quality of Whittier's work on the *Review* was out of all proportion to it. It is difficult to see how Whittier could, as he wished, reduce the mortgage on the farm at Haverhill; but on personal and professional grounds he matured markedly in Hartford. He made the *Review* for 1830–1831 distinctly superior to other political weeklies of the day.

Whittier learned quickly, from the Connecticut politicians who soon made a ward-room of his office, the political language of Connecticut.[14] On review, his Whiggism appears to have been a symptom of crudity, and so it was — of state and nation. This was the day when J. Q. Adams, Calhoun, Cambreleng, Clay, Hayne, McDuffie, and above all Jackson were having their brief hour on the stage, and the audience was hypercritical. Bowers has written of Jackson in the campaign of 1828 that "he had been opposed by two thirds of the newspapers, four fifths of the preachers, practically all the manufacturers, and seven eighths of the banking capital." [15] Whittier's editorial voice, if it took on partisan pitch, was relatively sweet in the midst of the political dissonances of the time.

It was September 20 before Whittier felt able to speak in his own right. Then in an editorial notice "To the Patrons of the N.E. Review" he made a statement of principles almost exactly like that of January 2 in the *Haverhill Gazette*, but more maturely written. Actually, the *Review* took on Whittier's character from his first day as editor, on July 19.

His conduct of affairs in Hartford almost precisely duplicated his Boston experience. He read the exchanges much more assiduously than his predecessor had done, and turned them to account in his own columns. This microscopic reading of prevailingly small type, which frequently bad press work did little to improve, must inevitably have strained Whittier's eyes. Very likely the lifelong abuse of his eyes, without the compensation of careful correction by eyeglasses, had much to do with the severe headaches which beset him at about this time and became chronic in his later years. At any rate, it is certain that Whittier's reading of exchanges became an increasing labor, for his exchange list grew with the quality of the *Review*. On February 21, 1831, he wrote: "Our list is already much too large for profit. Many papers reach us, with a request to exchange. . . . We would gladly exchange with every body, if it were possible to do so — although many with whom we *do* exchange neglect to give us credit for any thing, which they find in our columns, worthy of insertion in their own." [16]

Whittier always manifested great conscience toward his readers. Here he printed more news of general interest than Prentice had done, and page three of the *Review* now became a mirror of foreign countries and of distant States of the Union. And as always, Whittier quite exhausted himself in the production of editorials, prose articles, and poems. During his editorship the *Review* published forty-seven of his poems for the first time, of which number seven survived the winnowing of nearly sixty years and found their way into the Riverside Edition of Whittier's works in 1888.

The workaday mill of journalism, however, ground out principally chaff. In a typical issue of the *Review*, that of August 2, 1830, eight columns were devoted to advertising, the major revenues of which came from merchants of wines from Spain and from the south of France.[17] Yet there was much of Whittier himself in this issue of the *Review*. He published, for instance, a sentimental poem of some merit, "The Indian Girl's Lament," based upon the death, in the autumn of 1829, of the last of the Newfoundland Indians. Whittier was again working in native materials. He also began at this time, in a highly pontifical manner, a series of five editorials addressed "To the Electors of New England." [18] His thesis, long since reduced to a set speech, was that the danger to the Union was not external, but sprang from the corrupt leadership in the White House. While censuring Jackson he of course praised Clay.

Whittier's service at this time in the ranks of the oppositionist press — he was never a member of the ruling political party until Lincoln and the Republicans came to power in 1861 — trained him to the fiery and forthright expression of convictions which marked his career as an Abolitionist. To Whittier this was the particular value of his Hartford editorship.

## 2

It is a pleasant fact, however, that he enjoyed the city for itself. In an exuberant editorial, "Hartford," published on August 2, 1830, he revealed that he had explored the city and the surrounding countryside during his first two weeks. With relief he declared that the "view from Washington [now Trinity] College is enough to drive politics from one's head." And, antiquarian that he was, he reported with pleasure having visited the site of the old Dutch fort at the junction of the Little River with the Connecticut, in Hartford, "where even now we understand the ghosts of the Mynheers and Vrows of olden time, occasionally promenade." Whittier thriftily used this trifle; on August 22, 1831, he published in the *Review* his rollicking poem, unsigned but easily recognizable, "The Fort of Good Hoop."

The end of the editorial on Hartford was, however, of most biographical interest; it indicated a jovial, expansive tendency in some of Whittier's early writing which was plainly forced.[19]

> On the whole [he said], we like Hartford — "hugely" as Tristram Shandy's uncle said of Yorick's sermon, — our publishers are two as

fine fellows as ever accommodated themselves to the whims of an Editor; and our Landlord of the Exchange Coffee House furnishes us daily with a *Treat* which Epicurus himself might envy. Our brother editors may grumble as they please, and complain loudly and bitterly of the times — (not the Hartford Times — for no one ever supposed *that* worth grumbling about) — but we shall hardly join with them in their Jeremiads.

In contrast, there was nothing at all forced about Whittier's political pronouncements in the *Review*. They were numerous and hard-hitting, and they revealed a growing grasp of political technique. Since Jackson was a big target and easy to aim at, Whittier loosed his most pointed barbs at the President with a regularity which was as monotonous as it was futile. In "The Message," an editorial of December 20, 1830, Whittier thus undertook to defend Clay,[20] to whom Jackson had referred pointedly in his latest message to Congress:

> *We* say that it is a sentence which would disgrace the lowest politician who dabbles in the troubled waters of Jacksonism — a vile insinuation raked up from the depths of corruption — a response to the foul-mouthed presses of Duff Green and Isaac Hill!

There was dissent from this view, just as in 1836 there were to be objections to Whittier's excoriation, in the *Haverhill Gazette*, of Governor Edward Everett, of Massachusetts; for under the heading "Freedom of the Press" in the *Review* of January 10, 1831, Whittier stoutly defended himself for having spoken "freely, fearlessly and severely" of Jackson's message. Milton defended a free press with more power and grace, but not with more earnestness than his admirer, who concluded:

> Our press, we repeat, is FREE — free as the ocean wave — free as the winds of heaven — free as mind fresh from the hand of its Creator; and before God, while we are connected with it, it shall remain free, unbought, unshackled, and untainted by aught of servility or corruption.

It is doubtful that "Old Hickory" was aware of the Hartford stripling, or whether he would in any event have altered his course to benefit by the winds blowing from the *Review* office. Yet if he could have seen Whittier's final thrust at him as editor of the *Review* ("Political Credulity," November 28, 1831), he would have known that the young Quaker wafted no peaceful zephyr his way. The tenor of this blast, one and a half columns in length, may be judged by this passage:

> He has done every thing, in short, that could be done, by one whose ambition was his idol — whose passions were his rulers, and whose love of country was swallowed up in his supreme love of self. And yet, with all these facts staring them in the face, there are still persons who are credulous enough to believe Andrew Jackson to be the "greatest and the best of men."

Enough voters, indeed, so regarded Jackson as to re-elect him President in 1832, although Whittier had sounded his political doom in "Jacksonism" in the *Review* of February 28, 1831.

Whittier did no better in prophesying Van Buren's future. He wrote crisply of the Secretary of State on September 27, 1830, and on December 13, in "Martin Van Buren *versus* Republicanism," he handled him gingerly. "*What has Martin Van Buren done for his Country's good?*" Whittier asked. "NOTHING. . . ." Finally, on August 8, 1831, Whittier gave a long bill of complaints against the future President, as if to conduct his political funeral. Whittier was learning that political ambitions, shrewdly nurtured, can not be killed in the columns of a newspaper.

Still, it may be repeated, Whittier's training in oppositionist propaganda during his early editorial career had this value: it added trenchancy to his prose style, and it emboldened him, a naturally shy and gentle person, to knock heads together resoundingly if, by so doing, he felt that he could advance a cause in which he believed. How far he had developed this aggressive style, since his initiation to politics through the *Haverhill Gazette* and since he succeeded the mordant Prentice, may be best gauged by three notes early in 1831 in the *Review*. In "Fanfarronade" (January 3) he declared:

> The Message of His Excellency Governor Ray, of Indiana, recently promulgated, is, without exception, one of the most wishy-washy state papers that ever came under our observation. It is inflated beyond measure, and as full of bombast and fustian, as the composition of a Sophomore. . . .

On April 25, in "The Party," Whittier demonstrated his further increased proficiency in caustic writing.

> . . . Gideon Well[e]s, our own Gideon [he said], our peculiarly modest and honest hearted Jackson editor, is brought into the field. He cuts a sorry figure it is true, but that is not the fault of Gideon. The assinine

> propensities of a certain long-eared animal, when brought upon the list ground of the noble war horse, are always distinctly manifest in the light of contrast.

The third note, published on May 16, indicated that Whittier had recently had his second opportunity to hear Daniel Webster speak, for he rebuked Welles in these terms:

> The editor of the Hartford Times has seen fit to introduce the name of Daniel Webster, in his columns, and outrage the good sense and hospitable feelings of our citizens, by insulting him, and misrepresenting his motives, in reference to his late visit to this city. We know not how it may seem to others, but to us, this attack upon Daniel Webster looks marvellously like the oppugnation of a tom cat to an eagle, or the nibble of a mouse at the heel of an elephant.

Such captious self-confidence in political writing gave offense to Whittier's old friend Thayer. Absence from Essex County did not in the least diminish Whittier's interest in its affairs, and he voiced it strongly. Caleb Cushing, of Newburyport, had since 1826 been seeking election on the Whig ticket as Representative of "Essex North" to Congress, and Whittier, while in Hartford and afterward, favored his candidacy. In the *Haverhill Gazette* of January 8, 1831, Thayer answered Whittier's peppering of Stephen W. Marston, one of Cushing's several successive opponents for the Whig nomination. Thayer charged that his former protégé "seems to have entirely lost sight of that courtesy which is due to every respectable man, however obnoxious his political principles; and which Whittier's professed repugnance to meanness and scurrility gave us a right to expect he would rigidly observe." [21] Whittier replied sharply to Thayer, in the *Review* of January 31. Regardless of where he might be, he stated, he was determined to speak his convictions regarding the affairs of his birthplace. This controversy, at times acrimonious, extended into the Spring, and it strengthened Whittier's belief that Cushing deserved to be sent to Congress. Toward this end he was soon to work actively.[22]

Whittier was calmer in commenting upon the political issues of the day than upon personalities involved in them. He praised Calhoun's past services to the country, his promise of future usefulness, and his integrity; but he bade him drop Nullification.[23] Against this ogre, as against South Carolina and against the principle of the Hartford Convention of 1814,

Whittier had already spoken strongly. Quite as forcefully he had defended the Union.[24]

Naturally, Whittier continued to advocate the tariff,[25] and he was alarmed at Secretary McLane's policies bearing upon it. In "The West India Trade," for example (October 11, 1830), he asserted that McLane was playing into Great Britain's hands in permitting her ships to touch at United States ports in order to load for or to unload from the West Indies. Whittier further argued this point on January 17 and 24, 1831. In three other editorials[26] he commented pointedly upon the United States Bank, which he defended from Jackson's attacks. More heartily, Whittier pursued his old interest in labor. In "The Working Men's Party" he developed further the general aspects of the "Mechanics" series which he had published in the *American Manufacturer*, and in "The Working Man"[27] he maintained that the Jackson party was opposed to the interests of the laboring class.

This political education, added to the early tutoring by his father, gave Whittier a deep concern for politics and government — an interest which endured throughout his life. Even at this time he was clear-eyed about political motives and men, as he measured them later in life when he asked an Amesbury neighbor: ". . . has thee met many angels and saints in thy dealings with either of the parties [Democrats and Republicans]? Thy experience should teach thee not to expect too much of human nature."[28] For on July 11, 1831, in the story "Capo d'Istrias and Greece" in the *Review*, he had reached the conclusion that —

> . . . politicians are the camelions of mankind; they have *characters*, but no *character;* we are therefore determined to admire their hues, and let the animal[s] go. As they affect our happiness while on the stage, let us hiss or applaud them with due precision.

Whittier's readiness at this period to applaud Clay resulted in his first trip to New York, in January, 1831. He and Isaac E. Crary journeyed there together in order to supply material needed for Prentice's biography of Clay, approximately forty pages of which have been attributed to Whittier.[29] From Hartford to New Haven and thence down the Sound, probably on the steamboat *Hudson*, he and Crary made the two-day trip to New York. Never a good traveler, Whittier had a humorous loathing for his first voyage on the water.[30] With grateful relief he reached New York on New Year's Day, 1831.

The only known record of Whittier's work during the three weeks he spent in New York is preserved in three letters which he wrote to Jonathan Law. On January 5, in the second of them, Whittier related:

> I have reached N.Y. at last and am already surrounded with papers & musty documents. I find not so much difficulty as I anticipated. *The Ghent treaty is safe.* It was not among the missing.
>
> My first letter was dated on board the steam boat — that "floating Pandemonium" that pestilential hospital ship. — I shudder even now at the bare thought of it. We spent Friday night on the boat a few miles below the city. It was almost a sleepless one. . . .
>
> We are now sitting in our room — Crary and myself — there is a noble fire in the grate, and we are working away for dear life. We are in fact perfect hermits and we abide by our room, even as Diogenes did to his tub. * * * We have no news to relate — none in the world — and yet, as I promised to write I will fulfill my engagement. I have seen no one as yet. * * * The Editor of the N.Y. Mercantile Advertiser has just called on me, and invited me in the name of *Forrest* the tragedian of Halleck Wetmore and Leggett of N.Y. and of Hill of Boston, to attend a convivial meeting of the *Literati* this evening. I have declined. I have no idea of soaking my brains in champagne or Madeira, when I have so much use for them. * * * At present I must have a clear look-out, or all may go for the "old Harry" instead of our own Harry. * * * [31]

Whittier's third letter to Law, dated January 15, 1831, revealed his impatience with research, and the pains which the work cost him:

> I am yet in the land of the living, and would give half a kingdom to be in your goodly city of Hartford. We have had a wearisome time of it, and the end has not yet come. We have been sick, and given over to the buffeting of the "Indigo Demons." Verily we have seen enough of vexation, enough of agony, spiritual and bodily, to make our very hairs as white as those of Methuselah, when a thousand winters had gone over his venerable *occiput.*
>
> We have ransacked every street, we have turned over the huge folios of every Library, we have read, enquired, cogitated and written and rewritten, until our brains are in a worse state than Ovid's Chaos. * * * [32]

Back in Hartford in time to edit the *Review* of January 24, Whittier barely mentioned "our absence for the last two or three weeks." In the

*Review* of February 7, however, he expatiated for nearly one column on Prentice's biography of Clay, which Hanmer and Phelps, publishers of the Hartford weekly, printed with great speed. Whittier called Prentice's book "one of the finest specimens of beautiful composition, which we have ever read from an American pen. . . ." He promised his readers that on February 14 he would say still more about the biography, but he wisely failed to do so. His praise already far exceeded the modest merit of the work.

## 3

Meanwhile, Whittier's own first book, *Legends of New England*, was in press, and it appeared, also with the imprint of Hanmer and Phelps, on February 23. The volume had been advertised in the *Review* of September 13 preceding, and Whittier mentioned the project humorously in an editorial note. "If nothing else is gained," he said, "we shall, at least, have the satisfaction of ministering to our natural vanity. . . ." Of more significance was his preface to the book, which was in part a harvest of his writings in several newspapers. He said, of the seven prose and eleven verse pieces:

> In the following pages I have attempted to present in an interesting form some of the popular traditions and legends of New-England. The field is a new one — and I have but partially explored it. New-England is rich in traditionary lore — a thousand associations of superstition and manly daring and romantic adventure, are connected with her green hills and her pleasant rivers. I leave the task of rescuing these associations from oblivion to some more fortunate individual; and if this little volume shall have the effect to induce such an effort, I shall at least be satisfied, whatever may be the judgment of the public upon my own humble production. . . . A son of New-England, and proud of my birthplace, I would not willingly cast dishonor upon its founders. . . .

Whittier lived to deplore this excursion. Some years later he said that, when he examined the volume, "it seemed like somebody else." Such copies of the book as he could procure, in later life, he destroyed. In one instance, indeed, he paid five dollars for the pleasure.[33] Irving, the "somebody else" whose influence was painfully obvious in the book, would have been understanding; for the melodramatic flourishes that marred the *Legends* were not the best things an imitator could have learned from Irving.

In spite of its slender merit, *Legends of New England* was a significantly American book. Whittier was the first among the poets of "the flowering of New England" to publish a collection of writings based on native material. Of the importance of his emphasis on localism Constance Rourke has said:

> . . . the tendency to look backward with nostalgia upon the narrow local scene was new; Whittier and Mrs. Stowe as well as Bret Harte saw this as from a distance; they were bent upon a recovery of the past, upon saving the vestiges of a tradition.[34]

Whittier's saving candor in his preface was wise. He had not done extensive research, but had derived his materials chiefly from Cotton Mather's *Magnalia Christi Americana* and from Josselyn's *New-Englands Rarities Discovered*. For the rest, Whittier seems to have depended mainly upon Essex County folklore, into which he had delved earlier with the intention of writing a history of Haverhill. On March 27, 1830, in the *Haverhill Gazette* he had announced his plan, but it was B. L. Mirick who completed it, in 1832, with the aid of materials generously contributed by his friend. What these were is suggested by Whittier's treatment, in the *Legends*, of the Hannah Dustin story, under title of "The Mother's Revenge."

Whittier, just past twenty-three years of age, won little acclaim on his first bow before the American book-buying public. One critic, however, was aware that an American literary event had occurred. George P. Morris, of the *New York Mirror*, which was one of the leading magazines of the day, noticed the legends at length.[35] He commended Whittier for his enterprise and his subject matter, but censured him because the book

> . . . betrays that absence of literary enthusiasm, for which perhaps the public is more to blame than the author; and that exclusive devotedness to the mere business transactions of life, which may create good merchants and rich men, but which will never make successful writers. He is on the spot, and probably within reach of the best sources of information at present in existence, and is hardly excusable for having used so little research in preparing the present collection.

Morris concluded:

> . . . with only one or two exceptions, it is decidedly the most agreeable work of the kind we have read since the days of the Sketch Book. Before we opened it, from our previous knowledge of the literary abilities of the author, we anticipated much pleasure, but our expectations were more than realized; and though we will not, in the usual style, inform the public that he [Whittier] is equal to Scott or Irving, we can assure them that the "Legends of New-England" is no trifling addition to the stock of American literature.

A better literary service to his native region was Whittier's poem "New England," which appeared in the *New England Weekly Review* on October 18, 1830. He sang of its physical and moral beauty with a just and sure harmony, and he vowed that his poetry would always celebrate New England. Characteristically, he concluded the lyric with a restatement of his own ambitions, which, if they should one day lead to fame, would only yet more glorify his Yankee land.

Also characteristically, in an editorial entitled "New England" which was published in the *Review* on November 15, 1830,[36] Whittier made it clear that it was *old* New England which claimed his devotion. He was his essential self in pleading fervently for the election of *men* as New England's political representatives —

> . . . men of sterling principles and strong minds, who, when contending for the right would never quail at the time of trial — but would stand up in the struggle of mind with mind, unhumbled and unquailing, like the oaks of their own territory, when their brethren of the forest are bending like reeds before the whirlwind.

Could an inner voice have been telling Whittier that his own severest "time of trial" was only two and a half years away?

The "whirlwind" came on January 1, 1831, when William Lloyd Garrison first issued the *Liberator*, in Boston. Garrison's program, in the view of a social historian,[37] hit the South at the region's most sensitive four points. It was directed against the foundation of the South's whole economic and industrial system; it advocated direct action against property; it threatened a racial war or revolution; and it offended the psychology of the South — the people's sense of good breeding and true neighborliness and their religion, in the view of which "New England 'Come-

Outers' such as Unitarians" were "believed to have rejected the fundamental tenets of Christianity."

Whittier could not have understood, any better than Garrison, the psychology of the South, but not even a perfect grasp of it would have shaken his Quaker conviction that slavery was wrong. If he had not, in 1830–31, Garrison's fiery zeal for Abolition, his several pronouncements in the *Review* on the subject of slavery were nevertheless unalterably firm. On July 26, 1830, Whittier answered the *Sumterville* (South Carolina) *Gazette*, which had taken violent exception to an earlier editorial by Prentice in reply to the *Charleston Mercury*. Whittier defended the right of the North to speak its convictions about slavery. On January 10, 1831, there appeared in the *Review* another editorial on "Freedom of the Press." Again, the publication of Whittier's poem "To William Lloyd Garrison" in the *Haverhill Gazette* (November 26, 1831) was an important milestone in his own march toward Abolitionism.

But Whittier was far from certain, yet, precisely in what direction he would march. The yearning for fame was still strong in him, as he made repeatedly clear in the columns of the *Review*, and in April, 1831, he wrote to a literary lady in New Haven:

> Disappointment in a thousand ways has gone over my heart, and left it dust. Yet I still look forward with high anticipations. I have placed the goal of my ambitions high — but with the blessing of God it shall be reached. The world has at last breathed into my bosom a portion of its own bitterness, and I now feel as if I would wrestle manfully in the strife of men. If my life is spared, the world shall know me in a loftier capacity than *as a writer of rhymes*. There — is not that boasting? — But I have said it with a strong pulse and a swelling heart, and I shall strive to realize it.[38]

## 4

Certainly Whittier was in no mood for checks upon his ardor. At the start of 1831 he had come under the eye of William Joseph Snelling, whose satirical *Truth: A New Year's Gift for Scribblers* was a cold douche for more than one New England driver of the quill. Snelling chided Whittier for his too confident settlement of all questions: the meagerness of his culture and of his information would, in Snelling's judgment, have made it a more graceful thing for him to say, now and then, "I don't know." There was a modicum of truth in the satirist's lines. Whittier's rejoinder to these strictures was clear and curt as a dagger:

> "*Truth: a New Year's gift for scribblers.*" This is the title of a pamphlet, in imitation of "English bards and Scotch Reviewers," recently published in Boston. It possesses all the marks which distinguish its copy, except genius, spirit, satire, and poetry.[39]

In spite of Snelling's jibes, Whittier during his period with the *Review* did make progress in the writing of verse. He was himself more critical of it than he had been previously, as one amusing bout with J. T. Buckingham illustrates. In the *Review* of August 30, 1830, Whittier published "Rhymes," a neat thrust in prose at Buckingham, editor of the *Boston Courier*, who had reproved him for having dashed off Cavalier trifles. In this particular issue of the *Review* Whittier also published a weak poem of love, "To Mary," which had originally appeared in the *Courier* on June 13, 1829. He chaffed Buckingham for his want of critical taste in accepting such fare, and added that "we shall not again do outrage to the good sense of the public by anything of a like nature." Whittier gave notice, moreover, that he did not crave for the *Review* any verses written in the Cavalier manner.

Certainly the verses of love which Whittier now produced were an improvement over his past sentimental effusions. In two lyrics which were published in the *Review* on September 27 and October 18, 1830, and in which he was possibly reminiscing about his cousin, Whittier reduced his numbers to something like simplicity and harmony.

Whatever his present feelings about Mary were, Whittier threw a veil over them by repeated remarks, most of them plainly in jest, about celibacy and about love. He turned aside a reproach from the *Cincinnati Literary Chronicle* by saying [40] that he was "a bachelor not from principle but from necessity." But, in a letter to his friend F. A. P. Barnard [41] he remarked that "you know well I am no lady's man — and you know too that I am a bachelor in principle."

All of that talk was mere obscuration. Whittier might boast his indifference, but as editor of the *Review* he frequently bowed at that factitious "shrine" where all "radiant girls" dwelt. One reason for his paradoxical conduct was Cornelia Russ,[42] the daughter of his friend, Judge John Russ. Whittier's poem "To N. F. R." in the *Review* dated April 25, 1831, may have paid tribute to her charms. He had "a feeling holy, strong, benign" for her, but did not venture to call it love. His longer poem, "The Declaration," followed in the *Review* on August 8. By this time he was certain that his feeling for the lady was love — and certain that it would be unrequited.

If these lines were addressed to Cornelia Russ, they merely prefaced Whittier's real declaration. It is uncertain when he wrote to request the "interview" in order that he might ask for her hand, but the letter must have been composed in the autumn of 1831 just before Whittier left Hartford for Haverhill — virtually forever, as it proved. The courtly document read:

Thursday afternoon.

Miss Russ.

I could not leave town without asking an interview with you. I know that my proposal is abrupt — and I cannot but fear that it will be unwelcome. But you will pardon me. About to leave Hartford for a distant part of the country,[43] I have ventured to make a demand, for which under any other circumstances, I should be justly censurable. I feel that I have indeed no claims on your regard. But I would hope, almost against any evidence to the contrary, that you might not altogether discourage a feeling which has long been to me as a new existence. I would hope that in my absence from my own New England, whether in the sunny South or the "Far West," that one heart would respond with my own — one bright eye grow brighter at the mention of a — name, which has never been, and I trust never will be, connected with dishonor, — and which, if the Ambition which now urges onward shall continue in vigorous exercise, shall yet be known widely and well — and whose influence shall be lastingly felt. —

— But this is dreaming, — and it may only call forth a smile. If so — I have too high an opinion of your honorable feelings to suppose even for a moment that you would make any use of your advantage derogatory to the character of a highminded, and ingenuous girl ——

— I leave town on Saturday. Can you allow of an interview this evening or on that of Friday? If however you can not consistently afford me the pleasure of seeing you — I have only to resign hopes dear to me as life itself, and carry with me hereafter the curse of disappointed feeling.

A note in answer will be waited for impatiently. At least you will not deny me this.

Yrs. most truly

J. G. Whittier [44]

Only silence appears to have followed, and no heartburn on Whittier's part. His growing interest in politics gave him a quick release into sterner things than love, a fact which was to be good for his career.

Whittier's evident failure in love was abundantly offset by his success as editor of the *Review*. Despite gaps in his equipment, his product consistently outshone, both in quality and quantity, other New England weekly newspapers. This is not high praise until it is remembered that Whittier throughout his Hartford period was in frail health, and that he was not yet twenty-four when he gave up active charge of the *Review*. His awareness of current events and tendencies, particularly those of a political or literary cast, was exceptional. It was to remain so to the end of his life.

Travel was already another of Whittier's permanent interests. In proportion as his health declined, his interest in travel and far places increased. The subject evoked spirited and frequently humorous comment in the *Review*. On March 5, 1831, in a long letter to F. A. P. Barnard he discoursed amusingly on his protracted and disagreeable trip from Hartford to Haverhill. On May 9 Whittier related having spent, about a week since, a few hours in Springfield, and having been shown the "lions of the village" by the editor of the *Springfield Republican*. He recommended the return trip by steamboat, which "was accomplished in the short space of 2½ hours." Manifestly this outing was taken for reasons of health, and within a month Whittier went, from the same motive, to New Haven. In the *Review* of June 6 (probably in temporary charge of Barnard) there was a revealing note: "Our Editor is probably alive, breathing the pure, salt breezes in New-Haven, where he was sojourning a few days since, in search of health. His absence must account for our great lack of editorial [matter] this week and many other unmentionable defects." In the *Review* on July 18 Whittier mentioned this hegira in "A Week in New Haven," and in a letter from Haverhill on the fourteenth he revealed that he had just returned from "away 'Down East.' " [45]

It was ill health which finally forced Whittier to leave Hartford and the *Review*, apparently in October, 1831, when he was in such a delicate state that he had to be accompanied to Haverhill by Doctor John C. Crane.[45] On May 18 he had written to his mother that, so greatly was he suffering from kine pox and insomnia, he was forced to take laudanum.[46] By October 17 he felt obliged to apologize to his readers for the leanness of his editorial matter, although he remarked gaily that an editor had as much right to sickness as anybody else.[47] On November 7 it was announced in the *Review* that Whittier had been for some time absent from Hartford, and on November 21 that he had given Samuel Hanmer power of attorney over correspondence to the editor. Finally, in December, Whittier made a determined effort to go to Hartford; he had been appointed a delegate to attend, on December 12 in Baltimore, the convention of the National Republican party which was to nominate Henry Clay as a candidate for President. Whittier, alas, was unable to travel farther than Boston, and he was too exhausted even to return at once to Haverhill. On December 31 the *Philadelphia Album* began the chorus of compliments to him as retiring editor of the *Review*, and on January 2, 1832, Whittier's farewell "To the Patrons of the N.E.W. Review" was published.[48]

## 5

Whittier's physical debility, imposed upon his high ambitions, sat hard upon him; how hard, is shown plainly in his letter of January 5, 1832, to Jonathan Law:

> Well — I *have* at last written — or am a going to, — being the third time which I have actually written to you since I left Hartford, and delayed sending because I expected to be the bearer of my own epistle. I have been at home — that is to say in this vicinity all the time — half sick — half mad. . . . For the last fortnight I have been kept close. Mr. Barnard has doubtless told you that I started for H. about three or four weeks since, and was obliged to return —
>
> Now you may suppose that I have got the hypo. No such thing. It is all as real as the nose on my face, this illness of mine — alas, too real. Nor am I under the cerulean influence of the blue devils, *now*.

The last blue-visaged imp has departed with my exorcism ringing in his ears — "*Conjuro te sceleratissime* abire ad tuum locum."

But nonsense apart, my dear sir, what shadows we are, and what shadows we pursue! — We start vigorously forward with something for our object — up up among the very clouds — we toil on — we sacrifice *present* ease and *present* happiness — we turn from *real* blessings to picture *future* ones — unsubstantial as the fabric of the summer cloud or the morning mist. We press on for a time [,] the overtaxed nerves relax from their first strong tension — until the mysterious machinery of our existence is shattered and impeded — *until the mind realizes that chained down to material grossness and clogged with a distempered and decaying mortality it cannot rise to heaven!* Perhaps it is well — indeed we know it is — that this should be the end of human ambition. But, oh, how humiliating to the vanity of our nature! —

Now don't imagine for one moment, that I have become morose or melancholy. Far from it, I am among anxious friends. I have a thousand sources of enjoyment, even in the midst of corporeal suffering. I have an excellent society here to visit and receive visits from — my early companions — those who have grown up with me — who have known me long and well. I have spent some time in Boston, Salem, Marblehead, Andover etc, among "brave men and fair women" — have dabbled somewhat in local politics — and am extensively popular just now on that account. The girls here are fine specimens of what girls should be — excellent hearted creatures. You will find a description of one or two of them in a *poem* which I shall send you in a few weeks ["Moll Pitcher"] — perhaps in less time — a poem partly written at your house; and which is being published. It lay around in fragments, staring me every where in the face, and at last, to get rid of it I have given it over to the Book Makers — They will have a hard bargain of it.

Decency forgive me! I've filled up two pages with that most aristocratic little pronoun which represents the writer of this epistle. Misery makes a man an egotist, all the world over. *** [49]

That letter brought no answer, so on February 4 Whittier wrote Law again. "I have been quite ill," he lamented, " — and still am an invalid." One month later he sent Mrs. Sigourney, from Haverhill, a virtual "song of myself," written on a large scale. This letter read:

A thousand thanks for your kind letter which is now before me! — It has acted upon my melancholy feelings like a spell of exorcism. —

"Welcome as thy odours fanned
Around the weary seaman's keel
From some unseen and flowery land."

I say *melancholy* feelings — they are so only in consequence of ill health — and visit me only at intervals. In this vicinity I have every thing to make me happy — quiet, contentment — and a large circle of warm and kind-hearted friends. And yet, I long to visit Hartford — it has for me a thousand pleasant associations: — and the opportunity which my residence there afforded me of a personal acquaintance with yourself, is to me a constant source of self-congratulation. When your letter arrived, I had just been reading for the second time your admirable story in the "Amaranth." I know not what others may say, — indeed I care not, — but I do honestly think, that the short story of Jehiel Wigglesworth, aside from the laudable object which the author evidently had in view, contains more *nature* — a better delineation of New England character — and a closer imitation of the real Yankee dialect, than all the tales and novels, which have heretofore filled the circulating Libraries or the newspapers of this country.

I intended when I left Hartford to proceed immediately to the West. But a continuance of ill-health has kept me at home. I have scarcely done anything this winter. There have been few days, in which I have been able to write with any degree of comfort. I have indeed thrown together a poem of some length the title of which ("*Moll Pitcher*") has very little connection with the subject. You have doubtless heard of Moll Pitcher. This poem — I handed it to a friend of mine — and he has threatened to *publish* it. — It will not have the advantage or disadvantage of my name, however. — I have also written — or rather begun to write, a work of fiction, which shall have for its object the reconciliation of the North & the South — being simply an endeavor to do away [with] some of the prejudices, which have produced enmity between the Southron & the Yankee. — The style which I have adopted, is about half way between the abruptness of Lawrence Sterne and the smooth gracefulness of W. Irving. I may fail — indeed I suspect I shall — but I have more philosophy than poetry in my composition — and if I am disappointed in one project — I have only to lay it aside & take another up. If I thought I deserved half the compliments you have been pleased to bestow upon my humble exertions, I should certainly be in danger of becoming obnoxious to the charge of vanity. The truth is, I love poetry, with a love as warm, as fervent, as sincere, as any of the more gifted worshippers at the temple of the Muses. — I consider its gift as something holy and above the fashion of the world. In the language of Sir Francis Bacon "The Muses are in league with Time" — which spares their productions, in its work of universal desolation. But I *feel* and know that

> "To other chords than mine belong
> The breathing of immortal song" [50]

and, in consequence, I have been compelled to trust to other & less pleasant pursuits, for distinction and profit. Politics is the only field now open for me, and there is something inconsistent in the character of a poet & a modern politician. — People of the present day seem to have the ideas similar to those of that old churl of a Plato, who was for banishing all poets from his perfect republic.

— Did you ever read these lines from Halleck? —

> But when the grass grows green above me,
> And those who know me now & love me
> Are sleeping by my side,
> Will it avail me aught that men
> Tell to the world with lip & pen,
> That I have lived & died? —
> *No* — if a garland for my brow,
> Is growing let me have it *now*,
> While I am alive to wear it; —
> And if in whispering my name
> There's music in the voice of fame,
> Like Garcia's, *let me hear it!* [51]

Now I feel precisely so. I would have fame visit me *now*, — or not at all. — I would not choose between a nettle or a rose to grow over my grave. If I am worthy of fame, I would ask it now — now in the spring-time of my years — when I might share its smile with the friends whom I love, and by whom I am loved in return. But who would ask a niche in that temple where the *dead* alone are crowned — where the green & living garland waves in ghastly contrast over the pale, cold brow & the visionless eye; — and where the chant of praise & the voice of adulation fall only on the deafened ear of Death?

I have written to my frd B. on the subject of the Amaranth. — I will take care to do your other errand in Boston. I have a Work in my possession — the poems of Alonzo Lewis — who wishes me to hand it to you. — I shall be in Hartford as soon in the Spring as the travelling will admit. — Will you remember me kindly to my friend Stamiatides? — I am happy to see that the people of Hartford are alive on the subject of education in Greece. — My frnd Mr. Law will hand you this. Excuse this hasty — & I fear incoherent letter, and believe me that nothing would afford me greater pleasure than a speedy answer to it.[52]

Whittier had indeed had hopes of becoming an editor in Cincinnati, after leaving Hartford. As early as February 7, 1831, in the *New England Weekly Review* he had intimated [53] that "we intend to take a journey shortly to the 'far West.'" Evidently he proposed to go to Cincinnati in the following autumn or the early winter. At any rate, he was in correspondence with Isaiah Thomas, publisher of the *Cincinnati American;* and on May 5, 1832, he was further requested by Dexter and Bond, who had recently purchased the languishing newspaper, to come and put health into it.[54] They wrote, in part:

We should be happy to obtain your assistance upon any terms which should appear reasonable. It would not at present pay much; but we should hope it might soon afford a very liberal encouragement. If you should still feel inclined to try the western section of our country, I hope you will feel willing to make an arrangement with [us] upon terms mutually advantageous. We should at least try to accommodate ourselves to your own terms.

Whittier's own precarious health decided his course. He remained in Haverhill. "He worked between headaches," as George W. Cate remarked,[55] for the rest of his life; but he worked prodigiously.

During 1832 politics gained a firm ascendency in Whittier's mind over poetry. There was much evidence of that; almost none that a year hence he would firmly set his course and become an Abolitionist. On January 1, 1832, however, the New England Anti-Slavery Society was formed. Little by little, Garrison and Whittier were drawing together in the common cause to which both men dedicated so much of their life's work.

By this time Whittier had become independent of A. W. Thayer, and he contributed to the *Haverhill Iris*,[56] which was supporting Caleb Cushing for Representative to Congress, as well as to the *Gazette*. Whittier's enthusiasm for Clay waned noticeably after 1833, but during 1832 it had the further proof of his editorial, "Mr. Clay and the Tariff," which was published in the *Iris* on January 21, 1832. "If any man," said Whittier, "can reconcile the jarring interests of the country that man is Henry Clay." To the *Iris* of August 25 Whittier contributed his long poem, "Stanzas" ("Ay — stand erect! — the cloud is broken"), also written in honor of Clay. Like "Star of the West!" which Whittier had contributed to the *Cincinnati American* of May 3, 1830, these lines were widely circulated in the country as campaign propaganda for Clay.

Whittier's other political writings during 1832 were of varying tones. In the *Gazette* of March 17 was published an editorial philippic, "Martin Van Buren," two columns in length, to which Whittier signed his initials. This piece was conceived in a strain of high invective, and it foretold precisely in what terms Whittier was later to pronounce judgment upon politicians and other people who dodged what he considered their duty regarding slavery. Whittier asserted that recent developments in Washington

> . . . have numbered Martin Van Buren in the disgraceful catalogue of those exposed demagogues and baffled intriguers, who in all ages, and in all countries have been condemned to general and perpetual execration. . . . But the cowardly interloper — the stealing and crafty intriguer — the grovelling demagogue — the mousing politician — the ambitious hypocrite — however flattered and caressed in prosperity, in his downfall becomes the unpitied object of universal contempt and unbounded detestation. . . .

(In January, Van Buren, already in London as Ambassador to the Court of St. James, was refused confirmation when Calhoun, as Vice-President, cast the vote which broke a tie in the Senate.) Whittier accused Van Buren of capitalizing on the baser passions of human nature, and he ended by ranking him along with the Robespierres, the Polignacs, and the Burrs as "the deadliest enemies of republican freedom — deliberate and inexcusable conspirators against human liberty and happiness."

More astute judges of politics took another view of Van Buren's temporary reverse. G. C. Verplanck, Congressman from New York, remarked to William Cullen Bryant, "That makes Van Buren President of the United States." [57]

Whittier's references, in his attack on Van Buren, revealed something of his current study of the literature of politics. During 1832 he read Montesquieu, for one, and he re-examined Burke.[58] An unmistakable fruit of this study was Whittier's series of four articles entitled "The Veto and Its Doctrines," which appeared in the *Haverhill Gazette*. He signed himself "Eustis." [59] Whittier, intensely in earnest, spoke with unusual force and emphasis. Montesquieu gave him his text: "There is no liberty if the power of *judging* be not separated from the *Legislative* and *Executive* powers," but Whittier cited chapter and verse from Jackson's own pronouncements regarding his refusal to re-charter the United States Bank.

Whittier was less interested in the question of bank or no bank than in the basic equilibrium of the three branches of the federal government. This balance he considered to be in gravest danger; hence he believed the Constitution itself to be imperiled. Had not Burke sufficiently demonstrated the blessings of a Constitution, and the perils inherent in its violation? Burke's words were a kind of prophetic law to Whittier, who in these articles quoted almost verbatim, from passages which he had marked in his set of Burke's works.[60] Whittier's thesis was directly based on Burke's dictum that "a constitution is a thing antecedent to government; and . . . the constitution of a country is not the act of its government, but of a people constituting a government."

Whittier thus viewed with high concern Jackson's strong-willed course. To the opposition it was unconstitutional, and so opposed to the people themselves, the framers of the Constitution. The sanctity of ancestral custom and establishment was never stronger in Whittier than at this period.

Whittier asserted that Jackson also directly opposed the known will of the people in overriding the vote of the House of Representatives, who had favored the bank bill. Finally, in the fourth article of his series, Whittier summarized his objections in these terms:

> A great question, pregnant as I conceive, with the fate of the Republic is about to be decided. It will be for the people speedily to determine whether the institutions which our fathers founded and blessed, — our sacred Constitution, — our Union, — all that has made us glorious

among the nations of the Earth, shall be yet longer sustained, — a blessing for ourselves and a legacy for our children: — or, whether by countenancing past misrule and thereby inducing still greater for the future, they are prepared to establish Despotism on the ruins of constitutional liberty — Disunion in the place of Union — violence in the place of peace; and national misery and shame for our present happiness and honor.[61]

In our brief strictures upon the Veto Message it has been seen that the following are among the doctrines which it advances:

1. That the Constitution of the U.S. is not binding upon the officers who have sworn to support it.
2. Because *its principles are not definitely fixed:* inasmuch as each individual in the Confederacy may give them *a different interpretation,* and yet amidst all this multiplicity of opinions, *none can be wrong.*
3. That the Supreme Judiciary, the Constitution to the contrary notwithstanding, has no authority to decide upon the legality of public acts, beyond what is possessed by each individual in the Union.
4. That the confederated States have no common umpire; — no rights surrendered upon the altar of national Union as a pledge of their good faith.
5. That the Executive is independent of, and beyond the reach of the Judicial — the Legislative and the popular powers.
6. That Southern nullification is a justifiable resistance to the legislation of Congress.

"It requires no extraordinary discernment," protested Whittier in conclusion, "to perceive that the whole tendency of the present Chief Magistrate has been towards the possession of absolute dictation. His whole life has been marked by the exercise of arbitrary power and a violent disregard of the rights of his fellow men." [62] Whittier declared ominously that four more years of Jackson as President would leave little of value to defend; then he uttered prophetic words: "A nation divided against itself — a broken union — a dishonored name! With nations as with men the downhill road of ruin is rapidly trodden, even to its lowest abyss, after the first fatal steps are taken."

On October 11, five days after his fourth article on the veto had been published in the *Gazette,* Whittier attended the State convention of the

National Republican party,[63] at Worcester. Between five hundred and six hundred delegates listened to an address by Daniel Webster,[64] and Whittier, who elsewhere had heard him "sneered at by the *counterfeit democracy* of the day," rushed back to Haverhill and penned a glowing appreciation of Webster's various gifts. This encomium, over the signature "W," was published in the *Gazette* on October 20, 1832. It was significant because in it Whittier indicated that his current education in politics had included a reading of the orations of Brougham, Canning, Chatham, and other English statesmen besides Burke.

Whittier got his real political education, however, in active politics. He appears to have busied himself in Cushing's behalf soon after returning from Hartford, since on February 11, 1832, Thayer in the *Gazette* charged that Whittier's greatest fault was his attachment to Cushing. It was in fact enduring, as much so as the contest of 1831–1833 — which ran through seventeen ballots — for a Representative to Congress from Essex North. In March, 1832, Cushing withdrew his name momentarily from the lists.[65] Whittier, who so far had supported Cushing, was urged to run as a compromise candidate, partly with a view to drawing Thayer's support. This was enticing bait, and Whittier wrote to Harriman, probably in August, 1832, how he might be made "available":

> Since conversing with you yesterday, a new objection to our project has occurred to me, — the Constitution requires that the Representative shall be twenty-five years of age. I shall not be twenty-five till the 17th of December. So that I would not be eligible at the *next* trial in November. This, you will see, gives a different aspect to the whole affair. *Perhaps*, however, if the contest is *prolonged* till after the next time, the project might be put in execution.
>
> Suppose you advocate a holding on to Mr. C. in your Newburyport letter? Suppose, too, that you nominate in your paper Mr. Cushing without any one-sided convention? After the trial in November, you can *then* use the arguments in favor of our plan which you propose to do now; and if it suits Mr. C. he can then *request* his friends to give their votes for some other individual for the sake of promoting peace in the district. The Kittredge committee [66] would in that case probably nominate a candidate, — if one could be found, — but, I understand Mr. Thayer, not with the expectation of his being elected.
>
> If I were nominated after the November trial, Mr. Thayer, situated

as he and I relatively are, would support the nomination, and let the other candidate go, as he did John Merrill.[67] Purdy,[68] the "Telegraph," [69] and the "Essex Register" [70] would do the same.

The truth of the matter is, the thing would be peculiarly beneficial to me, — if not at home it would be so abroad. It would give me an opportunity of seeing and knowing our public characters, and in case of Mr. Clay's election might enable me to do something for myself or my friends. It would be worth more to me *now*, young as I am, than almost any office after I had reached the meridian of life.

In this matter, if I know my own heart, I am not entirely selfish. I never yet *deserted a friend*, and I never will. If my friends enable me to acquire influence, it shall be exerted for *their benefit*. And give me once an opportunity of exercising it, my first object shall be to evince my gratitude by exertions in behalf of those who had conferred such a favor upon me. . . . [71]

This maneuver, which came to nothing, represents one of Whittier's few lapses from a native idealism in his entire life. Place-seeking was alien to his nature, an appeal to self-interest even more so. Whittier's motive undoubtedly was his determination to have immediate and compensating success in politics, now that he had turned to it from six years of relatively fruitless versifying.[72]

One other excursion into office-seeking in 1832 also left Whittier unrewarded. On October 25 he was nominated on the National Republican ticket of four men as a candidate for Representative from Haverhill to the State legislature. This announcement appeared in the *Iris* of October 27, which on November 3 added that Whittier had withdrawn from the ticket. He escaped defeat, providentially for his frame of mind at the time, for, according to the *Iris* of November 17, the four National Republican candidates were defeated by four Jackson adherents.

Now it was on the side that Whittier wrote, a scrap of verse here, a bit of prose there. One elegiac poem — to the memory of Lucretia Maria Davidson — appeared in the *New England Weekly Review* on February 6, 1832, and "The Portrait" [73] in the *Haverhill Gazette* on February 18. Two prose articles of 1832 contain both more substance and more significance. "Powwow Hill" appeared in the *New England Magazine* in May, and "The Nervous Man" in August, with an added part in the issue of November, 1833.

"The Nervous Man," which Whittier evidently intended to publish in book form,[74] had more point and compression than most of Whittier's early prose articles, though at best it was a tenuous production. It did have the spice of variety, for Whittier's recent reading was reflected here: Coleridge, Domitian, Gall, Lavater, Pliny, Seneca, Spurzheim, Swedenborg, and numerous minor Latin writers.

Patently autobiographical touches in the article attract main notice. Whittier's friend, the nervous man, a bachelor, was full of melancholy and of notions about marriage. "Matrimony, after all," he said, "is but a doubtful experiment," a conviction which he enforced by quoting Bacon's aphorism: "He that hath wife and children hath given hostages to fortune." Such, it may be, were the consolations of philosophy to Whittier in 1832, for he wrote:

> It is unquestionably a propensity of the human heart, to seek to depreciate that, which it has in vain sought after; and it may be owing to this, that I take such malicious satisfaction in contemplating the character of our mother Eve. She loved Adam awhile in Paradise, it is true; but the very "first devil she saw, she changed her love." [75]

And as a token of Whittier's unrewarded feeling about poetry, there was this:

> Time has dealt hardly with my boyhood's muse. Poetry has been to me a beautiful delusion. It was something woven of my young fancies, and reality has destroyed it. I can, indeed, make rhymes now, as mechanically as a mason piles one brick above another; but the glow of feeling, the hope, the ardor, the excitement have passed away forever. I have long thought, or rather the world hath *made* me think, that poetry is too trifling, too insignificant a pursuit for the matured intellect of sober manhood. . . .

The second instalment of "The Nervous Man" likewise appeared to be vibrant with Whittier's own thoughts, given voice by his ventriloquistic friend. The first of the four parts was a protest against female vocal music, and the last was entitled "Coquets — Male and Female." It was virtually the same as "The Male Coquette," which Whittier had published in the *New England Weekly Review* on October 10, 1831, except that the second paragraph hit harder at this "anomaly in the human character, — a monster in the moral world. . . ."

So different from "The Nervous Man" was "Powwow Hill" as almost to have seemed the creation of another hand. In humor, diction, narrative skill, and management of material it was almost unique among Whittier's prose articles of this time. The story was based upon an Essex County legend, and, though slight, it was amusingly and swiftly told.

Whittier's other literary endeavors of 1832 culminated mainly in three books. In February or March appeared Mirick's *History of Haverhill*, some of the material for which Whittier had collected;[76] in April Whittier's "Moll Pitcher" was published; and in July his *Literary Remains of John G. C. Brainard* came from the press of P. B. Goodsell, of Hartford.

Pickard's report that Whittier felt himself deprived by Mirick of credit for his share in the Haverhill history is without foundation.[77] In the *Haverhill Gazette* of June 16, 1832, Whittier himself, in reviewing the book, struck the right note. He highly praised Mirick's researches and, in general, his writing. Whittier, without signature, established the authorship of this friendly review in the first paragraph, which reads:

> As a citizen of this town, I feel myself under many obligations to Mr. Mirick for his excellent History. It is not easy for a majority of its readers to form an adequate conception of the degree of labor and patient research expended upon so small a volume. The writer of this — in common with many others — believed it to be an easy task to collect and reduce to historical method the materials for such a history; and he had even proposed to undertake it himself — but he is free to confess that the many obstacles which unfolded themselves in the outset, were among the prominent reasons for his abandoning the idea.

"Moll Pitcher," which Whittier had begun writing in Hartford, was completed partly as an escape from the illness which probably kept him immured in East Haverhill during much of the winter of 1831–32. This poem, some eight hundred lines in length, sprang from an interest which his Uncle Moses had implanted in him — in spirits, spiritualism, and witchcraft. Whittier's early writings abounded with evidences of this special interest.

In the scales of today, "Moll Pitcher" holds interest simply because, like *Legends of New-England*, it shows Whittier again quarrying in native materials. Moll Pitcher was a fortune-teller, famous during the nineteenth century, who lived in that part of Lynn, Massachusetts, which is now Nahant.[78]

"Moll Pitcher" was a mélange; the narrative method strongly suggested Scott, the dominant tone was Byronic, and the occasional New England touches and the artistic blemishes were Whittier's own. His choicest poetry here was the lyric "New England," minus one stanza, which had been published in the *New England Weekly Review*.[79] As a whole, however, the production was inchoate versifying, and as he confessed in his quizzical preface, Whittier had no illusions about it.

The reviewers — a numerous company of them — quickly recognized the hand of the author, and shook it much too warmly. Two critics were more discerning. One, writing in the *New England Magazine* for May, 1832, chided the author for publishing a poem avowedly not his best. "He can do better," concluded the reviewer, "— the public and his friends, his *real* friends, expect him to do better. . . ." Mrs. Sarah J. Hale, in whose maternal phrases the review of Whittier's book for the *Ladies' Magazine* (July, 1832) was apparently couched, joined the other dissident critic in praising the lyric "New England."

> We do not, however [she concluded], give an unqualified approbation of this Poem. The beginning is not, as we think, in good taste, and there is a carelessness in the versification which at times is slovenly and unpardonable in one who could polish if he would take pains. It is no excuse to plead want of time. No poem should be given to the public till the author has finished it with all his skill. We are sick of this affectation of striking off works, as it were at a dash. It is no proof of genius, and it often injures, even ruins efforts that with care might be really excellent. Our most serious objection to this poem is, that by the author's confession, and its internal evidence, it was done in a hurry.

Whittier was less headlong in preparing the memoir and poems of Brainard for publication, but this work suffered acutely because of Whittier's absence from Hartford while it was being hastily printed there. He appears to have been in Hartford in May,[80] but from then until the book was put through the press in the summer his interest in the project languished.[81] In the autumn Whittier wrote to Jonathan Law:

> . . . I have not seen a copy of it — the proof wasn't read, and from an extract or two which I have seen, [I judge that] it is pretty well spiced with mistakes. If you ever see Mr. Goodsell will you be kind enough to tell him that I have not received a single copy of his Book?[82]

The significant part of *The Literary Remains of John G. C. Brainard, with a sketch of his life by J. G. Whittier* was the memoir, thirty pages long. Whittier greatly overpraised Brainard's verse, but he appropriately extolled the Connecticut literary pioneer for his use of native American material. This subject firmly engaged Whittier; virtually all the camouflage of imitation and literary affectation fell away from his style, in this longest piece of prose which he had so far published. He said now simply what he had to say:

> There is one important merit in his poetry which would redeem a thousand faults. It is wholly American. If he "babbles o' green fields" and trees they are such as of right belong to us. He does not talk of the palms and cypress where he should describe the rough oak and sombre hemlock. He prefers the lowliest blossom of Yankee-land to the gorgeous magnolia and the orange bower of another clime. It is this which has made his poetry popular and his name dear in New-England.
>
> It has been often said that the New World is deficient in the elements of poetry and romance; that its bards must of necessity linger over the classic ruins of other lands; and draw their sketches of character from foreign sources, and paint Nature under the soft beauty of an Eastern sky. On the contrary, New-England is full of Romance; and her writers would do well to follow the example of Brainard. The great forest which our fathers penetrated — the red men — their struggle and their disappearance — the Powwow and the War-dance — the savage inroad and the English sally — the tale of superstition, and the scenes of Witchcraft, — all these are rich materials of poetry. We have indeed no classic vale of Tempe — no haunted Parnassus — no temple, gray with years, and hallowed by the gorgeous pageantry of idol worship — no towers and castles over whose moonlight ruins gathers the green pall of the ivy. But we have mountains pilloring [pillaring] a sky as blue as that which bends over classic Olympus; streams as bright and beautiful as those of Greece or Italy, — and forests richer and nobler than those which of old were haunted by Sylph and Dryad.[83]

For this editorial labor Whittier received sixty dollars.[84]

His last significant literary work of 1832 was created in his own right — the prophetic poem, "To a Poetical Trio in the City of Gotham."[85] This purposeful and characteristic creation, ninety-six lines of brisk satire in *ottava rima*, was published in the *Haverhill Iris* on September 29. The piece indicated Whittier's now complete conversion to the principle of art for humanity's sake, and it denoted the last stage of change in him from the ambitious and vagrant versifier of 1826–32 to the social reformer of 1833–65 and later. The poem was slightly colored with Whittier's oppositionist propaganda, for in it he implored James Lawson, of the *New York Mercantile Advertiser*, and William Cullen Bryant and William Leggett, of the *New York Evening Post*, to forsake propagandizing Jacksonism and to write and work for the social amelioration of the nation. The last three stanzas show Whittier, who had now at last decided upon his mission in life, seeking also to recruit the New York editors for humanitarian works:

> Lost trio! — turn ye to the minstrel pride
> Of classic Britain. Even effeminate Moore
> Has cast the wine-cup and the lute aside
> For Erin and O'Connell; and before
> His country's altar, Bulwer breasts the tide
> Of old oppression. Sadly brooding o'er
> The fate of heroes struggling to be free,
> Even Campbell speaks for Poland. *Where are ye?*
>
> Hirelings of traitors! — Know ye not that men
> Are rousing up around ye to retrieve
> Our country's honor, which too long has been
> Debased by those for whom ye daily weave
> Your web of fustian: That from tongue and pen
> Of those who o'er our tarnished honor grieve —
> Of the pure-hearted and the gifted, come
> Hourly the tokens of your master's doom? —
>
> Turn from *their* ruin — dash your chains aside,
> Stand up like men for Liberty and Law,
> And free opinion: Check Corruption's pride —
> Sooth[e] the loud storm of fratricidal war; —
> And the bright honors of your eventide
> Shall shame the glory which your morning saw, —
> The patriot's heart shall gladden at your name —
> Ye shall be *blessed* with, and not "*damned to fame*"!

Whittier was finally on the highroad to his life's achievement. Among his traveling companions he was to have Bryant and Leggett [86] — and Garrison.

# VI

# No Sword but a Pen

FOR WHITTIER the step into Abolitionism was a natural one. As early as 1830, directly upon becoming editor of the *Haverhill Gazette*, he had pledged himself to support "the reforming spirit, which is abroad in our land." William Ellery Channing acutely observed "an age of great movements" which had shown an unprecedented "tendency and power to exalt a people." He declared: "Every age teaches its own lesson. The lesson of this age is that of sympathy with the suffering, and of devotion to the progress of the whole human race." [1]

Thus Samuel Gridley Howe gave seven years' active service to the cause of Greek independence, collecting money in the Boston area. Thus in 1832 he established the Perkins Institution for the Blind. Thus Dorothea L. Dix aroused public sentiment for the better treatment of paupers, prisoners, and the insane. Thus, too, the United States Temperance Union was formed in 1833.[2]

In the social movements of the decade from 1830 to 1840 the Quakers, "hereditary reformers," played a conspicuous part.[3] English Friends, likewise active in Britain's contemporary reforms, helped in particular to create the sentiment which in 1833 resulted in the law insuring gradual extinction of slavery from the colonies.

## 1

Whittier, as a member of the Society of Friends, was keenly aware of these contemporary social currents. If the overtones of his early verse were chiefly of love, of ambition, and of New England lore, the dominant note in his vast production of editorials was that of social justice. For the downtrodden of the earth, and especially for the Negro slaves, he had all of the Quakers' militant sympathy. When Garrison established the Bennington *Journal of the Times* in 1828, Whittier wrote "commending his views upon Slavery, Intemperance and War, and assuring him that he was destined to do great things." [4] When Whittier himself first became editor of the *Haverhill Gazette*, on January 2, 1830, he quoted from the *Portsmouth* (Virginia) *Times* a report of the execution of four Negro slaves for killing their master in an attempt to gain their freedom, and a description of their brave defense of this act, just before being hanged. Whittier's subsequent and numerous editorial comments upon slavery further enforced his conviction that it was inhuman and un-American, and that a day of atonement for the nation's sin of racial oppression must inevitably come.

Four years of advocating social causes had naturally tempered Whittier's finely ethical mind. Although he was a primitive Quaker, best circumstanced in his own quiet corner of Essex County, he readily met the summons of his conscience when, in March of 1833, he became an Abolitionist. He was unlike Philadelphia Friends in being never at home in the market place. "We hate excitements of all kinds," he wrote in the *Haverhill Gazette* of February 6, 1830, "— we like to see the world jogging on quietly and good naturedly — we hate mortally to see those who should live like brothers of one family fall to quarrelling and fist-clenching about religion, politics or anti-masonry." But injustice aroused his suppressed combativeness, and here was a cause to be championed. After three years' pursuit of fame, notably in Boston and in Hartford, and a brief moment's jockeying for political preferment in Essex North, Whittier during his sickness and farming of 1832 became again the unselfish humanitarian. Like a true Friend he had been deliberate in taking his course, but he took it resolutely. He reclaimed his Quaker birthright when he wholly espoused a cause.

At once Whittier forsook the quiet life, and embarked upon what Garrison rightly forecast as "a most tremendous excitement." [5] How unpopular and offensive this cause was, at first, has been lucidly explained by historians of the Abolition movement.[6] The reformers had to run the double gauntlet of Southern fury over the invasion of states' rights, and Northern fear of the unwelcome effects of this anger upon trade. Moreover, Garrison, as the assumed leader of the Abolitionists, aggravated the certain trouble by leveling measureless invective at foes who did not believe that the rooted evil should be plucked from the land, and equally against Abolitionists who did not agree with him how it should be uprooted. Even in New York and in the Middle West, where Garrison had no status as Abolitionist leader, anti-slavery speakers won for their portion stones and eggs. Theodore Dwight Weld, prime mover of the rebellious students who left Lane Theological Seminary in Cincinnati and enrolled at Oberlin College, the new Abolitionist center in the Middle West, became increasingly a man of heroic mold. Only he and "the gentle Whittier, his beloved friend, were unslandered by their co-workers"; but by the public he was given the title of honor, "the most mobbed man in the United States." In central Ohio and in northeastern New York, for instance, his potent anti-slavery work nearly cost him his life.[7]

Whittier, too, when he became an Abolitionist, furthered his education by exposure to the school of mobs. But persecution had long been the badge of his Quaker tribe, as Sewel and other historians of the Friends had told him. No less had he learned that the drive of a strong concern, not petty self-interest, is the mainspring of Quaker action. In *Margaret Smith's Journal* Whittier asked, "What avail great talents, if they be not devoted to goodness?" [8]

It is uncertain precisely how, in 1832 and early in 1833, Whittier determined to abjure his bogus Byronism and to devote his talents to a cause. One certain fact is that Whittier was most in character when he was in his proper milieu, rural New England. Another is that he considered false values a regrettable penalty of urban life. That several grew upon him, in Boston and in Hartford, only marks him the more definitely as human. In East Haverhill, Whittier could reflect and weigh values. He deplored the utter sterility of much that he had written, and he resolved to dawdle no more in verse over dreams of fair cousins and of other heart's desires.

To Jonathan Law he wrote, on September 13, 1832:

> . . . even if my health were restored, I should not leave this place. I have too many friends around me — and my prospects are too good to be sacrificed for any uncertainty. I have done with poetry & literature: I can *live* as a farmer — and that is all I ask at present. . . .
>
> 'Tis true I am in love — just now — deeply & desperately — but these things seldom last with me more than ten days or a fortnight at the most, so that I shall soon be "myself again." [9]

In truth, Whittier was more like himself when, having just turned twenty-five, he wrote to Mrs. Sigourney in January, 1833:

> Continual ill health, and natural indolence — and the daily duties devolving upon me in the care of a large farm, *must* be my excuse. Of poetry I have nearly taken my leave — & a pen is getting to be something of a stranger to me. I have been compelled again to plunge into the political whirlpool; — for I have found that my political reputation is more influential than my poetical: so I try to make myself a man of the world — and the public are deceived, but *I* am not. They do not see that I have thrown the rough armor of rude & turbulent controversy over a keenly sensitive bosom — a heart of softer & gentler emotions than I dare expose. Accordingly as Gov. Hamilton of S.C. says, I have "put on athletic habits for the occasion."
>
> . . . Have you seen Garrison's "Thoughts on Colonization"? I wish you would read that Book. I know your predilection for the Col. Soc.: but I regret it.[10]

## 2

In this mood Whittier was ripe for enlistment, and Garrison, who long since had marked the poet for his own,[11] now nudged him into the Abolitionist ranks. On March 4, 1833, he wrote to a group of Haverhill young ladies who styled themselves "Inquirers after Truth," soliciting their help in inducing Whittier to "devote his brilliant genius more to the advancement of our cause, and kindred enterprises, and less to the creations of romance and fancy, and the disturbing incidents of political strife." Next, on March 22, Garrison wrote a direct appeal: "Whittier, enlist! — Your talents, zeal, influence — all are needed." Finally, on March 30, Garrison lectured in the First Parish meeting-house, in Haverhill, and "fully demonstrated to our mind the obligation of the American people to urge the *immediate* abolition of slavery." Whittier seems at this time to have been won to active Abolitionism.[12]

The first fruit of his commitment to the cause was his brief pamphlet, *Justice and Expediency*, five hundred copies of which he published in May of 1833 at his own expense.[13] This document marked the turning point in his life, and was a clear proof of his newly won driving purpose, of his changed direction of energies. It was a cogent plea for immediate abolition, written in the trenchant style of many of Whittier's Hartford editorials. Since March he had obviously re-studied old literary materials and the Constitution, and had freshly examined anti-slavery writings. For his habit of mind in this work was vastly more thorough than it ever was in his researches into New England lore. In imposing array he cited his authorities, many of them English, like Lord Brougham; and he framed an almost unanswerable argument.

> I am not unaware [he wrote] that my remarks may be regarded by many as dangerous and exceptionable; that I may be regarded as a fanatic for quoting the language of eternal truth. . . . But if such are the consequences of a simple performance of duty, I shall not regard them.[14]

That Whittier did upset some comfortable delusions is most likely, for Property must have been disturbingly pricked by his seven main points:

1. That by tolerating slavery anywhere in the United States we "practically recognize the infernal principle that 'man can hold property in man.' "
2. That the American Colonization Society has failed to improve the lot of the slaves, but instead has increased the slave population of the United States via Sierra Leone and Liberia.
3. That the only just scheme of emancipation is the immediate emancipation of the slaves, starting first in the District of Columbia and the Territories of Arkansas and Florida — which are under Federal jurisdiction.
4. That we must give effect to the spirit of the Constitution, which is guardedly silent on the subject of human servitude. "The spirit of the Constitution should be maintained within the exclusive jurisdiction of the government." "The slave-holding states are not free. The name of liberty is there, but the spirit is wanting."
5. That it is to the South's economic interest to abolish slavery now; that St. Domingo's experience has demonstrated the practical wisdom of this course.
6. That feudal aristocracy and servitude belong to old Europe, and can not exist side by side with republican equality in the United States.

7. "The burning, withering concentration of public opinion upon the slave system is alone needed for its total annihilation. . . . Nothing unconstitutional, nothing violent, should be attempted; but the true doctrine of the rights of man should be steadily kept in view; and the opposition to slavery should be inflexible and constantly maintained."

Whittier was alert to the colossal difficulties which lay in the way of changing public opinion. He was by this time thoroughly schooled in human nature, and had learned not to expect too much from it. He was also acutely conscious of the temper of the South concerning restrictive legislation, as it had been exhibited during the furore over South Carolina's threat of Nullification in 1832; and he was under no illusion that the threat of civil war was permanently past. "The danger," he wrote, "has been delayed for a time; this bolt has fallen without mortal injury to the Union, but the cloud from whence it came still hangs above us, reddening with the elements of destruction." Indeed, he added, "A day of revolution must come, and it is our duty to prepare for it." [15]

Two ideas dominated *Justice and Expediency*. For both of them, at root, Whittier was indebted to Burke and to Milton, who were to serve him well as exemplars in politics and humanitarianism. Whittier argued in his pamphlet that the existence of slavery in a state robs that state of its essential justice and virtue, and that constitutional guarantees, including that of free speech, are sacred. In essence these two ideas powered all of Whittier's protests, in verse and prose, until emancipation became a fact.[16]

Whittier posted copies of *Justice and Expediency* to various editors, but the treatise does not appear to have caused at once any great excitement.[17] Yet Arthur Tappan, of New York, had five thousand copies of it printed at his own expense,[18] and he also caused it to be republished in the September, 1833, issue of the *American Anti-Slavery Reporter*. Moses Brown, the wealthy Quaker philanthropist of Providence, in July procured a five-column representation of the pamphlet in the *Providence Journal*. And once the American Anti-Slavery Society was established, it reprinted *Justice and Expediency* as one of its numerous tracts.[19]

One copy of the pamphlet reached the editors of the Richmond *Jeffersonian and Times*, who forthwith (probably in the issue of July 2, 1833) poured vitriol upon it and its author.[20] Whittier henceforth was probably anathema to the South, a fact which he could not disregard. On receipt of a copy of the notice in the *Jeffersonian and Times* he acted upon what became with him a fixed principle of shrewd propaganda. He countered the Richmond editors in lengthy, published letters, and for the next thirty years he seized every other opportunity to make public answers to proponents of slavery whose arguments reached his ears. Of retaliatory name-calling he was incapable; threats of violence he turned off with well bred appeals to the best in his opponents; misrepresentation he met with precise statements of fact, based upon the best information available to him; and to all humbuggery he opposed an air of inexorable reason.

The first two of a myriad such letters were published in the Salem *Essex Register* on July 25 and August 1.[21] In them Whittier elaborated his arguments of *Justice and Expediency*, that the self-interest of the South could be served only by the abandonment of slave labor in favor of free labor. As sanction for his determination to speak the truth as he saw it regarding slavery, he cited at the end of the second letter Milton's defense of free speech, in the *Areopagitica*.

Hardly a week now passed which did not test Whittier's patience, and his tenacious claim to the right of free speech. On June 27, Miss Prudence Crandall was arrested in Canterbury, Connecticut, for persisting, in the face of a special act of the state legislature, in admitting to her school Negro girls from outside the state,[22] and she was imprisoned in Brooklyn, Connecticut. Whittier, in a two-column letter published in the *Haverhill Gazette* of July 13, excoriated the authors of man-made laws "annulling the laws of God written upon the consciences of men."

There was Hebraic fire in his writing now, and he fed it with pointed quotations which testified to the breadth of his reading. All of this literary and moral armament he leveled at Doctor Ebenezer Porter, president of the Andover Theological Seminary, in a three-column letter published on August 31 in the *Haverhill Gazette*. Doctor Porter had recently visited the South, and the secretary of the American Colonization Society at the Seminary had requested a public expression of his opinion upon various aspects of the anti-slavery movement. (Doctor Porter's letter was published in the *Newburyport Herald* on August 9, 1833.) In all his intercourse with the South, said Doctor Porter, he had avoided discussion of slavery because of the peculiar delicacy of the subject; although he considered slavery a "national evil," he would eradicate it not by active opposition, but by "a wise system of moral influence."

Whittier's moral indignation erupted when he read the seeming acquiescence of a clergyman and a New Englander in the slave system as it existed. For once Whittier's pliancy of temper to human nature went cold and rigid, and he was provoked to unwonted asperity. Ranged against a theologian, he was equally skilled at argument based upon Scriptural authority; and he took higher moral ground than Doctor Porter. In the Miltonic vein, Whittier inquired whether, since Doctor Porter would not actively oppose the slave system, it was "then *unwise* to rebuke iniquity and testify in behalf of Truth! *Unwise* to apply the Gospel remedy to one sin as well as another?" Doctor Porter had featured the South's consent to the North's thinking for itself upon the subject of slavery, and Whittier derided the South's *granting* "the only right which man cannot be robbed of, by his fellow man."

How, Whittier asked pointedly, could the "prospective legislation" and the "change of habits" suggested by Doctor Porter be effected — "unless the consciences of the people are awakened to the *sin*, and their understandings convinced of the danger and impolicy of slavery? Are people usually reformed by apologizing for, and excusing, and upholding, that which needs the reformation?"

Whittier reduced to an absurdity Doctor Porter's statements that the Abolitionists sought the emancipation of the slaves in one month; that he and his fellow advocates were incendiaries or bloodthirsty men, as was widely charged, or that they had ever pursued any other than the "elevated, Christian course" recommended by Doctor Porter; that the Southern slaveholders were not reprehensible because they did not *create* the slave system; and that it was so interwoven with Southern social habits that its immediate abolition would uproot the foundations of society. Of this last argument Whittier said that it was simply not Christian.

By such documents, even before he began to write his flaming Abolitionist verses, Whittier "became the voice for which a few had been wearily waiting, yet which exasperated and terrified the whole country. To these few, therefore, Whittier at once became a prophet; to the many, an object of detestation." [23] But now he set no value at all upon the public's regard, and wished only to do his part toward displacing a system which he believed was foul with social injustice. And his choice was made the more easily because his mother and his sister Elizabeth, for whose support he was mainly responsible, approved of the decision which he had made. It was they for whom Whittier had so ardently desired early fame and its rewards.

# 3

His meager income during 1833 (and thereafter until 1866) bound them to a rigorous economy which was to last as long as they lived. In this first year as an Abolitionist he tended the farm; [24] he for a second time undertook odd jobs of bookkeeping; [25] and he contributed nine articles to the *New England Magazine*. Five of these were in prose, which, though it brought only half as much money by the page as verse, probably paid more by the piece into the needy Whittier's pocket.[26]

Without discarding old and tried *genres*, Whittier now added Abolition to his literary subjects. None of his other contributions to the *New England Magazine* during 1833 compared in interest or quality with the poem "Toussaint L'Ouverture," [27] which was published in the November issue. Whittier now had a suitable subject for poetry, and in nearly two hundred and fifty lines he told with skill, both narrative and descriptive, a heroic incident in the life of the Haytian Negro which proved his worth and stature. Gone now was Whittier's discursiveness; in its place was relatively condensed and pointed expression. Possibly excepting only "The Vaudois Teacher," [28] "Toussaint L'Ouverture" was the best poem which Whittier had yet written, and it accurately measured his progress since the adoption of a cause had begun to order his thoughts. Certainly it was better than "To the Memory of Charles B. Storrs," [29] which was published in the *Liberator* on November 30, 1833.[30]

Other activities during 1833 further prepared Whittier for his long career of political and humanitarian action. On March 2 the *Haverhill Gazette* published his two-column letter in defense of Henry Clay's policy respecting the tariff — one of Whittier's last utterances in behalf of "our Harry." On September 18 Whittier apparently attended in the company of A. W. Thayer, as a delegate from Haverhill, the convention in Worcester of the Massachusetts Society for the Suppression of Intemperance. Also in Worcester, on September 28, he was a Haverhill delegate to the State convention of the National Republican Party.[31] In November, Whittier was nominated as one of this party's four candidates for Representative to the State legislature from Haverhill, but he was defeated when Jacksonian candidates won all four seats.[32]

# 4

Career-wise, during 1833, it remained only for Whittier to become formally affiliated with Abolitionism by attending the convention in Philadelphia, from December 4 to 6, which established the American Anti-Slavery Society.[33] On November 12 he wrote to Garrison:

> I have as yet done nothing. I have had no leisure — my time is all occupied with the affairs of my farm; — I must work, or starve, — or do worse, plunge again into the seven times heated furnace of modern politics. I have strong temptations — very strong, to adopt the latter course — but Truth & Conscience & Duty are against it — for so soon as I should enter the lists of political controversy, my lips would be sealed up on the subject, dearest to my heart, the holy cause of Emancipation.
>
> I long to go to Phila: — to urge upon the members of my Religious Society, the duty of putting their shoulders to the work, — to make their solemn testimony against Slavery visible over the whole land, — to urge them by the holy memories of Woolman & Benezet & Tyson, to come up as of old to the standard of Divine Truth, though even the fires of another persecution should blaze around them. But, the expenses of the journey, will I fear be too much for me; — as thee know, our farming business does not put much cash in our pockets. — I am, however greatly obliged to the Boston Y[oung]. M[en's]. Association, for selecting me, as one of their delegates. I do not know how it may be, — but whether I go or not, my best wishes & my warmest sympathies are with the fr[ien]ds of Emancipation.[34]

The generosity of Samuel E. Sewall, of Boston, enabled Whittier — the youngest delegate — to attend the Philadelphia meeting, of which he served as secretary, and which has been called "a convention only in name." Garrison, full of zeal absorbed from his recent contact in England with Brougham, Buxton, and Wilberforce, seems to have forced the convention upon American Abolitionists who were not yet willing to advocate immediate emancipation. Leonard Bacon, one of the leading clergymen of New Haven and an anti-slavery writer, remarked acidly that Garrison was "the man whom they assembled a national convention to glorify." Short notice of the meeting, winter weather, and poor road conditions were other factors which prevented all except a fervent nucleus of Abolitionists from attending the Philadelphia meeting. And the Quakers were not out in numbers to satisfy Whittier, although twenty-one of the sixty-two delegates were Friends. Among the non-Quakers was Whittier's friend and former school teacher, Joshua Coffin, who signed the Declaration of Sentiments; and Whittier reported that there were "two or three colored members of the Convention."

Garrison seems indeed to have had his way at the three-day conclave. As author of the Declaration of Sentiments (although Samuel J. May and Whittier were appointed a committee with him to draft it), he gave to the Abolition movement its dominant character for some years to come.[35] He was firm and frank and acrid, too, in stating the principles to which he committed the American Anti-Slavery Society. Yet he specifically disavowed any intention to confront the slave system with physical force; he would uproot it by "the opposition of moral purity to moral corruption." Since he deemed the guilt of oppressing the Negroes "unequalled by any other on the face of the earth," the only way of repentance, he proclaimed, was "to break every yoke, and to let the oppressed go free."

Here, in bold terms, was the dread doctrine of immediacy. Garrison would not even compensate the slaveholders; to do so would be, in his judgment, "a surrender of the great fundamental principle that man cannot hold property in man. . . ."[36] He recognized the sovereignty of every State "to legislate exclusively on the subject of the slavery which it tolerated within its limits," and he acknowledged that Congress had no right, "*under the present national compact*," to interpose in this sphere. But he declared that Congress did have a right and a solemn duty to suppress interstate traffic in slaves, and "to abolish slavery in those portions of our territory which the Constitution has placed under its exclusive jurisdiction." Finally, Garrison avowed that the people of the free states were under the highest obligations "to remove slavery by moral and political action, as prescribed in the Constitution of the United States."[37]

Exactly one half of the delegates to the convention signed this declaration. Whittier, twelfth among the bold group, stated thirty years later, in a letter to Garrison, what that signature meant to him: "I am not insensible to literary reputation. I love, perhaps too well, the praise and good-will of my fellow-men; but I set a higher value on my name as appended to the Anti-Slavery Declaration of 1833 than on the title-page of any book."[38] The contemporary view of this commitment was less warming. In reporting the convention, the *Pennsylvania Inquirer* (Philadelphia) called the delegates "*a collection of visionary fanatics*, who know not what they do." [39]

Such sentiments were natural in Pennsylvania, which bordered upon the slave domain; but Whittier found, if not at first such bitterness, at least cautious mistrust of Abolition even in Essex County. On May 10 the *Salem Gazette*, published in the county seat, acknowledged that the North greatly desired to see the slaves set free, but declared that "the business of emancipation must be managed by those whose lives and property are staked on the event." On May 13 the *Essex Register* (Salem) asserted that "the people in this quarter are averse to any improper interference with the Southern institutions." The *Newburyport Herald*, which favored colonization, published an anti-Abolition editorial on June 24, and at the end of another on July 3 it confessed: "We look forward with intense, with almost fearful apprehension to the discussion of this subject. It is fraught with the most imminent consequences to the peace of the country." Finally, on December 21, the *Herald* discussed the Abolitionists' "Declaration of Sentiments," which, in its judgment ". . . must produce a deep impression at the South. The signers of it may say and think too, that the prosecution of their measures will not lead to any political concussions. For ourselves we cannot see, how it is possible to avoid it." [40]

In this unpromising area Whittier set about spreading Abolitionist doctrine — so far as his health and his farm work permitted — with unrelenting vigor. Better than most men he knew that New England was not soil which yielded rich or ready crops; that resistance to something was the law of New England nature. Only Whittier's tenacity, burning purpose, and sense of humor enabled him to succeed in his persistent mission of cultivation. That he was able to work at all, at times, was a sublimation of the will. But especially for the next fifteen years he did unflinchingly the prodigious work which came into his able and willing hands. What he wrote to Elizur Wright, Jr., on February 25, 1834, applied always to his work in Abolition: "I cannot as yet accuse myself of neglecting any opportunity for the dissemination of truth on the great subject of slavery." [41]

If Whittier could not go in person to perform a duty, he sent a letter in his stead — usually a long one. To Samuel E. Sewall, as secretary of the New England Anti-Slavery Society, he wrote such a letter in January,

1834,[42] the reading of which, Garrison reported in the *Liberator* on January 18, "created the liveliest sensations of heart-felt approbation in the minds of the numerous auditors." In February, Whittier's letter, written *con amore* about the reawakening of Friends to the cause of Abolition, was read in an anti-slavery address at Salem.[43] Again, although Whittier was unable to attend on October 1 a meeting held at Groton in order to organize the Middlesex County Anti-Slavery Society, he wrote at length from Haverhill on September 27, touching the familiar theme of Massachusetts' duty respecting Abolition.[44]

Whittier himself realized very clearly that his prime gift to Abolitionism was his pen. Early in 1834 he was appointed an agent of the American Anti-Slavery Society, and in his letter of acknowledgment (February 25) he fairly marked out his sphere of activity in the Abolition cause:

> Situated as I am, I can at present do but little. . . . The clergy in this vicinity are rapidly taking side with us. There is another class which might, I think, be easily moved. I allude to that class of politicians or civilians whose sphere of influence is limited to their town or county. These can take hold of our cause without essentially endangering their popularity, and through them the higher classes of our statesmen may be reached. I have some influence with this class. My exertions as a political writer for the last four years have gained me a large number of political friends. The columns of all the leading newspapers are open to me.[45] With many of the editors I am on terms of intimate personal acquaintance. All know me as a quondam brother. . . . Now if I were at leisure to reply to such misrepresentations and charges as occasionally appear in these papers — to visit personally gentlemen in my vicinity and engage their co-operation — and finally to combine the anti-slavery feeling upon some definite and practical object — such, for instance, as the election of members of the state legislature, who will bring forward and sustain resolutions instructing our Congressional delegation to urge the abolition of slavery in the District of Columbia — I have no doubt I could do good and efficient service.
>
> But I have really little leisure for such exertions. In the first place, my brother and myself are almost constantly engaged in the affairs of our small farm, which does not yield profit enough to enable us to hire labor: and I am obliged to occupy my evenings and other leisure

time in writing occasional articles for the "New England Magazine," for which I am paid. Besides this, I have felt myself under the necessity of applying myself to the study of constitutional law, political economy, etc. Whatever I have written on the subject of slavery has been an effort of extra exertion, and under circumstances of haste and constant interruption.

Now, if the Executive Committee of the American Anti-Slavery Society could assure me for the term of six months the sum of $150, I should be able to bend all the energies which God has given me to the great work before us; and I fully believe that at the end of that time we shall be able to lend both moral and pecuniary strength to the National Society. I have specified that sum as the smallest which could possibly meet my expenses, as I should be compelled to travel considerably from home, and owing to the consequent interruption of my labor on the farm, I should be under the necessity of hiring a person to supply my place.

I have been induced to make this proposal from a sincere desire of aiding in the advancement of a righteous cause. I have recently had an offer, highly favorable in a pecuniary point of view, to take charge of a political newspaper, but should I accept it, my mouth would be closed on the subject nearest my heart. The political idols of the day will accept of no divided homage. Every principle must be compromised — even holy truth suppressed — which does not tend to their elevation. Besides, I fear should I leave this place, that the leaven of anti-slavery, which is now working steadily and powerfully around me, will be checked by the strong counter influence of Andover Colonizationism.[46]

"Whittier tried an agency," wrote G. H. Barnes, "but he was too gentle for the needs of such work and he soon returned to his pen." [47] He was nothing of a revivalist, but he could do well what he had marked out for himself to do. Like his hero Milton, he was adept at written controversy: he addressed human reason rather than the emotions.

Whittier hit high. As he had previously reduced Ebenezer Porter, of Andover, so now [48] he singled out Leonard Bacon, of New Haven, for flagellation because of remarks made at the last annual meeting of the American Colonization Society and published in the New York *Evangelist.* In the guise of "Eustis," Whittier said, in part:

For the principle and practice of slavery I entertain no other feelings than those of disgust and abhorrence. A free citizen of that free state which rocked of old the cradle of American Liberty, I have a right to express those feelings. — For the two millions of my enslaved and outraged fellow beings, I feel a sympathy which I shall not seek to disguise, — a sympathy which should belong to every lover of freedom — every friend of suffering humanity, and for their relief I am ready to join in any measure *political* or otherwise, which is sanctioned by Religion and Humanity, and which involves no violation of the American Constitution, or the laws of my own State. Fully up to this point I am ready to go — heartily despising the miserable calumnies and misrepresentations of those, who, fearful themselves of doing their duty, are striving to prevent its performance by others, — of men who excuse themselves from any participation in the moral enterprises of the day, because somebody else has in their opinion, "*gone too far*," the loud denouncers of *evil* in the *abstract*, yet the timid apologists of *crime* in *practice*, ever in bondage to the opinions of others, with souls broken down to the true temper of mental slavery, and ready when duty demands an exertion of moral courage, TO PUT ON THE SPANIEL, AND PUT OFF THE MAN.

But deeply as I detest the system of Slavery, my political principles forbid me to seek its overthrow by advocating an unconstitutional interference with the slave-holding States. I would place no new power in the hands of the General Government. It has already as much as is compatible with the rights of the States. I believe I speak the sentiments of the anti-slavery portion of the community. . . .

Yet how often is the absurd objection raised against us, that we are hastening a dissolution of the Union and provoking civil war. Now for one I have never been able to see precisely how all this mischief is to be brought about by our peaceful opposition of truth to error, offering violence to no man and violating no law. Perhaps some of our wise and learned opponents can explain the *modus operandi*. What pretext will our Southern brethren have for dissolving the Union? Upon what will they make war? — Upon moral sentiment? — Upon free opinion? — Upon human sympathy for human suffering? — Will they undertake to obliterate moral Truth by the law of physics? — To revive in republican America the principles of that Ordinance which

Charles X. and Polignac could not sustain in Europe? — No — I will not so libel the high minded citizens of the South as to treat seriously this most ludicrous attempt to work upon the credulity and fears of the community. . . .

That was the essence of Whittier the controversialist. It is obvious that, remembering how newspapers widely copied his earliest writings, Whittier hoped that these published letters would likewise be circulated over the country. Whether they traveled as far as his Abolitionist verses were soon to do, is uncertain.

There is some doubt, too, about the effect of the personal letter which Whittier wrote on March 24, 1834, to William Ellery Channing, who is sometimes regarded as Whittier's prize recruit to Abolitionism.[49] Whittier, not yet acquainted with this most eminent of New England's clerical liberals — nearly twenty-eight years his senior — was emboldened by Channing's already expressed sentiments to urge his acceptance of the doctrine of immediate emancipation. At about this same time Lydia Maria Child, who knew Channing, also wrote him urgently; and Samuel J. May, who was close to him, strongly commended this course to him, in person. In December, 1835, Channing published his book, *Slavery*, which he had begun in 1831 in the West Indies; in 1836, *The Abolitionist*; and in 1842, the potent *Duty of the Free States*.[50] Whittier rejoiced in Channing's powerful agency.

Now, in 1834, Whittier's multifarious Abolitionist writings became more considerable in scope and harder hitting in effect. His long article on Daniel O'Connell, champion of Irish freedom and foe of slavery, was published in the *Haverhill Iris* on March 28 and April 4.[51] On April 12 Garrison published in the *Liberator* Whittier's letter addressed to him on the subject of Truth *versus* Slavery.[52] In August, Whittier felt obliged to pen a long and forceful "Defence of Abolitionists" in answer to misrepresentations which had appeared in the *Farmer's Cabinet*, of Amherst, New Hampshire. "I have neither leisure nor inclination to notice one half of those wilful mis-statements with which our enemies have flooded the newspapers and periodicals of the day," wrote Whittier, but "the highly respectable character of the paper and its editor" impelled him to speak. Whittier's remonstrance appeared in the *Haverhill Gazette* on August 16. Countering the charge that "the ground assumed by the leading Abolitionists is untenable and dangerous to the quiet and welfare of the community," Whittier blazed: "What worm of the dust, what being of a day, shall pronounce the Bible doctrine of immediate repentance 'untenable'?" Against the plea that "the sensitiveness of the public mind" should make the Abolitionists quiescent, Whittier cited the examples of Christ, Paul, Stephen, Luther, and the latter-day Friends in parallel circumstances. He charged that the allegation the Abolitionists were acting "without regard to public sentiment" was most unworthy of the New Hampshire editor. Popular sentiment, Whittier rejoined, is seldom right in progressive matters. With shrewd flattery he concluded that "the respectable Editor of the Cabinet" will, as a Christian, see the falsity of his present position: "Whatever others may do, he will not be found fighting shoulder to shoulder with infidelity, and hate, and prejudice."

Whittier's early masterpiece of controversy, however, was the six-column article, "The Constitution and Slavery," which was published in the *Haverhill Gazette* on September 20, 1834. His current study of constitutional law came out in fighting array in this cogent argument, bulwarked with the authority of Blackstone, Kent, and Justinian. Besides, Whittier had by now examined carefully the sentiments expressed upon the subject of slavery by Franklin, Jay, John Randolph, Washington, and John Wesley, precisely as he had studied those of Jefferson before he wrote *Justice and Expediency*. In "The Constitution and Slavery" Whittier fortified previously expressed convictions that "Congress has power under the express provisions of that Constitution, to virtually abolish the whole system of Am[erican]. Slavery, because

1. It can abolish slavery in the District and the Territories, and
2. It can abolish the domestic slave-trade. When these *constitutional* and necessary measures shall be carried into effect, the power of slavery will be prostrated forever."

Whittier proposed to accomplish these ends "by sending our strong and honest men into Congress, and leaving our 'dough-faces,' of all parties at home."

## 5

Whittier acted upon this proposal at once. As a political leader of the Abolitionists in Essex County, he sounded Caleb Cushing, who in the autumn of 1834 was again a candidate for Representative to Congress from Essex North, regarding his views upon slavery in the District of Columbia. On October 25, the day after he had attended at Danvers a meeting of the Essex County Anti-Slavery Society, Whittier journeyed to Newburyport to see Cushing. When he found Cushing absent, Whittier left a note requesting an expression of his friend's attitude to slavery, and telling him that he might win approximately three hundred anti-slavery votes if he favored abolition in the District of Columbia.[53] Then on November 3 Whittier wrote astutely to Cushing, from Haverhill:

> Several individuals personally & politically thy friends have suggested to me the idea of addressing thee in regard to thy sentiments in relation to the existence of Slavery in the Dist. of Columbia. From this I have uniformly dissuaded them by assuring them that, although friendly to Colonization, and consequently opposed to the Immediate Emancipationists, in many of their views, I could have no manner of doubt of thy willingness to do all in thy power to remove Slavery from the District, where it exists without warrant from the Constitution and in its most aggravated form. By this assurance I have, I believe, fully satisfied the individuals above alluded to. Perhaps in making it I have unintentionally misrepresented thy views and feelings. If so, I can only say that my motives, which will readily suggest themselves, were of the most friendly nature. In the present posture of affairs in this district any formal interrogation of candidates in reference to matters of this kind is certainly to be deprecated. But nothing is more certain than that the time is close at hand when it cannot be avoided. The spirit working deep in the heart of New England will not slumber. Party machinery will not much longer repress it.
>
> If I have rightly represented thy views, it would be a great satisfaction to myself to be able to put a line from thee to that effect in the hands of two or three gentlemen previous to the coming election. If, on the other hand, I have mistaken them, thee will oblige me by making no reply whatever, in reference to the particular subject of this letter.[54]

Cushing, who had no intention of becoming Whittier's agent in Congress,[55] answered him in this wise:

> Your letter dated the 3rd inst. and postmarked the 5th, did not reach me until this afternoon on my return from Salem, where I have

been attending the Supreme Court. I write a line of reply, in great haste, for the possibility of some private conveyance to Haverhill.

I profess that I think the situation of the District of Columbia, in respect of slavery and the slave traffic, is wholly indefensible; that I should heartily rejoice in any change for the better; and that I should, of course, wherever I may be, favor any feasible project for attaining so desirable an end. In so representing my opinion, therefore, you have but done me justice. At the same time, however, I should be unwilling to enter Congress *pledged* to INSTITUTE *a legislative* measure, either upon this or any subject of national policy and legislation, unless it were a point directly and publicly put in issue by my own constituents; in which case I should feel bound either to obey their instructions, or to yield my place to some other Representative.

I write you this frankly, because between you and me there should be no reservation of views on my part. But I have not time to weigh my language sufficiently for publication; and therefore commit these few lines, uncopied, to your discretion. . .[56]

Cushing was elected, and Whittier was to hold him to his engagement.

Politics and prose and farming quite filled up Whittier's normal day, and yet ringing lines in support of Abolition continued in 1834 to come from the farm in East Haverhill. His poem "Plead for the Slave!" appeared in the *Liberator* on April 26; and also in Garrison's weekly, on September 20, was published the famous poem variously called "Stanzas," or "Follen,"[57] or "Expostulation." Of this passionate plea for human liberty in the United States, which begins with the stirring line, "Our fellow-countrymen in chains!" Garrison prophesied accurately: "Our gifted brother has again seized the great trumpet of Liberty, and blown a blast that shall ring from Maine to the Rocky Mountains." Another of Whittier's best known contemporary poems against slavery, "The Slave-Ships,"[58] was copied in the *Liberator* on October 11 from the *Oasis*, an anti-slavery gift book published in Boston in 1834 by Mrs. Lydia Maria Child.[59] For a fee, that year, he managed to write only the poem "Lament,"[60] which appeared in the *New England Magazine*.

The remainder of Whittier's relentless energy during 1834 was expended upon attendance at anti-slavery meetings, and in the faithful discharge of offices to which he was elected. When the Haverhill Anti-Slavery Society was organized on April 3, he was elected its corresponding secretary.[61] Next day he was in Topsfield, secretary of a meeting of the Essex County Anti-Slavery Society.[62] When more than two hundred members of the New England Anti-Slavery Society convened in Boston on May 27–29, Whittier was one of a committee of five men appointed to prepare an "Address to the People of the United States." [63] Afterward, from Haverhill on June 3, Whittier penned a long report of this convention for the *Emancipator*, which the *Liberator* copied on June 21. In behalf of Abolition and Abolitionist institutions, he had become a high geared writing machine.

Yet again, when the Essex County Anti-Slavery Society met at Salem on June 11, Whittier was elected corresponding secretary.[64] Far more significant than this was his introduction of a resolution seeking the appointment of a committee to prepare a memorial requesting the next Congress to abolish slavery in the District of Columbia.[65] G. H. Barnes declares that "Whittier's insistence on petitions as 'the first measure of our cause' was sound statesmanship; for if petitions should provoke a discussion of slavery on the floor of Congress, the whole nation would give ear. Agitation could find no better forum." [66] Gradually Whittier's peculiar talent as an Abolitionist was unfolding; as both a forceful writer and a skillful politician, he was to make a unique contribution to his cause.

Gradually, too, his education in the school of mobs was developing. Misrepresentation and detraction he had learned to combat, but a harder lesson had to be mastered in 1835; the right of free speech had to be bought at the price of physical danger. The "Reign of Terror" which had tested the anti-slavery leaders in New York City and elsewhere was moving upon New England. Even the "land of steady habits" was to lose its equilibrium to the psychology of the mob.

# VII

# Men Who Labor for Humanity

IN THE FACE of the Essex North district's known preference for the principle of colonization, as against the abolition of slavery,[1] Whittier was elected, on November 11, 1834, a representative to the state legislature, from Haverhill.[2] Late in life he remarked that he had been sent to the House not as an Abolitionist, but as an ambitious young man whom "the people were willing to gratify." [3] Yet he contrived, while conscientiously attending the several sessions of the legislature in Boston, to maintain his Abolitionist activities. At this time he also got first hand political experience which for years he turned to excellent account in his strategic rôle as an adviser to John Quincy Adams, Cushing, Senators John P. Hale and Charles Sumner, and other members of Congress. The importance of political action in behalf of Abolition began, indeed, to be obvious in 1835 when the United States Post Office in Charleston, South Carolina, was prevented from delivering Abolitionist periodicals. It stood out even more clearly when President Jackson endorsed such local control of the functions of the Post Office.[4]

## I

In the state legislature Whittier had little direct opportunity to serve his chief cause. In the first place, a total of 609 Representatives attended at least the autumn session of the House,[5] and Whittier, never at his ease in a crowd, made no speeches during either that or the winter session. In the second place, the legislature was currently more concerned with pressing sectional matters than with slavery. The three-month winter session considered chiefly such matters as transportation, the revision of the paupers' laws, other social legislation such as that concerning the State asylum for the insane, the incorporation of various academies, the establishment of city fire departments, and the incorporation and regulation of banks and manufacturing concerns. During the autumn the legislature concerned itself mainly with the Revised Statutes of the Commonwealth.

Whittier was on terms of personal acquaintance with the Speaker of the House, Judge Julius Rockwell, of Pittsfield, but he was appointed to only two committees, both of them unimportant.[6] On January 13 he became one of the seven members of the Committee on Engrossed Bills, which evidently polished the text of legislation before its final reading and enactment; and on January 30 he was named one of the twelve members of the Committee on License Laws. Yet Whittier appears to have been an interested and observant member of this House, notably in relation to its consideration of capital punishment. Not even his ill health, which caused his temporary retirement to Haverhill in March, could prevent his attending a meeting of the House when the bill for abolishing capital punishment was to be considered. He wrote from Haverhill on March 17 to Robert Rantoul, with whom he was living at the Bulfinch Oval in Franklin Street, Boston,[7] to inquire "what day of next week the Bill for Abolish. Cap. Pun. is to be taken up — if indeed thee can *guess* anything near the precise time! — I wish to be with you if possible when that question is taken, — although my health is wretched & perhaps ought to place me *hors de combat.*" [8] This issue was carried over to the autumn session of the legislature, and on September 10 it was recorded in the *Journal* of the House that Whittier had presented a petition from fifty-eight citizens of Haverhill seeking the abolition of capital punishment.

During 1835 slavery was mentioned in the *Journal* only once, on October 13, when a petition from the American Colonization Society for the right to hold a meeting in the House chamber, was tabled. But during the winter session two things were considered which touched Whittier nearly. As a Quaker he had a natural interest in the deliberations of the House over means to eliminate war; and as an Abolitionist he was directly affected by a bill regarding riots. This was an omen. In September and October, in Concord, New Hampshire, and in Boston, Whittier was to have intimate personal experience with mobs.

## 2

He had merely to continue exercising the Constitutional right of free speech, writing about slavery as he saw it. But his other services to Abolitionism also exposed him to the growing public indignation in New England against the anti-slavery movement. In Boston, on January 21, he was elected a vice-president of the New England Anti-Slavery Society. When this body convened again in Boston in May, Whittier was active in committee work. By such means he became a potent force in the shaping of Abolitionist policies. When, on June 20, he was elected to the board of managers of the Essex County Anti-Slavery Society, he was also appointed to write an address to the electors of the County, which was published in the *Haverhill Gazette* on August 22, 1835. Whittier again urged the necessity of forcing Congress to exercise its Constitutional right in abolishing slavery from the District of Columbia. "We must," he said, "immediately circulate memorials to be presented to the next Congress."

Whittier's public utterances, more than his internal services in anti-slavery societies, made him a marked man. On February 11, in the New England Anti-Slavery Society's hall at 46 Washington Street, Boston, he even lectured on "The Constitution of the United States and the Declaration of the Philadelphia Anti-Slavery Convention compared." [9] This was one of perhaps three public addresses — and the longest — which he made in his entire lifetime. The seventh in a series of lectures arranged by the Society, it was mainly an elaboration of Whittier's article, "The Constitution and Slavery," which had been published on September 20 preceding in the *Haverhill Gazette*. Significantly, the eleventh and last of this lecture series was delivered on March 11 by Garrison, on the subject of "Political Anti-Slavery." Even so early he had set himself like a flint against the course of action to which Whittier and other Abolitionists were committed; and from this time the division in the ranks which occurred two years later, over this subject, was inevitable.

Chiefly, of course, Whittier's increasing flow of anti-slavery verse established him more and more prominently in the public mind as a leading Abolitionist. Indeed, he was fast becoming the leading mouthpiece of the anti-slavery movement. The *Liberator* was at this time his main sounding-board, and it sent his stirring notes echoing through the land. On January 31, 1835, for instance, the *Liberator* published Whittier's poem, "The Yankee Girl," [10] which ended with the lines:

Full low at thy bidding thy negroes may kneel,
With the iron of bondage on spirit and heel;
Yet know that the Yankee girl sooner would be
In fetters with them, than in freedom with thee!

Even the *New England Magazine* published his Abolitionist poem, "To Governor M'Duffie," [11] a strong address to the South Carolina executive denouncing him as "Last champion of Oppression's battle." Whittier's fieriest poem of 1835, however, was "Stanzas for the Times," [12] which appeared in the *Boston Courier* on July 25. He was deeply aroused by a pro-slavery meeting held in Faneuil Hall, Boston, at which a demand had been made that free speech be suppressed, "lest it should endanger the foundation of commercial society." To Whittier this sentiment was a red flag, and in part he wrote:

Shall tongues be mute, when deeds are wrought
  Which well might shame extremest hell?
Shall freemen lock the indignant thought?
  Shall Pity's bosom cease to swell?
Shall Honor bleed? — shall Truth succumb?
Shall pen, and press, and soul be dumb?

. . . . . . . . . . .

No; guided by our country's laws,
  For truth, and right, and suffering man,
Be ours to strive in Freedom's cause,
  As Christians may, as freemen can!
Still pouring on unwilling ears
That truth oppression only fears.

Such appeals to the public conscience fell mainly on deaf ears and stony hearts among the economically privileged classes of Northern society. "Respectability was founded on property," wrote Parrington, "and respectability was mightier in New England than even John Calvin." More: "The dominant commercial group would not tolerate a movement that was certain to alienate its southern customers." [13] This frightened, intolerant temper invaded even the centers of learning, as Charles Follen, German-born scholar, learned to his cost. At the meeting of the New England Anti-Slavery Society in Boston on May 25–28, 1835, Follen pointed out that "Europe, which had rekindled the extinguished lamp of liberty at the altar of our Revolution, still nourishes the holy fire; England goes before us as a torch-bearer, leading the way to the liberation of mankind. . . . Shall the United States, the free United States, which could not bear the bonds of a King, cradle the bondage which a King is abolishing? Shall a republic be less free than a monarchy? Shall we, in the vigor and buoyancy of our manhood, be less energetic in righteousness than a kingdom in its age?" [14] In August, 1835, Follen received his answer. He was not reappointed to his professorship at Harvard.[15]

A tactical error on Garrison's part merely aggravated the rising public temper in New England. While in England in 1833 he had sought the services of George Thompson, a gifted anti-slavery speaker. Against their better judgment, Joseph Sturge and other British humanitarians agreed to finance a three-year mission for Thompson in America. He began it apparently during the winter of 1834–35, in New England. In less than a year Thompson had to be smuggled on board ship and returned home. Several alleged blemishes upon his past record in England had been discovered, and the intrusion of a Briton in the domestic affairs of the United States was resented.[16] On January 11 and 12, 1835, Thompson lectured in Andover, and after appearances elsewhere in New England, he spoke before the first anniversary meeting of the Essex County Anti-Slavery Society, on June 10 and 11 in Haverhill.[17] Gradually Whittier was being drawn into Thompson's dangerous orbit. In two more months he came completely within it.

On August 5 when Thompson spoke in Lynn an unruly mob threw missiles and rotten eggs at the hall in which the meeting was held. After several more such disturbances, Thompson took refuge on the Whittiers' East Haverhill farm, where he arrived on August 21 and where he remained for four days.[18] On August 24 Elizabeth Whittier wrote in her diary:

> The three past day[s] have been full of incident and excitement. Oh! we have been too proud of our country — we have been flattered, inordinately flattered — 'till like the self-glorying Pharisee we have thanked God we "*were not like other nations.*" America is working *everlasting* disgrace for her future name — the shameful record must be writen down — that in this land of *bibles*, and *law*, and *learning*, and *freedom* a minister of Christ — a Paul, in his zeal for the promotion of every cause of righteousness and truth — a stranger — led by the holiest impulses of humanity, coming among us, to proclaim, in his own

> wonderful and fervid eloquence, the eternal principles of justice to mankind. that such a man — with such purposes was slandered by Americans! hated by Americans! and *mobbed* by Americans That in Massachusetts, thousands of dollars were offered for his assassination. Oh! I am sure I shall never be proud of my country. (I shall much sooner be ashamed of my "Father land" while it is thus unchristianized.)

Three days after this, on August 27, Whittier wrote from Salem, where he and his mother apparently had gone to attend a Friends' quarterly meeting, to his sister:

> I write by our good friend, Thomas Spencer, to request thee to welcome brother Thompson to our house, as his friends are somewhat fearful for his personal safety at this time. Mother and myself will be at home on Seventh day, if nothing happens. . . . Thompson will remain with us some days at Haverhill.[19]

On the next day, Friday, anxiously noting Thompson's failure to arrive, Elizabeth Whittier showed her colors by writing, "I wish I was good enough to be an Abolitionist." [20] On Monday she recorded, with relief, that Thompson and the Reverend Samuel J. May had safely reached the farm on Saturday evening.

Whittier and Thompson raked hay together, and went about the farm unmolested.[21] But when they set out on Sunday morning, August 30, to visit Nathaniel Peabody Rogers at Plymouth, New Hampshire, they left trouble behind them in Haverhill and ran into worse trouble ahead. That in Haverhill broke out first, on Sunday evening, and in her diary Elizabeth Whittier again made a good report of events, this time under date of August 31. An anti-slavery meeting which Samuel J. May was addressing in the Christian Church was broken up when a mob outside threw heavy stones and smashed windows. Whittier's sister made this characteristic note: "I am very sorry and ashamed for Haverhill — for my own dear and beautiful village. I hope they will never ring our bells again on the anniversary of our national *independence*. . . ."

Elizabeth modestly omitted from her account the sequel to this meeting. She and her friend Harriet Minot, both highly esteemed in Haverhill, took Mr. May by the hand, one on each side of him, and safely escorted him to Judge Minot's home through the boiling mob of two hundred men and boys. The trio were rudely handled but not injured. Their escape nullified the plans of the mob, who had removed the front steps of the church, with the expectation that the breaking of limbs and possibly the loss of lives would result from a panic following the discharge of a cannon. It failed to go off, luckily, and the removal of the steps was discovered in time to avert trouble when May's audience left the church. His safe escape through the menacing crowd was made certain when Rufus Slocomb charged furiously into it and cleared a path. "Old Sloc," a Gargantuan man who had once been a tavern keeper, was friendly to Elizabeth Whittier and Harriet Minot in their need.[22]

Whittier and Thompson, on the contrary, were opposed by unfriendly patrons of New Hampshire taverns who, as Whittier wrote good-humoredly, had drunk themselves into a high state of patriotism. In a letter published in the *Haverhill Gazette* on September 12, he described lucidly his and Thompson's encounter with a mob at Concord, the State capital. A meeting of the Concord Anti-Slavery Society was announced on the morning of September 4, and it was also given out that Thompson and Whittier would speak — a fact which he learned only in the evening. "I am, heart and soul, an Abolitionist," Whittier admitted in his newspaper report, "but by no means, a *speaking* one."

He would have attended the meeting if it had been held, but the Selectmen of Concord, alarmed by belligerent appearances in the streets, closed the doors of the town hall in order to prevent the gathering.

> But the sovereign mob [said Whittier] were not to be put off thus easily. They had gathered together for a mob — they had drunk themselves into a state of remarkable patriotism — they had come to the rescue of the Constitution and the laws of the land — they had sworn vengeance against the Abolitionists, and vengeance they meant to have.

At dusk, in company with a Concord Abolitionist named Hoag and the editor of the *Concord Herald*, Mr. J. H. Kimball, Whittier passed near a large group of people in the town's main street, frenzied and cursing the Abolitionists. Suddenly the cry was raised, "*to George Kent's and the wine in his cellar!*" (With Kent, brother-in-law of N. P. Rogers, Whittier and Thompson had stopped overnight on their way back to Haverhill from Plymouth, and Kent circulated the troublesome announcement of the anti-slavery meeting.) [23] When Hoag, Kimball, and Whittier turned back to warn Kent, the mob followed them, insisting that Whittier, in spite of his Quaker coat, must be "the identical incendiary and fanatic, George Thompson."

The rioters pelted Whittier with rotten eggs and soiled his coat so that it could never be cleaned.[24] Harmless curses followed, and an equally harmless shower of stones; but these, Whittier joked, were hurled with considerable force, and might have done injury except that the marksmen were somewhat "over-done" by their patriotic exertions in "*drinking* destruction to the Abolitionists."

> In order [continued Whittier] to escape this somewhat unique attempt to MacAdamize us — this *granite* specimen of the hospitality of the *Granite State* — we entered the house of the Hon Wm A. Kent, who, together with the Rev Mr Thomas, the Unitarian Clergyman, and an Abolitionist, assured the stormy and somewhat obstreperous multitude without, that they had mistaken their man, and that Geo. Thompson was not in the house.

Whereupon, related Whittier, the mob moved up the street to George Kent's mansion, yelled furiously, threw a few stones at the house, cursed a bit, and then retired. Thompson, out of the house at the time, now returned.

> After parading the town for an hour or two [Whittier went on], refreshed with "Deacon Giles' best" [25] and provided with drums, fifes &c. they once more returned and once more, to use the words of Milton,
>
> ——— "A furious noise environed us
> Of owls and cuckoos, asses, apes and dogs." [26]
>
> and then these guardians of constitutional rights retired upon their laurels —
>
> "The King of France with fifty thousand men
> Marched up the hill, and then marched down again."
>
> From 2 o'clock until nearly sunrise the glorious rescue of the Constitution from the onslaught of the Abolitionists, was celebrated by the discharge of Cannon! We left our kind and warm-hearted friends George Kent and his Lady with their amiable and excellent visitors, early in the morning in company with Rev Mr Putnam of Dunbarton; and all further proceedings, although unknown to myself, will doubtless be officially published in a glorious and glowing description of the preservation of the Union — by a *mob!*

Whittier ventured that this unruly affair did not betoken abstract hatred of Abolition principles, which, he said, were the principles of Jeffersonian democracy lying at the base of New Hampshire's own constitution. And it indicated no personal hatred of Thompson, whom the mob had never seen or heard. In Whittier's judgment, the riot was organized for political effect "to convince the South that the hard-working *democracy* of New Hampshire was hand in glove with the slaveholding democracy of Virginia and the Carolinas." Thus, said Whittier, the Abolitionists were caught between the fires of two political parties. With keen foresight he concluded:

> It will not avail. The South will not be deceived. The Slaveholder sees the true nature of the Northern mobs and Anti Abolition Meetings. He asks for more — he demands *legislative action.* This he cannot have. — Who dares in the Legislature of Massachusetts to attempt the resurrection of the OLD SEDITION LAW from its grave of ignominy — to call it out from its abode of curses to fetter the free soul of New England? No one. What then will all these wire-worked and heartless Anti-Abolition movements here amount to? — Depend upon it, they will but accelerate the cause of universal Emancipation!

Whittier's forecast of the revulsion of feeling against these political tactics showed, however, no maturer judgment in him than did his clear perception that human nature is frail, that no one should expect too much from it. What he realized at this time he phrased well ten years later in his poem "At Washington":

> Always he who most forgiveth in his brother
> is most just.[27]

It was utterly true that Whittier's "keen sense of the ridiculous kept him from being in the least degree 'cranky' in his philanthropy." [28]

Whittier, Thompson, and Mr. Putnam galloped out of Concord in a carriage while the mob was still milling around George Kent's house. The three men went by the Hookset bridge, left unguarded by the Concord rioters. When the weary travelers paused for breakfast at an inn, they found the landlord regaling a small band of coarse men with extravagant reports: that at an Abolition meeting in Haverhill on the preceding Sunday night Thompson and Whittier had been so roughly handled as to be out of action for some time, and that they had escaped into New Hampshire.

The landlord exhibited a circular which advertised the request for Thompson's apprehension. How, Whittier inquired, could the rascally Englishman be recognized? "Easily enough," responded the innkeeper, "he is a tonguey fellow." When the travelers were in the carriage and ready to leave, Whittier delighted in informing the landlord, "This is George Thompson, and my name is Whittier." The host was too confounded to give chase.

Nearly fifty years later, in Portland, Whittier learned from a man who had been one of the Concord mob that preparations had been made to tar and feather Thompson and himself.[29]

In her diary of September 10 Elizabeth Whittier set down a fervent chronicle of the events at Concord, and reported that Thompson had left Haverhill on Monday, the seventh. Whittier himself departed on the eighth to resume his work in the legislature, at Boston. There the public mind was being worked up to the fever pitch which was to cause the serious riot of October 21. Even Emerson, in his placid study at Concord, Massachusetts, realized the gravity of the social disturbance, for on October 7 he wrote to Carlyle:

> I read with interest what you say of the political omens in England. I could wish our country a better comprehension of its felicity. . . . We have had in different parts of the country mobs and moblike legislation, and even moblike judicature, which have betrayed an almost godless state of society. . . .[30]

This condition reached its nadir on the occasion of the meeting, on October 21, 1835, of the Boston Female Anti-Slavery Society. On this day "men of property and standing" led the mob which sought to manhandle Thompson, advertised as the main speaker, and instead apprehended Garrison. The incredible psychology which prevailed in Boston at this time was indicated by handbills, reading:

THOMPSON

THE ABOLITIONIST

---

That infamous foreign scoundrel THOMPSON, will hold forth *this afternoon*, at the Liberator Office, No. 48, Washington Street. The present is a fair opportunity for the friends of the Union to *snake Thomp-*

*son out!* It will be a contest between the Abolitionists and the friends of the Union. A purse of $100 has been raised by a number of patriotic citizens to reward the individual who shall first lay violent hands on Thompson, so that he may be brought to the tar kettle before dark. Friends of the Union, be vigilant!

*Boston, Wednesday,* 12 *o'clock.*[31]

Thompson did not appear, and Mayor Theodore Lyman ordered the meeting dismissed, but the infuriated mob, bound to have some sacrifice for their lust, seized Garrison. While he was being led through the streets with a rope around his neck, police intervened and took him under protection to the Leverett Street jail. The din of this mob in Washington Street, which is estimated to have included between two and five thousand persons, attracted Whittier and other members of the legislature, then sitting in the old State House.[32]

Once again Whittier was in the midst of a mob, and this one gave him anxiety on account of his sister Elizabeth, who was in Boston and who attended the anti-slavery meeting. With Samuel J. May he went to the jail to visit Garrison, who playfully invited them "to share the safe lodgings which the state had provided for him. . . ." [33] That night Whittier and May watched over Elizabeth, who had been removed to a place of safety when they were warned that the mob might attack the house at which they were staying.[34]

Public indignation in New England against the Abolitionists continued very high during the rest of 1835 and until the spring of 1837, but the danger of physical indignity, which Whittier did not relish, abated with the departure of George Thompson for England. On October 29 the *Haverhill Gazette* reported his will-o'-the-wisp manner of life; on November 21, the newspaper revealed that he was actually within twenty miles of Haverhill, but that he "will leave for England *soon* — probably within a year." He appears in fact to have withdrawn from the American scene before 1835 had passed.

# 3

Throughout the turbulent months of 1835 Whittier contrived time for writing, and he produced a few things besides Abolition pieces. His long poem, "Mogg Megone," [35] was published in the March and April issues of the *New England Magazine*. Whittier had started writing the verse narrative in 1830, but he finished it only in 1834, with the aid of two books of Maine history [36] which were published opportunely when he had penned only a few lines of the poem. Working once again in New England historical materials must have been a grateful change to Whittier from his unremitting Abolition work, but he did not measurably surpass his previous attempts to produce an adequate poem having a New England background. In the choice of his subject he was unlucky.

Mogg Megone, a leader of the Saco Indians, was murdered by Ruth Boniton, after he had become drunk on liquor given him by her father, the outlaw John Boniton. Thereafter Ruth sought in vain the peace of forgiveness at the hands of the Jesuit priest, Rallé, who was in turn killed when the British swooped down upon Norridgewock in 1724. In a subsequent spring, Baron de Castine came to Norridgewock with a searching party. Bleached bones revealed the fate of Rallé and his Indian converts, but the dead body of Ruth Boniton, found leaning against a maple tree, held its own secret.

"Mogg Megone" displays a feeling for nature, and it contains one of Whittier's best-reasoned statements against war, as well as intermittent flashes of descriptive power. The poem was, indeed, reviewed favorably by Professor C. C. Felton in the *North American Review* of April, 1837.[37] Yet Whittier was right in his low opinion of "Mogg Megone." When the book was issued in the spring of 1836, it was somewhat apologetically prefaced by Whittier, and thereafter he suppressed the poem, whenever possible, from his collected works. He permitted its inclusion, as a specimen of his early verse, in the Appendix of the Riverside Edition in 1888, but with faint praise: "Looking at it, at the present time, it suggests the idea of a big Indian in his war-paint strutting about in Sir Walter Scott's plaid." [38]

Aside from "Mogg Megone," Whittier's utterances during 1835 had a social or a political purpose. His poem, "The Prisoner for Debt," [39] appeared in the *Boston Pearl* on December 12. In the *Haverhill Gazette* on

March 21, A. W. Thayer published at Whittier's request[40] a le[illegible]
an English quarterly review regarding the polemical spirit in [illegible]
Whittier remarked the absence of this spirit in Europe, and saic[illegible]
lamentable that discussion on this all important subject is con[illegible]ted
with so much sectarian bitterness and want of charity and brotherly
kindness among those who assume to dispense the Gospel of Christ."
Five months later, on August 29 in the *Gazette*, Whittier turned to politics
and advocated the nomination of Daniel Webster by the Whigs as a
candidate for President. Then an admirer, Whittier wrote: "Daniel
Webster is the candidate not alone of Massachusetts, but of the true and
tried friends of Constitutional Liberty all over the country."

During 1836 Whittier held steadily to the course which he had now
defined so well. On November 7, 1835, in the *Haverhill Gazette*, he had
announced his decision to decline any renomination for Representative to
the State legislature,[41] and twice during this autumn he seems to have
refused to go to Portland, Maine, to become editor of an Abolitionist
newspaper which was to be founded there.[42] Whittier decided, rightly,
that he could better serve the cause of Abolition by remaining in more
populous Massachusetts, where he could be closer to political developments.

One such development was the inaugural message of Governor Edward
Everett, of Massachusetts, early in 1836. He asserted that when the
Constitution of the United States was adopted, the question of slavery
was left open, and that "the patriotism of all classes of citizens is invoked
to abstain from a discussion" of the subject of Negro servitude. For at
least three years Whittier had been highly sensitive upon these two points,
and equally well informed. His response to Everett was characteristic.
In a five-column letter addressed to Everett which the *Haverhill Gazette*
published on February 13, 1836, he castigated the Governor severely —
and then signed himself, also characteristically, "Thy friend and fellow
citizen, John G. Whittier." One of the sharpest letters that he ever wrote,
this blast had personal consequences for him. With bitter irony he said:

> What more does the Holy Alliance require! — What more does
> Gov. McDuffie demand? Is this the age — are ours the laws — are the
> sons of the Pilgrims the men — for advice like this? — *** Is it here
> alone, that Truth, which is abroad in the earth exposing and over-

turning the lies of ages, is to be put to silence? *** Is this the advice of a republican magistrate to a community of freemen? Far fitter is it for the banks of the Bosphorus and the Neva than for those of the Connecticut and the Merrimack. It is not suited to our hard-handed artisans and free farmers. . . . They see too clearly the peril in which their own liberties are placed by slave holding encroachment. They have not yet forgotten that the same Message of the Governor of South Carolina, whose *demands* may be supposed to have called forth the servile advice of obedience, from our own, contained also sentiments in the highest degree insulting to the working people of the North — intimating that they must be either held in check by an aristocracy or reduced to the condition of Slaves. . . . Holding with Milton that the liberty to know, to utter, to argue freely is above all other liberties, he cannot consent to "abstain from discussion," even though the advice to do so, comes backed by a cautious intimation of "prosecution for misdemeanor" or a revival of the old Sedition Law.

To the remark that the matter of slavery should be left where the Constitution left it, Whittier answered that the advice had come too late: the system which fifteen years earlier had embraced six hundred thousand "victims" now bound more than two million souls. To Everett's further plea that the matter of slavery should be left wholly to God, Whittier retorted acidly:

Yes — Slavery is in the hands of Providence, but that Providence often effects the removal of evil by the visitation of tremendous judgments. Slavery perished in St. Domingo in a storm of fire and blood. It may be so in our own country. . . . The hour of Emancipation is advancing in the march of time. It must come, if not brought on by the generous energies of our own minds it must come by the bloody process of St. Domingo.

. . . . . . . . . . . . . . .

The right of freely discussing any and every subject under Heaven, is not a thing to be surrendered. The talk of yielding it now as a sacrifice to patriotism is most manifest absurdity. It would be the immolation of the Goddess on her own altar. Yielding this right, we should have nothing left. . . . The true glory and interest of a nation consist in the secure and free exercise on the part of each individual of his natural rights, the humblest as well as the proudest.

. . . . . . . . . . . . . . .

The subject of slavery is now, owing in a great measure to the violence of the enemies of emancipation, fully before the people. Executive advice will not prevent its discussion! legislative enactments against the liberty of speech and of the press, cannot. Before God and the world, every man not ignorant of, nor blind to his own rights and duties as an accountable being, will hold the latter, if attempted, as utterly null and void.

Whittier never uttered words more full of passionate indignation than those with which he ended this letter:

Thus urged to action we cannot yield "the home bred right of free discussion" to the threats of Slave holders, or the demands of interested politicians. We can neither permit the GAG to be thrust in our mouths by others, nor deem it the part of "patriotism" to place it there ourselves. The more fiercely our rights are assailed, the closer will we hold them to our hearts, believing as we do, that the very existence of our country — the cause of human freedom abroad, and the welfare of the white man as well as the black man at home, depend, under God, mainly upon their preservation and untrammelled exercise.[43]

Whittier had not, however, formed a merely censorious habit of mind. He remained as quick to praise a man for opposing slavery as to condemn one for condoning it. On March 2, 1836, for instance, he wrote to a Boston friend, a member of the state legislature, rejoicing to find him "faithful among the faithless" and expressing the conviction that "thy noble example will not be lost upon the young men of Boston." More pointedly, as a New Englander proud of the fact that Massachusetts "from the first Pilgrim step on the Rock of Plymouth has been emphatically a *free state*," he remarked with delight: "I have just received a long letter from Gov. Davis [44] in relation to the P. Office censorship of the press. He writes as becomes a freeman representing the interests of a free state."

As a freeman's advocate, Whittier himself was praised in a poem, "The Bard of Haverhill," which William Comstock [45] contributed to the *Liberator* on March 12, 1836. The last three stanzas belong to the Whittier portrait at that time:

His reed wastes not its melody
  To lull to sleep a guilty land —
He flings his branching laurels by,
  To grasp the patriot's naked brand.

He climbed Parnassus' utmost height,
To thunder on a tyrant world,
And on that high and glorious sight,
The flag of LIBERTY unfurled.

Flash out again, thou orb of fire,
Which lately launched its scorching ray
Where "knapsack" priests preach Christ for hire —
For *office* barter him away.

Yet during 1835–36 Whittier received painful proof that his writings were aggravating already exacerbated Southern feelings. In his long letter of October, 1833, to Jonathan Law, he had said, among other things: "I have written some considerable upon Slavery & have been pretty roughly handled by the Southerners — but so long as I can entrench myself behind my Quakerism, as a tortoise does under his shell, I am perfectly safe." On the contrary, it was no jest for people to circulate Whittier's writings, and on August 10, 1835, Doctor Reuben Crandall, a Georgetown (D.C.) physician and a brother of Prudence Crandall, was arrested for lending his copy of the *American Anti-Slavery Reporter's* reprint of *Justice and Expediency* to a Mr. Henry King. Charged with "publishing and circulating seditious and incendiary papers," Doctor Crandall lay for eight months in the old city prison in Washington.

Then, beginning on April 15, 1836, he had the honor of a trial, in the United States Circuit Court, in which his conviction was sought by Francis Scott Key, who in happier days had written "The Star-Spangled Banner" and who was at this time District Attorney for the District of Columbia. Doctor Crandall was acquitted, only to die, after his liberation, of tuberculosis which he had contracted while in prison. In 1841, when Whittier was in Washington with Joseph Sturge, the English Quaker philanthropist, he visited this jail, and he mentioned the incident in one stanza of his poem, "Astraea at the Capitol," written in 1862 after slavery had been abolished from the District of Columbia:

Beside me gloomed the prison-cell
Where wasted one in slow decline
For uttering simple words of mine,
And loving freedom all too well.[46]

# 4

As editor of the *Haverhill Gazette* from May 7 to December 17, 1836, Whittier learned further how dearly free speech is bought in a time of social stress.[47] In a long exordium "To the Public" which was published on May 7, he avowed himself "the friend of Universal Liberty and the advocate of Free Discussion," and he invited his fellow citizens "to lend their patronage to an independent and unshackled Press." In his first issue it was manifest that he intended to scourge the apologists for slavery with nettles and scorpions. It was made equally clear that Abolition, whether or not his readers considered it to be news, would be persistently advocated in the *Gazette* by Whittier.

On May 7 he published a strong editorial entitled "Arkansas — A New Slave State!" and on July 16 he printed an entire speech, five and one-half columns long, by Caleb Cushing upon the Arkansas question. The issue of May 14 also contained five columns of impassioned argument against slavery. Also on this date, as in several subsequent issues, Whittier advocated the election of Daniel Webster as President.[48] On June 4 he printed an editorial protest, "The Right of Petition Gone!" Two weeks later he returned to an old favorite subject and wrote warmly on "The Freedom of the Press." He based this editorial upon Congress's rejection of Calhoun's so-called "Bill of Abominations." Whittier again invoked Milton's defense of a free press, and rebuked American newspapers for their supineness in the face of the fact that —

> TWENTY OF OUR SENATORS have voted for a Law to create *ten thousand* censors of the American Press — to subject our papers, and letters even to a search in every petty post-office — to exclude the *Holy Scriptures, the Constitution of Massachusetts, and the Declaration of Independence from the United States Mail*. . . . For ourselves, whatever others may do, we go for the full and perfect freedom of the Press as guaranteed by the Constitution of Massachusetts and of the United States. *We shall regard no law which nullifies that guaranty.* We will yield to no laws whatever our freedom of opinion, and constitutional right of expressing that opinion. We are for giving Truth full play. We believe with Milton, in his noble defence of the freedom of the Press.[49]

As the weeks passed, Whittier seemed steadily to gain boldness and to lose his sense of what would "go down." On June 25 he subjected Van Buren once more to cauterizing criticism, and condemned Van Buren's voting for Calhoun's bill as "one more evidence of the overmastering power of American Slavery." Whittier warned: "We must learn to distrust the policy of the world, and rely upon the single heartedness of Truth for success in the cause of humanity." Van Buren, whom he certainly distrusted, he castigated further, on August 27 and September 10, for his ambiguous attitude regarding slavery. Whittier remembered Everett, too, at whose heels he snapped like a terrier. In "The Response of the North," which appeared in the *Gazette* on July 2, he condemned Everett for his "threat of prosecution at common law" in an effort to silence the Abolitionists; and on September 17 he once more censured the Governor for his inaugural address. Again, in "A Scene in Congress in 1826," which was published in the *Liberator* on October 29, Whittier demonstrated that Everett's illiberal point of view concerning slavery represented a settled conviction of long standing.

The forging of these editorial thunderbolts, it is patent, demanded most of Whittier's energies, but he could at no time wholly neglect verse. In "Ruins of Egyptian Thebes," which he published in the *Haverhill Gazette* on June 25, he hazarded the guess that "The heir of Afric may not always be the 'lowest link' in this our being's chain." Already, in the *Gazette* of June 11, he had printed his powerful "Lines, written on the Passage of Pinckney's Resolutions in the House of Representatives, and of Calhoun's 'Bill of Abominations' in the Senate of the United States." [50] On July 30 Whittier published "The Cry of My Soul," which he had adapted from a poem by Lamartine, and on September 3 and 10, respectively, he gave out "Song of the Free" and the terrible indictment, "Clerical Oppressors." [51] This scathingly denounced the clergymen of Charleston who had joined in a public defense of slavery.

On a sweeter note, Whittier wrote "To the Memory of Thomas Shipley" (*Haverhill Gazette*, December 1) as a tribute to the Philadelphia Quaker, a lifelong philanthropist who had advocated emancipation. "The Frost Spirit," written six years earlier, was revived in a moment's cool detachment from Abolitionism and published in the issue of November 5.[52] And choicest of all the non-Abolitionist verses which Whittier published that season was the simple poem, "Who Is My Neighbor?" which was published in the *Gazette* on November 5. Whittier never showed better, in a few lines, his large and gentle humanity.

WHO IS MY NEIGHBOR?

Thy neighbor? It is he whom thou
Hast power to aid and bless;
Whose aching heart or burning brow
Thy soothing hand may press.

Thy neighbor? 'Tis the fainting poor,
Whose eye with want is dim;
Whom hunger sends from door to door;
Go thou and succor him.

Thy neighbor? 'Tis that weary man
Whose years are at their brim,
Bent low with sickness, care and pain;
Go thou and comfort him.

Thy neighbor? 'Tis the heart bereft,
Of every earthly gem —
Widow and orphan, helpless left;
Go thou and shelter them.

Thy neighbor? Yonder toiling slave,
Fetter'd in thought and limb,
Whose hopes are all beyond the grave;
Go thou, and ransom him.

Whene'er thou meet'st a human form
Less favor'd than thine own,
Remember 'tis thy neighbor worm,
Thy brother or thy son.

Oh! pass not, pass not heedless by;
Perhaps thou can'st redeem,
The breaking heart from misery;
Go share thy lot with him.[53]

Whittier's broad humanitarianism, to which he was constantly adding deeper comprehension, was further demonstrated in non-Abolition editorials which he wrote during his second tenure as editor of the *Haverhill Gazette*. In an article published on July 23, 1836, he defended the right of collective bargaining among workmen. If there had remained any doubt that he was thoroughly the friend of the common man, it would have been dispelled by the stinging editorial "Aristocracy," which appeared in the *Gazette* on September 17. Whittier assailed the economically privileged class in this country who, in his opinion, wished to substitute for our democratic institutions the "power and pomp of European Aristocracy." He flayed such people for upholding the rights of property as against the rights of man, and for defending slavery and opposing Abolition. Yet again, on September 24, he condemned the Jackson administration for exploiting and dispossessing the Indians of the South by military means.

These and other matters of the day Whittier saw out of the corner of his eye, but until the end of the Civil War it was Abolition which steadily occupied his attention. Even as editor of the *Haverhill Gazette* in 1836 he found time, as an agent for the American Anti-Slavery Society, to circulate petitions advocating the abolition of slavery in the District of Columbia.[54] This work, however, he was forced to give up in October, at which time he received one hundred dollars to pay expenses which he had incurred on account of it.[55] The effect of petitions such as he had circulated was plainly realized by the South as much as by his Society, for during 1836 the Southern delegation in the House of Representatives contrived to force the House to table Abolitionist petitions. Not until 1844 did the astute and tireless John Quincy Adams succeed in getting the taboo removed.[56]

Whittier even managed, with all else that he was driving himself to do at this time, to continue active work in the various anti-slavery societies of which he was a member. In January he was re-elected a vice-president of the New England Anti-Slavery Society, and in May a member of its standing committee.[57] At Newburyport on May 30 he attended a meeting of the Essex County Anti-Slavery Society, and was elected secretary of the group. Here his fire was drawn when a church committee which had first agreed to the convention's use of "Mr. Milton's meeting house" revoked its promise. The more than one hundred delegates then started their meeting in the garden of Mrs. Charles Butler, but "wharf rats" led by respectable "men of propitty" broke it up by raising great din and clamor with fish-horns and tin pans. H. B. Stanton, the main speaker, was assaulted and lost the buttons from his coat. Whittier wrote of this affair, the third anti-slavery riot in which he had been involved:

> As we were being assailed with decayed eggs, sticks, and light missiles, I thought discretion the better part of valor, and hurried away at what my friend N. P. Rogers called "an undignified trot," in company with an aged Orthodox minister, one of the few who had the moral courage to attend an anti-slavery meeting in those days, and who was settled in a neighboring town. *** [Probably the Reverend Gardner B. Perry, of Bradford, who was elected president of the Society at this meeting.] [58]

In his report on June 4 in the *Haverhill Gazette*, Whittier said wrathfully:

> As for Newburyport we shall remember it. We shall place it, as the Sandwich Islanders say, under *taboo*, until it comes to its senses. Nature has placed a bar in its harbor; let its self complacent aristocracy, see to it that they do not place a more effectual one against the approach of their country friends, upon land.

When the Essex County Anti-Slavery Society met again, on September 15 at Danvers, Whittier as secretary reported the convention in detail to the *Liberator*. Meanwhile, on July 4, he had been elected secretary of the Haverhill Anti-Slavery Society.[59]

## 5

At this very time Whittier and his mother, his sister Elizabeth, and his Aunt Mercy were on the point of removing from Haverhill, where his great-great-grandfather had settled in 1647, to Amesbury, near the spot where he had set down the family's roots in America in 1638. Amesbury was to be the poet's legal residence for the rest of his long life; and that town and Haverhill, it is worth remembering, approximately a dozen miles apart, described the geographical limits within which Whittier lived nearly all of his eighty-four years.

Several factors determined him to sell the old homestead, in April, 1836. There was no Friends' meeting house in Haverhill, and Whittier's mother, now about fifty-five years old, and his sister were unequal to making regularly the long drive to worship in Amesbury.[60] In the second place, Whittier's frail health and his increasing absorption with editorial and anti-slavery work weaned him inevitably away from farming. It also appears that his brother, Matthew Franklin, was ready to abandon the "hard and unthankful soil." On August 4, 1836, he married Abigail Poyen, daughter of Joseph Rochemont de Poyen, and he seems to have left farm work at this time, and to have removed to Dover, New Hampshire.[61]

The Whittiers' ancestral place in Haverhill was sold to the neighbor Aaron Chase for $3000, and for $1200 they purchased a cottage on Friend Street, in Amesbury, nearly opposite the old meeting house of the Friends.[62] On July 6, 1836, Elizabeth Whittier mentioned in her diary "the bustle & confusion of moving," and on August 23, in Amesbury, she made frank confession of the wrench which leaving Haverhill had caused her. She added: "I know scarce any of the abolition people here — I expect to like them all however or at least like their abolition."

Before long Whittier, too, found that leaving Haverhill was an ordeal. When he had scarcely become settled in Amesbury he discovered that a distinct cycle in his life was coming to an end. Abolitionism and political journalism could not be mixed together to the satisfaction of the *Gazette's* subscribers. When Whittier was faced with a choice between compromising his repeatedly stated editorial principles and resigning from his Haverhill charge, he did what a man would do. As early as August 27 he recognized the symptoms of dissatisfaction, and from Haverhill he wrote to the new co-owner of the *Gazette*, Doctor Jeremiah Spofford, of East Bradford (Groveland), in this vein:

> I have received a long letter in relation to Gov. Everett from one of his personal friends, who says that if the Gazette supports him after what I have said, it will surprise & mortify my friends every where. On this point I do feel as if it would not do for me to act inconsistently. I should lower myself in my own estimation; and in that of the public.
>
> It does seem to me that there are many advantages which will result from thy coming in *after* the election. If we bend our whole energies to the Whig cause — if we fill our paper with Whigism and resolve to sink or swim, live or die with it — why, if that cause is unsuccessful, we shall go down with it. If on the other hand, the paper pursues the even tenor of its way until after the election, on thy coming in, it can then, so far as is consistent with principle & truth, govern its course by the circumstances & results of the great struggle.[63]

The wound caused by Whittier's slashing Abolitionism proved to be more serious than he had suspected. Instead of waiting until November to join in the management of the *Gazette*, Doctor Spofford, to whom Jacob Caldwell had sold a half-interest in it to try appeasing friends of Everett,[64] took up his duties on September 17. It was then announced that in future the newspaper would be devoted more to commercial and political interests than it had been in the past, and that Doctor Spofford would be its political editor. Whittier was to conduct the literary department and others. In point of fact it developed that he could not dry his pen of slavery, occasional references to which appeared in the *Gazette* after Doctor Spofford's accession. Whittier was silent concerning Everett. But the situation was beyond saving, as Whittier recognized candidly when he wrote to Doctor Spofford, again from Haverhill, on November 23:

I have just learned that a good deal of dissatisfaction exists in this village in regard to my connexion with the Gazette. Many say they will not take the paper so long as I am the editor. They want a thorough-going exclusive Whig press. My aim has been to make the paper as interesting as possible, & at the same time temperately advocate my sentiments on the subject of Slavery. In so doing I have had no compensation except $90 from Mr. C. and the pay for my expenses in circulating petitions in Essex County. I did not expect to make money — on the contrary, I did not by any means consult my pecuniary interest in the matter. I am attached to Haverhill & would like to stay here — if my expenses could be paid. Of late however some of the Whigs have told Caldwell that he must get rid of me — that my abolition made me indifferent as to politics &c. Of one thing I am certain: the paper is now more than 120 advance[d] on its old subscription list — and if it were not for a few in this place all would go well. As it is however Caldwell is uneasy about it — but I cannot promise that next year I will go for Everett — on the contrary — I must oppose him. — Of the two I prefer Morton.[65] Situated as we are I have been willing to sacrifice many of my feelings, but on this subject I cannot. I wish thee would come up Friday morning & we will talk the matter over. I have had some idea of buying Caldwell's half myself — but if the Whig leaders are against me I should hardly have courage to do it — much as I wish to permanently locate myself in this village.

> I have written this note in great haste, as I did not understand that there was any particular opposition to me, before today. I thought it proper to mention the fact to thee.[66]

A few days more of reflection made it still clearer to Whittier that he was in an untenable position. One thing only remained for him to do, and he did it on December 1. His letter of resignation written then to Doctor Spofford is a record of high principles. Whittier said:

> I meant to have had a conversation with thee yesterday, but was not able to, having some business to transact with my brother from Dover, N.H. I have felt rather unpleasantly about leaving the paper, & could I, consistently with what I conceive to be my duty, take such a course as would be satisfactory to its patrons, I would do so. In regard [to] this matter, however, I am now persuaded that there are some persons in the village who will have nothing to do with the paper so long as I am connected with it; let my course be what it will. Capt. Caldwell, is a good deal disappointed, & no doubt thinks I have acted imprudently. As it is, I do not see how I could have done otherwise. I can now do no otherwise than yield to the pressure of circumstances, & give up my situation as joint editor. It is a very unpleasant & painful matter to me — but I have no complaint to make, — and, in case thee assume the entire control of the editorial department, it is important that it should not be supposed that there is any personal difficulty between ourselves. The truth is we have *always been friends* — & I trust we always shall be so. So far as my influence & exertions can go; I shall do all I can to procure thy election as a member of the Executive Council this winter. So far as I can judge few, if any of the anti-slavery folks *out of town* will drop the paper in consequence of my leaving it. Two or three individuals in the village, will probably discontinue it: But on the other hand from 20 to 30 will take hold of it. Our anti-slavery folks generally understand thee to be a friend of *Free Discussion*, although not an abolitionist, & that is sufficient, provided the paper does not say anything against them.
>
> Nothing ought to be said publicly about my being compelled to leave the paper as it would only irritate some of my friends. For my own part I shall have it understood so far as I am able, that it is only a business transaction between my brother in law & thyself, or others. From the estimate which I made recently the profits of the establishment

over the expenses is between $500. & $600. per year, at the present time. With a little exertion it might be raised to $800. or $1,000. — ****[67]

On Whittier's twenty-ninth birthday, December 17, 1836, his resignation as editor was announced over his own signature in the *Gazette.* He explained that he was "about to spend a portion of the winter in another section of the country," although he made it obvious enough that his "constant and consistent testimony" against slavery had motivated his leaving the newspaper. Characteristically, he ended his "Notice" with this brief paragraph:

> In retiring from his editorial duties, the subscriber would express his thanks to those patrons of the Gazette who have continued to support it, although differing from its sentiments, on the subject of Emancipation — thus proving themselves the friends of Free Enquiry and Discussion. He leaves with his enemies, if he has any, his hearty forgiveness; with his friends, his gratitude and love.

Whittier's fortunes seemed at this time to be straitened. In truth he had been through a hard school at Haverhill, but he profited by the chief lesson which he had learned through the *Gazette:* that the progress of the world is conditioned by the courageous championship of unpopular causes.

Out of Whittier's temporary loss of position came only increased commitment to the course he had chosen. In a letter to Garrison which was published in the *Liberator* on December 10, 1836, he reiterated his conviction that the best strategy for the Abolitionists was to convince the voters, and then to petition the legislators; and on December 19 he again wrote to Garrison, with decision:

> We are circulating petitions to the State Legislature. Will it not be well for the Mass. A.S. Society to print a circular & a petition & send it to abolitionists throughout the State? — It should be done at once. Pray see to it.[68]

Unable now to speak freely from an editorial forum, Whittier had resourcefully decided how, especially for the next year, to use his other talents in promoting Abolitionism.

"Life," declared one critic, "taught him deeper secrets than bookish ease could ever have imparted."[69] At the age of twenty-nine Whittier knew what it cost to be a friend of man.

# VIII

# Manly and Vigorous Battle

DURING 1837, a year of business decline in the United States caused by the orgy of speculation and overexpansion through which the nation had been passing, Abolitionism rose somewhat in public favor. On March 28, at Lynn, Wendell Phillips gave notice of his complete adherence to the movement. By April the legislative and popular tide in the North is considered to have begun turning toward the Abolitionists. By November there were more than twelve hundred anti-slavery societies in the United States.[1]

## 1

Whittier, momentarily a free agent and destined never again to be long bound to editorial desk work, became a convention-goer. His gift of expression, his sympathy with divergent points of view, and his incisive thinking made him a valuable committee man.

His first convention of 1837 took him to Harrisburg, where on January 31–February 2 the Pennsylvania Anti-Slavery Society was founded. On January 16 he wrote to Caleb Cushing, from Philadelphia: "I expected to have been in Washington ere this; but shall remain here until after the Harrisburg fanatical convention. . . ." Obviously Whittier, as journeyman Abolitionist, was dispatched to Harrisburg when his potential usefulness to John Quincy Adams and Cushing was cut off by the suspension of the right of petition in the House of Representatives.[2]

In the Pennsylvania capital Whittier, officially one of two delegates from the Massachusetts society, perhaps assisted the committee of seven men who were appointed to draft a constitution. When the convention weighed the subject of political action, Whittier spoke briefly to advocate it — and rarely in his life did he make such talks.[3] But for him the most exceptional event of the sessions must have been his meeting Governor Joseph Ritner, whose recent message to the legislature had so gratified the Abolitionists. Back in Boston, Whittier at once composed his spirited poetical tribute to "the independent farmer and high-souled statesman, . . . [who] alone of all the Governors of the Union in 1836 met the insulting demands and menaces of the South in a manner becoming a freeman and hater of Slavery. . . ."[4] The *Liberator* published the poem on March 24, 1837.

During that month Whittier was intensely active in the Abolitionist lobby in the State House at Boston. On May 9–11 he was in New York for the annual meeting of the American Anti-Slavery Society, took a leading part in committee work, and was continued as secretary of the Society's board of managers for the ensuing year.[5] In order then to confer with Garrison, he paused in Brooklyn, Connecticut, on his return trip to Boston.[6] And there he was a leader in the four-day convention (May 30–June 2) of the New England Anti-Slavery Society. He served on the committee on business, and put boundless energy into a long preamble — a bill of particular charges against the slave power — and resolutions which he introduced and the Society approved on the last day. How Whittier worked on the offensive was illustrated in the final resolution:

> That SLAVERY, and not *Anti-Slavery*, threatens the dissolution of the Union — that it has already virtually destroyed it, so far as regards all who believe in and cherish the inalienable rights of man — and that nothing but the speedy abrogation of the laws which sustain slavery can save from utter annihilation that Union, formed by our fathers, for the glorious purpose of securing to themselves and their posterity the blessings of liberty.[7]

## 2

Whittier might now have accepted in Portland, Maine, the editorship of a proposed Abolitionist paper which he had refused in the autumn of 1835,[8] but after a week's vigil in Boston he learned that the project was not even yet ripe. Opportunely, there was more important work for him to do in New York as one of the corresponding secretaries of the American Anti-Slavery Society, and thither he went on June 14 after having attended the Friends' yearly meeting in Newport.[9]

At Anti-Slavery headquarters, 143 Nassau Street, Whittier worked in a small office alongside other stalwarts of the movement, men whom Harriet Martineau met in that year and of whom she wrote in 1838: "A just survey of the whole world can leave little doubt that the abolitionists of the United States are the greatest people now living and moving in it." [10] Whittier worked with these colleagues:

JAMES G. BIRNEY, of Kentucky, future Liberal Party nominee for President, who had voluntarily freed his slaves and turned philanthropist and Abolitionist.

JOSHUA LEAVITT, Yale graduate and prospective editor of the *Emancipator*.

THEODORE DWIGHT WELD, one of Whittier's closest friends in the anti-slavery movement; a man of "marvelous eloquence which, in the early days of anti-slavery, shamed the church and silenced the mob." [11]

ELIZUR WRIGHT, JR., Yale graduate, former professor at Western Reserve College; founding member of the American Anti-Slavery Society; future editor of the *Massachusetts Abolitionist*.

With this hard-working staff Whittier was in his element. Besides editing the weekly *Emancipator*, the monthly *Anti-Slavery Record*, and four other serial publications, headquarters directly propagandized leading public men through personal letters; petitioned Congress against the interstate slave trade and the annexation of Texas, and for freedom in the District of Columbia; wrote tracts; operated an "underground railroad" for fugitive slaves; and employed lecturers and agents such as Whittier himself had been for a time in 1836. The main financial supporters of this work were four men of means: Gerrit Smith, Arthur and Lewis Tappan, and Joseph Sturge, the English Friend and philanthropist.

Whittier's main contribution to the pool of talents at headquarters was his occasional verse, his sage counsel, and his editorial skill. He guarded his health by avoiding now any regimen of close desk work, and he ferried at will between lower Manhattan and Brooklyn, where he stayed for a while. Yet he must have been, as always, on top of his job, in spite of New York's humid summer heat and an onset of "my old complaint of palpitation." On July 4, 1837, in a letter written to his sister he specified that he was overseeing the dispatch of petitions,[12] but he must also have had a hand in editorial work, of which there was so much to do.

In its plenitude Whittier seems to have found instant if temporary usefulness. From early June until August 17, when Leavitt became its editor, the *Emancipator* was in no one's stated charge, but Whittier's trained hand is discoverable in its conduct and contents. The weekly now published in serial form John Quincy Adams's letters to his constituents which in May had been printed as an anti-slavery pamphlet with "Introductory Remarks" by Whittier. Again, the *Emancipator* on August 10 published Whittier's hymn "O Holy Father" without signature — Whittier's accustomed way with his own compositions appearing in newspapers which he edited. Leavitt took charge of the *Emancipator* on August 17, and Whittier left New York — "a place which . . . I must consider unfit for Christian, or heathen even, to dwell in" — for Amesbury between August 21 and 27.[13]

Though his health suffered in New York, Whittier took away some pleasant memories of it and of work accomplished. He and Weld, another quiet dynamo of the Abolitionist forces, enjoyed a close intellectual companionship. One evening, on the balcony over the entrance to City Hall, they became so engrossed in a subject that they talked on, unconscious of passing time, from nine o'clock until the striking of the great clock overhead sent them home at nearly daybreak.[14] Whittier's home, late in his stay in New York, was with the family of Don F. Del Floys, a Spanish refugee, and there he got a fresh view of the "talkative sex" — whom, in a shy way, he found always engaging. In a letter to Harriet Minot he exulted: "I see all the French and Spanish ladies in the city. As a general thing they are not so beautiful as the American ladies. There is more dignity and haughtiness in the Spanish ladies; yet on acquaintance they are very agreeable. . . ."[15] Earlier, while living in Brooklyn, Whittier met the twenty-year-old poet Lucy Hooper, a native of Essex County. Her origin recommended her to him, and so did her writing, which he strongly encouraged and some of which he later published. They became warm friends, and Whittier was a frequent visitor at the Hoopers' Brooklyn home.[16]

Finally, in New York, Whittier wrote the brief preface to the pamphlet "Views of Slavery & Emancipation," eighty or so pages taken from Harriet Martineau's important two-volume *Society in America* in order to enable a numerous public to profit from "this able and impartial account of the state of society in the United States. . . ."

From Boston on August 27 Whittier sent a long letter of advice to Lucy Hooper about publishing her selected poems. He thought the present time favorable for publishing, since "there are few new books in the market." [17] One of the "few" was his own *Poems written during the Progress of the Abolition Question in the United States, between the years 1830 and 1838*, a collection of twenty-one pieces which had been advertised in the "Letters of John Quincy Adams to his Constituents." The book, Whittier's second compilation, was put through the press during his absence and without benefit of his habitual revising.[18] As Abolitionist propaganda the verses were potent, including, among familiar titles: "To William Lloyd Garrison," "Stanzas for the Times," "Clerical Oppressors," "Toussaint L'Ouverture," and "The Vaudois Teacher." The editor (perhaps Garrison) regretted Whittier's diversion from the writing of poetry —

> But he may derive satisfaction from the idea, that his labors for the honor of our nation, in a far nobler sense, will ultimately give freedom and life to her literature — now withering beneath the soul-enslaving censorship of a public, who exact of an author that he shall not *unreservedly* name the very name of Freedom. ***

## 3

For at least part of September, Whittier rested in Amesbury. One fruit of his moment's surcease from anti-slavery turmoil was the poem "Palestine," which appeared in the first (October–December) number of the Washington publication, the *Democratic Review*. (Through 1846 Whittier followed with twenty-two other contributions to this non-Abolition magazine which commanded some of America's best literary talent of the day.) But his rest at home was brief, for some time during the autumn of 1837 he was called to Philadelphia as assistant to Benjamin Lundy, of the *National Enquirer*. A Quaker and a pioneer Abolitionist editor who had recruited Garrison, Lundy died in 1839, a victim of long and hard battle against discouraging odds. On March 15, 1838, Whittier had succeeded him as editor of the weekly, renamed the *Pennsylvania Freeman*.

Whittier not only went to the aid of one of the first of Abolitionist editors, he went into the first line of battle against slavery. Pennsylvania was borderland. In Delaware, only a few miles from Philadelphia, Negroes were in bondage. Whittier was very conscious of his new situation, as he subsequently described it in a letter of August 16, 1838, to J. E. Fuller, of Boston:

> Our cause is slowly, and against unnumbered obstacles, going ahead. *You* in New England have got *pro*-slavery to contend with; *we* have got into a death-grapple with slavery itself. They leave no stone unturned to put us down. The clergy of all denominations are preaching against us. The politicians are abusing us in their filthy papers; and dirty penny sheets, with most outrageous caricatures of Garrison, Thompson, Angelina Grimké Weld, are hawked daily about the streets. But we shall go ahead nevertheless. We are slow-moulded, heavy-sterned, Dutch-built, out hereaway; but when once started on the right track, there is no backing out with us. The abolitionists of old Pennsylvania are of the right material; many of them don't believe in the devil, and those who do are n't afraid of him. I admire and honor their stern moral courage, in manfully maintaining their ground against a fiendish and bitter opposition.[19]

Whittier clearly realized that the Pennsylvania Abolitionists, although "of the right material," were a small band. In 1833 when he attended the founding convention of the American Anti-Slavery Society he was chagrined to find leading Quakers averse to Abolitionism because of their commercial interests. He found them still opposed five years later. In his first (March 15) issue as editor of the *Freeman* he mentioned having received a copy of the *Glasgow Argus* of December 28, 1837, in which the Society of Friends was praised for its action looking to the abolition of the apprentice system. Then he asked pointedly:

> When will the Society of Friends in our country merit such an eulogium? They have done well in times past, but we fear that at the

> present crisis they are, as a body, too lukewarm on this subject. Their ancient and excellent testimony against slavery has been, in too many instances, sacrificed to prejudice, mercantile connexions with slave-holders, and a somewhat inconsistent dread of association with other sects for any other purposes than those of worldly gain.

"Mercantile connexions with slaveholders" were at least as formidable in Philadelphia as in New York and in the Boston which, in 1851, wrung from Whittier the damning lines of "Moloch in State Street." In 1838 the issue of Philadelphia mercantilism and mobs *versus* Abolitionism was highlighted for all to see, two months after Whittier became editor of the *Freeman.* The forces of reform, including the Abolitionists, had at a cost of some $40,000 built Pennsylvania Hall, at the southwest corner of Sixth and Haines Streets, and in ceremonies beginning on May 14 the building was dedicated to liberty and free discussion. On May 15 a poem composed for the occasion by Whittier was read for him by C. C. Burleigh,[20] and the two men together wrote the "able and eloquent address" signed by eleven members of the executive committee of the Eastern District, Pennsylvania Anti-Slavery Society.[21] This group controlled the *Freeman*, whose offices were now located in Pennsylvania Hall.

Trouble brewed on May 16 when the Abolitionists began a series of scheduled meetings which attracted many of the leaders of the national movement. Garrison was there, and also Weld, who on the fourteenth married Angelina E. Grimké. On the afternoon of May 16 Whittier introduced his favorite resolution, that against voting for political candidates who did not favor the abolition of slavery in the District of Columbia and in the Territories. The evening session then brought an omen of what was to come. As Whittier reported in the *Freeman* of May 17, this meeting, attended by at least three thousand people, was early disturbed by a mob which threw stones and broke windows. But blinds drawn, on the order of the presiding chairman, saved the audience from injury; and Mrs. Weld continued with her address.

Next day the mob began to gather early, and it reached such portentous numbers that Daniel Neall (Whittier's friend, now president of the governing board of Pennsylvania Hall) invoked the aid of Mayor John Swift. This magistrate perpetrated a shameful double-cross, whose consequences Whittier reported indignantly in a postscript dated 7.30 A.M., May 18, which appeared in the *Freeman* of the seventeenth.

Pennsylvania Hall [Whittier wrote] is in ashes! The beautiful temple consecrated to Liberty, has been offered a smoking sacrifice to the Demon of Slavery. In the heart of this city a flame has gone up to Heaven. It will be seen from Maine to Georgia. In its red and lurid light, men will see more clearly than ever the black abominations of the fiend at whose instigation it was kindled.

We have only time to give a hasty sketch of the horrible proceedings of last night. All day yesterday a body of ill-disposed persons lingered around the Hall. The crowd increased towards evening. Between 6 and 7 o'clock, the mayor *for the first time* made his appearance, and met the managers of the Hall. He told them that he could not protect the building unless the keys of it were placed in his hands — and earnestly requested them to put the Hall under his control for the evening. This was acquiesced in. He then addressed the crowd, who answered him with cheers, but refused to disperse. About 8 o'clock the work of destruction commenced in the midst of assembled thousands. The doors were broken open with axes, — the Anti-Slavery Office in the lower story was entered and the books and pamphlets scattered among the crowd. Soon the cry of fire was heard, and flames appeared from the building.

It was set on fire in several places: and the engines of the firemen were not permitted to play upon the Hall. Piles of shavings from the cellar were brought up to the speakers' forum, placed upon it, and set on fire. The flames soon rose high above the roof, casting a baleful light upon the busy incendiaries — and the immense crowd of human beings who filled all the adjoining streets. From 15,000 to 20,000 persons stood gazing on the scene.

We have no time for comment. Let the abhorrent deed speak for itself. Let all men see by what a frail tenure they hold property and life in a land overshadowed by the curse of Slavery.

That was Whittier's fourth — and worst — encounter with an anti-Abolitionist mob, but he omitted to report that he had been at close grips with it. Under the disguise of a wig and a long white overcoat which he assumed at the home of his friend the Reverend Doctor Joseph Parrish, he went to his office in the lower story of the burning building to salvage what he could from the ransackers. His life might have been hard to save if they had recognized him.[22]

After a driven night of putting the paper (but not himself) to bed, Whittier attended the anti-slavery meeting held on the morning of May 18 in the open street facing the ruins of Pennsylvania Hall. That was a majestic spectacle; the brave bearing of the Abolitionists faced down the hovering mob, and Whittier pressed the political resolution he had offered previously. On May 24 in the *Freeman* he appropriately published an editorial entitled "The Work Going On." He reported that the mob uprising of the sixteenth and seventeenth had continued several nights more, had threatened to destroy the houses of Abolitionists, and had led to assaults upon colored people and whites of both sexes. He also deplored the hostile tone of the newspaper press, and said: "We ask the attention of our readers to the manly and noble tone of the Pennsylvanian, in regard to this outrage, as contrasted with that of the other city papers. Let the different city editorials of the past week be preserved, for future reference. . . ."

Gleeful reports of the Pennsylvania Hall fire printed in Southern newspapers [23] were barely endurable. Home evidence of the bond of Northern business and Southern slavery ignited a heavy blast which Whittier released in the *Freeman* on August 2, 1838, under the head of "Base and Contemptible Servility." He bitterly castigated Philadelphia merchants and manufacturers who were identified with the "Southern and Western Business Card," handsomely framed and colored, which was executed by a Philadelphia printer. Embellished with a cut of Pennsylvania Hall in flames and surrounded by a mob, the card bore the inscription: "Burning of the Pennsylvania Hall, erected by the Abolition Society, . . . Philadelphia. Destroyed by the People on the night of May 17, 1838." Whittier flared: "No one can mistake the object of this picture and inscription. . . . It is manifestly intended to convince the Southern slaveholder that the 'merchant-princes' of Philadelphia, are willing to sacrifice principle and humanity, law, order, and decency, for the sake of Southern trade." And Whittier advocated that those whose names appeared on the card should exculpate themselves.

He had a far more agreeable story to report in the *Freeman* on October 18, 1838. The Council-elect of Philadelphia on the first ballot retired from office Mayor Swift, whose continuance Whittier had opposed, and named Major Isaac Roach as his successor. Swift's failure to serve properly in the Pennsylvania Hall mob uprising came swiftly home to him.

## 4

Although he was now fighting slavery virtually on its borders, Whittier never lost sight of its vast ramifactions, or of the issues which it involved of property and law and order. In an editorial entitled "Cotton and Slavery" in the *Freeman* on October 24, 1839, he asserted clear-headedly that England, too, had a rôle to play in abolishing slavery in the United States. He could never have imagined, however, that on the threads of King Cotton the British would, on occasion, almost be drawn into the Civil War when it came, except for the skillful diplomacy of a son of his admired John Quincy Adams — and except for the efforts of John Bright and other Englishmen.

At home, Whittier repeatedly condemned slavery as a lawless force wielding power far beyond its domain. That was the broad point of his editorial "We Want Your Votes" in the *Freeman* of September 13, 1838,[24] and of another entitled "Mobs" which was published in the issue of June 20, 1839. Whittier rated the mobs of European cities as far more enlightened than our own: they would actually give their lives to advance the cause of human liberty, ours plainly sought to kill it. Whittier prophesied that the North would get revolution as its reward for tolerating mobs.

> The spirits of mobocracy [he reasoned] may yet tear in pieces the magicians who have raised them. The inventor of the brazen bull perished in his own instrument of torture: Haman mounted the gallows which he had set up for his neighbor: the hounds of Acteon devoured their own master. Let the instigators of mobs beware. What if it should be ascertained that it is as easy to destroy a bank as a Hall of Free Discussion: that deeds of warranty and mortgage are as combustible as anti-slavery papers: that the hoarded heaps of the capitalist are as accessible as the "incendiary documents" of the abolitionist.

## 5

Besides insisting upon the duty of government to protect guaranteed civil and human rights, Whittier referred often to the need for political action to eliminate slavery. Now and always he kept an intent watch on major politicians, and steadily insisted that the Abolitionists had a specific duty: to vote for no one who was not in favor of emancipation.

On January 10 and February 28, 1839, Whittier excoriated in turn Congressman C. G. Atherton, of New Hampshire, and Governor David Rittenhouse Porter, of Pennsylvania, in two of the merely six poems which he published in the *Freeman* while its editor. Atherton on December 11, 1838, introduced into the House of Representatives the "gag resolutions" which continued the practice of laying on the table, without consideration, all petitions relating to slavery; and Porter, who had defeated Joseph Ritner, in his inaugural address of January 1839 turned against the Abolition cause which, while in the State Senate, he had supported.

Later in the year, on December 19, under head of "A Word of Caution," Whittier weighed the larger question where William Henry Harrison, in his inaugural address as President, would stand on the slavery question. In brief, Whittier said:

> We should then [if Harrison spoke out against slavery] give our vote to General Harrison as an ABOLITIONIST, and not as a Whig, or anti-mason. But he must give us a decided and unequivocal testimony in behalf of Freedom to satisfy us.

Four weeks later, on January 16, 1840, Whittier in a leader entitled "General Harrison" said the assertion that bloodshed and massacres would result from agitation of the abolition question was disproved by the experience of England, France, and Germany. He always believed, he indicated, that emancipation in the United States could and should be effected peaceably. One week later in the *Freeman* Whittier argued that the mighty "slave power" must fall if Pennsylvania, the keystone State, voted solidly against it in Congress.

But if he now had high hopes of Congress, they were quickly dashed. On February 6 he published an editorial, "The Deed Consummated! The Right of Petition Gone!" saying that he had been in the House gallery "when this outrage was perpetrated." Eleven Northern Democrats and one Whig, he reported, voted for the resolution of William Cost Johnson, of Maryland, and it was carried by a majority of six votes. The lesson of this was clear to Whittier:

We have neither time nor space for protracted comment. We can only urge upon abolitionists a solemn consideration of the mighty responsibility now resting upon them. To them, for the time, is entrusted the preservation of constitutional freedom. The world demands of them, at this crisis, firmness, energy, and activity.

## 6

That was why Whittier decried the diversion of any Abolitionist energy and activity to other causes than Abolition. He would not admit that the cleavage over the issue of political action was serious, as it plainly was. The difference between Garrison and Whittier over it, dating back to 1834, now became a clean rift. Whittier constantly emphasized the need for Abolitionist unity, for effort aimed solely at emancipation. Other reforms, such as women's rights including suffrage, were secondary to Abolition in his present scales, although as a Friend he was literally born to the women's-rights principle which Garrison took up in the eighteen-thirties as a social issue — and, characteristically, as a very personal one.

While ill at his Amesbury home from October 1838 to April 1839, Whittier sent lengthy editorial correspondence to the *Freeman.* He acknowledged the division in the Abolition ranks in "New School Abolitionism" (January 17, 1839) and in letters appearing on February 14 (on dissension in the Massachusetts Anti-Slavery Society) and February 21 ("The Impartiality of Slavery"). Particularly in the second, Whittier prayed for a submergence of personal and partisan differences in the main stream of Abolitionism; as editor of the *Pennsylvania Freeman*, observing with perspective equal to his regret the troubles of the Massachusetts society, he addressed an appeal for conciliation to Garrison. An extract from this letter was published in the *Liberator* on February 22, 1839, and Garrison added the gratuitous comment: "All this is certainly in a very amicable spirit, but somewhat in the Henry Clay style, when Missouri was admitted into the Union as a slave State, for the sake of peace."

Whittier wrote from Amesbury two days later (the letter appearing in the *Liberator* on March 8) lamenting and rejecting Garrison's accusation as "far more injurious to himself than to his friend: and in the free spirit of an abolitionist, I tread it as the dust under my feet, and leave it." Whittier rejected also the possibility of a "quarrel with the friend of twelve years' standing." Garrison, however, was in a quarrelsome mood; to Whittier's letter he appended a half-column of accusations against the "political Abolitionists," and flung this barb at Whittier: "We sympathize with our dear friend in his illness. In our allusion to Henry Clay's manner of 'pacification,' we only meant that J. G. W. is for obtaining peace at the expense of consistency, if not of principle."

Whittier wisely let the matter rest there until he was well enough to return to Philadelphia. Then in "The Editor at His Post," published in the *Freeman* on April 11, 1839, he calmly reviewed his editorship and his exclusive concern with Abolition, not with other agitating questions of the day. Part of his statement read:

> For ourselves, we have with scrupulous fidelity endeavored to adhere closely to the original principles of the Anti-Slavery Association. We stand now precisely where we stood in the Convention of 1833, when the American Anti-Slavery Society was formed. We entered into the association and gave our name to the Constitution with no ulterior object of reform in church or in state, or in the general condition of the social fabric. We looked only to THE ABOLITION OF AMERICAN SLAVERY. We simply pledged our moral power as a man, and our political power as a citizen, for the overthrow of the abomination. *** No man can say in truth that we have ever, as *an abolitionist*, assailed the reserved mental rights — the varied opinions, prejudices, or partialities, of our brethren, on subjects apart from the single and well-defined one of our association.

So, Whittier explained, he had to reject some articles and resolutions submitted to the *Freeman* "touching the controversy going on among our Eastern brethren." Pennsylvania Abolitionists had a "border war with slavery" and no time for contention. "As abolitionists," he advised, "we have a single object: let us keep our eyes single towards it." And he ended, with cogent logic:

> Is the present harmony of feeling among the Abolitionists of Pennsylvania, to give place to personalities, invective, jealousy and evil surmisings? Will our McKims and Burleighs, our Coateses and Motts, turn away from the victims of the southern prison-house to

discuss the relative merits of William Lloyd Garrison, Henry B. Stanton, or Amos A. Phelps? We will not believe it.

Out of his willingness to go to any length for the sake of peace and harmony, Whittier in the *Freeman* of June 6, 1839, directly begged Garrison as editor of the *Liberator* to pass by irrelevant issues in favor of Abolitionism; and in the issue of September 5, in a letter sent from Amesbury, he again deplored the division in the ranks and pleaded for Abolitionist unity of spirit.

No one strove harder than Whittier to build and keep clear the road leading to emancipation.

## 7

For him it continued to go many places, and he continued to report to his readers the main events of major anti-slavery meetings. On May 10, 1838, and May 23, 1839, he reported on the annual business meetings in New York of the American Anti-Slavery Society. On May 20–21, 1839, he went to Norristown for a meeting of the Anti-Slavery Society of Eastern Pennsylvania, and served on the business committee. Then in the *Freeman* on August 8 and 15, 1839, Whittier's long letters from Albany and from Saratoga Springs told of signal events at the national meeting of the A.A.–S.S.,[25] and of the quarterly meeting of the Saratoga County group. At the famous spa he had an unexpected and welcome opportunity, which he described modestly:

> This place is now the great centre of the fashionable world. Its numerous Hotels are crowded to overflowing, and it may be safe to say that from one-third to one-half the visitors here are from the South — spending in fashionable dissipation the hard earnings of their slaves. I have had many opportunities of laying our principles before the minds of some of these men, — and, I fervently trust, not without producing a favorable impression.

Whittier was speaking in character, not at all idly. He despised the institution of slavery, but not individual slaveholders. Quakerlike, he would "deal with them in a spirit of Christian love and tenderness."

Toward the South, which he regarded as erring on the subject of slavery, he maintained a respectful and conciliatory attitude. He was firm but friendly in two *Freeman* editorials (December 6 and 13, 1838) addressed to the *Richmond Enquirer* and the *Richmond Whig*. In the *Freeman* dated October 17, 1839, he respectfully printed for the enlightenment of the misinformed *Louisville Bulletin* the significant fact that the first anti-slavery society was founded in New England in 1832, and had twelve members; currently, Whittier wrote, there were between fifteen hundred and two thousand anti-slavery societies extending all through the free states.

On the other hand, Whittier tore to shreds all Northern apologies for the South's "peculiar institution." If he had one favorite whipping-boy it was the Democratic *Washington Globe*, whose editor was Francis Preston Blair, Sr. On December 12, 1839, for example, he ripped to pieces, as a gross misrepresentation, the *Globe's* self-imposed duty of exposing the alleged alliance everywhere of Whiggery with Abolition. Whittier knew, no man better, how chary both major political parties were of his cause. His ideal conception of Democracy, which he stated repeatedly,[26] was leagues beyond that of the Democratic *Globe*. On February 13, 1840, in the next to last issue which he edited of the *Freeman*, Whittier sketched how paltry a thing "Democracy" was in this country, in contrast to what it ought to be; and the measure of the difference to him was the *Globe* itself, which he called "the unblushing advocate of slavery."

## 8

Whittier's manly and vigorous battle on the borders of slavery was frequently, because of his health, carried on from the rear. He was actually in Philadelphia only about half the time during his twenty-three months as editor of the *Freeman*. Yet he contrived to send abundant copy to the weekly, whether he was in Amesbury or Boston, New York or Albany, or in Pennsylvania cities other than Philadelphia. And in his absence the *Freeman* continued in good hands. Charles C. and William H. Burleigh, Thomas Earle, and Lewis C. Gunn substituted for him at various times, and Whittier's cousin Moses A. Cartland was in charge between July 11 and September 12, 1839. In announcing on June 27 that "protracted indisposition" obliged him to resign at least in part his charge of the *Freeman*, Whittier apologized: "We have not been able, for some months, to do justice to the great cause in which we have been engaged." Not until October 10 was "the editor at his post" again.

A regimen of editorial desk work was simply no longer possible for Whittier. How, from this time forward, at once to guard his health and serve his cause was a grave problem, aggravated by the fact that he needed a salary for the support of his Amesbury home. Whittier eked out his strength on the *Freeman* as long as he could, until he formally resigned on February 20, 1840, by interspersing with his desk work in Philadelphia rests in Amesbury and Abolitionist missions elsewhere.

His health and spirits seemed to rise automatically when he escaped from his office. This was never so true as when, in July and August of 1839, he went on a mission with H. B. Stanton through the beautiful Cumberland Valley of Pennsylvania, and soon afterward to the anti-slavery meetings in Albany and Saratoga Springs. From the spa Whittier wrote to a Philadelphia friend: "I am on the whole enjoying myself quite well, and my health is, I think, most decidedly improved, not by drinking the rascally drugged water here, but by travel, exercise, and open air." [27]

These he had certainly found also in his preceding trip of a week or so through Harrisburg, Carlisle, Chambersburg, and Gettysburg. Whittier seemed in altogether ebullient spirits as he reported his progress — in search of seventy speakers, like the equal band whom Theodore Dwight Weld had trained as anti-slavery agents in 1836–37 — to Elizabeth Neall, of Philadelphia.[28] Whittier and Stanton left Philadelphia early on the morning of July 7 by coach for the state capital. On the eighth, Sunday, Stanton lectured there twice. That evening Whittier wrote, in a letter which the *Freeman* published on July 11: "This section of the state has been much neglected. It needs the services of two or three able and active agents." And from Carlisle he wrote Elizabeth Neall of his and Stanton's progress, chiefly of their having learned of prospects "whom we hope to interest in our cause. We must get the Germans with us, by some means or other." [29]

Whittier and Stanton were entertained in Carlisle at the home of their Abolitionist colleague, the Reverend J. Miller McKim, and in that place Whittier began to be refreshed by "the great Cumberland valley," walled in by the Allegheny Mountains to the west and the Blue Ridges to the east. Characteristically, he remembered it in detail, as he remembered his view of the Susquehanna River in Harrisburg and, equally, the impending visit to Gettysburg. After a pleasant morning visit on July 9 to the farm of former Governor Ritner, nine miles from Carlisle, the Abolitionist "talent scouts" went on thirty miles southwest down the valley to Chambersburg. This old road junction and rich agricultural center (burned by the Confederates in 1864) proved to be the westernmost point reached by Whittier in his lifetime. It looked east twenty-five miles to Gettysburg, where he had the main engagements of this trip. In July twenty-four years later it was the terminus for another man born in 1807 — Robert E. Lee, who also reached it via Chambersburg.

Presumably Whittier and Stanton recruited some of their seventy anti-slavery agents among the students of the Lutheran institution, founded seven years before on Seminary Ridge, which is now Gettysburg College (and theological seminary). Certainly they were charmed with the soft landscape — and as certainly they could not have fancied that it was terrain which, in 1863, would be made "hallowed ground" by the Northern and Southern lives laid down in one of the most pivotal battles of all history.

Whittier's main report of this mission was his editorial "The Cause," which appeared in the *Freeman* on July 25, 1839. He underscored his earlier plea for anti-slavery work in Pennsylvania's central counties, and then reflected on the lot of Abolitionists doing that work:

> It is comparatively a small thing to suffer for a good cause, in the midst of sympathizing friends, and in common with a multitude of our fellow-laborers. Heart gathers from heart a strength for endurance even unto death. But the man who, alone and without sympathy, stands firmly up against the tide of popular prejudice, — with no voice of encouragement in his ear, — no kindly glance of approval resting upon him — but meeting, wheresoever he turns, an eye of hatred or contempt — the fingers of his neighbors pointing after him in scorn — the drunken howling mob in his track, or breaking the miserable repose of his afflicted family, — and who knows that for all this endurance he can acquire no earthly praise — that his thousand sacrifices and trials will find no record among his fellow-men — that, if he perishes in the struggle with his enemies, the verdict of his contemporaries will be, like that pronounced over the grave of the Israelitish warrior, "*Died Abner as the fool dieth*," — such a man, opposing his single breast to the

beating storm of universal censure — in opposition to the passions, the interests, the prejudices, of all around him — moving onward in his path of duty — uncheered even by any decided fruits of his exertions, and hearing on all sides, —

> "the world's dread laugh,
> Which scarce the firm philosopher can scorn,"

is the true martyr of our cause, and, even, while living, the crown is resting on his brow.

## 9

Whittier himself lacked neither friends nor appreciation in Philadelphia. The A. W. Thayers, once of Haverhill, were there, and he early made his home with them. Whittier esteemed Daniel Neall and, quite as much, an Essex County native, Joshua Coffin. Whittier's old schoolmaster was now active in anti-slavery work of a sometimes perilous sort. For the rest, Whittier mingled chiefly with a close circle of relatives and of Abolitionist friends from Bucks, Chester, Delaware, and Lancaster counties. With the family of his first cousin Anna A. Wendell he had affectionate relations, and also with the family of Joseph and Rachel Healy, with whom he lived at 72 North Seventh Street during part of his Philadelphia stay. Healy was financial agent for the Pennsylvania Anti-Slavery Society.

John Dickinson, active in Abolition, was a warm friend. William J. Allinson, of neighboring Burlington, New Jersey, was another Abolitionist intimate of Whittier's, in whose honor, partly, he named his son Francis Greenleaf Allinson.[30] Finally, Whittier enjoyed, in a reserved way safe for a now settled bachelor, the friendship of a cultured, attractive group of young ladies, among whom were Sarah Lewis, three Elizabeths — Lloyd, Neall, and Nicholson, — and his two cousins, Ann E. and Margaret Wendell.

These were the friends in whose company Whittier found solace and relaxation when, all too seldom, he could be free from the *Freeman*. His Philadelphia story was a tale of close work. But he delighted to get out of the city whenever he could. In a letter of August 3, 1838, he mentioned to his sister Elizabeth the inroads which his work was making on his health, and he added: "I have been out in the country frequently." [31] Manifestly, in spite of his yearning for Essex County and his home, Whittier became greatly attached to the Philadelphia countryside and its people. Some years later he wrote:

> I think the old Quaker settlements of Chester, Bucks, Delaware and Lancaster counties forty years ago were nearer the perfection of human society than anything I have since seen or had heard of before.[32]

A particular retreat to which Whittier retired with marked pleasure on more than one occasion [33] was Joseph Healy's place, "Spring Grove Farm," situated north of Philadelphia in Bucks County, on a high bluff above the Delaware River.

# 10

Healy was the kind friend who saw through the press, before Whittier's return to Philadelphia in November 1838 from an enforced rest in Amesbury, the fifty anti-slavery poems which Whittier himself had collected and edited during the summer. This edition was authentic even to the personal application of the quotation which Whittier took from Coleridge for the title page of the *Poems:*

> "There is a time to keep silence," saith Solomon. But when I proceeded to the first verse of the fourth chapter of the Ecclesiastes, "and considered all the oppressions that are done under the sun, and beheld the tears of such as are oppressed, and they have had no comforter; and on the side of the oppressors there was power," I concluded this was *not* the time to keep silence; for Truth should be spoken at all times, but more especially at those times when to speak Truth is dangerous.

It was Healy, too, who published in Philadelphia the revised edition of Whittier's *Moll Pitcher, and The Minstrel Girl* (April 1840).

Nothing in Whittier's character suggests that in the editorial, "The Cause," he was asking his Abolitionist friends to place any crowns on his brow. He deserved them abundantly, none the less, for his achievement in giving to the *Pennsylvania Freeman* such quality and influence as no borderland organ of the Abolition movement had yet had; and above all for his stature as a man. Happily, they were given from free hearts and minds. In taking temporary charge of the weekly on July 11, 1839, Joseph Cartland spoke particularly of "the unvarying prudence with which the paper has been guarded by his [Whittier's] watchful eye." On succeeding to the editorship of the *Freeman* on April 30, 1840, C. C. Burleigh referred to "the station . . . so brightly adorned by the genius, taste, and talent of your favorite Whittier. . . ."

Appropriately, the fullest measure of appreciation was expressed in resolutions of the Eastern District Executive Committee of the Anti-Slavery Society of Pennsylvania, on March 17, 1840:

> Whereas our friend & fellow laborer Jno. G. Whittier has been obliged by the delicate state of his health to retire from his place as Editor of the "Penn[a] Freeman"; and whereas an occasion is thus afforded us of publicly expressing the sentiments which while he was present with us a proper sense of delicacy obliged us to cherish in private, therefore,
>
> Resolved, that this committee have submitted with the deepest regret to the necessity which deprives us of the presence & cooperation in his capacity as editor, of our beloved friend John G. Whittier.
>
> Resolved that in the discharge of his duties as editor of the Freeman, and in all his labors among us in the cause of emancipation, as well as in the private walks of social life our friend has acquitted himself in such a manner & manifested such a spirit as to enhance our admiration of his talents, strengthen our confidence in his discretion, to renew our regard for his singleness of heart & purity of purpose, and to bind us to him by ties of the strongest friendship.
>
> Resolved, that our best wishes attend him during his retirement with our earnest desires for the renewal of his health and his restoration to the field of labor in the cause to which he has already rendered such invaluable aid.
>
> Resolved that as a testimony of our confidence & esteem Jno. G. Whittier be appointed to represent the Penn[a] A. S. Society (E. Dist.) in the convention to be held in London on the 12th of June 1840.[34]

# IX

# The Governing of Men

As a member of the Society of Friends, which from its earliest days had a strong and particular interest in democratic government, Whittier all his life was interested in politics. His newspaper writings of the years 1829–32 are full, by turns, of attraction and repugnance to it. In equal measure he was alternately drawn to and repelled by the works of Byron and Shelley — admiring their writings and their championship of a better estate for man, and detesting their respective social codes. On balance, Whittier regarded them as heralds of liberty.

Their preferences and his for a career ran a dead parallel. Byron in 1813 wrote to his future wife:

> I by no means rank poetry or poets high in the scale of intellect. This may look like affectation, but it is my real opinion. . . . I prefer the talents of action — of war, or the senate, or even of science, — to all the speculations of those mere dreamers of another existence (I don't mean religiously but fancifully) and spectators of this apathy.[1]

And Shelley said in a letter of 1819:

> . . . I consider Poetry very subordinate to moral and political science, and, if I were well, certainly I should aspire to the latter. . . .[2]

All three of these poets were in their mid-twenties when they caught the vision of government as an instrument to be used for raising man's estate in the world.

Even in his untimely reach for a place in Congress in 1832, Whittier was not wholly selfish. By the time he served in the Massachusetts House of Representatives in 1835, he knew as fact, tested by experience, what Burke had taught him years earlier: "There is no safety for honest men, but by believing all possible evil of evil men, and by acting with promptitude, decision and steadiness on that belief." [3] And Whittier had by that time become fixed in the conviction that his prime mission was to help free the slaves, with all the weapons ready to his hand. One of these was political skill of no mean order. He used it, under a sense of duty to his God, to fight a system which he considered a violation of all of God's ordinances for man.

## 1

Burke, as Whittier's first political mentor, left with him, or confirmed in him, a conservative set of values. Whittier's remark, "I reverence old-time faith and men," became wearisome by iteration. Burke's abhorrence of the French Revolution was taken over uncritically by Whittier and spread, all too often, before the eyes of his newspaper public in 1829–31. From Burke he acquired a blind spot: he failed at first to perceive that liberty, the very reason for the existence of constitutions, was more important than the preservation of established order. Burke refused to treat politics as an abstract science; he held duties rather than barren rights to be the true basis of political action, and wrote, "Principles should be subordinate." Logically, Burke held loyalty to his party to be the duty of every man "who believes in his own politics." And he gave deep root in Whittier's mind to the idea of "the most material of all social ties, the principle of our obligations to government." [4]

These concepts, rather than the valid inheritance of Jeffersonian Democracy which he derived from his father, determined most of Whittier's early political attitudes and pronouncements. In the Jackson administration he thought he saw a revolutionary movement, and he opposed it vehemently. Of Jackson himself, Whittier seldom spoke in temperate phrases. In truth, the mass of the people and the root causes which gave the Jackson party their power were the side on which Whittier belonged. With the banking, industrial, and mercantile class who constituted the backbone of the Whig party, he had no common cause. Burke's teaching, none the less, made of him at first a Whig party man, in a normally Whig district.

The spell did not last for long. In 1830 Whittier began to have doubts of party organization, and on December 6 he wrote in the *New England Weekly Review:*

> We are tired of the eternal cant of old party names. The time has been when these names signified something. They were signs of things — the rallying words of *principles*. It is not so now. ***

Again, in an article "Mr. Clay's Bill" which he contributed to the *Haverhill Gazette* on March 2, 1833, he declared: "I offer no blind homage to an individual, for I am more than ever disgusted with personal politics." By 1834 Whittier was out in the clear, away from Burke on most points and confidently creating his own school of political action.

It had a cause to serve. Whittier gave a lucid exposition of how he would make politics further it, when he wrote on January 10, 1834, to the New England Anti-Slavery Society, meeting in Boston:

> *** The people of the free states, with a perfect understanding of their own rights and a sacred respect for the rights of others, must put their strong shoulders to the work of moral reform, and our statesmen, orators, and politicians will follow, floating as they must with the tendency of the current, the mere indices of popular sentiment. They cannot be expected to lead in this matter. They are but instruments in the hands of the people for good or evil. . . . Be it our task to give tone and direction to these instruments; to turn the tide of popular feeling into the pure channels of justice; to break up the sinful silence of the nation; to bring the vaunted Christianity of our age and country to the test of truth; to try the strength and purity of our republicanism. If the Christianity we profess has not the power to pull down the strongholds of prejudice, and overcome hate, and melt the heart of oppression, it is not of God. If our republicanism is based on other foundation than justice and humanity, let it fall forever.[5]

As Whittier had expected, and as events proved, it was an exceedingly difficult business to get party to serve cause. Infinite patience and determination were first required even to get men, regardless of party, to take and hold freedom's line in the legislatures of State and nation. Equally, Whittier and others who advocated the use of political action as an aid to their cause had to overcome reluctance in the Abolitionist ranks, centering mainly about Garrison. But the political-action wing of the movement carried their strategy to triumph, finally, in the election of Lincoln to the Presidency in 1860, after their third-party tactics had directly influenced the results of five successive national campaigns.

## 2

Two lectures in the series sponsored by the New England Anti-Slavery Society in Boston during the winter of 1835 revealed currents which were running strong in the Abolitionist ranks. Whittier's address, already referred to, was delivered on February 11; Garrison's, the last of the series, one month later, on the subject of "Political Anti-Slavery." One passage in Whittier's rare utterance was this:

> When prejudice and oppression feel the influence of Truth, working their destruction, the cry is forthwith raised, that the world is about to be turned upside down — that every thing beautiful and sacred in ancient institutions is about to be offered up as a sacrifice to the spirit of reform. The law — the *law*, is pronounced to be in danger.

Whittier's steady argument, which became potent in the armory of Abolitionism, was that under the Constitution there was no warrant for the existence of slavery in the United States; that Congress had the right to abolish it by law in the nation's capital and prevent its spread by eliminating it as a condition to the admission of new territories as States of the Union.

In practice, this logic demanded that the North send men of firm purpose and of vision to Congress, determined to speak and act as free men in a free country. Whittier was resolutely opposed to appeasement of the slave power in Congress. He was particularly sharp in his comments of May 7, 1836, on becoming editor of the *Haverhill Gazette*. One burning passage in his editorial "To the Public" read:

> I regard the present struggle as the closing one between LIBERTY and SLAVERY in this republic. It is a contest of life and death. *** "The Whip of the South!" said senator Preston, in speaking of the Tariff compromise, "ay, the WHIP OF THE SOUTH has brought the North to compliance!" This whip is again brandished over our heads, and we are called upon to give up our own constitutional and natural rights and

seal our lips on the subject of human freedom, on pain of its infliction. For the preservation of peace and union, we have already made many heavy sacrifices, and if necessary, we can and ought to make many more. But in so doing let us not yield the rights of the free laborers of New England; let us not forget the outcast and down-trodden Slaves, nor the cause of holy liberty throughout the earth. In no spirit of menace or defiance, but calmly and firmly, as becomes men conscious of their own rights and respecting those of others, we must PUT BACK THE WHIP.

That kind of tough logic did not appeal to Garrison and others in the non-resistant wing of the Abolitionists. The divergence of opinion which had existed since at least 1834 was brought into sharp focus at the 1837 meeting of the American Anti-Slavery Society, held in New York. Whittier there introduced two resolutions, one calling on Congress to abolish slavery in the District of Columbia, the other exhorting the people of the United States to "pour in their petitions to Congress, year after year, until the seat of the national government shall become the habitation of freemen." After lengthy debate, these resolutions were referred to a committee of four men, three of whom were Garrison, H. B. Stanton, and Whittier. Garrison later submitted a weakened resolution, which was adopted, specifically barring the Abolitionists from creating a political party or attaching themselves to any existing party, but asserting that the people of *all* parties were bound to refuse support to any candidate who would not further the immediate purposes of the Abolitionists. These were three: to sustain freedom of speech and press and the right of petition, to abolish slavery and the slave trade in the District of Columbia and the territories, and to oppose the introduction of any new slave state into the Union.[6]

In 1879 Whittier explained simply: "I felt it my duty to use my right of citizenship at the ballot-box in the cause of liberty, while Garrison, with equal sincerity, judged and counselled otherwise." But in 1837 Garrison's stand caused a "new organization," favoring political action, to spring up around Whittier and Stanton, J. G. Birney, Joshua Leavitt, Amos A. Phelps, Samuel E. Sewall, Gerrit Smith, and Arthur and Lewis Tappan. Garrison and his adherents refused to recognize the possibility of abolishing slavery without the overthrow of the Constitution and the Church, and they advocated simultaneously such reforms, in addition to liberty in general, as peace and women's rights.[7]

Whittier, strongly deploring the diversion of Abolitionist energies to side issues, wrote an open letter to Garrison, which he published in the *Liberator* on October 27, 1837, regretting that the Massachusetts Anti-Slavery Society, which was financially responsible for that newspaper, had no control over it. Whittier added, in an editorial note of the period, "What an absurdity is moral action apart from political!" [8] And, since the contest went on with the establishment in 1839 of *The Non-Resistant* in Boston, to oppose political action,[9] Whittier in the *Pennsylvania Freeman* said on April 11, 1839: "As abolitionists we have a single object: let us keep eyes single towards it." On June 6, in "Politics and Non-Resistance," which he published in the *Freeman*, Whittier directly begged Garrison to stick to Abolitionism in the *Liberator*, not continue with controversial issues that did not relate to it. "In a word," Whittier implored, "let the SLAVE have the Liberator as his own."

## 3

For himself, Whittier held steadfastly to his set course of action. In national elections and state campaigns he labored astutely to throw behind dependable candidates all the support he could command for them. In equal measure he opposed candidates who had in any way opposed the Abolitionists or served the slave power. Until the Liberty Party was organized before the 1840 Presidential campaign, he coldly discounted any possibility of getting party help — from either the Whigs or the Democrats. He wrote succinctly in the *Haverhill Gazette* on June 25, 1836: "After all, the abolitionists . . . have nothing to hope for from either of the great political parties. They are joined to their idols — and one of these . . . is southern slavery. We must learn to distrust the policy of the world, and rely upon the single heartedness of Truth for success in the cause of humanity. . . ."

Whittier had a very long memory, the *bête noire* of politicians. When Edward Everett was running for re-election as Governor of Massachusetts in 1836, Whittier sent a one-column article, which the *Liberator* published on October 29, attacking his early record in Congress and also his late one in the State House. "Let that friend of liberty vote for him who can," Whittier warned. (Everett was re-elected.)

Clay, too, aroused his opposition, although Whittier clung overlong to his early admiration for "Harry of the West." From New York on June 5, 1837, he wrote a long letter to Clay, calling him "the advocate of universal liberty" and requesting him to oppose the annexation of Texas, as a prospective slave state. Whittier hopefully (not too hopefully) asked if Clay would "sustain the petitions," on the subject, which the Society of Friends "would be glad to entrust" to his care.[10] Respecting slavery, Clay cared only about colonization. When, on a visit to the Senate in June, 1841, Whittier met Clay, the Senator accused him of deserting an old friend. Whittier gave his Abolitionist reasons,[11] which were to the fore at the annual meeting of the American Anti-Slavery Society in Albany two months later. On August 15 in the *Pennsylvania Freeman* he reported the Society's decision to vote for no man who did not favor the principle of immediate emancipation. "It has sealed the fate of Henry Clay," he prophesied. Thus in the 1844 Presidential campaign Whittier rejected Polk only more strongly than Clay, whom, in the *Middlesex Standard* on August 8, 1844, he condemned as "a deliberate ROBBER OF THE POOR."

To Van Buren also Whittier applied the sting of his Abolitionist disapproval. In an editorial of June 25, 1836, in the *Haverhill Gazette* he accused Van Buren, as Vice-President, of having cast a tie-breaking vote in favor of the Incendiary Bill which was dictated by considerations of political expediency. Then on September 10, also in the *Gazette*, Whittier cast up the records on Abolition of Van Buren and of Harrison, one of whom would be elected President. In resignation Whittier concluded: ". . . verily — a pair of abolitionists!" One week later Whittier devoted a strong editorial note to the *Boston Atlas* and its attempt to identify Abolitionism with Van Buren. In the *Gazette* of November 12, two days before Van Buren's election, Whittier confessed that he "has seen too much of the hollowness and hypocrisy of political parties, to be deceived by empty professions held out on the eve of an election." And so it went, down to the year 1848, when, with a brave gulp, Whittier accepted Van Buren as the Presidential candidate of the Free-Soil Party.

Whittier's hopes of Webster, whom he first regarded as a titan, came to the same end of wrathful repudiation as his wavering confidence in Clay. In 1835 Whittier advocated Webster's nomination as Whig candidate for President, and in a letter of March 1, 1836, he advised Cushing: "A firm and steady support of Daniel Webster, without playing into the hands of the White and Harrison parties, or volunteering attacks upon the Van Buren party, is, it appears to me, the safest course for yourselves, and the best for the true interests of the State."[12] In the next decade Whittier's trust in Webster began to wane, and in 1847 he began to pepper the Senator with the disapproval which at last exploded in the cannonade of "Ichabod," after Webster's famous "Seventh of March" speech. Whittier's poem, which appeared in the *National Era* on May 2, 1850, was the bitterest denunciation he ever penned. It ranks with Browning's "The Lost Leader" as one of the most sorrowful testimonies in modern times of one man's loss of faith in another.

"Ichabod" represented the final crash of Whittier's trust in Webster; but there had been hints of its coming. On January 7, 1847, the *National Era* had published a long letter from Whittier which included this thrust at Webster:

> Thou wilt see, by the Boston Atlas and Advertiser, and by the speeches of Daniel Webster over his dinner and to the volunteers for the Mexican war, that all due care is taken to let the Southern wing of the Whig party understand that the Whigs of Massachusetts are "sound on the subject of Slavery," and the war now waged for its extension. ***

Also in the *National Era*, on October 28 of that year, Whittier was entirely negative to some one else's suggestion that Webster would be a suitable candidate for President. Whittier's opposition was specific. After paying the usual tribute to Webster's intellectual ability, he said that the "*Creole* case," along with Webster's attitude on the annexation of Texas, would not go down. Only complete repentance on Webster's part, Whittier added, would win his vote. On October 31, 1850, Whittier went all the way, in the *National Era*, and urged that Webster be defeated even in his campaign to return to the Senate. More than ever, Whittier then wanted dependable men representing Massachusetts at Washington.

## 4

In John Quincy Adams and, later, in Charles Sumner he found the perfect co-operators. Caleb Cushing, too, did all that he felt able to do, as a Representative of the people of the Essex North district, to help Whittier to activate Abolitionist measures in Congress. Robert Rantoul, Jr., Whittier's best friend among the Democrats, also gave aid to the cause, first as a member of the House of Representatives in Massachusetts and then at Washington.

Whittier's admiration for Adams as a man of principle and courage — and of Massachusetts — never abated. He had it in his youthful newspaper days,[13] and he had it in his experienced maturity. Chiefly he admired Adams because in the House of Representatives he fought for the free exercise of rights guaranteed by the Constitution, above all the right of petition. Strongly supported by Whittier, Adams exercised that right even when, occasionally, he disapproved of the petitions themselves. After the House suspended the right in 1836, Adams fought with tenacious ability to have it restored, as it finally was in 1844. That was Adams's laurel more than any one else's. In Whittier's book, *there* was a man. He knew what government was for.

Adams's view of it touched, at points, directly upon Whittier's concept, which he expressed lucidly in an editorial "We Want Your Votes," published in the *Pennsylvania Freeman* on September 13, 1838. Part of it read:

> Government is designed for the protection of the citizen in his natural and civil rights; and when this protection ceases to be given, government becomes a curse, and not a blessing. The abolitionists, in almost all parts of the Union, whether under the government of Whig or Democratic authority, *have been left unprotected;* their property destroyed; their lives hunted after; denied the constitutional right of peaceably assembling to discuss the great questions pertaining to human liberty; denied the right of petition; abused "*by authority*," in public and in private; and abandoned to the tender mercies of every ruffian who can wield a brickbat argument in favor of "the Union," or who takes upon himself to avenge, by ROBBERY and ARSON, insults offered to the "moral sense" of official dignitaries.
>
> The great question which comes home to the abolitionist is not therefore one in reference to the "currency," or the "Presidency," or "the Bank," or the "sub-treasury." It is a question of life and death; or freedom or slavery; liberty to speak and think, or the gag of penal enactments; security for person and property, or the delivery of both

over to the "regulation" of the mob. This is THE QUESTION brought home to the bosoms and the firesides of the friends of freedom in all parts of the country; and in an especial manner to those of Philadelphia abolitionists.

At any rate, as neither bounden Whig nor Democrat, Adams was independent and could put humanity above party. In Congress he became spearhead of the Abolitionist cause, and he carried the burden until, at the age of eighty, he died in 1848. Earlier in the decade Whittier is said to have written to Joseph Sturge describing Adams as, in effect, head of the American Anti-Slavery Society and of the Liberty Party.[14] Certainly his years of service to the Abolitionist cause had prime value. Beginning in 1834 he had manfully laid before Congress the petitions which Whittier and others fed to him, directly or through Caleb Cushing. This labor Adams is said to have regarded as "the crowning work of his long and useful life." [15]

In 1837 he wrote a series of cogent letters to his constituents telling plainly the story of his fight in Congress for the right of petition. These documents, first published in the *Quincy Patriot*, had more than a merely local application. When the Abolitionists determined to publish them in pamphlet form for wide circulation, Whittier as deputy conferred at Quincy with the former President, and then edited the letters with "Introductory Remarks" ending on this prophetic note: "Massachusetts will sustain her tried and faithful representative; and the time is not far distant, when the best and worthiest citizens of the entire North will proffer him their thanks for his noble defense of *their* rights as *freemen*, and of the rights of the SLAVE AS A MAN." [16]

On three of his visits to Washington — in January 1840, June 1841, and February 1848 — Whittier called on Adams. (In December 1836, when he had first started for the Capital, only to be headed off at Philadelphia, Whittier had intended to help Adams, Cushing, and other Massachusetts representatives prepare material for debate in the fight which they were then waging, and lost, to sustain the right of petition.) When he arrived in Washington on January 28, 1840, Whittier was just in time to take a seat in the House gallery and hear the Abolitionists specifically denied that right. To Joseph Healy, in Philadelphia, he wrote: "Northern subserviency has yielded *all* to the demands of the South." [17]

In June 1841, accompanied by Joseph Sturge, Whittier had a seat behind the Speaker's chair in the House during the bitter debate on the "gag rule." Whittier went with Sturge when the English philanthropist paid his respects to Tyler, who had declined to receive a memorial from British Friends, on the subject of slavery, which Sturge was commissioned to offer.[18]

But Whittier missed the scene caused in Congress in 1842 when Adams presented a petition, signed by forty-three citizens of Haverhill, which was devised to deflate Southern threats of dissolving the Union unless even the right of petition was denied upon topics which in any way touched slavery. The Haverhill petition, which Whittier must have had a hand in writing, read:

> The undersigned, citizens of Haverhill, in the Commonwealth of Massachusetts, pray that you will immediately adopt measures, peaceably to dissolve the union of these States: First, because no union can be agreeable or permanent which does not present prospects of reciprocal benefit; second, because a vast proportion of the resources of one section of the Union is annually drained to sustain the views and course of another section without adequate return; third, because (judging from the history of past nations) this union, if persisted in, in the present course of things, will certainly overwhelm the whole nation in utter destruction.

Tumult followed in the House of Representatives. Adams in submitting the petition had explained his lack of sympathy for it, but with the pertinacity which exasperated the Southerners he had demanded that all respectful petitions should be considered. Four days' fiery debate followed on a resolution to expel Adams from the House because, it was charged, he had offered the deepest indignity to the House and insult to the American people, and was even guilty of high treason.[19] Adams bravely rode out the eleven-day storm, and two years later, in 1844, he hoisted his own flag above this threat of ignominy when he won his eight-year fight to have the right of petition restored.[20]

Whittier saw the elder statesman of the political anti-slavery forces only a few days before Adams died, and reported the interview in the *National Era* on April 13, 1848. On the day Adams died, February 23, Whittier paid him this tribute in a letter addressed to Charles Sumner from Washington:

> Ere this thou has doubtless heard of the sudden illness of the vener-

able Adams. At a late hour last night he was still living, but sinking fast. I have not heard this morning. His death will be the fitting end of such a glorious life. Falling at his post, dying with his harness on, in the capitol so often shaken by his noble battle for freedom! My eyes fill with tears, but the emotion is not unmingled with a feeling of joy that such a man should thus pass from us. A few days ago I had a highly interesting conversation with him. All his old vigor seemed to reanimate him when he touched the subject of slavery. I shall never forget that interview. Even if now living, he cannot survive through the day.*** [21]

## 5

Caleb Cushing, unlike Adams, was in the period 1830–1850 young (only seven years older than Whittier) and full of personal ambition. He was, moreover, a Whig nearly as conscious as Henry Clay of the potent Southern wing of the party. When the Whigs came to power in 1841, his nomination as Secretary of the Treasury was three times sent to the Senate by President Tyler, and three times blocked by Southerners who chose to regard his anti-slavery record. Cushing then went on a special diplomatic mission to China, and afterward he served as an officer in the war with Mexico, by which time Whittier was opposed to him. Whittier acknowledged, however, in the *Pennsylvania Freeman* on November 29, 1838, that Cushing's whole course in Congress on the question of slavery —

> . . . has been honorable to himself — manly, open, and consistent. Whatever else the papers may say of him, they cannot accuse him of being a "dough-face." He has never betrayed his constituents, nor compromised the honor and dignity of the Pilgrim State, on the question of human liberty.

Cushing, not an Abolitionist, unquestionably gave the anti-slavery cause valuable service during his four terms in Congress. As a man of Massachusetts he had entirely valid sentiments against human slavery; and as a lawyer, a strong legal sense of the rights guaranteed to individuals under the Constitution. Whittier, coolly exploiting these two facts and the dominant drive in Cushing's make-up, the wish to hold public office, was able to make him in effect a highly useful aide to Adams — for eight years — in Congressional matters affecting Abolition. Frequently the relationship between Whittier and Cushing was a tussle between two strong men.

In 1832 Whittier canvassed "Essex North" in the interest of Cushing's ambition to go to Congress, as Cushing did go in 1834 and again in 1836 with the help of Abolitionist votes which, under exacting agreement, Whittier delivered to him. Likewise in 1838 Whittier got from Cushing a promise of aid to Abolitionism, although C. M. Fuess has been at pains to say that even without the votes of his anti-slavery constituents, Cushing (with a majority of 1800) would have defeated his Democratic opponent.[22]

The youthful careers of the two men were closely bound together, especially in 1832–34. Whittier helped to keep Cushing in the running for Congress in 1833, and had a direct hand in his success of 1834, his first. But in 1833 it was obvious that Cushing, favoring colonization of American slaves, and Whittier, then making his commitment to Abolitionism, would not go down the same road.[23] Whittier contrived very skillfully indeed to win from Cushing as much support as he did for his own high-minded concepts of government and of Democracy.

The considerable correspondence between the two men [24] shows how far they were able to travel together. Whittier made it altogether clear that the Abolitionists, whom he led in Essex County, were unwilling to support any man who would not uphold the right of petition and likewise vote for the abolition of slavery and the slave trade in the District of Columbia. In general, Cushing's anti-slavery constituency distrusted him. But in return for his pledges given to Whittier in 1834, in 1836, and (most reluctantly) in 1838, he did serve the Abolitionists. He confessed scant sympathy as he presented to Congress some of the flood of petitions received from Essex County, but he did submit them. He ably seconded Adams in his demand that *every* petition be received and referred with respect to the appropriate committee of the House. Like Adams, he spoke with fire and courage; when the Territory of Arkansas was being admitted as a slave State in the spring of 1836, he ably opposed it on the floor of the House, and Whittier in the *Haverhill Gazette* of July 16 that year was gratified to print the speech, five and a half columns long. Like Adams, again, Cushing fought hard against the "gag rule."

Whittier saw to it that Cushing earned the trust which had been given him, by getting petitions signed and sent from every possible locality in "Essex North" — more, naturally, from Amesbury and Haverhill than from other centers. He constantly briefed Cushing on the political state of the county, and with firm tact let him know that his services were both appreciated and watched. In the letter of March 1, 1838, previously referred to, Whittier included these remarks:

> Thy skirmish with Hardin, of Kentucky, and its triumphant result on thy part, has gained thee no small degree of credit among *all* parties here. It discovered an untrammelled and independent spirit, and a determination to defend the honor and the interests of thy constituents, irrespective of partisan feelings. I like the old-fashioned democratic tone of thy speech on the right of petition. The Van Buren organ in this district copied two paragraphs of it with approbation. On the right of free speech and communications there will be a splendid opportunity to maintain the vital principles of democracy; to hold up before the nation the now universally detested Sedition Law; to speak of those who suffered by it, and to set the Democrats of Virginia and South Carolina of 1800 in battle array against the position of these "chivalrous" sovereignties at the present time. It will be sport to see the "engineer hoist with his own petard." [25]

Earlier, on April 14, 1837, Whittier wrote to ask Cushing for a report, to be submitted to the impending quarterly meeting of the Essex County Anti-Slavery Society, on petitions from the County which Whittier had forwarded to him. (Cushing promptly furnished the list, indicating which petitions had been presented, which were yet to be offered.) Whittier also made this request:

> Could thee write me a letter in reference to the reception of the petitions, and permit me to read it as a private but not strictly confidential letter to myself? A similar request will be made of Mr. Phillips [Stephen C., of Salem]. Of course I do not expect you to avow yourselves to be other than what you are now understood to be, — anti-abolition. But as an abolitionist I am grateful to both of you for your defense of the character of the petitioners, and for your manly stand for the periled right of petition.[26]

There matters stood until the time of the war with Mexico, which Whittier opposed both as war and as an inevitable means of extending the slave domain in the Union. Then, in a letter from Amesbury which was published in the *National Era* on January 28, 1847, Whittier scoffed at

Cushing's effort to procure $20,000 from the Massachusetts Legislature for helping to equip a special Bay State regiment, of which he had already been named colonel. The significant part of the letter, striking a final balance in his attitude toward Cushing, reads:

> Seriously, it is a poor compliment to the civilization, religion, and humanity of our age and country, that a man like Caleb Cushing, with a mind highly gifted by nature, enriched by varied learning, and capable, if rightly directed, of exerting a healthful influence upon his country and the world, is able to find no better employment than that of leading off a company of deluded unfortunates thousands of miles, to shoot men with whom *they* at least have no quarrel, or be shot at by them; and this, too, without the plea that the welfare of the country requires or its true honor demands it. And, when we consider that it is manifestly the design of the promoters of this war to extend the curse of human slavery over whatever territory our arms may conquer, there really seems very little to be said in favor of transforming one's self into a mad Berserker, and, tucking up the sleeves of one's Christian garb, to do gratuitous butchering in its behalf. I remember a spirited reply which Cushing once made in Congress to the ridiculous threat of some exasperated member, that the law of slavery should be extended over the free North: "You may destroy," said he, "our manufactures, you may cripple our commerce, raze our cities to the dust, and lay our whole land waste; but you cannot, you shall not, introduce slavery into the heart of the North!" Is it possible that he is now prepared to do himself the very thing which he then so strongly deprecated, and to aid in introducing slavery into the heart of a free country?***

## 6

With Whittier the cause was the thing, and in his efforts to promote it regardless of party, he in 1837 appealed to his highly esteemed friend Robert Rantoul, Jr., then Democratic leader in the Massachusetts House of Representatives. March of that year was critically important to the Abolitionists, since Van Buren in his inaugural address veered so much to the side of the South. He declared himself "an uncompromising opponent of every attempt on the part of Congress to abolish slavery, in the District of Columbia, against the wishes of the slaveholding States," and he bade people to cease discussing the matter. Thereupon Whittier and his Abolitionist colleagues induced both Houses of the Massachusetts Legislature to pass resolutions (unanimously in the Senate, only sixteen members dissenting in the House) favoring the right of petition and the abolition of slavery in the District. Likewise, both Houses passed, almost unanimously, a bill which secured jury trial to runaway slaves caught in the Commonwealth. The *Atlas* of Boston, which, with other newspapers there had been opposed to the resolves, objected that Whittier and other anti-slavery men "were indiscriminately mingled with the members in the Representatives' Hall during the whole debate." [27]

Before going to Boston for four weeks of lobbying, Whittier on March 1 wrote from Amesbury to Rantoul pointing out that if the Democrats opposed the resolutions submitted to the Legislature, Governor Everett and the Whig Party would at the next election be stronger than ever. Then Whittier added cannily:

> Thousands of anxious eyes are watching the movements of both parties in the Legislature. The course of the Democratic members thus far has been in accordance with the true principles of Democracy. Let them sustain the Senate & their cause will prosper. At the late Quarterly Meeting of the Mass$^{tts}$. A Slavery Society held at Lynn on the 28th ult. — in the midst of an assembly of from 1000 to 1500 persons, Mr. Stanton denounced "the Defender of the Constitution," Daniel Webster, as craven, recreant, untrue to his professed principles & to the cause of liberty & equal rights. This I mention to show that the abolitionists have cut loose from party attachments, & will go with those only who are in favor of liberal principles & equal rights. *** [28]

In Boston, Whittier evidently talked with Rantoul often and unreservedly about slavery, and on March 13 he added weight to his sentiments by posting to him a letter which is a remarkably clear exposition of Whittier's concept of the governing of men. He said that he thought the resolutions then before the Legislature would pass even without Rantoul's aid, but that in such an event "there would be a *party* aspect given to the matter, which I should regret exceedingly." Whittier ended his appeal on this illuminating note:

> It does seem to me that the present responsibility of thyself in this

matter is very great. Thy talents, eloquence, and thus far steady devotion to equal rights, thy influence almost unbounded with the administrative party of the State, all combine to render thy decision, whatever it may be, of no trifling importance. Whatever may be thought of it now, the present is a crisis in the affairs of this State. Thy course on this question will be a matter of history. Never since Patrick Henry electrified the Assembly of Virginia has there been a nobler opportunity for advancing the cause of righteous liberty. What are the paltry offices which men contend for, which the vile, the imbecile, the sordid struggle for, as the *reward* of partisan fraud and management, to that which is received from a grateful, intelligent, and virtuous people, not for services rendered to themselves, but for those rendered to the cause of pure democracy, humanity, and truth!*** I feel assured that slavery, in any form, is odious to thy feelings. Why not, then, say so; carry out thy democratic principles, and insure the approbation of the wise and good, throughout the world, and for all time; nay more, secure that self-approval, that answer of a good conscience, which, when the exciting ambitions and hopes of the partisan are lost, in the hour of sickness, and in the decline of life, will be dearer than any earthly honor. Never had any one a more excellent opportunity of doing honor to himself and to the cause of republican liberty than thyself at this time. It would prove to the people of Massachusetts that thy democracy is not a partial and time-serving principle, but radical and based upon the equality of the human family, and zealous for the rights of all classes. In a word, it would prove that to be a friend of the policy and principles of Mr. Van Buren, as regards other matters, does not necessarily imply a slavish acquiescence in his extraordinary views on the subject of liberty and slavery. It would win the respect and command the admiration of all parties. It would *disappoint* thy enemies; it would increase the esteem of all thy present friends, and add to their number. It would do much for the cause of humanity, and truth, and justice. May we not hope that it will be done?***

Rantoul took the bit. On March 31 Whittier wrote joyfully to A. W. Thayer, then in Philadelphia, how the Abolition lobby had "caucused in season and out of season, threatened and coaxed, plead[ed] and scolded," until the resolutions were passed, and the Van Buren men "persuaded to look to the people of Massachusetts, and not to orders from Washington."

Whittier counted confidently on passage of the jury-trial-for-slaves bill, and he exulted that Rantoul would "make a great effort for it." One of Whittier's colleagues among the Abolition lobbyists was, like Rantoul, a Democrat — George Bancroft, historian and future Secretary of the Navy.[29]

So it went, by skillful improvisation and tactics, until 1839, when definite steps were taken to found the Liberty Party. Garrison considered H. B. Stanton to have led the movement — Stanton, "the Napoleon of our cause." [30] They and Whittier attended, at Albany, New York, the anniversary meeting of the American Anti-Slavery Society, which Whittier reported in the *Pennsylvania Freeman* on August 8 and 15, 1839. Whittier and Stanton were two members of a business committee which submitted a proposal looking to the nomination of candidates for President and Vice-President by the Abolitionists. Over the protest of Garrison, who had refused to serve on the committee, this resolution was finally passed by the convention. Thus was born the Liberty Party, which in 1840 nominated James G. Birney for President and Thomas Earle for Vice-President.[31]

That event, which he had helped to bring to pass, was to Whittier almost the realization of a divine ordinance. Here at last was a party dedicated to his idea of government: a means of raising man's estate in the world. With Charles Sumner, John P. Hale, and other men of heart and enlightenment he was to work directly and unremittingly for the only political ambition he now had. He phrased it precisely in a letter addressed to a Liberty Party convention held at New Bedford in September, 1843:

> I am with the Liberty Party because it is the only party in the country which is striving openly and honestly to reduce to practice the great truths which lie at the foundation of our republic: all men created equal, endowed with rights inalienable; the security of these rights the only just object of government; the right of the people to alter or modify government until this great object is attained. Precious and glorious truths! Sacred in the sight of their Divine Author, grateful and beneficent to suffering humanity, essential elements of that ultimate and universal government of which God is laying the strong and wide foundations, turning and overturning, until He whose right it is shall rule. The voice which calls upon us to sustain them is the voice of God. *** [32]

# X

# The Clear Vision

FOR WHITTIER extended travel was a fond dream, nothing more. From his Hartford period to the end of his days he had delicate health for his constant companion, and it was a rough arbiter. Whittier did not have the physical strength to go to London for the world's anti-slavery meeting; indeed, he was plainly warned by his physician against overactive public or social life. In July and again in September, 1840, he was unable even to make an ocean cruise from Boston to Halifax which was planned to bolster his health.[1] The final decision against attempting the trip to London seems to have been reached in Philadelphia several months after he had resigned his charge of the *Freeman* and returned to Amesbury. From the Healys' place in Bucks County, Whittier wrote to his sister Elizabeth in May:

> *** I expect myself to return by way of Newport, although my health is not equal to a constant attendance of the [Friends'] meetings. I think I shall go back to Philadelphia in a day or two, and after a short visit in Wilmington, return to New York. It is, I believe, well that I did not go to England. It was a great disappointment to me, but it is all right. I wish I could feel wholly resigned to all the allotments of All-Wise Providence, and be more thankful for the blessings still reserved to me. It sometimes seems strange that I cannot do as others around me, but I try to suppress any feeling of repining or murmuring. I feel that I have not deserved the least of the bounties bestowed on me.[2]

Whittier was not, in fact, knocked under by his ill health. Instead, he turned the hard necessity of his now restricted activity to clearly marked gain: as he withdrew from the feverish organizational work to which he had been so deeply committed since December 1833, he patently grew in inner strength and spiritual grace. With perspective sharpened by sitting momentarily in the stands of the battle arena, Whittier approached nearer to God as the only possible dependence of man and hope of the universe; and he won renewed faith in the mission of the Society of Friends.

## I

English Friends — Joseph John Gurney in 1840 and Joseph Sturge in 1841 — gave him the kind of strong lift that William Forster had given him in his youth.[3] It was a happy chance that put Whittier in the way of Gurney in June 1840, soon after the eloquent Englishman had been in the West Indies to see at first hand the results of emancipation, voted by Parliament in 1833. In New York, Gurney joined Whittier and other Friends bound for Newport; and there, in emphasizing the Society's distinctive principles, he spoke a devout eulogy of his departed Quaker friend, Daniel Wheeler, which held three thousand people in rapt silence. Soon Whittier indited lines to that exemplary soul.[4]

Very soon, too, Whittier had to clarify doubts in other people's minds about his future relation to the Abolition movement. On July 2, 1840, he wrote from Amesbury to his cousin Moses A. Cartland:

> I wish to contradict in terms as explicit as possible the rumor which thou mentions from Newport Yearly Meeting. It is most preposterously absurd. My abolitionism grows daily stronger, my faith in its principles is deepening amidst all difficulties and trials and perplexities and vexations of our organizations. Like the pine of Vich Alpine, "Firmer it roots the louder it blow." But I do fear that my faith in our organizations is not of the "saving kind." I have just sent a letter to Joshua Leavitt, declining to act as one of the executive committee of the American and Foreign Anti-Slavery Society, and another to the anti-slavery convention in this State, declining to allow my name to be on the electoral ticket for Birney and Earle. I am now free from all trammels, and I feel more at ease. Strong in my confidence in the

justice of our cause, in the beauty and excellence of our principles, and in the wisdom and expediency of our prominent measures, I am still, as far as my failing health admits of, ready to do and suffer, if need be, for abolitionism. As a man, if not as an abolitionist, I have a right to agree or disagree with the "no government" people, without giving up my faith that a man *is* a man, and not a mere thing! At Newport, and at Philadelphia, and at Lynn, I have spoken as freely in disapprobation of the lukewarm course of a portion of our Friends as the truth would justify, while at the same time I am not prepared to give up Quakerism, to throw myself body and soul into the antisectarian *sect* about Boston.[5] Free I am to say that I feel a deeper interest than formerly in supporting the religious doctrines and testimonies of our Society, and I hope I shall find strength to manifest that interest; but the cause of the slave still rises solemnly before me, and from the warfare of the oppressed I feel no release, I ask for none. For me, I am sick, but to see thee would get me well again almost. We have now a great excitement here about a parcel of blacks, supposed to be runaways, landed from some vessel on our coast, who are now in the great swamp in this town and South Hampton. I have been out to-day after them, and have seen a boy, but he refuses to tell where he comes from. Depend upon it, we shall get up a great negro hunt here, and try to catch and tame them.[6]

Whittier remained in Amesbury, inactive and reflective, during the winter of 1840–41, and in a letter of March gave a frank report of himself to Harriet Minot. "Too dull and stupid to feel any interest in things present," he had turned his mind back to "old familiar faces," as he was to do more and more after 1840. He mentioned the struggle to accept his lot, and then added significantly: "I think sickness has a wonderful effect in fanning into life the half-extinguished conscience. It is doubtless better for me and for my friends that the hand of sickness is sometimes laid heavily upon me.***"[7]

## 2

Whittier still had a healthy concern for the corpus of the anti-slavery movement, and in the next four months, as companion of the English Friend and philanthropist Joseph Sturge, he toured the Middle Atlantic and New England States in an effort to "fan into life the all but expiring embers of abolition." In April he escaped from "our east winds which I dread," and met Sturge in New York. A leader in the already successful fight for abolition in Parliament, Sturge doubtless knew that factional differences and the growing strength of local units had reduced the American Anti-Slavery Society to not much more than a name by 1840. He tried, with little success, to move American Friends to greater service in it, and to compose the differences between Garrison's "no government" faction and the "political action" group of Abolitionists. But Sturge was treated with respect, not to whipped-up mobs as George Thompson had been in 1835.

Whittier, as Sturge's traveling companion for a good part of four months (sent home to Amesbury by only two bouts of illness), had something to do with that fact. The two men lent each other prestige. Together they beat "the Quaker trail" to Philadelphia, Wilmington, Baltimore, Washington, and into New England — to Newport, New Bedford, Boston, Lynn, Worcester, and Lowell. They saw slavery at first hand, in the trading markets of H. H. Slaughter in Baltimore, in a slave-pen located within sight of the Capitol in Washington, and in the State of Delaware, where the institution still existed legally although sentiment for it had been waning for years. Likewise, Sturge and Whittier directly saw the forces at work against the Abolitionists and felt, in Philadelphia and in Newport, the apathy of many Friends to their cause. If Sturge wished a poll of sentiment and public opinion toward Abolition in the United States, eight years after the American Anti-Slavery Society was founded, this trip undoubtedly gave it to him.

In Baltimore, besides slave markets, Sturge and Whittier saw the unpleasant spectacle of the Triennial Baptist Convention, dominated by influential slaveholding ministers, voting to exclude Abolitionists from the Baptist board of foreign missions. Sturge considered this rather than the slave markets "the darkest picture of slavery." Returned to Wilmington in June, the two travelers attended a meeting of Abolitionists who were working on the plan of a slight land tax to enable purchase and emancipation of all slaves remaining in Delaware. In Washington, next place on the itinerary, Sturge was treated to a spectacle about which Whittier had written often in protest: a debate in the House of Representatives on one in the series of "gag rules" which, from the time the first one was passed on May 26, 1836, until December 3, 1844, prevented the discussion of anti-slavery petitions submitted to Congress. Sturge and Whittier conversed in the Senate chamber with Henry Clay, to whom Gurney had posted a copy of his *A Winter in the West Indies.* Clay accused Whittier of "deserting him, after having been his warm friend," and his frank doubt that Whittier's strong Abolitionism permitted him to be a good Friend caused Sturge to write: "The praise [of the Society of Friends, in the South] of such men is the strongest testimony that could be adduced of the declension of the Society of Friends in anti-slavery zeal."

President Tyler, the Virginia Whig, after ignoring Sturge's letter requesting an interview, received the two anti-slavery leaders on the introduction of a Congressman; but their call on a former President, John Quincy Adams, must have been by all odds the most agreeable they made in Washington.[8] Very different was the visit which they made to the grim city prison, in which Dr. Reuben Crandall had been held five years before.[9]

In Philadelphia again, on the way to New England, Sturge found, as Whittier had learned while editor of the *Pennsylvania Freeman,* that individual Quakers but not the Society of Friends as a whole would support his anti-slavery mission. The atmosphere in which he was received in Philadelphia was indicated in a letter which Whittier wrote to a cousin there some time after August, when Sturge returned to England:

> When [said Whittier] I was in your city last, I was so anxious about J. Sturge's visit, and the course of Friends, and the little difficulties which we met with, that I was hardly myself. I recollect calling at the Lloyds' some two or three times, when my mind was altogether away and dwelling upon other things. What they thought of me I have often marveled at since. It was not on my own account that I felt uneasiness, — I am used to such things, — but I felt keenly for my English friend.

Sturge while in Philadelphia expressed his own feeling briefly to Elizabeth Nicholson. "The most beautiful place in the world your city would be," he said, "if it were only Abolitionized." [10]

Whittier and Sturge next journeyed to Newport to attend the Friends' Yearly Meeting, and there the English philanthropist saw plainly revealed the guarded attitude of strong elements in the Society toward Abolitionism. They informed him and Whittier that the meetinghouse was not available for an anti-slavery meeting. Not even two warming calls on the Unitarian minister William Ellery Channing, still ardent in his

Abolitionism one year before his death, could have burned off the cold fog of that attitude. But in New Bedford, Sturge was cheered by attending a Friends' meeting in which Negroes and white persons sat together indiscriminately. It was his first experience of such equality in the United States.

After a rest of June 22–25 in Amesbury, which gave Elizabeth Whittier the particular pleasure of making Sturge's acquaintance, he and Whittier returned to Boston. Chiefly, Sturge wished if possible to reconcile the aims and methods of the two Abolitionist factions — Garrison's following and the group which had dissented from his leadership and his concern with reforms in addition to Abolition. A long interview with Garrison proved fruitless: he and Sturge differed widely on the pertinence of women's equal rights and other reforms, important and desirable in themselves, to the cause of Abolition.[11]

The Society's further usefulness must have seemed limited to a man of Sturge's clear vision, and the fact is that by 1848 the fundamental job of the Abolitionists had been done in the North. But Sturge, eager to help the organization to function as long as necessary, generously offered to underwrite continued Abolition work by his new friend. In Boston on July 30, 1841, he placed $1000 at Whittier's disposal for personal use or anti-slavery work in the next twelve months, and paid $130 of the amount then, the remainder to be procured as needed through Lewis Tappan. Sturge specifically recommended to Whittier a visit to a tropical climate for the sake of his health. An identical arrangement was made by Sturge, through Tappan, on April 21, 1847, and December 22, 1848, the money perhaps to be invested for the benefit of Whittier's mother and his sister Elizabeth. In 1852 and again in 1857 and 1858, Sturge offered $1000 to enable Whittier and Elizabeth to travel to England for their health. They could not make the trip, evidently, and they never saw Sturge again before he died in 1859.[12]

The Whittiers, undoubtedly grateful enough, however reluctant to accept help from Sturge in their real financial need, were on personal grounds drawn to him at once and permanently. Sturge and Whittier were in exact harmony on Abolition. Whittier expressed their common attitude when he said to his friend in a letter: "This cause has been to me what the vision on the house-top of Cornelius was to Peter — it has destroyed all narrow sectarian prejudices, and made me willing to be a man among men." Warmly appreciative after coming to know him, Whittier in the letter of May 12, 1841, described Sturge as "a fine, free-hearted nobleman of nature; no pretension; a clear-headed, stout-hearted, practical philanthropist; the 'Howard of our day,' as he is called in England." And Elizabeth wrote: "How we did love Joseph Sturge! His bland, kind face will be a joy in my memory forever.***" Moreover, she penned a poem to him at the end of his "gospel mission" here, whose purpose had been "to point the Pharisaic eye/Away from empty creed and form to where the wounded lie." [13]

## 3

Except for that trip and the firm friendship with Sturge, the year 1841 was uneventful for Whittier, mainly devoted to convalescence in Amesbury. From there as corresponding editor he contributed ten or so articles, chiefly on familiar topics, to the September and October issues of the *American and Foreign Anti-Slavery Reporter*, published in New York; and at the turn of the year he appears to have sat in, a month or more, for Joshua Leavitt as editor of the *Emancipator and Free American*, published in Boston, as he was to do again in 1844 "for a short period." [14]

That, for the next twenty-five years, was the essential pattern of Whittier's life. He no longer had the boiling energy to be traveling delegate of Abolitionism or

> To pour the fiery breath of storm
> Through the harsh trumpet of Reform; [15]

instead, he had to make his strong and reasonable voice, as in the poem "Massachusetts to Virginia," heard from Amesbury. He had earned that right, and he made wise use of it.

During the period 1841–44 Whittier wrote a number of "poems subjective and reminiscent," and he was deep in religious reflection.[16] He "thought some" of attending the national anti-slavery meeting at Buffalo, New York, on August 30–31, 1843,[17] but did not do so. His mind became completely clear as his efforts became channeled, not in the routine work of Abolitionism, but in the broader field of politics serving freedom. His political writing continued to be voluminous, and it gained hitting power as Whittier clarified his objectives.

# 4

Obviously, from the time the American Anti-Slavery Society in its Albany meeting of August, 1840, resolved upon taking political action, Whittier had little hope for the "Old Organization" led by the protesting Garrison. In a letter written from Amesbury in June 1841, Whittier warmly congratulated Frederick Palmer Tracy for having "firmly flung to the breezes of New Hampshire the *Independent* flag," and Whittier counseled: "Do try to get in the *old organization* folks as far as possible. Lay great stress on the fact that N.H. was the first to raise the [Abolitionist] standard of independent action." And in a postscript he added: "Dont spend your time in quarreling with the Old Organization. Let it fight alone." [18]

Whittier was now as free from the Whig Party as from the Garrison faction of Abolitionists, and he was a strong force in the Liberty Party until in 1852 it was absorbed in the Free-Soil Party. When in 1854 the Free-Soilers became part of the Republican Party, and Whittier a "founder" of it, the political action which he had long advocated to eliminate the evil of slavery became a reckonable force. In 1860 it came to ultimate power when Lincoln was elected President.

Whittier's influence on the growth of the "party of freedom" movement was plainly marked. In 1840 James G. Birney was made the first candidate of the Liberty Party for the Presidency. Five years earlier, on May 28, 1835, Whittier was one of five men [19] who asked their fellow Abolitionist seven questions. These and Birney's instant answers, summarized as follows, laid the moral basis for the Liberty movement:

1. Promulgation, in the North, of the doctrine of immediate emancipation would probably seem officious meddling to many persons, but would reach the best consciences of the South.
2. The knowledge that efforts were being made in their behalf would not incite the slaves to indiscretions.
3. Only the doctrine of immediate emancipation, founded on Christian principle, would serve the nation.
4. Emancipation of the slaves would not endanger the lives of their former owners, but would produce cordial reliance upon and friendship for them.

5. Manumitted slaves could provide for themselves and become good citizens.
6. Compensation should not be granted for giving up what was sinful. In freeing his slaves in 1834, Birney expected no compensation.
7. The "Colonization Society" had tended only to strengthen and conserve the system of slavery.[20]

Whittier succinctly described the third-party movement to Joseph Sturge as the result of "a growing determination in the Free States to meet the combination of slaveholders in behalf of slavery, by one of freemen in behalf of liberty; and thus compel the party politicians, on the ground of expediency, if not of principle, to break from the thralldom of the slave power, and array themselves on the side of freedom." [21] Whittier's preferred rôle in the councils of the Liberty Party was that of adviser and publicist, as he explained in a letter of July 1842 to his Philadelphia cousin Ann Wendell:

> *** I am not much affected by the whirl of politics. I act because I believe it to be my duty, decidedly and vigorously, but my inward self is calm. The ambitions and selfish hopes of other years do not disturb me. Why it is so, I know not, but I can mingle in the exciting scenes of an election without feeling the excitement to any considerable extent. My enthusiasm has been tamed down by that hard and cross-grained schoolmistress, Experience. . . .[22]

As an aid to his party, however, Whittier in November 1842 stood as a candidate for Representative to Congress from Essex North. He would far rather have thrown the Liberty vote to whichever major party candidate would engage to support anti-slavery measures in Congress. In Essex South a coalition, steered by Whittier, of Liberty votes with Democratic strength elected his friend Robert Rantoul, who in Congress gave strong backing to the Abolitionist bloc. In successive trials in Essex North, Whittier continued to split the vote and prevent any candidate from getting the required majority, until in December 1843 his withdrawal from the contest, because of his health, let the Whigs elect their man.[23]

On the same principle, Whittier campaigned for his Abolitionist friend Samuel E. Sewall, as Liberty candidate for Governor of Massachusetts, in the autumn of 1842. Sewall's strong fight hurt the Whig candidate and enabled Marcus Morton, for the second time, to win the Governorship. Whittier had respected Morton, like Rantoul a Democrat, since 1836.[24]

# 5

Whittier's writing for the cause of freedom was, in the period 1841–44, strictly occasional. A prime demand upon his reserve of Abolitionist fire was the case of George Latimer, an escaped slave who was arrested by Boston police late in 1842 and then claimed by his Virginia master. Here came into issue the Massachusetts statute, guaranteeing to escaped slaves a jury trial in the Bay State, which Whittier in 1837 had helped to press through the Legislature.[25] Latimer was refused trial after such a State law had been ruled unconstitutional by the United States Supreme Court.

The implications of this judgment were plainly of national significance: that the "slave power," now becoming odious especially to the conscience of New England, was protected by law even where slavery did not exist. Liberty leaders found general support for indignation meetings in Massachusetts, the most publicized of which was held in Faneuil Hall on October 30, 1842. Samuel Sewall presided, and potent addresses were made by Edmund Quincy and by Wendell Phillips. Phillips, a Garrison follower, here invoked his curse on the Constitution — which, with the Union based upon it, the "old organization" Abolitionists soon desired to see dissolved because slavery could exist under it.[26]

Breadth was added to the weight of that meeting by conventions, held on January 2, 1843, which friends of liberty arranged in each county of the Commonwealth. The meeting in Essex was held at Ipswich, from where the firm lines of Whittier's poem "Massachusetts to Virginia," written for that day, quickly went out to impress the mind of the North. Garrison helped to circulate them by printing — anonymously, in the *Liberator* on January 27 — the ninety-six lines of ringing hexameters. In them Whittier renewed his plea, already many times made, that Virginia, land of Patrick Henry, should reclaim the freedom for which the Colonies had fought together. And again he rejected, courteously but resolutely as he had done in his editorial of May 7, 1836, in the *Haverhill Gazette*, the notion that the North could be brought to comply with the slave power by "the whip of the South." [27]

Public sentiment was measured by the petition, signed by nearly 63,000 citizens, which protested to the Massachusetts Legislature against the possibility of Latimer's being remanded into slavery; and by another, signed by more than fifty thousand Bay State citizens, which called upon Congress "for such laws and proposed amendments to the Constitution as should relieve the Commonwealth from all further participation in the crime of oppression." Such indeed was the public temper that in the end Latimer's freedom was purchased, in Massachusetts, for four hundred dollars.[28]

"Massachusetts to Virginia" was easily one of Whittier's most moving Abolitionist verses. In others — like the series soon evoked by the probability of Texas' admission to the Union as a slave State — he similarly treated, with consistently great power, the salient events of what Henry Wilson called "the rise and fall of the slave power in America."

## 6

Into that struggle Whittier poured his best energies, without stint, until the end of the Civil War. It remained his chief cause. What energy he had left went mainly into the inescapable business of writing for income — in the *Democratic Review*, the *Knickerbocker*, Lowell's short-lived *Pioneer*, and other magazines. Yet in October, 1842, and May, 1843, in "The Gallows" and "The Human Sacrifice," [29] he once again spoke forcefully against capital punishment. In 1840 Whittier had written to and visited Governor Morton "and got him to recommend the abolition of capital punishment in his [inaugural] message." Entirely aware of the time factor involved in effecting reforms, Whittier said in writing to his brother on February 7, 1843: "I shall try for it this winter, not, however, with much hope of success." [30]

On personal and financially pressing grounds, Whittier greatly hoped for success in the publication of *Lays of My Home*, which appeared in June, 1843, under the imprint of William D. Ticknor, of Boston. This was the first collection of non-political verse by the mature Whittier, and he wished it to make amends, in format and appearance as well as in contents, for productions like *Moll Pitcher* and the 1837 edition of his early Abolitionist work. Whittier dealt with James T. Fields, whom he had known since at least 1839 and with whom he now established a long and satisfying relationship. Beginning with *Lays of My Home*, this publishing house, under its successive firm names, was to publish regularly the authorized editions of Whittier's writings.

On January 24, 1842, he proposed to Fields the title *Legends of the Merrimack*, and suggested "about 100 pages" of contents. Then he specified:

> I want it printed in first rate style or not at all. I am wholly unacquainted with booksellers, having never published anything of any consequence, and would be greatly obliged to thee if thee would take the trouble to negotiate for me, & let me know as soon as convenient the result of thy inquiry. I wish it to be done well or not at all.[31]

Fifteen months later, on April 6, 1843, when plans for the publication were taking form, Whittier again wrote to Fields, and again made clear his financial hopes of the venture:

> In regard to the matter of publication, — I know little or nothing about it. I shall leave it altogether to you, thinking that if the work meets with a ready sale, you will do me justice, as I should, I am free to confess, like to realize something from it. Will these terms answer? * * * [32]

Luck and public favor were not yet with Whittier. His letter of October 30, 1850, to Fields gave the sad accounting:

> Like a lady's P.S. the important matter of my letter comes last. By the act forwarded me I find some $60.56 due me. I am charged in that acct. with $8.20 in books which I had when the "Lays of Home" were published. As these books were all I recd from that publication I thought it might be suffered to pass. But I yield to yr judgement entirely. Would it be convenient to send me a check for the balance due? [33]

*Lays of My Home* was, actually, a book of considerable merit. Its twenty-four poems constituted "the complete Whittier" — in subject, metrical style, narrative power, simplicity of tone, and above all in atmosphere. The sounds and forms in which he set the experience of thirty-five years were all characteristically Whittier. He sang of subjects great and small: of the remembrance of his boyhood love and friendship for his cousin, in "Memories," and of his sorrow over Lucy Hooper's death in 1841; of his love and respect for manly men — Charles Follen, John Pierpont, and others — who fought, in God's right, to raise the estate of man; of the beauty of Nature, and its comfort to man, in "Chalkley Hall," a poem of deep and serene charm evoked by reflection on his days in Philadelphia, and in others, including "The Funeral Tree of the Sokokis"; and of gripping events in the history and legend of the Western World, especially the North Atlantic seaboard.

There, in firm line and pleasant tone, were songs of delight in his native New England and its history, such as "The Merrimack" and "The Norsemen," a poetic vision of the Past and a quest for "an immortal origin" of all things. There, too, was Whittier's fascination with foreign places which he was never to see except with the eye of his fertile imagination. "To a Friend [Elizabeth Lloyd], on Her Return from Europe," which first appeared in the *Pennsylvania Freeman* in 1841, is a delightful example of Whittier's "travel by proxy," and a skilled piece of versification lightly employing the seven-line tail-rhyme stanza of the British national anthem.

Whittier's humanitarianism, his dominantly serious side, also loomed large in *Lays of My Home*. Included in it, to bear his stout testimony against capital punishment, were "The Gallows" and "The Human Sacrifice"; and "Massachusetts to Virginia" and the sonnet "Leggett's Monument" stood his witness against slavery. But Whittier's strong hopes for the uplifting of man to his full stature, through freedom, had neither national bounds nor geographical limits. He wanted man everywhere to be free, as he made eloquently clear in "To the Reformers of England." And with strength and melody he voiced his devout belief that when men *lived* Christianity and did God's work on earth, all mankind would be free. That was Whittier's burden in "Democracy," in his finest ballad, "Cassandra Southwick," and in the important autobiographical poem "Ego," which he had composed for the *Pioneer* at editor Lowell's request.

*Lays of My Home* marks a very important stage in the development of Whittier's religious position. His letters record his religious meditation and growth during his illness and withdrawal from routine work in 1840 and following years, and numerous poems measure his newly fortified faith. The presentation piece, "To. —— With a Copy of Woolman's Journal," quietly reaffirms Whittier's simple Quaker belief. "Cassandra Southwick" contains a fervent protest against meaningless externals such as creed backed by the civil authority of men like "dark and haughty Endicott." More important still, in "Follen," in "Lucy Hooper," in "The Norsemen," and in "Raphael" Whittier sings out, in humble gladness, his now shining faith in immortality.

Significantly, Whittier was at this time searching widely for answers to his deep soundings of life, and this slender volume testifies to his avid combing of great books. He read, it is clear, critically and with absorption.

# XI

# Nation in the Shadows

GRAVELY IMPORTANT EVENTS happened in quick and ominous succession during the twenty years which preceded the outbreak of the Civil War. Whittier — just as for years he had surveyed the national scene — followed them with heightened interest, and commented on them in the rôle of acute observer. He became in effect a columnist, an editorial contributor speaking out from Amesbury on the history-shaping events of the eighteen-forties and fifties. Only for eight months in 1844–45, as editor of the *Middlesex Standard*, the Liberty Party organ in Lowell, did he stand in the middle of the arena where the battle over slavery was actually being fought.

Yet his trumpeting for the cause of liberty continued to be a powerful and moving note. It appears to have stirred the souls of men throughout the land, and to have won converts to the band of gifted men who were sounding the new call for mankind to be free. Lowell, Longfellow, and Emerson were three particular members of the "New England group" from whom Whittier requested specific anti-slavery labors. He very well knew the force which "a few assured voices," in Emerson's phrase, could give to a social movement; and he set a high value upon the poet's ancient rôle as *maker* or *doer*.

## 1

In anti-slavery feeling and action Whittier was closer to Lowell than to any other literary figure of the day, and it is manifest, from their exchange of letters, that Whittier — an Abolitionist since 1833 — helped to bring his well-placed friend into the growing Abolitionist chorus in 1843. He petitioned Lowell cannily. On November 18, 1843, for instance, he invited Lowell to speak at an anti-slavery meeting in Haverhill on the twenty-sixth — and complimented him on recently published sketches of Cromwell and Hampden. On July 14, 1844, Whittier requested a poem, to be read on August 1 at "a great anti-slavery meeting at Salem." He said in part:

> I think thee once promised me a Liberty song — & I now claim it for this meeting. Give me one which shall be to our cause what the song of Roget de Lisle was to the French Republicans. Such an one as the maiden may whisper in the —
>
> "asphodel flower place
> She walks ankle deep in"
>
> and the strong man sing at his forge & plough. Think of it, dear L. & oblige me, and do a great work for holy Liberty, by complying with my request. Let me have it soon, that I may hand it to the Com. of Arrangements.[1]

Lowell seems to have been unable to comply. He was busy during July with his *Conversations*, and he wrote "Stanzas on Freedom" for an anti-slavery picnic held at Dedham on August 1 to celebrate the anniversary of emancipation in the West Indies.[2]

On his part, Lowell on March 21, 1844, solicited a poem in which Whittier would "cry aloud and spare not against the cursed Texas plot." On the nineteenth Lowell had published anonymously in the *Boston Courier* his own "Rallying Cry for New England against the Annexation of Texas." Whittier's long concern over this issue yielded the stern "Texas: Voice of New England," which J. T. Buckingham published in the *Courier* on April 17 under Lowell's warm commendation:

> . . . In the present crisis of the fate of the Republic, New England listens for a trumpet-call from her Tyrtæus. Nor will she be disappointed. Whittier has always been found faithful to the Muses' holy trust. He has not put his talent out at profitable interest, by catering to the insolent and Pharisaical self-esteem of the times; nor has he hidden it in the damask napkin of historical commonplaces, or a philanthropy too universal to concern itself with particular wrongs, the

practical redressing of which is all that renders philanthropy of value. Most poets are content to follow the spirit of their age, as pigeons follow a leaky grain cart, picking a kernel here and there, out of the dry dust of the past. Not so Whittier. From the heart of the onset upon the serried mercenaries of every tyranny, the chords of his iron-strung lyre clang with a martial and triumphant cheer; and where Freedom's Spartan few maintain their inviolate mountain pass against the assaults of slavery, his voice may be heard, clear and fearless, as if the victory were already won. It is with the highest satisfaction I send you the inclosed poem, every way worthy of our truly New England poet. I trust that when this meets his eye, the few words which I could not refrain from adding by way of preface will not be deemed impertinent.[3]

Whittier, quite naturally, was always gratified by cordial, human warmth, and on April 18 he wrote to thank Lowell for the compliment — and to pass him an equal one. Whittier specified two of Lowell's poems which had given him particular pleasure, and added that he "half suspected *thee*" of writing the "Rallying Cry," which he had re-read with doubled pleasure.[4]

Lowell, Boston Brahmin, was less dedicated to "causes" than the Quaker Whittier. Made hospitable to reform in good part by Maria White, Abolitionist, whom he married in 1844, Lowell had virtually completed his contributions to causes when she died in 1853. But a sharp critic wrote of these contributions, "Their equal as a whole is not to be found in the work of other contemporary radicals," and he added: "The eager rhetoric of *The Present Crisis* was the high-water mark of Abolitionist argument in verse. . . ." [5] Whittier was happy to have Lowell for a colleague, and they remained warm friends always.

Longfellow, more placid by nature than either Lowell or Whittier, was not able to contribute, like them, "the flash and outbreak of a fiery mind" to the Abolition movement. His seven "Poems on Slavery," published in December, 1842, were the sum of his contribution to it. And it appears that these were evoked by Longfellow's reading, in London, the "grand chapter on slavery" in Dickens' *American Notes*. Whittier was already then acquainted with Longfellow; in a letter of August 14, 1840, he mentioned having had Longfellow with him "down east." [6] In 1844 Whittier aspired to have Longfellow with him in the Liberty Party movement, and on September 4 he addressed to his "Dear Friend" a letter of request whose tone betrayed the fear of a refusal. Whittier, then in Lowell, wrote:

> I do not know as thy views on the question of Anti-Slavery entirely coincide with mine: but I do know that thy little collection of poems on slavery have been of great & important service to the Liberty movement. From my heart I thank thee for them.
>
> I write now to enquire of thee whether thou art with us on the great question of Liberty which is about [to] be decided at the ballot-box; and if so, whether we may not present thy name as the Liberty candidate of the 4th Congressional District, at the Convention at Boston on the 16th. Our friends in the 4th say they could throw for thee 1000 more votes than for any other man. The cause is taking a deep hold on the best hearts & minds among us. A line from thee at thy earliest convenience would be acceptable.[7]

Whittier had not long to wait for an answer, which was addressed to him as "Dear Sir":

> It is impossible for me to accept the Congressional nomination you propose, because I do not feel myself qualified for the duties of such an office, and because I do not belong to the Liberty party. Though a strong anti-Slavery man, I am not a member of any society, and fight under no single banner.
>
> I am much gratified that the "Poems on Slavery" should have exercised some salutary influence; and thank you for your good opinion of them. At all times I shall rejoice in the progress of true liberty — and in freedom from slavery of all kinds; but I cannot for a moment think of entering the political arena. Partizan warfare becomes too violent — too vindictive for my taste; and I should be found but a weak and unworthy champion in public debate.[8]

Emerson was critic of slavery rather than fighter for its abolition. In 1837 at Concord he spoke on slavery in America, but not until August 1, 1844 (also in Concord), did he make a forthright plea for emancipation. Whittier at once knew the importance of the event; America's prime thinker, a philosophical champion of democracy, had at last advocated abolition of slavery. In the *Middlesex Standard* on September 12, 1844, Whittier published this grateful exultation:

> *** We had previously, we confess, felt half indignant that, while

we were struggling against the popular current, mobbed, hunted, denounced from the legislative forum, cursed from the pulpit, sneered at by wealth and fashion and shallow aristocracy, such a man as Ralph Waldo Emerson should be brooding over his pleasant philosophies, writing his quaint and beautiful essays, in his retirement on the banks of the Concord, unconcerned and "calm as a summer's morning." We were ready to expostulate with him in the language of Wordsworth's ballad:

"Why, William, on this grey old stone,
Thus for the length of half a day —
Why, William, sit you thus alone,
And dream your time away?"

Now, Whittier rejoiced —

With our whole heart we welcome him into our dusty and toil-worn ranks, where every man does battle with whatsoever weapon his hands find — where the extremes of individualism and unity meet and harmonize. Let him there find his own place, and assail the common enemy in his own way.

Emerson's way was, chiefly, that of the thinker and the lecturer. Even so, he attended a few Liberty meetings arranged in protest against the annexation of Texas. After one, held at Concord on September 22, 1845, Emerson was so disturbed by the *Emancipator's* introductory comment on a letter, published in the issue of October 1, which Whittier had written to him for that occasion, that on October 9 he sent Whittier a long and nervous account of its handling. Emerson ended on this note: "I am so seldom a mover in politics & so seldom honoured with a public letter, that I earnestly hope nothing indiscreet or unfortunate has attended my charge in this instance." [9] In April, 1847, Emerson made this honest and reflective entry in his *Journals:* "N. P. Rogers spoke more truly than he knew, perchance, when he recommended an Abolition Campaign to me. I doubt not, a course of mobs would do me much good. . . ." [10]

Emerson himself, without a doubt, did much good for the anti-slavery movement. Particularly after the passage of the Fugitive Slave Act he spoke with eloquent wrath, and his denunciation of Webster as agent of the "Cotton Whigs" was hardly less severe than even Whittier's. Parrington said justly of Emerson: "He never faltered, never compromised; the prophet of the ideal faced the real and told the truth about it, serenely and with clear insight." [11]

Whittier had rather better luck in getting the "assured voices" of Charles Sumner and John P. Hale to speak against slavery than in stirring his literary confreres to action. He followed intently the fortunes of Hale, the New Hampshire Democrat who was read out of his party for opposing, in 1845, the annexation of Texas, and who in 1846 was elected to the Senate as an insurgent. Whittier, delighted, chaffed the fallen "Concord Clique" in "A Letter," [12] which the *Boston Chronotype* published anonymously on March 19, 1846.

The significance of this "most notable anti-slavery success hitherto achieved" [13] was particularly obvious to Whittier. On September 16 of that year he wrote to his friend Hale:

> I see by the papers that thy lecture in Faneuil Hall takes place on the 18th. There is one point which I wish to call thy attention to. We want some common ground for all who love Liberty and abhor Slavery to unite upon. May it not be found in the following: —
>
> 1. Abolition of slavery the leading and paramount political question.
> 2. No voting for slaveholders.
> 3. No voting for men who are in political fellowship with slaveholders.
>
> Why can we not have a great League of Freedom, with the above for its watchwords and rallying cry? We have eighty thousand Liberty voters to begin with, and a majority of both the old parties are well-nigh ready to join in such a movement. Think of it. I notice that the English Liberal papers, Birmingham "Pilot," London "Non-Conformist," etc., have an eye on the New Hampshire movement, and think of it as a most encouraging fact in favor of the Rights of Man. In the late meeting of the British Anti-Slavery Society, Joseph Sturge, the President of the Free Suffrage Union, alluded to thy course with great satisfaction. The Editor of the "Democratic Record" has spoken of Sturge as the noblest and purest of the democracy of England.[14]

Four months later, on January 7, 1847, Whittier in the *National Era* wrote correctly that Hale's victory would have a salutary effect elsewhere in making people follow the "example of the safety of doing right." Whittier remarked the emergence of "a powerful anti-slavery party" from "the two great parties at the North," and in the *Era* of September 2, 1847, he went on to recommend Hale as "The Man for the Hour" for the Presidency. In brief, Whittier said:

In his triumphant struggle with the allies of the Slave Power, has he not indeed "given the world assurance of a man?" Are not the positive qualities he has manifested those which the occasion demands? *** Where is there to be found a man so well calculated to bring about that union among the Friends of Liberty which is so eminently desirable?

Hale was in fact nominated in 1847 as the Liberty Party's candidate for President, but he withdrew in favor of Van Buren when the Free-Soil Party absorbed the Liberty Party in 1848.[15] In 1852 he accepted the nomination of the Free-Soilers.

It was Charles Sumner, more than Hale, whom Whittier regarded as the chief legislative protagonist of Abolition, after the death of J. Q. Adams in 1848. Indeed, from 1845 onward — six years before Sumner was elected to the Senate — Whittier gave him sound counsel and admiring support for his stand on the subject of freedom. The two men first met, in 1829, casually in the office of the *American Manufacturer*. Their friendship and collaboration began only when Whittier wrote to congratulate Sumner on his address of July 4, 1845, upon "The True Grandeur of Nations." Sumner, boldly pleading for peace rather than war (then imminent) with Mexico, with one gesture turned down the proffered prizes of worldly success and joined the growing ranks of Reform. Whittier ardently welcomed him. In a letter of September 11, 1845, he said, in part:

I thank thee from my heart, for thy noble address. The truths are none the less welcome for the beautiful drapery in which they are clothed. It will do great good. I would rather be the author of it than of all the war eloquence of Heathendom & Christendom combined. . . . It will I doubt not be republished in Europe. I shall be in Boston, at the Liberty Convention, of the 1st of next month, and shall take some pains to procure an introduction to the author of the very best plea for peace which has ever fallen under my notice.[16]

Sumner strove manfully to win the Whig Party to support of Abolition. At a party convention held in Faneuil Hall, Boston, in September, 1846, he spoke in defense of an anti-slavery resolution, put forward by Stephen C. Phillips, which was defeated. Whittier quickly wrote to Sumner:

I have just read the proceedings of your Whig convention, and the lines enclosed are a feeble expression of my feelings. I look upon the rejection of S. C. P.'s resolutions as an evidence that the end and aim of the managers of the convention was to go just far enough to save the party, and no further. We shall have another doughface in the Senate for six years. As for Webster, — thy hopes and wishes to the contrary, — he is, I fear, no better on that question than a "colossal coward." All thanks for the free voices of thyself, Phillips, Allen, and Adams. Notwithstanding the result, you have not spoken in vain. If thee thinks well enough of these verses hand them to the "Whig" or "Chronotype." ["The Pine Tree" was published, unsigned, in the *Boston Daily Whig*, Sept. 24, 1846.]

Sumner on September 26 responded in this hopeful vein, wholly characteristic of his long correspondence with Whittier:

We do not despair. We are all alive to wage the fight another day, and feel that more was done than we had hoped to do.*** The ball has been put in motion; it cannot be stopped. Hard words are said of us in State Street. I am grateful to you for your note of encouragement.*** [17]

In 1850 Whittier induced Sumner to "carry the ball" for the antislavery forces in the Senate. Webster had resigned his seat there for a post in President Fillmore's cabinet. A "deal" between the Democrats and the Free-Soilers of Massachusetts had allotted the Governorship to the Democrats, whose George S. Boutwell was elected by the coalition; and the United States Senatorship and a few state offices to the Free-Soilers. Whittier had a hand in effecting that coalition, and afterward he visited Sumner at Phillips Beach, Swampscott, and persuaded his friend to stand for the Senate. It was to this visit that Whittier referred in the lines of "To Charles Sumner" (1854):

Thou knowest my heart, dear friend, and well canst guess
That, even though silent, I have not the less
Rejoiced to see thy actual life agree
With the large future which I shaped for thee,
When, years ago, beside the summer sea,
White in the moon, we saw the long waves fall
Baffled and broken from the rocky wall,
That, to the menace of the brawling flood,
Opposed alone its massive quietude,
Calm as a fate; with not a leaf nor vine
Nor birch-spray trembling in the still moonshine,
Crowning it like God's peace.[18]

But after the coalition had elected Governor Boutwell and his council, Democrats led by Caleb Cushing refused to vote for Sumner. Governor Boutwell's inaugural message, moreover, offended his Free-Soil allies. Robert C. Winthrop, the Whig candidate, firmly held his party's vote. Irate at the Democrats for their double-cross, Whittier — severely ill in Amesbury — wrote Sumner: "... I, who urged the nomination so strongly and imperatively, must now confess I see no other course for thee than to *decline at once*." Free-Soil Party leaders, on the other hand, who were actively in touch with the state legislature, kept Sumner in the race. Toward the end of March he spent a Sunday in Amesbury, consulting with Whittier. Finally, on April 24, 1851, the twenty-sixth ballot cast in the prolonged contest gave Sumner a majority of one and the Senate seat which he held until his death.

Whittier at once penned this joyous letter of congratulation to Sumner:

> I take the earliest moment of ability, after a sudden and severe attack of illness, to congratulate thee, not so much on thy election, as upon the proof which it offers of the turning of the tide — the recoil of the popular feeling — the near and certain doom of the wicked Slave Law. My heart is full of gratitude to God. For when I consider the circumstances of this election, I am constrained to regard it as His work. And I rejoice that thy position is so distinct and emphatic; that thy triumph is such a direct rebuke to politicians, hoary with years of political chicanery and fraud; that unpledged, free, and without a single concession or compromise, thou art enabled to take thy place in the United States Senate. May the good Providence which has overruled the purposes of thy life, in this matter, give thee strength and grace to do great things for humanity. I never knew such a general feeling of real heart-pleasure and satisfaction as is manifested by all except inveterate Hunkers, in view of thy election. The whole country is electrified by it. Sick abed, I heard the guns — Quaker as I am — with real satisfaction.

And in a letter written on May 18 to his friend Grace Greenwood, Whittier gave his accurate estimate of Sumner's potentialities as Senator:

> ... a man physically and spiritually head and shoulders above old hackneyed politicians of that body.*** I am proud of old Massachusetts, and thankful that I have had an humble share in securing her so true and worthy a representative of her honor, her freedom, and

intellect, as Charles Sumner. He is a noble and gifted man, earnest and truthful. I hope great things of him, and I do not fear for his integrity and fidelity, under any trial.[19]

## 2

Integrity and fidelity were Whittier's own code words in the fight against slavery. They bulked particularly large in his editorial pronouncement "To the Public," a characteristic paean to freedom which he published on July 25, 1844, in the first issue of the weekly *Middlesex Standard*. That set the seal to Whittier's editorship of the *Standard*, and it brought a favorable response. With pleasure he remarked in the issue of August 1 that "our subscription list is filling up with a rapidity far beyond our expectations."

In this second number of the weekly, Whittier began publishing the series of articles which were collected in book form in 1845 under the title, *The Stranger in Lowell*. Obviously his quick sympathies and observant eye found much that was engaging in the young manufacturing city. In two sketches, "The City of a Day" and "The Lighting Up," Whittier reported interesting aspects of the industrial revolution, especially the 12½-hour work day which was then in force throughout the year in the textile mills of Lowell. His personal interest was at once aroused by "the factory girls" and their "Improvement Circle," and by the *Lowell Offering* which published their writings. It was on invitation to a meeting of the "Circle" that Whittier met Lucy Larcom, whose compositions he admired and who was to become one of Elizabeth Whittier's dearest friends.

But local and personal matters in Lowell did not weigh in the same scale with Whittier's absorption in politics. His dominant concerns here were the Presidential election of 1844 and the hard fight then being waged in the North to curb the extension of slavery in the United States. All eyes and events seemed to focus on Texas. Whittier in the *Standard* published fifty or so editorial comments on the election, and at least five poems in various periodicals during 1844–46 on the Texas question. One of these was "To Faneuil Hall," which appeared in the *Standard* on January 2, 1845; another was "Texas," which the *Boston Courier* printed on

April 17, 1844. Whittier's tribute to John Pierpont equally fitted his own blazing lines written on this controversial topic:

> . . . even thy song
> Hath a rude martial tone, a blow in every thought! [20]

Whittier, indeed, had since 1842 been alert to the implications of the slave power's demand for enlarged territory, including Texas. In March of that year he wrote to Samuel E. Sewall:

> I fear we shall get dragged into a war after all, — a war in defense of the vilest negro traffic existing anywhere save on the African coast! It is unendurable! And if Texas is to be added to us, as there are no doubtful indications, let us say, Disunion before Texas! . . .[21]

By the winter of 1845, free men in the North were alarmed over the imminent admission not only of Texas but also of Florida as a slave State. Whittier, on January 2 in the *Middlesex Standard*, lashed out with a twin protest. He concluded a strong editorial entitled "Florida. More Slave Territory Knocking for Admission!" with this challenge:

> Just God! — is there to be no end to all this? Are we to go on year after year strengthening the stakes and lengthening the cords of slavery? Is there no limit to slaveholding aggression and northern servility? Have we no man in Congress to rise up with this infamous Constitution in his hand, and speak out in plain terse Saxon the honest truth about it? No man to rise up and tell the House or the Senate that slavery in Florida exists by the authority of Congress alone — that all the monstrous and brutal laws of the territory are sustained by the same authority — that the red-hot branding iron which sunk hissing into the flesh of Jonathan Walker was held by the arm of the General Government? Is there no one to demand in the name of God and humanity the repeal of these laws, and the instant withdrawal of the support and sanction of the General Government from Florida slavery?

With his other eye on Texas, Whittier published in the *Standard* of January 2 his poem, "To Faneuil Hall!" written on reading a call for a meeting there of Massachusetts citizens opposed to the annexation of Texas and in favor of decisive action against slavery. Whittier was one of the secretaries for this meeting, held on January 29–30 in Boston, and in an editorial published in the *Standard* on February 6 he commented joyously on the change in public sentiment which the years had brought. On August 21, 1835, Whittier had stood in Faneuil Hall and heard Harrison Gray Otis and Peleg Sprague, with popular acclaim, denounce the Abolitionists. Whittier now wrote revealingly:

> In the hope of a better day, when the judgment against us should be reversed, we left Faneuil Hall, to redouble our exertions in the cause of Liberty. — That hope was not in vain. Once more we have been in the "Old Cradle," not as proscribed, hunted and outlawed men, to hear slavery be praised, and Freedom mocked, but, with our right of free speech, acknowledged, to bear our part in the protest of Massachusetts against the extension of Southern slavery, and to hear the principles for which we have so long striven enunciated by those who have heretofore opposed us; to hear from the lips of distinguished civilians and divines the very language which these men, eight years ago, regarded as incendiary when uttered by ourselves. Who shall say, after this, that we have labored in vain?

Withal, Abolitionist opposition to the admittance of Texas and Florida as slave states availed nothing. Congress on February 28 authorized Texas' admission, on December 29 formally admitted the Republic as a state, and on March 3 brought Florida into the Union.

Whittier went to the Capital in December as a member of the commission which presented to Congress the remonstrance of Massachusetts against the annexation of Texas. In his poem, "At Washington," which was published in the *American Citizen*, Philadelphia, on February 7, 1846, he spoke pityingly of the Northern Congressmen groping for the largess of the slave power; mentioned almost ominously "the coming strife for Freedom"; and — in the light of it — begged that the Abolitionist factions would bury their small differences and measure up to their large responsibilities.[22]

The election of James K. Polk as President in November, 1844, had of course insured further expansion of slave territory. The Liberty Party were nowise fooled by him; they distrusted him only less than Clay. Their 62,300 popular votes gave them the balance of power in three important States, and if they had voted for Clay in only one of them, New York, its thirty-six Electoral College votes would have given him the victory over Polk. Whittier in the *Middlesex Standard* of November 14 analyzed the results in these clear terms:

> And the Democratic party — what has *it* gained? Its triumph is its defeat — its apparent victory, a hollow and miserable mockery. What has true and generous DEMOCRACY in common with such a man as James K. Polk, a practical slave-holder, living down in his daily conduct the doctrines of the Great Declaration? We speak advisedly when we say that the best portion of the Democratic party in the Free States feel no exultation or satisfaction at the election of such a man, whose only qualification for the office seems to have been his unscrupulous devotion to slavery. They rejoice over the defeat of Clay — but they feel no pride in the elevation of such a man as Polk as the representative of Democracy in the United States.

For Clay in defeat, Whittier had no sympathetic word. In the issue of November 28 he wrote, in part:

> So far as we were personally concerned, we had no disposition to exaggerate the faults of the Whig candidate. His brilliant talents, his early republicanism, his splendid eloquence, excited our boyish enthusiasm and admiration. We would not rob him of one tittle of his just fame as a statesman and man of genius. But, when his friends urged him upon us for the highest place in the gift of a free people, we felt bound to speak the whole truth of his present position and past history in relation to the cause of Freedom.

And Whittier advised finally: "Let him repent of the evil he has done to the holy cause of Liberty."

## 3

As editor of the *Middlesex Standard* until March 1845, Whittier was not always as deadly serious as that. In the Lowell "Liberty" sheet, as a fact, he laughed oftener than in any of his other nine editorial charges. And the flavor of his articles was as often literary as humorous. After Polk's election, Whittier had as associate in the editorship Chauncey L. Knapp; and when he left the paper four months later, before his last desk job could drag him down, Whittier had both his health and a new store of learning culled from steady reading. Both were to serve him well during the period 1847–59 when, living in Amesbury, he was contributing editor of the *National Era*.

Whittier produced some of his most eloquent Abolitionist verse and prose for that Washington weekly established by the American and Foreign Anti-Slavery Society. Far more distinction marked his work with the *Era* than his voluntary labors on the *Essex Transcript*, in Amesbury, during parts of 1844–46. As writer of special articles for the *Era*, Whittier surveyed the whole state of the nation; as informal editor of the Amesbury weekly, he looked at affairs necessarily in a smaller focus than he could have liked. On April 18, 1844, he wrote to Lowell:

> As for myself, what with cares of all sorts on my hands, the principal charge of our weekly paper here (weakly would be the better word), and the trouble and responsibility of an active politician of the Liberty stamp, as well as the constant draw-back of ill health, especially since these Eastern winds have been blowing, I can do little or nothing in the way of rhyme or reason.[23]

Whittier's increasing concern over national trends in 1845–46 was a beacon of sentiment among thinking people in the North. After Florida and Texas had been admitted to the Union, and after war had broken out with Mexico in May of 1846, a sense of inevitable conflict began to spread. The Wilmot Proviso of August 1846 — that slavery be prohibited in lands acquired from Mexico — was defeated in Congress, but it did help to arouse the country to the importance of the question of slavery in the Mexican cessions. The founding of the *National Era* was a token of mounting determination in the North to appease the slave power no further.

For nearly eleven years, from the first issue of the *National Era* on January 7, 1847, until the *Atlantic Monthly* appeared in November, 1857, Whittier spoke his mind chiefly in the Washington weekly. In all, he contributed 109 original poems and 275 articles or editorials to the *Era* alone. This voluminous output contained work of considerable quality — and payments for it held body and soul together during some of Whittier's leanest years.

At the outset, there was the ugly spectacle of the Mexican War to draw his fire. His shame and indignation were hardly overmatched in the utterances of the Hebrew Prophets. As a prime instance, Whittier on May 20, 1847, in "Dancing and Sabbath Breaking," directed the attention of clergymen then absorbed with such matters to the dance of death then going on in Mexico, "with the whole universe for spectators." This long article, probably his bitterest excoriation of war and war-makers, ended with the cannonade:

> We venture no opinion in respect to it, but would simply suggest, with the deference befitting one of the laity, that its attention might be very profitably turned to some recent transactions of our Christian army and navy, engaged in opening the way for the introduction of the Gospel into Mexico. If our Almanac does not deceive us, our navy spent a Sabbath at Tabasco some months ago, and performed "services" of an impressive but somewhat equivocal kind, sending messengers of peace and good will among the poor benighted Catholics, in the shape of red hot balls and shells. More recently, Gen. Scott has "kept the Sabbath" on the heights of Cerro Gordo, storming batteries, blowing whole squadrons into eternity, impaling men on bayonets, and tearing off their limbs with cannon shot. We should like to know what General Assemblies and Conferences think of this way of spending holy time. The occasions referred to were doubtless solemn enough to satisfy a Puritan tythingman — so much so, in short, as dying groans and ghastly corpses could make them. But, apart from this, we cannot see that the storming of forts, and slaughter of women and children on their own hearths, or while kneeling in their places of worship, is a more appropriate Sunday business than the running of the United States mail or the delving of a Seventh-Day Baptist in his potato field. We respectfully refer the whole matter to the Tennessee Methodists, who have made Capt. Walker, of the Texas Rangers, and the leading heroes of Monterey, life members of their Missionary Society; and to the Western Home Missionary Society of Baltimore, of which Gen. Taylor has just been made a life member; and to the Old and New School Presbyterian Assemblies — subject, as a matter of course, to the final action of the Evangelical Alliance.

In "Piety and Justice," which the *Era* published on June 3, 1847, Whittier leveled another blast of irony at the war, which he summed up as "a grim farce, the plot of which must have been borrowed from beneath."

Luckily, Whittier's faith always kept him from despair, and these two bitter denunciations of the war and its managers were followed, on July 1, 1847, in the *Era*, by his characteristic poem "Forgiveness":

> My heart was heavy for its trust had been
> Abused, its kindness answered with foul wrong;

So, turning gloomily from my fellow men,
One summer Sabbath day I strolled among
The green mounds of the village burial place;
Where, pondering how all human love and hate
Find one sad level — and how, soon or late,
Wronged and wrong-doer, each with meekened face
And cold hands folded over a still heart,
Pass the green threshold of our common grave,
Whither all footsteps tend, whence none depart,
Awed for myself, and pitying my race,
Our common sorrow, like a mighty wave,
Swept all my pride away, and trembling I forgave!

Whittier took heart, also, from the acts of other men. In "The Heroism of Philanthropy," published in the *Era* on January 14, 1847, he wrote glowingly of the recent trip of James Richardson "for the purpose of ascertaining, from personal observation, the actual features and extent of the slave trade, carried on between the Great Desert and Tripoli. . . ." Richardson's report to the British and Foreign Anti-Slavery Society exhilarated Whittier, who, at the end of his long article in the *Era*, fashioned a precise "character" of the modern reformer:

> We hope the entire journal of this heroic philanthropist will be published. He deserves the highest commendation for his disinterested and noble efforts. He belongs to that new and glorious band of Christian knight-errants — the chivalry of humanity — who, in generous endeavors to ameliorate the condition of their fellow-men, have associated with their names that romance of personal peril and intrepid adventure, which has been too long monopolized by those who have added to the afflictions of our race, and stained our common inheritance with the blood of brethren.

In the *Era* of February 11, 1847, appeared Whittier's memorial tribute to Alexander Pushkin, whose works he praised and equally his pride in the blood he inherited from "the black sea captain." Whittier considered that the lives and works of Pushkin and other famous men who had in them Negro blood drove home "the truth of the inspired Apostle's language — 'GOD HATH MADE OF ONE BLOOD ALL THE GENERATIONS OF MEN.' "

The utter denial of this truth by John Caldwell Calhoun, for example, saddened Whittier as much as the labors of the James Richardsons of the world encouraged him in his hopes for mankind. On August 2, 1847, in the *Era*, Whittier published a half-admiring denunciation of Calhoun, saying in sum: "... History might safely antedate its record, that the mightiest intellect in the New World, in the first half of the nineteenth century, was devoted to the last to the extension and perpetuation of human slavery." (Calhoun died in 1850.)

Calhoun's stature and the "bad eminence" upon which he resolutely stood were among the causes of Whittier's firm grasp of the critical nature of the times. He was himself, candidly and ably, a propagandist for an attitude to life which was leagues apart from Calhoun's; and never more so than in "The Mission of Democracy," which appeared in the *National Era* on April 20, 1848. The last part was no less eloquent than ominous:

> *** The simple question of Slavery or Freedom, stripped of all extraneous matters, and in some measure placed above the influence of party, is now fairly before the Democratic masses of the free States. Party hacks, men without faith in right and truth, hangers-on of the Government, greedy for spoil, will undoubtedly take the side of Slavery. But the generous and humane, the clear-sighted and hopeful, the men of Progress and Christian Reform, all who believe the Declaration of Independence, and who comprehend and love the Democratic principle — the great idea of the world's future — will count it a privilege to stand on the side of Liberty. Our brethren of the South cannot complain that we are aggressors. They have provoked the contest by efforts to extend and perpetuate slavery. They have interfered, in so doing, with the interests of free labor. We would only retaliate by returning good for evil. The Democratic doctrines, which with them unhappily have fallen on stony places, took root in the congenial soil of free labor, and are there producing their proper fruits. The North owes a debt of gratitude to the South, for the benefits, neither few nor trifling, which have resulted from these doctrines. We would pay it by applying them, as Jefferson did, to the relation of master and slave; and, by so doing, confer a lasting blessing upon both classes. Already the work of a practical application of Democracy has commenced at the South. Noble hearts there sympathize with us; and voices from Virginia and Kentucky call upon us to persevere. The non-slaveholders — the poor whites — writhing under the aristocracy of slavery, are prepared to unite with us. ***

Let, then, the great contest come — the sooner the better. Free Labor against Slave Labor; Democracy against Serfdom. The struggle may be sharp, but it is thrust upon us. We cannot avoid it — we would not, if we could. In the memorable words of Adams, "*Let it come!*"

That statement was the essence of Whittier's consistent stand against slavery. Opposition to its extension was the steady and informing principle of all of his Abolitionist articles in the *Era*. He was not, he made plain in the issue of February 15, 1849, opposed to the extension of American territory — "the annexation of Cuba, under circumstances compatible with justice, national honor, and the cause of freedom we are prepared to regard with favor." But he begged Providence to save us from Cuba with its slaves and its slave traffic protected, as it then was, by the American flag.

## 4

Paradoxically, Whittier's fear that the slave power, if curbed, would spill over into conflict with the Union of States seldom lessened his belief in the power of political action to hold it within bounds. He at no time gave in without protest to the "inevitable conflict." Right up to the moment Fort Sumter was fired upon, he held to the humanitarian's concept of a reasonable society of men living in harmony. On the part of all extremists, whether Abolitionists or defenders of slavery, he advocated moderation. It is true, however, that Whittier himself was not always moderate in his expressed views: he would denounce utterly Northern men like Webster who endeavored to "make a deal" with the expanding slave power, but would at least understand, if not approve, the position of Calhoun and other Southerners.

Whittier always held rigidly to his belief that the last way to get along with the slave power was to appease it. Year after year, in the *National Era*, he cannily marked the growing strength of the Liberty Party and of the Free-Soilers, certain that it would mount to final success at the polls — if the anti-slavery forces held their line steadily. In 1848 Martin Van Buren polled nearly 300,000 votes as the Free-Soil candidate for President, and Whittier, commenting on "The Election in Massachusetts" in the *Era* of November 16, concluded:

> The Free Democracy have made a good beginning. They have tried the strength and temper of their principles, and the result has given them new hope and stronger faith. They have proved the safety and expediency of boldly taking a right position in the outset — of planting themselves upon the absolute truths of Freedom. They have obtained no votes by concealment, double-dealing, or subterfuge — they have not abated one jot of the righteous demands of Justice and Humanity for the sake of a temporary success. Their appeal has been made to the noblest attributes of man's nature — to Reason and Conscience. All that they have gained is therefore real and abiding. The prophecy of John C. Calhoun bids fair to become history in 1852, by the election of the candidate of the Free Democracy to the Presidency.

The anti-slavery forces supporting Van Buren held the balance of power in eleven northern states, as compared with three in the election of 1844.

At Webster and his part in the Compromise of 1850 Whittier vented the flame of his indignation in the poem "Ichabod," which the *National Era* published on May 2, 1850. Already, in "Settling the Slave Question" in the issue of March 28, he had reiterated that appeasement merely keeps the system alive. "Confine it, limit it," he reasoned, "and it dies." When in September the Compromise bills — eliminating slavery in the District of Columbia but writing into law a new and drastic Fugitive Slave act — were passed by Congress, Whittier was irate with Webster. In the *Era* of October 31 he urged the Senator's defeat at the polls, and on November 21, in "The Election in Massachusetts," he concluded gladly:

> It is indeed a singular and not uninstructive coincidence, that the three great Northern Compromisers on the Slave Question, Webster, Dickinson, and Cass, are in a condition to condole with each other upon the votes of censure which their respective States have passed upon their action in the Senate at its late session. Let us not despair. The recuperative principle of democracy survives; the heart of the people is sound.

Whittier's abiding distrust of what, on February 18, 1847, he called "the great overshadowing interests of trade and manufacture" which Webster represented, took final shape in "Moloch in State Street." This calm but lethal indictment in verse, provoked by the controversial arrest in Boston of the fugitive slave Thomas Sims, was published in the *National Era* on May 22, 1851. State Street put greed above humanity, Whittier lamented, but Massachusetts remained what she had been: "Her inland hills, her seaward plains,/Still nurture men!"

He never, in fact, lost faith in the people; always he felt that they would respond to able leadership. He was not discouraged even by the Free-Soilers' temporary reverse in the election of 1852, in which the people seemed to declare for the finality of the Compromise of 1850. John P. Hale lost nearly half of the Free-Soil strength of 1848, but Franklin Pierce, New Hampshire Democrat, defeated General Winfield Scott, his commander in the War with Mexico. Commenting in the *National Era* of January 27, 1853, on "Our Prospects and Our Duties," Whittier took lively pleasure in the "unprecedented sale" of *Uncle Tom's Cabin;* for it showed, said he, that —

> The public ear is open. Whatever politicians may resolve, or clerical conservatives preach, the heart and conscience of the nation are with us. It is our business to give direction and practical efficiency to this popular sympathy, and point out legal and constitutional channels wherein it may act upon the politics of the country. * * *

Whittier dismissed with contempt the "pointless witticisms of our opponents," and rejoiced that the "heaviest blow which Slavery has received for the last half century has just been struck by a woman. . . ."

The *National Era* itself had helped to increase *Uncle Tom's* immense circulation by printing the book serially from June 5, 1851, to April 1, 1852.

Charles Sumner's election in April 1851 to the Senate seat vacated when Webster became Secretary of State in President Fillmore's cabinet was, manifestly, the answer of people in Massachusetts to the Compromise of 1850. For nine months following, both of the major parties conspired to deny Sumner the occasion of speaking his sentiments against slavery. Whittier, not at all astonished, wrote him that the Senate was "simply carrying out the resolutions of the two Baltimore conventions," and he counseled patience. Time, he felt certain, would be on Sumner's side. On the other hand, he was sorely grieved to learn that another valued friend and political co-worker, Robert Rantoul, had died on August 7, 1852, while representing the Essex South district in Congress.[24]

The passing of two years merely brought the sectional tension over slavery to a new pitch, a fact which Whittier recognized in the article

"The Occasion and Its Duties," published in the *National Era* on April 6, 1854. Whittier asserted that the defeat of the Kansas-Nebraska Bill — which, violating the Compromise of 1820, would leave the determination of slavery to the local settlers — was of the utmost importance, and he added that the time had come for Congress to form a League of Freedom having for its watchwords:

> No Slave Territory.
>
> No more slave States.
>
> The General Government relieved from all responsibility for Slavery.
>
> No interference by the General Government with Slavery in the slave States.
>
> No interference with the right of jury trial, the writ of habeas corpus, and other guarantees of life, liberty, and the pursuit of happiness, in the free States.
>
> Slavery left to itself in the States which cherish it, without any extraneous aid or comfort, to reconcile itself as best it may to the progress of civilization and Christianity, and to the liberal spirit of the age.

Whittier was convinced that the people of the free states would join such a movement, and that it required a leader to embody its idea. Here was an invocation to Lincoln:

> The Divine Providence does not mock us in presenting these great opportunities for the advancement of humanity. It gives the Man for the Hour — the strong, bold hand, to grasp the forelock of the passing Occasion. When such a man shall unmistakably reveal himself, whatever may have been his party name or connection, whether his home is in New England or the Empire State, by the Mississippi or the Colorado, all who love liberty, and desire the peace, honor, and prosperity of the several States, and the permanence of their Union, will naturally rally about him. ***

President Pierce signed the Kansas-Nebraska Act on May 30, 1854, and Whittier urged "Union Now" even more pressingly in the *National Era* of June 29: "If anything is to be done to save the country from the perdition to which it is tending, now is the time for it." Indeed, after the election for Governor in the preceding autumn, he had written to Sumner on November 15: "This must be the end of *coalition* except on anti-slavery grounds. It becomes us now to take our stand on the old platform, with *inexorable firmness*." [25] After the Kansas-Nebraska Act became law, he pleaded still more insistently that Whigs and Democrats alike join the Free-Soilers.

History was, indeed, then recording the death of the Whigs and the formation of the Republican Party (February and July, 1854). As an original Liberty Party man, Whittier came to be considered one of the Republican "founders."

The settlement of Kansas, inevitably, resolved itself into a bloody struggle between North and South to get there first with the most men. Northern determination was hardened in particular by the opening up to "squatter sovereignty" of land which, by the terms of the Missouri Compromise, had in 1820 been closed to slavery. Senator John J. Ingalls, writing in *Harper's Monthly* for April 1893, caught the spirit of perilous romance and of emotional stir in Northern souls which animated the settlement; and, no less, the moral force of the emigrants of many nations who flocked to Kansas as agents of freedom. Anti-slavery verse and oratory in the North rose in force and volume over the Kansas crusade. "Whittier," Senator Ingalls specified, "was the laureate of the era. His 'Burial of Barber' and 'Marais du Cygne' seemed like a prophet's cry for vengeance to the immigrants. . . ."

Those two poems, appearing respectively in the *National Era* and in the *Atlantic Monthly*, were matched by two others from Whittier's pen during the struggle. The *Era* published also "The Kansas Emigrants," which Edward Everett Hale said a company of the settlers sang when they left Boston, as they journeyed, and in their new home.[26] The dramatic monologue, "Letter, from a Missionary of the Methodist Episcopal Church, South, to a Distinguished Politician," appeared unsigned in the Amesbury *Villager*.

In July 1854, probably at the very time he was writing "The Kansas Emigrants," Whittier was invited by Ralph Waldo Emerson and others to attend a meeting in Boston of men of all parties who were determined to resist the encroachments of slavery. From Amesbury he wrote Emerson on July 3:

> The circular signed by thyself and others, inviting me to meet you at Boston on the 7th inst., has just reached me. If I am able to visit

Boston on that day I shall be glad to comply with the invitation. Your movement I regard as every way timely and expedient. I am quite sure good will come of it, in some way. I have been for some time past engaged in efforts tending to the same object, — the consolidation of the anti-slavery sentiment of the North. For myself, I am more than willing to take the humblest place in a new organization made up from Whigs, anti-Nebraska Democrats, and Free-Soilers. I care nothing for names; I have no prejudices against Whig or Democrat; show me a party cutting itself loose from slavery, repudiating its treacherous professed allies of the South, and making the *protection of Man* the paramount object, and I am ready to go with it, heart and soul. The great body of the people of all parties here are ready to unite in the formation of a new party. The Whigs especially only wait for the movement of the men to whom they have been accustomed to look for direction. I may be mistaken, but I fully believe that Robert C. Winthrop holds in his hands the destiny of the North. By throwing himself on the side of this movement he could carry with him the Whig strength of New England. The Democrats here, with the exception of two or three office-holders and their dependents, defend the course of Banks [Nathaniel Prentiss Banks, Representative from Massachusetts], and applaud the manly speeches of Sumner.[27]

Two years later, on June 13, 1856, Whittier wrote to urge Emerson to attend the Philadelphia convention of the new Republican Party, as a substitute for the ailing Governor Boutwell. "It is a great occasion," declared Whittier, "the most important public duty which can occur in a lifetime. . . ." [28] General John C. Frémont became the Party's first nominee for President, and the campaign waged in his behalf reached a pitch, at times, of almost religious fervor. Whittier, captivated by the cross-continent exploits of Frémont "the Pathfinder" and urged also by Charles A. Dana, composed an unusually large number of campaign songs. In Amesbury he was of course active, and once during the campaign he wrote in hopeful vein to his cousin Moses Cartland:

Ah me! I wish I had the strength to do what I see should be done! But all I *can* do shall be done. I am not apt to be very sanguine, but I certainly have strong hopes of Frémont's election. I think I see the finger of Providence in his nomination. It appeals to all that is good and generous in Young America. It touches the popular heart.[29]

But James Buchanan, Philadelphia lawyer, former ambassador, once Secretary of State, got the electoral vote, 174 to 114, over Frémont. He was the last of three successive Northern Presidents, following Fillmore and Pierce, who occupied the White House thanks to Southern votes. Whittier's hopes of the election of Frémont, whose administration of affairs in California had been open to question, were not unreservedly high. In the poem "What of the Day?" [30] which was published in the *National Era* on September 4, 1856, Whittier again — as he did at intervals — admitted a doubt whether slavery in America could be beaten at the polls. On a note of prophecy he wrote, in part:

> I fain would thank Thee that my mortal life
> Has reached the hour (albeit through care and pain)
> When Good and Evil, as for final strife,
> Close dim and vast on Armageddon's plain;
> And Michael and his angels once again
> Drive howling back the Spirits of the Night.
> Oh for the faith to read the signs aright
> And, from the angle of Thy perfect sight,
> See Truth's white banner floating on before;
> And the Good Cause, despite of venal friends,
> And base expedients, move to noble ends;
> See Peace with Freedom make to Time amends,
> And, through its cloud of dust, the threshing-floor,
> Flailed by the thunder, heaped with chaffless grain! [31]

Whittier took courage at least from the fact that New England went for Frémont. If, he asked in "A Song Inscribed to the Fremont Clubs," so much Republican ground could be gained in a few months, "What may not four years do?" In 1860 the new party of liberty, with Lincoln, won 180 electoral votes and the Presidency.

## 5

In the last five years before the Civil War broke out, Whittier particularly observed the ripening seeds of it in events involving individual persons. By his thrust at the settlement on Osawatomie Creek, in Kansas, on May 24, 1856, John Brown became nationally known, and he made his celebrated raid on the arsenal at Harper's Ferry on October 16, 1859.

Whittier perceived the purpose of Brown's mad stroke — to create a refuge in the hills for slaves — but disapproved, as always, of extremism. These sentiments he made clear in a letter written to a friend on December 2, 1859, the day Brown was hanged for treason: "What a sad tragedy to-day in Virginia! I feel deep sympathy for John Brown, but deplore from my heart his rash and insane attempt. It injures the cause he sought to serve." [32]

For the caning and nearly mortal injury of Charles Sumner, as he sat at his desk in the Senate chamber on May 23, 1856, two days after delivering his speech "The Crime Against Kansas," Whittier had only outright condemnation. It was directed not against the South Carolina Congressman, Preston S. Brooks, who made the assault, but against the slave power that motivated it. As he affirmed clearly in a statement to a citizens' meeting in Amesbury-Salisbury, on June 2, Whittier felt that the only weapon the North could wield in defense against Southern actions was united political strength. He wrote:

> Fearing I may not be able to attend the meeting this evening, I beg leave to say a word to my fellow-citizens. I need not say how fully I sympathize with the object of the meeting, nor speak of my grief for the sufferings and danger of a beloved friend, now nearer and dearer than ever, stricken down at his post of duty, for his manly defense of freedom; nor of my mingled pity, horror, and indignation in view of the atrocities in Kansas. It seems to me to be no time for the indulgence of mere emotions. Neither railing nor threats befit the occasion. It is our first duty to inquire, why it is that the bad men in power have been emboldened to commit the outrages of which we complain. Why is it that the South has dared to make such experiments upon us? The North is not united for freedom, as the South is for slavery. We are split into factions, we get up paltry side issues, and quarrel with and abuse each other, and the Slave Power, as a matter of course, takes advantage of our folly. That evil power is only strong through our dissensions. It could do nothing against a united North. The one indispensable thing for us is Union. Can we not have it? Can we not set an example in this very neighborhood, — Whigs, Democrats, Free-Soilers, and Americans, joining hands in defense of our common liberties? We must forget, *forgive*, and UNITE. I feel a solemn impression that the present opportunity is the last that will be offered us for the peaceful and constitutional remedy of the evil which afflicts us.

> The crisis in our destiny has come: the hour is striking of our final and irrevocable choice. God grant that it may be rightfully made. Let us not be betrayed into threats. Leave violence where it belongs, with the wrong-doer. It is worse than folly to talk of fighting Slavery, when we have not yet agreed to vote against it. Our business is with poll-boxes, not cartridge-boxes; with ballots, not bullets. The path of duty is plain: God's providence calls us to walk in it. Let me close by repeating, Forget, *forgive*, and UNITE.[33]

On March 6, 1857, two days after Buchanan's inauguration, Whittier's "solemn impression" was doubly underscored by the Dred Scott decision, the first judgment which the Supreme Court had to deliver on the case of an escaped slave. The decision was, in effect, a complete victory for the Southern Democrats and the planting interest, for it gave judicial sanction to the extreme theory of unlimited expansion of slavery in the territories. If the North needed shock treatment to goad it into taking a united stand, this was it. In the Congressional elections of 1858 the Republicans consequently made significant gains in the North, and Lincoln, while losing the Senatorial race in Illinois to Stephen A. Douglas, became a national figure and leading advocate of preserving the Union.

Toward Lincoln, in his rise to the Presidency, Whittier had not a clear and firm attitude. It required an even more perceptive person than Whittier to foresee that Lincoln would rise to such stature in the office as to make it again internationally important, and himself an international figure. In 1860 the New England Abolitionist looked for a moment past the Illinois lawyer again to California and Frémont, even then of faded glamor. But when nominated by the Republicans, Lincoln received Whittier's full support. And the "strength and wisdom and moderation and firmness" [34] which Lincoln demonstrated on so large a scale in the White House were, in their sphere, simply the main personal qualities which Whittier had brought to anti-slavery work dating from 1833.

Whittier's contributions to Lincoln's first campaign were mainly two poems: "The Summons," which appeared in the *Atlantic Monthly* in October 1860, and "The Quakers Are Out," written to be sung at a political rally in Newburyport on October 11. The Friends' turn-out for a Pennsylvania election had just helped to carry the State and forecast national Republican success in November; hence Whittier proclaimed, ". . . Lincoln goes in when the Quakers are out!"

When Lincoln actually was *in*, Whittier joined Lucy Larcom in a Hallelujah.[35]

# 6

The vigor and bite which featured Whittier's anti-slavery work from 1840 to the outbreak of the Civil War betokened a central fact: his mental activity was at its highest in these middle years of life. Frail health was no bar to enormous productivity. An even dozen books and a large number of leaflets bearing his name were published between 1844 and 1860, including three — *Ballads, and Other Poems*, *The Supernaturalism of New England*, and *Poems by John G. Whittier* — which were also issued in England. J. T. Fields, ever glad to publish work of merit for which he saw an assured (if delayed) market, was more than a routine editor; his warm friendship for Whittier and his wise criticism helped immensely to bring Whittier the high success which he had coveted early and then sacrificed to his anti-slavery work.

Whittier's writing of 1840–60 had, as a matter of fact, much more than a merely Abolitionist flavor. A close look at his prose and verse of the period reveals a broad range of interests: intenser cultivation of some which were present even in his earliest writings, and the plumbing of a mind and spirit tempered by significant experience of the world and men. Whittier now wrote —

Songs of labor and of reform other than Abolitionist.

Poems personal and reminiscent.

Poems and the prose history, *Leaves from Margaret Smith's Journal*, of rural New England.

Religious lyrics.

Verses written in reverence of "old things" showing, beneath his reformer's mantle, a conservative side which helped to give him the well balanced character he had.

Tributes to individuals.

Poems of legends and romance.

During 1845–47, in the *Democratic Review* and the *National Era*, Whittier published six "songs of labor" — honoring shoemakers, fishermen, lumbermen, shipbuilders, drovers, and huskers — which betokened his lifelong championship of people who work with their hands.[36] These were heartfelt pieces, of no great poetic merit, bodying forth his old conviction that "life is wisest spent/Where the strong working hand makes strong the working brain." [37] And likewise on the side of the angels Whittier counted those people who worked against war. This article in his Quaker creed he had early set to verse. Now, from the time of the War with Mexico to the outbreak of the Civil War, he wrote some of his strongest protests against armed means of settling disputes. Here were poems which became at once well loved and are still well remembered: "The Angels of Buena Vista" and "The Pipes at Lucknow," which appeared in the *National Era;* and others which rang with ironical protest — "To Pius IX" and "The Dream of Pio Nono," "From Perugia," and "The Conquest of Finland." In particular, Whittier rejected utterly the notion, sanctified by history, that religion had need to crusade and was justified in taking up the sword.

For institutions and customs, for all social thinking that prevented man from standing up to his full height, Whittier expressed his strong distaste in "The Reformer," written in 1846. This poem, he later said, "embodies my sentiments." [38] The last stanza reads:

> God works in all things; all obey
> His first propulsion from the night:
> Wake thou and watch! the world is gray
> With morning light! [39]

Of poems personal and reminiscent, Whittier wrote many after he was forty and could afford what previously, for him, would have been the indulgence of tranquil reflection. In 1851 he indited the lines of "Remembrance" to a woman friend "whose lot was cast/ With me in the distant past"; and in the same year he wrote "To My Old Schoolmaster," a tribute of ripe sentiment to Joshua Coffin — "genial pedagogue," co-worker in Abolitionism, and antiquarian. This aboundingly cheerful man assisted Whittier with the research for his historical novel, *Leaves from Margaret Smith's Journal, in the Province of Massachusetts Bay, 1678–9,* which was published serially in the *National Era* during 1848 and in book form in 1849.[40]

The poem "My Namesake," which *Harper's Weekly* published on May 23, 1857, was addressed to Francis Greenleaf Allinson, the son of Abolitionist friends of Whittier's Philadelphia period. It is a graceful salute to a youth, but even more it is Whittier's fragment of an autobiography

— a quick tracing of his career and a modest, thoughtful accounting of the forces which made him what he was. An equally charming evocation of sentiment is "My Playmate," a remembrance of his cousin Mary Emerson Smith,[41] which appeared in the *Atlantic Monthly* in May 1860.

That poem, reaching out to Mrs. Smith in her Kentucky home, yet was a fresh record of Whittier's delight in the golden mean of life in Essex County — of being "content to breathe his native air, in his own ground." He became now, at least as much as Lowell and more than any one else, the poet of rural New England. Song after song, contributed to the *National Era* from 1847 to 1857 and to the *Atlantic Monthly* in 1857–58, gave out to a widening circle of readers Whittier's sensitive perception of the people, the customs, and the seasons in the New England countryside that was his milieu. In simple rhythms but with sure hand he set to music the feelings of genuine Yankee folk. Here — in "A Dream of Summer," "Autumn Thoughts," "The Lakeside," "Summer by the Lakeside," and "The Last Walk in Autumn" — was the joy of him and his kind, and of generations down to our own day, in the smiling months when Nature gave fruit and leaf to the land. Here, too, was chilled awe of winter's blasts and "the white pagodas of the snow."

Whittier's oft-mentioned preference for the bland months was manifest in his poems of rural New England. His choicest inspirations — aside from "Snow-Bound" — were songs and ballads like "Maud Muller," "The Barefoot Boy," and "Telling the Bees" which had upon them the light of "the June warm sun."

These pieces Whittier wrought from his own time, but he was never more felicitous than when he worked in materials drawn from *old* New England. Its history held endless fascination for him, and in 1857 alone he published poems narrating incidents in the lives of three historical characters. "The Sycamores," light with the Celtic air of Hugh Tallant himself, told of this early Irish settler's planting of buttonwood trees along the Merrimac at the eastern edge of Haverhill. "Mabel Martin" was a sad tale, with a happy ending, of the witchcraft craze. But it was in "Skipper Ireson's Ride," published in the *Atlantic Monthly* for December 1857, that Whittier turned history to best account. The ballad registered the wrath of people of the port town toward a captain who was said (incorrectly) to have deserted his sinking ship. Lowell, as editor of the *Atlantic*, helped Whittier to reproduce perfectly the dialect of the Marble-headers. Then, of Whittier's version of "old Floyd Ireson's" tarring and feathering by the women of Marblehead, he generously wrote that it is "by long odds the best of modern ballads." [42]

Whittier was also writing, in these two turbulent decades, some of his best-known poems of faith — and he probably still ranks as the most deeply religious poet in American literature.[43] His search for meaning in life led him back, more and more firmly, to the God of his fathers. As the outward storm of events mounted, so his inner calm increased. "A Voice grows with the growing years," he avowed in "The Shadow and the Light" (1860). A long series of poems written in the period 1845–60 — "My Soul and I," "What the Voice Said," "The Angel of Patience," "Questions of Life," "The Over-Heart," "My Psalm," and others — revealed clearly Whittier's deepening faith that God is man's only dependence. In "The Wish of To-Day" (1848) he specifically disavowed Fame, which up to 1833 had been a particular goad and lure to him; and in "First-Day Thoughts," written in 1852, he prayed for renewed strength to "restrain the sore disquiet of a restless brain." For him, life now consisted precisely of

> Doing God's will as if it were my own,
> Yet trusting not in mine, but in His strength alone! [44]

The changes which were taking place in Whittier were not unnoticed. Longfellow paid him what must have been a compliment when, on December 4, 1857, he noted in his journal: "Met Whittier at the publisher's. He grows milder and mellower, as does his poetry." [45] It is certainly true that, at this time, Whittier devoted more of his verse than previously to subjects other than slavery. He lost none of his intense absorption in national events, but progressively with the years he turned from them to reflect upon the past. Much that was in it he found good.

If in one way Whittier was a political and social radical, equally he was a conservative who clung to roots which he thought sound. In "The Men of Old" (*National Era*, June 14, 1849) he bade his contemporary reformers to bow to the "old confessors" in "the solemn Pantheon of the Past." It was like Wordsworth invoking the spirit of Milton. Whittier said that soft words and smooth prophecies are doubtless well —

> But to rebuke the age's popular crime,
> We need the souls of fire, the hearts of that old time! [46]

With Whittier this was a familiar theme. He thought always that the

Society of Friends in his day had lost its first strength, and a constant note with him was of praise for the "Quakers of the olden time," above all George Fox and John Woolman. Later, in "The Meeting" (1868), he said precisely, "I reverence old-time faith and men." And in "To My Old Schoolmaster" Whittier particularly praised Joshua Coffin for "teaching reverence for the old" in an age obsessed with immediate things — "Mad for party, sect and gold." [47]

Occasional poems, dedicated chiefly to individuals, also helped in the two decades before the Civil War to give balance to Whittier's verse. When Kossuth, the great Hungarian patriot, came a fugitive to America in 1851, Whittier hailed "the coming of the noblest guest/The Old World's wrong has given the New World of the West!" In 1853, on the passing of his old friend Robert Rantoul, Whittier paid him warm poetic tribute, also in the *National Era*, because "he died at his post in Congress, and his last words were a protest in the name of Democracy against the Fugitive-Slave Law." [48] Twice in five years Whittier gave his meed of mature praise to Burns, first in the *National Era* on February 13, 1854, and again, on the occasion of the Boston celebration of the one hundredth anniversary of the birth of Burns, on January 25, 1859. (Whittier was unable to attend in person, and Emerson read the lines.)

When Joseph Sturge died in 1859, honored internationally as a humanitarian, Whittier bowed to the memory of his English friend and Abolitionist co-worker with reverential lines which appeared in the *Independent*, New York, on July 21. His, said Whittier, was "a life of duty transfigured into love," and that fact was the bond between these kindred spirits.

Whittier's fascination with legend and romance, especially if it was grounded in Christian chivalry, did not yield even to his intense antislavery labors of 1840–60. Five poems in particular sprang from that lifelong interest — "Barclay of Ury," "The Legend of St. Mark" (suggested by Charles Sumner), "The Gift of Tritemius" (which appeared in the first issue of the *Atlantic Monthly*, November 1857), "The Red River Voyageur," [49] and "On Receiving an Eagle's Quill from Lake Superior." Furthermore, "The Cable Hymn," which appropriately was published in the *Atlantic* in October, 1858, gave new proof of Whittier's imaginative optimism — and that of Emerson, Thoreau, and many other thinking men on both sides of the Atlantic — that, with the laying of the cable at last,

> The hands of human brotherhood
> Are clasped beneath the sea.[50]

Whittier was localized by circumstances in Essex County, but he had an unusually alert national vision, illustrated by the lines written on receipt of the eagle's quill from Lake Superior. In imagination he flew to the Northwest, and he wrote exultantly:

> The rudiments of empire here
> Are plastic yet and warm;
> The chaos of a mighty world
> Is rounding into form.
> * * * * * * * * * *
> And, westering still, the star which leads
> The New World in its train
> Has tipped with fire the icy spears
> Of many a mountain chain.[51]

This same breadth of vision informed an editorial, obviously written by Whittier, which was published in the Amesbury and Salisbury *Essex Transcript* (or *Villager*) on November 19, 1846. Under the headline "Stupendous Project! A RAIL ROAD TO THE PACIFIC," Whittier praised the campaign of a Mr. Whitney to persuade the people and members of Congress to undertake the building of a railway from Lake Michigan to the mouth of the Columbia River. The last two paragraphs of the editorial are an essence of Whittier's social thinking:

> Of the advantages likely to accrue to the whole country from such a road, it is scarcely possible to speak in a tone of exaggeration. It would open to us a boundless commerce with China, and the East; and bring Boston and Pekin as near each other, as Boston and Liverpool were twenty years ago.
>
> Of course the cost of such a work must be in proportion to its magnitude, and at first view has an appalling appearance. But, with a less sum than has already been expended on the Mexican and Florida Wars — Wars disgraceful in their origin and productive of nothing but evil in the increase of Slave-territory — THE WORK MIGHT BE DONE. When will statesmen learn what constitutes the true glory and real prosperity of nations?

# 7

Finally, Whittier in this period observed closely the literary work of friends, and commented from time to time, in the *National Era*, on specific works. In 1848, for instance, he gave warmly appreciative notices to Lucy Larcom and (posthumously) to Lucy Hooper, and on November 25, 1847, he expressed his keen relish for Longfellow's "Evangeline." "Here, then," he said, "we have it at last. An American poem, with the lack of which British reviewers have so long reproached us." And he went on to praise Longfellow's character portraits.

Ten years later, Whittier and Longfellow were among the goodly company of liberty-loving writers of the North whose talents were assured an unobstructed outlet when the *Atlantic Monthly* was founded. Francis H. Underwood, who in 1883 was to write an extremely readable "biographical sketch" of Whittier, originated the plan; it was perfected at a dinner given in the summer of 1857 by the publisher Moses Dresser Phillips and attended by Emerson, Holmes, Longfellow, Lowell, Motley, Edmund Quincy, and other literary personages of New England; Lowell was acclaimed as editor-in-chief; and Holmes suggested the title the *Atlantic Monthly*.[52]

Wisely the editors so framed their policies that belles-lettres provided entertainment and information, and political discussion, free but temperate, was kept in the hands usually of Lowell or of Parke Godwin. From the outset the *Atlantic* enjoyed prestige. And Whittier in particular had, at last, a free outlet in a New England magazine of liberal tendencies. Moreover, the *Atlantic* paid him more liberally for his contributions than any periodical had ever done before. This new income, added to gradually increasing royalties from his books, had by the end of 1860 begun to lift from Whittier the shadow of financial need — a shadow as persistent, if not as ominous, as that which had hung over the nation for three decades before the issue of Civil War was joined.

# XII

# Wild War's Desolation

THE OUTBREAK of the Civil War was to Whittier more unwelcome than unforeseen. As early as 1829, in the *American Manufacturer*, he had published his reasoned fear that, for countenancing the system of slavery, the nation would bring down upon its head a "fatal catastrophe." In 1833, in *Justice and Expediency*, he clearly stated his conviction that the nation must prepare itself against "a day of revolution." In 1836, protesting Governor Edward Everett's soft attitude,[1] Whittier recalled that slavery perished in Santo Domingo "in a storm of fire and blood," and he prophesied: "It may be so in our own country." War, however, was a loathsome thing to him, and in the *Pennsylvania Freeman* on April 12, 1838, he proclaimed: "We are fully and entirely, as an individual, opposed to all violence for the redress of injuries." Ten years later, in the glare of the conflict with Mexico, Whittier was too clear-eyed and realistic to doubt that the issue between slavery and freedom in the United States would have in time to be resolved by a "great contest"; and in the *National Era* on April 20, 1848, he said, "*Let it come!*" — the sooner the better.[2]

## 1

Yet while believing that the nation would suffer for its sin, Whittier held firmly to the Quaker principle of non-resistance. Toward the greatest question of his day his feeling was torn, for his detestation of slavery was matched only by his hatred of what, he realized, must be the ultimate purge for the nation. In the 1850's his hope for a settlement by reason was overmatched by his fear of a decision by war. His state of mind under the cruel dilemma shows plainly in a letter which he wrote to Lydia Maria Child on October 21, 1859:

> I was glad to get a line from thee, and glad of the opportunity it affords me and my sister to express our admiration of thy generous sympathy with the brave but, methinks, sadly misguided Captain Brown. We feel deeply (who does not?) for the noble-hearted, self-sacrificing old man. But as friends of peace, as well as believers in the Sermon on the Mount, we dare not lend *any* countenance to such attempts as that at Harper's Ferry.
>
> I hope, in our admiration of the noble traits of John Brown's character, we shall be careful how we encourage a repetition of his rash and ill-judged movement. Thou and I believe in "a more excellent way." I have just been looking at one of the *pikes* sent here by a friend in Baltimore. It is not a Christian weapon; it looks too much like murder.
>
> God is now putting our non-resistance principles to a severe test. I hope we shall not give the lie to our life-long professions. I quite agree with thee that we must judge of Brown by *his* standards; but at the same time we must be true to our settled convictions, and to the duty we owe to humanity.
>
> Thou wilt see how difficult it is for me to write as thou request. My heart is too heavy and sorrowful. I cannot write now, and can only *wait*, with fervent prayer that the cause we love may receive no detriment.[3]

Whittier's fear that calamity impended must have been increased by an interview in Boston, evidently during 1860, which was arranged on the request of a Southern planter come to test sentiment in the North. They exchanged views freely. The planter reported that there was in the South a strong feeling of hate toward the North and Northern men, and that the "Southrons" were determined to fight. Plainly the Alabaman was astonished to find Whittier "so mild mannered a man," and he ac-

[3] From: pp. 78–79, T. W. Higginson, *John Greenleaf Whittier*. Copyright, 1902, by The Macmillan Company and used with their permission.

knowledged that, generally, he did not perceive that the feeling of the North toward the South was bitter and unfriendly, as Southern politicians represented it. He himself had been treated only with courtesy and civility.

One other unexpected treat Whittier arranged for him — an opportunity to see at its worst the anti-slavery phase of "Northern fanaticism." They concluded their tour of Boston by calling at the *Liberator* office, where they found Garrison, Wendell Phillips, and Frederick Douglass, and where they enjoyed a "precious season of conversation." The planter returned south with precisely Whittier's feeling: mourning for the condition of the country, he could only pray for its betterment.[4]

It was, of course, by then clear that the mounting issue of war or no war would be settled by men less zealous to understand than Whittier and the planter were. Whittier's foreboding and his stubborn hope bulked larger than ever in a letter which he wrote on November 22, 1860, to Elizabeth Lloyd:

> What an excitement arises at the South from the election of Lincoln! I cannot bring myself to look upon it as really in earnest. Lincoln is a very conservative, cautious & moderate man; and he will do nothing rash or illegal. If South Carolina dissolves the Union on so flimsey a pretext, she will not carry anybody else with her. God grant that this awful question of Slavery may have a peaceful solution! It is perhaps too much to expect that so great a wrong should pass away without convulsing the nation which has so long cherished it.[5]

Events thereafter sped at an accelerated pace. South Carolina formally seceded from the Union on December 20; in January, Kansas was admitted as a free State; and on February 4, six other States joined with South Carolina in organizing the Confederacy. In "A Word for the Hour," which appeared in the *Boston Evening Transcript* on January 17, Whittier lamented the fatal trend. His counsel, however, remained strongly against war. Characteristically he believed that the old Union would better hold fast to principle and be smaller in numbers than

> . . . leap
> On one hand into fratricidal fight,
> Or, on the other, yield eternal right. . . . [6]

Other people than Whittier, of course, advocated trying all means "which truth can sanction," and proposals, many and fervent, were advanced in the North during this fateful winter to prevent the sectional breach. William H. Seward, as putative spokesman for the incoming Administration, made two propitiatory speeches, in neither of which he ruled out the possibility that war might be the necessary cost of preserving the Union. Whittier's poem "To William H. Seward," which the *New York Evening Post* published on January 28, was partly thanks and partly remonstrance — thanks for "wise calm words" and remonstrance against admitting the thought of war.

On February 1 Whittier wrote to W. S. Thayer, son of his old friend A. W. Thayer and Washington correspondent of the *New York Evening Post*, to say, among other things:

> Tell Mr. Seward I have bound him to good behavior in my verse — and that if he yields the ground upon which the election was carried and consents to the further extension of slavery he will "compromise" *me* as well as the country and himself. God give him strength and wisdom and moderation and firmness! *** The South by their madness are assuming all the *responsibility* of whatever painful duty may be imposed upon the government. It may be the will of God that slavery shall perish through their folly and crime. . . .[7]

Charles Sumner deplored both of Seward's speeches, and on February 5 he wrote to Whittier:

> *** The true-hearted here have been filled with grief and mortification. People are anxious to save our forts, to save our national capital; but I am more anxious far *to save our principles*, which leaders now propose to abandon, as Mr. Buchanan proposed to abandon Fort Sumter. The public pride arrested the latter; I hope the public conscience may arrest the former. My old saying is revived in my mind. *Backbone*, — this especially is needed here. If we are saved, it will be by events, and not by man. *** Pray keep Massachusetts firm and strong. She must not touch a word of her personal liberty laws. The slightest act of surrender by her would be a signal for the abasement of the free States.[8]

Whittier in the next two days wrote to Sumner and to C. C. Washburn, respectively, showing a cool head held above the smoldering fire. In his letter of February 6, which probably crossed Sumner's in the post, he said in part:

> If I recollect rightly, in a speech of thine some time ago, thee suggested the plan of compensation on the part of the general government for the emancipation of slaves in any State that might undertake to throw off the burden and curse of slavery. *** Would it not be well, while calmly and firmly maintaining on our part the principles of freedom, to renew the offer, as a pledge and proof of our willingness to make great sacrifices in behalf of those of the slave States which are disposed to rid themselves of the dangers and guilt of slavery? It may be that the offer would be rejected by all, but the moral effect of it would not be lost. It would show the slaveholders that we do not hate them, but slavery only. . . . For the sake of the *truly* Union men of the Border States, I would do everything short of abandonment of principles to extricate them from their unhappy position. They need our kindest regards and sympathy. *** [9]

And to Representative Washburn, Whittier avowed:

> Come what may I w$^{d}$ yield not one inch of territory to Slavery. I would do nothing to irritate; I would go far in the way of pressing sacrifice to aid any State in Emancipation, but I could never yield the preamble of non-extension.
>
> At the same time I could not agree with those who talk of *forcing* the seceding States back into the Union. This is madness & folly.[10]

Finally, in a letter written a few days before February 6, Whittier specified again that the apprehension of runaway slaves was altogether impossible for Northern people. "But we are ready to pay for them," he added, "and that ought to satisfy anybody outside of South Carolina." [11]

Manifestly Whittier believed now that the decisive step would be taken by the Confederate States. His apprehensive wait was punctuated by a letter of March 29 in which he told Sumner:

> I have a good degree of confidence in Lincoln, but my trust is rather in the Divine Providence than in man. The current of events seems to be running towards the separation of the free & Slave states. Better this than the sin & dishonor of bearing yet closer to the Evil Spirit of Slavery.[12]

## 2

After the dread war was begun, Whittier penned the famous nine stanzas which he set to Luther's hymn, "Ein Feste Burg Ist Unser Gott," and which *The Independent* published on June 13, 1861. Here, in notes firm and clear, he sounded the call for believers in freedom to "endure and wait and labor!" It was a fervid statement of Whittier's faith that God in his goodness would put down the evil of slavery, and in the shifting tides of the war it evidently gave hope and courage to all ranks of people in the North. It received the seal of Lincoln himself, who overrode the judgment of Generals Franklin, Kearney, and McClellan and renewed the permit for John Wallace Hutchinson and his family to return and sing to Union soldiers encamped on the Virginia side of the Potomac. On one occasion following the first Battle of Bull Run the Hutchinson singers rendered the hymn — which they called "The Furnace Blast" — before an audience of two thousand Federal troops. One soldier created a disturbance by hissing the lines

What whets the knife
For the Union's life? —
Hark to the answer: Slavery![13]

General Franklin considered the hymn incendiary, and General McClellan revoked the Hutchinsons' permit to sing to the troops.

In Washington, Mr. Hutchinson related the story to Secretary of the Treasury Chase, who at the next meeting of the Cabinet exhibited a copy of the banned hymn. Lincoln decided that stirring songs like Whittier's "were just the songs he wanted his soldiers to hear," and with his permission the Hutchinsons visited the Army of the Potomac again.[14]

The episode of this song symbolizes Whittier's war service particularly well. Other and younger Friends took up arms to help put down slavery; Whittier's weapons were words. In verse and in voluminous letters published in the North or addressed to leaders in British public life he bolstered morale, built faith in the survival of the Union which he had always reverenced. Whittier spread one abiding message: the Union would live because it was good; slavery would die because it was evil.

And what might Quakers in general do to serve the Union cause? On June 18, 1861, Whittier from Amesbury addressed a circular "to the Members of the Society of Friends," in which he declared:

> We have no right to ask or expect an exemption from the chastisement which the Divine Providence is inflicting upon the nation. Steadily and faithfully maintaining our testimony against war, we owe it to the cause of truth, to show that exalted heroism and generous self-sacrifice are not incompatible with our pacific principles. Our mission is, at this time, to mitigate the sufferings of our countrymen, to visit and aid the sick and the wounded, to relieve the necessities of the widow and the orphan, and to practice economy for the sake of charity. Let the Quaker bonnet be seen by the side of the black hood of the Catholic Sister of Charity in the hospital ward. Let the same heroic devotion to duty which our brethren in Great Britain manifested in the Irish famine and pestilence be reproduced on this side of the water, in mitigating the horrors of war and its attendant calamities. What hinders us from holding up the hands of Dorothea Dix in her holy work of mercy at Washington? Our society is rich, and of those to whom much is given much will be required in this hour of proving and trial.[15]

Whittier had not the physique to become a nurse as Walt Whitman, also of Quaker parentage, did; nor could he assume the duties of a chaplain, which he was reported to have said he would undertake if he went into the service at all.[16] As a citizen of Amesbury, however, he found effective ways of helping the Union cause. Nationally he was a leading builder of morale; locally a potent raiser of money. He had a strong interest in the gift boxes which were sent from Amesbury, as from other towns, to soldiers at the front. On at least one occasion when, at a town meeting, subscriptions were being raised for soldiers' boxes and for support of the work of the Sanitary Commission, Whittier's words sharply spurred a lagging effort. Seldom in his life did he speak in public. Now he rose to his full five feet ten and a half inches and said, the lines of his mouth resolute and his dark eyes flashing: "If this sum needed is not raised by this meeting, I shall write to Salmon Chase [with whom in fact Whittier corresponded] to have your exemption money on the next draft of men put up to seven hundred dollars instead of three hundred, as it is now." The money was subscribed without further delay.[17]

At another time during the war, while riding in a train in New Hampshire, Whittier encountered a Quaker whom he knew, a man then on his way to enter into what he feared was a war contract. His Quaker conscience appeared to be bothered by the belief that his lot of oak timber would go into a warship then under construction at the navy yard in Kittery, Maine. Whittier perceived that his friend had, in truth, quite resolved to sell his timber to the government. Teasingly Whittier stressed the violation of principle in a Friend's helping to build a vessel of war. His canny advice to ease the Quaker conscience of a business man was: "My friend, if thee does furnish any of that timber thee spoke of, be sure that it is all sound!" It was, and it became part of the strong frame of the *Kearsarge*, victor over the English-built *Alabama* off Cherbourg.[18]

Whittier's attitude toward the Civil War was turned into a neat jest by his witty friend Gail Hamilton (Mary Abigail Dodge). She fashioned for him a pair of slippers — in material of peaceable Quaker drab — with a belligerent American eagle on each, its eyes vigilant for defense or attack, and its talons clutching a sheaf of thunderbolts. As he loaned these slippers to visitors at his Amesbury home, Whittier smiled at the implication. His literary friend's needle, he would say, almost matched her tongue or pen in sharpness.[19]

## 3

Whittier followed the course of the war with rapt interest, if seldom with gratification. For him the only point and reason of the conflict was the advancement of freedom. He was sorrowed by the disadvantage of the North in the first summer's campaigns, and, writing to Sumner on August 20, he confessed in a postscript: "The sky looks dark now — God grant that we may see light soon. I am sorry the Baltimore Convention was held so soon — and fear the result will be bad for freedom." [20] But the note of hope for liberty sounded clear and strong in "Thy Will Be Done," which *The Independent* published on September 19, 1861; and it was raised to a joyful key in the poem "To John C. Frémont," which appeared in the *Boston Evening Transcript* on September 28. Whittier praised General Frémont's proclamation of August 31 (countermanded by Lincoln as premature), which first announced emancipation — in Missouri. Mixing prophecy with his pleasure, Whittier rejoiced:

> * * * God has spoken through thee,
> Irrevocable, the mighty words, Be free! [21]

For the Lincoln administration's conduct of the war Whittier — no authority in such matters — had far more sympathy and understanding than Horace Greeley, for instance. But he lashed out at Cabinet members whose acts seemed to jeopardize the cause of freedom. He was particularly severe in commenting on an act of Gideon Welles, his editorial opponent in Hartford days and now Secretary of the Navy. When he wrote to J. T. Fields on December 20, 1861, about literary matters, Whittier characteristically added this political comment:

> Our government needs more wisdom than it has thus far had credit for to sustain the national honor and avert a war with England. What a pity that Welles indorsed the act of Wilkes in his report. Why couldn't we have been satisfied with the thing without making such a cackling over it? Apologies are cheap, and we could afford to make a very handsome one in this case. A war with England would ruin us. It is too monstrous to think of. May God in his mercy save us from it! [22]

During 1862, of course, Whittier was gladdened by Lincoln's immediate use of Northern victories as a means for starting emancipation. When, in April, Congress abolished slavery in the District of Columbia, Whittier wrote to Sumner, on the 11th:

> Glory to God! Nothing but the hearty old Methodist response will express my joy at the passing of the bill for the Ab. of Slavery in the Dist. in the Senate of the U.S. I hail it as the first of the "peaceable fruits of righteousness" which are to follow the "chastening" of war which now for the present "seemeth grievous."
>
> It is a great event, — a mighty step in the right direction. As an American I can now lift up my head without shame in the face of the world. ***
>
> It is hard to be a mere looker on at a time like this. But, such is my condition. I am not allowed to write — indeed I *cannot* without great suffering. But the good cause goes on — & I bless God that I am permitted to see it.[23]

When on January 1, 1863, the Emancipation Proclamation itself became effective, the cause to which Whittier had devoted his life for thirty years seemed to have been brought to final and ennobling success. Fitly, Whittier's mood was not one of exaltation; instead, in "The Proclamation," he soberly bade the freed slaves —

To bless the land whereon in bitter pain
Ye toiled at first,
And heal with freedom what your slavery cursed.[24]

Also appropriately, the American Anti-Slavery Society convened in Philadelphia in December 1863 to survey its thirty years' painful toil. There Whittier's many services were listed and praised. Ill health kept him in Amesbury, but he wrote Garrison his sentiments; and in this letter, more precisely than anywhere else, Whittier set his quiet personal value on his fight for freedom:

I must not close this letter without confessing that I cannot be sufficiently thankful to the Divine Providence which, in a great measure through thy instrumentality, turned me away so early from what Roger Williams calls "the world's great trinity, pleasure, profit, and honor," to take side with the poor and oppressed. I am not insensible to literary reputation. I love, perhaps too well, the praise and good-will of my fellow-men; but I set a higher value on my name as appended to the Anti-Slavery Declaration of 1833 than on the title-page of any book. Looking over a life marked by many errors and shortcomings, I rejoice that I have been able to maintain the pledge of that signature, and that, in the long intervening years,

"My voice, though not the loudest, has been heard
Wherever Freedom raised her cry of pain." [25]

His voice, it may be repeated, sang during the Civil War almost solely of freedom; and, though fatigued and much of the time unwell, he spoke on fit occasions with his old fire and conviction. Illness prevented his writing a song requested for the second anniversary of the fall of Sumter, but he wrote a letter which included this typical statement:

* * * We must sink party (in the old acceptation of the term) out of sight, and make fidelity to "Liberty and Union" the only test.

It is of small consequence who have the *offices*, so that the country is saved.[26]

Whittier began the year 1864 by re-inscribing, on January 16, eleven lines in partial sonnet form which elaborated the thought expressed in his recent letter to Garrison, and which also acknowledged his frail health and his now less active anti-slavery rôle. He said:

I, who have striven for Freedom at the cost
Of some weak friendships, or some paltry prize
Of name or place, & more than I have lost
Have gained in wider reach of sympathies
And free communion with the good & wise, —
May God forbid that I should ever boast
Such easy self-denial, or repine
That the strong pulse of health no more is mine!
That, ever worn at noon-day, I must yield
To other hands the gleaning of the field,
A tired looker-on through the day's decline! [27]

Among the "other hands" Sumner was foremost, and Whittier's steady correspondence with him shows often the warm love and admiration he had for his friend in the Senate. In June 1864, when Congress killed the Fugitive Slave Law — long anathema to both men — Whittier wrote Sumner:

> Thank God! for the final Repeal of the accursed law.
> What a satisfaction it must be to thee who have labored so long & so well for its overthrow! Let events now turn as they will something has been gained for freedom & humanity. * * * [28]

To Whittier the abolition of slavery (officially proclaimed by the Secretary of State on December 18, 1865) was the positive gain which alone justified the war. The passage by the Senate, on January 31, and Lincoln's approval next day of the resolution proposing to the states the Thirteenth Amendment, evoked Whittier's paean "Laus Deo!" His jubilant response to the news on Thursday, February 2, as he sat in Friends' meeting at Amesbury while cannon and bell raised tumult outdoors, has been often told. After the poem was published in *The Independent* on February 9, Whittier responded to Lucy Larcom's praise of it by saying, "It wrote itself, or rather sang itself, while the bells rang." Whittier in fact penned "Laus Deo!" from memory after returning from Friends' meeting to the "garden room" in his home and there reciting the fervent lines to members of his dwindled household.[29]

Two months to the day after "Laus Deo!" was published Whittier realized, under the shock of Lincoln's death, that even the fall of the Confederacy was only "something gained for freedom," not the final victory over slavery. Six days after Lincoln died, Whittier wrote W. J.

Allinson: "The assassination of the President has painfully affected me. I have been hardly able since to collect my thoughts, to fathom the extent of our loss, or to forecast the consequences. I bow, humbled and awed before the mysterious providence." [30] Whittier went on to say that he believed Andrew Johnson "will be found a true man," and he prayed that in the justice meted out to the South there would be no excess.[31] Then, on May 11 in the Amesbury *Villager*, Whittier in "The Lesson and Our Duty" pleaded still more strongly, "We must forgive their past treason." But for him the main lesson to be learned from Lincoln's assassination was that slavery was not dead. By now full of the prevalent indignation, he wrote:

> * * * Wherever God's children are despised, insulted, and abused on account of their color, there is the real assassin of the President still at large. I do not wonder at the indignation which has been awakened by the late outrage, for I have painfully shared it. But let us see to it that it is rightly directed. The hanging of a score of Southern traitors will not restore Abraham Lincoln nor atone for the mighty loss. In wreaking revenge upon these miserable men, we must see to it that we do not degrade ourselves and do dishonor to the sacred memory of the dead. We do well to be angry; and, if need be, let our wrath wax seven times hotter, until that which "was a murderer from the beginning" is consumed from the face of the earth. As the people stand by the grave of Lincoln, let them lift their right hands to heaven and take a solemn vow upon their souls to give no sleep to their eyes nor slumber to their eyelids until slavery is hunted from its last shelter, and every man, black and white, stands equal before the law. * * * [32]

## 4

Taken all in all, Whittier's service to his cause and to his fellow men during the Civil War was considerable. When late in 1862 the flow of cotton from the South to English textile manufacturers was blocked off, subscriptions were taken in New England manufacturing towns for the relief of sufferers in affected English cities. Whittier led the campaign in Amesbury and Salisbury, and he wrote the resolutions of the Amesbury meeting published in *The Villager* on December 18, 1862. A month later he sent the total contribution to his friend John Bright, with this message:

> I take pleasure in inclosing to thy care for the benefit of the unemployed people of your manufacturing districts, a bill of exchange on Tallmont, Brothers & Co., of London, for £32 14s 1d ($238 of our money), the sum contributed by the people of the villages of Amesbury and Salisbury for that purpose. I also inclose the proceedings of the meeting which originated the subscription. With a grateful appreciation of thy generous efforts to promote good feeling between the people of England and the United States, and of thy eloquent and truthful presentation of the great questions involved in our terrible arbitrament, I am very truly thy friend.[33]

The English statesman's warm acknowledgment was sent from London on February 27:

> Thy letter has given me much pleasure. The contribution inclosed in it I have paid over to the secretary of the Lancashire relief fund in Manchester. Thy letter and the report of the meeting at Amesbury have been published in the Manchester "Examiner and Times," the most widely circulated paper in the north of England. I am sure the kindness towards our people indicated by the contributions has given much pleasure in many quarters. . . .
>
> I have been a warm admirer and a constant reader of thy poems for many years, and I can imagine something of the deep interest which the great conflict must excite in thee. It seems as if a peaceable termination of the great evil of slavery was impossible — the blindness, the pride, and the passion of men made it impossible. War was and is the only way out of the desperate difficulty of your country, and fearful as is the path, it cannot be escaped. I only hope there may be virtue enough in the North, notwithstanding the terrible working of the poison of slavery, to throw off the coil, and to permit of a renovated and restored nation. . . .
>
> With us, we are witnessing a great change of opinion, or opinions hitherto silent are being expressed. In every town a great meeting is being held to discuss the "American Question," and the vote is almost everywhere unanimously in favor of the North. The rich and the titled may hate the Republic, but the *people* do not. . . .

My daughter sometimes sends thee a newspaper with a report of some speech of mine. She is as much an American in sympathy as I am, and she wishes me to say how much pleasure she has derived from thy poems, and how much she hopes all thy noble words for freedom may soon bear fruit throughout your country. I await tidings from the States with anxiety — but I have faith in freedom and in good. With many thanks for thy kind note, and for the sympathy with our people manifested by the Amesbury contribution, believe me always thy sincere friend.[34]

Whittier, it is clear, helped to build and sustain Bright's confidence in the Northern cause; and Bright's great influence with the plain people of England was as clearly sobering upon Palmerston and Russell, both unfriendly to the North.

At home, Whittier's "words for freedom" were widely circulated in anthologies and in his own books, particularly *In War Time, and Other Poems*, which was published in November, 1863. In a large number of collections circulated in the North to keep the issues of the war vividly before the people, Whittier was drawn on for both verse and prose. His "Ein Feste Burg Ist Unser Gott" and his "Song of the Negro Boatmen" (from "At Port Royal") appeared quite as often as Lowell's "The Present Crisis" — in such patriotic books as *Chimes of Freedom and Union* (Boston, 1861), *Only Once* (New York, 1862), *The Patriotic Glee Book* (Chicago, 1863?), *Trumpet of Freedom* (Boston, 1864?), *The Freedmen's Book* (Boston, 1865), and successive editions of *The Rebellion Record* (New York).

Whittier's most famous single poem inspired by the Civil War was, beyond comparison, "Barbara Frietchie," which first appeared in the *Atlantic* in October, 1863. Northern newspapers at once recopied it widely; publication in leaflet form followed, probably soon after its first appearance; it was included in *In War Time;* and a German translation in leaflet form was brought out in 1865. Of the ballad's popularity, arising from the aged Barbara's patriotic fervor and from the sheer dramatic quality that Whittier gave to the narrative, there seems never to have been any doubt. Of the literal accuracy of all the facts of the story, originally sent to him by the novelist Emma D. E. N. Southworth, of Georgetown, D.C., Whittier had no proofs. All the controversy over the question simply slid off the obvious truth that imaginative art is seldom anchored in precise fact; and that Shakespeare was not less a poet for ascribing a seacoast to Bohemia, or Keats for calling Cortez rather than Balboa the discoverer of the Pacific.

Whittier contented himself with two utterances on the subject. First he remarked: "That there was a Dame Frietchie in Frederick who loved the old flag is not disputed by any one. As for the rest I do not feel responsible. If there was no such occurrence, so much the worse for Frederick City." Then when, in June 1886, the writer of an article in the *Century* denied to "Barbara Frietchie" any factual basis at all, Whittier said, in a letter to the editor which was published in the September issue:

> Those who know me will bear witness that I am not in the habit of boasting of anything whatever, least of all of congratulating myself upon a doubtful statement outliving the possibility of correction. I certainly made no "boast" of the kind imputed to me. The poem of "Barbara Frietchie" was written in good faith. The story was no invention of mine. It came to me from sources which I regarded as entirely reliable; it had been published in newspapers, and had gained public credence in Washington and Maryland before my poem was written. I had no reason to doubt its accuracy then, and I am still constrained to believe that it had foundation in fact. If I thought otherwise I should not hesitate to express it. I have no pride of authorship to interfere with my allegiance to truth.

It is still of interest that J. T. Fields, in accepting the ballad for the *Atlantic*, wrote Whittier on August 24, 1863, in part: "You were right in thinking I should like it, for so I do, as I like few things in this world. . . . Inclosed is a check for fifty dollars, but Barbara's weight should be in gold." [35]

Gold followed, somewhat to Whittier's embarrassment. Possibly because the volume included "Barbara Frietchie," or possibly because all of its twenty-eight collected poems appealed to Northern readers, *In War Time, and Other Poems* brought Whittier larger royalties than he had previously known. He received a payment on January 28, 1864, and at once responded to Fields:

> Thy favor, with remittance of $340, is received. It makes me rich as Croesus. I am like one who counting over his hoard finds it double what he expected. From a merely shoddy point of view the sum might seem small, but we did not cheat the government out of it —

that's some satisfaction. . . . I have just sent what I think is a hymn to T. S. King for the opening of his new steeple-house. It was kind and like thyself to tell me that my rhyme ["Barbara Frietchie"] found much approval. It is only when they are blamed or praised that we fully realize how much we love these bantlings of ours.[36]

In the months immediately following, Whittier was at least twice invited to visit Northern soldiers fighting on the Southern fronts. His health and his sister Elizabeth's obliged him to decline both invitations. On March 20, the wife of Joseph Roswell Hawley, Colonel commanding the Seventh Connecticut Regiment and editor of the *Hartford Press*, wrote from Hartford on her return from nursing in Beaufort, S.C., urging Whittier to go and see for himself the sacrifices which Union soldiers were making for the North. And in the same month he was invited by Brigadier General J. C. Rice, of the Fourth Division, to visit the Army of the Potomac. General Rice, in writing the invitation, expressed what seems to have been a widespread sentiment: "Your loyal verse has made us all your friends, lightening the wearisomeness of our march, brightening our lonely campfires, and cheering our hearts in battle, when 'the flags of war like storm-birds fly!' "[37] Whittier, as he revealed in a letter of 1876, saw only one regiment during the war — the 54th, colored, under command of Colonel Shaw, when it departed for the South.[38]

In the summer of 1864 Whittier, with quiet effectiveness, performed one of his most valuable war services by helping to clear the way for Lincoln's renomination. For essentially negative reasons, dissident elements in the Republican Party appeared to desire the nomination of some one like Frémont. Whittier had retained his romantic fancy for Frémont, but an extremely candid letter of June 20, 1864, from his old Philadelphia friend Hannah L. Neall, then residing in California, must have crystallized doubts in Whittier's mind that Frémont was of Presidential stature.[39] Promises of preferment for the General's friends, from the chairman of the Republican national committee, did not persuade him to withdraw. But Whittier's declaration to Mrs. Frémont, at the family's summer cottage in Nahant, was decisive. In a letter of November, 1889, she wrote Whittier:

Among the words I remember from you are: "There is a time to *do*, and a time to *stand aside*." I never forgot your saying this to me at our Nahant cottage (in 1864), where you had come to say them to

Mr. Frémont. Wendell Phillips, who saw the "do" more clearly than the "stand aside," insisted I had dreamed your visit. "Whittier goes nowhere — he *never* visits — his health does not let him," and other laughing arguments against your wise and necessary view of what the time demanded of Mr. Frémont — to renounce self for the good of the greater number. Do you not remember it, too? It was a deciding word coming from you. And how we have outlived all of that time![40]

Whittier was unreservedly glad to have supported Lincoln in both of his Presidential campaigns. On September 2, 1865, he wrote to an inquirer, enclosing on request a copy of "The Lesson and Our Duty," to say, among other things:

I never knew our good President personally, but I had learned to love him, as well as honor him. It was my good fortune, alone of all others in the country, to vote legally for him *four* times, [I] having been a member of both Electoral Colleges.[41]

The flares of war were dying, in the winter of 1865, but the demands on Whittier resulting from his long-time enlistment in the fight for freedom never ended. On January 21, 1865, for instance, he was asked by Robert C. Waterston, president of the Massachusetts Historical Society, for a tribute to the memory of Edward Everett. In 1836 Whittier had flayed Everett, then Governor of Massachusetts, whose attitude to slavery he considered erroneous; now he paid him warm tribute for his later devotion "to the great cause in which we had a common interest."[42] And when the firing had stopped, Whittier was one of the vice-presidents of a meeting convened in Faneuil Hall, and one of a committee of eight delegated to prepare an address (dated June 21, 1865) on the reinstatement of the Southern states, and above all on the question of Negro suffrage.[43] Whittier's personal sentiments on reconstruction he expressed in the poems "The Peace Autumn" and "To the Thirty-Ninth Congress."[44] He rejected all proposals except such as would insure freedom now to all men in the land.

His attitude was stated most clearly in a letter of June 20, 1865, to R. H. Dana:

I did not get thy note until late last Evng: and I greatly regret that illness prevents me from being with you this morning.

I read carefully the proceedings of the Faneuil Hall meeting: & I

think I shall have no difficulty in giving my full sanction to the address, which I presume will embody the sentiments of the meeting. I think it best to pretend that the President's views are mainly in accordance with ours, or at any rate not to make any direct issue with him. A simple expression of our view of the matter, and an appeal in this behalf to the people I presume is all that we can do. The position of affairs just now is critical — the enemy north & south are watching us, & it becomes us to act wisely & cautiously as well as firmly. Experience has taught us that Vice Presidents elevated to the Presidency are, as Walter Scott has it, "kittle cattle to shoo behind."
[P.S.] It seems to me [we] should urge the suffrage for the freedmen on high moral & Christian ground, rather than on that of expediency, and political policy. We lose strength in descending to that lower atmosphere.[45]

Whittier's citations for war service were of a kind which a fervently patriotic Friend must have liked. For instance, in his review of *In War Time* for the *North American Review* (January 1864), Lowell wrote, in part:

It is a curious illustration of the attraction of opposites, that, among our elder poets, the war we are waging finds its keenest expression in the Quaker Whittier. Here is, indeed, a soldier prisoner on parole in a drab coat, with no hope of exchange, but with a heart beating time to the tap of the drum. Mr. Whittier is, on the whole, the most American of our poets, and there is a fire of warlike patriotism in him that burns all the more intensely that it is smothered by his creed.

Perhaps even more felicitous was a portion of the letter which R. C. Waterston sent Whittier on February 4, 1865 — four days after the Senate had resolved in favor of the Constitutional amendment abolishing slavery:

Providence works in mysterious ways but we will rejoice in the grand results. — You have done all that a human being could do to bring it about. Perhaps you do not know how much, for these words which you have given to the country have given impulse to who can say how many hearts. They have stirred the Conscience. They have strengthened Faith. They have awakened Zeal. They have inspired Patriotism. They have set the whole soul on fire. They have breathed into multitudes a higher Life. They have helped — greatly — to re-mould the Nation. * * * Not one syllable has lost any of its power.[46]

# 5

All the insensate cruelty of the war, and in particular the loss of young lives, was repugnant to Whittier. Still more acutely, if possible, he felt the natural deaths of persons immediately dear to him — Doctor Elias Weld at Hudson, Ohio, on May 4, 1863; A. W. Thayer at Northampton, Massachusetts, on April 24, 1864; Thomas Starr King in California on March 4, 1864, and Joshua Coffin at Newbury, Massachusetts, on June 24, 1864; and, most of all, Elizabeth Whittier (injured in a fall in June, 1863) at home on September 3, 1864. For Whittier, who was in his 58th year when the war ended, and increasingly conscious of his own waning strength, these losses only heightened his sense of the desolation of war. But Whittier accepted these sore separations with the serene faith that "God *is* good; He *is* our Father!" and that, because He is Love, He will not leave us comfortless.[47]

"The wise old Doctor" Weld died without having seen the poem "The Countess," which appeared in the *Atlantic* in the month of his death and which Whittier affectionately inscribed to him.[48] One month after the aged physician had died, his niece wrote to Whittier to say, in part: "I suppose Uncle would have been familiar with the story of your beautiful ballad. I do not recollect it but should like to know the name of the 'Countess.' "[49] Doctor Weld undoubtedly had known the incident of Essex County history from which Whittier fashioned the ballad and which he described in the notes of the Riverside Edition of his works.[50]

Between Whittier and Thomas Starr King, whose ardent ministry carried him from New England to California, there was unaffected love and friendship. In November, 1855, on Whittier's request, King enthusiastically read for him the poem "The Panorama" following Horace Mann's lecture on slavery in Tremont Temple, Boston.[51] Whittier remembered that incident, and during the Civil War sent him, for use in California, copies of the kind of songs which made up *In War Time.* Then when, in January 1864, the great church built for King's ministry in San Francisco was dedicated, Whittier at the request of Mrs. Hannah L. Neall (speaking for King) wrote at once but with trepidation the hymn mentioned to Fields.[52] In a few months King was dead, and in sorrow Whittier wrote Sumner: ". . . Was there not something triumphant & glorious in the death of Starr King? He had done his great work so manfully & well."[53]

Joshua Coffin's death touched Whittier even more nearly than King's. In education, Abolition, and historical research their lives had long run close together. Coffin's impaired eyesight evidently handicapped his life, and on occasions when he was in financial need Whittier from his own slim resources and from the contributions of other friends gave him grateful relief.[54] When Coffin died Whittier was mainly worried by the steady decline in the condition of his sister, whose life lasted little more than two months longer; but he remarked in a letter to Harriet Minot Pitman:

> Another of the old landmarks of the past has been removed. My old schoolmaster, Joshua Coffin, died last week. While he lived he served to connect me with my early boyhood, or rather childhood. I shall miss him. He lived at Newbury and often visited us. I found a letter of his awaiting me on my return from Yearly Meeting. * * *

As a final tribute, Whittier at the request of Coffin's daughter wrote this inscription for his stone in "the old grave-yard" in Newbury:

> Teacher and Christian, rest!
> Thy threescore years and ten,
> Thy work of tongue and pen,
> May well abide the test
> Of love to God and men!
> Here let thy pupils pause, and let the slave
> Smooth with free hands thy grave! [55]

Elizabeth Whittier's death marked a sharp turn in her brother's life. Henceforth it was a journey of twenty-eight years paced with growing honor and acclaim, and with the literary success which had been the dream of his youth. All these things he accepted in his firm stride; but mainly he regretted that his mother and sister who had so long needed his support — and given him theirs, of inestimable value, in his Abolitionist work— were no longer present to enjoy them. On the day Elizabeth died, Greenleaf wrote to Lucy Larcom, probably her dearest friend:

> Our dear Lizzie is no longer with us. She passed away this morning. Notwithstanding her great weakness, I find I was not prepared for the event. It is terrible — the great motive of life seems lost.[56]

And to Grace Greenwood, Whittier confessed:

> My dear sister's illness was painful and most distressing, yet she was patient, loving, and cheerful even to the last. How much I miss her! how much less I now have to live for. But she is at rest; surely, few

needed it or deserved it more, if it were proper to speak of *desert* in that connection. A pure, generous, loving spirit was hers. I shall love all her friends better for her sake. The autumn woods are exceedingly beautiful at this time. I miss dear Elizabeth to enjoy them with me, but even now I realize the truth of Keats' line, "A thing of beauty is a joy forever," and I am thankful that I can still find peace in communion with outward nature in this season of glory and beauty. I wonder sometimes that I can be cheerful and attend to my daily duties, since life has lost so much of its object. But I still have many blessings, — kind friends and books, and the faith that God is good, and good only.[57]

Whittier drew at once, in letters to numerous friends, the style of life he would have to lead now that "Lizzie" was gone. He prayed that they would continue to come, "the old familiar faces" she had loved, to cheer the Amesbury home with their presence. They in turn lured him from there oftener, perhaps, than before — to Boston, and in summer to New Hampshire and to Maine. To the Isles of Shoals, where on their first visit, in the summer of 1863, Elizabeth's fall on the rocks had hastened her decline,[58] Whittier went on occasion to join the pleasant company which Celia Thaxter attracted. With the Fields and other friends he went more and more to upland places in New Hampshire, and to the Boston homes of the Fields and the Governor Claflins he was always a heartily welcome visitor. On September 21, 1864, as she acknowledged receipt of a memento of Elizabeth's, Mrs. Fields added warmly:

We hope, in the hours that are left to us we may perhaps meet oftener — that you will remember there is always a bed and a quiet room ready for you here and a warm welcome. We who have known the riches of her love can never feel poor even in her absence but remembering our treasure find all true affection in some way allied to her.[59]

It was thus a meaningful coincidence that Whittier and the Union he always loved had almost simultaneously, after desolating losses, to set about reconstruction. Whittier at once proved his recuperative powers by having his New England idyl, *Snow-Bound*, in his publisher's hands by October, 1865. Here was provided a hint of what became one of the most significant facts of his life. Whittier's creative powers were never higher than in the dozen or so years following the end of the Civil War.

# XIII

# The Farm Wagon and Buckboard of Verse

*I am not a builder in the sense of Milton's phrase of one who could "build the lofty rhyme." My vehicles have been of the humbler sort — merely the farm wagon and buckboard of verse, and not likely to run so long as Dr. Holmes's "One Hoss Shay," the construction of which entitles him to the first place in your association. I shall not dare to warrant any of my work for a long drive.*

So wrote Whittier, late in life, to acknowledge his election to honorary membership in the National Carriage Builders' Association.[1] He was here enforcing a truth in which he believed — as he often did — by adding to it the salt of his humor.

Lowell, too, spoke truly and often humorously of Whittier's work (that was their friendly way with each other), and he repeatedly stressed the indigenous quality of it. In his review of *Home Ballads and Poems* which appeared in the *Atlantic* in November 1860, Lowell declared:

> He is, on the whole, the most representative poet that New England has produced. He sings her thoughts, her prejudices, her scenery. * * * Whatever Mr. Whittier may lack, he has the prime merit that he smacks of the soil.

Whittier's new birth of freedom, in the release of his energies following the end of the Civil War, he devoted in good part to literary cultivation of his native ground — to long-time interests, "warmed into life once more," which he mentioned in the proem of *The Tent on the Beach.* With his mission now fulfilled, he again set his hand, which for thirty years had been on "the crank of an opinion-mill," to the service of his rustic muse.

# 1

*Snow-Bound* was a sublimation of the subjective. It sprang immediately from Whittier's reflections on his departed mother and his sister, from the conviction —

> Yet Love will dream, and Faith will trust,
> (Since He who knows our need is just,)
> That somehow, somewhere, meet we must.[2]

But its larger inspiration was "the household it describes," to the vivid memory of which Whittier dedicated the poem.

The chief distinction of it, for the attentive ear and eye, is its lyrical intensity. Whittier had for nearly thirty years been removed from the rural birthplace when he began writing *Snow-Bound*, which he first mentioned in a letter of August 28, 1865, to Fields as "a homely picture of old New England homes."[3] The motif of the idyl, however, appears to have been forming in him even ten years before the family's removal to Amesbury. He sounded the tonic chord in the *Newburyport Free Press* in 1826, and developed it into the full song under the impulse of a keen memory which in fact did lead "the harass'd mind back to the scenes it lov'd" in bygone years.[4]

Whittier's intense feeling for his birthplace and his family — now reduced to himself and his brother "Frank" — welled up into an undoubted masterpiece when at last it found issue. To the large body of criticism which the poem has called forth little can be added, except that the universality of its appeal betokens a fit poetic subject treated by Whittier in a genuinely poetical way. He was himself, for once, instantly certain that his touch had been accurate and the tone right, even though he missed Elizabeth, "who might have tuned my song/ To sweeter music by her delicate ear."[5] And Lowell, noticing the poem in the *North American Review* of April 1866, remarked among its many excellences "that kind of spiritual picturesqueness which gives so peculiar a charm to his verse."[6] Later critics ranked *Snow-Bound* as prime among the "Flemish pictures" of New England country life which might survive longest among Whittier's poems.[7] And there is a solid basis for the belief of Henry Seidel Canby and others that Whittier in *Snow-Bound* made a permanent record, unsurpassed in beauty, of a very important stage of American life in the nineteenth century.[8]

The popular reception of the poem was immediate and, to Whittier, incredibly rewarding. At least twenty-five thousand copies were required during 1866, ten thousand of them within a month and a half of the publication date, February 17. On April 2 Fields reported in a letter to Whittier: "We can't keep the plaguey thing quiet. It goes and goes, and now, today, we are bankrupt again, not a one being in crib. I fear it will be impossible to get along without printing another batch! I do indeed. Pity us! Your 'mitten-hooded' [line 444] is capital and will go into the next issue." [9] By July 14 Whittier was able to acknowledge the congratulations of his friend Margaret Burleigh by saying that *Snow-Bound* had given or would give him about two thousand dollars; and from the multiple-issue first edition Whittier earned altogether ten thousand dollars.[10]

These gains he considered simply the largesse of Providence. His own needs were all his life simple, but he was happy now to be able to send his niece Elizabeth (the future Mrs. Pickard) to Ipswich Seminary, and to have one hundred dollars a year left for charities. Whittier was happy, too, that now at last his works could stand on their merit and not be discounted by his Abolitionism. He closed his letter to Mrs. Burleigh on this note:

> * * * So that I am satisfied — more would only be burdensome, as it is now too late for me to make a display with money, or attempt a fast life. When it pleases the Lord to call me, I shall leave little to quarrel about among my relatives. If my health allowed me to write, I could make money easily now, as my anti-slavery reputation does not injure me in the least, at the present time. For twenty years I was shut out from the favor of booksellers and magazine editors, but I was enabled by rigid economy to live in spite of them — and to see the end of the infernal institution which proscribed me. Thank God for it.[11]

Whittier, in a word, was now acclaimed on ground of his own choosing. He had long ago,[12] during his first editorship, advocated the use of native artistic materials. Although in both verse and prose he left many records of his gift of imaginative projection into distant places, he excels as a regional and religious poet. On the occasion of Whittier's seventieth birthday, Holmes appropriately called him "the wood-thrush of Essex." [13]

# 2

J. T. Fields, who was as well able to exploit a market as to recognize an exceptional talent, now encouraged — nay, drove — Whittier to produce. The first new fruit of this friendly teamwork, probably seldom equaled and hardly surpassed in the history of author-publisher relations, was *The Tent on the Beach*, published in February, 1867. On April 2, 1866, Fields urged Whittier:

> Don't fail to have your new vol. ready *early* for the press. I shall start with a good large ed$^{n}$ of the "Tent on the Beach" and be in the market before the leaves are off and the sea is chilled.[14]

In essence, the volume was a collection of twenty-two of Whittier's poems which, since *In War Time* was brought out in 1864, had appeared in the *Atlantic*, the *Independent*, and other magazines. Almost no new fabric went into the making of the "Tent" except three songs, two of them revisions, which were sung as pieces to bind the whole together. Whittier regarded the performance quite lightly as a "poetical picnic" in which Fields and Bayard Taylor passed two days with him in a tent on Hampton Beach, New Hampshire, where the Hampton River flows into the Atlantic.[15] There Whittier read his poems to his critical companions.

The book vexed him considerably, both in its assembling and by its success. During the summer of 1866 his recurrent illness made careful work on it regrettably impossible, for, as he wrote Fields on August 18, "I meant to have made it better than 'Snow-Bound.' "[16] When on January 2, 1867, he acknowledged Fields' enthusiastic reception of copy for the "Tent," he was still unsatisfied with it, though he ventured, "It is better than 'Snow-Bound' now."[17] Even after he and Fields polished it in proof, Whittier disparaged the book. On February 15, 1867, he responded to Lucy Larcom:

> My head is getting better — Thanks for what thee say of my new book. But, it don't convince me. I rather think I have made a failure of it. My only hope is that the public won't find it out.

And on February 17 he wrote to another friend, "My 'Tent' will get itself pitched, I hear the last of this month," and he went on to say that it "was written under sad disadvantages, but that is no valid excuse."[18]

On the next day Whittier bared an uneasy mind in writing Fields; for he thought his own part needed "some corrections and emendations," and he feared that his friend's printing of ten thousand copies would prove a losing venture. Whittier enforced his fear by adding, "It will never come to a second edition."[19] But Fields again had judged the market right — twenty thousand copies of *The Tent on the Beach* were quickly bought by the public — and Whittier was confounded. On February 28 he sent this humorous protest to Fields:

> I got thy note last evening. Think of bagging in this "tent" of ours an unsuspecting public at the rate of a thousand a day! This will never do. The swindle is awful. Barnum is a saint to us. I am bowed with a sense of guilt, ashamed to look an honest man in the face. But Nemesis is on our track; somebody will puncture our "tent" yet, and it will collapse like a torn balloon. I know I shall have to catch it; my back tingles in anticipation. If a promise of never doing such a thing again would avail, I am more than ready to make it. . . . I thank thee for H. W. L's [Longfellow's] note, and thank him for his kind word and invitation. I would accept the last if I were in a bodily condition to do it.[20]

Whittier's doubts about the nine poems which made up the title section of the book were justified. None of them was itself notable, but the taste of his public must have been pleased by the "home-brewed" and the "foreign wine" served in the "Tent." Here were American narrative and legendary tales deriving from Hampton River, from Lake Winnipesaukee, and from Hampton, New Hampshire; from Amesbury, from Harpswell, Maine, and Long Island Sound; and from colonial Connecticut. (The last, "Abraham Davenport," is one of Whittier's relatively rare excursions in blank verse, and a good one.) Here side by side with them were two foreign pieces — one "The Brother of Mercy," a dramatic monologue of Tuscany, with Browning touches, and the other "Kallundborg Church," a Norse tale in verse. The Proem, the new song "Her window opens to the bay," and revisions of "The Cable Hymn" and of "The Worship of Nature" (which fitly stood an excellent and emphatic last in the title part) completed the first section.

But the ribs and supports of *The Tent on the Beach* were the five national lyrics and the eight occasional poems with which Whittier rounded out the collection. Here reappeared "Laus Deo!" the essence of Whittier's broad humanity and one of the noblest poems called forth by the Civil War. Here also was "The Mantle of St. John de Matha," white with the heat of patriotism, eloquent of the fact that the battle for freedom is never wholly won but needs, in the cycle of time, to be taken up and waged again and again by the brave and courageous.

And in characteristic union with Whittier's championship of democracy was his firm belief in God, its protector.[21] Among the occasional poems stood two of his finest religious lyrics, "The Eternal Goodness" and "Our Master." All the waste and ruin of the Civil War merely buttressed Whittier's fundamental stand in life — that God is in it and of it, proof that it is good and a means of doing good.

## 3

That note, a constant throughout Whittier's adult life, became only firmer and deeper with the years. Along with his countless utterances on the delights of friendship, it was dominant in the twilight period of which the appropriate coda was "At Sundown." The years 1832–65, which have been too often considered as merely an interruption in Whittier's career, actually gave direction to his life and point and force to his pen. In the introduction to the Riverside Edition of his works, Whittier himself felt moved to explain "a class of poems" written in mid-career as "the earnest and often vehement expression of the writer's feeling at critical periods in the great conflict between Freedom and Slavery." And he remarked in particular the want of "the finish and careful word-selection which reflection and patient brooding over them might have given." The lack of condensation which marred nearly all of his early work Whittier never overcame; but in his devotion to his Cause he developed vividness of imagery, a keen awareness of the need for the telling and forceful word, and all in all a gift for imparting the veritable sound and rhythm of music to his simple lyrics. That is why, ironically, so much that has survived of his voluminous work is the hymns, drawn from his religious poems, which were easily adapted to music. Whittier, a non-singing Quaker, held his gift too cheaply.

Signs abound that he was relieved to turn at last from the trumpet and again take up the lyre. He returned happily to themes on which he had previously written, even in a measure during the three decades of what T. W. Higginson called his "reformatory journalism." [22] What Whittier wrote after the Civil War was, in the main, an extension and a refinement of his earlier verse. He produced narrative and legendary tales, mostly native; religious lyrics; poems occasional, or personal and reminiscent; hymns to nature, and paeans to freedom everywhere. He intensely cultivated well-traveled and loved ground.

His work was thus all of a piece, and his personal fame and the triumph of his cause added to the public interest in it, even abroad. Bayard Taylor wrote Whittier from Gotha on March 19, 1867:

> Here in my German home, I take a leisure evening to tell how much I value the introduction into such a sedate company as are gathered together in the tent by the seaside. Of course, there was no difficulty in recognizing my companions. If my picture be drawn with an over-kindly and affectionate pencil, I would not change it if I could. The words which came to me like a "God-speed!" at parting still echo in my heart. It is a pleasant thought that our names should be thus connected, if only to prove to the world that there *may* be faithful friendship between poets. The surprise and delight made me happy for many days. . . . Marie and I spent a day and a half with Tennyson. He gave us a cordial welcome, and in the evening read to us his "Guinevere." He had Whittier, in blue and gold, on his writing-desk, and asked me a great many questions about the poet, which I was glad to answer. It seems that the success of "Snow-Bound" in England has recalled attention to your other poems. While I was in London, I was more than once asked where they could be had. My friend Graham sent a number of copies to English and Scotch authors.[23]

It was not that Whittier rested on old laurels gathered late; he added to them. Straight along the line of "Maud Muller" (1854), "Skipper Ireson's Ride" (1857), and "Telling the Bees" (1858) followed "The Witch of Wenham" (1877), "How the Women Went from Dover" (1883), and "The Captain's Well" (1890). On this ground, the narration in ballad form of American (and sometimes foreign) legends, Whittier was and he remains unsurpassed among the writers of his time. Again, no other poet of his day (or later, except Robert Frost) wrote with such felicity of the natural charms of New England, and of peculiarly attractive aspects of life there. On this ground, Whittier long put to capital use the lesson he learned early from the writings of Burns,[24] and until he was past seventy he continued to produce verse of notable quality. Here in simple distinction stand "Among the Hills" (1868), "In School-Days" (1870), "Sunset on the Bearcamp" (1875), "St. Martin's Summer" (1880), and "Storm on Lake Asquam" (1882). All in all, *this* class of poems gives an unexcelled record, compiled with hard and clean artistry, of the life in New England that Whittier found both stimulating and humanely gratifying.

Of the godlike in man that gives him his better nature, Whittier with almost no interruption wrote a lifelong series of religious poems that continue to stand unmatched in American letters. If anything, they mounted in quiet intensity after the Civil War and until he contributed "At Last" to the *Atlantic* in 1882. After "The Eternal Goodness," perhaps his most famous and characteristic affirmation of faith, appeared in 1865, there followed with sustained power "The Meeting" (1868), "My Triumph" (1870), "The Brewing of Soma" (1872), "The Prayer of Agassiz" (1874), "The Vision of Echard" (1878), and other religious lyrics of marked excellence. Currier lists ten hymns drawn from "The Eternal Goodness," nine from "Our Master," and a total of nearly one hundred taken from sixty different poems that Whittier wrote. Many of them, like "Our Master," came after the end of the Civil War. And it is a curious twist of fate that, in the last six stanzas of "The Brewing of Soma," this unmusical Friend who disbelieved in church singing furnished one of the best-loved two or three hymns now sung throughout the English-speaking world — "Dear Lord and Father of Mankind."

Occasional verse was not Whittier's forte, but he was — like Holmes in particular, Longfellow, and Lowell — frequently requested to "give" for specific events. After 1866 the requests were many and importunate. Whittier, never able like Emerson to say No easily,[25] too often gave with unfailing courtesy what considerations of strength should have forbidden. And when a friend died, or a public figure with whom Whittier had been associated, he was quick with voluntary tribute. The body of his occasional verse is consequently large.

No single piece of it nearly approaches Lowell's "Commemoration Ode," and as a whole this class of Whittier's work nowise compares with Holmes's in ease and felicity. Whittier of course realized his preference for other concerns, as he made clear in 1875 when he declined J. R. Osgood's invitation to write a poem for the Bunker Hill centennial.[26] (Whittier had already written one for the observance at Lexington.)

More effective than "Lexington, 1775" was the "Centennial Hymn" that Whittier wrote for the opening of the International Exposition at Philadelphia on May 10, 1876. For this labor he was waited upon by his Hartford friend General Hawley and by the chairman of the Centennial Committee, who desired him to "write the ode or poem for the grand occasion, Longfellow having given it up." Whittier declined, "not feeling able to go through the nervous strain of such an effort." But he acceded to later urging that he write the hymn,[27] which was an instant and popular success. Currier notes that it "became public property at once and was reprinted widely, appearing in the form of sheet-music, small hand-bills, advertising fliers, and as an adjunct to souvenir pamphlets, maps of the exhibition grounds, and the like." [28] The flurry astonished Whittier, who wrote to Mrs. Fields:

> It was very kind in thee to think of me in the midst of emperors, and mandarins with their buttons, and pachas with many tails, and all that grand show and world display at Philadelphia. I sent my hymn with many misgivings, and am glad it was so well received. I think I should have liked to have heard the music [by John K. Paine], but probably I should not have understood. "The gods have made me most unmusical." . . . I don't expect to visit Philadelphia. The very thought of that Ezekiel's vision of machinery and the nightmare confusion of the world's curiosity shop appalls me, and I shall not venture myself amidst it.[29]

Four years later, in the *Atlantic* for April 1880, Whittier weighed impressively in "The Lost Occasion" the public service of Daniel Webster, "New England's stateliest type of man." Exactly thirty years earlier Whittier had seared Webster in the lines of "Ichabod." [30] Now, long after the war which Webster unluckily had done nothing to avert by his "sad concessions vainly made," and then had not lived to see, Whittier averred that if Webster had been on the scene in 1861 —

> No stronger voice than thine had then
> Called out the utmost might of men,
> To make the Union's charter free
> And strengthen law by liberty.[31]

Bad rhymes mar this stately if not warm tribute, but in the main the lines measure up to Whittier's high estimate of Webster's natural powers —

now fitly represented for all time by the naming for him of a peak in the Presidential Range of his native New Hampshire.

Holmes, writing Whittier on March 6, 1881, to acknowledge receipt of a copy of *The King's Missive, and Other Poems*, commented particularly upon "The Lost Occasion" — "that generous tribute to the man whom living we so longed to admire without a reservation — of whom, dead, you write with such a noble humanity." [32]

## 4

Whittier's immense popularity after the Civil War was not a result merely of Fields' astute management of his publications. That was effect. The cause was Whittier's own stature as a man: a mind and a nature disciplined in the kind of hard school which always confers its honors late and discriminatingly. The plain fact is that he was long in learning to write well, long in raising natural fluency to the simplicity of art. The handsome editions in which Ticknor & Fields brought out many of his later books, and re-issues of earlier ones, were in their way merely elegant tokens of Whittier's "humbler sort" of art and its creations. And the public's overwhelming acceptance of them betokened a clear recognition of what he was: an exemplar of human life aspiring to reach its finest level, a representative man who perceived essences and made of them art which the many recognized and embraced. His voice was heard most sympathetically in the northeastern United States, but the accents of it were caught in far places.

Even in the South there were admirers of Whittier. From an unknown correspondent, William J. Duprez, of Savannah, he received this letter of May 4, 1866, mainly concerned with *Snow-Bound:*

> I have long been an admirer of yours, although disagreeing with you in politics. I found many gems in your recent popular poems, and a few things which, abstractly right, seemed a little harsh to me from one so palpably kind at heart. I have just read another of your poems in the Daily News & Herald, published by a thoroughly loyal man, who has met me twice on the battlefields, while I was supporting the "lost cause." Will you accept my sincere tribute of admiration and

allow me to say that Southern men, as well as Northerners, appreciate your genius.[33]

When he was in his seventy-fifth year Whittier in "At Last" gave out the living testament of a man who, under stiff handicaps, had met the world and taken its measure. Once more he affirmed his deep faith in God. The burden was familiar, but here was conveyed in lines so effortless as to stamp it at once for permanence in American letters. Whittier wrote:

When on my day of life the night is falling,
And, in the winds from unsunned spaces blown,
I hear far voices out of darkness calling
My feet to paths unknown,

Thou who hast made my home of life so pleasant,
Leave not its tenant when its walls decay;
O Love Divine, O Helper ever present,
Be Thou my strength and stay!

Be near me when all else is from me drifting:
Earth, sky, home's pictures, days of shade and shine,
And kindly faces to my own uplifting
The love which answers mine.

I have but Thee, my Father! let Thy spirit
Be with me then to comfort and uphold;
No gate of pearl, no branch of palm I merit,
Nor street of shining gold.

Suffice it if — my good and ill unreckoned,
And both forgiven through Thy abounding grace —
I find myself by hands familiar beckoned
Unto my fitting place.

Some humble door among Thy many mansions,
Some sheltering shade where sin and striving cease,
And flows forever through heaven's green expansions
The river of Thy peace.

There, from the music round about me stealing,
I fain would learn the new and holy song,
And find at last, beneath Thy trees of healing,
The life for which I long.[34]

Frederic W. Farrar, Dean of Canterbury, summed up what, evidently, men in many walks of life have felt about Whittier and his work:

> . . . He was one of the most modest and most saintly men I ever saw. The deepest, yet most tolerant, religious feeling breathes through all his poems, from those of his early youth to those written in advanced age. I was further drawn to him by the noble passion with which, all his life long, he had thrown himself into every movement in the cause of humanity and mercy. Further, I found in his writings a far nearer approach to the true religion of Christ than I did in most books professedly religious.[35]

And as for Whittier's poems which bear the distinctive mark of nineteenth-century New England, Holmes hazarded the opinion that "In School-Days" is "the most beautiful school-boy poem in the English language."[36] Among its other admirers has been Matthew Arnold, who recognized it, Mrs. Fields wrote, "as one of the perfect poems which must live."[37]

A respectable portion of Whittier's work appears to carry its own warrant for a drive in the equipage of time.

# XIV

# Fixed to a Spot

WHITTIER'S CHARACTER as a representative New Englander was a natural thing which he maintained and accepted with grateful pride. In a long letter of October 1833 to Jonathan Law, of Hartford, he remarked: "I am fixed at Haverhill, as Pope says, —

> 'Fixed as a plant to one peculiar spot,
> To draw nutrition, propagate and rot.' "[1]

From 1836 to his death in 1892 his fixed spot and legal residence was Amesbury, eight or nine miles east of his birthplace. In a word, Whittier, though a citizen of the world, was all his life an Essex County resident, and of that part of Essex which lies north of the Merrimac River.

## I

Here was no Salem, briefly made a cosmopolis by the Clipper trade; and from Essex North, even from Newburyport, no Frederick Townsend Ward went out to link the ancient and cultured East with the young and vigorous West. Still, Whittier throughout his long life found nurture in his native ground, and by a kind of intellectual osmosis he drew into himself the vitalizing blood also of the world at large.

New England was itself then astir with new currents of thought, and especially to native eyes its past was honorable and full of achievement — omitting the Puritans' persecution of the Quakers in the colonies. That for Whittier was the only black page in a book of history which gave him particular pride of place. What he wrote in an editorial of 1830 for the *Haverhill Gazette* [2] represented the fixed attitude of a lifetime toward that place.

In verse and in prose Whittier gave a reasoned and voluminous accounting of his taste for New England, especially for Massachusetts. He began early with versifying, weak in technique but strong in admiration of colonial heroes (mostly anti-Calvinist religious zealots) who gave backbone and brain to the Commonwealth. His first editorial utterances, in newspapers published in Boston and Haverhill and Hartford, put rational planks under his devotion to New England. Later prose articles and poems maintained the steady flame, which erupted in righteous wrath whenever, during his Abolitionist career, Massachusetts and New England in any way faltered in the fight against slavery.

Whittier read avidly in curious and almost forgotten volumes of New England lore, especially the *magnalia* of the Puritan settlers and histories and other records of the Quakers. Southern taunts like those flung at him by the Richmond *Jeffersonian and Times* following the publication of his *Justice and Expediency*, brought from him quick and articulate replies.[3] He became in fact a firm exponent of the New England point of view, and he spoke oftener than merely once in the tone of the poem "Massachusetts to Virginia." Even the shortcomings of the Puritans, which he often deplored or condemned, he regarded as only human perversity in a system of human society which aimed to let every man grow up to the highest possible level of life. That to him was real democracy. In "Our State" (1849) appeared these typical thoughts:

> The riches of the Commonwealth
> Are free, strong minds, and hearts of health;
> And more to her than gold or grain,
> The cunning hand and cultured brain.
>
> For well she keeps her ancient stock,
> The stubborn strength of Pilgrim Rock;
> And still maintains, with milder laws,
> And clearer light, the Good Old Cause! [4]

Other articles of Whittier's faith in Massachusetts were prose pieces like "The Pilgrims of Plymouth," "Governor Endicott," *Leaves from Margaret Smith's Journal*, "A Chapter of History," and "Peculiar Institutions of Massachusetts." Plymouth Rock was not more solidly based than Whittier's belief in the institutions and the people of his corner of the world.

## 2

But he found more than historical sanctions for it. Life round about him, even in what he called in 1833 "the narrow limits of my immediate neighborhood," [5] felt the pulse of industrial and other changes. C. R. Fish described them well: "New England was like a well-made engine into which an electric current was newly turned, increasing its power of production." [6]

Transportation was being spread and speeded. Even the waters of the "tranquil Merrimac" helped to bear the steamboat traffic which "doubled or tripled the commercially profitable areas of the United States." [7] In April 1828 "the first Steam boat ever borne on the bosom of the Merrimack" made the trip from Haverhill to Newburyport, saluted with cannon and huzzas by the inhabitants of the villages along the way.[8] By 1836, the year the Whittiers removed to Amesbury, Haverhill had twice-daily train service to Boston,[9] and between 1840 and 1850 the nation's greatest railroad development took place in New England.[10]

The *Salem Gazette*, in a review of salient events of 1830, reported that "literature and science are receiving more of the public attention than formerly." [11] In Haverhill the public interest in books had already been many times demonstrated. As an instance, a citizens' committee in 1827 called upon others to contribute to the Apprentices' Library, already very useful but obliged to send away unserved many of the apprentices on their fortnightly calls for books.[12] In the next year, local awareness of the industrial revolution then upon the country was indicated by the topic chosen for discussion at a meeting of the Haverhill Literary Society: "Have large Manufactories a demoralizing tendency?" By 1830 Haverhill had its lyceum,[13] one in the long New England chain, and the zeal for civic improvement also embraced anti-alcohol and anti-tobacco campaigns. The purely humanitarian impulses of the people responded to Samuel Gridley Howe's labors to relieve the suffering in Greece which resulted from the war with Turkey.[14]

That, briefly, was the kind of *aspiring* society in which Whittier lived and delighted. It does not appear that he ever regarded it complacently, and it is known that on at least two occasions — in 1831 and 1845 — he seriously considered moving to Cincinnati and elsewhere in the West.[15] Essex County held him. To his frank preference for it were added cogent reasons of health which set regretted limits even to his travels: Portland to the east, the White Mountains to the north, Chambersburg, Pennsylvania, to the west, and Washington, D.C., to the south.

## 3

Whittier found stimulation and congenial friends also in Hartford and particularly in "the City of Brotherly Love." For New York and for large cities in general he cared little. Wherever he was, however, he proudly wore the badge of "a very decided Yankee." In a characteristic letter, written from Philadelphia to Caleb Cushing on April 4, 1839, appeared these home thoughts from abroad:

> * * * I am glad thou hast undertaken to say something of our own Merrimac, endeared to me by all the recollections of childhood, and the ripple of whose waters I still hear in my dreams, even on the banks of the Schuylkill and the Delaware. Some time ago I wrote a prose tale called "Passaconway," the scene of which is on the banks of the Merrimac. I long to return once more to New England, but when I shall it is out of my power to decide. I like the Quaker purity of this city, and its Quaker hospitality, but I would rather live as an obscure New England farmer. I would rather see the sunset light streaming through the valley of the Merrimac than to look out for many months upon brick walls and Sam Weller's "werry beautiful landscape of chimney pots." * * *[16]

In verse Whittier so often sang the same theme as to make it a virtual refrain, which he rendered with particular sentiment in "The Last Walk in Autumn." There he wrote imaginatively of the pleasures and stimulation of travel to the far places of the world, and then lucidly sketched the peculiar attraction of New England for him:

> Then ask not why to these bleak hills
> I cling, as clings the tufted moss,

> To bear the winter's lingering chills,
> The mocking spring's perpetual loss.
> I dream of lands where summer smiles,
> And soft winds blow from spicy isles,
> But scarce would Ceylon's breath of flowers be sweet,
> Could I not feel thy soil, New England, at my feet! [17]

Whittier was an exponent of New England's point of view in his day, but never an apologist for its climate. He felt somewhat like the Maine man who jested, "We have two seasons here, Winter and July." All his life Whittier writhed under "the needles of this goading air," [18] and his comment in a letter written from Amesbury to Edna Dean Proctor on February 22, 1877, was typical: "The winter has been very trying to me, wearing, & exhausting. One deserves great credit for patriotic love of New England in spite of its awful climate." [19] Earlier, on September 22, 1870, he had felt obliged to decline Elizabeth Stuart Phelps's offer of the use of a cottage in Florida. He explained: "I must live if I can, and die if I must, in Yankee land." [20]

At all events, Whittier reveled in the blessings which Nature measured out to New England in summer, and in the occasionally long Indian summers which New Hampshire in particular enjoys. For the rest of the year he took pleasure in people, the farmers and artisans and tradesmen who were Essex County. His regard for them was as strong as Wordsworth's for the folk of the Lake Country. In a salute to the Essex County Agricultural Society written in 1888, Whittier made the point abundantly clear:

> * * * I have lived to see a great and favorable change in the farming population of Essex County. The curse of intemperance is now almost unknown among them; the rumseller has no mortgage on their lands. As a rule, they are intelligent, well informed, and healthy, interested in public affairs, self-respectful and respected, independent landholders, fully entitled, if any class is, to the name of gentleman. It may be said that they are not millionaires, and that their annual gains are small. But, on the other hand, the farmer rests secure while other occupations and professions are in constant fear of disaster; his dealing directly and honestly with the Almighty is safer than speculation; his life is no game of chance, and his investments in the earth are better than in stock companies and syndicates. As to profits, if our

farmers could care less for the comfort of themselves and their families, if they could consent to live as their ancestors once lived, and as the pioneers in new countries now live, they could with their present facilities, no doubt, double their incomes. But what a pitiful gain this would be at the expense of the delicacies and refinements that make life worth living. No better proof of real gains can be found than the creation of pleasant homes for the comfort of age and the happiness of youth. When the great English critic Matthew Arnold was in Essex County, he remarked that while the land looked to him rough and unproductive, the landlords' houses seemed neat and often elegant. "But where," he asked, "do the tenants, the working people live?" He seemed surprised when I told him that the tenants were the landlords and the workers the owners.[21]

In Amesbury, whose population in 1890 was 9798, Whittier lived unpretentiously, a national figure happy among neighbors whom he liked and respected. The cottage which in 1836 he bought on Friend Street was a modest structure of four rooms and an attic chamber. Over the next eleven years Whittier enlarged the house, chiefly by adding the ell on whose ground floor is located the "garden room" — his study — in which for forty years he carried on his writing. This modest expansion was made possible by the generosity of Joseph Sturge.[22]

Whittier's interest in Amesbury people and institutions was active and characteristic. He was chairman of the committee responsible for building in 1851 the new Friends' meeting house, still in use nearby on Friend Street. He made certain that in plainness it would satisfy "Quakers of the olden time" by employing as carpenters a venerable Quaker minister and two elders of the Society of Friends.[23] The Quarterly Meeting held in Amesbury in the month of May was a point about which Whittier's life turned. So it had been with his mother and his sister Elizabeth. No matter where he was, and no matter what the engagements of his later years, Whittier always during his life returned to Friend Street for the meeting, and gave the hospitality of his house to his friends.[24]

He was, in addition, a trustee of the Amesbury Public Library from 1856 to 1889. His interest in local and county politics was also alert, though he held no office. To the J. T. Fields, who visited him often in Amesbury, he remarked once, evidently during the eighteen-seventies, that it had become "large enough to be a city, but I am not fat enough to be an alderman." [25] During at least his early years in Amesbury, however, he liked to "talk shop" with the men who gathered at a local store to trade news and views, and Mrs. Fields noted that "he was able to put in many a word to turn the vote of the town." [26] Whittier is also said to have spent considerable time in the back room of an Amesbury tailor shop maintained by John Hume, a Scot, who became one of his trusted political lieutenants. [27]

And Whittier had a strong weakness for odd characters of the village. Henry Taylor was one, an eccentric, home-bred philosopher drawn to lofty discussion. Whittier once invited Taylor to meet Emerson, then visiting in the house in Friend Street, and Taylor evidently provided amusement. Emerson listened attentively to the high thoughts expounded at length for his benefit. Whittier next morning called on Taylor to inquire what was his opinion of Emerson. "Oh," he condescended, "I find your friend a very intelligent man. He has adopted some of my ideas." [28]

When in 1876 Whittier's niece became Mrs. Samuel T. Pickard and moved to Portland, Maine, he left the Amesbury household of which, since his sister's death, she had been head; and by invitation he made his home part-time for the next fifteen years at Danvers. There his three cousins, Mrs. Abby J. Woodman and the Misses Johnson, had the year previously bought "the old Nathaniel Putnam place," a sixty-acre farm estate for which Whittier suggested the name Oak Knoll.[29] Whittier found seclusion and congenial life at Danvers, but as the years passed he spent less and less time there and, naturally, gravitated oftener to Amesbury, where members of his family lay buried, and to Newburyport. To his Amesbury home, maintained for him by the Honorable and Mrs. George W. Cate, and to the lovely Newburyport home of his Cartland cousins, in which he was to spend the last winter of his life, he was bound by close personal ties.

These became more magnetic with his advancing years, and they give particular personal significance to his lifelong residence in Essex County. But it is also significant that Amesbury, Danvers, Haverhill, and Newburyport are all of Essex. It was the quality of life and of people generally there that gave him such a comforting sense of peace and roots. He felt it nowhere else, and this was one of the governing facts of his life.

# XV

# Travel by Proxy

New Englanders coming to maturity in Whittier's time rediscovered the Old World and came to know the East. Bancroft and Longfellow and others from Harvard chose to continue their studies in Europe; Melville wrote that "a whale ship was my Yale College and my Harvard." Knowledge of the world and of men was ardently sought — so the record shows — by a very large number of New Englanders, nourished on industrial and commercial innovations and a thirst for new ideas. One either traveled to get them, or one stayed at home and read.

Emerson tried it both ways, and concluded that travel was an illusion. In his companionate *Journal* he said:

> My friend expects with travelling to learn human nature, as if to become acquainted with man it were necessary to know all the individuals upon earth. Were it not wiser to let God judge for us in this matter? He has provided every man with twenty or thirty companions, and two or three hundred acquaintances, by way of specimen of the varieties of human character, and as a large book wherein he may read his own nature *in extenso*.[1]

And again:

> The charm of Italy is the charm of its names. I have seen as fine days from my own window. Then what Boswellism it is to travel! Illustrate, eternize your own woodhouse. It is much cheaper, and quite possible to any resolute thinker. * * * Let the soul be fully awake, and its thought is so much that the place becomes nothing.[2]

Thoreau reached the same conclusion directly, without any foreign travel.

> I am afraid [he wrote] to travel much or to famous places, lest it might completely dissipate the mind. Then I am sure that what we observe at home, if we observe anything, is of more importance than what we observe abroad. The far-fetched is of the least value. * * * A wakeful night will yield as much thought as a long journey.[3]

Whittier differed from both Emerson and Thoreau. He traveled by proxy.

Whittier's interest in seeing foreign places, at first hand, was lifelong and fervent. In his boyhood, the book in his father's library which he found most fascinating was James Bruce's *Interesting Narrative of Travels into Abyssinia, to Discover the Source of the Nile;* when he was thirty-two, and greatly desired to go to London for the world anti-slavery meeting, the plague of frail health had caught him; [4] and thereafter, to the end of his days, he looked upon foreign places through his friends' letters, and through his own absorptive reading. He never crossed a national boundary, and in person he was able to see little even of the United States. Withal, he was a well-traveled man.

Both his feelings and the service of his friends are made clear in Whittier's letter of August 15, 1882, from Oak Knoll to Mrs. Fields, then in Europe:

> * * * I almost complained to the Fates that made it impossible for me to be with you. But on second thought, I have no reason for repining, for am I not travelling by proxy — seeing with your eyes & hearing with your ears, lacking only your fatigue and small discomforts, such as with inns, and Norwegian thunder & hail-stones? You are *my* travellers! [5]

## 1

Whittier's interest in places beyond his orbit was intense. He seems never, in Holmes's phrase, to have regarded the State House in Boston as the hub of the solar system; and, though a New Englander without capital to invest until late in life, he was fascinated with the vision of what the development of the West and the Northwest would mean to his country. His mind and heart went out, but his feet were stayed in Essex County by his physical inability to travel.

Washington interested Whittier not as the Capital merely, but as the center-front of the fight against slavery. He managed to go there exactly four times — in 1840, 1841, 1845, and 1848. New York, as the financial and commercial metropolis of the country, was of less concern to him. His bad opinion of it, formed during two months' work there in the summer of 1837,[6] was not improved by a visit of several weeks in New York with his friend Colonel Julian Allen in the spring of 1870. (Allen was a native Pole who commanded a New York regiment in the Civil War. His wife was a relative of Whittier's.) When he returned to Amesbury, Whittier wrote pertinently to Celia Thaxter: "I ought to have told thee before how welcome were thy letters, but I have been in Babylon for some weeks, and have had to see and talk to so many people that I am very weary, and have not yet been able to attend to my letters. * * *[7]

Philadelphia, as "the Quaker City" and the home of friends whom he loved, had a better claim on Whittier's regard. He always delighted in the memories of his personal associations there while he edited the *Pennsylvania Freeman* in 1838–40. Yet, though he often longed to return and visit in Philadelphia, he seldom did.

Newport, Rhode Island, continued until very late in Whittier's life to see him at the time of the New England Friends' Yearly Meeting — usually in May or June when he was able to travel in relative comfort. And Portland, Maine, attracted him often, and at least as late as 1889.[8] His brother Matthew Franklin lived there twenty-odd years, and after 1876 again his niece, "Frank's" daughter Elizabeth, whose husband was an editor of the *Portland Transcript*.

Late in life Whittier, upon whom New England's winter weather was a progressively increasing weight,[9] had to resist the temptations of relief in the milder climates of Florida and California — with what reluctance it is easy to conjecture. Harriet Beecher Stowe and her family were among other friends who invited Whittier to Florida,[10] and in 1887 a township in Southern California was named for Whittier. Its Quaker founders gave him the deed of a parcel of land on the central square — possibly as something more than an eightieth-birthday gift. In his warm letter of acknowledgment, Whittier gave no hint of an impulse to go and see.[11] That fact, all things considered, was only natural.

## 2

Still more natural was the fact that foreign travel, genuinely enticing to him, was even less possible. That is why his response to foreign letters from his more mobile friends was generally ecstatic. To Bayard Taylor he was particularly grateful, as a letter indicates, written in response to the Taylors' invitation to visit them in Pennsylvania:

> I have told Elizabeth so much about thy Marie that she wants to see her exceedingly. I hope almost against hope that we shall be able to visit you in your new home this fall, where we will plant our trees of friendship and enjoy ourselves. I wish I was a better traveler; if I could keep pace with you I would join you at the mountains instead of sending this note. I travel a great deal, however, by proxy. I have had thee in my service for many years, very much to my satisfaction. Dr. Booth has been to Timbuctoo for me, and Burton to Mecca. Atkinson has been doing Siberia for me. I think (if thy Marie does not object) of sending thee off again to find Xanadu and Kubla Khan.[12]

Whittier's friendship with Taylor began in 1847 when in the *National Era* he praised "The Norseman's Ride," which he reprinted from the *Democratic Review*.[13] Again, in the *Era* of July 4, 1850, he commended Taylor's new book *Eldorado*. By then the two poets had become acquainted,[14] and thereafter, on several occasions of returning from foreign travels, Taylor readily agreed to Whittier's request that he lecture before the Amesbury Lyceum and be his guest to recount for him privately the stories of his trips to distant lands. These intimate travelogues gave Whittier great joy.

So it was, for example, in 1853 when Taylor returned from Africa, China, and Japan, and in 1858 when he lectured in New England following his visits to Russia and Norway.[15] In one stanza of "The Last Walk in Autumn" Whittier tells what value he set on these visits from Taylor:

> Here too, of answering love secure,
>     Have I not welcomed to my hearth
> The gentle pilgrim troubadour,
>     Whose songs have girdled half the earth;
> Whose pages, like the magic mat
> Whereon the Eastern lover sat,
> Have borne me over Rhine-land's purple vines,
> And Nubia's tawny sands, and Phrygia's mountain pines![16]

When in 1869 Taylor determined to cease writing books of travel, Whittier sent him an appreciative and understanding letter on the theme "I thought of my sister, how she and I had followed thee in all thy wanderings, so happy and so grateful for the privilege. There must come an end to all things — and I am not surprised at thy final decision, but I am none the less sorry for it. . . ." [17] Finally, ironically, Whittier had a hand in sending Taylor on the trip from which he never returned. He brought his influence to bear on President Hayes, who early in 1878 appointed Taylor as United States Ambassador to Germany. Taylor died in Berlin in December of that year.[18]

Other close friends who reported faithfully to Whittier on their journeys abroad included Mrs. J. T. Fields. In the summer of 1882 she wrote often and at length while touring through England, Ireland, Switzerland, and other countries. Ten years later she again sent regular dispatches to satisfy Whittier's never-ending curiosity. In the spring and summer of 1892 she and Sarah Orne Jewett wrote of the local scene in Italy, France, and England. Faithful to the last, Mrs. Fields from London on August 30 acknowledged a letter which Whittier wrote from Hampton Falls, and Miss Jewett dispatched another dated September 9.[19] Whittier had died two days earlier.

## 3

Served so excellently by his friends, among whom must be mentioned Mrs. Lucia Gray Alexander, who lived in Italy, Whittier traveled in his writings. His pictorial imagination enabled him, far better than the average stay-at-home, to project himself into both the physical presence and the intellectual atmosphere of foreign places. And so he rationalized himself into a paradoxical attitude. The fascination of alien lands and people laid hold of him early and never released him from its grip. The personal wish to travel had necessarily to be subordinated to his constitutional inability to stand the rigors of travel. He ended by professing, often and amusingly, an indifference to it. This was a thin and probably an unconscious pretense.

In 1851, in the prose sketch "My Summer with Dr. Singletary," Whittier said in effect that one's own little sphere of human life represents the cosmos.[20] Two years later (on October 21) he wrote to Emerson, in Emerson's own language:

> What marvelous weather! Amidst the autumnal opulence of the last two weeks, I have lived more than royally. How poor and mean in comparison seem all the pomps and shows of kings and priests! And what folly to run abroad over the Old World, when all that is beautiful may be seen from our own doorstone! Munich, the Louvre, and the Vatican are doubtless well worth seeing, but I fancy I see all and much more in my own painted woodlands. At any rate, I am satisfied. Oh, that I could put into words the hymn of gratitude and unspeakable love which at such a season as this is sung in my heart. I wish thee could have been with us the other day on the Merrimac. We wanted an interpreter of the mystery of the glory about us.[21]

Again, in 1881 Whittier asserted in a letter to Celia Thaxter (then in Europe), "I do not care at all to see Rome, or Paris, or London. . . ." [22]

"The Last Walk in Autumn" is a literal spelling-out of how Whittier turned the necessity of his fixed position to the gain of his native song. Over against it, however, stand numerous poems in which he writes with feeling and pictorial clarity of foreign places which his traveling corps of correspondents had described to him, or of which he had read penetratingly in books. Asked once by the Fields why he did not go up from the White Mountains to visit in Quebec, Whittier answered, "I know it all by books and pictures just as well as if I had seen it." [23]

There is no evidence that Whittier ever saw a cathedral, but in the poem "Tauler" he gave this happy vision of Strasburg Cathedral:

> . . . he saw, far down the street,
> A mighty shadow break the light of noon,
> Which tracing backward till its airy lines
> Hardened to stony plinths, he raised his eyes
> O'er broad façade and lofty pediment,
> O'er architrave and frieze and sainted niche,
> Up the stone lace-work chiselled by the wise
> Erwin of Steinbach, dizzily up to where
> In the noon-brightness the great Minster's tower,
> Jewelled with sunbeams on its mural crown,
> Rose like a visible prayer. * * * [24]

With the same gift of imagination Whittier wrote frequently and feelingly of the East — in "Palestine," "The Holy Land," " 'The Rock' in El Ghor" (inspired by Bayard Taylor), and "Song of the Slaves in the Desert." In "Naples" he caught quite well the appearance and feeling of the ancient port city, and in "The Cry of a Lost Soul" he gave a sharply moving representation of the effect on explorers of the cry of an accursed bird in the wilderness of the Amazon. (Of this poem there were many translations, notably one by Dom Pedro II of Brazil, a friend and admirer of Whittier's.)

Whittier traveled, beyond the trace of a doubt, widely and very observantly in the world of his extraordinary imagination. It was the poet's way. His journeys into the world were precisely as wide as his interests and sympathies, and these were world-wide.

# XVI

# Whittier's One World

DESPITE HIS ROOTED LIFE in Essex North, Whittier had a world vision, derived in part from his Quakerism. Men everywhere, he believed, were brothers. And he realized, more than a century before Franklin D. Roosevelt dramatized the fact and made it a truism, that when freedom is threatened anywhere in the world, it is threatened everywhere. His conviction was in print when he was not yet twenty. The experience of riper years taught him that liberty, both personal and national, is not always a birthright freely exercised, but often a right won in the world only by arduous battle. Whittier thus hit hard, throughout his life, at forces anywhere and everywhere which threatened to keep men in bondage. The one world which he considered tolerable and always found strength to fight for was a world in which all men would be free.

## 1

Whittier's early attitude toward the freedom of mankind was, as shown in two poems of 1827, "The Switzer's Song" and "Montezuma," [1] romantic and influenced by Byron. His reasoned conviction and his feeling were sound, if his expression in verse was not. With the years, both became refined and pointed, and his comprehension of liberty took in all the world. It was natural that he fought longest and hardest for freedom in his own country, but in both fiery verse and prose he also attacked the agents or forces, at large in the world, which threatened human liberty in Brazil, Greece, Hungary, Ireland, Italy, Mexico, Switzerland, and other countries. "In freedom's manly part" he was endlessly active.

As in the American war against Negro slavery, Whittier seized instantly upon events in the international news whose broad significance was clear to him. He had manifestly taken a heart interest in the career of Bolivar, who had brought it to pass that in a whole continent "Freedom's loosened avalanche hurled down the hosts of Spain." Whittier was deeply grieved by news of Bolivar's death on January 17, 1831, and in a poem written to his memory and published in the *New England Weekly Review* on February 21, 1831, he deplored the fact that —

> Alone he perished in the land he saved from slavery's ban,
> Maligned and doubted and denied, a broken-hearted man! [2]

In the face of contemporary opinion, Whittier prefaced his warm tribute by declaring that Bolivar was "an honest patriot." Two years later, in *Justice and Expediency*, he added: "The departed Bolivar indeed deserves his glorious title of Liberator, for he began his career of freedom by striking off the fetters of his own slaves, seven hundred in number." [3]

As for Europe, Whittier somehow learned early how difficult it was, under the weight either of imperialism or of kingly power, for the mass of men to be free and to exercise the natural rights of human beings. Poland, a land of tragedy for centuries down to our own time, attracted his special interest and provided a plain illustration of the acute difficulty of achieving liberty. In an editorial on Poland published in the *New England Weekly Review* on May 2, 1831, Whittier appeared to feel so strongly as to run counter to his Quakerism. There may, he said precisely, be justice in a war fought against oppression or for liberty. About Poland he wrote, in brief:

> I consider this her present struggle [the Rising of 1830 against Russian rule] as *tending* to advance her liberties, but do not feel confident that *one* effort will suffice, but of *this* I feel confident, that the God of Nations will not see her part with her blood and treasure in a righteous cause without recompense.

For Ireland, Whittier felt an even greater concern, and during the particularly troublesome eighteen-thirties and forties he was a consistent friend of Ireland and an advocate of her freedom. He admired Daniel O'Connell unreservedly, and wrote a long and detailed tribute to him which the *Haverhill Iris* first published on March 28 and April 4, 1834. Whittier principally undertook to defend O'Connell's name and mission against the calumnies of English Tories and the remarks of Henry Clay. What he wrote was actually a full-scale statement of the case for reform. The kernel of it is this:

> But who is Daniel O'Connell? Ireland now does justice to him, the world will do so hereafter. No individual of the present age has done more for human liberty. His labors to effect the peaceable deliverance of his own oppressed countrymen, and to open to the nations of Europe a new and purer and holier pathway to freedom unstained with blood and unmoistened by tears, and his mighty instrumentality in the abolition of British colonial slavery, have left their impress upon the age. They will be remembered and felt beneficially long after the miserable slanders of Tory envy and malignity at home, and the clamors of slaveholders abroad, detected in their guilt, and writhing in the gaze of Christendom, shall have perished forever, — when the Clays and Calhouns, the Peels and Wellingtons, the opponents of reform in Great Britain and the enemies of slave emancipation in the United States, shall be numbered with those who in all ages, to use the words of the eloquent Lamartine, have "sinned against the Holy Ghost in opposing the improvement of things, — in an egotistical and stupid attempt to draw back the moral and social world which God and nature are urging forward." [4]

Whittier deplored any outside interference whatever in the domestic concerns of the Irish people, and he contended in a number of editorial opinions that Ireland's greatest need was the free exercise of its natural right to work out its own problems. One noteworthy utterance was "Ireland. The Pope *vs.* O'Connell and Reform!" which he published in the *Middlesex Standard* on February 27, 1845. Whittier concluded:

> What will be the final result of this "foreign interference" with the politics of Ireland, it is now difficult to conjecture. Unless the two delegates to Rome succeed in changing the views and purposes of the Pontiff, the question will come home to the Irish Repealers, whether they will obey the command of a petty sovereign of a small European State, wholly dependent for his temporal authority upon the Emperor of Austria, to submit their necks again patiently to the yoke which they

have so nearly shaken off; or whether, by hurling back the infamous requisition, and asserting their complete political independence, they will persevere in demanding full justice to Ireland. For the sake of plundered and outraged humanity, and for the sake of the cause of civil and religious liberty throughout the world, we fervently trust that when thus called upon to decide between liberty for Ireland, or blind subjection to papal authority, every Irishman will stand by his Fatherland.

Again, in a letter published in the *National Era* on February 11, 1847, Whittier made a plea which attested his alert sympathy with the Irish people. This time his note was grim: he advocated the sending of American aid to a starved people whose plight stemmed ultimately, he believed, less from the potato blight than from the fact that they were not masters of their own destiny.

## 2

For the Italian people Whittier had equal sympathy, and for Garibaldi he had unbounded admiration. Whittier perceived and unhesitatingly said that the Italian people, too, needed both political and religious freedom. Very early, in his poem "The Vaudois Teacher," which appeared in the *New England Weekly Review* on April 25, 1831, he celebrated the determined exercise of freedom of worship by members of the Waldensian church in the Cottian Alps. Translated into French and into Italian, this poem became a household favorite among the Waldenses; but not until 1875 were they aware that an American, "Jean Greenleefy Vittier," was its author. S. T. Pickard relates [5] how the Reverend J. C. Fletcher, while studying at Geneva under D'Aubigné, discovered the popularity of "The Vaudois Teacher" among his fellow students; in 1857 called on Whittier, who he learned was the author of the poem; and on returning to Italy in 1875 wrote the facts to the Moderator of the Vaudois Church. Whittier in turn received this letter, written from Torré Pellicé in the Italian Piedmont on September 13, 1875:

DEAR AND HONORED BROTHER, — I have recently learned by a letter from my friend, J. C. Fletcher, now residing in Naples, that you are the author of the charming little poem, "The Vaudois Colporteur," which was translated several years ago in French by Professor de Felicé, of Montauban, and of which there is also an excellent Italian translation, made by M. Giovanni Nicolini, Professor of our College at Torré Pellicé. There is not a single Vaudois who has received any education who cannot repeat from memory "The Vaudois Colporteur" in French or in Italian. The members of the Synod of the Vaudois Church assembled to the number of about seventy at a pastoral banquet, on Thursday evening, the 9th inst., and unanimously voted the motion which I had the honor of proposing, viz.: That we should send a very warm Christian fraternal salutation to the author of "The Vaudois Colporteur." I was intrusted with the duty of conveying this salutation to you — a duty which I fulfill with joy, expressing at the same time our gratitude to you, and also our wish to receive, if possible, from yourself the original English, which is still unknown to us, of this piece of poetry, which we so justly prize. Accept, dear and honored brother, these lines of respect and Christian love, from your sincere friend in the Lord Jesus,

J. D. CHARBONNIER,
Moderator of the Vaudois Church.[6]

Whittier's interest in the struggle for political liberty in Italy was also very strong, and for his cheering utterances on the subject he received Garibaldi's personal thanks. In his poem "The Prisoners of Naples," which first appeared in the *National Era* on October 16, 1851, Whittier cried out against the temporary fate of partisans fighting for Italian political freedom. Even more bitter and ironical was the protest in "The Dream of Pio Nono," originally published as "The Pope and Saint Peter" in the *National Era* on August 25, 1853. Here Whittier unsparingly attacked the league existing between the Pontiff and "the holy Bourbons," and the use of French troops in "the crusade Pio Nono preached" and the Oudinot ministry carried out by repressive measures. When in 1859 Whittier's English Quaker friend Joseph Sturge died, King Bomba of Naples also lay dead. Whittier at once wrote the poem "In Remembrance of Joseph Sturge," which *The Independent* first published on July 21, 1859. Whittier acidly contrasted the sorrow of the people of Birmingham over Sturge's death with the thrills of "mute Thanksgiving" which the Neapolitans felt; the simple burial of a commoner who had wrought well for humanity, in England and in other countries, with the ceremonial rites performed over Rome's "foulest gift to Heaven."

A still more bitter blast against tyranny was "From Perugia," which appeared in *The Independent* of October 27, 1859, as "Rome, 1859" and which later was lengthened from nine to thirteen mordant stanzas. Whittier's ire was here at white heat, fanned by the attitude of the Pope toward the officer who had supervised the slaughters at Perugia.[7] Finally, in the poem "Italy," which *The Independent* carried in its issue of November 22, 1860, Whittier once again admitted reluctantly that some evils in the world are so great as to force into play God's ordinance of war —

> that Nature must
> The balance of her powers adjust,
> Though with the earthquake and the storm.[8]

Over the years Whittier watched with rapt interest Garibaldi's determined fight to uproot tyranny from Italy. In his steady exchange of letters with Mrs. Lucia Gray Swett Alexander, of Boston and Florence (wife of Francis, the famous American artist), Whittier repeatedly lauded the great patriot. From Amesbury on March 4, 1867, he wrote to thank Mrs. Alexander for the souvenirs of Garibaldi and the pictures of Hiram Powers and his daughter, and he declared, "Garibaldi is one of my great enthusiasms. . . ." On June 5, 1867, he gratefully acknowledged Mrs. Alexander's procuring and sending the portrait and autograph of Garibaldi, and enclosed his own as requested. Whittier added that he was impatient to see Garibaldi replace the Pope at Rome,[9] and he must have inscribed his own picture with lines to Garibaldi, for Mrs. Alexander wrote from Abetone on July 13, 1867:

> * * * The lines to Garibaldi were magnificent — Mr. Alexander immediately learned them by heart, and often repeats them to us in our walks. * * * Garibaldi had left Florence, and gone to the grotto of Monsumauno, to try the baths for his inflammatory rheumatism, and I did not dare to trust it directed to him through the post office, so I sent the photograph with the poetry to Dolfi, who has offered to send any thing safely for me to Garibaldi. I sent him your address, for I knew he would like to write to you himself if possible, but his hands have been so much swolen, and writing very difficult, so he has desired me to express to you on his behalf, his thanks, and gratification, he seems to have been very much pleased, both with your presents, and your attentive consideration. * * *[10]

To Mrs. Alexander Whittier again, on November 22, 1869, wrote at length about Italian independence and about Garibaldi, "the true king of Italy."[11]

Finally, all of these sentiments went into the composition of Whittier's triumphant poetical tribute "Garibaldi," which was first published in the *Atlantic* of October 1869. Whittier on August 4 had transmitted an advance copy of the lines to Garibaldi through Mr. Alexander, then visiting in America,[12] and he received his reward in a letter from Mrs. Alexander dated Florence, March 16, 1870. Garibaldi had responded in his own hand to the copy of the poem which Mrs. Alexander had sent:

> Thanks for your precious letter of the 7; and for the most beautiful poetry of M. Whittier. I will express my gratitude to the great poet on the first opportunity, and with a dear salute to your family from your [Garibaldi].[13]

Because of his champion's interest in the cause of Italian independence, Whittier was asked to attend a meeting held in New York on January 12, 1871, to celebrate the freedom of Rome and the "complete unity of Italy." He sent a letter instead, as he so often had to do on such occasions. He rejoiced that the freeing of Rome and the political unification of Italy had been achieved at last without more bloodshed; that the French republic of 1849 which had crushed the Roman republic formed under Mazzini and Garibaldi was still (in the Franco-Prussian War) paying for its rottenness; and that the temporal power of the Pope had been curbed so that the people of Rome were free to choose their own government. Whittier summed up in one paragraph the reasons for his close vigil over events in Italy:

> For many years I have watched with deep interest and sympathy the popular movement on the Italian peninsula, and especially every effort for the deliverance of Rome from a despotism counting its age by centuries. I looked at these struggles of the people with little reference to their ecclesiastical or sectarian bearings. Had I been a Catholic instead of a Protestant, I should have hailed every symptom of Roman deliverance from Papal rule, occupying, as I have, the standpoint of a republican radical, desirous that all men, of all creeds, should enjoy the civil liberty which I prized so highly for myself.[14]

# 3

Whittier had an equal and long-sustained interest in the cause of freedom in Brazil, whose Emperor Pedro II started as an admirer of his writings and became a devoted friend of his. It was Dom Pedro's father who in 1822 proclaimed Brazil's independence of Portugal. The reign of Dom Pedro II, beginning in 1840 and lasting nearly a half century, was marked by enlightenment and by determined efforts to raise the level of the people. In 1830, under British pressure, Dom Pedro I had declared the slave traffic to be piracy, but the laxity of local authorities required further action in 1850, on the part of Dom Pedro II, to suppress decisively the still flourishing slave trade. Thereupon the planters and the mine owners cried out that this decision was a national calamity. With the Hydra-headed interests of the slave traffic Dom Pedro II continued to wage a hard battle, and it was necessary for the Brazilian Chambers, in 1871, to declare that slavery should be abolished throughout the empire. In 1888 the Chambers did decree total abolition.[15]

Whittier was particularly attracted to this final assault on slavery in the Americas. On his part, Dom Pedro seems to have found moral support for his fight in Whittier's writings, with which he became acquainted in 1855. He is said to have rejoiced, all his remaining years, in each new volume of Whittier's work to appear.[16]

Dom Pedro II translated into Portuguese Whittier's poem "The Cry of a Lost Soul," which made its first appearance in *The Independent* on Christmas Day, 1862, and at one time presented to him a stuffed and mounted specimen pair of the birds whose weird cry gave rise to the Indian tradition embodied in the poem.[17] Another translation into Portuguese was made by M. Pedro Luiz, and a rendering also of "The Red River Voyageur" by M. M. Lisboa, lately Brazilian Minister to the United States.[18] These facts were sent to Whittier by his friend J. C. Fletcher, writing from Boston on March 20, 1865, along with a specific request that he write a poem especially to help the anti-slavery cause in Brazil. Fletcher pleaded:

> Only if you can send a poetical word for Brazil, Pedro Luiz who translated (even better than the Emperor) & published the *Alma Perdida* (which I will send to you) will send it broad cast through out

> the Empire. He is one of the most promising of the Deputies. You to day preach for the Bible in Italy and France by the *Vaudois Colporteur*. Preach for the slave by some new poem in Brazil. . . .[19]

Whittier's "Freedom in Brazil" was published in the *Atlantic* in July 1867.

This and Whittier's other "preachments for the slave" singled him out for special attention by Dom Pedro when the Emperor came to the United States in 1876. T. W. Higginson met him at the home of George Bancroft in Newport, Rhode Island, and remembered Dom Pedro's eagerness to see Whittier, his comparative indifference to other matters.[20] Whittier equally looked forward to meeting the statesman-philanthropist, and on June 8 he wrote to J. T. Fields:

> Will the Atlantic Club have Dom Pedro as its guest? It has occurred to me that he would like it better than being toted about, looking at Boston public buildings. I would like very well to meet him, though I don't speak any language but my own, and that not very well. If he could only do as other folks do, I should like to have thee and Mrs. F. escort him here [Oak Knoll, Danvers], where we could see him apart from the fuss and feathers of ceremony, for an hour or two. But owing to the "divinity that doth hedge a king," that can't be, of course. . . . I shall not try to reach him through the double wall of Boston and court etiquette. He is a splendid man, let alone his title and rank.[21]

The reception honoring Dom Pedro was held actually by the Radical Club at its parlors in the home of the Reverend and Mrs. John T. Sargent, on Chestnut Street. Boston celebrities including the literary were there in full panoply, and various accounts of the reception were written. Mrs. Sargent best described the meeting between Dom Pedro and Whittier:

> When the Emperor arrived, the other guests had already assembled. Sending up his card, his Majesty followed it with the quickness of an enthusiastic school-boy; and his first question, after somewhat hastily paying his greetings, was for Mr. Whittier. The poet stepped forward to meet his imperial admirer, who would fain have caught him in his arms and embraced him warmly, with all the enthusiasm of the Latin race. The diffident Friend seemed somewhat abashed at so demonstrative a greeting, but with a cordial grasp of the hand drew Dom Pedro to the sofa, where the two chatted easily and with the familiarity of old friends. —
>
> * * * *

The rest of the company allowed them to enjoy their *tete-a-tete* for some half-hour, when they ventured to interrupt it, and the Emperor joined very heartily in a general conversation. . . . As he sipped his coffee, he noted the hour. "It is five o'clock, Mrs. Sargent; not my fault, only my misfortune," and, rising, he placed his arm round his brother poet's waist and gently drew him downstairs.

* * * While this tale was told, the parting of poet from poet took place unseen by any curious observer. Some did suspect that, in the privacy of that farewell, Dom Pedro asserted the continental manners; and, as Blücher kissed Wellington the evening of Waterloo, in the same way Dom Pedro celebrated his achievement in securing an interview with the poet of the Merrimac. What the company actually saw was the delighted Brazilian potentate standing erect in his open barouche, waving his hat with a seeming hurrah at the house which held his venerable friend.[22]

The surmise was right. Dom Pedro in fact did embrace his friend warmly, as Whittier, with characteristic modesty, reported incidentally in a long letter written on June 16, 1876, from Oak Knoll to Louise Chandler Moulton:

* * * I was in Boston yesterday & saw Dom Pedro. He is a very handsome man and learned & intellectual. He met me in the style of Brazilian friendliness, with a hug; and was exceedingly cordial & complimentary. * * *[23]

Miss Sparhawk adds one item which is further characteristic of Whittier. When Dom Pedro had left the Club parlors, the other guests joked Whittier about his embrace. He turned in a flash to Mrs. Sargent and said, "That was meant for thee."[24]

At any rate, Whittier himself was held firmly in the grip of the cause in Brazil which he had aided so obviously well. Ten years after he had met Dom Pedro, and two years before slavery was at last abolished in that vast domain, he received a letter of March 5, 1886, from A. J. Lamoureux, editor of *The Rio News*, Rio de Janeiro. Senhor Lamoureux regretted to report that abolition in Brazil was progressing so slowly that further help from North America would be welcomed. He implored Whittier to suggest the name of a young man who could carry on the work to which he himself had given impetus.[25]

## 4

When Kossuth, the Hungarian patriot and orator, fled to the United States in 1851, Whittier acknowledged his arrival with glowing lines published in the *National Era* on December 4. But they contained frank recognition of the fear that this son of liberty — who, while breaking "the Austrian yoke from Magyar necks," also freed the serfs and reared "the altar of his Fatherland on the firm base of freedom" — might be an embarrassment to the Abolitionist cause in this country. "Who shall be Freedom's mouthpiece?" asked Whittier — who welcome Kossuth? Not Clay and not Webster, Whittier wrote; rightly it should have been John Quincy Adams, "last of the Puritan tribunes and the best," now lying at rest in Quincy.[26] Whittier could have paid no higher tribute than this to Kossuth, whose services to freedom he fully understood and appreciated.

At the same time, remembering the lessons learned from the visit of the English Abolitionist, George Thompson, in 1834–35,[27] Whittier and others became concerned after Kossuth's first speech in New York, at Castle Garden. Whittier's concern dictated this letter which he wrote to Sumner in the same month, December 1851:

> On thy way to Washington pray see W. C. Bryant, Seward, and some other leading men, — Greeley, for instance — and caution them to see to it that the "Union savers" do not thrust their notions upon Kossuth, and call out from him speeches of the Castle Garden stamp. Naturally he would deprecate a dissolution of this Union — but he ought to understand that it is not in the slightest jeopardy — that the solicitude of the "Union savers" is all for political effect. I wish he could have a half hour's talk with Benton. I do not wish him to be mixed up in *any way* with our domestic matters. He has his mission; we ours. I hope thou wilt see the great Hungarian's reception in New York, and take part in it. I have just finished reading his English speeches, and I am deeply impressed by his wisdom and ability. God bless thee, my friend, in thy new and difficult, but glorious position.[28]

Kossuth's bearing appears to have been above reproach. When in the following spring he came to Boston, Whittier was invited by Samuel Gridley Howe to meet Kossuth. In his letter of April 30, 1852, Whittier regretted that illness kept him at home, but he now said without reservation what he thought of the Hungarian patriot: "On this wide earth there is but one Kossuth — the true hero of the time. God bless him." [29]

## 5

Such were Whittier's heroes, then, men who had a high sense of the worth of the individual; men who knew how indissolubly the liberties of people the world over are bound together in one cause. In complete contrast, he had only bitter contempt for Carlyle and Carlyle's values in "heroes and hero-worship." On May 2, 1850, the *National Era* published Whittier's article "Thomas Carlyle on the Slave Question" — an unreserved repudiation of Carlyle's sentiments expressed in "An Occasional Discourse on the Negro Question," which appeared in *Fraser's Magazine* in 1849 [XL: 670–79].

Whittier prefaced his analysis and detailed comment by saying that the discourse bore "the unmistakable impress of the Anglo-German peculiarities of Thomas Carlyle." Then he came to close grips with Carlyle for his point of view on Negro emancipation in the West Indies, and with the logical reasons supporting it. Seldom are two fundamental and diametrically opposite outlooks on man in the world better illustrated than in Whittier's central comment:

> It is difficult to treat sentiments so atrocious and couched in such offensive language with anything like respect. Common sense and unperverted conscience revolt instinctively against them. The doctrine they inculcate is that which underlies all tyranny and wrong of man towards man. It is that under which "the creation groaneth and travaileth unto this day." It is as old as sin; the perpetual argument of strength against weakness, of power against right; that of the Greek philosopher, that the barbarians, being of an inferior race, were born to be slaves to the Greeks; and of the infidel Hobbes, that every man, being by nature at war with every other man, has a perpetual right to reduce him to servitude if he has the power. It is the cardinal doctrine of what John Quincy Adams has very properly styled the Satanic school of philosophy, — the ethics of an old Norse sea robber or an Arab plunderer of caravans. * * * [30]

Whittier liked better, far better, the concept of human dignity and freedom held by another Scot who lived centuries before Carlyle's time — John Bruce, archdeacon of Aberdeen, author of *The Bruce*. In the *National Era* on January 7, 1847, Whittier wrote in encomiastic glee of "the brave old minstrel-monk." He said that in lately looking over some fragments of the poetry of England in the Middle Ages, he was "struck with the following animated and really beautiful apostrophe to Freedom":

> Ah! Fredome is a nobill thing!
> Fredome mayse man to half liking!
> Fredome all solace to man gives;
> He levys at ease who freely levys.
> A nobill heart may haif nane ease,
> Nor nocht els that may hen plese,
> Gif Fredome failyth: for free liking
> Is yearnet for ower all other thing.
> And he, that ay hase levyt free
> May nocht know weill the properte
> The angyr, nor the wretchyt doome
> That couplyt is to foule thraldome!

Bruce's lines carried over the centuries to Whittier not only a free man's sentiments which he himself always held to be true, but the basic historical fact of which he had long been aware: that brave hearts and strong wills are needed in all ages and all parts of the world to wage the common fight for freedom. In his own day Whittier fought the long fight at home, and he held up the hands of men everywhere who believed that liberty is possible for all of the sons of Adam.

# XVII

# Friend of Labor

WHITTIER'S INTEREST in the improvement of mankind had the added and particular point of an abiding concern with the welfare of men who work with their hands. He was himself born to life on the farm, and as long as he lived he had a deep-based respect for it. Like his father, and like other worthy men of Haverhill, he fashioned slippers in odd moments, when he was young, as a means of getting funds for special needs. Partly from youthful pride but chiefly from a genuine and, as it proved, a life-long partisanship for working people, Whittier in the period of his first editorship declared himself militantly on their side.[1] There, on fundamental principles, he remained always.

If in late life he was not a paladin of labor — no longer indeed, because of declining energies, a militant crusader in any cause — it remains true that he was a faithful friend of the workingman. It is further true that in management-labor disputes, which arose even before the Civil War, he was pro-public. His sympathies as between labor and management were unequivocally on the side of labor, but on grounds of reason he believed that legislation should be passed which would protect the consuming public, *and* capital *and* labor. He believed, in short, that strikes are futile and wasteful, that they should if possible be prevented.

Whittier's guide in this matter, as in so many which were important in his life, was his Quaker dislike of strife; his belief in the ability of government, representing the will of the people, to protect the interests of all of them peaceably.

# 1

Whittier's brief term as editor of the *American Manufacturer* in 1829 gave him a close-up view of the "American System," and he grasped clearly the fundamental nature of manufacturing and industry. He regarded it as inevitable that the future economy of New England should be based on manufacturing, and in turn he reasoned that the strongest asset of any industrial establishment must be its trained workers. Here he was acutely aware of the probability and the dangers of exploitation.

The tone and point of the six editorials in his "mechanics" series, and of another entitled "Aristocracy," [2] was anti-capitalist and pro-workingman. Whittier said explicitly that entrenched wealth, waxing upon the labor of diligent craftsmen, was anti-democratic. He was entirely aware that, even then, cheap labor was being imported from Europe, and that the health, security, and general welfare of the workers was of far less concern to "the manufacturing interest" than the demand for profits. Whittier's heart and his native common sense taught him his labor economics. In his view, nothing that was not fair and equitable to the workers who produced goods would in the long run profit the manufacturers either.

Along with Bryant and other sharp observers of the time, Whittier very early approved of the principle of collective bargaining. He followed intently the campaign in the courts (including the Supreme Court) in 1835–36 which momentarily curbed the union movement. In particular he was alert to the significance of the decision rendered on June 6, 1836, by Judge Ogden Edwards, of New York, against the Society of Journeymen Tailors, who had struck to win recognition of an increased wage scale. Judge Edwards levied total fines of $1150 against the twenty leading tailors who had been arrested on charges of criminal conspiracy, for striking; and he stigmatized the unions as "illegal combinations." [3]

Whittier on July 23 in the *Haverhill Gazette* spoke his sentiments in biting terms:

> We have been desirous for some time past to say a word or two in regard to the decision of Judge Edwards of New York, in the case of certain journeymen tailors, who have been indicted, tried and convicted before the criminal court of the city, of New York for a con-

spiracy to procure higher wages. The crime is thus described by Judge Edwards. "These men are charged with entering into *a conspiracy not to work for any master which did not give them certain rates which they demanded*, or for any master who employed men that worked for a less rate, or who were not members of their society." In favor of this most absurd charge of "conspiracy" the judge argues at length. So then it has come to this, that in a land of equal rights a laborer cannot fix the amount of his wages in connection with his fellow laborer, without being charged as a criminal before our courts of law. The merchants may agree upon their prices; the lawyers upon their fees: the physicians upon their charges: the manufacturers upon the wages given to their operatives; but the LABORER shall not consult his interest and fix the price of his own toil and skill. If this be LAW, it is unjust, oppressive and wicked. It ought not to disgrace the statute book of a republican state. It places the Northern laborer too nearly upon a level with the SLAVE of the South. According to the argument of Judge Edwards a refusal to work unless for certain wages, on the part of the journeymen, would materially affect the *convenience* and *advantage* of the employer, and is *therefore* to be considered as criminal. — We will put a parallel case. In this town and vicinity, a large number of our shoe-makers quit their workshops during the haying season, and our manufacturers are subjected to no small inconvenience and difficulty by the loss of their workmen. According to Judge Edwards' opinion; the latter are to be considered as criminals, for abandoning their employers in the summer season. The whole doctrine is borrowed from the feudal aristocracy of Europe. If carried into practice generally, as it has been in New York, the condition of the free and happy laborers of our country will be little better than that of the Hungarian Miner, or the Polish serf. — We are no advocate of disorderly conduct on the part of any portion of the community. — But to brand laborers as criminals for *peaceably* requiring an increase of their wages, we hold to be an outrage on the rights of man, and a disgrace to a community professing to be free.[4]

In Lowell, vastly better than in Haverhill or in Boston, Whittier was able to see manufacturing at close range, with all of its features in clear relief. This "City of a Day," created almost over night by the magic of power looms, both attracted and repelled him. In spite of the fact that "marvellously here have art and labor wrought modern miracles," and that a stranger "seems treading on the outer circle of the millennium of steam engines and cotton mills," Whittier was true to his nature in weighing the spectacle of the city of Lowell in human terms. Plainly he doubted that industrialism would be able to transform "the great forces of Nature" into the means of relieving all of man's wants and the ills of his existence. Whittier frankly raised the question:

> * * * Grinding on, each in his iron harness, invisible, yet shaking, by his regulated and repressed power, his huge prison-house from basement to capstone, is it true that the genii of mechanism are really at work here, raising us, by wheel and pulley, steam and water-power, slowly up that inclined plane from whose top stretches the broad tableland of promise?

And he answered with a firm negative the related question whether work, a gospel to Poor Richard and a deity to Carlyle, was "precisely calculated for the redemption of humanity." Whittier was decades ahead of professional economists in emphasizing the serious issue of the relief and leisure, rather than wage slavery, which man ought to expect from the machine. He declared:

> * * * Labor, graduated to man's simple wants, necessities, and unperverted tastes, is doubtless well; but all beyond this is weariness to flesh and spirit. Every web which falls from these restless looms has a history more or less connected with sin and suffering, beginning with slavery and ending with overwork and premature death.[5]

These were first thoughts, published in the *Middlesex Standard* in August, 1844, in the second and third issues of the Liberty paper which Whittier edited. Closer acquaintance with industrialism and serious reflection upon it evoked "The Lighting Up" in the October 24 issue of the *Standard.* Whittier wrote the article on the evening of the twentieth after having seen, from the northern end of the bridge over the Merrimac to Dracut, the brilliant effect of the season's initial illumination of the mills for night work. He said at once that the beauty of the spectacle was an illusion. The hard reality was that now "for half a weary year, from the bell-call of morning twilight to half-past seven in the evening, with brief intermissions for two hasty meals, the operatives will be confined to their tasks." For Whittier the issue was utterly clear: whether man was to be the master or the slave of the machine. He went on:

> In this way the working-day in Lowell is eked out to an average throughout the year of twelve and a half hours. This is a serious evil, demanding the earnest consideration of the humane and philanthropic. Both classes — the employer and the employed — would in the end be greatly benefited by the general adoption of the "ten-hour system," although the one might suffer a slight diminution in daily wages and the other in yearly profits. . . . Health is too often a matter of secondary consideration. Gain is the great, all-absorbing object.

Whittier blamed the operatives almost equally with the operators for prevailing conditions. Most of the workers, he regretted, had come to Lowell from many points, with no regard for it as their "continuing city," and solely in the hope of quick gain. What Whittier felt in 1844 a weighty part of twentieth-century economic thinking has attempted to prove — that the drawing of farmers and of people from small towns to overcrowded industrial cities is in most cases a human mistake, and all in all a national disservice. Among the "undoubtedly many evils connected with the working of these mills" Whittier saw only one genuine virtue — the fact that "here, more than in any other mechanical employment, the labor of women is placed essentially upon an equality with that of men." [6] As a Friend he was born to the principle of equal rights among the sexes. Now, from experience and conviction, he became an articulate advocate of the rights of the workingman.

## 2

It would be wrong, however, to think of Whittier as in fact or by profession a leader in the labor movement. That he was not. In the fight for his concept of a democratic society, his chief interest and commitment was to the cause of Abolition — eliminating the injustice of Negro slavery. That undemocratic system he fought with a reformer's passion and zeal and with moral strength which always far outran his physical limits. He deprecated "wage slavery" but thought it the less immediate evil; argued against the unequal rewards of the industrial system, but chiefly upheld the dignity and worth of the labor of free men.

This was his precise purpose in writing the six "Songs of Labor" which he contributed to the *Democratic Review* and to the *National Era* in 1845–47:

"The Shoemakers," "The Fishermen," "The Lumbermen," "The Ship-Builders," "The Drovers," and "The Huskers" — all of whom, significantly, were manual laborers. In these imaginative and sympathetic pieces Whittier was ahead of Whitman in celebrating the American workingman. The burden of the series, and proof of the touch of Yankee strenuosity in Whittier himself, appeared in "The Drovers":

> There's life alone in duty done,
> And rest alone in striving. [7]

He emphasized the purpose of these poems in writing to a friend on November 8, 1845: "My 'Songs of Labor' are written for the working, *acting*, rather than *thinking* people. I wish to invest labor with some degree of beauty." [8]

To this theme he returned often, as for instance in the *National Era* of May 25, 1848, in a notice of Lucy Larcom's latest book of poems. Whittier again elaborated upon the dignity of labor, and once more sounded the anti-aristocratic note.

Four years later Whittier had a prime opportunity, in the Amesbury-Salisbury mill strike, to publicize his convictions on the subject of labor and to speak for the ten-hour day for factory hands — a subject then being agitated in Massachusetts. The agent of the Salisbury Manufacturing Company resigned after thirty years' service, and a man from Vermont took up his duties on May 1, 1852. On May 31 the new agent had notices posted in the several mills which lengthened the already long work day by a half-hour. For twenty-five years the mills had opened at 5.00 A.M. and closed at 7.00 P.M., allowing recesses of a half-hour for breakfast, one hour for dinner, and (for male workers only) the privilege of leaving the mills for fifteen minutes both forenoon and afternoon, nominally for luncheon. The new agent's order, effective at once, abolished the luncheon privilege.[9]

On June 1 about one hundred men left the mills as usual for luncheon, and on their return were all discharged. The ensuing excitement caused a succession of public meetings to be held, both in Amesbury and in Salisbury (in effect one town, separated only by the narrow Powow River). There were also fruitless conferences with the company's directors in Boston and its agent in Salisbury. In sympathy with the discharged men, the girls employed in the mills also quit work.

On June 5 a mass meeting of citizens adopted five resolutions which, according to a descriptive pamphlet, were "drawn up by John G. Whittier." The last and most significant of the five reads:

*Resolved*, That the citizens of this village, hitherto justly proud of the reputation of its manufacturing establishments, showing as they did that humanity and liberality towards the operative is the best economy for the capitalist, have rejoiced in the high character of the men and women employed, and it would be a matter of serious regret on the part of all classes of our citizens if the present policy is persisted in, and a proportion of those whose industry and good conduct have enlarged the dividends and established the honorable reputation of the Salisbury Company, are driven elsewhere for labor and their places supplied by a vagrant and unsettled class.

Other resolutions were passed at a June 15 meeting of the qualified voters of Amesbury, and the stiffening of tone which they reveal was heightened in a final circular drawn up subsequent to a voters' meeting in Salisbury. Whittier's name heads the list of Amesbury members of the joint committee which prepared and signed the circular, and the tone of the whole and the special diction of particular passages suggest the measure of his active interest in its preparation. The circular was a plea for political action, in which Whittier always deeply believed. In order to cure "the evils growing out of the unrestricted hours of daily labor in manufacturing corporations," the Amesbury-Salisbury committee solicited "the aid of their fellow-citizens throughout the state" in seeking regulatory action by the next general session of the legislature.

Attention was directed especially to a minority report and a bill, submitted to the most recent General Court by a member from Lowell, "which embodies substantially our own views." By three graduated steps the bill would have enforced the ten-hour work day, after July 4, 1853, on all companies incorporated by or under the laws of Massachusetts. The Amesbury-Salisbury committee cited precedent for a prohibitory law by the General Court — law which would regulate the conduct of both capital and labor. The last sentence of the circular, however, was conciliatory, and it had a tone characteristic of Whittier:

Actuated by no feeling of hostility to the manufacturing interest, and considering that the interests of the employer and laborer are identical, we ask for nothing more than the exercise of that true conservatism, which, while carefully guarding the interests of CAPITAL, does not neglect the higher obligation of the protection of MEN.

This circular accomplished nothing immediately, for the directors and the agent of the Salisbury Manufacturing Company were adamant in their stand against the strikers. Judge Cate recalled fifty years later that the strike resulted only "in the old operatives leaving, and in the employment of a large number of foreigners, which entirely changed the character of the operatives in Amesbury." [10]

Whittier, on his part, took the long-term view of the strike which experience had taught him to take in matters of social change. In a letter of July 8, 1852, to Ophelia Underwood, Secretary of Female Operatives of Salisbury Manufacturing Company, regretting his inability to attend their levee arranged for the relief of the discharged workers, he said:

> I have received thy note of this morning, inviting me to attend the Levee this evening. I regret that I am obliged to decline the invitation, and yet I am not the less gratified by it, and the kind terms in which it has been conveyed. So far as intention goes, this does me no more than justice, since, in my efforts against the great social and political wrong of the country, I have not overlooked more immediate evils.
>
> I have long been convinced that the term of daily labor in manufacturing companies should be abridged. I would prefer that it should be done by the voluntary action of owners and directors, but as this is scarcely to be hoped for, the legislature must provide a remedy.
>
> If the unpleasant state of things in this place shall have the effect to call the attention of the people to the subject, and bring about the ten hour system, I am persuaded none of us will regret any temporary inconvenience or loss, in consequence of it. With a very few exceptions, the operatives have the cordial sympathy of our citizens. This fact is a strong testimony to their good conduct and respectability. It shows, too, that ours is essentially a republican community. We have no privileged class, no petty village aristocracy, proud of its own worthlessness, and despising the more useful and, in all practical matters, more intelligent members of society. In this respect ours is a model manufacturing village. Long may it continue so.
>
> With kind wishes for the welfare of thyself and thy friends, and that, in your present position, you may know how to "*overcome evil with good*," and temper the firmness of principle with charity, courtesy and Christian forbearance, I am very truly thy friend.[11]

## 3

That letter precisely indicates both the strength and the weakness of Whittier's thinking on the complex problems implicit in an industrial society. For their solution he set too large store by faith and reason; took altogether too little into account the driving power of the profit motive upon human conduct. His conception of "a model manufacturing village" was ideal, but he was uneasily aware that even now in Amesbury the very forces were hard at work which he had condemned repeatedly since 1829 — economic forces which bred an aristocracy of wealth based on maldistribution of the goods and profits created by industry. Whittier saw the old stability and beauty of life in Amesbury dissipated under the impact of it. Clearly, not alone the breaking of his home ties, in 1864 and 1876, but the increasing "factory atmosphere" of Amesbury made him seek haven at Oak Knoll.[12]

Nothing in the record, however, indicates that he ever wavered in his sympathy for people who work and produce. His sense of belonging to them was strong and natural. As farmer, as shoemaker, as editor he had won a union card for his lifetime. None of these employments gave him wealth, and he lived more than two thirds of his eighty-five years in comparative poverty which at times was grim and pressing. He knew what it was to live on five hundred dollars a year while supporting his mother, his aunt, and his sister Elizabeth, and even in his later years he said, "A dollar has looked large so long that I cannot get over the feeling."[13] But the fact is that Whittier, with only limited aid on possibly two occasions, managed by careful economy to stave off extreme poverty. And far from ever being out of work, he had for sixty-five years of his life the quite unmanageable problem of doing all of it which came to his able hands.

One other fact is significant. Whittier disliked extremes. He distrusted ultimate things, barring only natural death. He was unalterably opposed to capital punishment. He thundered against the ousting of the Indians from their lands. By birth and by religious conviction he opposed war. Even the abolition of slavery he at times thought could be accomplished without extreme measures, and in fact he witnessed its final condemnation by a decree of the President and the action of state and national legislatures. These were deliberate processes of government.

The war which made it possible to carry them out was an extreme measure which Whittier deplored. ("Their senseless brawl," he called it in "The Watchers.") Eight years after it had been ended he wrote to Elizabeth Stuart Phelps:

> * * * The war has demoralized all — the contagion of its shoddy extravagance has reached everybody. The church and the world are alike infected. It has entered cradle and nursery, and turned the sweet simplicity and grace of childhood into a fashionable scarecrow. * * *[14]

So with the problems of capital and labor. Whittier plainly saw on the one hand the accumulation of extreme wealth, on the other the low wages and bad working conditions — above all the insecurity of employment. He yet preferred to believe that faith and reason would solve all problems of human relations, and he was reluctant to admit the fact of economic class warfare. The point of view which he expressed in 1830 ("... we hate mortally to see those who should live like brothers of one family fall to quarrelling and fist-clenching. ...")[15] was in truth his permanent outlook on life.

Hence industrial strife and the necessity of the strike never appealed to his reason. Evidently some time in the eighteen-eighties when great strikes were raging he wrote to his friend Daniel Ricketson, of New Bedford:

> My sympathies are naturally with the laboring class, amidst which I was born and grew up to manhood. But I confess that I have never known much benefit to result to that class from "strikes." I do not know enough of this particular movement to feel authorized in expressing a decided opinion.[16]

If by "this particular movement" Whittier meant the labor-union movement generally, his attitude is understandable, perhaps even praiseworthy. He was never a man to set his hand to things which he did not feel competent to carry through to accomplishment. In spite of his wish that capital and labor might get on together productively and peaceably, his hard common sense must have told him that vast problems were involved which defied easy solution and forbade careless talk. What he did venture on the subject late in life — as, for example, the double sonnet "The Problem" which he wrote in 1877, the year in which the deadly general strike broke out against the railroads[17] — was in the main uninspired, and no social contribution. "Poetic insight" failed him here, just as all solutions put forward by socio-economic experts for one hundred years or more have had only temporary effect or none. Even these specialists might at times be persuaded he had a point in suggesting that the Son of God alone was wise enough to be conciliator between capital and labor:

> * * * Solution there is none
> Save in the Golden Rule of Christ alone.[18]

It may be said with confidence, then, that Whittier knew his limitations, and with certainty that, after expending enormous strength on the Abolition cause, he was tired. He confessed in a letter of April 7, 1878, to Elizabeth Stuart Phelps:

> * * * Against all my natural inclinations, I have been fighting for the "causes," half my life. "Woe is me, my mother," I can say with the old prophet, "who hast borne me a man of strife and contention." I have suffered dreadfully from coarseness, self-seeking vanity, and asinine stupidity among associates, as well as from the coldness or open hostility, and, worst, the ridicule of the outside world, but I now see that it was best, and that I needed it all.[19]

And in the same key and year he wrote Gail Hamilton:

> * * * I read thy political papers with a rather confusing sense of admiration and regret, wonder and pride in the power exhibited, but with frequent misgivings as to the justice of some of thy strictures. For myself, I do not feel called upon to enter into these present contests. The game seems to me hardly worth the candle. The issues seem small and poor. I suppose I am growing old, and am disposed to ask for peace in my day. I have had enough of fighting in the old days.[20]

Few people will assert that Whittier had not earned "peace in his day," or quarrel overmuch with William Dean Howells's comment:

> In the quiet of his country home at Danvers he apparently read all the magazines, and kept himself fully abreast of the literary movement, but I doubt if he so fully appreciated the importance of the social movement. Like some others of the great anti-slavery men, he seemed to imagine that mankind had won itself a clear field by destroying chattel slavery, and he had no sympathy with those who think that the man

who may any moment be out of work is industrially a slave. This is not strange; so few men last over from one reform to another that the wonder is that any should, not that one should not.[21]

Whittier, it is only fair to say, did not believe that industrial slavery was admissible in a system of "free enterprise." A strong part of his argument against Negro slavery was that, economically, it was ruining the South, and that "in the free states labor is reputable." [22] So he replied in 1833 to the editors of the Richmond *Jeffersonian and Times* who had attacked him and his pamphlet *Justice and Expediency*, and so he always believed. In the final paragraph of his editorial announcement "To the Public" on July 25, 1844, in the first issue of the *Middlesex Standard*, he said:

> * * * It is to us a source of real satisfaction to know that we are in the midst of a community of working men and women, who know how to appreciate the great anti-slavery truth that the laborer is worthy of his hire, and to apply it to the condition of the slaves of the South. With such a community our habits and associations enable us heartily to sympathise. We aim to promote the prosperity of the Northern laborer, by removing its greatest obstacle — that system of coerced labor, the evil influences of which reach every section of our country, and are felt upon every farm and in every workshop. To the Liberty-loving citizens — the working men and women of Middlesex, we appeal for support in our enterprize, in the hope and belief that they will rally around a *Standard* which bears for its motto, "FREE LABOR AND EQUAL RIGHTS."

It is noteworthy that Lincoln, in his message to Congress in December, 1861, took precisely the stand on free labor that Whittier long had taken: "labor is prior to, and independent of, capital." Lincoln's argument, which had world-wide effect, went on:

> Now, there is no such relation between capital and labor as assumed, nor is there any such thing as a free man being fixed for life in the condition of a hired laborer. Both these assumptions are false, and all inferences from them are groundless.[23]

Whittier, in brief, decried injustice and inequality among the partners of industry, capital and labor; but he believed, as Lincoln did, that enterprising workers could get ahead and win rewards. And he believed in collective bargaining — that is, in unionism — if not in costly and bloody strikes employed as a weapon to enforce wage demands.

Viewed under this aspect, Whittier merely acted according to his lights — as his lifetime practice was in all matters — in declining to join other public figures in petitioning the Governor of Illinois to commute the sentences of certain anarchists who had been condemned to death. During the Chicago Haymarket riot of May 4, 1886, bombs had been thrown and human lives taken. The anarchists at the scene of the bombing were arrested, tried by jury, and convicted and sentenced for murder. On some of them the sentence was carried out. People on the spot, however, were of two minds whether the men should have been tried for murder or for conspiracy.

At a distance of a thousand miles Whittier was asked, on the basis of evidence which he did not possess, to request the Governor to give clemency to those of the anarchists who had not already been executed. On November 1, 1887, Howells wrote Whitter:

> I enclose a paper on the anarchists by a very good and very able young minister of Chicago. The conclusions reached there I reached many weeks and even months ago. The fact is, those men were sentenced for murder when they ought to have been indicted for conspiracy.
>
> I believe the mind of the Governor of Illinois is turning towards clemency; several things indicate this.
>
> A letter from you would have great weight with him. I beseech you to write it, and do what one great and blameless man may do to avert the greatest wrong that ever threatened our fame as a nation.
>
> Even if these men had done the crime which our barbarous laws punish with homicide, should a plea for mercy be wanting from *you?* * * * [24]

This astute letter put Whittier in a dilemma. It appears that his repugnance for labor agitation ending in public violence outweighed even his lifelong stand against capital punishment. He at any rate penned no letter; he deferred to Howells's ability to write the Governor with better heart and effect. But nothing happened until more than eight months after Whittier had died. It remained for John P. Altgeld (later justly celebrated by Vachel Lindsay in "The Eagle That Is Forgotten") to act, on June 26, 1893, very soon after his inauguration as governor. He commuted the sentences of the anarchists still in prison, convinced that the jury had not been fairly picked and that the condemned men, far from having been proved guilty of instigating or committing the crime, had been made scapegoats.[25]

A *New York Tribune* reporter interviewed Whittier, and one part of the published conversation brought a friendly letter of objection from Howells. Whittier replied, two days after his eighty-first birthday:

> I have not the "Tribune" letter to refer to. I saw it & hastily glanced at it in the midst of interviewers and callers on my birthday, and do not recollect the exact words of the passage referred to in thy note.
>
> I see that I should have stated so clearly that I could not be misunderstood the facts of the case, as I remember them, viz: that I was asked to join thee in petitioning the Governor of Illinois to commute the sentence of the anarchists. I think thee stated that thee thought they had not had a fair trial, and that this induced thee to urge the petition.
>
> In conversing with the writer of the letter, I think I said that I supposed thee thought that the extreme penalty of death might cause the victims to be regarded as martyrs; and I mentioned that thy interest in Count Tolstoi's non-resistance views, with which I have much sympathy myself, may have influenced thee in this case.
>
> The writer of the "Tribune" letter is a truthful & honorable gentleman, and if his version of the matter is incorrect it is doubtless owing to a lack of explicitness on my part, in a desultory conversation.
>
> Our relations as authors and friends have been too intimate and pleasant to allow me to even unintentionally misrepresent thee. I would be the last person to believe that the crime charged upon the accused persons is less detestable and awful to thee than to myself.[26]

## 4

Whittier in 1887 wrote to a friend: "I feel sometimes that I have a word to say that is needed, but I have not felt strong enough to write, so the world must get on without my shoulder to the wheel, and I guess it will." [27] Even so late in life he spoke firmly on matters of governmental policy and on public issues, especially to Republican officials who, he had reason to believe, might heed advice or warning which came from him. His dominant modesty did not blind him to the fact that he was himself now an "assured voice," listened to with respect which was at times deferential. He had earned this respect by the breadth of his attitude toward social reform, and by his avoidance — so far as he himself could manage — of personal animosities among colleagues, in the interest of concentrating on the issues and causes at stake. Barrett Wendell concluded later that

". . . although a lifelong and earnest reformer, he is the least irritating of reformers to those who chance not to agree with him." [28]

Whittier himself followed the advice which he gave to General Frémont in 1864: there is a time to act, and a time to stand aside. In effect, during the period of the nation's great industrial expansion following the Civil War, he professed no competence to deal with the vastly complicated problems of social justice which, under a capitalistic economy, seemed to multiply endlessly. What he really craved, deep in his heart, was simplicity — the simplicity, now forever gone, of "the olden time." Then at least, he knew by the experience of his own life, no man who was willing to work would want for work. Few who had the old virtues of thrift and sobriety would be without means, at the mercy of other people or of society. What Whittier really thought of industrial society is illustrated with particular clarity in a letter which he wrote to Mrs. Fields on November 7, 1889:

> There is very little of actual suffering which may not be traced to intemperance, idleness, and utter lack of economy, wasteful and careless of the future when wages are good. We need the gospel of Poor Richard's Almanac sadly. Last summer, in Conway, I found a town without a poor-house, because there was nobody that needed it. There were no rich men, but the village was a model of neatness, every house freshly painted and comfortable. The young clergyman had a salary of $400 a year, and I was told that the cost of living was less than $300 per family. There was no liquor allowed in the place. The small savings bank had a deposit of $80,000. With economy, sobriety, and the absence of ostentation, display, and extravagance, the example of Conway might be imitated in our country towns, and to some extent in our cities. But I suppose this is not to be expected. The poor we shall always have with us — until Bellamy's millennium.[29]

The echo of these words did not die when they were uttered. It came full-voiced, a half century later, from Henry Ford — prime exponent of American industrialism, but also a firm believer in a simple life rooted in the soil, and in precisely the kind of personal habits that Whittier himself possessed and advocated. There, perhaps, the comparison ends. But if Whittier did not confidently advance prophetic proposals which might solve the unprecedented problems of the new industrial society, all the evidence shows clearly that he was a profound believer in the dignity of labor, and that he was the unwavering friend of the man who works with his hands.

# XVIII

## Gentleman of the Press

WHITTIER'S ATTITUDES on social questions and public issues were manifested at least as much in his newspaper prose as in his letters and his verse. This body of his writing was voluminous — he once remarked, correctly, that he thought it would fill ten octavo volumes [1] — and in a sense it was an exhibition rack of his social opinions. Like Henry Adams, who regarded the press as a pulpit for men who would be neither preachers nor professors,[2] Whittier used it as a vehicle of opinion primarily, and after that as a conveyor of news. He was ten times an editor, half of the number as conductor of or regular contributor to anti-slavery media, and not once was he connected with a daily newspaper chiefly concerned with the round-the-clock grist of news.

With few breaks, Whittier served the periodical press over a span of thirty-one years, and in these rôles:

*American Manufacturer*, Boston. Editor. January 8–August 6, 1829.

*Essex Gazette*, Haverhill. Editor. January 2–July 10, 1830.

*New England Weekly Review*, Hartford. Editor. July 19, 1830–January 2, 1832.

*Essex Gazette*, Haverhill. Editor. May 7–December 17, 1836.

*The Emancipator, and Anti-Slavery Record*, New York. Acting Editor. June–August, 1837.

*The Pennsylvania Freeman*, Philadelphia. Editor. March 15, 1838–February 20, 1840.

*The American and Foreign Anti-Slavery Reporter*, New York. Contributing Editor. September–October, 1841.

*Middlesex Standard*, Lowell. Editor. July 25, 1844–March 13, 1846.

*Essex Transcript*, Amesbury and Salisbury. Acting Editor. 1844–1846.

*The National Era*, Washington. Contributing Editor. January, 1847–January, 1860.

# 1

Whittier's settled practice, on assuming charge of a paper, was to make a clear statement of his editorial creed. Six times he did so. The half-dozen leaders which he thus wrote were, though generally long, signally lucid; and they make a credo which does as much honor to American journalism as the famous "Here shall the Press the People's right maintain, unawed by influence, and unbribed by gain." In Whittier's code, *right* became simply *freedom*.

His grasp of the function of a free press in a free society was as firm and clear as that of Jefferson, to whom as authority he delighted to refer. In essence, this function was to promote and support right, while in all things opposing and exposing wrong. Whittier made it clear that on stated principles he would conduct his business without fear or favor, but he also made clear the need for criticism. On a wave of it, which he recognized frankly, he bowed out at the end of 1836 from his second brief editorship of the *Haverhill Gazette*.

Whittier believed that in this country an editor was obliged to make his paper the "vehicle of correct and honorable principles," [3] to —

Print the important news of the day, political or otherwise.

"Speak with entire freedom and frankness of all parties," approving as far as possible, censuring only when censure is believed warranted, and not being merely a partizan of the Opposition.

Stand firmly for the preservation of guaranteed human rights.

Promote the welfare of mankind.

Produce a clean sheet and aid public morality and the cause of "rational religion," without sectarianism.

Print nothing but the truth, and that resolutely.

Whittier's longest and most typical "exposition of views and purposes" was published in the *Haverhill Gazette* on May 7, 1836, and it ran the gamut.[4] But not less significant was his earlier editorial "To the Public," which he published on January 2, 1830, at the start of his first tour of duty on the *Gazette*. Two parts of it are particularly illuminating. Whittier first stated his political position, and then continued:

> On subjects connected with morality, I shall never hesitate to speak openly and firmly, whenever the occasion may require it — whenever it is probable that my humble exertions may facilitate the progress of the reforming spirit, which is abroad in our land.

And he ended, with meaning and emphasis:

> Enough — if I have promised little, there will be less room for disappointment. Dependant as I feel myself upon the public, and desirous as I am of securing the good will of all; I shall never forego my deliberate opinions, and settled purposes, to insure the favor, or escape the enmity of any individual.

Whittier's social philosophy, spread to view times without end in his newspaper writings, was indeed too active to be generally ingratiating. His chosen task was not merely to comfort the poor and weak but —

> To brave Opinion's settled frown,
> From ermined robe and saintly gown,
> While wrestling reverenced Error down.[5]

From his anti-slavery experience — especially in 1833 when his pamphlet *Justice and Expediency* raised a storm among Southern editors, and in 1836 when his forthright advocacy of Abolition cost him local Whig support and his editorship of the *Haverhill Gazette* — he knew how unpopular reform can be. In "The Scottish Reformers," which he first published in the *Middlesex Standard* on November 21 and 28, 1844, he commented:

> . . . it is evermore the case that the right word when first uttered is an unpopular and denied one. . . . there is, after all, but one way of doing the world good, and unhappily that way the world does not like; for it consists in telling it the very thing which it does not wish to hear.[6]

The trumpet blast against slavery did not, for many years, resound sweetly in the public ear, even in the North, but Whittier saw it at last become a triumphant strain. His first tentative soundings in the *American Manufacturer* reached a majestic pitch in his contributions to the *National Era*. That main concern of his "reformatory journalism," however, did not hinder him from speaking forcefully, again and again, on other subjects which also concerned him from the time of his first appearance in the columns of the *Newburyport Herald* in 1826. The range of his interests in reform, distinctly marked out from the time of his editorial bow on the *American Manufacturer* almost to the end of his life, was broad. Especially in that Boston Whig sheet and in the *Haverhill Gazette* he spoke often in behalf of temperance.[7]

In addition, Whittier was stern in his editorial pronouncements against war, imprisonment for debt, the denial of the vote to women, capital punishment, unjust treatment of the Indians, and neglect of the blind. All of these were among the "benevolent reforms" such as engaged the attention of other public figures of the time, including Walt Whitman.[8]

In fighting for the causes and principles in which he believed, Whittier was no "gentle Quaker." Eminently in his Hartford days when he edited the *New England Weekly Review*, he knocked opponents in the head with flinty paragraphs which gave off the sound of clashing steel. As shepherd of his reforms he was objectively willing to risk enmity, though he was far from welcoming it. He specified, at the end of "To the Public" in the *Haverhill Gazette* on May 7, 1836:

> In pursuing the course I have marked out, I may give offence to many — but, if I know my heart it shall not be intentionally. And, if causelessly excited, it is my fervent prayer that their enmity may occasion themselves as little uneasiness as I feel assured it will myself.

That was his way. Whittier could be combative over issues, but not with persons. He stood apart from the practitioners of the "personal journalism" in his time, and governed his own editing by a high ethical code distinguished, among other things, by generosity to opponents.[9] Of this canon of good journalism, from which he departed seldom, an especially good statement appeared in the *Middlesex Standard* on August 1, 1844, the second issue which Whittier edited:

> Our acknowledgments are due to the organs of the Whig and Democratic parties in this city for their personally kind and respectful notices of our sheet. We trust that however widely we may feel ourselves called upon to differ with them on matters pertaining to the great question of Slavery, we shall not on our part be found wanting in personal good feeling towards honorable opponents, nor in that courtesy which ought to characterize the conducter of a public press, under all

circumstances. Earnest, ardent and enthusiastic in our support of sentiments sincerely entertained, we may at times forget the true Christian rule of action, but, if we know our own heart, we shall stand ready to acknowledge our errors, whenever they are made apparent to us.

Very quickly he had occasion to make good his promise, and to demonstrate one more of his editorial canons which stand out from ordinary practice. On September 26, 1844, in the *Standard* he published a full and frank *erratum*, an admission which is an interesting journalistic document, very nearly unique:

CORRECTION

The Philadelphia Gazette and other journals concur in pronouncing the extract to which the annexed note refers, a sheer forgery. The body of the extract, according to the Bay State Democrat, was taken from Featherstonhaugh's Excursion through the Slave States, Harpers' edition, page 36, with the fraudulent addition of the branding story. We take the earliest opportunity our columns afford to put the matter right with our readers, by re-publishing the following note:

*To the Editor of the* [Lowell] *Advertiser:*

In the Middlesex Standard of last week, I copied, with such indignant comments as the atrocity related naturally called forth, an article from the Ithaca, N.Y., Chronicle, in which was given what purported to be an extract from the journal of a gentleman traveller in the U.S., charging the Hon. James K. Polk with branding his slaves with the initials of his name, and I have just learned that the whole matter is a FORGERY. Unwilling to do injustice to any man — and believing that, as a slave-holder, James K. Polk, in common with Henry Clay, has already sins enough to answer for, without charging him falsely — I wish to avail myself of the earliest issue of thy paper to make a prompt correction of the error into which I have been led by the authors of this base forgery.

As a Liberty man, I have no motive to misrepresent either the Whig or Democratic candidates. — Both are slave-holders — both are hostile to emancipation in any form, and as such they are on a perfect equality with each other, and have no claim to abolition support.

Respectfully, thy friend,

JOHN G. WHITTIER.

50 Merrimack st., 23d, 9th mo., 1844.

## 2

Whittier's grasp of the responsibilities of the press in a democracy was something more than matched by his insistence upon exercising the guarantee of its freedom under the first article of the Bill of Rights. He knew Milton, in particular the *Areopagitica*, and in 1866 he had the pleasure of writing: "Let me thank the publishers of 'Milton's Prose,' for the great compliment of the dedication. Milton's prose has long been my favorite reading. My whole life has felt the influence of his writings." [10] If not with the same surpassing skill, Whittier blew the trumpet of freedom with quite as much zeal as Milton.

During the three decades preceding the outbreak of the Civil War, probably no voice in the North was raised more forcefully than Whittier's against even the thought of curbing freedom of expression and freedom of assembly. Whittier's many utterances on the subject were hot and piercing, at times sulphurous. Whoever — president, governor, religious leader, any one at all — proposed restrictions on freedom of expression was berated by Whittier as an enemy of democracy.[11] He returned, with a persistence which the nature of the times warranted, to the danger of losing *all* civil rights guaranteed by the Constitution if the people of the North gave up the first of them. At least seven times as editor of the *Haverhill Gazette* Whittier vehemently called for defense of the right of free discussion, in assembly or in press; and likewise in the *New England Weekly Review* and the *Pennsylvania Freeman* he advocated a resolute stand upon it.

From tough reality, from the experience of himself and other Abolitionists, he knew at first hand the prime difficulty, in times of stress, of exercising the right of free assembly to discuss public issues. In Boston, Concord (New Hampshire), Haverhill, Newburyport, New York, and Philadelphia he saw embittered opposition to peaceful assembly and free discussion, and he lashed at it with fierce vigor. What in essence he wrote for the public prints he summed up lucidly in writing Garrison on May 13, 1850:

> I have just laid down a New York paper giving the disgraceful details of the outrage upon Free Speech at your late meeting in New York; and I cannot resist the inclination to drop a line to thee, expressive of

my hearty sympathy with thee in this matter. We have not always thought alike in respect to the best means of promoting the anti-slavery cause, and perhaps we differ quite as widely now as ever; but when the right to advocate emancipation in *any* shape is called in question, it is no time to split hairs, or to be fastidious in our exclusiveness. Wendell Phillips, Frederick Douglass, and thyself were assailed, not because of any peculiarities of opinion which you may entertain on other subjects, but because you were abolitionists and practical believers in the doctrine of the Declaration of Independence. So understanding it, I thank you for your perseverance and firmness in vindicating rights dear to us all.

The great battle for free speech and free assembling is to be fought over. The signal has been given at Washington, and commercial cupidity at the North is once more marshalling its mobs against us. The scandalous treachery of Webster, and the *backing* he has received from Andover and Harvard, show that we have nothing to hope for from the great political parties and religious sects. Let us be prepared [for] the worst, and may God give us strength, wisdom, and ability to withstand it.[12]

## 3

Whittier's sense of responsibility to his readers for the "important news of the day" was very strong. The spread of news by telegraph, which became a possibility in 1844, was not a reality until after he had given up his last editorial charge, the *Middlesex Standard*. But the kind of service which is now abundantly provided by the news associations and radio networks Whittier gave to his readers at the cost to himself of exceptional industry, and by the exercise of scrupulous judgment in the combing of available news sources. These for the most part were metropolitan newspapers, American and British, and special publications devoted to "causes."

His zeal for human improvement imparted to his columns a marked sobriety which he had the good judgment to leaven variously. His humor, a poor and forced thing in his first trials of it in Boston and Haverhill and Hartford, became a light and pliant aid by the time, aged thirty-six, he went to Lowell to edit the *Middlesex Standard*. In many of the contributions which he sent, later, to the *National Era* he added the edge of irony to his humor.

In addition, so far as assiduous reading could effectively support his own alert interest in the wide world, Whittier gave to the newspapers which he edited a somewhat cosmopolitan air. "Foreign intelligence" lent weight and balance to the run of domestic news that Whittier set before his readers; and among the spate of editorials and special articles which he wrote there appeared, now and again, one which was international in flavor. His prodigious output of material in both prose and verse, added to his meticulous "proofing" of small, hand-set type, gave point and reason to his frequent enforced absences from his editorial desk. The machine simply ran down at times.

Whittier's interest in the United States and its development never flagged, however, nor did his faith waver that it would become great among the nations of the world. His eyes looked often westward with hope, and southward with appreciation tinged with despair. The somewhat bumptious editorials such as "American Genius," "Our Prospects," and "American Literature" which he published in the *American Manufacturer* in 1829 [13] were not mere chauvinism, but intelligent declarations of the faith which he held always. He looked again into the future in the editorial "Our Country" in the *New England Weekly Review* of August 23, 1830. This was a dissertation in optimism, based upon the outgivings of the cosmopolitan John Neal, Portland editor, whose conception of America's future was enlarged by his late residence in England and by foreign travel.

Whittier, however, in his frequent editorializing upon the Union and its prospects, had one worry. He rightly feared the potential effects of sectionalism. In a pessimistic editorial on "The Union" which he published in the *Haverhill Gazette* on April 17, 1830, there was a portent of what Carl Sandburg has called "the Second American Revolution":

> * * * Alas! — if by the extension of our borders, the feeling of fraternal love is to be extinguished; — if the distinct and peculiar interests of the different and remote portions of this great family, render them forgetful of their mutual reliance upon each other, — if the jealousies which now embitter us, are increased into open hostility, — it were better that our territory were circumscribed as at the time of the Revolution — better even that the battles of our independence had never been fought; and that we were still overshadowed by the power of the foreign oppressor and fixed in our allegiance to the sovereignty of England.

The politics of the period, with its already ominous overtones, early won and held Whittier's absorbed interest. His New England Whig affiliation was his "original sin," and it aligned him illogically against the Jackson administration and the popular roots from which it sprang. The youthful Whittier's own economic sectionalism blinded him to the democratic force which gave the Jackson party its power. But his myopia began to fade by 1830; on December 6, under head of "Parties," in the *New England Weekly Review*, he declared that he was "tired of the eternal cant of old party names," now signifying nothing.[14] And by the end of his second editorship of the *Haverhill Gazette* and of Jackson's second term as President, he was entirely free from illusions about both major parties. In the *Gazette* of November 12, 1836, two days before the election of Van Buren, he repeated that he had "seen too much of the hollowness and hypocrisy of political parties, to be deceived by empty professions held out on the eve of an election." [15] From that time until the Republican Party came into being, Whittier was for twenty years a third-party man, an acute and vocal protestant against both the Whigs and the Democrats.

Whittier, in "temperately advocating his sentiments on the subject of slavery," [16] employed too zealously the political action which he believed to be the chief hope of Abolitionism. He was very far, however, from neglecting the basic issues which stemmed from the fight to preserve the Union of States. He seemed to be — and he made certain that his readers became — well aware that these issues were of global significance. Lincoln, in the early weeks of the Civil War, summed them up masterfully in describing to John Hay what he considered the key to the crisis:

> For my own part, I consider the first necessity that is upon us, is of proving that popular government is not an absurdity. We must settle this question now, — whether in a free government the minority have the right to break it up whenever they choose. If we fail, it will go far to prove the incapability of the people to govern themselves. There may be one consideration used in stay of such final judgment, but that is not for us to use in advance. That is, that there exists in our case an instance of a vast and far-reaching disturbing element which the history of no other free nation will probably ever present. That, however, is not for us to say at present. Taking the government as we found it, we will see if the majority can preserve it.[17]

Seldom a significant political event of 1830–60 passed without comment by Whittier in a newspaper. His standard practice was to editorialize on spot topics, and on occasion he set his political-humanitarian feelings to verse. Fundamental issues he gave proper weight by the printing of pertinent documents. Thus in February and March of 1830 he reprinted in the *Haverhill Gazette* considerable portions of the Webster-Hayne debate; and characteristically, while lauding Webster, he spoke in genuine admiration of Hayne's "exalted talents." Likewise Whittier discoursed frequently upon Nullification, and regretted the able Calhoun's advocacy of it. Calhoun's speeches, and those of Jackson, Everett, and other political leaders of the three decades were given space by Whittier in keeping with their relative importance to the nation's brewing struggle to live and be strong.

Few contemporary editors of periodicals reached nearly Whittier's stature as a political analyst and a commentator of force and lucidity.

## 4

It is altogether possible, indeed, that as an editor of weekly newspapers Whittier was unique. There is no evidence of his having performed regularly, during any of his editorships, as "leg man," as business manager, or as printer; but he seems to have been everything else, even office boy of the *New England Weekly Review*. (In the issue of November 21, 1831, under head of "Mysterious Disappearance of Newspapers," Whittier remarked the pleasure it gave him "to see a group of friends around our Editor's table of a morning, cracking jokes and conning over the latest news." But the "men of Clay" carried off so many of the exchanges that Whittier found it "impossible to lay our hand upon one in ten of the periodicals called for" when he was getting up the Weekly Review.) He was more than a newspaper man, he was a whole staff.

Few such newspapers as Whittier edited, it is true, could afford the luxury of an editorial "staff," and that is why the paste-and-scissors technique and the widespread appropriation of material, especially column-fillers such as verse, appear to have been common. It is likely that most editors of weeklies were, in the style of Whittier, all-in-one — editor-in-chief, managing editor, editorial writer, exchange editor, foreign editor, and copy and re-write editor. In addition, Whittier was book review editor, staff poet, and feature writer or steady contributor of prose fiction. His excellence in filling all these rôles was acknowledged and pointed to with pride by able colleagues such as John Neal, N. P. Willis, G. D. Prentice, and also fellow craftsmen outside of New England. By the time he became editor of the *Middlesex Standard* and contributing editor of the *National Era*, he had fulfilled their early prophecies that he would bring honor to American letters.

Hawthorne and Poe, too, learned part of their craft by editing and contributing to periodicals; and Hawthorne, like Whittier, was interested in the politics of his day. But neither Hawthorne nor Poe had nearly Whittier's journalistic versatility. Neither, in truth, could have aspired to it or have had the spur of a cause like Whittier's.

Workaday journalism was not at all their concern, and with Whittier it was chiefly a means of leverage to help lift the burden of slavery from the country. His major rôle was that of humanitarian. His editorships were all sub-parts of it, and so was the writing of prose tales — yes, even the composition of verse. This fact was made manifest, if not earlier, then certainly during the eight months of 1836 when he returned to edit the *Haverhill Gazette*. Even as a staff member *in absentia* of the *National Era*, to which he contributed well remembered verse and prose not inspired by Abolition, his primary concern was the furthering of his cause. It is simply a measure of the dynamo which drove him that, in addition to the copious political news and comment which he wrote for his newspapers, Whittier also gave his readers verse and fiction of which a full and accurate tally can never, in all probability, be made.

His writing in the *New England Weekly Review* in particular reveals plainly his zeal and conscience toward his readers — and his deliberate self-discipline through steady, voluminous production. During the eighteen months of his editorship he published forty-six of his poems in the paper, and forty-two essays, tales, and sketches which he did not sign but which bear his fairly identifiable stamp in subject, style, and general workmanship.[18] These were not examples of the plain, perspicuous prose which hard schooling enabled Whittier to write later, but the readers of the *Weekly Review* could have found them interesting. Many of the tales, like "The Plague-Stricken," "The White Rose of Scotland," "The Gondolier's Story," "Polar Seas," and "Salicetti" [19] bore upon them the obvious marks of English and Continental Romantic writers. Others were based upon New England lore — "The Quilting Party," "The

Catamount Hunt," "The Ghosts of the Island," and "A North East Storm." [20] But whether he worked in foreign or in native material, Whittier had an eye on the home quality of his newspaper.

## 5

Fellow editors commented often upon his work, and liked it. Some fancied it inordinately well, and "lifted" it without making acknowledgment to their readers. This was a practice that Whittier, though generous, disliked, if indeed he did not regard it as unethical. He had several times during his early days as editor to chide colleagues who gave him no credit for material which they had appropriated from his columns.[21] But these somewhat immature complaints had disappeared by the time he returned to the *Haverhill Gazette* in 1836. He had evidently learned to like it that his newspaper was liked.

A better test of popularity, as Whittier showed signs of having learned once and for all on the *American Manufacturer*, was the "box-office take" — the number of subscribers. Especially on the *New England Weekly Review* he showed plain signs of the kind of sense that business managers think no editor possesses and that all need acutely. Without catering to the "business interest," which Whittier flayed rather than endeavored to please, he appears to have attracted subscribers. He watched the list, which in no instance was large by newspaper circulation standards of the twentieth century, with a careful eye.

On January 29, 1829, in his fourth number as editor, he announced in the *American Manufacturer* that "we now have upwards of eight hundred subscribers." As editor of the *New England Weekly Review* he kept a sharp watch on the subscription list, and in the issue of January 24, 1831, he applied to delinquent subscribers this novel needle:

TO OUR SUBSCRIBERS

We despise the idea of dunning our patrons. * * * It may perhaps, be well to state, that we have made it a rule to consider every wilful delinquent subscriber as a Jackson man — an incorrigible and "whole hog" Heroite.

Toward the end of his second editorship in Haverhill, Whittier pointed out that the *Gazette* now had more than a hundred and twenty more subscribers than it had when he began in May — even in the face of local opposition to his outspoken Abolitionism and his whacking of Whigs who were against it and him.[22] So, too, in his second issue of the *Middlesex Standard* he was gratified to be able to announce: "Our subscription list is filling up with a rapidity far beyond our expectations."

But such gratification constituted the largest part of Whittier's pay as a newspaper man. His real reward came from the satisfaction of having, in that character, struck a blow for freedom. And always the hard pace he set himself while in charge as editor exacted the penalty of retirement from his post — with little money saved from the small salaries he was paid.

For his labors on the *American Manufacturer* he was paid at the rate of nine dollars a week. The proprietors of the *New England Weekly Review* got his services at a bargain for $500 a year. As editor of the *Haverhill Gazette* from May 7 to at least November 23, 1836, Whittier received the staggering sum of $90 — all the current salary he had, aside from compensation for his expenses in circulating anti-slavery petitions in Essex County.[23] It is hardly believable that he was well paid in Philadelphia or in Lowell, and it appears that as contributing editor of the *National Era*, while living at home in Amesbury, he was paid at piece rates by Lewis Tappan, his friend and one of the financial props of the *Era* as of the Abolitionist movement generally. On January 3, 1850, for instance, Tappan sent Whittier a check for $125 at the request of Doctor Gamaliel Bailey, editor of the *Era*, and on May 14, 1855, Tappan wrote that Whittier might draw on him for the $300 payable at Doctor Bailey's request.[24]

Whittier, with almost no exception, carried his underpaid and overloaded editorial jobs without relief until his health cracked. So it was in Hartford, particularly, and so it proved in Philadelphia. Only in Lowell did he have an associate editor, C. L. Knapp, who relieved Whittier of routine duties after the presidential election in November, 1844, and until Whittier left the paper in March following, his stipulated Liberty Party service in Lowell completed.

He was too painfully much a gentleman of the press to look to it for financial reward. He regarded journalism as a high calling, and he had occasion to underscore the fact after having described himself in a passage in "The Tent on the Beach" (1867):

> And one there was, a dreamer born,
> Who, with a mission to fulfil,
> Had left the Muses' haunts to turn
> The crank of an opinion-mill,
> Making his rustic reed of song
> A weapon in the war with wrong.[25]

E. L. Godkin, who as editor of *The Nation*, in New York, had so well demonstrated that journalism could be raised to the dignity of a profession, read into this passage a low estimate on Whittier's part of his work as an editor. Whittier set the scales right by writing Godkin as follows:

> In the half playful lines, if I did not feel at liberty to boast of my anti-slavery labors and to magnify my editorial profession, I certainly did not mean to underrate them or to express the shadow of a regret that they had occupied so large a share of my time and thought. The simple fact is that I cannot be sufficiently grateful to the Divide Providence that so early called my attention to the great interests of humanity, saving me from the poor ambitions and miserable jealousies of a selfish pursuit of literary reputation. Up to a comparatively recent period my writings have been simply episodical, something apart from the real object and aim of my life; and whatever favor they have found with the public has come to me as a grateful surprise rather than as an expected reward. As I have never staked all on the chances of authorship I have been spared the pain of disappointment and the temptation to envy those who, as men of letters, occupy a higher place in the public estimation than I have ever aspired to.[26]

# XIX

## Learning Self-Acquired

WHITTIER differed from such fellow poets of New England as Holmes, Longfellow, and Lowell in having small experience of the academy, either as student or teacher. He was not Harvard-educated, but he was like Thoreau at least in having taught very briefly and in having disliked the experience utterly.[1] Whittier felt acutely the need for patience, which he esteemed the sovereign and almost God-given quality of a good teacher. But he had it eminently in tutoring himself — patience doubly reinforced by determination. He and Lincoln were alike in acquiring a wide and useful fund of knowledge by the exercise of self-discipline. With Whittier, as with Lincoln, it was a conscious design to acquire working tools for the business of life. To it both men applied, with capital effect, what they learned and retained by teaching themselves. They richly cultivated their own minds.

### I

In nearly all aspects of his life Whittier was the practical economist *par excellence*. His self-cultivation, it is clear from his writings and from the books remaining in his library, gave him what Huxley termed "the most important portions of that immense capitalised experience of the human race which we call knowledge of various kinds." [2] And Whittier's special interests developed almost in a direct line from the meager library of his father's farm home. He read little science and relatively little fiction, but fed himself heartily upon history and political science, philosophy and religion, travel and romance, biography, and poetry. His habit was to turn to account the information which he acquired, so much so that his writings yield records from which the lifelong course of his self-education may be traced.

It was, in the beginning and briefly, rather helter-skelter than well ordered. On the magic carpet of Byron and the Continental Romantics, and of the Orientals who even then attracted him, Whittier broke the bounds of his New England environment and flew off into the world of the mind. In his prose sketch entitled "The Nervous Man," which appeared in the *New England Magazine* in August 1832 and November 1833, he obviously charted his own course. Whittier, professing that the prose and verse manuscripts which he submitted to the editors were the literary remains of his friend the Nervous Man, said of him:

> My friend made no pretensions to genius. He was a hard student, but the world has been little wiser for it. His literary appetite, like his physical, exceeded his digestion. He always seemed to me, like a volume of miscellany, without an index — or rather like a dictionary, to be looked into on occasions, but without any connexion. The following sketches I have extracted from his Diary, — a very wilderness of unintelligible chirography. I think there is some merit in them. There is, at least, originality.

Whittier's diet of reading was more than original, it was unique. In it were Romantic first courses, classical solids, and the variegated and novel junk which delights the palate of youth. Byron sat at the head of the table, with Coleridge on his right hand. Nothing spread upon it was light. "Coleridge says," wrote Whittier, "that the mind gives nature its gloom and its beauty — its light and sombre coloring. No such thing. Nature colors the mind. I feel at this moment her shadows closing around me." And in the Byronic mood the "old and single misanthrope [Whittier] at home on a rainy April day" complained: "Is it a light thing that I have suffered a daily martyrdom through life. . . ?" With romantic bravura he concluded, "*Manhood in its desolation has no tears.*"

Like wraiths of waiters catering to his tastes there appeared also an international force almost too numerous to capture. Whittier had read and he quoted pertinently from these, among others: Pliny, Seneca,

Domitian; the Physiognomists (whom he rejected), especially Lavater, Gall, and Spurzheim; Godwin, La Rochefoucauld, Shakespeare, Bacon (on marriage), Swedenborg; and a curious company from antiquity — Paracelsus, Harmolaus, Barberus, Joubertus, Licetas, Cardan, Olympiodorus, Aelian, and yet more. Lord Chesterfield carried all away at the end with a flourish of elegant immorality (which violated Whittier's taste).

Such was the sampling that nourished Whittier's fancy through 1832, or up to the time he began to school himself thoroughly in writings on politics and government, and gave hand and heart to the cause of Abolition. But from 1828 until that time he feasted mainly upon lighter fare. He was fascinated, for example, by legends of the devil, and particularly by the Faust theme. In his juvenile tales and sketches written for the *Haverhill Gazette* and other publications there appeared early glimmerings of his growing grasp of the agency of evil in the world. (Other signs of it showed in numerous youthful verses which he wrote about persecution of Quakers in the Colonies.) Among these were "Der Frieschutz [*sic*]; or the Magic Balls," and "The Everlasting Taper."

Whittier somehow got into his hands a copy of Johann August Apel's *Tales of the Wild and Wonderful*, translated into English and published in London in 1825 and in Philadelphia the following year. "The Freischütz; or, the Magic Balls" was one of the tales fashioned by this writer of the German Romantic school. In the *Haverhill Gazette* of September 27, 1828, Whittier gave part synopsis and part direct quotation from this story, a piece of German folklore about a hunter whose compact with the devil procured for him precisely sixty bullets with which he could hit unerringly any object selected. To Whittier the reading of the tale was a revelation, and he wrote in awe of the "wildness of conception," "the awful grandeur of its descriptions," and the "strange and fearful intensity" which begot in the reader almost a feeling of horror.

In another guise Lucifer dominated the story "The Everlasting Taper," which Whittier first published in the *New England Weekly Review* on September 5, 1831. Its setting was ancient Amiens, not a romantic German town, but Whittier's bow to Goethe appeared early in the tale. He said, "It is an old narration, and would figure well in an improved edition of the doings of Faust's Mephistopheles." Here the Devil appeared "in the shape of a respectable looking monkey" to Christopher, a simple carpenter, and snared him with the offer of as much gold as he desired for thirty years. In the end Beelzebub was outwitted by "a crafty monk."

Certain aspects of the brief tale attested Whittier's acquaintance with several versions of the Faust legend.[3]

A further mark of Whittier's youthful taste for odd volumes was the article "Spectral Illusions," which appeared in the *Haverhill Gazette* on November 22, 1828. He quoted an article from the *Edinburgh Phrenological Journal*, after a long introduction in which he said that, despite "the strong arguments of philosophy and reason, it is impossible to wholly withstand the pervading influence of a vague and undefinable dread of supernatural power." Here and in the later tale "The Opium Eater," published in the *New England Magazine* in March, 1833, Whittier indicated his youthful interest in a subject which engaged his fancy for a good part of his life. He had delved into the works of DeQuincey, Coleridge, Nicolai of Berlin, the memoirs of Maria Eleonora Schoning, William Hone's *Every Day Book*, and again Swedenborg.

Whittier, in a word, was in his mid-twenties engaged by the unfathomed mysteries of life — by hidden things of the mind and the spirit more than by the perceptible realities, even nature itself, which immediately surrounded him. He was quick to lose his taste for Walter Scott and the Gothic romances, under the impulse of which he wrote many youthful pieces like "The Holy Vehme" and "The Deformed Girl," and for Oriental tales which influenced the writing of such bagatelles as "The Young Bramin," "The Forsaken Girl," and "The Two Bridegrooms."[4] His sense of selection and direction led him early to firm ground on which he stood throughout his life.

## 2

He was weaned away from melancholy Byronism, but he caught the torch of Byron's fight for freedom — and that of Shelley and Milton and all other men, regardless of place and time, who held a godlike concept of the destiny of man. The question of how to achieve that, and truth and justice in human society, was one of the two principal concerns of his life. In the search for answers he examined intently, not the American state alone, but ancient states and civilizations — Egypt, and Greece and Rome in their flower — and England in the seventeenth and eighteenth centuries. He got, if not answers, at least confirmations or shadings of the ideal Quaker concepts to which he was born and bred.

His thinking and the reading which nourished it all bore upon the problem of fulfilling the hopes and plans of the Founding Fathers. They were his own political progenitors. He knew and loved their works well — Franklin, Jefferson, Jay, Washington and their compatriots — and the human service to which these works were later put by statesmen like Monroe and, primarily, John Quincy Adams, "our own venerable Apostle of Freedom." Whittier felt, like Whitman and Clemens after him, that his country was far from achieving the ultimate possibilities of democracy.

More than any other American writer of his day, he believed that "equal opportunity for all" according to their abilities was a myth as long as slavery, marked for elimination by Jefferson and other framers of the Constitution, was suffered not only to continue but to strengthen its hold on the American state.

In a succession of able utterances, in both cogent prose and blazing verse, Whittier declaimed that no democracy which tolerated chattel slavery had in it either truth or justice. During the eighteen-thirties he read or reread widely in the works of the lawgivers of the western world. What he already held as conviction he there found authoritatively written as fact. What his head and heart told him was true he found sanctioned by statesmen and political economists of America, England, and France: that slavery was not only undemocratic and inhuman, it was economically unprofitable.

Whittier brought in the testimony of Franklin's *The Peopling of Countries;* the memorable speeches of John Randolph of Roanoke, and his even more eloquent act, in his will written in 1821, of freeing his nearly four hundred slaves; the pertinent opinions of Chancellor Kent in his *Commentaries on American Law.* He cited the example of acts of Justinian the Great, Byzantine emperor of the sixth century. The German Humboldt, the Englishman Coxe, the Frenchman Brissot, and other observant travelers yielded their testimony that all countries which had not prohibited slavery were economically and socially backward. Whittier appealed to his widening audience through the authority of Blackstone's *Commentaries* and his *History of the Commonwealth;* of Brougham's *Colonial Policy;* of Burke, and Buxton, and Canning; of Lord Nugent and the elder Pitt; of Adam Smith and yet others in the Empire which by act of Parliament in 1833 decreed the gradual extinction of slavery in the colonies.

To France likewise Whittier turned, for the opinions of Montesquieu and of Marquis de Chastellux, from whose *De la Félicité publique* he quoted; and for the objective truths of de Tocqueville's masterpiece, *Democracy in America*, one in particular:

> The events which are taking place in the Southern States of the Union, appear to me to be at once the most horrible and the most natural results of slavery. When I see the order of nature overthrown, and when I hear the cry of humanity in its vain struggle against the laws, my indignation does not light upon the men of our own time who are the instruments of these outrages; but I reserve my execration for those who, after a thousand years of freedom, brought back slavery into the world once more.[5]

Whittier, in fact, read with such breadth and discrimination in politics and government that, by July, 1833, he was able to say, with quiet confidence: "Political economy has been the peculiar study of Virginia. But there are some important truths connected with this science which she has hitherto overlooked or wantonly disregarded." [6]

History, too, held many lessons for a self-taught humanitarian eager that all men should make the most of themselves and their world. First of all, Whittier knew American colonial history well, and that of the British Isles — England, Ireland, and Scotland equally. He made himself familiar with the modern history of the Papacy, and became thoroughly versed in the events and the significance of the French Revolution and the Napoleonic wars. Of ancient history aside from that of the Bible, and of the countries of the eastern Mediterranean and the land bridge to the Orient, he had a good grasp if not, evidently, a broad mastery.

Whittier's favorite historical period of modern times was, past all comparison, England in the seventeenth century. Milton, his nearly ideal hero, was living in that hour; George Fox in his unorthodox preaching gave rise to the Society of Friends; a titanic struggle, waged over human liberties, called up strong men only less in stature than Milton; and Whittier found heart's delight in writers of the period to whom his spirit flew as to its natural home — Bacon, Sir Thomas Browne, Bunyan, Fuller, Herbert, Marvell, Pepys, Quarles, Vaughan, Walton, with Milton himself in a timeless class all alone. Around some of his most admired figures of the time, both political and literary, Whittier wrote a series of readable "Old Portraits" which originally appeared in the *National Era* and the *Democratic Review* in the period 1846–50. In the article on John Bunyan appeared this forceful opinion, the essence of Whittier:

> The English revolution of the seventeenth century, while it humbled the false and oppressive aristocracy of rank and title, was prodigal in the development of the real nobility of the mind and heart. Its history is bright with the footprints of men whose very names still stir the hearts of freemen, the world over, like a trumpet peal. Say what we may of its fanaticism, laugh as we may at its extravagant enjoyment of newly acquired religious and civil liberty, who shall now venture to deny that it was the golden age of England? Who that regards freedom above slavery, will now sympathize with the outcry and lamentation of those interested in the continuance of the old order of things, against the prevalence of sects and schism, but who, at the same time, as Milton shrewdly intimates, dreaded more the rending of their pontifical sleeves than the rending of the Church? Who shall now sneer at Puritanism, with the *Defence of Unlicensed Printing* before him? Who scoff at Quakerism over the *Journal* of George Fox? Who shall join with debauched lordlings and fat-witted prelates in ridicule of Anabaptist levellers and dippers, after rising from the perusal of *Pilgrim's Progress?* "There were giants in those days." . . .[7]

With very close interest Whittier had read Carlyle's *Letters and Speeches of Oliver Cromwell*, but found the volumes disappointing, not nearly up to the mark of his *History of the French Revolution*. The Friend revolted at Carlyle's handling of "that moral phenomenon," the English revolution, in such a way that "the grim image of the colossal Puritan" became the face of the "hero of the great event." Whittier regretted, precisely, that as a writer of history Carlyle in his "blind admiration and adoration of mere abstract Power" sank at times to "nothing less than devil-worship," and minimized such figures as Henry Vane.

Whittier countered with his own interpretation of the significance of men of strong faith who resisted the Protectorate. He took for example "some pains to collect and embody the facts" [8] of the life of James Nayler, a Quaker persecuted with especial cruelty. He wrote tenderly of Thomas Ellwood, Quaker friend and companion of the blind Milton who suggested the subject of *Paradise Regained*, and he drew up the debt of gratitude and admiration which the present generation owed to Ellwood and other Friends who had suffered from the bigotry of the times.

> For [wrote Whittier], in an age of hypocritical hollowness and mean self-seeking, when, with noble exceptions, the very Puritans of Crom-

well's Reign of the Saints were taking profane lessons from their old enemies, and putting on an outside show of conformity, for the sake of place or pardon, ye maintained the austere dignity of virtue, and, with King and Church and Parliament arrayed against you, vindicated the Rights of Conscience, at the cost of home, fortune, and life. English liberty owes more to your unyielding firmness than to the blows stricken for her at Worcester and Naseby.[9]

Other persons sketched in this skillfully written series of articles included Andrew Marvell, John Roberts, farmer, and Richard Baxter. Whittier found Marvell a man of strong appeal, not simply as the author of verses which he affectionately quoted but as "one of the inflexible defenders of English liberty," outshone as a political controversialist only by Milton. A solid part of Marvell's charm for Whittier lay in the fact that he was "light, playful, witty, and sarcastic," and Whittier made him this grateful bow:

> It is the peculiar merit of Milton and Marvell, that in such an age they held fast their integrity, standing up in glorious contrast with clerical apostates and traitors to the cause of England's liberty.[10]

One more paper that Whittier contributed to the *National Era* [11] significantly shows his absorbed reading of English history of the seventeenth and eighteenth centuries, and the kind of lessons he drew from it. Reviewing at length Macaulay's *History of England from the Accession of James II*, Whittier came down to a closely analytical commentary on the chapter (I, 260–398) which described the condition of England when in 1685 James succeeded Charles II on the throne. Whittier saw in England's sorry state simply the results of bad government and the disregard of the rights and interests of five million people. Then, looking at the American scene twelve years before the outbreak of the Civil War, Whittier plainly stated his faith in the potential increase of right and justice among men in society:

> We no longer sigh for "the good old days." The most confirmed grumbler is compelled to admit that, bad as things now are, they were far worse a few generations back. Macaulay, in this elaborate and carefully prepared chapter, has done a good service to humanity in disabusing well-intentioned ignorance of the melancholy notion that the world is growing worse, and in putting to silence the cant of blind, unreasoning conservatism.[12]

In the processes of democratic evolution in France, whose history from 1789 on held him awed and at times embarrassed, Whittier had much less faith. Around 1830 he twice read Burke, and was persuaded to believe that the lawless terror of the Revolution in 1789 had robbed the people's uprising of all basis in truth and justice. This belief colored the frequent references to the French Revolution which appeared in the editorial pages of the newspapers conducted by Whittier at the outset of his career. He regarded the evil events which flowed out of the Revolution as an ironic commentary on the unpredictability of human affairs. Chiefly he deplored, as a gross miscarriage of justice, the rise of Napoleon and the wars that he waged.

But further reading must have done something to set the events of 1789 in more accurate perspective for him. Whittier began his prose sketch "James Nayler" with this tribute to Carlyle, whose view of life differed so sharply from his own:

> "Would that Carlyle could now try his hand at the English Revolution!" was our exclamation, on laying down the last volume of his remarkable *History of the French Revolution* with its brilliant and startling word-pictures still flashing before us.[13]

And in the library of his Amesbury home Whittier had copies of Thiers' *History of the French Revolution* (Philadelphia, 1842) and of Guizot's *General History of Civilization in Europe* (New York, 1862).

At all events, Whittier followed with unquenchable faith the overturns which in 1830 brought Louis Philippe to the throne, and in 1848 erected the Second Republic, with Louis Napoleon as president. In 1830 Whittier's intent watch on the course of events resulted in the editorial "Napoleon," which appeared in the *Haverhill Gazette* on March 13, and in a second, "France," published in the *New England Weekly Review* on September 13. In 1847–48 his stubborn hopes and unwilling doubts of democracy in France persisted in his reviews of Lamartine's *History of the Girondins* which he contributed to the *National Era* on November 4, 1847, and February 17, 1848; and in the article on Lamartine himself, much admired by Whittier, which the *Era* carried in the issue of April 6, 1848.

Three weeks later the Washington weekly published the article "Labor — the French Revolution," which effectively summarized Whittier's doubts and hopes of a people's government in the Second Republic:

Now, while we have reason to fear that many of the men upon whom the responsibility of the French Government rests have never passed through the deep spiritual baptism which prepared the humble philanthropist [John Woolman] above alluded to for his work of love; while we see much to excite our apprehensions in the extravagant expectations of the People, relying too much upon the amelioration of outward circumstances, and too little upon that inward purification of soul, without which there can be no true happiness — we still reverently recognize in their aims and purposes the influence of that Divine Spirit which, in all ages, has prompted and promoted the reformation of abuses in human society, and which will continue to turn and overturn until the Right is everywhere established, and the will of God is done on Earth as in Heaven.

## 3

In Whittier's view the ideal and the practical were, if not identical, then certainly halves of the same thing. Bred to Quaker faith in a good world and in human improvability, he knew very well both how men act and how they ought to act. As he approached middle life and became more and more engrossed in reflecting on the idea of life and of its final realization in death, he dwelt much upon the perfect commonwealth. Systematically and critically he weighed the ideas of the *Timaeus* of Plato and the *Cyropaedia* of Xenophon, of More's *Utopia* in particular, and of others coming up the centuries to his own time — Bacon's *New Atlantis*, Campanella's *City of the Sun*, Harrington's *Oceana*, Fénelon's *Telemachus*, and Saint-Pierre's *Arcadia*. Whittier regretted Plato's approval of slavery and his gradation of society in the ideal republic. That, seemingly, was his only serious reservation in a course of reading which he manifestly relished.

Fruits of it appeared steadily in his writings and enriched them. Finally, in a carefully composed article "Utopian Schemes and Political Theorists," which he contributed to the *National Era* of September 7, 1848, Whittier weighed the fate of these "practical visionaries" in their own day over against their long-term contribution to the world. All of them, he hazarded, like Bacon and Harrington, were ridiculed or called lunatic in their own times; and some of their notions doubtless were absurd. But he said that truth, in whatever guise it is introduced to the world, "never fails in the end of finding a lodging-place in the popular mind." His own opinion of the political theorists whose works he had considered was this:

> * * * They have entered into and become parts of the social and political fabrics of Europe and America. The prophecies of imagination have been fulfilled; the dreams of romance have become familiar realities.
>
> What is the moral suggested by this record? Is it not that we should look with charity and tolerance upon the schemes and speculations of the political and social theorists of our day; that, if unprepared to venture upon new experiments and radical changes, we should at least consider that what was folly to our ancestors is our wisdom, and that another generation may successfully put in practice the very theories which now seem to us absurd and impossible?

And he ended on a familiar chord: "Temporally and spiritually, the declaration of inspiration holds good, 'We are saved by hope.' "[14]

## 4

Whittier's salvation as a teacher of himself was that he read as much for pleasure as for purposeful fact. Francis Bacon was his obvious master. All of Whittier's writings — verse, prose articles, and letters — bespeak the fullness of his self-education, but also the social quality of his mind as well as the intellectual discipline which he derived from it. He was always aware that in the great books of modern times, as in the Bible, the substance and savor of life was preserved.

Whittier read the English classics with absorption and lasting profit. His introduction to them through Lindley Murray's *English Reader* and other such books [15] led to permanent friendships and to wide acquaintance. Whittier referred often, and with delight and point, to Shakespeare — and to Milton and Marvell, Sterne and Dickens, Tennyson and Arnold and the Brownings, and to the myriad company of gifted souls in Britain and America who had caught the spirit of the free peoples of the English-speaking world. What they meant to him he described simply in the

"Proem" which he wrote in 1847 and which he was to place first among his works in the Riverside Edition of 1888:

> I love the old melodious lays
> Which softly melt the ages through,
> The songs of Spenser's golden days,
> Arcadian Sidney's silvery phrase,
> Sprinkling our noon of time with freshest morning dew.
>
> Yet, vainly in my quiet hours
> To breathe their marvellous notes I try;
> I feel them, as the leaves and flowers
> In silence feel the dewy showers,
> And drink with glad, still lips the blessing of the sky.[16]

The works of Whittier's best-loved authors became veritably part of the clothing of his mind. His abounding allusions to Burns and to Lamb (who had on occasion written so affectionately of "the gentle Quakers") were as natural as they were apposite. And his delight in great characters like Falstaff, Yorick, and Pickwick who walked out of classic pages back into the lives of people where they were bred, knew almost no limits. In his writings Whittier showed a lively acquaintance with the works of all of the great English writers of the Renaissance and of the Romantic period, and of American authors beginning with Cotton Mather and his fellows; but his favorites among the poets remained Milton and Burns, and among the novelists Sterne and Dickens. Pickwick, as he told Dickens when they met in 1867, was his companion during many a night's vigil, until sheer entertainment banished thought and care and brought the relief of sleep.[17]

Whittier met Charles Kingsley, too, among the numerous company of English and Continental writers with whom he was to become acquainted on their visits to New England after the Civil War. How far literature was a reading of life to Whittier is lucidly shown in a letter which he wrote to Mrs. Kingsley in 1876 after her husband's death:

> In this country thy husband's memory is cherished by thousands, who, after long admiring the genius of the successful author, have learned, in his brief visit, to love him as a man. I shall never forget my first meeting with him in Boston [in 1874]. I began, naturally enough, to speak of his literary work, when he somewhat abruptly turned the conversation upon the great themes of life and duty. The solemn

questions of a future life, and the final destiny of the race, seemed pressing upon him, not so much for an answer (for he had solved them all by simple faith in the divine goodness) as for the sympathetic response of one whose views he believed to be, in a great degree, coincident with his own. "I sometimes doubt and distrust myself," he said, "but I see some hope for everybody else. To me the gospel of Christ seems indeed good tidings of great joy to all people; and I think we may safely trust the mercy which endureth *forever*." It impressed me deeply to find the world-renowned author ignoring his literary fame, unobservant of the strange city whose streets he was treading for the first time, and engaged only with "thoughts that wander through eternity." All I saw of him left upon me the feeling that I was in contact with a powerfully earnest and reverent spirit. His heart seemed overcharged with interest in the welfare, physical, moral, and spiritual, of his race. I was conscious in his presence of the bracing atmosphere of a noble nature. He seemed to me one of the manliest of men. I forbear to speak of the high estimate which, in common with all English-speaking people, I place upon his literary life-work. My copy of his "Hypatia" is worn by frequent perusal, and the echoes of his rare and beautiful lyrics never die out of my memory. But since I have seen *him*, the man seems greater than the author.[18]

Whittier's fascination with men who created letters was consistently shown in his references to Boswell and Johnson, and to other *lives* almost to the end of his own. Likewise he was fascinated with books of romance and travel — with the legends of Ariosto and with *Amadis of Gaul*, with novels like Charles Brockden Brown's *Wieland*, with Macpherson's *Ossian*, and with the old exploits of Marco Polo and Magellan and others who looked for the secrets of the universe. Narratives of travel in Arabia and Spain and other distant lands always found a ready reader in Whittier, and the *Arabian Nights* provided him with perhaps not less than a thousand and one nights' entertainment, as frequent lively references in his works suggest.

If not so much influenced by it as by the literature of the Bible, which he knew so well,[19] Whittier obviously had drunk deep of the records of classical civilization. The roster of the ancient great from the Mediterranean Basin was given in his pages, and Dante was there with "the rayless atmosphere" of the Middle Ages.[20] Latin civilization of no time was as engrossing to him as that of England in the seventeenth century, but Whittier knew and with appreciation often alluded to Montaigne, Molière, Corneille (*Le Cid*), Rousseau, and particularly to Saint-Pierre, whose works he admired and loved. Voltaire was not at all to Whittier's taste, though he read him.

In contrast, Scandinavian folklore and mythology was vastly interesting to Whittier, and inspired numerous poems or gave characteristic gray tinges to passages in his prose articles, especially "The Poetry of the North," which was first published in the *National Era* on August 19, 1847. He seems to have been acquainted with few of the Russian writers except Gogol, Pushkin, and Tolstoi, and of the works that he read, *War and Peace* appealed most naturally to a Friend.

Of German writers, thanks to his translator friends Charles T. Brooks and Thomas Tracy, he knew rather more. His writings and the books in his library testify that Whittier had read many of Goethe's works and was acquainted with those of Chamisso, Fouqué, and Uhland; of Heine, Novalis, and Richter; and of Lessing and probably Schiller. It is manifest, however, that the two books on German life and literature which he consulted most often in his library were Merle D'Aubigné's *History of the Great Reformation of the Sixteenth Century in Germany, Switzerland, etc.* (New York, 1843), and the Susanna Winkworth translation of *Theologia Germanica* (London, 1874). Whittier, like Luther, was strongly attracted to the unknown author of this fourteenth-century work; to the mystics Echard, or Eckhart (?1260–1327) and Tauler (1300?–1361); and to Jacob Boehme (1575–1624), father of the chief development of mysticism in modern Germany.[21]

## 5

But it was the literature and philosophy of the Orient that laid the firmest hold on Whittier's imagination after he had reached middle age. As early as 1847, during the decade when he was making his deepest soundings for the meaning of life, he referred to "the Persian seer" meditating upon the legions of light and darkness.[22] And as the years passed, it became clearer that the second great concern of Whittier's life was the question what life meant, and death after it; clearer, too, that he answered it for himself by faith in the way that Kingsley did.

Sir Edwin Arnold, author of *The Light of Asia*, is said to have introduced Whittier to the Persian and Hindu translations which he used. Emerson for a certainty did help to acquaint him with the wise men of the East, as a paragraph in Whittier's letter of December 12, 1852, to Emerson indicates: "I feel guilty in respect to the *Bhagvat Gita:* but it is too late to repent: & I will een keep it until I restore it to thee personally in exchange for Geo. Fox. It is a wonderful book — & has greatly excited my curiosity to know more of the religious literature of the East." [23] Later, on November 10, 1888, Celia Thaxter wrote to suggest with enthusiasm that Whittier procure a copy of Mohini's translation of the *Bhagavad Gita*, the great religious classic of the Hindus.[24] From time to time other friends catered to his known interest by sending him copies or suggesting the titles of books on the Orient which they thought he would like to know. William R. Alger, of Boston, remarked in a letter of February 16, 1869, "I have just got a little book, of great interest, on '*Oriental Mysticism*,' which I will lend you." Evidently it fascinated Whittier, for a year later, on February 23, Alger had to request the return of the book.[25]

In brief, Whittier during the latter half of his life, reading carefully the religious books of the Orient and the works of German mystics, made the same kind of use of them that he had made earlier of great works in history and government. He enlisted authority in support of beliefs which he already held. Emerson, it is said, was considered by the Hindus to be one of them. Whittier, Christian humanitarian rather than philosopher, took from the Oriental influence upon the thought of his time the ethical and moral principles with which he sympathized. His works are said to include more poems on Oriental themes, more paraphrases on Oriental maxims, and more imitations of Oriental models than may be found in Emerson, the one American poet in whose philosophy and art Orientalism is inextricably woven.[26]

In Whittier's library at his Amesbury home there were found (in 1936) only a few Oriental books, and these of a secondary nature. They could, however, have afforded him a general exposition of Asiatic life and culture. Among them were:

William Rounseville Alger, *The Poetry of the Orient*, 1874.

Lydia Maria Child, *The Progress of Religious Ideas through the Successive Ages*, 1855.

James Freeman Clarke, *Ten Great Religions*, 1883.

Charles C. Coe, *General Gordon in a New Light*, 1885.

Evariste Huc, *A Journey through the Chinese Empire*, 1855.

Richard Henry Stoddard, *The Book of the East, and Other Poems*, 1871.

Bayard Taylor, *Poems of the Orient*, 1855.

Charles Dudley Warner, *In the Levant*, 1877.

Whittier's writings, however, indicate a close knowledge of other books bearing upon the Far East. He knew the works of the English Orientalist, Monier-Williams, and those of Max Müller, including *The Sacred Books of the East*, which he edited. He was well acquainted with the *Laws of Menu;* two works by the Orientalist John Muir — *Sentiments Metrically Rendered from the Sanskrit*, 1875, and *Metrical Translations from . . . Sanskrit Writers, with an Introduction, many Prose Versions and Parallel Passages from Classical Authors*, 1879; W. H. Drew's translation of *The Cural of Tiruvalluvar*, generally esteemed in India the best book of morals written by a Hindu; and N. E. Kendersley's *Specimens of the Hindu Theatre*. It is also clear that Whittier read in the files of *The Journal of the Asiatic Society of Bengal*, upon which he based his poem "The Dead Feast of the Kol-Folk."

In addition, he had acquired a knowledge of Hafiz, of the Zoroastrian scriptures, of the Koran, of Samuel Lee's translation of the *Travels of Ibn Batuta*, and of the Sufi poets in general. Whittier's writings show, beyond this, that he had amassed considerable information in Buddhist lore; and they and his library show that he was deeply interested in Near Eastern or biblical themes. Above all, he read the *Bhagavad Gita*, and as a matter of course he was acquainted with the *Analects* of Confucius.[27] In his own day, Whittier had an absorbed interest in Mozoomdar, whose Hymns of the Bramo Somaj (the "Congregation of God") he paraphrased in a poem of that title written in 1885. On October 13, 1883, he wrote enthusiastically to Mrs. Fields: "I hope thee and Sarah [Orne Jewett] will see the wonderful Prophet of the Bramo Somaj — Mozoomdar, before he leaves the country. I would have seen him in Boston, but for illness last week. That movement in India is the greatest event in the history of Christianity since the days of Paul." [28]

More than most of his New England co-fraternity, — whether consciously or not is unclear — Whittier seemed to attempt to achieve a synthesis of quietism and of American nineteenth-century strenuosity and belief in work. So often as to make it appear, in his own thinking, a natural fusion, he fashioned poems out of both Christian and Buddhist or

Hindu elements. He might, as in "The Cypress-Tree of Ceylon," start with a passage in Oriental literature, restate or rework it briefly, and conclude with a Christian moral; or he might follow the style of "Disarmament," in which he begins with Christ's injunction "Put up the sword!" and ends with a Buddhist birth-story to illustrate the efficacy of the Christian principle of love. He at any rate made a practice of isolating unusual passages in Oriental books from their contexts, and of adapting them to his own purposes.

Whittier's most significant uses of Oriental thought are found in two poems, "Miriam" and "The Over-Heart." In them he reveals his peculiar interest in the ancient faiths of the East and the extent to which he accepted the basic principles of the Vedanta. It is a fact worthy of particular remark that the most famous of the many hymns drawn from his works appears in "The Brewing of Soma," which he based on a passage from the Vedas, in Georg Bühler's translation of the *Vashista* (included in Müller's edition of *The Sacred Books of the East*). The hymn is "Dear Lord and Father of Mankind," the last six verses of the poem, and the Christian moral of it is that libations, incense, vigils, music are of no consequence. Whittier, by the time he wrote his now famous lines in 1872, made a rule of his own life the quiet resignation he besought for all men:

> Drop Thy still dews of quietness,
> Till all our strivings cease;
> Take from our souls the strain and stress,
> And let our ordered lives confess
> The beauty of Thy peace.
>
> Breathe through the heats of our desire
> Thy coolness and Thy balm;
> Let sense be dumb, let flesh retire;
> Speak through the earthquake, wind, and fire,
> O still, small voice of calm! [29]

"The Brewing of Soma" first appeared in the *Atlantic* for April, 1872, and in November of that year Whittier's old Amesbury friend Henry Taylor died.[30] Whittier's obituary notice of him, published in the Amesbury *Villager* on November 28, revealed the breadth of his own Oriental reading. The lines of it sprang from the same quiet faith that gave out "Dear Lord and Father of Mankind." Whittier said of Taylor:

> * * * He was Oriental in his cast of mind; he would have been quite at home with Chinese benzes, Buddhist priests, Mohammedan dervishes, and Christian monks of Mt. Athos. . . .
>
> He had somehow reached a state of absolute quietude — a region of ineffable calm, blown over by no winds of hope or fear. All personal anxieties and solicitudes were unknown. The outward world was phantasmal and unreal — he was utterly beyond its common temptations, and looked with simple wonder upon the struggle for wealth and place — the strifes and ambitions of sects and parties about him.

And in ending his explanation of Taylor's mysticism, Whittier said:

> He used to quote with much intensity of meaning, the words which Prof. Plumptree attributes to the founder of Buddhism, on reaching the condition of absolute rest.
>
> It was a description of his own state — in which the Nirvana of the Buddhist — the mystic suicide and self-abnegation of the Moslem Sufi — the absorption into the Divine Will of the Christian mystics, and "the rest which remaineth for the people of God," — seemed to him but different names for the same spiritual experience.[31]

## 6

Whittier, in a word, distilled wisdom from the knowledge which he acquired of books and, more important, of the world of affairs. No baccalaureate degree would have measured even remotely the intellectual accomplishments of the man. It remained for Harvard University, appropriately, to give public recognition to these accomplishments. The oldest university in the country bestowed upon him the degree of Master of Arts, *honoris causa*, in July, 1860, and the ultimate Doctor of Laws, *honoris causa*, on November 8, 1886, at exercises in commemoration of Harvard's two hundred and fiftieth anniversary. "John Greenleaf Whittier, poet," the Records of the Overseers of Harvard University reveal, was one of three recipients of the LL.D. "who are prevented by distance or infirmity from attending this Festival." If he had presented himself at Cambridge, Whittier would have sat in the company of such professional Doctors as Timothy Dwight, president of Yale; Basil L. Gildersleeve, the eminent classicist; and S. Weir Mitchell, Philadelphia author and physician.

This academic accolade was fitting. On February 16, 1858, Whittier was one of five Overseers of Harvard elected by both branches of the Massachusetts legislature, and at the meeting of the board on March 10 following he was appointed chairman of the special examining committee in modern languages. At this time Charles W. Eliot, Master of Arts, formerly a tutor, was elected an assistant professor of mathematics and chemistry. Twenty-eight years later Eliot, as president, signed with pleasure the certificate that admitted the self-schooled Whittier to "all the rights and privileges" of the society of learned and accomplished men.[32]

# XX

## The Constant Drawback of Ill Health

WHITTIER'S STRONG MIND and brave spirit were, unluckily, not matched by a strong body. The driving force in him was vastly better than the machine. No man, or woman either, has been able to produce a convincing explanation of the fact, which may be very simple. Little more can be done, indeed, than to state the known facts upon which even a speculation can be based, and to hope that a clear medical case-history may yet be compiled which will forbid misinterpretation.

S. T. Pickard, Whittier's authorized biographer, makes it clear that Whittier himself "was accustomed to attribute the delicacy of his health throughout life to the methods of toughening the constitution when he was a lad." By the time he was fifteen years old he had reached his full height, five feet ten and one half inches, and he was slender.[1] He lacked altogether the powerful frame of his six-foot, three hundred-pound ancestors.[2] Life on a Massachusetts farm obviously worked a hardship upon him, no matter what the strength of his belief in tilling the soil, and no matter how frequent his reiterations of it in later years.

Farming was not for him. His sale of the one hundred and forty-eight acres in East Haverhill in 1836, in his twenty-ninth year and six years after his father's death, was not soon enough. Clothing of the kind that was available in his youth did not shield him against the winter climate of his native heath, and it left him with a bronchial ailment for life. Farm labor demanded tougher muscle than he possessed, and overexertion when he was seventeen — perhaps with the heavy flail — resulted in injuries, Pickard writes, "from the effects of which he never fully recovered."[3] From that time until 1836, Whittier's labors when he was at the birthplace seem to have been governed by the rule of physical economy which proved to be a lifetime imposition. Like a President of the United States in the nineteen-twenties, he on occasion "raked the meadow sweet with hay," but the sustained work of his life had necessarily to be performed in other fields.

## I

Whittier appears to have had to learn by experience that limits were set to his exertions which bound him rigidly, regardless of the kind of work he did. As editor he could never stand the regimen of desk work for many months in succession. That was a discovery of the eighteen-thirties, in Hartford and in Philadelphia. Even steady travel dragged down the state of his health, and that was a discovery of 1841 when he accompanied Joseph Sturge to various cities of the eastern seaboard.[4]

By that year Whittier had fairly well realized the cast of the die, and in March he wrote to his school friend Harriet Minot:

> Thy letter was heartily welcome, for I had been for some days too stupid and dull to feel any interest in things present, and naturally enough my mind wandered back to the past, and scenes which are now but memories and the old familiar faces have been with me. I should have been glad to make Haverhill a visit in the winter, but the extremely delicate state of my health has compelled me to forego the pleasure. I feel now somewhat better, but I have little confidence in it. Well, I am in God's hands, and striving to resign myself to his will, not how-ever, I fear, as I ought to. With all my suffering, I have many blessings, infinitely more than I deserve. . . . I now think some of going next week to New York and Philadelphia, partly to escape our east winds which I dread. I think sickness has a wonderful effect in fanning into life the half-extinguished conscience. It is doubtless better for me and for my friends that the hand of sickness is sometimes laid heavily upon me. Who knows what either thou or I should have been had we always enjoyed good health? [5]

Whittier came to that state of sober acceptance only by degrees; learned the hard way how to do his chosen work without being knocked completely under by it. During the eighteen-thirties, in the swirl first of competing ambitions and then of unreserved dedication to anti-slavery work, he almost burned out his dynamo. The law of compensation which fascinated Emerson held Whittier tight in its grip. For his every action there was an opposite and equal reaction. Hard service on the *New England Weekly Review* and on the *Pennsylvania Freeman* compelled frequent periods of rest and final retirement to Essex County for recovery. Whittier's letters to his friends in Hartford and Philadelphia reveal his awareness that he could not drive himself relentlessly.

In his newspaper columns, however, he for a time put on a jocose front. Through it could plainly be seen the fact that even momentary release from desk routine, with its inevitable hard strain on his eyes, gave him relief. He found it during one week in New Haven in June of 1831, whither he went from Hartford, even despite temperatures of ninety to one hundred degrees.[6] The fact is significant only because Whittier always was so much a weathervane, highly sensitive to extremes. But by autumn he was out of action once more, and in the *New England Weekly Review* of October 17, apologizing because illness had again resulted in leanness of his editorial matter, he bantered: "We shall pen nothing lugubrious on the subject, — for we have 'a melancholy of our own' — perfectly original, — a non-descript sorrow, which this lubberly affair of a world has nothing to do with."

His tone was soberer during the period 1838–40 when he conducted the *Pennsylvania Freeman.* Then his "editorial furloughs" were frequent, his adieux serious. On June 27, 1839, he announced to his readers that a "protracted indisposition" forced him to give up the editorship, at least temporarily. In Philadelphia the struggle between his physical delicacy and his sense of duty was virtually a draw: he was resident in the city about twelve months out of twenty-three during which he was editor of the *Freeman.* His disturbed state of mind at this time seems to fit a passage in the reflective prose piece, "My Summer with Dr. Singletary," which Whittier contributed later to the *National Era:* "In the midst of duties and responsibilities which I clearly comprehended, I found myself yielding to the absorbing egotism of sickness. I could work only when the sharp rowels of necessity were in my sides." [7]

It was in Philadelphia that Whittier was told, after an examination by a noted physician, that with care he might live to be fifty years old.[8]

So admonished, and with the lessons of his own experience entirely plain to him, Whittier during the eighteen-forties revised his way of life. The pendulum swung on the side of enforced calm. Whittier now turned his necessity to capital gain, and made the decade the most fruitful of his life in study and thought, and in the intellectual growth which resulted from it. "The constant drawback of ill-health" which he remarked in writing to Lowell on April 18, 1844,[9] was, in the long view, less that than it was a limitation. Whittier was obliged to give up certain things that he liked — public functions and private receptions, for example, which after 1840 he attended less and less often. His counterbalancing gain was time free from tension and far better opportunity to increase his power to do the work to which he had set his hand. In the period 1840–50 it became firmer in grasp than it ever was before, and from his study windows in the "garden room" of the home at Amesbury his view of the world and of men gained in penetration and in scope.

## 2

Most of the friends and other persons whom he wished to see came to him in Amesbury or in Danvers. There was, however, no falling off in requests that he attend this function or do that favor, and in the last thirty years of his life the weight of his correspondence became very formidable. Yet he disciplined himself to decline most invitations which would have overtaxed his strength, and only the most extraordinary attraction called him forth from the semi-retirement of his home — apart from voluntary journeys to see personal friends in Boston, or the Pickards in Portland, or to be with summer companions in the White Mountains. He never liked crowds, and avoided them increasingly as he grew older.

Pickard wrote that Whittier was quite unable to attend public affairs "unless an opportunity was given him to retire without notice, and without causing disturbance. A continuous mental strain of two hours was intolerable to him." Even from celebrations arranged in honor of his birthdays he frequently and adroitly disappeared. Pickard went on:

> The more highly prized and interesting the guest he was entertaining, the greater the necessity of getting an occasional brief respite from his conversation. His intimate friends understood this, and would leave him to himself, at short intervals, and it was interesting to see the in-

genuity with which he would escape from a bore, who did not appreciate or consider his infirmity.[10]

Weather was a stern governor of his venturings forth — weather and his sense of duty. He made it a practice to attend the New England Annual Meeting of Friends, at Newport, Rhode Island, generally held in June. But he attended only one meeting, on June 30, 1870, of the board of trustees of Brown University, in neighboring Providence, during his membership (1869–92).[11] As a member of the Board of Overseers at Harvard from 1858 to 1871 he was present at only four meetings — two of them, remarkably, in winter in the Senate Chamber, Boston, and one in Cambridge in June. Characteristically, he avoided commencement meetings of the Board, and the crowds he would have encountered in Cambridge.[12]

Two proposed journeys to London, in 1840 and 1849, had to be abandoned by Whittier because it was considered certain the weight of public and social engagements would overbalance the benefits of the sea voyage. In 1840 his fellow Abolitionist and friend and physician, Doctor Henry Ingersoll Bowditch, advised him to cancel the passage which had already been booked.[13] He feared serious consequences from any serious mental or physical exertion on Whittier's part. In 1849 Whittier himself decided against attempting the visit to England which Joseph Sturge had offered to underwrite. On July 14 he confided to Lewis Tappan:

> I have been spending some weeks in the northern part of New Hampshire, and thy kind note relative to our friend Sturge's proposition, receives my earliest notice on my return. I wish it were possible for me to avail myself of so generous an offer; but in my present very weak state of health, I could be of no real service to the cause, without making exertions to which my strength is inadequate. If I could visit Europe as a mere looker-on, careless and indifferent in respect to the great questions which agitate it, I might possibly be benefited by it. But this I cannot do, and I can ill bear any additional excitement. * * * I am glad thou art able to bear what Charles Lamb calls "the dull drudgery of the desk's hard wood." [14]

# 3

The specific symptoms and the causes of Whittier's infirmity are suggested in a letter which he wrote on November 14, 1842, in response to Doctor Bowditch's request which, evidently, later resulted in Whittier's writing the poem "Massachusetts to Virginia." (It was evoked by the capture in Boston of the runaway slave George Latimer, and Bowditch himself read the poem at a citizens' meeting in Ipswich.)[15] Whittier explained to Doctor Bowditch:

> Thy letter of the 11th instant has been received. From my heart I thank thee for thy kind and flattering notice of my anti-slavery rhyme. As to thy particular request, I feel too deeply on the subject to attempt it in the present state of my health. Protracted illness has shattered my nervous system, and I cannot bear any strong emotion. Any intellectual effort in which the *heart* participates is attended with pain and with distressing and suffocating sensations in breast, throat, and head. I must, therefore, crush down my feelings and remain silent. * * *[16]

Whittier appears to have consulted a number of physicians, including at least a few of the ablest in their time. Pickard said that some believed Whittier's trouble was a heart affection, and that it annoyed him less in late life than it did during the middle years. Evidently rest and care were already then known to be a relief for certain heart ailments.

Now and then, also, Whittier was laid low by fevers, presumably related to his chronic bronchial ailment. One such bout of illness caught him in the winter of 1867–68, and on January 18, unable himself to hold a pen, he dictated a note to Fields. Whittier related that for four weeks he had been unprecedentedly ill with a slow fever which left him without appetite, and very weak. Ten days later, in writing to Lucy Larcom, he reported, "It will . . . be a good while before I shall get up even to my usual very moderate degree of health and strength."[17]

More persistent than either of these trials, and nearly as painful as his heart trouble, was the succession of shattering headaches, evidently of the unfathomed kind called *migraines*, that Whittier had during most of his life. He once said, "I inherited from my parents a nervous headache, and on account of it have never been able to do all I wished to do."[18] Judge Cate testified, "He worked between headaches,"[19] and Pickard added the fact that Whittier in middle and later life was unable to write continuously for even a half-hour, without severe pain in the head. The close work, for example, of seeing *The Tent on the Beach* through the press was taxing, and he had to decline Fields's invitation, at about the time the book was published, to visit him. Whittier pleaded:

> Solitude as such has few charms for me. But I am and have been for many days unfit and unable to make any change. A miserable, inexorable headache engrosses me. I am a bundle of nerves for Pain to experiment upon, and I can think of nothing else until this subsides. I may as well be here as anywhere, since I should be neither useful nor ornamental, and I love my friends too well to inflict something which is not myself upon them.[20]

Beyond this, steady eyestrain and possibly insufficient correction by spectacles must have aggravated his condition. His brother "Frank" wrote him from Boston on September 6, 1882, to report that Doctor B. Joy Jeffries had diagnosed his trouble as akin to Whittier's.[21] It was "over-sight," or what Doctor George M. Gould, writing in 1903, called "hyperopic astigmatism," with the added strain of "presbyopia" as his years increased. Doctor Gould believed that Whittier's palpitation of the heart was probably due to a reflex from eyestrain, and he was convinced that the lack of special diagnostic skill in the medical profession at a time when it would most have helped Whittier, hid the facts of his trouble.[22]

That is plausible. It is true, at all events, that since Whittier's death in 1892 no new and solid information has been discovered that would support convincing new theories about the reasons for his bad health. All that matters is this: in spite of his burden Whittier worked prodigiously through a life span of nearly eighty-five years, and he accomplished much for his fellow men. It is a mark of his stature that his mind and spirit grew in health and robustness as he ran the handicap-course of his life. Even when his infirmities combined to plague him with sleeplessness, which was at times chronic, he retained his faith in his world, and in himself as a human being with a duty to perform. On October 13, 1883, after a particularly trying bout of insomnia which lasted 120 hours ("an experience I would not like to try again"), he indicated to Mrs. Fields that his world was on its sound foundations and not running down hill to any slough of despond.[23] Because he had faith he was able to bear trial, and at the same time achieve.

In this there is no mystery, no war with nature. Doctor Gould has rightly made the point that Whittier's ill health, so far as the known facts go, was very much like that of E. B. Browning, Carlyle, Huxley, and other creative souls. He could have added Wordsworth and Proust. And one always remembers Stevenson, racked with tuberculosis, writing to George Meredith in 1893:

> For fourteen years I have not had a day's real health; I have wakened sick and gone to bed weary; and I have done my work unflinchingly. I have written in bed, and written out of it, written in hemorrhages, written in sickness, written torn by coughing, written when my head swam for weakness; and for so long, it seems to me I have won my wager and recovered my glove. . . . I was made for a contest, and the Powers have so willed that my battlefield should be this dingy, inglorious one of the bed and the physic bottle.[24]

# XXI

# The Grace of Humor

WHITTIER was able to bear his infirmities because he had, along with faith, a pervasive sense of humor. In March, 1875, he wrote typically in a long letter to Celia Thaxter: "I remember Lindley Murray's Grammar defined a verb as 'a word signifying to be, to do, or to suffer,' which is just my predicament, leaving out the 'to do.' " [1] His predicament was never so sore that a laugh would not lighten it, and the fact is that life in nearly all of its aspects fascinated him because it was, in one way or another, laughable as well as "real and earnest." His salvation was partly the fact that he could see the humor in incongruities, in things of fair seeming which barely concealed the ridiculous.

Among professional Down East humorists Whittier holds no rank. He created no Yankee characters, no "Jack Downings" or "Sam Slicks," which Seba Smith, Charles A. Davis, and Thomas Chandler Haliburton made familiar and loved in the eighteen-thirties and forties; nothing like Lowell's Hosea Biglow or even "Frank" Whittier's Ethan Spike.[2] But with his *Legends of New-England* (1831) and his early prose tales published in newspapers and magazines, he was among the first American writers to use "local color." His humor, moreover, was distinctively Yankee, usually on the side of the dry and underdone. Constance Rourke has pointed out, in addition, that Whittier, "even in the elegiac mood, could portray local character trenchantly, and kept a low-keyed native satire." [3] In "Among the Hills," for instance, he twitted

> Church-goers, fearful of the unseen Powers,
> But grumbling over pulpit-tax and pew-rent,
> Saving, as shrewd economists, their souls
> And winter pork with the least possible outlay
> Of salt and sanctity.[4]

Again, much of Whittier's humor issued in witty allusion. It was pervasive in his prose, especially his letters to familiars, and it was a happy feature of his direct personal relations. Here it issued in smiling laughter, and many people of his acquaintance made particular note of the fact that he smiled often. Humor instantly broke his characteristic sternness in repose, and danced from his eyes all over his face. His laugh was a play upon his facial features, not a vocal response. Particular amusement brought him forward in his chair, and he slapped his knee. One chronicler explains that Whittier smiles often because —

> he is always awake to the humorous side of things, and you cannot entertain him in any way more certainly than by telling him bright, witty stories. He catches the point instantly and eagerly. But the wit must be of a quiet order, — no roystering for him![5]

## I

In the first place, Whittier delighted in the humor which stemmed from unexpected twists in the roots of his own prime concerns. A Quaker businessman profiting from war drew from him Chaucerian laughter rather than moral condemnation.[6] Whittier never blinked the fact that many Friends were exceptionally astute businessmen, but he as often threw darts of humor as bursts of displeasure at the spectacle of "plain people" amassing wealth and devoting themselves to propertied interests rather than to the Society's concern for the relief of the poor.[7] He was also highly amused, as Lincoln was, by the occasional profane Friend. Carl Sandburg ably tells a type story:

> Lincoln had stood with two umbrellas at an imaginary rat hole, impersonating Sam'l, the Quaker boy whose father wanted to stop the boy's using swear words. The two umbrellas were blacksmith tongs. Sam'l's father had said, "Now, Sam'l, thee will sit here until thee has a rat. If I hear thee swear, thee will sit here till thee has another." And Sam'l had sat there for hours, snipping the tongs a few times, but no rat caught. At last one came out from the rat hole, the whiskers peeping up, then the black nose, and the eyes blinking. And the two umbrella tongs snapped together in a flash. And Sam'l yelled, "By

God, I have thee at last!" And Lincoln with a shaking, swaying frame let out a squeal and stood holding an imaginary wriggling rat between the two umbrellas.[8]

Whittier is remembered by his grandnephew, the scientist and inventor Greenleaf Whittier Pickard, to have been amused greatly by the story of the Quaker card player who quaintly reproached his partner: "Damn thee, thee trumped my ace." [9]

Again, as a believer in "Quakerism of the olden time," Whittier preferred silent meetings to those in which there was any singing or much speaking. His attitude toward Quaker singing, often expressed in terms of humorous deprecation, was summed up in the remark that "two hundred years of silence have taken all the sing out of our people." [10] Mrs. Fields never heard of Whittier's speaking in a Quaker meeting,[11] and Pickard perfectly illustrated his feeling on the subject:

> I once accompanied him to a devotional meeting, where many of the leading Friends of the Society were present, and as the papers had announced the names of several speakers from distant States, he expressed the fear that there would be no opportunity to get "into the quiet." As the speakers followed each other in rapid succession, he asked me if I had a bit of paper and a pencil with me. Then he appeared to be taking notes of the proceedings. I fancied some of the speakers noticed his pencil, and were spurred by it to an enlargement of utterance. When we were at home, I asked what he had written. He smiled and handed me his "notes," which are before me as I write. "Man spoke," "Woman sang," "Man prayed," and so on for no less than fourteen items. Being slightly deaf, he had heard scarcely anything, and had been noting the number and variety of performances. It was his protest against much speaking. At dinner the same day, his cousin, Joseph Cartland, commented upon the inarticulate sounds that accompanied the remarks of one or two of the speakers. "Let us shame them out of it," he said, "Let's call it grunting." "Oh, no, Joseph," said Whittier, "don't thee do that — take away the grunt, and nothing is left!" [12]

Whittier himself adhered scrupulously to "old school" Quaker habits of dress, but he was endlessly amused by the plain bonnets which like-minded women of the Society wore. In a quippish youthful letter which he wrote from Boston on May 18, 1829, to Edwin Harriman, of Haverhill, he lamented, "The worst of it is — if I ever get married I must marry a Quakeress with her bonnet like a flour dipper, and a face as long as a . . . yawl." [13] Pickard gives several later instances of Whittier's wry humor over Quaker bonnets, and in particular one episode of "mistaken identity" which resulted in the temporary carrying-off of a bonnet of Whittier's mother by a visitor from Danvers, the eminent Quaker minister Sophronia Page.[14] On another occasion he joked about the antique sameness of the bonnets of Lydia Maria Child, a non-Quaker whose rejection of fashions was wholly in the spirit of the Society. After she had left he mused and soliloquized: "It must be so; I cannot be mistaken!" "What must be so?" asked his hostess. He went on, "Yes, I know I must be right — certainly I have made no mistake!" Finally he exclaimed triumphantly, "Our friend, Mrs. Child, has a new bonnet!" [15]

In a similar vein, Whittier was able to see humor even in hard experiences in reform. Pickard summed up what many of Whittier's fellow-laborers for "causes" appear to have felt: "His keen sense of the ridiculous kept him from being in the least degree 'cranky' in his philanthropy." [16] With barbed humor Whittier reported the prevention of a proposed anti-slavery meeting in Concord, New Hampshire, in September, 1835, by a dangerous mob that "drank destruction to the Abolitionists." [17] In Philadelphia later, when an Abolitionist meeting obliged him to cancel a social engagement with his Wendell cousins, he sent as an apology this light verse:

To cousin Margaret Wendell, greeting:
This may inform thee that to-night
There'll be an anti-slavery meeting,
To set the world and so forth right!
And I, bear witness all slaveholders,
Must hold therein a lofty station —
A moral Atlas on whose shoulders
Shall rest the ark of reformation.
And therefore, cousin Margaret, seeing
My present duty — pardon me!
Since nothing but the *world's* well-being
Shall keep me, dearest coz, from *thee*.[18]

Whittier applied the same light touch to the world's honors, as two incidents related to Harvard University illustrate. On February 16, 1858, he sent Lowell the manuscript of the poem "Telling the Bees," and on the same day the state legislature elected him to the Board of Overseers of Harvard College. Writing on February 22 to suggest revisions in the manuscript, he told Lowell, who then was a professor at Harvard as well as editor of the *Atlantic:*

> I wish to hear from thee in regard to the piece — if thou hast any doubts about it, send it back to me, without troubling thyself to explain why or wherefore. I shall be sure it is for good and sufficient reason. But at any rate let me hear from thee in some way. If thee fail to do this, I shall turn thee out of thy professor's chair, by virtue of my new office of overseer.[19]

In November, 1886, when Harvard added an LL.D. to the honorary Master of Arts degree which it had conferred upon him in 1860, Whittier wrote to a friend, "I suppose thee has seen in the newspapers that Harvard has given me the nickname LL.D." [20]

Again, although the success of *Snow-Bound* relieved his poverty, Whittier's comment upon the worldly reward was characteristic. He explained to Charles Brainard, "Since 'Snow-Bound' was published, I have risen to the dignity of an income tax." [21]

In politics, which he took with sober-citizen earnestness, Whittier learned to laugh also at indignity. On election day in 1832 or 1833, when he was an unsuccessful Whig candidate for the state legislature, he took along to the town house in his wagon a neighbor who requested a ride and vowed he was going to vote for Whittier. Whittier knew he was a Democrat, and determined to watch him closely. The neighbor left home drunk, stopped for refreshment along the way, and had to be supported by Whittier to the ballot box. There he used an Opposition ballot that was handed to him at the last second. When afterward he told the story Whittier was asked, "Did not take the man home, did you?" His reply was: "Oh yes, I did; I promised his wife I would see him home safely, and I had to do it. I took him home dead drunk in the bottom of my wagon!" In 1842 Whittier was again a defeated candidate — Liberty Party nominee from his district for a seat in Congress — and he referred to the campaign humorously, years later, in a letter of November 29, 1880, to his niece: ". . . Thy friend B. has written me saying he is done with politics. He feels rather sore about his defeat; but I told him I had been in the same predicament as a Free-Soil candidate for Congress, and got abused worse than he did, for I was charged with ill-treating my wife!"[22]

## 2

Whittier probably thought more and did less about marriage than about anything else in life. It is entirely clear that in his early twenties he considered it natural that a man should marry, but it was only a passing phase on the way to his serious resolution that marriage was not for him. Humor was an obvious aid to his reflections on the matter. Upon it he touched repeatedly, and invariably in the light vein, in the three newspapers which he edited in the period 1829–32.[23] And as late as October, 1833, he wrote to his Hartford friend Jonathan Law, as he did many times after leaving Hartford, in high humor about the institution of marriage and himself as a possible recruit to it.[24] After 1833 his remarks about it fell under head of the kind of humor which George Eliot defined as thinking in jest while feeling in earnest. But at any time he would have been delighted with the ultimate comment said to have been made by a Cambridge schoolboy to his teacher: "John Greenleaf Whittier was a Quaker. He was born in Haverhill. He never married — he hated slavery."[25]

Once he had accepted singleness as his lot, Whittier became humorous advocate of marriage for others — a paradoxical rôle whose seriousness appears to have amused him. When in 1850 James T. Fields married, Whittier added, in a characteristic postscript to a letter about his forthcoming *Songs of Labor:*

> And now, business over, let me in all sincerity, bachelor as I am, congratulate thee on thy escape from single misery. It is the very wisest thing thee ever did. Were I autocrat I would see to it that every young man over twenty-five, and every young woman over twenty, was married without delay. Perhaps, on second thought, it might be well to keep one old maid and one old bachelor in each town, by way of warning, just as the Spartans did their drunken Helots.[26]

Whittier evidently felt as kindly disposed toward the marriage, on

May 14, 1838, of his Abolitionist colleagues Theodore Dwight Weld and Angelina Grimké, although his Quaker scruples kept him from attending their wedding at the home of a friend.[27] (Miss Grimké, a Quaker, was being married "out of meeting" to Weld, not a member of the Society.) In 1837 Weld and Whittier had together vowed perpetual bachelorhood, and Whittier, in the ominous days just before the burning of Pennsylvania Hall on May 17, 1838,[28] composed a humorous arraignment of his beloved friend Weld, and delivered it in person at the house in which the wedding was held. The lines, lacking one that Weld inadvertently omitted in copying them very late in life, run in this light key:

Alack and alas! that a brother of mine,
A bachelor sworn on celibacy's altar,
Should leave me to watch by the desolate shrine,
And stoop his own neck to the enemy's halter!
Oh the treason of Benedict Arnold was better
Than the scoffing at Love, and then *sub rosa* wooing;
This mocking at Beauty, yet wearing her fetter —
Alack and alas for such bachelor doing!

Oh the weapons of Saul are the Philistine's prey!
Who shall stand when the heart of the champion fails him;
Who strive when the mighty his shield casts away,
And yields up his post when a woman assails him?
Alone and despairing thy brother remains
At the desolate shrine where we stood up together,
Half tempted to envy thy self-imposed chains,
And stoop his own neck for the noose of the tether!

So firm and yet false! Thou mind'st me in sooth
Of St. Anthony's fall when the spirit of evil

. . . . . . . . . . . .

Filled the cell of his rest with imp, dragon and devil;
But the Saint never lifted his eyes from the Book
Till the tempter appeared in the guise of a woman;
And her voice was so sweet that he ventured one look,
And the devil rejoiced that the Saint had proved human![29]

In 1867, when a newspaper report represented Whittier as at last "human," he wrote jocularly (March 5) to his friend Mrs. Apphia Howard, who had sent him her congratulations. Of course, he said, she did not believe "the silly story," and he concluded: "I don't care much about it, but I should be sorry to have to read congratulations upon it by every mail. I wish the newspaper scamp who started it nothing worse than to be an old bachelor like myself, or to have a wife like Mrs. Caudle." [30]

Whittier probably smiled still more wryly when he wrote, in a book containing the autographs of authors who frequented the Old Corner Bookstore in Boston:

Ah, ladies! you love to levy a tax
On my poor little paper-parcel of fame,
Yet strange it seems that among you all
No one was willing to take my name,
To write and re-write, till the angels pity her,
The weariful words,
Thine truly,
Whittier.[31]

Humor also served Whittier as a fence — surmountable, unfortunately — against what he was accustomed to call "pilgrims." From 1850 or earlier down to his last days, people from many walks of life and mostly unknown to him found the way to his door, some just to satisfy their curiosity by seeing him, others to make requests that oftentimes were importunate demands. Elizabeth Whittier, on a visit with her brother to Lydia Maria Child's home in 1860, explained: "Thee has no idea how much time Greenleaf spends trying to lose these people in the streets. Sometimes he comes home and says, 'Well, sister, I had hard work to lose him, but I have lost him. But I can never lose a *her*,' said Whittier; 'the women are more pertinacious than the men; don't thee find them so, Maria?' I told him I did. 'How does thee manage to get time to do anything?' said he. I told him I took care to live away from the railroad and kept a bulldog and a pitchfork, and I advised him to do the same." [32]

This sound advice Whittier's kind humility stood in the way of his taking. Part of a letter which he addressed to a friend on September 5, 1870, read: "I have no company now, always excepting 'pilgrims' going and coming, on their summer tramps, and 'doing' me as they do the beaches and hills." [33] He was somewhat better able to fend against strangers who made the weight of his correspondence — nearly all of which Whittier managed in his own longhand — intolerably heavy in the last thirty years of his life. Reasonable requests for financial help he met if they seemed to him worthy,[34] but he recoiled, generally in humor, from insolent demands made upon him. Some time probably in the eighteen-eighties he wrote from Amesbury to Mrs. Woodman at Oak Knoll: "I had a letter night before last from a woman in Ohio asking for $10, which she said it was the Lord's will that I should give. I must tell her that the Deacon here anticipated her." [35]

## 3

No bulldog but a parrot was Whittier's guardian and companion, and it amused all members of the household by its antics. Gail Hamilton described it amusingly: "They had a parrot which kisses and snuggles up and walks over the house and asks for water and eats peach preserves." [36] "Charlie" was king of the succession of domestic pets — cats, dogs, and even a bantam rooster — which the Whittiers had in their Amesbury home, and he possessed in the beginning a sovereign command of the language. Years of residence in the Quaker household toned down the vivid vocabulary which he had acquired, probably from a ship's crew putting into Newburyport. But he was now and then a backslider, to the Whittiers' embarrassment. On a certain Sunday morning "Charlie," whom Whittier refused to have caged, elected the church-going hour to escape up the chimney and regale passers-by in the street below with a wondrous eloquence. Even so, there was no "language barrier" between Whittier and the personable gray bird. "Charlie" at mealtimes perched on the back of Whittier's chair, and manifestly exchanged with him the drollery and teasing and tricks which were the communication system humorously operating between Whittier and all of his pets.

Once "Charlie" saved his amused master from an extremity of boredom inflicted by a haranguing "pilgrim." The parrot nipped the visitor's trouser leg when, by excited rocking in his chair, he worked it above his boot top. Very gratefully Whittier took command of the conversation to apologize for his sympathetic pet.[37]

On February 7, 1866, Whittier sadly communicated to Lucy Larcom the news of Charlie's death:

> I have met with a real loss. Poor Charlie is dead. He has "gone where the good parrots go." He has been ailing & silent for some time:

and he finally died. Do not laugh at me — but I am sorry enough to cry if it w$^{d}$ do any good. He was an old friend: dear Lizzie liked him. And he was the heartiest, jolliest pleasantest old fellow I ever saw.

And speaking of him reminds me of a little verse I have had by me suggested by one of his sayings. I enclose it. Perhaps it might fill a corner of O.Y. Folks. But I am by no means sure that it is fit for such a place.[38]

The poem appeared in *Our Young Folks*, edited by Miss Larcom, in June, 1866, under the title "The Bird's Question." In the Riverside Edition of his works Whittier called it "The Common Question." It was a serious reflection upon what man wants here below, induced in Whittier by the humorous query of Poor Poll, "What does Charlie want?".[39]

To sum it all up, the grace of humor deeply overlay Whittier's rich and strong personality. It marked him out as exceptional among fellow reformers, and as distinguished — along with Emerson and Lowell and Holmes — among the New England school of writers in his day. And even though it ran through many prose pieces like the article on Richard Baxter and poems such as "The Double-Headed Snake of Newbury," it was only to his intimates that he uncovered the full vein of his humor. This was a pity.

Once, after a joyous outing at the Bearcamp River House in West Ossipee, New Hampshire, in September, 1876, with friends of his election, Whittier showed his own humorous solicitude for the uninitiated public by writing to Mr. Pickard:

Don't print in thy paper [the *Portland Transcript*] my foolish verses, which thee copied. They are hardly consistent with my years and "eminent gravity," and would make "the heathen rage, and the people imagine vain things." [40]

# XXII

## A Man among Men

As THE YEARS PILED UP on him, Whittier's physical delicacy, coupled with a touch of shyness which he often exhibited in the company of large groups of people or of strangers, obliged him for the most part to be a stay-at-home, except in summer, at Amesbury or at Oak Knoll in Danvers. He had neither the excessive sociability of a Browning nor the reclusive bent of a Thoreau; nor had he the establishment or the zest of Longfellow which would have enabled him to conduct a salon. Yet people of exalted and of humble station alike sought him out in his relatively rustic homes because he was not solely a man of power but, surpassing all else, an exceptionally attractive human being.

It was not the "pilgrims" merely who sought to "collect" him. People busy with the world's affairs journeyed to his home to enjoy his conversation and unpretentious hospitality, or wrote letters which plainly manifested the regard of their authors for the man who received them. It was a convincing, well-based record and reason of Whittier's having so abundantly, in his ripe years, the blessings of "honour, love, obedience, troops of friends." Whenever he fared forth to Boston and other metropolitan places to be publicly honored or privately entertained, the manifestations were the same.

What, after the merely fulsome was cast out of the balance, did these amount to under careful assay?

# 1

With men of letters in New England and New York — "a goodly number of coevals," in Holmes's phrase — Whittier had happy and affectionate relations. He was probably closest in feeling to Holmes, the only one of the famous band to outlive him; but he was admiringly and unselfishly devoted to Bryant, Emerson, Longfellow, Lowell, Harriet Beecher Stowe, Thoreau, and others. W. D. Howells wrote that "Whittier was one of the most generous of men towards the work of others, especially the work of a new man. . . ." T. B. Aldrich remarked the same fact; and once, having just read Lowell's letters, he commented to a friend on October 31, 1893: "Emerson and Whittier are about the only men in that famous group who are not thinking about themselves the whole while. They were too simple to pose, or to be *intentionally* brilliant." [1]

Unexceptionably, although frank to point out his technical deficiencies, Whittier's coevals perceived the special New England quality of much of his verse, and all acknowledged his power as a man. E. C. Stedman got to the substance of the matter when he ventured the prophecy:

> We already see, and the future will see it more clearly, that no party ever did a vaster work than his party; that he, like Hampden and Milton, is a character not produced in common times; that no struggle was more momentous than that which preceded our Civil War, no question ever affected the destinies of a great people more vitally than the antislavery issue, as urged by its promoters.[2]

Whittier, it bears repeating, described himself to F. H. Underwood as "a *man*, and not a mere verse-maker." [3] About the *Atlantic* coterie he held the same sentiment, which he expressed in a letter of July, 1875, to Mrs. Fields:

> How good Longfellow's poem ["Morituri Salutamus"] is! A little sad, but full of "sweetness and light." Emerson, Longfellow, Holmes, and myself, all are getting to be old fellows, and that swan-song might serve for us all — "we who are about to die." God help us all! I don't care for fame, and have no solicitude about the verdict of posterity.
>
> . . . What we *are* will then be more important than what we have done or said in prose or rhyme, or what folks that we never saw or heard of think of us.[4]

Whittier knew well what he admired in the way of men, and in *Margaret Smith's Journal* he suggested his standard: "What avail great talents, if they be not devoted to goodness?" [5] His unreserved praise and affection went to men and women who put the service of mankind above personal concerns. Seldom, down to the time of the Civil War especially, were his prime heroes popular favorites. Whittier was most naturally attracted to men like John Quincy Adams, William Leggett, Robert Rantoul, William Ellery Channing, and Charles Sumner — individuals who saw clearly what they believed to be right and did it without compromise, without regard for personal consequences. He was himself four times gravely endangered by anti-slavery mobs, and he lauded for their physical courage Garrison, May, and other Abolitionists who also experienced outbreaks of popular unreason. Moral courage was yet the higher virtue, in Whittier's judgment — that kind of fortitude which dictates selfless choices and desires in favor of resolute, imaginative work to improve human society.

In applying his standard, Whittier was prim but not narrow. No other writer among the *Atlantic* contributors gave himself as freely as Whittier to the cause of Abolition, but nearly all took it up, in varying degrees, by the time the Fugitive Slave Law was legislated upon the North. Whittier welcomed any utterance, any action against slavery by Longfellow or Lowell or especially Emerson, but he did not in any way make Abolitionism a test of his attitude and feeling toward them or other writers. Indeed, he was the least warm and sympathetic to Whitman, of all the major writers of his time. Whitman, with whose philosophical conceptions of democracy his own had many points in common, he regarded as unwashed, in spite of the fact that Walt was anointed in war service of a kind which Whittier was bound as a Friend to admire. That, in Whittier, was simply and very regrettably a blind spot.

W. D. Howells remarked the reservations which Cambridge felt about Whittier as a poet, and he said: "Whittier in fact had not arrived at the clear splendor of his later work without some earlier turbidity; he was still from time to time capable of a false rhyme. . . ." [6] That was Lowell's standing complaint, echoed by others, and Whittier was well aware of the reason for it. When in 1888 he was reading proof for the Riverside Edition of his writings, he commented in a letter to Mrs. Fields: "I hope I am correcting a little of the bad grammar and rhythmical blunders which have so long annoyed my friends who have graduated at Harvard instead of a district country school." [7]

Yet the critical praise which Holmes, Longfellow, Lowell, E. P. Whipple, and others of the Cambridge and *Atlantic* coterie gave Whittier — and which he returned in kind and at least equal measure — plainly betokened the affection and admiration which the "goodly number of coevals" had for him both as poet and man. He was not so isolated by illness that he could not go to visit Longfellow in Cambridge and at his summer retreat in Nahant, or Emerson at Concord, or to meet visiting celebrities in Boston. And at his home in Amesbury or at Oak Knoll he received Emerson, Holmes, Lowell, and others of his literary contemporaries, in addition to Phillips Brooks, Sumner, Frederick A. P. Barnard (president of Columbia College), and Englishmen like Matthew Arnold, Archdeacon Farrar, Edmund Gosse, and Joseph Sturge.

On all of them the dominant impression that he made was that of vibrant strength, of being what he himself called Charles Kingsley — "a manly man." [8] Along with Lowell, E. P. Whipple was among the first of ranking critics to single him out for his distinctive qualities. As editor of the *North American Review*, Whipple in January, 1844,[9] warmly commended Whittier on the basis of poems included in Rufus W. Griswold's *The Poets and Poetry of America*. Forty years of friendship solidified Whipple's good opinion, and when the Edgar Parker portrait of Whittier was presented to what is now the Moses Brown School, in Providence, on October 24, 1884, he wrote:

> I have had the privilege of knowing him intimately for many years, and of doing all I could through the press to point out his exceptional and original merits as a writer. My admiration of his genius and character has increased with every new volume he has published and every new manifestation of that essential gentleness which lies at the root of his nature, even when some of his poems suggest the warrior rather than the Quaker. One thing is certain: that the reader feels that the writer possesses that peculiar attribute of humanity which we instinctively call by the high name of soul; and, whether he storms into the souls of others or glides into them, his hot invectives equally with his soft persuasions mark him as a man; a man, too, of might; a man whose force is blended with his insight, and who can win or woo his way into hostile or recipient minds by innate strength or delicacy of nature.[10]

That was the prevailing sentiment among people who knew him well — that in an unusual degree he combined gentleness and dignity with force.

It is of interest, but of less consequence, that his colleagues spoke of some of his individual works in superlative terms.[11]

Emerson, in Whittier's estimation, stood first among native writers. He said, "I regard Emerson as foremost in the rank of American poets; he has written better things than any of us." [12] Whittier admired the *Essays*, too, and Mrs. Fields tells of a Sunday occasion at the Isles of Shoals when he asked Celia Thaxter to read one to which he opened, and then himself "talked long and earnestly upon the beauty and necessity of worship — a necessity consequent upon the nature of man, upon his own weakness, and his consciousness of the Divine Spirit within him." [13]

The two men met at intervals. They worked together, for example, in anti-slavery affairs, which Whittier took up in 1833, eleven years earlier than Emerson. From their correspondence it is clear that Emerson twice was Whittier's house guest and twice spoke before the Amesbury Lyceum in the season of 1852–53. Emerson in turn was cordial in his invitation to Whittier to visit him in Concord, as in this letter written to acknowledge receipt of a copy of *The Pennsylvania Pilgrim* (1872):

> I have never thanked you for the kind welcome home [from an extended trip abroad] [14] you sent me under the best form of the book of poems, which we presently found time to read through, — my wife and daughters assisting. I confess to the frivolity of liking "King Volmer and Elsie" the best, if only because the reader's voice broke suddenly at the summit of the story. But we will talk of this and much more, if you will in your lifetime come to Concord, as you once promised to do. My dame will not forget it, nor will let me if I could. Now, a week from to-morrow is the meeting of the Saturday Club, which you might honor oftener than you do. I pray you to come and spend Friday with us, and we will carry you down to the Club on Saturday.[15]

In September, 1873, Whittier wrote in part to acknowledge another invitation from Emerson:

> Thy kind note, and that of my friend John M. Forbes, are before me. I cannot tell thee how glad I should be to accept so kind an invitation. The reason, the place, above all the company, attract me strongly; and it pains me to know that I must forego the pleasure. * * * [16]

The remainder of the letter touched upon political matters which concerned both men.

In addition, Emerson and Whittier over the years met at occasional dinners in Boston — as when, in the summer of 1868, they joined Sumner and Whipple. At other times they were guests together in the Fields' home in Charles Street.[17]

When it was that Whittier saw Emerson in Concord, and whether he was then a guest in the Emerson home, is not clear. But it is a reasonable conjecture that the meeting took place when Emerson's "mental mist" was lowering upon him.[18] Robert S. Rantoul recorded Whittier's account of the meeting thus:

> . . . Mr. Emerson told him that he had concluded he must give up all hope of a place among the poets. He said he could not see that he did not write as good verses as some of the rest of them, but the public would not buy his poems, and he did not care to read them, and there was an end of it. . . . He seemed for the moment to feel that there was no appellate tribunal beyond the judgment or lack of judgment of his contemporaries. Mr. Whittier thought this amusing and said so. . . .
>
> Before leaving Concord on this visit Mr. Whittier had said to Mr. Emerson: "Some time, I want to sit down with you and compare views about immortality." Mr. Emerson replied: "I should like that, — but not today, — not today. Come round here next Monday morning at ten o'clock and we will drop the bucket away down into the well and see what we may bring up." Mr. Whittier added that he had been obliged to leave Concord and was unable to meet the appointment, so he lost that opportunity and no other ever came to him.[19]

That was not the natural tone of relations among the *Atlantic* writers, and it affected Whittier not at all. His personal delight in the company of his literary fellows was steady and unexceptional. When in 1882 both Longfellow and Emerson died and he himself became seventy-five, he felt seriously the weight of years. In 1887 he wrote to his friend Daniel Ricketson, of New Bedford, "that Boston had lost much of its old attraction for him, since Emerson, Longfellow, Fields, and other friends had passed away. . . ." [20] The immediate blow of their deaths was accurately measured in two letters which he wrote in March, 1882, the first of them to his niece, Mrs. Pickard:

> The death of a man like Longfellow is a national loss. He had been an influence for good; all the Christian virtues, his verse and his life

exemplified. Pure, kindly, and courteous, simple yet scholarly, he was never otherwise than a gentleman. There is no blot on the crystal purity of his writings. His fame is secure, and is likely to increase in the future. I cannot imagine a time when his songs shall cease to be loved and cherished. "Peace to the good man's memory! Let it grow green with years and blossom through the night of centuries."

And on March 28, while Emerson lay ill with pneumonia which took him off in April (the result of exposure to weather when Longfellow's body was interred), Whittier confided to T. B. Aldrich:

It seems as if I could never write again. A feeling of unutterable sorrow and loneliness oppresses me. I must leave to thee or Dr. Holmes the poem for the "Atlantic." I have written a few verses for the next number of the "Wide Awake," in reference to the celebration of Longfellow's last birthday by the children, and do not feel that I can do any more at present, if ever. Our circle is awfully narrowing. We must close our thinned ranks and stand closer to each other. As Wordsworth says: —

"Like clouds that rake the mountain's summit,
As waves that know no guiding hand,
So swift has brother followed brother,
From sunshine to the sunless land!" [21]

## 2

Whittier's seventieth and eightieth birthdays in particular were made the occasion of organized jubilation. His peers had then full play to voice in public the sentiments which they entertained for him in their direct relations. Two magazines, the *Literary World* and the *Atlantic Monthly*, led in organizing a parade of praise on his seventieth anniversary which was to keep step with him through the fourteen more which he passed in his life. Whittier's response to all the outpouring of affection for him as man and critical approval of him as writer was one of diffident pleasure. He wrote wryly to his niece, when he learned of plans for the banquet which the publishers of the *Atlantic* gave on December 17, 1877, in his honor: "They are wanting to make a fuss over my birthday on the 17th.

I think I have put a stop to it. It is bad enough to be old, without being twitted of it." [22] But the *Literary World* had set an unstoppable force in motion when in its issue dated December 1 it dedicated a number of pages to Whittier. The roster of contributors to those pages and of the seventy or so men who gathered to honor him at the *Atlantic* dinner, was a literary and political *Who's Who* of the time.

Among the contributors of verse to the special section of the *Literary World* were Longfellow with the sonnet "The Three Silences," Bayard Taylor with "A Friend's Greeting," Holmes with "The Golden Calendar," Edmund Clarence Stedman with "Ad Vatem," and so on through a numerous list that included William Lloyd Garrison, the Southern poet Paul Hamilton Hayne, and also the women writers Charlotte Fiske Bates, Lydia Maria Child, Lucy Larcom, Elizabeth Stuart Phelps, and Celia Thaxter. From other well-known friends and admirers came letters bearing affection and solid respect — from George Bancroft, William Cullen Bryant, George William Curtis, Richard H. Dana, Charles W. Eliot, T. W. Higginson, Francis Parkman, Harriet Beecher Stowe, and yet more.

In merit the various pieces were uneven, but in tone remarkably steady. Bancroft the historian and Mrs. Stowe the novelist gave the distinctive note of all of them. The kernel of Bancroft's tribute was this:

> As a poet he is a New England man of the sharpest outline, and at the same time a cosmopolite militant, doing battle with spiritual weapons for liberty and humanity, regardless of continent, color or creed.

And Mrs. Stowe held the note of praise through this passage:

> It has been his chief glory, not that he could speak inspired words, but that he spoke them for the despised, the helpless, and the dumb; for those too ignorant to honor, too poor to reward him. Grace was given him to know his Lord in the lowest disguise, even that of the poor hunted slave, and to follow him in heart into prison and unto death.

To the dinner arranged by the *Atlantic Monthly* at the Hotel Brunswick in Boston, on his birthday, were invited the leading writers of New England and New York. Whittier, prevailed upon to attend and to sit at the head table along with Emerson, Holmes, Howells, Longfellow, and Charles Dudley Warner, was introduced by H. O. Houghton, senior publisher of the twenty-year-old magazine. The seventy guests rose and cheered. Embarrassed by the unaccustomed display, Whittier could only say:

You must know you are not to expect a speech from me tonight. I can only say that I am very glad to meet with my friends of the "Atlantic," a great many contributors to which I have only known through their writings, and that I thank them for the reception they have given me. When I supposed that I would not be able to attend this ceremony, I placed in my friend Longfellow's hands a little bit of verse that I told him, if it were necessary, I wished he would read. My voice is of "a timorous nature and rarely to be heard above the breath." Mr. Longfellow will do me the favor to read the writing. I shall be very much obliged to him, and hope at his ninetieth anniversary some of the younger men will do as much for him.[23]

Longfellow read the "Response," in which Whittier happily acknowledged, with a generous discount, "your words of cheer and praise."[24] Emerson, one of several who were unable, like Bryant, to arrange on call "the thoughts and words fitting for such an occasion," read Whittier's "Ichabod." Howells ran gracefully over the *Atlantic's* two decades; Charles Eliot Norton spoke for Lowell, then Minister to Spain; and Holmes rose to his reputation as prime occasional poet by reading lines which accurately characterized the works of Emerson, Longfellow, Lowell, and Whittier. Here it was that he called Whittier "the wood-thrush of Essex."

Other speeches and readings followed, in Whittier's honor, and there was one sketch — by Mark Twain, up from Hartford — which by its "celebrated jumping frog" kind of originality must have appealed to his sense of humor. Clemens greatly ruffled Boston dignity, however, by sketching Emerson, Holmes, and Longfellow as masqueraders in the guise of California roughs. Five or six years later, in his "biographical sketch" of Whittier, F. H. Underwood (assistant editor of the *Atlantic*, who attended the dinner and who knew Whittier well) wrote of Twain's contribution: "It was audacious, and perhaps in questionable taste; but nothing more comic was ever conceived. The manner in which the poets were supposed to have pelted each other with quotations was wholly irresistible."[25]

There was rejoicing in the land, moreover, that Whittier had reached seventy full of honor. The voices raised in his praise in Boston became a chorus elsewhere in the United States, and in England as well. Underwood gathered in a scrapbook seventy solid pages of tributes, in prose and verse, which had appeared in newspapers. One particular editorial, published in the *New York Evening Post* on December 17 and perhaps written by Bryant, sounded the general key. Whittier was honored for his achievements in verse, but principally because they were grounded in strong humanity.

> For ourselves [the article read] we find the chief source of his poetic power where it is pleasantest to find it, in the intense truthfulness, naturalness and simplicity of his poetry. He is a bard of human nature, and he has helped human nature in honoring it.

Whittier now, precisely as in his newspaper-editing days, liked it that his work was liked, but he was quite able to distinguish between deserved praise and empty adulation. In the wake of the seventieth-birthday celebration, he confided in a letter to Julia A. Hodgdon:

> Of course, I prize highly the love and good will of others, but the thing was too pretentious, and had too much publicity to be altogether pleasant. Over-praise pains like blame. I know my own weakness and frailty, and I am humbled rather than exalted by homage which I do not deserve. As the swift years pass, the Eternal Realities seem taking the place of the shadows and illusions of time.[26]

And that was the genuine tenor of his grateful response to his Amesbury friends and neighbors, whose over-the-back-fence view of him, steadied by forty years' close observation, had prompted the sending of a warmly appreciative letter to him. This was Whittier's response, published in the Amesbury *Villager* on December 27, 1877:

> Forty years ago I came to dwell among you, although the place of worship which I have always frequented, within the bounds of the village, had made me familiar with it from early childhood. I can testify to the uninterrupted kindly and friendly relations which have existed between us during that long period. You have known me thoroughly; my whole life, with its faults, follies, and better characteristics, has been before you in the daily intercourse of citizens and neighbors; and qualified as you are to judge of it, it is an unspeakable satisfaction to know that you can render so favorable a verdict. You will, I know, pardon me if I say that while the praise, which in the excess of your kindness you have bestowed upon me, has been very grateful to me, it

has awakened a painful sense of my unworthiness to receive it without great qualification. I beg you, my old friends of Amesbury and Salisbury, to accept my warmest thanks for this testimonial, and for the delicate and considerate manner of its presentation. Circumstances may make our intercourse somewhat less constant and familiar than in former years, but your interests and welfare are mine; there is not a face among you that I shall not always be glad to see; not a rod of soil on the Merrimac or the Powow that I shall not be happy to retread; and about my hearth-fire in the old house on Friend Street I shall still hope often to meet you, as long as Providence, which has spared me hitherto, shall prolong my days.[27]

At Oak Knoll in Danvers, after 1877, Whittier in all except three years received a strong tide of birthday gifts and greetings which rolled in upon him from near and far. On December 17 of 1882, 1889, and 1891 he was elsewhere. Obviously the world loved a winner, and Whittier was twice triumphant — in his great cause and in his reception by the book-buying public after 1865. Yet it was equally obvious that the widespread popular appreciation of him was based on his personal qualities. He fought the good but long unpopular fight for freedom. He had the common touch. Somehow, perhaps even more than Longfellow, he reached the heart of man because his homely themes and simple lines touched a fundamental chord of man's aspiring.

So spoke the testimonials, and they were multitudinous. That which marked his eightieth birthday was almost overwhelming, and would have been except that Whittier chanced to be in vigor and good spirits for the occasion at Oak Knoll. Five weeks in advance of it the Essex Club, at a banquet in Boston (November 12, 1887), began a celebration which became national in scope. Whittier's friend, Senator George F. Hoar, made what was in effect a keynote speech, on the theme that Whittier was the third and most distinguished of three great advocates of liberty who sprang from Essex County in three memorable periods. In colonial times Nathaniel Ward, of Ipswich, had written the "Body of Liberties"; in 1848 Nathan Dane, of Beverly, had written the ordinance which excluded slavery from the Northwest Territory. Senator Hoar lauded these two men and their works, and then said:

The third, which I should place highest in the list, is the name of our living fellow-citizen, John G. Whittier. I wonder if Mr. Whittier

> knows how much his countrymen love him. The service he has rendered in our great anti-slavery struggle is one with which I think that no orator can be compared. The speech of Webster or Sumner is heard but by few. How soon, after all, it is forgotten! But the musical arrow of the poet pierces the heart of the whole people. It stirs the blood. It dwells in the memory. It springs to the lips in the time of deepest emotion. The figure of the orator is forgotten when his own passes away. But Whittier sits, and for centuries will sit, by millions of American firesides, a beloved and perpetual guest. . . . The love of liberty will not die out in the land while the youth of America learn and love the verse of the poet who combines the lofty inspiration of David with the sweet simplicity of Burns.[28]

The testimonial which the Essex Club prepared for Whittier on his birthday was an omnibus portfolio which contained, among other matter, an engrossed copy of Senator Hoar's speech; hundreds of autographs representing all elements of the people in Massachusetts; the signatures of Washington officials — the whole membership of the Supreme Court headed by Chief Justice Waite, fifty-nine Senators, Speaker Carlisle of the House and 333 Representatives coming from every State and Territory in the Union; and the autographs of private citizens like George Bancroft, James G. Blaine, Frederick Douglass, and Whittier's friend of fifty years' standing, Robert C. Winthrop, with whose politics he seldom agreed.

When he received the testimonial, Whittier responded:

> I really know not how to acknowledge a testimonial of such proportions and character, the magnitude and value of which I fully appreciate. I can only say that I accept it with profound gratitude. I am deeply moved by the fact that political and sectional differences seem to have been wholly set aside by the signers, and that those from whom I have felt compelled to dissent in times past have cordially joined with my personal and political friends in this tribute of respect to a private citizen, who loves his whole country, and is devoutly thankful that the sun of his closing day shines upon a free and united people.

December 17 was a day of celebration at Oak Knoll featured by the arrival of a special train from Boston bearing Governor Ames, his executive council, and well known citizens of Massachusetts and other States.

Mrs. Woodman noted that during the day Whittier received between five and six hundred guests. There was what Hawthorne would have called a choice collation, and Governor Ames cut the large birthday cake.

In Boston, the *Advertiser* published a birthday number which contained letters and poems of tribute addressed to Whittier by fellow writers, generous and admiring Walt Whitman among the number. Some appeared to say now again what had been proclaimed in 1877, and what Whittier himself in 1864 had written of Bryant on his seventieth birthday:

> His life is now his noblest strain,
> His manhood better than his verse! [29]

## 3

But the stuff of Whittier's life was not birthday celebrations, and he did not often, in his days of sorest battle, have governors on his side. The man who fought chattel slavery so hard was not physically able all his life to campaign for causes. He became a national symbol of the liberties which he did all that he could do to help solidify, but he was not a symbol merely. His stern sense of duty and his devout loyalty to people and principles in which he believed remained active as long as he lived. These, the chief qualities which marked him out among men, were permanent.

From Oak Knoll he wrote to Elizabeth Stuart Phelps on March 7, 1879:

> Back from my home in Amesbury. What a pity it is that we cannot shut down the gate, and let the weary wheels rest awhile! For myself, I have to work hard to be idle; I have to make it a matter of duty to ignore duty; and amuse myself with simple stories, play with dogs and cattle, and talk nonsense. Dr. Bowditch says that a man of active brain ought to make a fool of himself occasionally, and unbend, at all hazards to his dignity. But to some of us life is too serious, and its responsibilities too awful, for such a remedy. The unsolved mystery presses hard upon us.[30]

Politics and politicians often disgusted Whittier, but he neither recoiled from them nor ever ceased acting personally in behalf of good government. He was often extremely impatient with Republican Party politics and candidates, but kept his belief in the party's mission. He never forgot that the Democratic Party had been the instrument of the slave power, nor ever ceased liking individual Democrats or Southern friends on that account.[31] Whittier's friendship for the Carolina-born poet Paul Hamilton Hayne, who twice visited him in Massachusetts after the Civil War, had a more than ordinary warmth, in spite of Hayne's earlier bitterness against the North and especially the Abolitionists.[32]

Regardless of their party, Whittier was attracted to men by their quality. His invariable attitude was suggested by his adverse comment on one particular politician whom he distrusted: "I shouldn't wonder if he were willing to sell out. He had not much character to lose, and what little he had was hardly worth the trouble of keeping." [33]

Whittier's own attitude toward individual Southerners, and his post-war feeling about the South, was "correct." Vice-President Henry Wilson, writing Whittier on July 10, 1874, gave him this tribute: "Of all the actors in the grand struggle no one has been so unambitious, so moderate, so just, and so uniformly correct in judgement." [34] Whittier was glad that his country was cleansed of the stigma of chattel slavery, but always deplored the blood bath of the Civil War. Years lessened neither his sorrow over it nor his conviction that only wise measures of reconstruction such as Lincoln had had in view would "bind up the nation's wounds." Whittier stood for general amnesty, as he made clear, for example, in a letter of March 21, 1871, to Charles Sumner.[35] But chiefly he looked to the future. As his kind of democracy dictated, he stood for fair treatment and equal rights of all people, black as well as white. He was far-sighted enough to know that until there were full educational and other advantages of citizenship for the Negro population, no American society could inherently be either democratic or strong. Whittier never underestimated the problems involved in the reconstruction. He did ardently advocate that they be approached with good will and intelligence.

That is why, when the Civil War was over, Whittier was more active than ever to see that able candidates were nominated and elected. In the Presidential elections of 1872 and 1876 he was particularly energetic, and his feeling about men and issues involved is of pointed interest. Sumner, addressing the Senate on May 31, 1872, flagellated President Grant and his administration, and opposed his re-election. As a cushion and courtesy, Sumner wrote a letter of explanation to Whittier, who on June 12 replied to say, in brief: ". . . I am sorry for some parts of it, as I think its effect would have been better if it had been less severe." And he enclosed a copy of a letter which he had sent to the *Boston Transcript* and which was published on June 6:

. . . As regards the senior Senator of Massachusetts I have no change of opinion to record. I have not forgotten his long and brilliant services in the cause of freedom and the best interests of his country and mankind. I know him well. I have stood side by side with him for thirty years, and it requires something more than a mistake on his part to make me desert an old friend. I confess that I have seen with some impatience men, whose republicanism seems mainly to consist in their readiness to grasp the spoils of a victory won in a great measure by others, maligning, insulting, and displacing a man whose integrity, intellect, and acquirements are a standing reproach to themselves. I am no blind advocate of Senator Sumner, or any other man. I expect to see faults and frailties, and to grieve over the mistakes of those I love and respect. I regret the late speech, as it exposes the author to the charge of personal resentment, and because it seems to me unduly severe in its tone and temper. The Republicans of Massachusetts may, and probably will, dissent from its conclusions, through the press and at the ballot-box, but they have no occasion to question his sincerity or to charge him with abandoning any of the great principles which he has so nobly asserted, and for which he has suffered more than martyrdom.[36]

In 1872, also, Whittier leaped to Sumner's defense when the Massachusetts legislature passed resolutions of censure against him for proposing that the flags of national regiments should not bear the names of the Civil War engagements in which they had been carried. Whittier waged a one-man campaign to have the resolutions expunged. His personal reputation, as well as his standing with editors and public officials in other states to whom he wrote, finally won the fight early in 1874. It was full-scale, and Whittier pushed it deftly and with the old "Berserker fury" which he had often remarked in his heritage. He won the energetic support of his own State Representative, and of Governor William Claflin. To his friend Claflin, in whose Boston home he was many times entertained, Whittier at one point wrote:

The great and general court have acted like fools and worse, in denouncing Charles Sumner. I begin to hate parties and politics! I have sent to Hon. Willard P. Phillips, our representative, a draft of a petition for rescinding the odious resolution passed by the late extra session in censure of Charles Sumner. I made the movement not merely for Sumner's sake, but for the sake of the honor and goodness of our dear old Commonwealth. Sumner's fame is beyond its reach, but we cannot afford the disgrace on our records. I have not found one intelligent and respectable man who approved of that resolution.

Whittier also reported his tactics directly by letter to Sumner. In the spring of 1873 he described a hearing on petitions which he had got select members of all parties to sign. He wrote:

I have just got back from the hearing of the petitioners for rescinding the vote of the extra session of the legislature. The great Green Room was packed full of the noblest men and women of Boston and the State. Governor Claflin opened the matter in a brief but admirable speech, and was followed by ex-Governor Washburn, in a long and eloquent argument and appeal. James Freeman Clarke followed, earnest and able, and John C. Park had the floor when I left, making one of his best speeches. The hall rang with applause of the various speakers. The whole thing was well done, and I hope for the best results. The reports of the speeches will reach thee as soon as this, but I could not refrain from dropping a line. Governor Claflin has worked most actively and efficiently in the matter.

That session of the legislature did not budge, so Whittier stepped up his campaign on the next. The last letter he wrote to Sumner, on February 17, 1874, gladdened the last days of the dying man with the news that both houses of the legislature had voted decisively to annul the resolutions of censure. Whittier rejoiced:

The record of the Bay State is now clear. The folly of the Extra Session of 1872 is wiped out. I am especially pleased, as, like Senator Benton, on a former occasion, "solitary & alone I set the ball in motion."

When he learned of Sumner's death, Whittier wrote to Mrs. Claflin:

I have just received a telegram announcing the death of our dear and noble friend, Charles Sumner. My heart is too full for words. In deepest sympathy of sorrow I reach out my hands to thee and Governor

> Claflin, who loved him so well. He has died as he wished, at his post of duty, and when the heart of his beloved Massachusetts was turning towards him with more than the old-time love and reverence. God's peace be with him!

And when Massachusetts held commemorative services for Sumner on June 9, 1874, Whittier contributed fifty-three stanzas of elegiac verse, his last tribute to this man who "hated only wrong to man." [37]

In the 1872 election, Sumner had in effect bolted the Republican Party, but Whittier remained loyal to him. And Horace Greeley, another old friend, had been nominated by the Democrats to oppose President Grant. This was a strange pass, and many of the leaders with whom Greeley had for so many years worked in the Republican ranks employed every device to discredit him. He, too, found Whittier a steady friend and defender. On May 14, 1872, the *Boston Transcript* published a letter in which Whittier protested:

> . . . The poor attempts to ridicule him, and to underrate his eminent ability at the present time, on the part of some of our Republican papers, are best answered by the eulogiums bestowed upon him in their own columns heretofore . . . I have no wish, as I have no reason, to withhold my good opinion of my old friend, at a time when so many Republicans deem it advisable as a party expedient to assail him personally as well as politically.

Greeley failed to live out the year. When Whittier learned of his death, he wrote to the Reverend Doctor E. H. Chapin how much he had delighted in his thirty years' friendship with Greeley.

> All that time [he continued] I have known him as the educator of a people in liberty, temperance, integrity, economy, and industry, vigorously taking the side of the poor, enslaved, or suffering of every color and nationality. When I heard of his death, there mingled with my grief a feeling of gratitude, that I had been preserved from saying one word which could add bitterness to his life; that I had none of the late remorse over the dead for unkindness to the living, which is one of the saddest burdens of humanity.[38]

In 1876, Whittier, as he reported in a letter of April 26 to Celia Thaxter, faced "the worst east wind that ever blew in Boston" in order to attend the

Republican state meeting for the choice of delegates to the national convention to be held in Cincinnati.[39] He followed the campaign with his usual absorbed interest, and on November 4 said in a letter to Edna Dean Proctor:

> I feel anxious about the election. I think Hayes would be a safer man than Tilden, for the next four years. Tilden, however he might feel and wish, could not control his party. I hope I shall be able to vote, for I would n't like to lose my vote at this time. * * * [40]

Whittier's feelings about that acrimonious election were mixed. Tilden, the Democratic candidate, he had known for years to be an able and courageous man. Evidently he had given both aid and sympathy to Whittier in his anti-slavery labors. When Tilden died in 1886, Whittier was at Centre Harbor, New Hampshire. Without hesitation he wrote on August 4 the twenty-line tribute which was published in the *Boston Transcript* on the eleventh and in other newspapers immediately afterward. Certain Republican friends of Whittier's who remembered too well the bitterness of the election in 1876 were puzzled. When he returned to Oak Knoll he was asked how he came to write the lines to Tilden's memory. Whittier, Mrs. Woodman relates, said with emotion, "Why, I had to do it. It was due him, from me." [41]

Robert C. Winthrop and George F. Hoar were two other men in public life whose stand upon well defined principle won Whittier's respect. From the time they served together in the Massachusetts legislature in 1834–35, Whittier and Winthrop had a desultory correspondence. They seldom worked together or even stood together, and Whittier often regretted Winthrop's persistent Whiggery and his refusal to act with Liberty and Free-Soil leaders on specific anti-slavery issues. Yet their firm attitudes left ample room for respect and pleasant relations. Two of Whittier's many letters to Winthrop illustrate his feeling. In a note of February 26, 1859, he said in part:

> * * * It has been a matter of real pain to me to feel compelled to differ in some respects, upon public matters, with thyself & others whom I greatly esteem. All we can do, in these conflicts of opinion is to season our dissent with charity, & emulate the forbearance of Sir Thomas More, who could "hear heresies talked & yet let the talkers alone."

And again, in a letter of March 9, 1874, he expressed this sentiment:

* * * It gave me great pleasure to meet thee last week. Since our first meeting in the General Court nearly forty years ago, the respect I felt for thee as a worthy representative of the noblest historical name of Massachusetts has not been lessened by any differences of opinion on the questions which have engaged our attention. Thy speech against the Fugitive Slave Bill was a brave & noble utterance, & proved that the old Puritan Governor's love of liberty & justice lived in the heart of his descendant.[42]

Senator Hoar was much younger than Whittier, and their impersonal relations were founded merely upon solid respect. In December, 1882, Whittier gave a ready hand to the successful contest to re-elect Hoar to the United States Senate. The letter which he wrote on December 9 and which the *Boston Daily Advertiser* published on the twentieth was wholly typical of Whittier's lifetime interest in governmental affairs. The gist of his message was this:

I need not tell thee that I should regard it as a serious misfortune for Massachusetts to lose the services of Senator Hoar. I do not know him personally, and I am no man's partisan, but I have watched his course with great satisfaction. I regard him as one of the ablest members of the Senate, where his integrity and loyalty to the best traditions of his State have been abundantly manifested. He is a ready and able speaker, sound in judgment, and when once satisfied of the correctness of his position, he has the courage and firmness of his Puritan blood in maintaining it. It seems to me that it would be little short of political suicide for the legislature to set aside such a man. . . . It is neither safe nor just to discard without excuse or reason a faithful and efficient public servant.

Senator Hoar declared later that when four trusted advisers were on his side, he was always certain that "the wisdom and conscience of Massachusetts would be there also." Of Whittier in particular he said: "He added to the great genius which made him a famous poet the quality of being one of the wisest and most discreet political advisers and leaders who ever dwelt in the Commonwealth."[43]

Finally, among the many public men who were persuaded to address the Amesbury Lyceum on Whittier's invitation, he was attracted by the unusual force of Henry Ward Beecher. A likeness of him was in the "garden room" of the Amesbury home. When Beecher was made the subject of detraction and calumny, Whittier wrote to Elizabeth Stuart Phelps, on July 14, 1874:

> I love Beecher and believe in him. He has done good to thousands. If he has fallen into temptation I shall feel grieved, but would be ashamed of myself were I less his friend.[44]

When Beecher died in 1887, Whittier expressed his sense of acute loss, and again his admiration for Beecher, in a note to Mrs. Fields. Whittier closed with the remark: ". . . I think he could say, with David of old, that he would rather fall into the Lord's hands than into the hands of man." [45]

## 4

Whittier's belief in the mission and principles of the Society of Friends was, it may be said again, one of the fundamental drives in his life. His acceptance of old-school Quakerism's testimonies against some of the graces of life, including the arts of music and the theater, was narrowing. But in practical affairs Whittier at times took an independent stand upon principle which he thought even higher than the testimony of the Friends. He detested war, but thought that some blows struck for freedom and justice were warranted.[46] He had, besides, open admiration for at least two of the great soldiers of his day — William Tecumseh Sherman and Charles George ("Chinese") Gordon. Whittier in a letter of July 21, 1866, to Celia Thaxter, gave this opinion: "I hope you enjoyed the visit of Gen. Sherman. He seems to me the man of genius among our great soldiers." Of Gordon he said, in writing to Edna Dean Proctor on January 26, 1884: "I am deeply interested in the struggle going on in Upper Egypt. I am glad General Gordon is going there. At one time his bravery and sagacity nearly abolished the slave trade, and pacified the wild tribes of the Soudan." [47] And Whittier's public praise for Gordon and his works in Egypt brought him into disagreement with John Bright, English Friend, who held strictly to the Society's testimony against war. Even this difference of views did not destroy the respect and affection which the two men felt for each other.

Gordon died in 1885, Bright in 1889, and Whittier honored the memory of both men. After Bright's death Whittier, writing to Mrs. Fields on April 3, 1889, gave this affectionate summary of his feelings:

> * * * It seems strange to me that I am here alive to welcome her [the spring], when so many have passed away with the winter, and among them that stalwartest of Englishmen, John Bright, sleeping now in the daisied grounds of Rochdale, never more to move the world with his surprising eloquence. How I regret that I have never seen him! [48] We had much in common — in our religious faith, our hatred of war and oppression. His great genius seemed to me to be always held firmly in hand by a sense of duty, and by the practical common sense of a shrewd man of business. He fought through life like an old knight-errant, but without enthusiasm. He had no personal ideals. I remember how he remonstrated with me for my admiration of General Gordon. He looked upon that wonderful personality as a wild fighter, a rash adventurer, doing evil that good might come. He could not see him, as I saw him, giving his life for humanity, alone and unfriended in that dreadful Soudan. He did not like the idea of fighting Satan with Satan's own weapons. Lord Salisbury said truly that he was the greatest orator England had produced; and his eloquence was only called out by what he regarded as the voice of God in his soul.[49]

After Gordon's death, Whittier had been requested by Charles C. Reed, of London, to write an ode honoring his memory. He replied on March 4, 1885, saying that he had already been pondering the subject, but that he did not then dare to "undertake the eulogy of such a man with a feeble hand." On Whittier's suggestion, transferred by Mr. Reed, Tennyson wrote the four lines which became inscribed on Gordon's cenotaph in Westminster Abbey (and which he sent directly, with a note, to Whittier). Whittier's admiration for Gordon was expressed in this passage:

> For years I have followed General Gordon's course with constantly increasing interest, wonder, and admiration, and I have felt his death as a great personal bereavement. A Providential man, his mission in an unbelieving and selfish age revealed the mighty power of faith in God, self-abnegation, and the enthusiasm of humanity. For centuries no grander figure has crossed the disk of our planet. Unique, unapproachable in his marvelous individuality, he belongs to no sect or party, and

defies classification or comparison. I should be sorry to see his name used for party purposes, for neither Conservative nor Radical has any special claim upon him. . . . We Americans, in common with all English-speaking people, the world over, lament his death, and share his glorious memory.

When an extract from this private letter was sent, with Whittier's permission, to an English paper, Bright at once remonstrated. On March 18, 1885, he painfully wrote Whittier an eight-page letter, protesting that his admiration for Gordon was not based on facts. Bright felt so strongly about the English campaign in Egypt that in 1882 he had resigned in protest from Gladstone's cabinet, and he lamented the fact that "our Christian Poet" should by so much as a line add lustre to the memory of Gordon.

Whittier's firm but peaceful rejoinder was dated March 31, and its essence is this:

My dear Friend, — I regret the publication of my hasty private note to C. C. Reed, as it has occasioned thee uneasiness. I quite agree with thee as regards the armed interference with Egypt and the Soudan, and I think one of the best acts of thy life was thy withdrawal from the ministry in consequence of it. But as respects Charles Gordon, I cannot withdraw my admiration from the man, while I disapprove of his warlike methods. I learned much of him from my friend Dr. [Channing M.] Williams, who knew him well in China, and who thought him one of the most generous and self-sacrificing men he ever knew. Still later, I have read of his labors in the Soudan to suppress the dreadful slave trade, and it seems to me that he went to Khartoum once more really on an errand of peace, and I am not sure that he would not have succeeded if the English army had not invaded the Soudan. It is not probable that I shall write a poem on his life and death, but I thought of it, and intended to express my admiration of his faith, courage, and self-abnegation, while lamenting his war training and his reliance on warlike means to accomplish a righteous end. As it is, he was a better man than David or Joshua — he was humane and never put his prisoners into brick-kilns nor under hammers. And he believed in a *living* God, who reveals himself now as in the old time. . . . Hoping that thy own health is good, I am with love and sincere regard thy friend.[50]

This exchange of views between Bright and Whittier in no way shook

Whittier's conviction that Gordon, too, was a stalwart and admirable man. Whittier's portrait of him, in the red coat of a British soldier and the fez of an Egyptian officer, was never jarred from the wall of the study — the "garden room" — in the home at Amesbury, and it may be seen there today.

Whittier, indeed, was particularly attracted — and attractive — to strong men in England. He never met Tennyson, whose work he relished, but Bayard Taylor (in 1867) and other intermediaries testified to the warm regard which Tennyson had for Whittier and his writings.[51] Matthew Arnold met Whittier when he came to America in 1883, and on November 28 he wrote to his younger daughter: "Dear old Whittier came to meet me at luncheon yesterday. I have got his autograph for you, Holmes's and Hawthorne's. . . ." [52] Their personalities were sympathetic, and likewise their regard for each other's way of life and set of values. Mrs. Fields wrote that Whittier "had followed Arnold with appreciation from his earliest appearance in the world of letters, and knew him . . . 'by heart' long before a personal interview was possible." And, she added, Whittier wrote to her after Arnold had returned to England:

> I share thy indignation at the way our people have spoken of him — one of the foremost men of our time, a true poet, a wise critic, and a brave, upright man, to whom all English-speaking people owe a debt of gratitude. I am sorry I could not see him again.[53]

Dickens was another of England's stellar figures whose strong vitality won an automatic response from Whittier. His writings had for years been sprinkled with allusions to the life with which Dickens's pages teemed, when in 1867 Whittier met and heard him. For once Whittier faced the ordeal of two hours' sitting in a hall, and implored J. T. Fields to find him a place, in spite of the "crazy rush for tickets." Both Mrs. Fields and Pickard wrote that on the day of the evening Dickens was to give the reading, December 21, Whittier sent Fields a note excusing himself most reluctantly from the performance. "I would so like nevertheless," Whittier added, "to see Dickens, and shake that creating hand of his." Pickard went on that Whittier, who came in from Amesbury especially for the event, stayed the two hours of the reading in his room at the Marlboro Hotel — his usual Boston haunt — but afterward met Dickens at a private reception.[54]

In truth, Dickens lectured in Boston six times during December, 1867, his biographer John Forster wrote — on the second, third, fifth, sixth, twenty-third, and twenty-fourth.[55] Whittier, perhaps cajoled by Fields or some other friend, attended the reading on December 6. For on the fourteenth, from Amesbury, he sent this exceptionally vivid piece of reporting to Celia Thaxter:

> I have "made an effort" as Mrs Chick would say, & have heard Dickens. It was his last night in Boston. I found myself in the packed hall, sandwiched between Ricd. H. Dana Sen. & Longfellow with Mrs Fields one side of us & Mrs Ames the other. We waited some half hour: a slight brisk man tripped up the steps, sparkling with ring & chain — tight vested wide bosomed, short dress coat, white choker; tight pantaloons enclosing, as the Prairie girl said of Judge Douglass's — "a mighty slim chance of legs!" Somehow a slight reminder of his own Tim Tappertit in Barnaby Rudge. Face marked with thought as well as years — head bald or nearly so — a look of keen intelligence about the strong brow, & eye — the look of a man who has seen much & is wide awake to see more. I dont think he shows the great genius that he is — he might pass for a shrewd Massachusetts manufacturer, or an active N.Y. merchant. But his reading is wonderful, far beyond my expectations. Those marvellous characters of his come forth, one by one, real personages, as if their original creator had breathed new life into them. You shut your eyes & there before you know are Pecksniff, & Sairy Gamp, Sam Weller & Dick Swiveller & all the rest. But it is idle to talk about it: you must beg, borrow, or steal a ticket & hear him. Another such star-shower is not to be expected in one's life-time. After the reading I called on him with Longfellow & the Fields. * * *[56]

Whittier, after all, recognized good theater when he happened upon it — good theater and a man charged full with life.

Dickens's death, in 1871, did not take him out of Whittier's life. On a summer afternoon before long Whittier turned up at the Fields' home to talk about Dickens. Whittier remarked his gratitude for the light that Dickens brought into his quiet life at Amesbury, "and what grateful love he must ever bear to him. He wished to hear all that could be told of him as a man." Tea came, the sun went down, and still Whittier clung to the life of Dickens. Mrs. Fields recorded that after a long silence he broke out:

What's he doing now? Sometimes I say, in Shakespeare's phrase, O for some "courteous ghost," but nothing ever comes to me. He was so human I should think thee must *see* him sometimes. It seems as if he were the very person to manifest himself and give us a glimpse beyond. I believe I have faith; I sometimes think I have; but this desire to see just a little way is terribly strong in me. I have expressed something of it in my verses to Mrs. Child about Loring.[57]

So it was that Whittier long was drawn to Dickens the man. Only Milton, it may be, appealed to him more strongly as a vivid man powerful in his works and life. It was fitting and not merely fortuitous that, on the verge of becoming eighty, Whittier was asked to write the inscription for the Milton memorial window in Saint Margaret's Church, London. In 1880 and again in 1885 Whittier had met Archdeacon Frederic W. Farrar who, with Phillips Brooks, called upon him at Oak Knoll. Both churchmen greatly admired Whittier. Bishop Brooks conveyed his own sentiments in a letter deferentially dated 11th mo., 11, 1885:

* * * Archdeacon Farrar left me on Monday. He will never forget — as I surely shall not — the kind and cordial welcome which you gave us, and the time which it was our privilege to pass with you. I have had much to thank you for before, very much indeed. Now it is a pleasure to assure you most earnestly of my respect and deepened gratitude.[58]

Two years later Mr. George W. Childs, of Philadelphia, offered to meet the costs of installing a Milton memorial window in the famous London church, and his offer was accepted. In October, 1887, Archdeacon Farrar reported to him:

The Milton window is making good progress. It will be, I hope, magnificently beautiful, and both in coloring and design will be worthy of your munificence, and worthy of the mighty poet to whose memory it will be dedicated. The artists are taking good pains with it. I sent you an outline of the sketch not long ago. Before the end of the year I hope to send you a painting of the complete work. Messrs. Clayton and Bell are putting forth their best strength, and promise me that it shall be finished before the end of the Jubilee Year.[59] When it is put in, I shall make your gift more universally known. Mr. Lowell wrote me a quatrain for the Raleigh window. I can think of no one so suitable as Mr. J. G. Whittier to write four lines for the Milton window. Mr. Whittier would feel the fullest sympathy for the great Puritan poet, whose spirit was so completely that of the Pilgrim Fathers. I have always loved and admired Mr. Whittier's poems. Could you ask him as a kindness to yourself and to me, and as a tribute to Milton's memory, if he would be so good as to write this brief inscription, which I would then have carved in marble or otherwise under the window. The same tablet will also record that it is your gift to the church of the House of Commons, which was dearer to Milton than any other.

Whittier acquiesced in the double request conveyed by Mr. Childs, and composed these lines:

The new world honors him whose lofty plea
For England's freedom made her own more sure,
Whose song, immortal as its theme, shall be
Their common freehold while both worlds endure.

Whittier transmitted the quatrain to Doctor Farrar through Mr. Childs, with one textual comment. He used *freehold* rather than *heirloom* because Milton himself had used it: "I too have my chapter and freehold of rejoicing!" [60]

Archdeacon Farrar's acknowledgment, dated January 2, 1888, was choice — something like an ultimate measure of Whittier's place among men. He wrote:

First let me express the wish that God's best blessings may rest on you and your house during this New Year. My personal gratitude and admiration have long been due to you for the noble influence you have exercised for the furtherance of forgotten but deeply needed truths. I have myself endeavored to do something to persuade men of the lesson you have so finely taught, — that God is a loving Father, not a terrific Moloch. Next let me thank you for the four lines on Milton. They are all that I can desire, and they will add to the interest which all Englishmen and Americans will feel in the beautiful Milton window. I think that if Milton had now been living, you are the poet whom he would have chosen to speak of him, as being the poet with whose whole tone of mind he would have been most in sympathy. . . . Unless you wish "heirloom" to be substituted for "freehold," I will retain the latter as the original.[61]

# XXIII

## A Man among Women

WHITTIER was also attracted — and attractive — to women. Among his numerous company of friends and admirers, he was proud to count a long and distinguished company of women. This was an aspect, merely, of a well-balanced personality. Whittier's nearly lifelong physical delicacy and his partial deafness in his late years made him averse to crowds, but by all accounts he was a companion of much more than ordinary charm. His sober common sense left him open to relatively few illusions about himself, and he spoke "scholarly and wisely" when he said in a letter of August 29, 1886, to Lucy Larcom (who had been enjoying resort-hotel life in New Hampshire): "It is possible to be too quiet, and a change from solitary Nature to human contact and voices is sometimes desirable." Then he touched a main truth about himself: "There are always nice people to be found in any crowd. For my own part, I like folks generally. Very few come amiss to me." [1]

By nature and by religious precept Whittier believed in the equality of women with men. Long before George Meredith wrote the lines in 1877, Whittier felt that "there never will be civilization where comedy is not possible; and that comes of some degree of social equality of the sexes." And Whittier's practice of life showed his grasp of the truth that "the comic Muse is one of their [the women's] best friends." [2]

His enjoyment of their company, taking into account the wit and humor of his own make-up, was natural and in good part blithe, with an element of pleasant contest in it. Robert E. Lee, joyous in his marriage and his family life, delighted in the company of women in his natural circle for precisely the same reasons and in the same way. His unfailing courtesy toward them was matched with courtly quipping. That was Whittier's way also, after he had matured emotionally under the brief distress of several unsuccessful bouts of young love.

## 1

Personal appearance was a thing that Whittier noticed. His own was always scrupulously neat. To begin with, he was handsome — quite as well made as well mannered. He described himself to an inquiring Detroit artist, in a letter of March 6, 1878, as five feet, ten and a half inches tall; in weight, 150 or 155 pounds, according to the season; in figure perfectly straight and what the tailor would call well proportioned.[3] Whittier's striking dark eyes, quick and nervous movement, pleasant speaking voice, and vivacious humor were remarked by many people all through his life, not least by his women friends. And nobody described his countenance better than Lyman Abbott, who called on him at Amesbury in 1879. Later he wrote:

> No one could call his face handsome; it was better, it was beautiful. The features were homely, though the forehead was high and the eyes were luminous. Photographs but illy represent him. For his face was a transparency; the spirit within lighted it up; and photographs rarely, the older photographs never, interpret the spirit. His illuminated face has made quite real to me the picture in Exodus of Moses when he descended from the mount where he had talked with God and "his face shone." Whittier's was a shining face.[4]

In the second place, Whittier took quiet care in matters of dress. He adhered throughout his life to old-style Quaker garb, simply impressive as he wore it. In the late eighteen-thirties, when he edited the *Pennsylvania Freeman*, he discovered in Philadelphia a tailor who periodically renewed Whittier's plain wardrobe as long as Whittier lived.[5] During his Philadelphia period Whittier sat for his portrait to Bass Otis, a student of Gilbert Stuart's and first lithographer in America, and is represented as very handsome indeed. How attractive he appeared to people in Amesbury at this time was made clear by his friend James Neall, in a letter written to S. T. Pickard on August 10, 1892: "I can well remember the sensation, created in Amesbury meeting, occasionally as a tall black eyed whiskered young gentleman, dressed in the correct and Orthodox Quaker fashion of Philadelphia, flashed in upon us in the house of worship. . . ." [6]

The years took from Whittier his health but not his attractive appearance and personality. When Edmund Gosse, the English author, came to visit in America in 1884, he wrote down this vivid impression after calling upon Whittier:

> . . . The peculiarity of his face rested in the extraordinary large and luminous black eyes, set in black eyebrows, and fringed with thick black eyelashes curiously curved inwards. This bar of vivid black across the countenance was startlingly contrasted with the bushy snow-white beard and hair, offering a sort of contradiction which was surprising and presently pleasing. . . .
>
> He struck me as very gay and cheerful, in spite of his occasional references to the passage of time and the vanishing of beloved faces. He even laughed, frequently and with childlike suddenness, but without a sound. His face had none of the immobility so frequent with very aged persons; on the contrary, waves of mood were always sparkling across his features, and leaving nothing stationary there except the narrow, high, and strangely receding forehead. His language, very fluid and easy, had an agreeable touch of the soil, an occasional rustic note in its elegant colloquialism, that seemed very pleasant and appropriate, as if it linked him naturally with the long line of sturdy ancestors of whom he was the final blossoming. In connection with his poetry, I think it would be difficult to form in the imagination a figure more appropriate to Whittier's writings than Whittier himself proved to be in the flesh. . . . [7]

There is the sum of it. Whittier was created personable and attractive, and so he remained.

He idealized love during his days at the Haverhill Academy and until after he returned from Hartford — that is, until he was about twenty-five. He admired a number of young ladies and was in turn much admired, but marriage he avoided. It is plain that, in his conventional terminology of the day, he "worshiped at the shrine" of young love, twice. His remote cousin Mary Emerson Smith and Evelina Bray, both enrolled with him at the Academy, were his young fancies. Both, it is clear, regarded him as attractive but evidently not as marriageable. Both retained agreeable sentiments about him, and his own steadfast attachment to old friends led to fitful correspondence and an occasional meeting with both of them, late in life.

While his feeling for his cousin was astir, Whittier wrote her from Boston on June 6, 1829, to say that matrimony was for him out of the question — unless he married a Quaker. "But such *must* be my lot," he emphasized, "unless, indeed, I come to the conclusion to lead a life of 'Single Blessedness.' "[8] He may, in fact, have known a sufficiently attractive Friend, for Mrs. Woodman hints at one whom he met —

> Then and always the most beautiful woman he ever saw. Had he then been in circumstances to have engaged her affections for him, his life would doubtless have been different in many ways. In youth and in old age, the lady in the case was ever a most lovely and beautiful woman."[9]

In Hartford, where his work on the *New England Weekly Review* kept him hard driven, Whittier was obviously more sought than seeking. His later correspondence with Jonathan Law, which is now in the Houghton Library at Harvard, includes several references to young ladies of Hartford who fervently remembered that he had been there, and been busy. In turn, Whittier's letters to Law contain items of evidence that, forced back to Haverhill to rest mind and body, he could not keep his heart still.

And then in 1833 he wedded himself to a cause. He was not yet twenty-six, but the possibility of marriage was for him nearly ended.

After Whittier's death, Mary Emerson Smith Thomas wrote to Mr. Pickard two revealing letters. The first, dated December 13, 1892, contains the query: "Why did he never marry? I believe it was best for him, he did not." And in the second, written November 16, 1894, on receipt of a copy of Pickard's authorized *Life* of Whittier, she said:

> I always revered Whittier. I don't know that I ever loved him any better than I do now. What youth of twenty and twenty one in these days, would write such letters of wisdom and humor, so full of pure Love, without passion or prejudice, as were those he penned after we left school. *Why* I kept them I know not. I did not read them for forty years. I knew he was unlike other young men, but I was surprised at the strength, dignity, and beauty of his language — and am not surprised at the beauty of his life.[10]

## 2

Even while the spell of young love was upon him, Whittier fenced against his situation by the use of humor. Bachelordom became an honorable state to which he referred often in the columns of his newspapers,[11] even as late as 1844 in the *Middlesex Standard.* He seemed to operate on the adopted principle that a bachelor is a man who never makes the same mistake once. In the Lowell paper on July 25, 1844, commenting on a report of the local high marriage rate, he said that the fact the epidemic (Leap Year) was half over gave hope to "such of us as, in view of what has happened, may, like Mr. Weller, Senior, entertain fears of being married 'by force and arms.' "

Whittier had decided, plainly, that a bachelor's life only was possible for him, and he took scrupulous pains to avoid the embarrassment of attracting any one who might think him interested in or eligible for marriage. He abjured it on grounds of his health, his financial obligations in the support of three women of his family after his father had died in 1830, and, in a measure, his full commitment to anti-slavery work. (The practical effect of this was to limit his income, often, to as little as five hundred dollars a year. Pickard said that Whittier's finances were at their lowest ebb about 1857, when Joseph Sturge again came to his relief. Whittier himself confessed, in a letter of October 5, 1857, to Lowell regarding payment for "Skipper Ireson's Ride": "I have suffered in my small way in these hard times, and am beginning to feel that my creditors will not have the Christian grace to forgive my debts.") When asked why he never married, Whittier was explicit:

> Circumstances — the care of an aged mother, and the duty owed to a sister in delicate health for many years — must be my excuse for living the lonely life which has called out thy pity. It is some, if a poor, consolation to think that, after all, it might have been a great deal worse. My life has been on the whole quite as happy as I deserved, or had a right to expect. I know there has something very sweet and beautiful been missed, but I have no reason to complain. I have learned, at least, to look into happiness through the eyes of others, and to thank God for the happy unions and holy firesides I have known.[12]

Elizabeth Whittier's death in 1864 left her brother, then in his fifty-seventh year, for the moment alone in the Amesbury home. One friend hinted for many that now he might marry. Whittier answered decisively, "No. I have not married a wife. I will not marry a nurse." [13] There remained to Whittier then the support of Bacon, upon whose wisdom he drew often, and of the wise man quoted by Bacon on the time a man should marry: "A young man not yet, an elder man not at all." A far greater support was the company of gifted women as well as able men, friends to whom Whittier gave his affection unreservedly. The special quality of his feeling was made unmistakably clear in one part of a letter which he wrote to Mrs. Fields on November 26, 1886: "I am thankful that the right to love is a right which nobody, not even its object, can deny. 'If I love you,' said Spinoza, 'What is that to you!' " [14]

## 3

Among the women, Whittier was most naturally attracted to those alongside whom he worked in the anti-slavery ranks, those whom he met in literary circles, and those with whom he had bonds of blood or place. He was drawn always to those in whom wit was wedded to purpose. He found the Grimké sisters, Angelina and Sarah, Quakers of South Carolina, not merely eloquent Abolitionists but people distinguished in mind and manner. Lucretia Mott, Philadelphia Friend present when the American Anti-Slavery Society was founded in 1833, was marked by grace and dignity of presence. One of his favorites was Charlotte Forten, later Mrs. Francis J. Grimké, in whose education Whittier took an interest. In 1863, when she was teaching the children of freedmen at that place, Whittier on her request wrote the "Hymn Sung at Christmas by the Scholars of St. Helena's Island, S.C." With the poem he sent this sentiment:

> I send herewith a little song for your Christmas festival. I was too ill to write anything else, but I could not resist the desire to comply with thy request. . . . Most sincerely, dear friend, do I rejoice at the good providence of God, which has permitted thee to act so directly for the poor, yet deeply interesting people of the Sea Islands.

Miss Forten reported happily the effect of the poem:

. . . I read it to the children, and showed them his picture, and told them about him; and they were much delighted, and proud to think the hymn was written especially for them. They learned it readily, and sang it with great spirit on that bright, beautiful Christmas Day, in the old church, amid grand, moss-draped live oaks. It was a scene I shall never forget.

Whittier admired not only Miss Forten and her work, but her inheritance of freedom. In 1870 he wrote about her to Charles Sumner: "She is slightly colored; her grandfather, James Forten, of Philadelphia, was a friend of Rush and Franklin, served in the revolutionary war, and was a prisoner in the Jersey prison ship — a noble old man!" [15]

None of these women Abolitionists, however, enjoyed quite the esteem and affection that Whittier had for Lydia Maria Child. They probably worked together from as early as 1834, when in Boston Mrs. Child edited *The Oasis* and included in it Whittier's "The Slave-Ships." They remained warm friends until Mrs. Child died in 1880. Two years later Whittier, on request, wrote the biographical introduction to the *Letters of Lydia Maria Child*,[16] and there gave his generous measure of her as a person and a friend. He admired her courage in sacrificing literary reputation and income to the fight for Abolition. He praised her because "she was by no means a reformer of one idea, but her interest was manifested in every question affecting the welfare of humanity." But for this, chiefly, he loved her: "Her philanthropy had no taint of fanaticism; throughout the long struggle, in which she was a prominent actor, she kept her fine sense of humor, good taste, and sensibility to the beautiful in art and nature."

Following the Civil War, Mrs. Child and Whittier shared a common, active interest in the work of the Hampton Institute. It was a bond, too, that she aided at every opportunity "the greatest social reform of the age, which aims to make the civil and political rights of women equal to those of men." In 1874 her husband died, and thereafter Mrs. Child went from her Wayland home to spend several of the winter months in Boston, and there see old friends. Mrs. Fields has described delightfully the happy sessions which Mrs. Child and Whittier had at the homes of friends. Wit and humor and a rich store of reminiscence brought on high festival, proof that people could grow old gracefully.

Together, in serious mood, they often weighed the mystery of the afterlife. Both accepted the fact of it on faith. Soon after Mrs. Child had died, Whittier wrote to Mrs. Fields, exactly as he had done after the passing of Charles Dickens: "My heart has been heavy ever since I heard of dear Maria Child's death. The true, noble, loving soul! *Where* is she? *What* is she? *How* is she? The moral and spiritual economy of God will not suffer such light and love to be lost in blank annihilation. She was herself an evidence of immortality. . . ." [17]

Whittier's general interest in the growth of society bound him in interest and affection to other able women, not least among them Dorothea Dix. During the Civil War, Whittier bade the Society of Friends to support her work in Washington, she sent him a portrait of Barbara Frietchie, and from that time they were admiring friends. After Whittier took up residence at Oak Knoll in 1876, Miss Dix spent one summer at a Danvers hospital, and was an occasional guest in the Woodman-Whittier household. In a letter written on June 29, 1883, from Trenton, New Jersey, she summed up her gratitude for his work in the world, and she said, especially: "How well I remember with comfort and cheer your calls when I was at Danville. You did not suspect the good you were doing me; . . ." [18]

In her waning days Miss Dix wrote to Oak Knoll to request a penned copy of Whittier's "At Last." This she kept in her hands or under her pillow during the last two years of her life, Mrs. Woodman noted, and from the worn copy the lines were read at the burial service for Miss Dix in Mount Auburn Cemetery, Boston.[19]

Whittier's friendship and correspondence with friends of his youth in Haverhill, and with others whom he met in Hartford and in Philadelphia, was often as blithe as his association with Mrs. Child. Several of these friends, especially Harriet Minot Pitman, of Haverhill and Cambridge, seemed to delight in writing him partly to twit him upon his singleness. And with his Wendell cousins, the Neall sisters, Elizabeth Nicholson, and Elizabeth Lloyd Howell, all of Philadelphia, he had, over a long term of years, an intermittent exchange of letters which was affectionate and often lively and needling.

Mrs. Pitman had been with Whittier in Haverhill Academy, and with her as with all persons he knew "in school days" he maintained a warm and unflagging friendship. Many of the letters which Mrs. Pitman and Whittier exchanged have been published, but others show even better the delightfully teasing tone in which she often wrote. Her mentor's mantle lies over a characteristic letter which she sent him from Cambridge on April 9, 1884:

> . . . One passage in your letter moved me a good deal: You wondered whether any one grew better with old age. Haven't you grown better, with years? You had not always the beautiful, wide-embracing charity, which now characterises you — and, I suppose that your desire to make others better has become a steadfast principle, and hasn't the thinking of the Lord and His ways, made you more spiritual? I suppose that the best are not free from temptations whilst they live here. . . . If you really think, that marriage would make you better, why not marry? "Whilst the lamp holds out to burn," it is not too late. It might bring to light, latent, unsuspected evils, & give you a chance to overcome them. Perhaps it is a little too late, for any moulding influence.
>
> . . . Haven't I often spoken to you more freely than to any one else! Does not the custom of laying my burdens upon you, give me a prescriptive right to do so. Are we not *very old* friends? and have n't you done me good all my life? . . .[20]

Precisely that kind of relationship was enjoyed also by Whittier and Elizabeth Lloyd, one of the lively group of young Friends whom he came to know in Philadelphia between 1837 and 1840. She was four years younger than Whittier. Theirs was a choice friendship, into which Elizabeth Whittier entered equally, and the letters exchanged between Amesbury and Philadelphia for a quarter century bespoke common interests, minds that sparked, and hearts that beat closely together. Elizabeth Lloyd was undoubtedly the Friend whom Mrs. Woodman called "the most beautiful woman" Whittier ever saw.[21] The sparkling letters which Marie C. Denervaud collected in *Whittier's Unknown Romance* (1922) and T. F. Currier in *Elizabeth Lloyd and the Whittiers* (1939) indicate that the "circumstances" mentioned by Whittier himself and others made any thought of marriage between the two friends impossible when "it might have been."

It is clear that in 1859–60 they seriously discussed marriage, but agreed against it. By then Elizabeth Lloyd had been married, in 1853, and in January 1856 brought so low by the sudden death of her husband, Robert Howell, that for at least two years she was inconsolable. In Amesbury, Whittier's family circle dwindled with the death of his Aunt Mercy in 1846, of his mother in 1857, and of his older sister Mary in January, 1861.

By the time correspondence was resumed between Mrs. Howell and Whittier, the bloom on life's prospects had been lost. The affectionate tone of their exchanges — as when on March 24, 1861, Whittier reported the death of his sister Mary [22] — was more one of "laying my burdens upon you" than of heart's interest.

In the spring of 1859 Whittier paid his last visit to Philadelphia, and, declining the hospitality offered by friends, stayed at Girard House, "a fashionable, uncomfortable Hotel in the City of Penn!!" [23] He saw Mrs. Howell on various occasions over a period of three weeks, and then, on May 14, just before leaving Burlington, New Jersey, for home, he wrote her a very affectionate letter in which these lines appear:

> My thoughts dear E. have been with thee, and if my prayers have not been availing in thy behalf they have been, at least, fervent. The sweet remembrance of our communion during the past three weeks, dwells with me — a dear & sacred possession. I am better and happier for it — rich beyond my hopes.[24]

Some time during the summer of 1860 Mrs. Howell visited the Whittiers in Amesbury, and Greenleaf perhaps saw her again in Boston or in Salem in September, 1861.[25] Then, on a March day some time after 1866, Mrs. Howell wrote him from London a letter tingling with recovered spirits and with the lively personality that made her, beyond any doubt, the most attractive woman outside his own family whose life touched Whittier's. The last part reads:

> I am sorry thee has decided to be such a very ancient man. My dear mother never liked any allusions to her years — & always insisted upon it that she was not old — & never expected to be. And she never was — She perfectly fulfilled her being's end & aimed to be lovely & beautiful — always — & to the end of life.
>
> I inherit — a good deal of her temperamental nature & warmth — & love & enjoyment & many good things come in to me — making me very thankful to live — even in my lonely lot.
>
> It is delightful to me to be here — I have a charming circle of English friends — good, intellectual & living true lives in the midst of the world & every elegance & refinement that wealth & culture, supposes.
>
> It is a high privilege — to be in the way of *learning* — One sees so many people who dwindle & repeat themselves — for want of making

a little effort to get into the realms of attrition & movement that I appreciate more & more, an enlarged horizon.
* * * [26]

When Mrs. Howell visited the Whittiers in the summer of 1860, she and Whittier, as her letter of September 13 from Princeton reveals, together climbed Wachuset, the two-thousand-foot "mountain" near Fitchburg, Massachusetts. A year later Whittier wrote, as the second part of "Mountain Pictures," the poem "Monadnock from Wachuset." It was a Turner landscape, but he regretted that he lacked the skill to do justice to —

> . . . . . her who led,
> A fitting guide, with reverential tread,
> Into that mountain mystery. * * * [27]

Elizabeth Lloyd Howell was the "fitting guide." Serious students of Whittier can only think, with regret, how much richer his life might have been if she had been his companion in climbing all the mountains which lay across his path leading to pleasant valley.

## 4

In the critical way, Whittier was not himself always a "fitting guide" for the many women writers whom he befriended. His generosity toward the work of others, remarked by Howells, betrayed him occasionally into giving greater encouragement than the merits of a piece of writing deserved. Whittier had to learn to give encouragement without seeming to let his heart go with it. For he might — and several times he almost did — get either way into an uneasy position. In commenting on the first chapter of Underwood's *Life* of Whittier, a copy of which had been sent to her, Edna Dean Proctor on July 3, 1883, wrote Whittier: "I have always been impressed by the mingled volcano and iceberg of your character." [28]

It was to Miss Proctor that Whittier wrote, on November 10, 1860: "If I had not many things to teach me lessons of humility, the kind & flattering words of thy letter might cause me to overestimate myself & my writings. As it is, there is no great danger; & from my heart I thank thee." [29]

It is of fleeting interest that Whittier had many times to thank his New Hampshire friend from his heart — for scarfs which she was pleased to knit for him, out of a thoughtful generosity which could not be misinterpreted.[30]

Whittier, on the evidence of letters published in Pickard's *Life*,[31] was fond of Lucy Hooper [32] and he helped her to publish a few of her poems. He was eight years older than she; when they met in New York he was in his thirtieth year. With the heady generosity of youth he undertook to be sponsor for her work. In a letter of August 21, 1837, he encouraged her to attempt to write a long poem rather than merely fugitive pieces. Then, as editor of the *Pennsylvania Freeman*, he invited contributions from her and published two of her poems, with favorable comment, in the issues of April 19 and August 16, 1838.

That the two young writers found each other attractive is obvious; so is the fact that serious love between them was impossible. Lucy Hooper was not a member of the Society of Friends, although she was an Abolitionist. On an August afternoon in 1839, back in her native Essex County, she walked with Whittier along the Merrimac, a pleasant episode that he wove into his elegy written after her death, from tuberculosis, at Brooklyn in August, 1841.[33] In the *American and Foreign Anti-Slavery Reporter* of September 1, Whittier praised her as —

> a friend of the oppressed — as one who, with the simplicity of a child and the shrinking modesty of a sensitive woman, had yet the firmness to defend and advocate the cause of Emancipation — to throw her literary reputation on the altar of reform — and to consecrate youth, beauty, genius, to the vindication of unpopular truth.

What she meant to Whittier he indicated exactly when he wrote to Elizabeth Lloyd, on August 28, 1841: "Didst thou get a paper from me containing a notice of the death of Lucy Hooper? She was one of my dearest friends — a noble girl — in heart as well as intellect." [34] Finally, in the *National Era* of September 7, 1848, he reviewed her collected poems, just published in New York, and said that her "life, indeed, was in itself a psalm of beauty."

With variations, that was the pattern of Whittier's association with a number of women writers — among them Charlotte Fiske Bates, Alice and Phoebe Cary, Elizabeth Jones Cavazza, Grace Greenwood (Mrs.

Sara J. Lippincott), Gail Hamilton (Mary Abigail Dodge), Harriet McEwen Kimball, Lucy Larcom, Louise Chandler Moulton, Nora Perry, Elizabeth Stuart Phelps, Edna Dean Proctor, Harriet Beecher Stowe, and Celia Thaxter. Out of principle, because they were women, he praised and encouraged them in their work. If they needed help he gave it, and for some of them he took pains to find publishers. He was the devoted friend of all of them indifferently, the married as well as the unmarried. He lent his hand to all but gave it to none, for "circumstances" possessed it.

With Lucy Larcom, from the time they met in Lowell in 1844, he had a close literary association which was cemented by the even closer friendship arising between her and Elizabeth Whittier. After his sister's death in 1864 Whittier at least twice wrote to Miss Larcom in the vein of "I hope thee and other friends will feel the same freedom to visit me as heretofore." [35] As personal and literary friend he was unselfish and appreciative. When Fields, Osgood & Company published a volume of her poems in 1868, Whittier wrote a generous "estimate" of them for advertising purposes. When in 1871 she helped him to edit *Child Life: A Collection of Poems*, in 1873 *Child Life in Prose*, and in 1875 *Songs of Three Centuries*, Whittier in his prefaces acknowledged his special indebtedness to Lucy Larcom. Moreover, he gave her the solider thanks of financial arrangements in her favor. On May 6, 1871, he ordered his publishers to pay her three hundred dollars for editorial collaboration on *Child Life*, and insured her part of the copyright returns. On March 22, 1877, he wrote to Mr. Osgood: "Pay to Miss Larcom, one-half of the sum due, as percentage on 'Songs of Three Centuries,' 'Child Life,' and 'Child Life in Prose,' which is owing to her on my part." Finally, Whittier willed her the copyrights of the first and third of these books.[36]

In the eighteen-eighties, when Miss Larcom's frail health reduced her to financial need, Whittier led in arranging an annuity to which her friends contributed. He wrote to Mrs. Fields on October 22, 1883, in part:

> I have now the facts of birth &c necessary, & am ready for the money. Lucy has been very ill at Bethel. She spent two or three days at Portland and gained strength to go to Beverly last week. My niece with whom she stopped thought her quite sick. If her illness is really serious I think it would be better to put the money in savings banks for

> the present. We have now a sum sufficient to give her about $118 on an annuity. I had to tell her that a sum had come into my hands the source of which I could not divulge even to her, but that it was the outgrowth of love & friendship, & she need have no misgivings about it.[37]

Again, on December 31, 1883, Whittier informed Mrs. Fields: "Lucy Larcom is very grateful for the annuity & the $221. She cannot conjecture where it comes from — thinks the Lord did it!" [38]

Meanwhile, Miss Larcom on November 7 wrote to thank Whittier for the more personal gift of the copyright returns:

> I think your "annuity" is more valuable to me than any other I am likely to receive, for it stands to me for the continued generosity and friendship of years. But I hope you have not given me more than what you judge a fair share of the spoils. I am glad the books sell so well — and for the check, I thank you sincerely.[39]

All in all, that was the quality of the friendship between Whittier and Lucy Larcom, although at times a note of irritation crept into it when seemingly he was asked to do or be more than was possible. He was not by nature patient, and what appeared to be his natural self-restraint was cultivated. On one occasion following a misunderstanding and the exchange of sharp words, Whittier was quick to write Miss Larcom this apology:

> Thee are right in thinking that I don't know much about what was said on the evening thee refer to. . . . If I remember rightly thee was unreasonably persistent in thy contention. When one is unreasonable himself, he is in no mood for tolerating the same thing in others. I dare say that I was a fool, but that is no reason thee should make thyself one, by dwelling on it. Lay it all to dyspepsia, Ben Butler, or anything else than intentional wrong on the part of thy old friend. We have known each other too long, and done each other too many kind offices, to let it disturb us.[40]

And Miss Larcom herself, in a letter of April 25, 1883, gave a hint of the flicks and flaws in this kind of friendship, by protesting against Whittier's refusal to turn out some amusing lines for the occasion of a picnic. "You have never refused before," she twitted him. "You should not be weary in well doing." Then, on a note of reflective appraisal, she added:

> Those lines to Allen Dodge & Eliza were very good. You need not be ashamed of them now. They were written before you were 25. — It was a great thing to me to know you then, although you were then, much more than now, very provoking, *at times*. On the whole your influence was a great good, for which I am sincerely thankful.[41]

A still better estimate of the value of Whittier's friendship to her is given by a diary entry, once after Whittier had visited her: "I have more admiration and reverence for such a man, from having found a higher standard in life for myself from which to look across and up to him." [42]

With a full regard for his circumstances and his choice, Whittier found a kind of relief in the game of parrying which he carried on with Alice and Phoebe Cary and with Gail Hamilton, and in the lively correspondence and society of Mrs. Fields and her close friend Sarah Orne Jewett. He found the Cary sisters, of New York, "noble and richly gifted, lovely in person and character," as he said in the headnote to "The Singer," [43] written after the death of Alice Cary in 1871. But in their eagerness for his company they at times became "pilgrims" to Amesbury. After a visit there in 1850 Phoebe Cary tried, without luck, to cajole him into returning the visit. (Whittier disliked New York.) The fourth of four letters on the subject was dated December 26, 1850, and in part it reads:

> I think now I may make my visit to the friend of whom I told you the second or third week in January, but will not promise certainly to come to Amesbury unless I can bring you home with me, and you do not give me much hope of that. So you see my visit all depends on yourself. * * * [44]

Gail Hamilton (1833–96) was a distant cousin of Whittier's esteemed friend Allen W. Dodge, Harvard graduate and man of many rôles.[45] Whittier was one of many friends who found her letters, especially those from Washington, vibrant and informing. Even in writing to Henry James she acted the conscious rôle of "the saucy fly with her jests and jeers." [46] Whittier's discerning comment of May, 1865, earned first place in H. Augusta Dodge's *Gail Hamilton's Life in Letters* for this note: "I was a little *blue* this morning, but thy letter was just the tonic I needed. If anybody is out of sorts and *hypped* I shall prescribe for him a course of thy letters. And now, God bless thee!" [47]

To those who knew her, Gail Hamilton's effervescence did not hide her discernment. With her sharp eye and independent mind she saw the captains and kings in Washington and elsewhere, but reserved for Whittier this judgment, in a letter in 1863 to another friend: "He is the king of men and what is the good of talking?" Whittier, in turn, knew Mary Abby Dodge very well. He met her retort that he didn't trust her by the friendly comment, "Yes, I do trust thee, but thee has great audacity — great audacity." [48]

They treated each other as equals, and that was the security of this charming friendship. After she had received an inscribed copy of *The Tent on the Beach* from Whittier, she said pointedly in a letter of February 20, 1867, to a correspondent:

> ... I have not read it, but I know the best part of it is what he has written on the fly-leaf. I suppose the great mass of persons in the world are really incapable of friendship. No otherwise can I account for the clouds that seem to hang over so many. I am as far as possible from believing that friendship should, or can, encroach upon love. It seems to me they may run in parallel lines forever, since parallels never meet. I have a very great scorn for the notion you often find afloat that propinquity is the — what do the theologians call it? — predisposing cause of love. . . . And I wish there were high living enough in the world to be at least recognized as a ponderable and visible and appreciable thing in its own right.[49]

Whittier and Gail Hamilton were able to recognize it, knew that their friendship was of a kind rare in the world.

Among his numberless friends she was, in fact, unique. He vastly relished her gayety. For him she was the feminine personification of the Comic Muse. She explained to him once: ". . . don't mind my adjectives, which won't suit your Quakerly reticence, but they are the sweetest matter-of-fact." [50] That was her license to start many of her letters to Whittier with endearing salutations — such as "Dear little darling (You know I have to be demonstrative for two)," "My dear Sheikh," "The dear," "Dearly beloved," and "Dear Angel" — and she filled them with wit and persiflage often mixed with serious discussion of current issues. Whittier now and then reduced her pose as the Comic Muse by such comments as these in a letter of March 1, 1872, written after reading her *Woman's Worth and Worthlessness:*

> . . . I shall not put my quarrels on paper, but when a kind Providence gives me an opportunity I shall "withstand thee to thy face." I will simply say that my old bachelor reverence for woman has been somewhat disturbed by thy revelations. *I* am not going to condemn her because thee turn State's evidence against her. Voter, or non-voter, I have faith in her. Mrs. G. gave me the history of thy shawl hunt in Boston. I shall not waste my sage advice on thee any more. I don't see but thee are just as much given to worldly vanities as if thee had never had the benefit of a Quaker's counsels and example.[51]

It was a pleasant contest, played for sheer enjoyment because each so well understood the other's position. From Hamilton, Massachusetts, Miss Dodge wrote Whittier on February 14, 1866:

> . . . and by the way I have found you out, Mr. For she [Lilly Gillette, whom Whittier knew in Hartford] is telling about Fanny Hess and says she is the one of whom you said when learning that she was not married as you supposed "Ah! it might have made a great difference with me had I been a younger man." Now you make great boast of what you might could would have done were you a younger man, but I can't find out that you ever did anything to signify when you *were* a younger man and my conviction is that that is only a pretext and that, young or old, you never did and never would care very much about any of us. . . .[52]

In truth he cared greatly, as Whittier said in a letter to her written at Holderness on July 13, 1883: "Through all the fun and bantering and unreason of thy letter, I discern the true, good and noble woman, whose friendship has been so much to me. I am quite willing to be laughed at or criticized by her. 'Faithful are the wounds of a friend.' "[53]

Whittier cared greatly, too, for the friendship of Celia Thaxter, whom he met on his first visit to the Isles of Shoals, in 1863. She was twenty-seven years younger than he. Her marriage to Levi Lincoln Thaxter, student of Robert Browning and much her senior in years, was clouded. In the literary life she made for herself, with "Appledore" in the Isles of Shoals as her center, she particularly valued "the most delightful friendship" of Whittier, and gratefully wrote, after his death: "His sympathy and interest in all I did were invaluable to me."[54]

In a letter of March 4, 1869, Whittier spoke of her to Charlotte Forten as "our mutual friend Celia Thaxter — one of those rare people whom not to know would be a real loss, and whom not to love would be simply impossible. She has plenty of faults enough to make her friends at times sorry and anxious, but not the less attached to her." [55] What could have been the impact on Whittier of the letter which Mrs. Thaxter wrote him on September 9, 1881? She spoke warmly of his recent visit at the Shoals, and then described her feeling when he departed by steamer:

> . . . do you know you looked so finely, so full of life & of power, all my heart was stirred looking up at you, thinking of all you are & of all you have done. — Great heaven, what eyes you have got in your head! — Now I hear you say, "Hush, thee foolish woman!" But I shan't hush. * * *

She signed herself "Ever & ever your audacious & affectionate CT." [56]

## 5

It remained for Annie Fields (Mrs. James T.) and Sarah Orne Jewett to give Whittier what was, in many ways, his most nearly perfect friendship with women. Mrs. Fields was twenty-seven years his junior, Miss Jewett forty-two. With them he was altogether relaxed. They were gifted, cosmopolitan souls, well aware of the humor in life, and on their occasional meetings with Whittier in Boston, in Amesbury, and in southern Maine (Miss Jewett lived at South Berwick), the two women called up in him a joy of life quite unlike any other that he knew. The same spirit breathed through their correspondence, which lasted to the day of Whittier's death. From South Berwick, in 1889, Miss Jewett wrote him, "I think that you and Mrs. Fields are my two youngest and growing-est friends!" [57]

Despite temperamental tensions which now and then arose in the Fields' home in Boston, Whittier was a warm friend of both the publisher and his wife. It was his novel habit to call on them, when he was at the Marlboro in Boston, at the breakfast hour. He was a bad sleeper, he knew that the Fields "were not late people, and that his visits could never be untimely," and he delighted in their company at a time when they could talk uninterruptedly of books and life. Mrs. Fields, in her pleasant book of reminiscences of Whittier, said, "We owe much of the intimate friendship of our life to these morning hours spent in private, uninterrupted talk." [58] On his part, Whittier wrote to her on January 2, 1882: "Life is brief, and nothing is of any real value but love and friendship." [59]

To Miss Jewett, even more than to most younger authors, Whittier gave friendly criticism and support. In 1879 he wrote her, characteristically:

> I am glad to get thy charming book from thy own hand. I have read "Deephaven" over half a dozen times, and always with gratitude to thee for such a book — so simple, pure, and so true to nature. And "Old Friends and New" I shall certainly read as often. When tired and worried I resort to thy books and find rest and refreshing. I recommend them to everybody, and everybody likes them. There is no dissenting opinion; and already thousands whom thee have never seen love the author as well as her books.[60]

After J. T. Fields's death in 1881, Miss Jewett was more than ever a frequent guest of Annie Fields in Boston. From anxiously attending his brother "Frank," then seriously ill in East Boston, Whittier in the winter of 1882 gave himself the relief of occasional calls at the home in Charles Street. In February, from Danvers, he wrote Miss Jewett:

> I wonder how I can reconcile myself to the old, customary life here, after my pleasant stay in Boston, and our delightful companionship there. I cannot make thee understand how grateful and refreshing it all was and how much I thank thee for it. I did not leave the city until Thursday morning. My brother has been very ill, but is now somewhat, though I fear not permanently, better. The last of our family, he is a kind, unselfish man, whose way of life has been hard and difficult. For the last fifteen years he has been connected with the Naval Office in Boston. . . .[61]

Whittier was called to his brother's bedside soon again, and Miss Jewett on February 21 wrote from South Berwick:

> . . . I am so glad that you are to be in Boston again early in March and I have already made a plot to go down for a day and night, and perhaps we will have another twelve o'clock breakfast [at Mrs. Fields' house], and tell some new ghost stories, and be otherwise dismal! [62]

During the summers of 1882 and 1892 Mrs. Fields and Sarah Orne Jewett journeyed abroad together, and their periodic letters to Whittier, which were entertaining as well as informative, enabled him very gratefully to "travel by proxy." From New Hampshire, on July 14, 1882, Whittier acknowledged Mrs. Fields's letter describing their visit to the Isle of Wight, and he went on: "Since reading it, I seem to have been with you all the way. Did John Oak or his uncle seem aware that they were carrying a third passenger, like the boatman in Uhland's ballad, and did you pay double fare on my account?" [63]

That was the distinction of this particularly rich friendship. The three equal partners were in it together "all the way." After his last birthday, observed in the home of his Cartland cousins in Newburyport, Whittier wrote to Mrs. Fields on December 29, 1891: "The best thing on my birthday was to meet thee and our dear Sarah on the stairs, and the worst was that you went away so soon. . . ." [64] So they expressed themselves, after his death, about all of their meetings together.

Whittier, clearly, was happiest in his friendships with women who regarded him as an equal — who neither looked up to him as superior because he was a man and strong, nor down upon him because he was a faithful Quaker.

## 6

The best and truest aspect of Whittier as a man among women was that in practice he held scrupulously to the Quaker precept that the sexes are equal. He published his belief as early as 1827,[65] and he held fast to it always.

As an Abolitionist he ably advocated the equal status of women with men in the councils of the movement, and in his poem "The Pastoral Letter" (1837) he ridiculed the sense of the General Association of Congregational Ministers in Massachusetts that the lectures there of the Grimké sisters seemed "to threaten the female character with widespread and permanent injury." [66]

In Lowell, he considered the essential equality of men's and women's wages and working conditions one of the few good aspects of the factory system.

In his writings and in practical action he supported the cause of equal suffrage for women, although he did not at all fancy Bloomer Girls — "grotesque caricatures of womanhood at the ballot-box," as he dubbed them in a letter written in 1873.[67]

And in his interest in Wellesley College and in what became Pembroke College of Brown University, Whittier manifested his strong belief in educational opportunities for women equal to those provided for men.

Short of being a joiner, Whittier gave all the support he could to the suffrage movement. He attended in person a convention held in Boston in the summer of 1868,[68] he contributed to the *National Era* on November 6, 1851, a long article on the convention held at Worcester, and he wrote a skilled "brief of reasons" to another held in Newport in August, 1869, and to yet another which met in Washington in 1888.[69] Whittier told the Newport convention simply that "the steady friendships which have inspired and strengthened me, and the reverence and respect which I feel for human nature, irrespective of sex, compel me to look with something more than acquiescence on the efforts you are making." His sober conclusion, however, was this:

> On the other hand, I do not see that the exercise of the ballot by woman will prove a remedy for all the evils of which she justly complains. It is her right as truly as mine, and when she asks for it, it is something less than manhood to withhold it. But, unsupported by a more practical education, higher aims, and a deeper sense of the responsibilities of life and duty, it is not likely to prove a blessing in her hands any more than in man's.[70]

Whittier's interest, then, in Pembroke College and in Wellesley was logical. As a trustee, he was one of the five Quaker members of the board whose initiative, in 1881, finally in 1891 opened the doors of Brown University to women. On August 10, 1881, he transmitted a letter to Richard Atwater, one of his fellow members of the board, in which he said:

> I hope the time is not far distant when Brown University will be open to women. The traditions of the noble old institution are all in favor of broad liberality and equality of rights and privileges. The state of my health and the increasing weight of years may prevent me from taking an active part in the matter, but it would be a great satisfaction to give my voice in behalf of a measure which I feel certain

would redound to the honor, and materially promote the prosperity, of the college. Brown University cannot afford to hesitate much longer in a matter, like this, of simple justice. No one who has felt the pulse of public opinion can doubt that the time has come when a liberal educational policy irrespective of sex is not only a duty, but a necessity.[71]

Wellesley, opened in 1875, was the women's college located nearest Whittier's home, and from September 16 of the next year, when President Henry Fowle Durant issued him an invitation,[72] he was often urged to visit the college. That he was never able to do so was a penalty of his illness, as he frequently regretted. President Durant's successor, Alice E. Freeman (afterward Mrs. George Herbert Palmer, wife of the distinguished philosopher at Harvard), became his warm friend, and was among the company who went to greet him on his last birthday, in Newburyport.[73]

In April, 1886, unable to respond in person, Whittier sent a sonnet [74] which Miss Freeman read at the time Norumbega Cottage was dedicated. Of more pointed interest was "A Birthday Prayer," which Whittier sent in an autographed copy on his birthday in 1881. Then on his next, the perceptive Miss Freeman in her official greeting defined — only less specifically than Lucy Larcom did — the quality of Whittier's influence upon women. She wrote:

> I have hesitated on the verge of sending you a note many times since I saw you, because I know how many are eager to gain your audience just now. And so when these girls have turned from your "Birthday Prayer" to ask with serious faces, "Is there nothing we can do for Mr. Whittier?" I have wished many things in my heart, but have only said, "Live as long and as well, with such prayers on your lips. . . ." [75]

Whittier, strong exponent of standards and believer in a future life, could only have replied, "Amen."

# XXIV

## A Poet's Revisions

WHITTIER has often been called, not inappropriately, "the American Burns." But in two major points he and Bobby Burns were leagues apart — in their attitudes toward women, and in their methods of work. With Burns the two were mixed. Whittier, except in "My Playmate," very rarely found any deep release of feeling in praise or contemplation of fair women.

Burns once told George Thomson, for whose *Select Collection of Scotish Airs* he wrote, under persuasion, many of what became his most famous lyrics:

> Whenever I want to be more than ordinary in *song;* to be in some degree equal to your diviner airs; do you imagine I fast & pray for the celestial emanation? — Tout au contraire! I have invented a glorious recipe, the very one that for his own use was invented by the Divinity of Healing & Poesy when erst he piped to the flocks of Admetus. — I put myself on a regimen of admiring a fine woman; & in proportion to the adorability of her charms, in proportion you are delighted with my verses.[1]

Whittier had no pat way of creating in himself the unfathomable stir that issues in poetry. He steadily disliked calls upon him to write against deadlines for occasions, but he now and then responded with fervor to subjects such as the Barbara Frietchie story which were suggested to him by friends. That poem he completed within two weeks of the time he received the material from Mrs. Southworth.[2] On the other hand, he wrote many of his New England ballads and other poems after long periods of gestation. The idea of *Snow-Bound* was at work in him for nearly forty years before he wrote the idyl.

What was most absorbing about his writing of verse was, simply, the way he got his material down on paper and then prepared it for publication.

## 1

Whittier's friends and his publishers alike were glad to get from him the voluminous pages turned out at high speed in a fine script which he produced always with a steel pen. Pickard said that Whittier "wrote rapidly a clear, legible hand," but it was not always that. Pickard rightly adds that Whittier's "first drafts of poems and letters are exceedingly difficult to decipher." Under the relentless reign of time Whittier wrote rapidly but not clearly — ran words together, did not stop to cross *t's* or dot *i's*, and ended with "a bewildering network of interlineation and erasure." [3] He was well aware of his unintentional cruelty to compositors. In the *National Era* of April 22, 1847, he assumed all the blame for errors in the printing earlier of his article on John Bunyan "because our hieroglyphics are sometimes complained of, as scarcely less difficult to decipher than the plates of the Mormon Bible."

And it is a curious fact that Whittier himself, when he had completed a piece of writing for publication, could not immediately see by the longhand shapes of the words and the lines whether he had got the effect which he desired. This was all the more significant because, as he said candidly, he lacked the keen musical ear which his sister Elizabeth possessed. With Whittier in his writing the visual sense was much the most acute of the five, in spite of his color-blindness.[4] The form rather than the sound or "color" of words was what mattered to him.

For his uses the typewriter was brought to perfection a trifle late. A machine equipped with jumbo display-type would, it is likely, have served him admirably when he made his revisions. As it was, he required to see his poems in proof before he could judge how nearly he had hit the mark. Then he got down to hard revising. At one point in the publication of *The Tent on the Beach*, Whittier remarked to J. T. Fields, "When it gets in type, if it ever does, we shall see what it looks like." And in submitting "In School-Days" to Lucy Larcom, he said, "When I get a proof I may see something to mend or mar." [5]

Like most poets, Whittier knew that he practiced an exacting craft and that the first article of it was hard self-schooling. Along with Holmes and Emerson and other New England brethren, he was called upon almost constantly by unknown correspondents to read and criticize verses which they poured in upon him. To one aspirant, J. S. Cutler, of Woodford's Corner, Maine, Whittier in a letter of June 28, 1878, furnished the kind of service which he felt it a duty to give if it was requested. He wrote a paragraph of criticism of the lines which Mr. Cutler had sent to him, and then counseled:

> The only secret of writing poetry or prose is in long study & meditation, great patience, & unsparing criticism of one's self. For myself I regard good prose writing as really better than rhyme: at any rate I prefer to read it: and the public, at large, certainly do. It pays much the best in a pecuniary point of view.
>
> Few men can be poets in the true sense of the term. I certainly dare not claim to be. . . .[6]

Whittier here was deferring to the acknowledged master-poets whom he named in his "Proem." As a writing man, none the less, he knew that he had gifts, especially as a composer of ballads and other verses which, in a plain language, spoke to the popular heart. But the generally limpid simplicity of his work is deceptive. On one occasion Whittier had to assure even his friend and physician, Doctor Thomas Sparhawk: "Everything is labor to me. I don't know any easy writing." [7] He wrote with pains so that other people could read with ease.

Whittier's newspaper prose gave him little difficulty, and a compositor on the Amesbury *Villager* described how Whittier swiftly turned his ideas into exact copy. Mr. Stephen Lamson told the result:

> When the written pages went into the copy drawer, it [the copy] would be found in a beautiful flowing hand, with seldom an emendation or any interlining, he held his ideas in such perfect form and control. I used to call it a "lightning hand," so rapidly did the pen fly over the paper. . . .[8]

But in writing verse Whittier was much less facile. Here his capital difficulty was with poetic diction. Hitting upon the just word was always hard for him, an initial obstacle which even with years of practice he never entirely conquered.

His authorized biographer gives a fascinating account [9] of Whittier's peculiar problems in composing verse. The "nervous headache" which he inherited from his parents made long concentration at his desk impossible. He was not at any time able to set himself a daily writing schedule and keep it, although he attempted to answer his correspondence (sometimes up to fifty letters a day) before breakfast. Inevitably the hard condition imposed by his infirmity restricted him to composing his poems verse by verse, in intervals of strong vitality.

It has to be repeated that he was a poor sleeper. Mrs. Fields wrote that in forty years he had rarely missed seeing a sunrise. Pickard adds, not surprisingly, that while lying awake at night Whittier got some of his best ideas for poems. As the lines shaped themselves in his mind he said them aloud, and at the first opportunity he wrote them down.

These initial conceptions, Pickard goes on, were usually written on odd scraps of paper, on backs of letters, on whatever was readiest to hand. Some first drafts Whittier even made on the fly-leaves of books and in the margins of printed pages. He alone could decipher some of the words. Fair copies, when he started them, quickly became illegible with interlineations. Printing was his solution, and it was sovereign good luck as well as necessity that brought him to it.

Mrs. Woodman carefully observed his habits of work at Oak Knoll. They were of course well formed by 1876, when he went to live with his cousins and when he had won great popular success. She was aware that his poems still came hard, and that his difficulty was with exact diction and with keeping his material tightly condensed. Seldom did Whittier lay his work down willingly. He often tinkered so long with it, grafting afterthoughts or suggested incidents upon ballads, for instance, that they needed to be almost entirely reconstructed. Yet, Mrs. Woodman emphasized: "It was never the poem, existing in his inner consciousness, which halted and marked his manuscript with changes, but the lack of fitting words wherewith to clothe the conceptions of his mind." [10]

So Whittier worked and reworked his diction and his lines, and, it appears, during the process "often enjoyed listening to the reading of them, commenting upon them, and relating some circumstances of their conception, &c." He remarked to Mrs. Woodman that the poem "What of the Day?" — a forceful prophecy of the Civil War — laid hold of him one day when he was hoeing in his garden at Amesbury. He went at once to his desk, wrote the thirty lines, and after reading them over several times asked himself what they meant. For two years they lay in his desk drawer. When he looked at them again during the 1856 presidential campaign, they had meaning and were published in the *National Era* on September 4.[11]

Two other quick products of Whittier's imagination were "Laus Deo!" and "Abram Morrison." The first "sang itself" to Whittier in Quaker meeting while bells in Amesbury, in February 1865, celebrated news of the Senate's and President Lincoln's action leading to the constitutional ban on slavery; [12] and the other, in 1879, composed itself in his mind, during First-Day (Sunday) meeting, twenty-four hours before he had promised it to the managers of a charitable fair being held in Amesbury.[13] "Laus Deo!" was published unchanged, in the form in which Whittier wrote it from memory.

## 2

With such notable exceptions, Whittier's poetical production was assiduous labor. It was seldom he had strong confidence in his own results. On occasion he would send a poem in tentative form to a fellow craftsman for criticism, as he sent the nettlesome "Marguerite" to Celia Thaxter. More often he looked for — and got — help from his incomparable critic and publisher, J. T. Fields. Of him E. C. Stedman said: "Fields was the only editor I ever knew, who, while not a leading author himself, *always* improved the *poetry* of any writer to whom he made his wise suggestions before publication." [14]

Fields and Whittier worked long together, from at least 1839, when Fields contributed a poem to the *North Star*, anti-slavery gift book edited in Philadelphia by Whittier, down to Fields' death in 1881. Fields, a partner in the firm of William D. Ticknor from 1845, in 1843 saw through the press *Lays of My Home*, the first of Whittier's books published by that house; and as long as he remained active in Ticknor & Fields he seems always to have given personal attention to Whittier's volumes. Likewise, as the potent editor of the *Atlantic* from 1861 to 1870, Fields shepherded thirty-five or more of Whittier's poems into print. Whittier also highly esteemed Doctor Gamaliel Bailey, his friend and editor of the *National Era*, but remarked in a letter of 1847, "I write but little for it, and have not been able to revise or correct that little." [15] Fields knew Whittier's strong literary conscience, and genially held him to close revision.

The Fields-Whittier teamwork was effective, good-humored, and unexceptionably friendly. When *The Chapel of the Hermits* was in the manufacturing stage, Whittier wrote Fields giving the corrected spelling for the title of the poem "Astraea," and he added this comfort:

> I am sorry to trouble thee in the midst of thy business with these small matters of proof reading, which might be settled between me & the printers. Never mind it will soon be over. Thank thy stars I am not "a ready writer," getting up a volume semi-monthly like the Great Hindly.[16]

Two years after the subject had been suggested to him by his friend J. C. Fletcher, Whittier wrote "Freedom in Brazil," and received this advice from Fields, to whom he had sent it, in a letter of May 15, 1867:

> Thank you for sending me "Freedom in Brazil." It is a most timely and admirable poem. I think all the double rhymes you have employed in the piece take from the dignified movement of the poem [it is written in four stanzas, in iambics, with five- and three-stress lines alternating] and if I were you I would change them. They are as follows:
>
> Environ
> Iron
> ———
> Curses
> Rehearses
> ———
> A/ringing
> Swinging
> ———
>
> I wait to hear from you before I put the piece in type. . . .[17]

Whittier accepted Fields's advice, and the poem, improved, appeared in the *Atlantic* in July, 1867.

Under the testing of Fields's criticism, Whittier took one year to get "Marguerite" ready for the *Atlantic*, which published it in March, 1871. He first submitted it and Fields returned it with comment in November, 1869. On the last day of that month Whittier responded: "I was by no means satisfied with the 'French Neutral' [as he first called it], when I sent it, and had misgivings about it afterwards. I shall let it lie by awhile, and then see if it can be made anything of. In the mean time, I am glad to have it again in my possession. The subject is a good one if treated rightly."[18]

Whittier had thought so, indeed, for more than twenty years. He had studied the banishment of the Acadians and intended writing about it, before Longfellow, acting on Hawthorne's suggestion, in 1845–47 wrote the sustained narrative of "Evangeline." Whittier gave the poem an ecstatic notice in the *National Era* on November 25, 1847,[19] and said privately:

> Longfellow was just the one to write it. If I had attempted it I should have spoiled the artistic effect of the poem by my indignation at the treatment of the exiles by the Colonial Government, who had a very hard lot after coming to this country. Families were separated and scattered about, only a few of them being permitted to remain in any given locality. The children were bound out to the families in the localities in which they resided, and I wrote a poem upon finding, in the records of Haverhill, the indenture that bound an Acadian girl as a servant in one of the families of that neighborhood. Gathering the story of her death I wrote "Marguerite."[20]

But that poem was two decades growing in him. Soon after his *Leaves from Margaret Smith's Journal* was published in February, 1849, his friend Theodore Parker wrote requesting him to —

> furnish for the "Massachusetts Quarterly Review" a paper on the Servants, i.e., the *White Slaves*, which our fathers brought to New England, or otherwise acquired, and held in most wicked bondage. I know how well you have studied the subject of our early history, and suppose that it would not be so laborious for you as for me to do the work. The subject is new; the matter little known, little thought of, yet it is interesting and highly important. If you will be good enough to inform me whether you will do so or not, you will much oblige me. I should not want the paper before the middle of October.[21]

Whittier was unable to "give" by that date, and even twenty years later his first version of "Marguerite" was rejected. Then in November 1870, on the day he sent a copy of the poem to Celia Thaxter (because she had lived nearly all her life on the Atlantic coast and knew its history well), Whittier resubmitted it for publication, with this note to Mrs. Fields:

> Some time ago I sent the first draft of this little ballad to J. T. F., and he, rightly considering its incompleteness, returned it. I have just been reconstructing it, and I send it, in the hope that it is better for my tinkering. You know that one thousand of the Acadians were distributed among the towns of Massachusetts, where they were mostly treated as paupers. I am not sure that I have succeeded in my attempt to recall the too probable scenes of a century ago. Read it, and let thee or J. T. F. tell me what it amounts to.[22]

It was Fields's day when "Marguerite" appeared in the *Atlantic*.

He had others in abundance, and Lowell, his predecessor, also had a few. At the suggestion of Lowell and his assistant, F. H. Underwood,[23] Whittier in revising proof adopted the use of the provincial Marblehead dialect in the burthen of "Skipper Ireson's Ride," and wrote it —

"Here's Flud Oirson, fur his horrd horrt,
Torr'd an' futherr'd an' corr'd in a corrt
By the women o' Morble'ead!"

This three-man board also made ready for publication in the *Atlantic* such of Whittier's poems as "The Old Burying Ground," "Telling the Bees," "Le Marais du Cygne," "The Cable Hymn," and "My Playmate." [24] Whittier as often as not would send revised lines or improved passages to Lowell or Underwood before they had had an opportunity to acknowledge receipt of the manuscripts. Sometimes, on reflection, he recalled them promptly for more appropriate placement elsewhere, as he did "The Pipes at Lucknow," which finally appeared in the *National Era* on February 4, 1858. On January 20, 1858, Whittier wrote Underwood to suggest changes in the lines of one stanza and the interpolation of another, and he ended: "If friend Lowell, however, thinks the lines not quite up to the subject, or to his estimate of my ability, he is a true man and a true friend, and will act accordingly." [25]

Whittier was seldom as exercised as Lowell was about perfect rhyme, a critical point which Lowell made sharper with the years in commenting on his friend's verse. Underwood, however, said later and with authority, in his biography of Whittier: "His care over the productions of his brain never ceased, and it was seldom that a poem was printed as originally written." [26]

That was true, certainly, of Whittier's productions which came under Fields's acute but friendly eye. Whittier, in fact, looked to Fields not merely as editor but as judge, and zealously sought his criticism. Much of it was fundamental, some of it touched merely upon titles of poems and upon diction. Between them the two men put Whittier's creations over the jumps of hard revision, and it is clear that Fields held him up to his highest level of effort.

When he returned to Fields on December 20, 1861, a proof sheet of "Mountain Pictures," Whittier referred humorously to a passage, marred by overplay of imagery, which first had read:

> Last night's thunder-gust
> Roared not in vain: for where its lightnings thrust
> Their tongues of fire, the great peaks seem so near,
> Lapped clear of mist. . . .

Fields had come down upon it, and Whittier mused:

> See what it is to trust an author with his own proofs! I defer to thy judgment. I shrink from the feline suggestiveness of my figure of speech. The tongues of fire shall *burn* up the mist, and not *lap* it. For the rest, I hope the poem is none the worse for the changes I have thought it best to make. How would it do to strike out these lines:
>
> Tangling the dusky woods with silver gleams;
> And far below the dry lips of the streams
> Sing to the freshened meadow-lands again;
>
> and substitute these:—
>
> Making the dusk and silence of the woods
> Glad with the laughter of the chasing floods,
> And luminous with blown spray and silver gleams;
> While, in the vales below, the dry-lipped streams
> Sing to the freshened meadow-lands again.[27]

These changes were made, and the *Atlantic* published the two parts of "Mountain Pictures" in March and April, 1862.

Early in this year Whittier confided to Fields: "Some time or other if I can get a day of health I hope to write something better than I have yet for the Magazine. It is in me, but, as Thersites says of the wit of Ajax, it lies as coldly as fire in flint. I would not mind suffering if I could but *do* something." Soon the germ of "Andrew Rykman's Prayer" was at work in him, and in June, 1862, he reported to Fields: "I have by me a poem upon which I have bestowed much thought, and which I think is in some respects the best thing I have ever written. I will bring it or send it soon."[28]

What followed was typical. In November he sent the manuscript of the poem to Fields, who suggested changes, and on December 2 Whittier responded, interestingly:

> I return Mr. Rykman. I know that "pearl" and "marl" do not jingle together well — but the lines have a meaning in them, and if the reader will roll his r's a little they will do. I add a verse at the tail of it. John de Labadie was a devout "come-outer" in Holland two centuries ago. . . . Abraham's message is a great improvement in point of style. Its conclusion is really noble.[29]

A close student of prose writing, Whittier was here referring to Lincoln's message to Congress delivered on December 1, 1862 — the "we cannot escape history" address. Whittier's critical sense of the merits of both verse and prose was good and was improving.

By the summer of 1865, when he was writing *Snow-Bound*, Whittier felt sure of his touch and taste, as his first announcement of it to Fields on August 28 and his note of October 3 accompanying the manuscript indicate. His letter of transmittal read:

> I have thy note of this date. In answer I send "Snow-Bound" to do with as seemeth best in thy sight. I shall see some things wrong when I get the proof, — as it is now I cannot do much more with it, owing to illness. I think thee will like some parts of the conclusion. The portrait of that strange pilgrim, Harriet Livermore, the erratic daughter of Judge Livermore of New Hampshire, who used to visit us, is as near the life as I can give it.[30]

Fields read the long narrative poem minutely, and recommended at least nine changes involving whole passages or precise diction. Whittier accepted most of the suggestions; especially he reworked the conclusion. And when he returned the corrected proofs to Fields early in November, he commented generally:

> I thank thee for looking over my poem. I have acted as well as I could on thy hints, but I have left one "bad rhyme," *heard* and *word*, to preserve my well-known character in that respect. . . . I think I have not injured the piece by my alterations, — that on the second page of the proof is rather improved than otherwise; and I have added two lines to my slightly *lackadaisical* reference to the boys and girls, in road-breaking. Don't send the poem to me again. I shall tear it all to pieces with alterations, if thee do. In the picture of the old home, the rim of

hemlocks, etc., at the foot of the high hill which rises abruptly to the left, is not seen. They would make a far better snow picture than the oaks which are in the view. Don't put the poem on tinted or fancy paper. Let it be white as the snow it tells of.[31]

But Whittier was not yet done. At least twice more he wrote Fields about the proof, in the one instance agreeing with Mr. and Mrs. Fields "that the poem is (though I say it who shouldn't) good," and again, on November 3, suggesting a change in one passage near the end of the poem.[32] And Mr. Currier noted: "Four passages were changed, and ten verbal variants introduced after the first printing" [33] — one of them in 1894, two years after Whittier's death.

Whittier bestowed equal pains on "Our Master," another poem brought out in 1866 and now famous as a hymn. Pickard described Whittier's zealous recasting of the verses and lines before they were sent to *The Independent* and published on November 1. Originally he entitled the poem "The Master," and the opening stanza, as first amended, began: "O Love of God, forever full." On a second try Whittier wrote it: "O boon of Love, forever full," and probably not until he sent the late copy to *The Independent* did he achieve the now widely recognizable line: "Immortal Love, forever full." In his almost endless revisions, incidentally, he expanded the poem from twenty-five stanzas to the present thirty-eight.[34]

What his habits of work entailed upon other people Whittier grasped with imagination and humor. When on July 13, 1871, he returned to W. D. Howells the proofs of a poem in which Fields had indicated the need for changes, Whittier joked: "I hate to trouble publishers & printers but I fear I was born to do so. I only hope that I may not be held responsible for any language more emphatic than polite which my blunder may call out." [35]

## 3

Fields retired both from his publishing firm and from the *Atlantic* in 1870, to devote himself to writing and lecturing. Thereafter, with the passing years, Whittier devised his own personal machinery to preserve the painstaking techniques of revision which he had developed with the aid of Lowell, Underwood, and Fields especially. He formed the habit of giving manuscript drafts of his poems to local printers (probably those at the office of *The Villager*), who made galley proofs, saved him much manual labor in copying, and enabled him at the same time to "see what the poem looked like." This was a practice of Whitman too.

Whittier's long memorial ode to Charles Sumner, read by Professor J. W. Churchill at the commemorative services held in Boston on June 9, 1874, was evidently revised in three proofs, one broadside, and one preliminary pamphlet before it was put in the form used in the 316-page "Memorial of Charles Sumner" published by the Commonwealth of Massachusetts.[36] Whittier's exceeding care in the preparation of this ode befitted his regard for Sumner. He threw out or added in longhand whole stanzas, and made numerous verbal corrections. He appears to have sent copies of the second proof to Longfellow and other friends for comment, and even after the ode had been read at the exercises in Music Hall, Boston, he tinkered with the copy being prepared for the "Memorial." He dropped one stanza and added seven others which were an apparent afterthought.

Whittier's late habit of having his poems set in type before he sent them to magazine editors led him to a pleasant and close friendship with a young fellow townsman, Frederick Augustus Brown (1859–1924). Fred Brown mastered the printer's trade in the office of *The Villager*. When he died, Judge Charles I. Pettingell prepared a tribute to him, part of which reads:

> Between John Greenleaf Whittier and Mr. Brown there was a personal relation that was unusual. In Mr. Brown's capacity as printer he was frequently called upon by Mr. Whittier to set up from the poet's manuscripts galley proofs which could be sent to the publishers in Boston. Thus it was, that almost everything which Mr. Whittier wrote in his later years passed first to Mr. Brown, and thus it was, in many instances that Mr. Brown retained the manuscript as a gift from the poet. But their relationship went further and contained a more personal touch. They were neighbors, and for many years almost nightly engaged in a friendly game [high low jack] which ran along without end accumulating an enormous score, all the while accompanied by conversation and discussion.[37]

The Whittier-Brown team appears to have been formed in the early eighteen-eighties, and to have continued to function until Whittier died. Brown was reported to have struck off only two or three copies of a Whittier work in galley form, though it is evident that Whittier in some instances requested extra copies of the corrected proofs, for distribution to friends. Mr. Currier, who has made a careful study of items assignable to Brown, reaches the conclusion:

> These advance printings have far greater interest than ordinary proof sheets since they have the nature of early manuscript drafts. Not only do they frequently have variant words and passages, but often contain whole stanzas which were later rejected, and they usually bear in their margins corrections and additions in Whittier's own hand. There are sometimes successive printings of one and the same poem, the new printings incorporating the corrections, being in their turn duly provided with a new crop of alterations, thus presenting a vivid picture of the development of each poem as Whittier worked at it.[38]

One of the manuscript poems of which Fred Brown made an advance printing is "The Vow of Washington," which Whittier was prevailed upon to write for the celebration, on April 30, 1889, of the one hundredth anniversary of Washington's first inaugural. Brown made two proofs. Then from Oak Knoll on January 31, 1889, Whittier posted a copy of the revision to Clarence W. Bowen, secretary of the committee on arrangements for the centennial, with this message:

> I enclose the poem I have written for the Inauguration Centennial. I am not very sure it is equal to the occasion. But put it in clear large type, and return it to me for a final look at it. I will send it back without delay. Perhaps it will not be best to show it to your Committee in its present shape. If the Com. have any doubts about it let the whole matter drop, and return the poem to me. I shall be satisfied any way.

When the proof began to come, Whittier had a kind of chain-reaction to it. On February 18 he returned the first impression, with his revisions, to Mr. Bowen — and with a virtual promise to call it a day. On the nineteenth he returned another proof with the assurance that now it was "precisely in the shape I wish it," and that if Bowen would "send me the poem as a fixed fact I promise you I will not change it in word or letter." On the twentieth he was vexed by an afterthought — that several verses and one pivotal word which he had deemed it necessary to add were really superfluous. Mr. Bowen received thanks for his patience. Finally, on February 21, Whittier wrote, in part:

> Thine just rec'd. Need not send any further proof. The proof I returned yesterday is all right. I am sure thee will be glad as I am that

the "long agony" is over. I hope the thing will be satisfactory to the Committee and to the audience on the 30th of April. I shall never undertake such a thing again.[39]

## 4

That was Whittier's habit of work, not alone in his eighty-second year but in all others after he ceased, around 1860, being primarily an Abolitionist writer. He looked long and acutely at the "shape" of his poems, and recast them with zeal and patience. He was a far sharper self-critic than Wordsworth, for one, but he neither cared nor was able to achieve the skill in rhyming of a Pope — or a Lowell. Whittier did not worry excessively about perfect rhyme if his lines had other beauty, meaning, and easy flow.

And it is likely that his unmusical ear and his use of the provincial (sometimes archaic) New England pronunciation of certain words put exact rhyming beyond his reach. Whittier knew this limitation, and referred to it often, as when he wrote J. T. Fields:

> See what thy good nature in sending me a proof has come to. I yield the rhyme of *martyr* and *water* to please thee; but reluctantly, for it is no time now to give up our Yankee rights of pronunciation. I should be hung for my bad rhymes anywhere south of Mason and Dixon's line. My "speech bewrayeth me." . . .[40]

A student of Whittier's rhymes [41] points out that some of his pronunciations did not pass out of the New England of his day, but are still heard along the Atlantic seaboard. In "The Merrimac" he rhymed *banner* with *Susquehanna*, and whether he dropped the *r* from *banner* or added it to *Susquehanna*, he was in keeping with New England practice. Often, Yankee-like, he "softened" or dropped the *r*, and used a number of words in *–orn* to rhyme with words ending in *–awn* (*scorning* and *fawning*, *morning* and *dawning*). Likewise he rhymed words ending in *–arm* with others ending in *–alm*, and made other such combinations as *law* and *war*, *saw* and *for*.

Even in curious-sounding vowel combinations in his rhymes (*toil* and *isle*, *soil* and *while*) Whittier had honorable precedent, for interchange of pronunciations like *join* and *jine* was standard from the sixteenth century into the eighteenth. It is found in a whole range of English authors from Shakespeare through Dryden, Pope, and Gray, to Wordsworth, Coleridge, and Byron. Selections from their writings, found by Whittier in Lindley Murray's *English Reader*, were, if one omits the Bible, the first literary works whose influence he felt. In a literary way, he seldom lost what he had acquired by reading.

Others of Whittier's vowel combinations indicate merely archaic pronunciation: *haunt* and *chant*, *want* and *aslant*, *wants* and *grants*, and *hearth* with *earth*, *dearth*, *mirth*.

So viewed, they were probably not so bad as they sounded to Lowell and others whose ears were more strict than Whittier's. To the question whether Whittier's rhymes were "careless," or "slovenly," or "excruciating," the best answer seems to be the comment of C. F. Richardson: "Whittier's rhyme-derelictions are more famous than they deserve to be, and mostly fall into some freedom of earlier English verse, rather than a wild hunt for some passable rhyme." [42]

To sum it all up: if Whittier's ear at times betrayed him, he was always able to see what his faults were, and what his virtues. That is why his revisions hold particular interest. Whittier knew that there were flaws in his technical equipment, and that, in strictness, no amount of revising would bring him to a perfectly hard and clean artistry. He anticipated by half a century an American prose writer who, with a nod toward the critics, published in the covers of a book his own criticism of it. In 1883 when Francis H. Underwood was preparing his biographical sketch, Whittier on July 21 wrote to him:

> I am grateful for thy generous estimate of my writings in "Characteristics" but I fear the critics will not agree with thee. Why not anticipate them, and own up to the faults & limitations which every body sees, and none more clearly than myself. Touch upon my false rhymes, and Yankeeisms: confess that I sometimes "crack the voice of Melody, & break the legs of Time." Pitch into Mogg Megone. That "big Injun," strutting around in Walter Scott's plaid, has no friends and deserves none. Own that I sometimes choose unpoetical themes. Endorse Lowell's "Fable for Critics" that I mistake occasionally, simple excitement for inspiration. In this way we can take the wind out of the sails of ill-natured cavillers. I am not one of the master singers & don't pose as one. By the grace of God I am only what I am, and don't wish to pass for more.
>
> I return the sheets, with this note. Think of my suggestions and act upon them if it seems best to thee.[43]

# XXV

## Among the Hills

WHITTIER penned the letter of July 21, 1883, to Underwood from Asquam House, Holderness, New Hampshire. Here among the hills and upland lakes he spent parts of several summers, free from the heat of eastern Massachusetts and, in the main, from the intrusions of "pilgrims." Until the Bearcamp River House, in West Ossipee, burned down in 1881 it was Whittier's summer favorite, and there he spent many vacations. In turn, after Holderness, he found refreshment for his spirit at Sturtevant House, in Centre Harbor. Once at least — in 1849 — he went to northern New Hampshire in search of health. With his Cartland cousins, his usual companions, he enjoyed rest during the summer of 1881 at Intervale and in 1889 at Conway. From both places he had a broad view of the land formation rising to its crest in Mount Washington (6288 feet) and other peaks of the Presidential Range.

Consciously or not, Whittier as he grew older made of these upland visits a symbol of the aspiration and rise of his life. There, amid the choicest manifestations of Nature which he knew, he felt that he was coming closer to God. In "The Lakeside" (1849) he made himself one with the Indian of old who "through the sunset air looked down/ Upon the Smile of God" — that is, upon Lake Winnipesaukee. Whittier ended:

Thanks, O our Father! that, like him,
Thy tender love I see,
In radiant hill and woodland dim,
And tinted sunset sea.

. . . . . . . .[1]

As boy and man Whittier always knew New Hampshire and Maine, and had both the White Mountains and the seashore within ready view or easy reach. The border of New Hampshire lay just north of the Whittier homestead in East Haverhill, and in his youth, when his parents first took him for a visit among the hills, Whittier received a soul-filling impression of "the great wooded slope of Agamenticus" which he never lost.[2] And he knew closely the coast of Massachusetts, New Hampshire, and Maine as far as Portland; knew "the tremulous shadow of the Sea" before "the shadows round the inland sea." [3] His writings teem with references and historical incidents related to coastal places all the way from Salisbury Beach, above the mouth of the Merrimac, to Grand Manan Island.

## I

For the "far islands looming tall and high" which he mentioned in *The Tent on the Beach* Whittier had, chiefly, the attachment of a warm personal friendship which began in 1863. In the summer of that year he and his sister Elizabeth went to the Isles of Shoals for the first time, and it was a fall on the rocks there which at last broke the frail reed of her health. She died in September, 1864. Thereafter Whittier returned often to "the Shoals," one of many writers and artists attracted to the spacious resort hotel on Appledore Island, and to the salon of Celia Thaxter. (Her father, Thomas B. Laighton, had the hotel built in 1848.)

Whittier delighted to begin letters addressed to Mrs. Thaxter, "Po Hill [Amesbury] sends Appledore good-morning," and the fact that on clear days one could see from there the distant islands, ten miles off the shoreline border of New Hampshire and Maine, was a comfort to him when the summer heat of the Merrimac Valley became oppressive. On July 24, 1870, he wrote her:

> Be thankful for sea-surrounded Appledore! We are literally baking alive here. Yesterday the thermometer went up to 98° — making our ashen earth (we have had no rain for 3 weeks) too hot to tread on. In the evening it cooled down to 90° *& stuck there.* I spent the night like a wandering ghost, going from room to room, trying sofas and floors, & getting no sleep out of them. We have had a splendid day-break, but there is now a fierce menace of heat, and *not* "tenderly the haughty

day fills its blue urn with fire." Over Po Hill the sky looks cool & hard, refreshing to eye & spirit, & the two great rustic baskets full of bloom & greenery, with their fresh luxuriance make a pleasant contrast to the hot street and the dusty trees & shrubbery in the front yard. My little room is quiet enough. — Lizzie is at Seabrook — and I am all alone. The sweet calm face of the pagan philosopher & emperor, Marcus Antoninus, looks down upon me on one hand, & on the other the bold, generous & humane countenance of the Christian man of action, Henry Ward Beecher; and I sit between them as a sort of compromise. It is very still — the leaves move softly without sound — I can hear my own thoughts. How I thank thee for thy letter just received, bringing me the sweet breath of wild rose & mignonette. It is as if the cool, soft, sea air of the islands blew over this feverish inland, & I bathe my hot, aching brow for a moment in the dream of a milder atmosphere. * * *

Pilgrims come & go, as usual, and now & then old friends. Mrs. Pitman spent most of two days with me, & Lucy Larcom one. An old bachelor friend came to tell me of his newly resumed hopes of matrimony. It was very droll. * * *

Monday morning.

Yesterday the thermometer ran almost to 100, and this is likely to be another hot day. I find the extreme heat affects me so much that I shall be obliged to try some cooler region. I suppose you are over-full by this time at the "Shoals." I have been really sick for the last few days, and if this terrible weather continues I must find some place of refuge.[4]

For Whittier, the charm of "the Shoals" and of all other vacation places to which he went in his life was double. He loved to be closer to the beauties of Nature than urban life permitted, and, only less, he reveled in the companionship of special friends. Mrs. Fields and Lucy Larcom were among others who occasionally joined him in the Thaxter circle at "Appledore," and also his cousins, Joseph and Gertrude Cartland — his summer companions *par excellence.* Whittier wrote Mrs. Thaxter on August 12, 1869:

* * * I am so sorry my good cousins the Cartlands did not reach the island before we left. They are very dear to me. I wish thee could have known Moses A. Cartland. There are so few like him now left in the world! I am almost tempted to run the gauntlet of your great

> crowd on the island for the sake of seeing them, and bringing them so near to thee as to make thee know & love them as I do, for there are few better people in the world than Joseph & Gertrude Whittier Cartland. * * *[5]

Whittier's summer vacations with these particular friends became fairly regular after the end of the Civil War, and were an important part of his life. But he at no time thought of them as placing him on a magic mountain, detached from the life down below among other valued friends in the workaday world.

None the less he got something more than the invigoration of sea or mountain air. Mrs. Fields pictured his style of life at "Appledore," both conversing with his friends in quiet corners of the great piazzas of the hotel, and again sitting with them in the parlor of Mrs. Thaxter's cottage. He might pass whole days watching her at her painting in the window, and listening attentively to what was on the minds of others in the circle. It was on a particular summer Sunday, when all spark and spirit had gone out of the company, that Whittier suddenly asked Mrs. Thaxter to read from Emerson.[6] When she had finished he picked up the discourse. "His whole heart was stirred," Mrs. Fields noted, "and he poured himself out towards us as if he longed, like the prophet of old, to breathe a new life into us."[7]

From the sea, it is obvious, Whittier got pleasure but no great promptings to write. None of the New England poets, indeed, had the genuine infection of "sea fever" — only R. H. Dana and Herman Melville. Whittier was the poet of the mountains, of the White Hills.

## 2

His spirits perceptibly rose with the land. As early as 1831, Ernest Poole writes, Whittier went to Plymouth.[8] With the Cartlands he visited during the summer of 1842 in Lee, New Hampshire, but he became a regular summer visitor to the State only later, as his means allowed. Yet the fragrance of life among the hills had penetrated thoroughly into his system, and his joyous response to it is marked in a letter written by Mary Rogers Kimball, daughter of his early friend and Abolitionist colleague Nathaniel Peabody Rogers. She said:

We all loved Mr. Whittier, and before we left our home near Plymouth, N.H., for the West, in 1853, I think, he spent a week with us. With what delight we wandered, talked, read, and played with him. We sang to him; and of all the songs, English, Scotch, or Irish, he loved the negro melodies best. How well I remember his creeping softly behind me and shaking into my neck the dew from a branch of cinnamon rose he had picked and carried a long distance that early morning, "for this express purpose," as he said. I cherished the precious twig for many years. . . . The little poem entitled "A Memory" was of my next older sister, Ellen, who was spending a few days with friends at Wolfborough, N.H. She was a singer, and one evening the poet wrapped a white shawl about her, and put a Quaker bonnet on her head, and made her sing through the long twilight the songs he loved. The little event is immortalized; the Singer and the Poet have "passed on." [9]

And Whittier professedly had no ear for music!

On one occasion Whittier was with the Fields at Campton, just north of Plymouth. And very likely in the summer of 1861 he visited, still farther north, the valley of the Pemigewasset, and afterward wrote the poem "Franconia from Pemigewasset," the first part of "Mountain Pictures." [10] A far better piece of art, which gave capital prominence to the Franconia Notch country, was Hawthorne's prose tale "The Great Stone Face." Whittier's verse was significant mainly as an invocation to the "Mountains of the North" to fill him so richly with their "calm and strength" and "unforgotten beauty" that he could draw upon this reserve in the "common life" of his "lowland home." [11]

By all odds the best, Whittier came to love the lower country between Campton and Laconia, just south of a parallel drawn through Sandwich Notch. Here, in a square twenty-five miles along the side, were Holderness (on Squam Lake), Lake Winnipesaukee, and West Ossipee and Bearcamp River. And here at South Tamworth is the mountain now named for him. It was this region of abounding lakes and of rangy, green-belted hills traced against the sky that was most congenial to Whittier's nature. Mount Washington was more majestic, but Whittier vastly preferred Chocorua (3475 feet) to it and to all others. The view of it and its bald granite crown, lofting over placid Lake Chocorua, was one of the attractions which drew him, for many summers, to Bearcamp River House. This place he described to Gertrude Cartland in August, 1875:

"We have been here for the last three weeks. It is a quiet, old-fashioned inn, beautifully located, neat as possible, large rooms, nice beds, and good, wholesome table. . . ." [12]

Thither went various of Whittier's friends, including, Ernest Poole writes, the painter George Inness.[13] For Chocorua was and is often called "the most beautiful mountain in America," and to the natives and the initiated it came almost to signify what Fujiyama does to the Japanese.

## 3

To Whittier the visits to the White Hills signified three things. He went, first of all, for reasons of health. Again and again he returned for a deep draft of beauty, when —

> the stress and strain
> Of years that did the work of centuries
> Have ceased, and we can draw our breath once more
> Freely and full.[14]

And increasingly he lifted up his eyes to the hills because they were the creation of God, who was sensibly present to him there more than anywhere else.

If Whittier went to Plymouth in the summer of 1831, he went certainly for the benefit of his health. Its weak state had driven him home from his editorial duties in Hartford, and on July 14 he wrote Jonathan Law that he had been "away Down East." On July 14, 1849, he had to decline, through Lewis Tappan, Joseph Sturge's offer to pay the expenses of a trip to England, and said that he had been "spending some weeks in the northern part of New Hampshire." [15] Whittier thrived on the cool, clean air of the upland country, and particularly on the quiet of the inns to which he customarily went. He had nearly always the company of the Cartlands or other relatives and friends, and consequently freedom from the intrusion of curiosity-seekers. With strangers he enjoyed chatting, but when "pilgrims" spotted him at Bearcamp House or at his other haunts, he vanished into favorite lanes or retreats of the woods he knew so well. Unluckily he was not able to climb Chocorua or other peaks in the Sandwich Range. Of one loquacious admirer who trapped him

Whittier remarked afterward, with a smile, "He extravagantly praised my work and all the time called me Whitaker." [16]

When the Civil War ended, and his freer and fuller life began, Whittier found "the pervading symphony of peace" [17] in the White Hills. He described himself precisely in "An Autograph" (1882):

> Hater of din and riot
> He lived in days unquiet;
> And, lover of all beauty,
> Trod the hard ways of duty.[18]

For beauty he went, with the deep fervor of a pilgrim, to the White Hills — "To feel, from burdening cares and ills,/ The strong uplifting of the hills." A half-century had passed since he had first seen the Sandwich country, with companions now gone. But he wrote:

> Still, when the sun of summer burns,
> My longing for the hills returns;
> And northward, leaving at my back
> The warm vale of the Merrimac,
> I go to meet the winds of morn,
> Blown down the hill-gaps, mountain-born,
> Breathe scent of pines, and satisfy
> The hunger of a lowland eye.[19]

And, once Whittier has arrived in the hill country —

> Life's burdens fall, its discords cease,
> I lapse into the glad release
> Of Nature's own exceeding peace.[20]

When work or other cause anchored Whittier at home, his spirits fell to the level revealed in a letter of August, 1868, to Lucy Larcom:

> I am doing nothing at a great rate; come and help me. I, too, have dreamed of the Shoals and the hills — but they must come to me. They must return my visits now. Bring thy painting traps with thee; perhaps we may find a flower in despite of the drought. . . . Everything seems returning to its original dust. We are eating our bushel instead of our "peck of dirt." We can't lay the dust of the streets for fear the water will turn to steam, and blow up the cart.[21]

The White Hills, in fact, did return Whittier's visits: he always took home with him vivid memories, and he put into words, better than any one else has done, the emotions which these particular hills stir in people who love them. From Whittier they called forth, after "The Lakeside," a long succession of charming pictures, the last of which was, fittingly, "The Wood Giant" (1885). His delight, and his answered prayer, was that the beauty of the hill country would last through and brighten his winter's hibernation. He said rightly, in "Summer by the Lakeside":

> But none shall more regretful leave
> These waters and these hills than I:
> Or, distant, fonder dream how eve
> Or dawn is painting wave and sky; . . . [22]

For emphasis, this sentiment stood at the end of his choicest poem of the White Hills — "Sunset on the Bearcamp."

## 4

Whittier's eye, as he looked about him in "these smiling hills," was no less discerning than fond. He observed sharply, came to know all of the various moods of Nature, and recorded them joyously in verse which, if not touched with the genius of Byron's pictures of the Alps, had at least something of Wordsworth's power to describe softer landscapes. (Tennyson told an American visitor that Whittier's "My Playmate" was "a perfect poem" — that "in some of his descriptions of scenery and wild flowers he would rank with Wordsworth.") [23] That was particularly true in "Among the Hills," a simple story idealizing New England farm life as Whittier perceived it, in the summer of 1867, in Sandwich vale.

In spite of his strong preference for the warm months, he wrote no single poem of summer that compares with *Snow-Bound*. But he caught the charm of that favored region in "Summer by the Lakeside," "The Last Walk in Autumn," "St. Martin's Summer," and "Storm on Lake Asquam" among others in a list headed by "Sunset on the Bearcamp." Whittier in this group of poems excelled in flashes, in single or grouped images which in effect are nearly always lovely and often striking. In "Among the Hills" he described lucidly the spectacle of clearing after a storm, and "the purpling lights of heaven" which marked the sunset. Even better was a sundown picture in "Sunset on the Bearcamp":

Touched by a light that hath no name,
A glory never sung,
Aloft on sky and mountain wall
Are God's great pictures hung.
How changed the summits vast and old!
No longer granite-browed,
They melt in rosy mist; the rock
Is softer than the cloud;
The valley holds its breath; no leaf
Of all its elms is twirled:
The silence of eternity
Seems falling on the world.[24]

Whittier in "Summer by the Lakeside" skillfully painted the rise of the moon and the silver of its sheen on lake, isle, and mountain side; and equally the moment when the "pale ghost of the setting moon" —

Shall hide behind yon rocky spines,
And the young archer, Morn, shall break
His arrows on the mountain pines,
And, golden-sandalled, walk the lake! [25]

Stars and Northern Lights were represented with crystal clarity in "Among the Hills." In "The Seeking of the Waterfall" he saw that the water "whirled in mad dance its misty hair," and he imagined that the fall "its white scarf flutters in the air!" [26] Finally, his luminous figure of "the rainbow's angel" at the end of "Storm on Lake Asquam" was excellently conceived.

But it was to Chocorua that Whittier returned again and again, deftly depicting it in its varied aspects. In "Storm on Lake Asquam" he pictured "Chocorua's tall, defiant sentinel" standing above the "wraith of tempest" and finally blotted out from sight.[27] In the vision of "A Mystery" he felt delightedly —

One sharp, tall peak above them all
Clear into sunlight sprang:
I saw the river of my dreams,
The mountains that I sang! [28]

He sketched in "Among the Hills" the phenomenon in which —

. . . once again Chocorua's horn
Of shadow pierced the water.[29]

Chocorua had for Whittier another and particular meaning. It became, by an odd twist, a symbol of the rest, relaxation, and fun which he found in the White Hills. His party, filling nearly every room in Bearcamp House, included many young people, chiefly his niece "Lizzie," Addie Caldwell, wife of his nephew Lewis, and friends of theirs. Whittier could merely admire Chocorua. They climbed it. In the evening, by the inn fire which he tended as zealously as his own in winter in the "garden room" at Amesbury, Whittier relished their exuberant reports of the day's outing.

In September, 1876, a party of seven of them spent one night on the summit of the mountain, conducted there by two young farmers of West Ossipee, the Knox brothers. These youths had a flair for bear-hunting, and supplied the inn with sweet steaks that Whittier enjoyed eating. The young ladies of the party, which camped for the night among the bear traps on Chocorua, reported next evening to Whittier that they had heard the growling of bears and other horrendous noises.

Soon afterward the entire Whittier entourage were guests at a husking party given by the Knox brothers. Whittier composed for the occasion, and Lucy Larcom read as the composition of an unknown author, a string of twelve verses, product of a very light touch, entitled "How They Climbed Chocorua." For the party of which she had been a member Lucy Larcom countered with equally joshing verses addressed "To the Unknown and Absent Author of 'How They Climbed Chocorua.'" Whittier ended the festival with the pure fudge of "The Last Will and Testament of the Man in the Bear Trap," and even added a codicil which S. T. Pickard found next morning tucked under his breakfast plate. It was to this hilarious "poetry contest" that Whittier alluded when he asked Mr. Pickard not to print in his paper "my foolish verses." [30]

## 5

To an inquirer Whittier wrote on May 11, 1881:

The lady of the poem "Among the Hills" was purely imaginary. I was charmed with the scenery in Tamworth and West Ossipee, and tried to call attention to it in a story. My old haunt there, the Bearcamp House, is burned down, much to my regret. . . . I hope another house will be built on its site. With the long range of the Sandwich Mountains and Chocorua on one hand, and the rugged masses of Ossipee on the other, it is really one of the most picturesque situations in the State. . . .[31]

That summer Whittier spent several weeks with the Cartlands at Intervale, and thereafter passed part of every vacation with them until he died.[32] They visited at Holderness during the next four summers, and then in 1886–88 at a quiet farm home, Sturtevant House, a mile above Centre Harbor, which is on an arm of Winnipesaukee reaching toward Squam Lake. It was about an immense pine in the Sturtevants' pasture that "The Wood Giant" was written.

All of these places delighted Whittier. At Intervale he had Mount Washington, patched with snow streaks above the tree line, to watch, and thick pine woods to walk and talk in. At Holderness he loved the view northeast across Squam Lake toward Chocorua, and in a letter written from Asquam House on July 14, 1882, he feelingly described the pleasures of the situation to Mrs. Fields, then traveling in England.[33]

In all of his New Hampshire and Maine vacations after mid-career, it is manifest, Whittier derived his chief pleasure from the closeness to God and Nature. His sense of it was deep and significant. All his life he believed in the immanence of God; here He could be seen and His presence felt. Whittier loved the Indians' belief, implicit in the name, that Lake Winnipesaukee was "the smile of the Great Spirit." So, too, for him, were the trees and flowers, the myriad other lakes, the mountain walls and passes.

Whittier's expression of his feeling became progressively stronger with the years, after "The Lakeside" appeared in 1849. In "Summer by the Lakeside" (1853) he wrote a clear statement of his belief in the Eternal Goodness, for here —

> The Shadow which pursues us all,
> Whose ever-nearing steps appall,
> Whose voice we hear behind us call, —
>
> That Shadow blends with mountain gray,
> It speaks but what the light waves say, —
> Death walks apart from Fear to-day! [34]

This sentiment he intensified and heightened in "The Last Walk in

Autumn" (1857) and in "Sunset on the Bearcamp" (1876). And by 1880, in "St. Martin's Summer" (i.e., Indian Summer), he felt that he was in tune with the infinite, and wrote:

O stream of life, whose swifter flow
Is of the end forewarning,
Methinks thy sundown afterglow
Seems less of night than morning!

Old cares grow light; aside I lay
The doubts and fears that troubled;
The quiet of the happy day
Within my soul is doubled.[35]

Finally, "A Summer Pilgrimage" (1883) is at once a plain statement and a song of joy that God is in Nature: that Whittier's sense of worship which, in its presence, takes possession of him is the —

Soul of the mountain, lake, and wood,
Their witness to the Eternal Good!

The White Hills are proof to him that "eternal verities remain," and they lead him to the happy conclusion:

But let me dream that hill and sky
Of unseen beauty prophesy;
And in these tinted lakes behold
The trailing of the raiment fold
Of that which, still eluding gaze,
Allures to upward-tending ways,
Whose footprints make, wherever found,
Our common earth a holy ground.[36]

That belief, even more than his assurance of the love of friends, was the main prop of Whittier's late years, and indeed the guide of his long life. His stout conviction was that life had meaning only if God was in it. For him, as for so many devout souls back to the beginning of time, the surest proof of the eternal goodness of the world and its design was Nature itself. His comment to Grace Greenwood in a letter of October, 1886, had pointed meaning: "I spent last summer among the New Hampshire hills, as I have done for several years. Nature never disappoints me. . . ."[37]

# XXVI

## The Afternoon Slope of Life

As he approached and then passed the Scriptural span of seventy years, Whittier imagined himself on "the afternoon slope of life." For a man whom experience had made so well acquainted both with the valleys and the peaks, this was a choice figure, but not wholly applicable. The quality of Whittier's life became so widely known and admired, during the eighteen-seventies and eighties, that his reputation and influence continued to grow as his merely physical energies waned. Old friends and colleagues fell away — Sumner in 1874 and then in the next decade Bayard Taylor, Garrison, Fields, Longfellow and Emerson, and Samuel E. Sewall — but new friends and admirers, many times multiplied, stepped into Whittier's life. He was often and greatly honored by men and women close at hand and far away.

Whittier was as full of humility as of thanks. His strong belief in the perfectibility of man only made him, the higher the praise, the more acutely aware of his shortcomings. How high he aspired he very often made clear, as he did in part of a letter of September 22, 1870, to Elizabeth Stuart Phelps:

> . . . The foundations seem breaking up. I only hope that if the planks and stagings of human device give way, we shall find the Eternal Rock beneath. We can do without Bible or church; we cannot do without God; and of Him we are sure. All that science and criticism can urge cannot shake the self-evident truth that He asks me to be true, just, merciful, and loving, and because He asks me to be so, I know that He is Himself what He requires of me.[1]

How modestly Whittier rated his performance is plainly shown in another letter, addressed to Mrs. Pitman in 1879:

> I am greatly pained to hear of the illness of our old friend Garrison. For how many years he has been an important part of our world! Much of my own life was shaped by him. It is very sad to think I shall see him no more. The next mail may bring tidings of his death. I have been thinking over my life, and the survey has not been encouraging. Alas! if I have been a servant at all I have been an unprofitable one, and yet I have loved goodness, and longed to bring my imaginative poetic temperament into true subjection. I stand ashamed and almost despairing before holy and pure ideals. As I read the New Testament I feel how weak, irresolute, and frail I am, and how little I can rely on anything save our God's mercy and infinite compassion, which I reverently and thankfully own have followed me through life, and the assurance of which is my sole ground of hope for myself, and for those I love and pray for.[2]

These were the sentiments which he checked and weighed in the reflective poem "At Eventide," published, significantly, in *Youth's Companion* on September 19, 1878. He asked clear-eyed Justice, i.e., God, to "judge our frailty by the life we meant." [3]

## I

In the eyes of his fellow men it was a strongly encouraging example of what a man could do with his life. Some time late in the course of it Whittier revealed his conviction that he gave core and purpose to it when (in 1832–33) he renounced political ambitions and enlisted in the anti-slavery ranks. And having been asked to counsel a lad of fifteen, Whittier said to him gently: "My lad, if thou wouldst win success, join thyself to some unpopular but noble cause." [4]

To Whittier's highly ethical mind that was the essence of beauty — to love God and serve His creatures. In "Fame and Glory," a tribute to Sumner published in the *National Era* on December 30, 1847, Whittier expressed his conviction that "no true and permanent fame can be founded except in labors which promote the happiness of mankind."

In 1857, at the age of fifty, Whittier was in poverty because of the choice he had made for his career. At sixty he was free from financial want, and for the rest of his life he received back, many times compounded, the love of men and even the literary favor he had craved when young. He was rich because, on "the afternoon slope," with all obstructions to the view swept away, he saw that essentially "love is about all there is worth living for, and I thank our Heavenly Father for the capacity to love my friends, & the joy of being loved in return." [5] That was the happy burden of many of his letters written after 1870.

Whittier's correspondence during the last fifteen years of his life was varied and revealing. From many lands and from close home, affectionate voices spoke to him. They were a joint chorus of the mighty and the humble, all one to Whittier, and of strangers and familiars. Annie Fields and the feminine literary group were steady correspondents, and among the company of "old boys" with whom Whittier exchanged heart-warming letters, almost to the end, were Henry Ingersoll Bowditch, Boston friend and physician; William Henry Furness, Unitarian clergyman and early Abolitionist, of Philadelphia; and the aged Quaker, Daniel Ricketson, of New Bedford. None loved him better, however, or saw more clearly the secret of his appeal to so many people, than O. W. Holmes, for whose eighty-third birthday Whittier was to write his last fragment of verse.

Out of Whittier's yearly mass of correspondence, his portion of which poured in on him at the rate of a thousand pieces or more a month, two letters perfectly sound the tonic chord. He wrote one to Annie Fields and received the other from Holmes.

In 1885, from Danvers, he sent birthday congratulations to Holmes, who on September 15 wrote from Beverly Farms saying, "I do seriously threaten you with a visit before I return to Boston," and asking directions to Oak Knoll.[6] Whittier entertainingly described his general situation and Holmes's visit, in a letter written to Mrs. Fields on October 2:

> I have been thinking of thy gracious and generous proposal of hospitality. It has made me very happy, though I have not been able to see how I can avail myself of it. I find that I am unable to bear the excitement of city life for any length of time, however carefully I may be shielded by my friends. I am unhappily notorious, and cannot hide myself. My deafness [7] makes me confused and uncomfortable when strangers are present. The great and really painful effort I am com-

pelled to make when in company, to listen and try to understand, and make fitting replies, and the uncertainty I feel, when I venture to speak, whether I have heard aright — all this affects my nerves, and costs me nights of sleeplessness and days of weariness. In fact I am what the Turks call "a cut-off one," so far as society is concerned. . . . As soon as it is known that I am in your premises a steady stream of interviewers, autograph-hunters, and people with missions will flow in upon you. It would be like having a waif from Barnum's Museum shut up in your library, and people coming in to see what it looks like. It would make your life miserable. Sarah's dog could not keep them off. You would have to get out a writ of ejectment and set me and my carpet-bag into the street — and yet how I wish I could say "yes"! I thank the good Providence that has given me such a friend, dear as Vittoria Colonna to Michael Angelo. I wish I could look forward to the enjoyment of such friendship for many years in this life, but when one is approaching fourscore that is not to be expected. Though for that matter, I see that Senator Hoar, in his great speech of day before yesterday at Springfield, took occasion to deny the self-evident fact that I am an old man! . . . I had a rare good visit from Dr. Holmes and his wife the other day. We two old boys wandered about in the woods, talking of many things — half merry, half sad. We were stranded mariners, the survivors of a lost crew, warming ourselves at a fire kindled from the wreck of our vessel. . . .[8]

And when Holmes had reached eighty, he wrote Whittier on September 2, 1889, a letter which was as much a mirror of Whittier as of himself. He said:

Here I am at your side among the octogenarians. At seventy we are objects of veneration; at eighty, of curiosity; at ninety, of wonder; and if we reach a hundred we are candidates for a side show attached to Barnum's great exhibition. You know all about it. You know why I have not thanked you before this for your beautiful and precious tribute, which would make any birthday memorable. I remember how you were overwhelmed with tributes on the occasion of your own eightieth birthday, and you can understand the impossibility I find before me of responding in any fitting shape to all the tokens of friendship which I receive. . . . I hope, dear Whittier, that you find much to enjoy in the midst of all the lesser trials which old age must bring with it. You have

> kind friends all around you, and the love and homage of your fellow-countrymen as few have enjoyed, with the deep satisfaction of knowing that you have earned them, not merely by the gifts of your genius, but by a noble life which has ripened without a flaw into a grand and serene old age. I never see my name coupled with yours, as it often is nowadays, without feeling honored by finding myself in such company, and wishing that I were more worthy of it. . . . I am living here with my daughter-in-law, and just as I turned this leaf I heard wheels at the door, and she got out, leading in in triumph her husband, His Honor, Judge Holmes of the Supreme Court of Massachusetts, just arrived from Europe, by the Scythia. I look up to him as my magistrate, and he knows me as his father, but my arms are around his neck and his moustache is sweeping my cheek — I feel young again at fourscore.[9]

Whittier always delighted in his relationship with "young" Doctor Holmes, and in the freely exchanged esteem of all of his New England fellows. But he was as deeply moved by the manifestations of affection which came to him in a flood from the youth of the land. He was impressed by the fact that in his birthday celebrations after the eightieth, the accent was as much on youth and the future as on the steady affection of old friends. After his eighty-first birthday he wrote to Mrs. Fields that "among the many tokens of good will from all parts of the country and beyond sea, there were some curious and amusing missives." One Southern woman included him in her curse upon the "mean, hateful Yankees." But as an offset to this, the Southern Forestry Commission, assembled at De Fanick Springs, Florida, informed him by telegram that "in remembrance of your birthday we have planted a live-oak tree to your memory, which, like the leaves of the tree, will be forever green." [10]

Just before his eighty-second birthday Whittier wrote to Mrs. Fields, on December 12, 1889:

> I came to Amesbury yesterday, where I hope my birthday will pass quietly. As life draws nearer the close, one feels desirous to be near the old home and the unforgotten landscape of youth, and to muse by the same fireside where our dear ones used to sit.[11]

Whittier had his wish. The day was quiet, but it was, Pickard noted, quite generally observed in the nation's schools. Students in Amesbury marched in a procession to the house in Friend Street, and Whittier (no public speaker) gave them warm but brief greeting. And among the usual tide of letters and gifts which came in from all parts of the United States and from other nations, Whittier was touched by none more than by the tokens of affection from students in seminaries for the colored people of the South. For him they had gratitude and reverence, and they gave particular demonstrations of their feeling. On a number of occasions, for example, Whittier received barrels of pitch-pine kindlings for the fire in his study, sent by Negro students of Alabama and the other Gulf States.[12]

Other honors, less substantial, seemed likely to stand as perpetual monuments to his name and his life. Two colleges, both in the West, have been called Whittier. When in 1868 the Quaker settlers of Salem, Iowa, determined to found a college for the benefit of the youth of the area, they gave it his name. Whittier was happy to help in giving the young institution the best of all possible starts, and he sent fifty books, each inscribed with his own name, which became the nucleus of "a really good library." [13] Luck did not favor the Iowa institution, which was closed in 1885, one of a number of other sectarian colleges, founded during the westward expansion, whose managers failed to find the large means required for the development of an institution of higher education. But the second Whittier College, opened in 1896 in the Southern California community whose Quaker leaders named it for him in 1887,[14] is today in thriving condition.

Finally, on this head, it is a curious fact that Whittier was so often elected to honorary membership in student literary societies and authors' leagues and historical associations. As early as 1831, when he was editing the *New England Weekly Review*, he was honored by the perhaps perspicacious young men of the Franklin Society of Brown University.[15] At later dates he was elected to — among others — literary societies at Colgate and at Cazenovia Seminary (of which his friend Charles Dudley Warner was a graduate). And in 1889 he was made an honorary member of the Cliosophic Society at Princeton, one of the oldest of its kind in the country.[16] Whittier was humbly grateful for these tokens of esteem and affection from young people.

Of the adult organizations which elected him to honorary membership — the Authors Club, New York, the Massachusetts Historical Society, the Western Reserve Historical Society, and others — only one attracts particular notice. By letter of November 1, 1887, from the Secretary, Alfred J. Weyman, Whittier along with Holmes was offered and he accepted the position of Honorary Corresponding Member in the Scottish

Society of Literature and Art, "a distinction that as yet has only been conferred on Mr. Jules Verne and 'Mark Twain.' "[17]

Whittier's work and his lifelong labors as a friend of man had become well known in the British Isles and in various parts of Europe, as various friends, beginning with Bayard Taylor in 1867, had the pleasure of assuring him. F. H. Underwood remarked in a letter to Whittier from Glasgow, on December 3, 1889:

> Your reputation in Great Britain is rapidly growing. I suppose you know that for a long time it was mainly confined to Friends, to Reformers, and to those especially interested in the literature of the U.S. It is no longer so. I find that your poems are known everywhere, and any reference to your name brings applause from audiences. . . .[18]

## 2

Whittier capitally demonstrated the truth of Emerson's dictum that "men of character are the conscience of the society to which they belong."[19] More than most men of letters he became a Public Man because what he was exceeded in importance even what he wrote. Because he was "a man, and not a mere verse-maker," he realized painfully well the price of publicity. Much oftener than he wished, he had to decline appeals to him as the conscience of too many parts of society. If he would do this or write that he would, because he was Whittier, give an air of quality, nay, almost of divine sanction, to an event or a cause near to the heart of some one. Even his dearest friends forgot at times his essential character. Mrs. Fields, for instance, wrote him on September 3, 1868, to suggest a poetry-reading evening or evenings as a means of raising five thousand dollars to support the work of certain schools in the South. If Whittier would read "Maud Muller" or whatever else he chose, Bryant would come to read "Thanatopsis." Mrs. Fields told Whittier, "I am obliged to make it clear that Mr. Bryant will not consent unless you will assist, and without either, we must give the project up altogether." Whittier replied, on September 9:

> Thee ask a miracle of me. Anything within the bounds of my possibilities I would do, as thee very well know, not only for the cause's

sake, but for thine. Ask me to dance the polka, or walk a slack rope from the Park Street steeple to the State House dome — but don't ask me to stand up and read my rhymes to a Boston audience. I fancy I see myself doing it! And yet, how I wish I could! I am so sorry to have to say no, and disappoint thee. But it would be utterly impossible. I could not do it if I tried.[20]

In truth, Whittier gave more strength than he was well able to spare to the writing of forewords or biographical introductions to the *Lives* or published letters of friends, as for example Oliver Johnson's *William Lloyd Garrison and His Times*, 1879, and the *Letters of Lydia Maria Child*, 1883. If he had met all such requests, which in general were made by the widows or other relatives of deceased friends, they would have absorbed his time and energies completely. Thus Whittier felt obliged to decline to write, for instance, the biographies of John Pierpont, George D. Prentice, Robert Rantoul, and Charles Sumner, or to edit the writings of the Cary sisters.[21]

He did contrive to produce a large number of personal and occasional poems, in the eighteen-seventies and eighties, particularly "The Vow of Washington," 1889, and the lines for three centennial celebrations — of the Battle of Lexington, 1875, of the convening of the Continental Congress which made the Declaration of Independence, 1876, and of the siege of Yorktown, 1881. But he declined to write a poem for the Bunker Hill centennial, and explained to J. R. Osgood in a letter of May 1, 1875:

I stretched my Quakerism to the full strength of its drab in writing about the Lexington folks who were shot and did not shoot back. I cannot say anything about those who *did* shoot to some purpose on Bunker Hill. These occasional poems are fatal to any poet save Dr. Holmes. He always manages to come off safely. I am sorry I cannot oblige thee in this matter, but I don't think any verses of mine could add lustre to the memorial.[22]

Such calls upon Whittier were multifarious and often vexing. He was asked to write "a battle-cry or a chant, for the future of Woman"; "a few ringing verses" to advance the cause of women's suffrage in Michigan; lines for a New York song writer, eager to create a new national anthem in time for the centennial celebration at Philadelphia; poems for special meetings devoted to education, juvenile affairs, peace, race relations, and temperance; paeans for the semi-centennial celebrations of Haverford and Oberlin colleges, as well as a commencement poem for Dartmouth (1876); and so on endlessly. Also in 1876, a Baltimore man even wrote to suggest the topic for a poem about Roger B. Taney — as if Whittier could ever have forgotten that the Chief Justice wrote the Dred Scott decision! [23]

Quite unable to keep up with the heavy traffic upon his time, Whittier remarked in a letter of January 26, 1884, to Edna Dean Proctor that "all the world has been writing to me, and making all manner of unreasonable demands & sending innumerable axes to grind." [24] But the nature of his character compels the belief that he must have laughed when he received certain kinds of requests. There was the one from a lady of Indianapolis ("write a piece for me . . . when you are at leisure"), and another from a gentleman of trade, in Oak Park, who desired a poem, written with the light touch, to describe the merits of "Old Country Soap" as "a strictly pure & superior article." He expansively offered to pay Whittier — a strictly commercial proposition.[25]

Whittier's conscience could not have been troubled by refusal of most of the requests made of him. But many letters, although requests, were also plain manifests of the extent to which he was esteemed "the conscience" of American society. One letter in particular gives an exact illustration. Whittier was requested to write a poem for a women's party to be held in the rotunda of the Capitol, in Washington, on the centennial of the Boston Tea Party. The occasion was trivial. The letter written by Olive Risley Seward, adopted daughter of Lincoln's Secretary of State, who had met him at the home of Governor and Mrs. Claflin, in Boston, was not. She said, in part:

> I have hesitated very much before venturing to ask the great favor, and if it seems bold, I beg you to remember that my generation has been fed on the "voices of freedom," that we have looked to you, many of us, for all our patriotic inspiration, and that you have never failed us.[26]

Precisely that attitude prevailed also among editors, who in effect regarded Whittier as Public Man and Sir Oracle. Whatever he wrote, it appears, was regarded as good "copy," and after the publication of *Snow-Bound* he came to be well paid for his work. How fervently it was desired a careful reading of his correspondence makes clear. Theodore Tilton, editor of *The Independent*, New York, on October 21, 1889, sent a typical request:

Will you write a poem for Thanksgiving, and another for Christmas? I like to see our paper keep the festivals of the year.

I hope you do not think you write as often as we would like.

We shall not hear from you often enough until we have a new manuscript every week.[27]

That pace would have required turning the clock back to the days of Whittier's apprenticeship, when in fact he did write and publish at least one piece of verse a week. Now, in his eighties, he wrote only six or eight poems a year for publication, and in *The Independent* there appeared only one in each of the last four years of his life.

But by garnering poems like these in new volumes, from time to time, and by bringing out re-issues of old ones or collected editions of his poetry and prose, Whittier's publishers met the demands of the reading public for his outgivings. Ticknor & Fields (and the firm under its successive names) managed these affairs to his entire satisfaction, particularly from the time when in 1857 J. T. Fields obtained the copyrights for his work and collected it in the Blue and Gold Edition. While negotiating for those copyrights, Fields reported accurately to Whittier, "In whatever I have attempted to do, I have had your interest in mind," [28] and that principle happily governed the long span of Whittier's relations with the publishing house personified to him by J. T. Fields. It has been pointed out, fitly, that Tennyson and Whittier both showed lasting gratitude to their respective publishers for skillful handling which helped to establish them solidly in the favor of book-lovers.[29]

Between 1870 and the time of his death in 1892 Whittier was brought out in a half dozen or so American collected editions — in 1873, 1874, 1876, 1880 and twice in 1888, the year of the standard or Riverside Edition — and nine English, collected or selected. The English edition issued in the series of Moxon's Popular Poets had an appreciative critical introduction by William Michael Rossetti, and four of the collected editions, brought out in the two years 1890 and 1891, seemed an unmistakable token of the regard of the English for Whittier's life and work.

In this country, Ticknor & Fields or its successors brought out during 1870–90, in addition to others already mentioned, these particular volumes of Whittier's writings:

*Ballads of New England*, 1870.

*Miriam and Other Poems*, 1871, dedicated to F. A. P. Barnard.

*The Journal of John Woolman*, 1871, with introduction by Whittier.
*The Pennsylvania Pilgrim, and Other Poems*, 1872.
*Hazel-Blossoms*, 1875.
*Mabel Martin. A Harvest Idyl*, 1876.
*The Vision of Echard and Other Poems*, 1878.
*The King's Missive, and Other Poems*, 1881.
*The Bay of Seven Islands, and Other Poems*, 1883.
*Saint Gregory's Guest and Recent Poems*, 1886.
*The Captain's Well*, 1890.
*At Sundown*, 1890.

Most of these books were very handsomely made and illustrated, notably *Mabel Martin*, and Whittier's publishers engaged some of the best known artists of his day to assist in bringing out his works most appropriately. Among a group of twenty illustrators appear the names of F. O. C. Darley, E. H. Garrett, Howard Pyle, Frederic Remington, and W. T. Smedley.[30]

## 3

Whittier's books carried his peculiarly American and democratic message to English-speaking peoples everywhere and to many places wide apart. From the Duke of Argyll came a letter of February 27, 1875, in which he acknowledged receipt of a copy of *Hazel-Blossoms*. It had, obviously, been sent because of Argyll's friendship for Charles Sumner, and because Whittier's poem to the memory of Sumner stood at the head of this volume. Argyll responded that he and his Duchess had long been familiar with Whittier's poetry, and now were especially grateful for the lines to Sumner and for "The Prayer of Agassiz," whom also they knew. In 1884 and years following, Whittier received a great tide of mail from admirers in England, and a substantial volume even from the colonies "down under." One Australian on his way to England wished to call on Whittier and deliver the respects of himself and many of his fellow countrymen, and late in 1891 Whittier received "fan mail" from young admirers in New Zealand. Editors from England and Holland and Germany, moreover, wrote for material out of which to fashion biographical articles about Whittier or for the right to publish volumes of his selected writings.[31]

It was his neighbors in Amesbury and Danvers who saw him most clearly, in the afternoon of his life, and the plain record is that he lived out his years in his "lowland home" on the high plane to which he always had aspired. His natural sense of kinship with unpretentious people, and the same quality of kindliness and tenderness which in Lincoln particularly became a supreme virtue, made him less a "first citizen" than merely a comfortable neighbor. This character was dominant in him — as Stephen Lamson, the printer, saw it in 1844–46 [32] and as Whittier demonstrated by his acts as long as he lived.

By post he received seemingly never-ending requests for financial aid, chiefly from young people struggling to get an education — whom he generally helped — and elder folk, dogged by illness and poverty — whom he almost invariably aided. In Amesbury he practiced a discerning kindness which his fellow villagers remarked and admired. He was drawn chiefly, it appears, to people humble in means who had personal distinction. The village philosopher, Henry Taylor, was one of his favorites.[33] Another was a poor and aged Englishman, James Standring, for whom also Whittier contributed an obituary notice to *The Villager* (January 13, 1870). Part of Whittier's tribute was this:

> He was a man not to be overlooked or ignored in any community. He was always comparatively a poor man, earning his daily bread by constant toil; he had little or no learning, and there was nothing conciliatory or prepossessing in his appearance or manners. Sturdily independent, he exercised the fullest freedom of speech; flattered nobody; and would have burned like a candle for opinion's sake had it been necessary. He had no disguise or reticence — his few faults and his many virtues were open as the day. His distinguishing trait, that which made him a marked man in a community which has deservedly a reputation for liberality, was his abounding generosity. None who was poor, none who suffered whether providentially or from his own folly and crime, ever appealed to him in vain. After exhausting his own slender means, he had no hesitation in levying contributions upon his neighbors. He took the first man he met by the button, told the story of the want and suffering he had witnessed, and if he did not obtain assistance, he at least made refusal impossible without an uneasy conscience, and a sense of meanness on the part of the refuser.[34]

Whittier, still more, was interested in the good fortune and personal welfare of Amesbury friends. When his laundress thriftily achieved the building of a home for her family, he evidently was the prime mover in a generous house-warming. Whittier attended that event of January 9, 1873, spoke words of congratulation to Mrs. Choate on her success, and read a piece of "machine poetry" (his own composition) with which he said he had been charged for the occasion.[35] And over many years' time he steadily concerned himself with the comfort of the James Squires. When in 1870 his niece Elizabeth, later Mrs. S. T. Pickard, was teaching at a school for freedmen in Charleston, South Carolina, Whittier wrote her:

> We had a grand surprise party at Uncle Squires's, — fifty present, H. C. and J. H. spoke, and J. W. C. [Horace Currier, John Hume. Jason W. Cowden] presented in behalf of the company a purse of $130. Several persons sent money, and messages, which I read on the occasion, and I took the liberty to put in some money and good wishes from thee, as I knew thee would like to do it. Don't let Uncle Squires know that thee did not know of it, as I should have written thee if there had been time. It was a very lively and merry occasion.[36]

Even after he had gone to Oak Knoll in 1876, Whittier kept an affectionate eye on his aged friends, and he returned to Amesbury often to see and help them. The Squires are mentioned in many of his letters to Mrs. Woodman. On April 29, 1879, as an instance, he reported that he had been enjoying "so bad a cold that I am unable to get out," and yet —

> I have got the *Squires'* folks settled in their house in Amesbury — and a girl comes in two or three times a day to sweep and wash dishes &c. They are both feeble, but I think they will get along for the present. I have had some others to look after also.

And when Whittier was on the verge of eighty he wrote Mrs. Woodman from Amesbury, in November, 1887:

> I have been wanting to see Oak Knoll for the last week, but have not been able to leave here. Yesterday the Doctors pronounced James Squires in the way of recovery from his accident. I am very glad I came here as it was a comfort to him. . . .[37]

Whittier's humane and humorous ease with his fellow citizens was particularly shown in his friendship with Isaac and Mary Barnard, brother and sister, marked characters by whom he was greatly engaged.

He was concerned that in the face of very advanced years and the possession of a competency, they overworked. When he suggested that they ought to hire young help, the sister demurred. "We must lay something by for our last sickness, and have money enough left to bury us." Whittier's reply was, "Did thee ever know any one to stick by the way for want of funds?" [38]

Young friends, too, concerned him deeply. He had an exceptionally warm friendship with Horace H. Currier, for one, a lawyer of Amesbury who on occasion was a member of the youthful group accompanying Whittier to West Ossipee in summer. Whittier's solicitude for young Currier was almost that of a father, and when in 1879 his health broke completely, Whittier kept a very close and tender watch upon him. Two letters — one dated March 19 at the New Marlboro Hotel, Boston, and the other written from Oak Knoll on July 9 — typically show Whittier's eagerness to do all that he could for his friend.[39] On August 27 he went to Bearcamp River House to be with Currier, stayed longer than he had planned,[40] and from there wrote sorrowfully to Lucy Larcom: "I am feeling sadly about Horace. But he is only going the common way of all, sooner or later, and 'who knoweth which is best?' . . ." [41] On October 23 Whittier's warm letter to his memory, characteristic of others written after the death of valued friends in Amesbury, appeared in *The Villager*.[42]

That was the uprising angle of Whittier's later years, in his "lowland home" — that modest frame house in Amesbury and the small farm-estate of his Johnson cousins in Danvers. Examples abound of his zealous care for his neighbors and visitors, and of his lifelong concern with the great issues of the world. He delighted particularly to welcome old friends who visited him in Amesbury, where he liked nothing so much as lively conversation in winter before the fire in his study which he alone tended, ever so carefully.[43] With him that was almost a rite, the one thing that he would share with nobody. But it was his natural habit to give quickly whatever help he could to people who genuinely needed it. A choice illustration appeared in the *Literary World's* pages dedicated to Whittier on his seventieth birthday. A person signing himself "C. M." related:

> When I was a young man trying to get an education, I went about the country peddling sewing-silk to help myself through college; and one Saturday night found me at Amesbury, a stranger and without a

> lodging-place. It happened that the first house at which I called was Whittier's; and he himself came to the door. On hearing my request he said he was very sorry he could not keep me, but it was quarterly meeting, and his house was full. He, however, took the trouble to show me to a neighbor's, where he left me; but that did not seem to wholly suit his idea of hospitality, for in the course of the evening he made his appearance, saying that it had occurred to him that he could sleep on a lounge and give up his own bed to me, — which, it is perhaps needless to say, was not allowed. The next morning he came again, with the suggestion that I might perhaps like to attend meeting, inviting me to go with him; and he gave me a seat next to himself. The meeting lasted an hour, during which there was not a word spoken by any one. We all sat in silence that length of time, then all arose, shook hands and dispersed; and I remember it as one of the best meetings I ever attended.[44]

Whittier, it may be said in passing, was happy in the possession of this home, but not covetous of it or of property in general. He *was* proud of the grapes in his garden.[45] To him the chief value of the house was sentimental: he had lived with his mother and sister here to the end of their days. And when accidents befel the place in 1871 and 1872, Whittier was only concerned about their portraits and about his nieces. He wrote Edna Dean Proctor on October 30, 1871:

> My place here came near burning up a week ago. I was roused at midnight by the alarm of fire. The house & barn next but one to mine was burned, & the intermediate house caught fire. I stood guard over my mother's & sister's portraits, as the two valuables to save.[46]

Pickard described the effect of a bolt of lightning which struck the house during a storm of August 13, 1872. Whittier was on his way from the Garden Room to warn his nieces away from the windows in the sewing-room, on the far side of the house. The bolt floored Whittier and stunned the two young ladies. But all soon recovered, their momentary deafness wore off, and only slight damage was done to the house. Whittier, however, from that day lost faith in lightning-rods, which he ordered stripped from the house, and he acquired a lasting dread of thunderstorms.[47]

These, however, were among the very few things that Whittier did fear. The scales were tipped far on the side of things that he loved, and his love of these grew as his years increased. It was the power of custom and memory which gradually drew him back from Oak Knoll, "my half-way house," [48] to Amesbury, where his roots went all the way down. The Merrimac Valley was his native ground, rich in customs as well as human relationships which he built into his life. One particular gathering of friends which for many years he enjoyed attending was the "laurel party" for which he wrote occasional pieces, including "Our River," "Revisited," "The Laurels," and "June on the Merrimac." These spanned the years 1861–78, and the parties which they celebrated were described by Mrs. A. B. Bassett, of Newton, Massachusetts:

> My dear father and mother [Mr. and Mrs. William Ashby] gave these parties annually for twenty-one years. They were very pleasant occasions, and became notable, as the years passed on, increasing in attendance, and including many distinguished visitors. The first was a small party of friends from out of town, invited to visit the Laurel Grounds, in the perfection of the laurel bloom. This proved so enjoyable that it was repeated with additions, year after year. To many, old and young, it was a red-letter day in the year's calendar. Occurring the last of June, the weather, with but one exception, was perfect. The arrival and meeting of old friends, the repast at our house in Newburyport, the sail up the Merrimac to the grove on its banks, the redolent pines, the beauty of the laurels, the appetizing lunch at noon followed by speeches and songs, made the hours pass quickly, and the time for the good-bys came all too soon. Interesting and distinguished visitors were often with us. Whittier was always present, when his health and other circumstances permitted, and frequently wrote poems for the occasion. . . .[49]

In September, 1885, Whittier went to Haverhill for an hour's pleasant reunion with fifteen of his Haverhill Academy schoolmates, Mrs. Evelina Bray Downey among them. O. W. Holmes sent a letter of greeting, Mrs. Woodman read the verse which Whittier wrote especially for the occasion, and Thomas B. Garland, down from Dover, New Hampshire, noted this impression:

> His pictures hardly do him justice. They lack the cheerful, animated look of the poet himself. Mr. Whittier appeared to be in excellent health and spirits. The fire is not yet, by any means, burnt out from his

dark, expressive eyes, and he is not at all the dreamy-eyed, pale-faced being a poet is supposed to be; but he is a simple gentleman, upright in form, active in manner, and forceful in look.[50]

None of these personal associations, and nothing in Whittier's habits, was altered by his life at Oak Knoll in Danvers. The outward aspect of it was fairer — that was all. When manufacturing had transformed Amesbury from a fair village into a bustling town, Whittier was grateful for the quiet of Oak Knoll. The spacious house, standing behind its Doric pillars at a good distance from the road, was set in extensive, well landscaped grounds featured by the grassy knoll in a curve of the drive and by tall trees. Some of these were unusual for New England. The "oak knoll" was crowned actually by both an oak and a hickory. Carefully spaced about the grounds Whittier found and loved a magnolia, a tulip-tree, a purple beech, English elms and oaks, and chestnuts, hemlocks, pines, and indeed nearly all trees hardy enough to stand the climate. To an immense Norway spruce Doctor Holmes gave the name, "The Poet's Pagoda." And in addition there were apple and pear orchards, a fruit arbor, and, near the eastern piazza of the house, a large flower garden enclosed in a circular hedge and with a high-spraying fountain at the center of the circle.

Here, in brief, Whittier had seclusion and he was once more close to the soil. In the warm months he could "farm" again. He could walk in the gardens, nurse the plants and flowers, have that close community with Nature which was a need of his soul. Of the dogs and other pets upon the place he made friends. Phebe, young adopted daughter of Mrs. Woodman, became a brightly eager companion, and in late years an occasional helper with his correspondence.[51]

All of these things were a solace, and for several years they held Whittier most of the time at Oak Knoll. But his fixed ties remained at Amesbury — the right to vote, other civic duties, the nearly lifelong habit of open house at the time of Quarterly Meetings, his old and intimate friendships and his solicitude for those who needed his help. Above all, there was the constant tug of Family. He confessed to Mrs. Pickard, in a letter of November 29, 1880: "I thought of thee on Thanksgiving Day, and wondered if thee was at the table. It was a rather dull day to me, for on such occasions I always think of the old days in Amesbury, when my mother and sister were with me. . . ." [52]

This was Whittier's dominant thought as the years sped by. His "half-way house" did not hold him, and Boston ceased to attract him overmuch after the death of J. T. Fields in 1881, of Longfellow and Emerson in 1882, and of "Frank" Whittier in January, 1883. Once, in 1871, Whittier remarked to Bayard Taylor: "I feel myself the need of coming into nearer relations to the great life of our centres of civilization and thought, and if I were younger and stronger I should certainly spend my winters in Boston." [53] Actually, Whittier never became a steady attendant at meetings of the Atlantic Club, the Radical Club, or the Saturday Club; and in the normal course of events his visits to the Claflin and Fields homes fell off and then stopped.

Withal, the cycle of sentiment which brought him back to Amesbury in his late years never at any point closed out Whittier's abiding interest in world affairs and domestic issues. He was intensely interested, for example, in the reconstruction of the South, and especially in Negro education. An admired friend, General Samuel Chapman Armstrong, was president of Hampton Institute, and Whittier annually contributed to its budget and procured funds from other people. As early as 1873 he wrote to a friend in Lynn, "I think well of the Hampton enterprise, & have great confidence in Gen. Armstrong." [54] In 1889, on Whittier's birthday, both as a tribute to him and an aid to a cause in which they knew him to be greatly interested, Algernon P. and Mary Nichols, of Haverhill, placed a check for one thousand dollars in Whittier's hands to be transmitted to Hampton Institute. On October 9, 1891, General Armstrong acknowledged receipt of Whittier's personal gift of one hundred dollars to the Institute — perhaps the last annual contribution which he had an opportunity to make to Hampton. And in 1890–91, aware of Whittier's interest in Negro education, Booker T. Washington directly solicited his financial aid for the Tuskegee Normal and Industrial Institute.[55]

Whittier also continued to be an active advocate of the education of American Indians. In a letter, published in part in the *Danvers Mirror* on May 5, 1883, which he addressed to a meeting called in Boston to consider the problem, he concluded:

> The work of education and civilization must be done. The money needed must be contributed with no sparing hand. The laudable example set by the Friends and the American Missionary Association

> should be followed by other sects and philanthropic societies. Christianity, patriotism, and enlightened self interest have a common stake in the matter. Great and difficult as the work may be, the country is strong enough, rich enough, wise enough, and, I believe, humane and Christian enough to do it.[56]

In November, 1879, Whittier received an immeasurable "return" on his heart-interest in the education of the two races who knew him as their friend. Just returned from Europe, where they had sung before seven kings and emperors and dined with Gladstone, the Jubilee Singers of Fisk University called upon Whittier. He was fascinated by the story of their tour, they by meeting him. Just before departing they sang four songs for him, the last of them "Swing Low, Sweet Chariot," including the ancient benediction —

> The Lord bless thee and keep thee.
> The Lord make his face shine upon thee,
> And be gracious unto thee.
> The Lord lift up his countenance
> Upon thee, and give thee peace. Amen.

Whittier was so touched that, for once, he cried. Mr. F. J. Loudin afterward said for the Fisk Singers:

> It was with great difficulty we could sing, so deeply were we touched by the experience of this hour now closing. I shall never forget the expression upon that illumined face at that parting moment. Then he stepped forward and shook hands, but so deep were his feelings that he never spoke a word until he came to the two last. I was the last to shake hands with him, and as he did so, he said, "Good-by; God bless you all!"

The next morning he wrote four stanzas in Mr. Loudin's album, dating them November 7, 1879, to which he afterward added two more and gave the title "The Jubilee Singers." [57]

Education was a fundamental and ongoing interest of Whittier's, but he also met, actively and often, special appeals for relief. In 1888, for example, he contributed to "the relief of the brave old patriotic town of Marblehead," to an aid fund for "the forlorn Quakers at Juneau," in Alaska, and again to Haverhill Hospital.[58] And it is worth notice that Whittier's rule of giving for relief was self-denying. At a time when certain repair work had been planned at Oak Knoll, he wrote Mrs. Woodman from West Ossipee on September 16, 1878:

> I am, on the whole, glad you have not disturbed the house. It is quite as good as we deserve now. It would be better to send something to the fever-sufferers at the South than to spend money "for the looks of it. . . ." [59]

## 4

Whittier, with progressive faith, regarded life on earth as a preparation for a future life. For one inquirer he spelled out his creed precisely, in a letter written from Oak Knoll on January 8, 1879:

> I presume I meant to say that the Present is all we have to do our work in, holding as it does the Past & shaping the Future. That behind the elusive & perishable things of time & sense, the *real* things, God, truth, goodness, remain: The things seen are temporal but things unseen eternal: That Heaven and hell are not so much *places* as *conditions* and are not limited in space or time.[60]

Particularly after 1870, Whittier's letters reveal his firm faith in immortality, and an Oriental resignation to whatever was reserved for him. In 1890 he wrote, characteristically, to Louise Chandler Moulton:

> My dear cousin Gertrude read in her beautiful way thy poems under the head of "The Still Hour," and was greatly moved by their pathetic power. I wish thee could have her serene, clear faith in the future life. But I think it will come to thee some time. Emerson once said to me, "If there is a future life for us, it is well; if there is not, it is well also." For myself, I trust in the mercy of the All Merciful. What is best for us we shall have, and Life and Love are best.[61]

Whittier's certainty still left room for curiosity, and he never lost altogether a lurking interest in spiritualism. But it left him strongly skeptical. Neither the publications of the Society for Psychical Research nor the beliefs of Garrison and other friends persuaded him in the least degree. His comments enlivened many letters to Mrs. Fields in particular, with whom he often weighed eternity, and one of them, dated March 24, 1882, summed up all:

> With regard to modern Spiritualism I have had a feeling that it was not safe or healthful for mind or body to yield myself to an influence the nature of which was unknown. There is a fascination in it, but the fascination is blended with doubt and repulsion. I am disgusted with the tricks and greed of these mediums; their pretended spiritual intercourse has none of the conditions which Tennyson's "In Memoriam" describes, and I do not know that I really need additional proof of the life hereafter. I think my loved ones are still living and awaiting me. And I wait and trust. And yet how glad and grateful I should be to *know!* I must believe that our friends are near us — that they still love and watch over us.[62]

All else he judged spurious. Once at a tea in the Boston home of the John Sargents, the conversation turned upon Robert Dale Owen and his report of "some very remarkable spirit appearances." Whittier, attentive but skeptical, now and again made the alert query: "Is thee sure there was no door here, and no opening there?"[63]

Ultimately, Whittier's inquiries only strengthened his belief in the one thing of which he was certain, and which he stated, never more clearly, in a letter of February 22, 1887:

> Some of my friends in Boston are puzzling themselves with the Buddhist Theosophy, and have got a Hindoo adept, one Mohini, a solemn-faced Oriental, to expound its mysteries. And the Society for Psychical Research are gathering up all the stories afloat of signs and omens and apparitions, witchcraft, and spiritualism — a competitive examination of ghosts! I have rather enjoyed reading the reports of a similar society in England. The investigations are conducted on strictly scientific principles. I hope some clue may be found to the great mystery of life and death — and the beyond! But I scarcely expect it. We shall still have to trust and wonder, and keep our faith, with Emerson, that "whatever is excellent, as God lives is permanent."[64]

## 5

To Whittier's admirers, throughout the English-speaking world, even while he lived, what was permanent and excellent in his own life was no mystery. He possessed and he used the common touch.

People mighty and humble alike responded to the chords that he touched. His constant emphasis on the nearness of God, his inevitable belief in the dignity of man, his broad and tolerant spirit, and his deep human sympathy all made him a symbol and an actual rock of faith. In that light, Lincoln during the Civil War turned to his writings, and found strength and comfort.[65] In that light, fifty friends and admirers in Great Britain and Ireland sent him a joint letter of gratitude in 1882, and Whittier's response, from Amesbury on October 30, conveyed both his thanks and a beautiful reiteration of his faith.[66] In that light, John White Chadwick, when in March 1881 he asked Whittier to prepare (as he did, for the Riverside Edition in 1888) headnotes for his individual poems and especially those of the anti-slavery period, ventured the prophecy: "Your poems will be read much more than any history. . . . I am sure you could do nothing that would so much increase the debt of gratitude we owe to you already." [67]

Holmes proved to be the most discerning and accurate prophet of them all, with John Bright and Archdeacon Farrar in England as his echo. As early as 1878 Holmes said in a letter to Whittier:

> I was going to say, I thank you, but I would say rather, I thank God that He has given you the thoughts and feelings which sing themselves as naturally as the wood-thrush rings his silver bell, — to steal your own exquisitely descriptive line. Who has preached the gospel of love to such a mighty congregation as you have preached it? Who has done so much to sweeten the soul of Calvinistic New England? You have your reward here in the affection with which all our people, who are capable of loving anybody, regard you. I trust you will find a still higher, in that world, the harmonies of which find an echo in so many of your songs.[68]

Then in an article entitled "The Pulpit and the Pew" and published in the *North American Review* in February 1881, Holmes wrote, with particular reference to the poem "The Minister's Daughter":

> . . . kind Nature . . . sent as his counterpoise the inspired plowman, whose songs have done more to humanize the hard theology of Scotland than all the rationalistic sermons that were ever preached. Our own Whittier has done and is doing the same thing, in a far holier spirit than Burns, for the inherited beliefs of New England and the

country to which New England belongs. Let me sweeten these closing paragraphs . . . with a passage or two from the lay-preacher who is listened to by a larger congregation than any man who speaks from the pulpit.[69]

In 1884 John Bright expressed the same sentiment in broader terms, on the occasion when the portrait of Whittier by Edgar Parker was presented to the Friends' School, Providence. (The main address was made by President Thomas Chase, of Haverford College, and Lowell, then Minister to England, addressed a letter and a sonnet to "New England's poet, rich in love as years.")[70] Bright, who never visited America, said in part, in his letter of regret:

"The Eternal Goodness" is another poem which is worth a crowd of sermons which are spoken from the pulpits of our sects and churches, which I do not wish to undervalue. It is a great gift to mankind when a poet is raised up among us who devotes his great powers to the sublime purpose of spreading among men principles of mercy and justice and freedom. This our friend Whittier has done in a degree unsurpassed by any other poet who has spoken to the world in our noble tongue.[71]

That year, in England, Garrett Horder included in his *Congregational Hymns*, evidently for the first time anywhere, the hymn "Dear Lord and Father of Mankind," the words of which were derived from the last six stanzas of "The Brewing of Soma."[72] Frederick Charles Maker, English organist and composer of many church anthems and choruses, wrote the music to which Whittier's verses of intercession and entreaty are now sung everywhere in the English-speaking world. An English writer, just after Whittier's death, attributed the widespread love of hymns drawn from his poems to the fact that they are free from unction, on the one hand, and from denunciation of man, on the other.[73] "Dear Lord and Father of Mankind" in particular has come to be one of the most popular hymns, in the hymnals of many denominations, because it is based upon a clear and serene statement of personal faith in the Eternal Goodness which appeals to the common sympathies of men. In English eyes it has something of the strength of Clough's poem "Say Not the Struggle Naught Availeth" — a moral prop and comfort to a sturdy people in 1914–18 and again in 1939–45.

It is a curious example of the force of indirection in life that Whittier, on "the afternoon slope" of it, should have been solidly lodged at the peak of American hymn writing. His lifelong and unwavering belief in the immanence of God, preceding by decades its acceptance by religious leaders such as Henry Ward Beecher and Horace Bushnell, won him the love of people who yearned for songs of faith and trust. His unimagined gift as a "hymnist" is measured by Henry Wilder Foote, who declares that "with the passing years his hymns have become more widely used and dearly loved than those of any other American hymn writer"; and, again, that "he stands in the front rank among American hymn writers of the nineteenth century by virtue of what may be called his unintended hymns, made up of stanzas quarried from his poems like jewels cut out of their matrix, in many cases with some adaptation to fit them for use." Still more conclusively, Mr. Foote writes:

> ... his fame as a hymn writer has stood the test of time better than that of almost any other [Victorian-period writer]. Indeed, if wide-spread and continued use of an author's hymns be the test, he would doubtless be ranked, both in this country and in England, as the fore-most American hymnist of the nineteenth century.[74]

Whittier, quite in character, rated his talent very modestly. He re-sponded to an inquiry:

> I am not really a hymn-writer, for the good reason that I know nothing of music. Only a few of my pieces were written for singing. A good hymn is the best use to which poetry can be devoted, but I do not claim that I have succeeded in composing one.[75]

His real deficiency, as Mr. Foote indicates, is his unfamiliarity with the limitations of form imposed by congregational singing. Despite occasional attempts, as early as 1833, to write hymns in precise form, he never succeeded in writing religious songs equal to the thirty or so for which editors and tune-writers took centos from his poems and which, with variant readings and arrangements, have come into common use.[76]

Whittier, quite possibly, has been assured of a lasting audience by the work of these perceptive folk. Two young Harvard Divinity School students, Samuel Longfellow (younger brother of Henry Wadsworth) and Samuel Johnson, brought out in the year of their graduation, 1846, a new type of hymnal, *A Book of Hymns.* (When Theodore Parker received a copy, he is reported to have said, "I see we have a new book of Sams!")

In this, for the first time, Whittier's poems were used for hymnody, and the young editors were the first to see in them the possibilities for hymns. Later editors and denominational groups have eagerly accepted them — the Episcopal and the Presbyterian, and the English other than the Unitarian and the Congregational, somewhat later than others. As an example, a collection of sixty-six hymns prepared for the Parliament of Religions in Chicago, in 1893, contained nine adapted from Whittier's poems, the largest number from any author. The undenominational *Songs of Praise*, edited in 1926 by Canon Percy Dearmer of the Church of England, contained eleven of Whittier's choicest hymns. The Unitarian *Hymns of the Spirit* (1937) contained eighteen.[77]

It is significant that the best loved of them are centos — the six stanzas from "The Brewing of Soma" and others from "My Psalm," "The Eternal Goodness," and "Our Master." [78] Hence, it is of peculiar interest that "At Last" (1882) has found its way in its entirety into some hymnbooks. Its seven stanzas bar it from frequent congregational use, and the noble French melody, *Christe Fons Jugis*, to which it is beautifully adapted, is not easily sung. But, Mr. Foote emphasized, "for a funeral or memorial service it is of great beauty. It is our American equivalent of Tennyson's 'Crossing the Bar,' and in its contrast with the appalling hymns about death, 'calculated to strike terror in the heart of the sinner,' so popular in some circles at the beginning of the century, marks the progress which had been made in religious thought." [78]

William McKinley, fond of hymns, particularly loved one drawn from "Seed-Time and Harvest." On his request it was sung in the First Methodist Episcopal Church, Canton, Ohio, of which he was a member, at regular service on the Sunday morning before he set out for his inauguration at Washington.[79] Not he alone found comfort and strength and faith in Whittier's work, and in the example of his life. A writer in the *London Quarterly Review* for January, 1893, seemed to state the general view of it when he concluded: ". . . and whether, or not, he lives as a poet in the memory of future ages, he has earned at any rate this praise — than which there is no greater — that he "served his generation by the Will of God." [80]

# XXVII

# The Soul's Anchor of Faith

"As the swift years pass," Whittier wrote to his friend Julia A. Hodgdon soon after his seventieth birthday, "the Eternal Realities seem taking the place of the shadows and illusions of time." [1] Seldom a week passed now, beyond the biblical term, that did not find Whittier deep in reflection on the Ultimate. He was calm and resigned, sure of an Eternity under God's grace, just as he had discovered God surely in a life of service. Whittier's faith was anchored in a timeless sea.

His religious certitude was not, however, an easy prize of fair sailing under always cloudless skies. Over his early course in life there had been shadows and illusions. Whittier's first twenty-five years had not taken him into clear water, or under any favorable star. In 1840 he confessed himself still rather at sea, certain by now that the true course in life was in God's way, but certain, too, that he was not himself wholly on it.[2] When to his native faith Whittier added works as he conceived them to be ordained by God, then he felt borne over serene waters home to his Maker.

Whittier, as a Quaker, got his bearings somewhat more directly than other men about him. In a New England struggling, with great labor, to break the bonds of severe Calvinism as drawn by Jonathan Edwards, the Friend had an advanced position. Men like William Ellery Channing went to French philosophy to learn the dignity and perfectibility of man. Henry Ward Beecher (in 1835) and Horace Bushnell (in 1849) broke out of "the iron cage of Calvinism" with the aid of ecstatic personal experiences which discovered to them faith, "a sense of the freeness of God and the ease of approach to Him." Whittier was born and bred to that. In 1853 he wrote that at his mother's knee he had learned that —

All is of God that is, and is to be;
And God is good.[3]

Whittier's religious position was founded on the will to believe what history had accepted and man had then forgotten. He believed that:

God is good.

God is immanent to man, and Christ is about him — the revelation of God and the assurance of the Trinity.

Man's task is to do God's will on earth, after the example of Christ.

Death is not the end of life.

There is a future life, an Eternity.

Personal faith, not formal creeds and priests' offices, is the true testimony of these beliefs.

# 1

Whittier was an optimist; his faith in the goodness of God required that he be. Men and measures might go wrong, and Whittier lose faith in a Clay, a Cushing, or a Webster. Yet he made constantly clear — in verse, article, and letter — his unwavering trust that God was good, and that He wished only the best for man. Augustine, fourteen centuries before in his *Soliloquies*,[4] had lighted up this simple conviction, which Whittier in 1860 elaborated in "The Shadow and the Light."

Four years later Elizabeth Whittier was dead, and, as Whittier had said in the bereavement following his mother's death in 1857, ". . . the great motive of life seems lost." [5] His grief was genuine and deep, but his faith was deeper. In 1865 he gave out "The Eternal Goodness," his most fervent utterance of faith in the Fatherhood of God. Whittier wrote:

. . . . . . . .

To one fixed trust my spirit clings;
I know that God is Good!

And, four verses later

> I long for household voices gone,
> For vanished smiles I long,
> But God hath led my dear ones on,
> And He can do no wrong.[6]

In letters Whittier's refrain was the same, notably when he wrote to Lydia Maria Child on November 15, 1864:

> * * * How strange and terrible are these separations — this utter silence — this deep agony of mystery — this reaching out for the love which we feel must be ever living, but which gives us no sign! Ah, my friend! What is there for us but to hold faster and firmer our faith in the goodness of God? that all which He allots to us or our friends is for the best! — best for them, for us, for all. Let theology, and hate, and bigotry talk as they will, I for one will hold fast to this, God *is* good; He *is* our Father! He knows what love is, what our hearts, sore and bereaved, long for, and He will not leave us comfortless, for is He not Love? * * *[7]

Time's flight only exalted Whittier's faith, which evoked these lines of October, 1876, written from Danvers to his and Elizabeth's lifelong friend Harriet Minot Pitman:

> * * * For as the years pass and one slides so rapidly down the afternoon slope of life, until the dark and chill of the evening shadows rest upon him, he longs for the hands and voices of those who, in the morning, went up on the other side with him. The awful mysteries of life and nature sometimes almost overwhelm me. "What, Where, Whither?" These questions sometimes hold me breathless. How little after all do we know! And the soul's anchor of Faith can only grapple fast upon two or three things, and first and surest of all upon the Fatherhood of God. * * *[8]

Whittier by no means closed his eyes to the evil which is in the universe. Like his mentor, Milton, he believed that good and evil exist side by side in the world, but that good — and Truth — will win the ultimate triumph. Whittier perfectly expressed this sentiment in the *Middlesex Standard* on September 19, 1844, after he had attended a Second Advent camp meeting near Lowell. In part he said:

> And after all, is the idea itself a vain one? Shall to-morrow be as to-day — shall the antagonism of Good and Evil continue as heretofore, forever? — Is there no hope that this world-wide prophecy of the human soul, uttered in all climes, in all times, shall yet be fulfilled? Who shall say it may not be true? Nay, is not its truth proved by its universality? The hope of all earnest souls *must* be realized. That which through a distorted and doubtful medium shone even upon the martyr-enthusiasts of the French Revolution — soft gleams of heaven's light rising over the hell of man's passions and crimes — the glorious ideal of Shelley, who, atheist as he was, through early prejudice and defective education, saw the horizon of the world's future kindling with the light of a better day, — that hope and that faith which constitute as it were the world's life, and without which it would be dark and dead, cannot be in vain.

Sharply conscious as he was that evil is in every man, Whittier believed that God alone can judge a soul's good or ill. It was like him to say, "Be thou, in rebuking evil, conscious of thine own," and, no less, "Always he who most forgiveth in his brother is most just." [9]

All his days, though he recognized that "good and evil interflow," [10] Whittier clung to his sublime faith that God, supremely understanding but utterly inscrutable, is all good. When he was seventy he reiterated that "I do not believe it possible . . . to be sinless." On the verge of eighty he still proclaimed his rationale to be the faith that

> The darkness of His providence
> Is star-lit with benign intents.[11]

## 2

"We pity the man who has no religion in his heart," Whittier wrote in the *Haverhill Gazette* on March 13, 1830. Obviously he had added the sanctions of reading to his inborn Quaker conviction of the immanence of God; for he plainly referred to the "Chain of Being" conception of the universe — originating with Plato and Aristotle and systematized by the Neoplatonists — which was widely diffused and accepted in the eighteenth century.[12] Of that period Addison, Akenside, Pope, and Young, with some of whose writings Whittier became acquainted at home through Lindley Murray's *English Reader*, wove the Chain of Being into their writings. Whittier, though never a pantheist, very naturally absorbed the concept of God's revelation in nature, which he made manifest in many of his poems. From his writings about nature it was almost never absent.

Part of his article in the *Gazette* read:

> To limit our hopes and aspirations to this life and this world is like remaining forever in the place of our birth, without ever lifting the veil of the visible horizon, which bent over our infancy. . . . There is religion in every thing around us; — a calm and holy religion in the unbreathing things of Nature, which men would do well to imitate. It is a meek and blessed influence, stealing in, as it were, unawares upon the heart. . . . It is the poetry of Nature.

Other writings of Whittier's early years likewise bodied forth his conviction of God in Nature. One choice example in prose was "Hanging Hills," which he published in the *New England Weekly Review* on September 12, 1831. Whittier declared that it is well "to go out occasionally from the dusty city and look on nature in its calmness and its grandeur. . . . It brings us nearer to the presence of Him, whose immediate works are around us." This theme Whittier set to the music of "Summer by the Lakeside" (1853) and other poems.

Years added only conviction and grace to Whittier's acceptance of an immanent God. Later he wrote:

> The central thought — the root-idea of Quakerism, so-called, is as old as human needs. Not only is it affirmed in the venerable Jewish Scriptures, but with more or less distinctness, also, in the remarkable Vedas of India, coming down to us from the solemn remoteness of ages; & in those utterances of prophets, poets, priests & philosophers, of all peoples & times, which remain to testify that at no period & in no nation, God hath left himself without witnesses. Its fitting expression may be found in the word *Immanuel:* God with us.
>
> God is One; just, holy, merciful, eternal & almighty Creator, Father of all things — Christ, the same eternal One, manifested in our Humanity, and in Time, — and the Holy Spirit is the same Christ, manifested within us, — the Divine Teacher, the Living Word, the Light that lighteth *every* man that cometh into the world. * * * [13]

Whittier's "view of Christ as the special manifestation of the Love of God to humanity" was repeatedly given fervent expression in his verse. He himself particularly mentioned "Our Master" (1866),[14] a song of warm and appealing simplicity whose dominant motive appeared and reappeared in the compositions, of increasingly deep religious fervor, which he produced after the death of his sister. Of the fact of the Trinity, Whittier had no doubt at all. He resolved the problem by faith, evidently not without first having made soundings for a logical basis. He wrote:

> I shut my grave Aquinas fast;
> The monkish gloss of ages past,
> The schoolman's creed aside I cast.
>
> And my heart answered, "Lord, I see
> How Three are One, and One is Three;
> Thy riddle hath been read to me!"

So it was, in Whittier's own time, with Beecher and with Bushnell, too.[15]

In 1877 Whittier added a plain note concerning the complex problem of the tri-personality of God. He had just read Gail Hamilton's *What Think Ye of Christ?* and on July 15 he wrote her about it, with approval but with one reservation:

> * * * My own mind had, from the same evidence that thee adduce, become convinced of the *Divinity* of Christ; but I cannot look upon him as other than a man like ourselves, through whom the Divine was made miraculously manifest. Jesus of Nazareth was a man, the *Christ* was a God — a new revelation of the Eternal in Time. * * *[16]

As a Quaker, then, Whittier from very early in his life rejected the Calvinistic doctrine of man's alienation from God. He believed that God is with man; and as a Friend he believed that God is *within* man. The belief in God's love for man was the core and base of the tenets upon which, in the seventeenth century, George Fox established the Society of Friends. William Sewel lucidly explained that the Friends' "chief principle, in which they differ from the generality of modern Christian societies, is, That every man is enlightened with the Divine Light, according to the evangelist John, who . . . in speaking of Christ, as he was from eternity with the Father, calls him the Word, and saith, 'That the

Word was God, that all things were made by him, that in him was life, and the life was the light of men.' " [17] Thus the doctrine of the Inner Light had a scriptural foundation.

Whittier accepted and practised it without the shade of a doubt. From first to last this aspect, too, of his religious belief was manifest in his writings. In the last stanza of some lines based on Mark IV. 39, which were published in the *Haverhill Gazette* on February 9, 1828, Whittier prayed:

> O, thou! whose power could rule the sea,
> Extend thine influence e'en to me!
> Control my will, and lay to rest
> The stormy passions of my breast;
> Check there, each wild discordant mood,
> And grant an humble quietude,
> To list, amid earth's jarring din,
> The teachings of *thy voice within.*

At all stages "The Voice" spoke in Whittier's verse, but he made it most articulate in two late poems, "The Vision of Echard" (1878) and "The Word" (1881). In the later work Whittier proclaimed that "the unpardonable sin is to deny the Word of God within!" [18]

## 3

Whittier's ardent conviction, if not his early practice, was that man should seek close communion with God and do His work on earth. But in 1837, when he was in his thirtieth year, and as late as 1840, the world was too much with Whittier to permit complete subjugation of his hot ambition to the service of his God. He plainly said that he saw the light, but that his infirm humanity made his feet stray from the highroad which it clearly revealed. Whittier lamented:

> I feel that there are too many things of the world between me and the realization of a quiet communion with the pure and Holy Spirit. Why is it that we go on from day to day, and week to week, in this manner? Alas for human nature in its best estate. There is no upward tendency in it. It looks downward. It is indeed of the earth.[19]

Clearly, Whittier knew what his duty was, and he believed, moreover, that —

> The tissue of the Life to be
> We weave with colors all our own,
> And in the field of Destiny
> We reap as we have sown.[20]

That state of mind, in 1842, was proof of progress, and in 1843 there was more. Whittier indicated further his belief in the "doctrine of future retribution, — the accountability of the spirit for the deeds done in the body. . . ." [21]

Before the end of the decade, Whittier had buttressed his well-defined religious position and made his practical work pivot upon it. In a letter published on March 11, 1847, in the *National Era*, he said that ". . . I am constrained to believe, with him [Milton], that that Truth which can alone cure the ills of humanity is 'bred up between two grave and holy nurses, the doctrine and practice of the Gospel of Christ.' " On December 30 of that year, also in the *National Era*, Whittier warmly commended Charles Sumner for his strong utterances against slavery, and he hit at "perfectionist reformers as well as religionists" who would cure the evil by soft opposition. Then Whittier added, revealingly:

> The emblem of practical Christianity is the Samaritan stooping over the wounded Jew. No fastidious hand can lift from the dust fallen humanity, and bind up its unsightly gashes. * * * Our faith in a better day for the race is strong; but we feel quite sure it will come, in spite of such abstract reformers, and not by reason of them. The evils which possess humanity are of a kind which go out not by their [the abstract reformers'] delicate appliances.

That, then, was the duty of man — to be a practicing Christian and son of God. For himself Whittier set a standard of perfection, and he reached it, if not earlier, then indubitably in 1848. "The Wish of To-Day," as he expressed it in the poem of that title published in the *National Era* on November 30, was for "a will resign'd, Oh, Father, to Thine Own." Whittier now abjured fame and the tinsel of earth's strivings. He craved only peace and rest:

> And now my spirit sighs for home,
> And longs for light whereby to see,
> And like a weary child would come,
> Oh, Father, unto Thee.[22]

This it was to be a man traveling the highroad of life.

Thereafter "the godlike power to do, the godlike aim to know" [23] became virtually Whittier's dominant motif. Like a man truly bred on the Bible, he never became weary of singing God's praises or of laboring in His vineyard. In poem after poem he sang the paean — in "The Angel of Patience" and "My Soul and I" (both of 1847), "First-Day Thoughts" (1852), "Andrew Rykman's Prayer" (1863), "Our Master" (1866), "At Last" (1882), and "Adjustment" (1885), among numerous others.

And what would be a man's reward? That was for God to say:

> Suffice it if — my good and ill unreckoned,
> And both forgiven through Thy abounding grace —
> I find myself by hands familiar beckoned
> Unto my fitting place.[24]

# 4

Advancing years brought not only an increase of beauty to Whittier's concept and practice of life on earth, but increased conviction that it was a preparation, an aspiration; that death is a rising from life. Whittier reached that belief after labor. At the outset, in his early stage of Byronic versifying and editorial writing, death was a dread specter to him. In "The Thought of Death," which he published in the *American Manufacturer* on January 15, 1829, he admitted:

> There is to us, something terrible in the idea of death, even in its mildest and most gradual approach — something in its dim and uncertain horrors, that steals darkly and drearily among the pleasant images of life — a spectre in the midst of its beautiful forms, and a shadow on its sunshine. * * *

In 1830 Whittier's father died, peacefully and naturally, five months short of seventy years. By 1843 Whittier was writing that in death —

> The soul may know
> No fearful change, nor sudden wonder,
>
> . . . . . . . .
>
> But with the upward rise, and with the vastness grow.[25]

On September 5, 1844, in the sixth of his "The Stranger in Lowell" series published in the *Middlesex Standard*, Whittier said that we do not know "what it is to pass from this state of being to another," but that Christ has made the journey, and "the light of His footsteps lingers in the path." [26]

As he so often did in his writings, Whittier was talking subjectively. He believed that a man should live his life on an ascending scale, and as his own years increased he more and more regarded death as a rising from life. In his poem "The Shadow and the Light" he wrote that "a Voice grows with the growing years. . . ." It is particularly significant that in the green trails and upland pastures of New Hampshire, where he began to go in summer during the eighteen-forties, Whittier became ultimately and eloquently certain of the eternal oneness of God, Nature, and man. In 1876, in "Sunset on the Bearcamp," [27] he gave the loftiest expression of his belief that God and Nature furnish to man the proper tone and scale for his life. A key passage reads:

> But beauty seen is never lost,
> God's colors all are fast;
> The glory of this sunset heaven
> Into my soul has passed,
> A sense of gladness unconfined
> To mortal date or clime;
> As the soul liveth, it shall live
> Beyond the years of time.

Whittier's sense of the aspiration of life, his conviction that a man must live ever more up to the exalted level of God's example, was stated almost as a credo in "The Clear Vision" (1868):

> Strike when thou wilt the hour of rest,
> But let my last days be my best!

Whittier here spoke the same optimistic language as Robert Browning.

Thus, very simply, a life lived after God's example "shall live beyond the years of time." Whittier in 1863, writing to comfort Lucy Larcom after the death of a sister, quoted a heathen stoic: "Death is according to Nature, and nothing is evil which is according to Nature." [28]

## 5

As years and honors piled up on him, Whittier often and yet oftener directed his thoughts to "that bourn [whence] no traveller returns." It was the question of the ages, answerable only by faith. Whittier seems always to have believed that there was life after death. In inchoate form his faith in it was a gleam in some of his youthful writings, as early as 1827; and in "The Norsemen" (1841) [29] Whittier gave a rounded conception of "the Eternal will . . . , whose impulse fills anew with breath the frozen solitude of Death. . . ." In 1863 he gave a complete avowal of his faith in immortality in "The Answer," [30] to which he referred in answering a friend:

> I think I understand thy inquiry. I am not a Universalist, for I believe in the possibility of the perpetual loss of the soul that persistently turns away from God, in the next life as in this. But I do believe that the Divine love and compassion follow us in all worlds, and that the Heavenly Father will do the best that is possible for every creature He has made. What that will be must be left to his infinite wisdom and goodness. I would refer thee to a poem of mine, "The Answer," as containing in few words my belief in this matter.

After the death of his mother in 1857, his sister Mary in 1860, and his favorite sister Elizabeth in 1864, Whittier became profoundly absorbed in meditation — which he knew could yield no logical answer — on the future life. He had never the trace of a doubt that they and his father and his Aunt Mercy would be waiting for him. In *Snow-Bound* (1866) he spoke in pity of that man —

> Who hath not learned, in hours of faith,
> The truth to flesh and sense unknown,
> That Life is ever lord of Death,
> And Love can never lose its own!

By Love he meant God, and fervently he hoped that he would be found acceptable to God.

In 1875 Whittier wrote to his cousin Mrs. Cartland that he was little interested in current negotiations for the repurchase of the old homestead at East Haverhill. To people at seventy, he explained, "the mansions of the earth are of small importance, in comparison with those spoken of by our Lord, where only true rest can be found." [31] And to such, time after time and with mounting resignation, even eagerness, Whittier said that he was ready to go, with God's blessing, and join his "dear ones." In 1879 he wrote a particularly revealing letter to his friend Charlotte Fiske Bates, giving in large scope his sentiments about many matters of faith. Primarily, Whittier doubted the *facts* upon which Garrison supported his faith in Spiritualism — a topic which greatly engaged Whittier, as it had his mother.[32] But, Whittier demurred:

> I am slow to believe new things, and in a matter of such tremendous interest, I want "assurance doubly sure." I wonder whether, if I could see a real ghost, I should believe my own senses. I do sometimes feel very near to dear ones who have left me — perhaps they are with me then. I am sure they would be, if it were possible. Of one thing I feel sure: that something outside of myself speaks to me, and holds me to duty; warns, reproves, and approves. It is good, for it requires me to be good; it is wise, for it knows the thoughts and intents of the heart. It is to me a revelation of God, and of his character and attributes: the one important *fact*, before which all others seem insignificant. * * *
>
> I have no longer youth and strength, and I have not much to hope for, as far as this life is concerned; but I enjoy life: "It is a pleasant thing to behold the sun." I love Nature in her varied aspects; and, as I grow older, I find much to love in my fellow-creatures, and also more to pity. I have the instinct of immortality, but the conditions of that life are unknown. I cannot conceive what my own identity and that of dear ones gone before me will be. * * * [33]

Future identity thus baffled him, but not the future place of any one who rightly lived his life on earth. Whittier simply negatived Hell out of his conception of the Eternity of God-serving people. In late life Joshua Coffin, Whittier's fellow Abolitionist and school-teacher, usually a man of bright outlook, needed strong reassurance about his prospects in the future life. Whittier, in a characteristic way, once talked Coffin out of a bout of religious depression, in which he was convinced that he was predestined to perdition. Their conversation ran this way:

WHITTIER — Joshua, don't thee hate God, who has doomed thee to everlasting torment?

COFFIN — Why, no, it is for the good of all, that some are punished.

WHITTIER — Joshua, thee has spent thy life doing good, and now thee is of course getting ready to do all the hurt thee can to thy fellow-men?
COFFIN — No, indeed, my feelings have not changed in the least in this regard.
WHITTIER — Thee is going to hell, then, in this mood?
COFFIN — Why, yes, I am reconciled to the will of God, and have no ill feelings toward Him or my race.
WHITTIER — Now, Joshua, thee is going to hell with a heart full of love for everybody — what can the devil find for such an one as thee to do?

Whittier won. Coffin at once got back his old cheerfulness.[34]

In the eighteen-seventies and eighties the subject of immortality was ever present to Whittier's mind. To Edna Dean Proctor he said in a letter of February 22, 1877: "After all, there is no great use in arguing the question of immortality. One must feel its truth. You cannot climb into heaven on a syllogism." Mrs. Fields has left a further record of Whittier's reflections, about 1885, on the unseen world, and two years later he confided to Harriet Pitman, "The great question of the Future Life is almost ever with me. I cannot answer it, but I can *trust*." A fit conclusion of these reflections was his poem "At Last" (1882), which he sent to Thomas Bailey Aldrich for the *Atlantic Monthly* "as the expression of my deepest religious feeling. . . ." [35] The last stanza of this moving prayer to God reads:

There, from the music round about me stealing,
I fain would learn the new and holy song,
And find at last, beneath Thy trees of healing,
The life for which I long.[36]

## 6

Whittier's religious position, in summary, was founded on the will to believe. The credo which he worked out for himself, with no trace of direct influence from any quarter, is that of extreme individualism — as befitted a Friend. From the quietistic meeting at Amesbury of which he was a lifelong member, and from his home life, he must have learned the virtue of faith; but the planks of his faith were solidly laid before he could have become acquainted with the writings of Horace Bushnell, whose religious position was so much like his own. (The celebrated Hartford minister had his mystical experience in 1849, and in the same year brought out his *God in Christ.*)

If not a mystic in the way that John of the Cross was, Whittier yet was a man of extraordinarily penetrating vision, in practical as well as in spiritual matters. In the instalment entitled "Modern Magic" of his "The Stranger in Lowell" series, published in the *Middlesex Standard* on October 10, 1844, Whittier wrote revealingly:

> * * * For myself, I am not willing to reject at once everything which cannot be explained in consistency with a strictly material philosophy. Our whole life is circled about with mystery. Who knows the laws [of] his own spiritual nature — who can determine the precise conditions of the mysterious union of soul and body? It ill becomes us, in our ignorance and blindness, to decide that whatever accords not with our five senses, and our every day experience, is an impossibility. There is a credulity of doubt which is more to be deprecated than that of belief.

In an earlier article of that series, "A Mormon Conventicle," published in the *Standard* on August 22, 1844, Whittier had spoken kindly of the basic purpose of "these modern prophets" — to give to weary hearts assurance that "in these latter days Faith is again in the world; that the universe is not a blind, dark mechanism; but that God's spirit moves in it yet. . . ."

Of infidelity Whittier had already spoken plainly, very early in his career. Three editorials under that head were published in the *American Manufacturer* on February 19, 1829, and in the *Haverhill Gazette* on January 23 and February 6, 1830. Hence, thirty years later, he was prepared to solve for himself the questions which science raised, by standing on the rock of his faith. He was keenly aware of the impact, on the mind of the times, of Darwin's *On the Origin of the Species by Natural Selection* (1859) and of Spencer's *Programme of a System of Synthetic Philosophy* (1860). For himself he took, and for the Society of Friends he advocated, a firm stand on the principles of Fox and Woolman. A clear and resolute faith dictated the letter which he sent to Haverford College, in September, 1884, on the occasion of its fiftieth anniversary:

> * * * Holding fast the mighty truth of the Divine Immanence, the Inward Light and Word, a Quaker college can have no occasion to renew the disastrous quarrel of religion with science. Against the sublime faith which shall yet dominate the world, skepticism has no power. No possible investigation of natural facts; no searching criticism of letter and tradition can disturb it, for it has its witness in all human hearts. * * * [37]

In such matters, then, Whittier's advice to any individual would have been: love God and do His work. His own credo was direct and personal. There was no place in it for elaborate church organization or for priests, although on numerous occasions Whittier rejoiced in specific good fortune which had come to the Roman Catholic Church, for example; and he wrote, correctly, that "I have learned with John Woolman to find 'no narrowness respecting sects and opinions.' " At an earlier time he told a friend that to him "Quaker and Catholic are alike, both children of my Heavenly Father." He added that the creed which separated them was, in his judgment, "frail and slight as a spider's web." [38]

Nevertheless, Whittier constantly reiterated his belief that religious faith was a direct matter between a man and his God; equally, his disbelief in the need for intercessors. In the *National Era* of October 7, 1847, on the subject of "The Clergy and Reform," Whittier said that he always judged men by a single standard, the clergy on an even basis with all others. He felt genuinely that priests did not stand in any preferred relation to God. In the *Era* of January 25, 1849, he defined in warmly human terms the duties of a "true preacher for our age." In verse he spread the same message — in "The Story of Ida," in "Adjustment," and in other poems — and in "Worship" he wrote that the service which God desires from His children is —

> Not the poor offering of vain rites, but rather
> The simple duty man from man demands.[39]

By upbringing and by preference Whittier found his spiritual home climate in the Society of Friends. Always he turned away from "priests, sacrifices, and ghostly mummery and machinery," of which he wrote to Lucy Hooper in 1843:

> * * * To me it seems to bid fair to swallow up everything save Quakerism of *the old stamp*, which has this advantage, that its distinctive characteristic is the entire rejection of *all* ceremonial, the total disbelief in

the power of pope, priest, or elder to give a ransom for the soul of another. * * * I have a strong faith — it seems almost like prophecy — that the result will be, ere the lapse of two centuries, a complete and permanent change in the entire Christian world. * * * Love will take the place of fast, penance, long prayers, and heathenish sacrifices; altar, church, priest, and ritual will pass away; but the human heart will be the Holy of Holies, where worship will still be performed, not in set forms, and on particular occasions, but daily and hourly a worship meet and acceptable to Him who is not deceived by the pomp of outward ceremonial, and who loves mercy better than sacrifice. . . .[40]

Whittier was completely fair-minded in his attitude toward clergymen. He felt as warmly toward them as toward all other men; but he distrusted *church organization* with its hired ministry. He wrote mordantly and perhaps too often about the Calvinists' persecution of the Quakers in the American colonies; a long list of poems and articles in prose bespoke his burning resentment of the old New England theocracy. Yet he said that if he could persuade himself that a hired ministry and a written creed were essential to his moral and spiritual health, he would "prefer to sit down at once under such teachers as Bushnell and Beecher." (He regarded both men highly.) And he went on: "If I must go into the market and buy my preaching, I should naturally seek the best article on sale, without regard to the label attached to it." [41]

Always, however, Whittier turned to "an unshaken faith in the one distinctive doctrine of Quakerism — the Light within — the immanence of the Divine Spirit in Christianity." [42] The Inner Light was the beacon which regulated all the traffic of his long life.

His manner of living it was not for all men to follow. Few could. Whittier wrote in 1870, "I believe that the world needs the Society of Friends as a testimony and a standard." [43] He was taking account of the Society's numerically small membership, stemming from a fact noted by C. R. Fish: "The uncompromising maintenance of a rigid standard frightened the weak. . . ." [44]

Whittier himself, by the faith which he forged and by the signal triumph to which he brought it in practice, left a strong testimony and a standard. He and John Woolman are considered "the finest product of Quakerism on our American soil," and he himself as the strong exemplar who "gave the inner life and central conception of Quakerism their most adequate interpretation." [45]

# XXVIII

# The White Summit

WHITTIER'S DEDICATION to the better life which he demonstrated so convincingly as a standard for all men, and his resolute faith in immortality, carried him in peace through his last years. The physical machine ran down, but his mind remained alert and his spirit serene. Mrs. Fields reflected, "It was not, however, until 1890 that we could really feel he had left the years of active service and of intellectual achievement as things of the past." [1]

He took his accustomed interest in "old things" — the various causes which he had fought for, his attachment to friends and theirs to him, and even in the correspondence entailed. And because he was interested, he continued to be interesting. Calls upon him, by "pilgrims" in person and by letter, never ceased. Miss Sparhawk took note of his remark in a letter of about 1889 that he had been "miserably ill in August and September," unable to read or write much. "My eyes fail me," he reported, "and I cannot use them without pain." [2] He had a way to keep up, however. On October 22, 1889, he wrote from Amesbury to Phebe Woodman, at Oak Knoll: "I have got so many letters on hand that I cannot get through them; and if thy mother is willing I wish thee could come up tomorrow or next day, & help me. Come & spend the day & stop over night, & return in the morning, as the days are so short, and I can't hurry in dictating." [3]

One of Whittier's exchanges of letters is richly illustrative. In the eighteen-thirties he had been interested in Samuel Gridley Howe's work in America for the relief of the Greeks, and he became even more interested in Howe's lasting monument — the Perkins Institution for the

Blind, established in 1832. Selections from Whittier's works came in time to be reproduced in Braille for the use of students there. In the summer of 1890 he sent a note of encouragement to Helen Keller, already a marked person there because deaf as well as blind, and on his eighty-third birthday, in December following, he received a reply written in her own hand, in square characters. Whittier's typical letter of thanks [4] resulted, in the summer of 1891, in a call upon him at Amesbury from her and her tutor. Miss Keller left a grateful record of it:

> One beautiful summer day, not long after my meeting with Dr. Holmes, Miss Sullivan and I visited Whittier in his quaint home on the Merrimac. His gentle courtesy and quaint speech won my heart. He had a book of his poems in raised print from which I read "In School Days." He was delighted that I could pronounce the words so well, and said that he had no difficulty in understanding me. Then I asked many questions about the poem, and read his answers by placing my fingers on his lips. He said he was the little boy in the poem, and that the girl's name was Sally, and more which I have forgotten. I also recited "Laus Deo," and as I spoke the concluding verses, he placed in my hands a statue of a slave from whose crouching figure the fetters were falling, even as they fell from Peter's limbs when the angel led him forth out of prison. Afterward he went into his study, and wrote his autograph for my teacher and expressed his admiration of her work ["With great admiration of thy noble work in releasing from bondage the mind of thy dear pupil, I am truly thy friend, John G. Whittier"], saying to me, "She is thy spiritual liberator." Then he led me to the gate and kissed me tenderly on my forehead. I promised to visit him again the following summer; but he died before the promise was fulfilled.[5]

Other "pilgrims," with marked exceptions, rather tried Whittier's self-developed patience than gratified him. They gave him, obviously, too much the sense of being a museum piece soon to be retired from exhibition. At Danvers he had a devoted group of protectors, but not at Amesbury, from where he wrote often to the Oak Knoll household in this vein:

[5] From: p. 136, *The Story of My Life*, by Helen Keller, copyright, 1903, 1931, by Helen Keller. Reprinted by permission of Doubleday and Company, Inc., and Curtis Brown, Ltd.

*July 15, 1885* — I am not feeling very well in the change of weather. I have had a great many callers, and just now am pestered by a travelling *crank* who has been all over the world, and has come here to finish up. When he found that this was not the place of "Snow Bound" he started off this morning for Haverhill, but will no doubt return.

*October 21, 1887* — I have been sadly beset with company. Everybody seems after me; the world is too full and is flowing over.

*April 29, 1889* — The great Methodist Conference met here and a hundred & fifty ministers are calling on me.

*November 11, 1889* — The "pilgrims" still keep coming. On First Day a "*Millerite*" Quaker came and preached. I was not able to attend meeting, so he came to see me — an awful specimen of a *bore* of the podanger kind.

*July 29, 1890* — I am beset by callers. On Saturday in spite of the rain they came all day, one from Philadelphia, one from Portland, Oregon, two from Haverhill and three from Lawrence, and I am quite exhausted by them. I shall have to get away from them if possible.

*Newburyport, February, 1891* — A woman pilgrim from New York is here and I must stop writing and see what she wants. — My pilgrim has just left. She proved to be a very lovely woman — the wife of Gov. Cooper of Colorado — bright and genial.

*October, 1891* — The Gov of N H and his aids in full uniform called on me yesterday.

*November 8, 1891* — Too many people are constantly coming, and they tire me more than I can well bear. * * * (November 12.) I have just got rid of six Californians.

*Newburyport, April 3, 1892* — I had Lady Somerset here on Thursday, — a very bright, handsome woman, with fine speech and manners, — the best specimen I have ever seen of British womanhood, very pleasant, easy, and conversational.[6]

Old friends yet remained to Whittier, and his devotion to them was steadfast, as he declared in a letter of October 22, 1884: "I am not an 'Independent' in politics, or anything else, but confess that I am very *dependent* upon the love and friendship of thyself and other good folks." [7] When, in July 1890, he was with the Cartlands at a quiet place on the Piscataqua River, in Eliot, Maine, Grace Greenwood spent a day on visit from Philadelphia, and Governor and Mrs. William Claflin and Alice Freeman Palmer were among veteran friends who called on him at Amesbury.[8]

With the private printing of *At Sundown* in December, 1890, Whittier's literary work was done. Lowell wrote to him in particular praise of the poem "The Captain's Well" — and in August, 1891, the shadows fell on him at "Elmwood," in Cambridge. On January 14, 1892, Doctor Henry Ingersoll Bowditch, with whom Whittier had just exchanged affectionate letters on the occasion of his own eighty-fourth birthday, was dead; [9] and on August 31 of that year, George William Curtis. Whittier, drawn ever closer to the dwindling group of his special friends, had written to Holmes on August 18, 1891:

> Ever since I heard the sad news of Lowell's death, I have been thinking of thee, and longing to see thee, for we are now standing alone. The bright, beautiful ones who began life with us have all passed into the great shadow of silence, or rather, let us hope, in the language of Henry Vaughan, "They have gone into the world of light, and we alone are lingering here!" Well, I at least shall soon follow them, and I wait the call with a calm trust in the Eternal Goodness. I have been ill all summer, but the world is still fair to me; my friends are very dear to me; I love and am loved. And it is a great joy to me that I can think of thee as well, and in the full enjoyment of all thy gifts and powers, surrounded still with friends who love and honor thee.[10]

Holmes and Whittier both wrote verses in memory of Lowell,[11] and Whittier that summer contributed one more sun-down poem, "Between the Gates," to *The Independent* (September 10).

Whittier looked to the White Hills, then, but was unable to undertake to travel farther than Wakefield, New Hampshire. There on the southern tip of his beloved upland country he stayed for a time with the Cartlands at a quiet hotel. But as it had done two summers before, at Conway, increasing feebleness compelled him to return ahead of schedule to the Cartlands' home in Newburyport and to the care of a physician.[12]

There he spent the last winter of his life. He rose to full enjoyment of his friends' observance of his eighty-fourth birthday, in the Cartlands' beautiful home. Sixty members of the Whittier Club of Haverhill who called in the morning brought eighty-four roses encircled in a scarf, upon the ends of which were designs of Whittier's birthplace and the schoolhouse of "In School-Days." Even three of his fellow students at Haverhill Academy appeared to greet him. In one of his very rare addresses, Whittier acknowledged the congratulations of the Whittier Club delivered by their president, and showed a lively interest in the traffic — friends and messengers and gifts — which coursed through the rooms of the spacious house. The last guest left in the evening. Whittier then joined the Cartlands at the tea-table, reviewed with pleasure the events of the day, and said that he had passed no birthday more comfortably and happily.

Particularly he had enjoyed the personal calls of Charles F. Coffin, of Mrs. Fields and Sarah Orne Jewett, of Mrs. Claflin and Alice Freeman Palmer, of Francis J. Garrison, and of Harriet McEwen Kimball. And two especial messages, both in their way prophetic, sensibly touched him. Phillips Brooks, who had just become, as Whittier put it, "bishop, not only of the Episcopal Church, but of all New England!" [13] wrote:

> I have no right, save that which love and gratitude and reverence may give, to say how devoutly I thank God that you have lived, that you are living, and that you will always live.[14]

Holmes, always felicitous, sent a long letter, saying in part:

> I congratulate you upon having climbed another glacier and crossed another crevasse in your ascent of the white summit which already begins to see the morning twilight of the coming century. A life so well filled as yours has been cannot be too long for your fellow-men. In their affections you are secure, whether you are with them here or near them in some higher life than theirs. * * * Of these many dead you are the most venerated, revered, and beloved survivor; of these few living, the most honored representative. Long may it be before you leave a world where your influence has been so beneficent, where your example has been such inspiration, where you are so truly loved, and where your presence is a perpetual benediction.[15]

Two other greetings, both from Canada, were less directly personal but none the less representative in feeling. The Indian poet of Ontario, E.

Pauline Johnson, said in a telegram: "Your young Mohawk friend asks for you to-day the Great Spirit's blessing." Then by letter from James W. Taylor, United States Consul at Winnipeg, Manitoba, Whittier learned that at the last stroke of the clock at midnight of December 16–17, the bells of Saint Boniface, which he had commemorated in his lyric "The Red River Voyageur," rang a peal of joy. Lieutenant-Governor John Schultz had so suggested, and Archbishop Tâché had so directed. Whittier made this acknowledgment:

> During my illness from the prevailing epidemic, which confined me nearly the whole winter, and from which I am but very slowly recovering, a letter from the United States consul at Winnipeg informed me of thy pleasant recognition of my little poem, "The Red River Voyageur" (written nearly forty years ago), by the ringing of the bells of Saint Boniface on the eve of my late anniversary. I was at the time quite unable to respond, but I feel that I should be wanting in due appreciation of such a marked compliment if I did not, even at this late hour, express to thee my heartfelt thanks. I have reached an age when literary success and manifestations of popular favor have ceased to satisfy one upon whom the solemnity of life's sunset is resting; but such a delicate and beautiful tribute has deeply moved me. I shall never forget it. I shall hear the bells of Saint Boniface sounding across the continent, and awakening a feeling of gratitude for thy generous act.[16]

Whittier explained his illness — grippe — when he wrote to Mrs. Fields on January 29, 1892. The meaning of it he grasped clearly: "I have been very near the border-land, — so near that the world seemed to drop away from me, and nothing was left but trust and love. I am still very weak, though I sit up several hours a day." [17] When, during the spring, Whittier was able to leave his room and rejoin the Cartlands in the library, he declared that he had had "not an anxiety, not a care; it was not ecstasy, but inexpressible peace." [18]

Spring brought Whittier his usual refreshment of spirits, but not again his strength. He had what was to be his last look at familiar places — Oak Knoll for a few weeks, then Amesbury in May at the time of Quarterly Meeting. Centre Harbor, where he aspired to go in the summer, he had already seen for the last time. He went instead to "Elmfield," home of his family friend Sarah Abbie Gove, at Hampton Falls, New Hampshire, nine miles from Amesbury.[19] The Cartlands were with him, and Mrs.

Pickard joined the group. All thought was of going to Centre Harbor later, if Whittier regained enough strength for the trip.

He improved somewhat, walked or was driven to points near by which he had known since boyhood, and was beyond reach of "pilgrims" — or almost. On August 2, 1892, he sent this letter to Mrs. Woodman:

> I wrote a line to Phebe at the Cape, but perhaps she had left before it got there. The rain which is falling was greatly needed here, and doubtless at Oak Knoll. I feel the change of weather a good deal but I have tried to be very careful. We have an open fire when we need it, in the sitting room. Abby Gove is a nice little hostess, and spares no pains to make us comfortable. We have been free from visitors here — only two or three since we came.
>
> My chamber opens upon a balcony which looks over a wide horizon with the sea in view. On the lawn near the house are two huge elms — one 16½ feet in circumference, and the other 18. Lizzie Pickard is now here and will probably stay some time.
>
> Has thee heard anything more from Alaska?
>
> I hope you are all well and none the worse for the terrible heat. I felt that very much, but the change was harder. I think I took a little cold but on the whole am better than I feared. * * * [20]

Whittier loved the place, for its own charm and for the views out over the Hampton meadows toward the ocean and the shore on which he had based various of his poems. With enthusiasm he said, "This is a very sweet spot to me: I used to come here with my mother." [21] One friend who spent a week here with him reported his fondness for T. B. Aldrich's "Memory" — his standing request to have the lines read, and his repeating them:

> My mind lets go a thousand things,
> Like dates of wars and deaths of kings,
> And yet recalls the very hour —
> 'Twas noon by yonder village tower,
> And on the last blue moon in May —
> The wind came briskly up this way,
> Crisping the brook beside the road;
> Then, pausing here, set down its load
> Of pine-scents, and shook listlessly
> Two petals from that wild-rose tree.[22]

Now he reveled in the quiet and peace of "Elmfield," wrote few letters, and composed only the four lines of verse addressed to Holmes on his eighty-third birthday (and published in the *Boston Journal* on August 27, 1892). But this effort, on "the hottest day of the season," was the last that he had strength to make.

When illness laid hold of him, nothing availed to revive his physical being. A paralytic stroke, on the morning of September 3, aggravated his condition. For four days he lingered, calm and resigned, solicitous only of the strength of his three attending physicians and his nurses. "You have done all that love and human skill could do; I thank you." When medicine was brought he managed to say, "It is of no use; I am worn out." And often he would breathe, "Love — love to all the world."

On the morning of September 6, when the nurse moved to draw the shades of his room so that at last he could sleep, he was able only to motion with his hand. He wished to see the sunrise. It was his hallowed custom, the one blessing of his sleeplessness.

His last words, spoken to his niece Mrs. Pickard that afternoon in a flash of recognition, were at once a release and a joining. Did he know her? she asked. "I have known thee all the time," he said. Then he felt for the hand of his Maker. At four-thirty on the morning of September 7, he learned the mystery of "the life for which I long." [23]

As stipulated in his will, Whittier was buried with simple Quaker rites in the Friends' section of Union Cemetery, in Amesbury. Under plain markers in the hedge-bordered burial plot which he had arranged, down the years, now lie Joseph and Gertrude Whittier Cartland, Samuel T. and Elizabeth Whittier Pickard, Whittier himself, his Aunt Mercy and his Uncle Moses, his parents, his two sisters, and his brother.

The arrangements that Whittier had made for burial caused no surprise. The size of his estate did. Royalties from the sale of his books after 1865, and investments which he had made, swelled to nearly $134,000 the value of his worldly accumulations. He bestowed all upon friends, relatives, and philanthropies. In his distribution of cash bequests to relatives and friends Whittier was generous. He made token gifts also to the American Peace Society, of which he had been a vice-president, and to the Amesbury Charitable Society. And his abiding care for people who particularly needed help caused the assignment of one half of the residual estate to the Amesbury and Salisbury Home for Aged Women, the Anna Jaques Hospital, in Newburyport, and Hampton Institute — for Negro and Indian students — in Virginia.

# *Notes*

Books frequently referred to in the following notes, under short titles only, are:

BENNETT: Whitman Bennett, *Whittier, Bard of Freedom* (Chapel Hill: University of North Carolina Press, 1941).

CARPENTER: George Rice Carpenter, *John Greenleaf Whittier*. American Men of Letters (Boston: Houghton Mifflin Co., 1903).

CLAFLIN: Mary B. Claflin, *Personal Recollections of John G. Whittier* (New York: Thomas Y. Crowell & Co., 1893).

CURRIER: Thomas Franklin Currier, *A Bibliography of John Greenleaf Whittier* (Cambridge: Harvard University Press, 1937).

FIELDS: Mrs. James T. Fields, *Whittier, Notes of His Life and of His Friendships* (New York: Harper & Bros., 1893).

HIGGINSON: Thomas Wentworth Higginson, *John Greenleaf Whittier*. English Men of Letters (New York: The Macmillan Co., 1902).

KENNEDY (1): W. Sloane Kennedy, *John Greenleaf Whittier: His Life, Genius, and Writings* (Chicago: The Werner Co., 1895 ed.). First issued in Boston, 1882.

KENNEDY (2): William Sloane Kennedy, *John G. Whittier, The Poet of Freedom*. American Reformers (New York: Funk & Wagnalls Co., 1892).

MORDELL: Albert Mordell, *Quaker Militant: John Greenleaf Whittier* (Boston: Houghton Mifflin Co., 1933).

PICKARD: Samuel T. Pickard, *Life and Letters of John Greenleaf Whittier* (Boston: Houghton Mifflin Co., 2 vols., 1894). The authorized biography. Unless otherwise indicated, reference is made to the 1-vol. 1907 revised edition.

POETICAL WORKS: Riverside Edition, *The Writings of John Greenleaf Whittier* (Boston: Houghton Mifflin Co., 1888).

PROSE WORKS: Vols. 1–4 include *Poetical Works;* vols. 5–7 the *Prose Works.*

Sparhawk: Frances Campbell Sparhawk, *Whittier at Close Range* (Boston: The Riverdale Press, 1926).
Underwood: Francis H. Underwood, *John Greenleaf Whittier* (Boston: James R. Osgood Co., 1884).
Whittier-Land: Samuel T. Pickard, *Whittier-Land, A Handbook of North Essex* (Boston: Houghton Mifflin Co., 1904).
Woodman: Mrs. Abby J. Woodman, *Reminiscences of John Greenleaf Whittier's Life at Oak Knoll* (Salem: The Essex Institute, 1908).

Short titles for libraries or collections most frequently referred to in the notes are as follows:

HPL: Whittier Collection, Haverhill (Mass.) Public Library.
HUL (Houghton): Collections, including the Pickard-Whittier papers, in Houghton Library, Harvard University.
Oak Knoll Collection: Special papers in the library of the Essex Institute, Salem, Mass.

## CHAPTER I

1 A *Farmer's Almanac* of 1807, kept in neighboring Newburyport by a person named Moody, recorded a fall of one-half inch of snow on December 9 and of three-quarters of an inch on the 19th. The *Almanac* is now in the possession of the Essex Institute, Salem.

2 I have been unable to confirm this belief by means of official records, since there was at that time no governmental registration of any kind for physicians. Nor are there records of any kind which would show whether or not Dr. Weld was a Haverhill resident in 1807. However, it is considered certain by Mrs. Phebe Grantham, the adopted daughter of his Johnson cousins, at Danvers, and by persons in Haverhill that Dr. Weld attended Whittier into the world. He was the Whittiers' physician for many years.

For biographical notes on Dr. Weld, see Appendix C.

3 In the U.S. Census of 1810, Essex County had a population of 71,888, an average of 150 a square mile, as compared with less than 59 for Massachusetts generally.

4 Carpenter, 298.

5 Based on *Vital Records of Haverhill, Mass., to the End of the Year 1849*

(Topsfield, Mass., 1911), vol. I; George Wingate Chase, *The History of Haverhill* . . . (Haverhill, 1861), *passim;* and statements made in 1936 by Mrs. Emma S. Elliott Coté, who knew the Whittiers, and Fred N. Noyes, an antiquarian, both of Haverhill.

6 On the statement of Mrs. Phebe Grantham. Cf. Clifton Johnson, *The Farmer's Boy* (New York, 1907), in which the style of life fits the known pattern of Whittier's boyhood; Harriet Beecher Stowe, *Old-town Folks* (Boston, 1881), ch. XXII; and Pickard, 14.

7 Pickard, 19.

8 On the statement of Mrs. Grantham, to whom Whittier described his boyhood tastes.

9 Pickard, 19; Higginson, 17. The will of John Whittier listed the following livestock: one horse, four swine, one yoke of oxen, six cows, one pair of yearling steers, one three-year-old steer, one yearling heifer, one two-year-old heifer, one calf, and twenty sheep.

10 Pickard, I, 20–21, says that Whittier as a lad used to sit astride the forehead of one of the oxen while it chewed its cud, under "The Oak" on Job's Hill. Pickard also tells this story (p. 21): "Although always disposed to tease his pets, Whittier secured the love of every living thing that came under his care. Old Butler once saved his life by a remarkable exhibition of strength, and by what would be called 'presence of mind' if shown by a man. One side of Job's Hill is exceedingly steep, — too steep for such an unwieldy animal as an ox to descend rapidly in safety. Greenleaf went to the pasture one day with a bag of salt for the cattle, and Old Butler from the brow of the hill recognized him and knew his errand. As the boy was bent over, shaking the salt out of the bag, the ox came down the hill toward him with flying leaps, and his speed was so great that he could not check himself. He would have crushed his young master, but by a supreme effort, gathering himself together at the right moment, the noble creature leaped straight out into the air, over the head of the boy, and came to the ground far below with a tremendous concussion and without serious injury to himself."

11 This sketch is based on Pickard, 19, and *Whittier-Land*, 48; Rebecca I. Davis, *Gleanings from Merrimac Valley*, Sheaf Number Two (Haverhill, 1886), 15; Stowe, *op. cit.*, 265; and C. R. Fish, *The Rise of the Common Man, 1830–1850*, 64–65.

12 Carpenter, 298.

13 *Whittier-Land*, 4–6.
14 "My Namesake," *Poetical Works*, II, 119.
15 Pickard, 29–30.
16 *Prose Works*, I, 323. Chase, *History of Haverhill*, xv–xvi.
17 Pickard, 12, and *passim*. Cf. Fields, 90. Great Hill lies northwest of the Whittier homestead, at the junction of North and East Parishes, on the New Hampshire border, north of Lake Kenoza.
18 *Poetical Works*, IV, 161.
19 Pp. 37–38.
20 Chase, *op. cit.*, 444 ff.
21 Pickard, 737.
22 *Prose Works*, I, 365.
23 Sparhawk, 173–174.
24 In Charles Edward Banks, *The Planters of the Commonwealth* (Boston, 1930), 96, Whittier's age on his arrival in America was given as eighteen. As a court witness on June 29, 1674, he was "aged about fifty-four years." *Records and Files of the Quarterly Courts of Essex County, Massachusetts* (Salem: Essex Institute, 1911), V, 330.
25 "English Ancestry of the Whittier and Rolfe Families," *New England Historical and Genealogical Register*, LXVI, 244–257.
26 Manuscript material in possession of Earle O. Whittier, Washington, D.C.
27 Pickard, 1.
28 Bernard B. Whittier, *The Ancestry and Descendants of Edmund Whittier* (East Lansing, Mich., 1917), 7.
29 Pickard, 2.
30 He settled in that part of Salisbury which is now called Amesbury. *Whittier-Land*, 14.
31 Joseph Merrill, *History of Amesbury, 1637–1880* (Haverhill, 1880), 10, 16–32 and *passim*. This seems the better authority, though Pickard, 2, and in *Whittier-Land*, 14, says: "He was sent as deputy to the General Court from Salisbury, and served his town in other offices of trust."
32 *Whittier-Land*, 38.
33 Pickard, 1–2; Merrill, *op. cit.*, 9.
34 Chase, *op. cit.*, 67.
35 Pickard, 5–6.
36 Manuscript material in possession of Earle O. Whittier, Washington, D.C. For further facts about Thomas Whittier, see Appendix A.

37 Quakerism is considered to have originated with George Fox's first preaching, in 1647. William Sewel, *The History of the Rise, Increase, and Progress of the Christian People Called Quakers* . . . (New York, 1844 ed.), I, 28. The first two Quakers on American soil landed in Boston in 1656. Thomas Whittier lived 1620–1696; George Fox, 1624–1691.

38 On April 19, 1676, King Philip and his allies appeared near Haverhill and Bradford, and killed two or three settlers. Herbert Milton Sylvester, *Indian Wars of New England* (Boston, 1910), II, 292–294.

39 Pickard, 3–4; Underwood, 11–12. Whittier mentions the general facts in "The Boy Captives," *Prose Works*, II, 399.

40 *Prose Works*, I, 320.

41 Manuscript material in possession of Earle O. Whittier, Washington, D.C.

42 Underwood, 11; Pickard, 5.

43 See Appendix A.

44 *Whittier and His Schoolmates, 1827–1885; Re-union of the Schoolmates of John Greenleaf Whittier at St. John's Rectory, Haverhill, Mass., September 10, 1885* (Haverhill, 1886), 37. For notes on the Peasley family, see Appendix A.

45 See Rufus M. Jones, *The Quakers in the American Colonies* (London, 1911), Book 1, ch. IV, "The Martyrs."

46 Whittier's fragment of a ballad about Sarah Greenleaf appears in Pickard, 10.

47 *Ibid.*, 6. See also Appendix A.

48 *Prose Works*, I, 346–347.

49 See Roland H. Woodwell, "The Hussey Ancestry of the Poet Whittier," *Essex Institute Historical Collections*, LXX, 58–68 (Jan., 1934).

50 See, e.g., Kennedy (1), 24 ff.; Pickard, 1894 ed., 1, 10 ff. To the end of his life Whittier himself believed his ancestry on his mother's side could be traced back to Bachiler. Pickard, 761.

51 Mordell, *Quaker Militant: John Greenleaf Whittier*, esp. pp. 2–3, 244.

52 An examination of the portraits of Whittier's mother, his sister Elizabeth, and himself leaves no reasonable doubt on this point. The first two may be seen at the Whittier home, Amesbury. The poet's eyes may have been like his father's, but no portrait of John Whittier is known to exist.

53 Pickard, 1894 ed., I, 52 n.

54 and 56. See Appendix A.

55 Carpenter, 297.

57 In *Prose Works*, I, 323, Whittier says, in speaking of "our bachelor uncle": ". . . there has always been one of that unfortunate class in every generation of our family."

58 "Snow-Bound," *Poetical Works*, II, 146.

59 Woodman, 25.

60 Claude Moore Fuess, "What Is a Yankee?" *Yankee*, I, 14–17 (Dec., 1935).

61 Bliss Perry, ed., *The Heart of Emerson's Journals* (Boston, 1926), 247.

## CHAPTER II

1 Carpenter, 297; Underwood, 43–45, 77.

2 Pickard, 25. Whittier had from his father this anecdote, which amused him, of a visit to the Canadian frontier: "He joined a party of horsemen and they rode through the wilds up to Lake Memphremagog. There they met a tribe of friendly Indians. The country was wild. No settlement had been made there by the whites. On the day of my father's arrival there these Indians had gone on a spree, and every man in the camp was tipsy, with but one exception, and he was kept busy looking after his companions to prevent them from rolling into the lake, and getting into mischief. My father asked the sober Indian if he never got drunk. He replied, 'Oh, yes; me get drunk some time; not now; me keep watch this time; next time me get drunk.' "

3 Pickard, 24–25; Sparhawk, 94–95.

4 Underwood, 57; Pickard, 34. Cf. *Rules of Discipline of the Yearly Meeting, Held on Rhode Island, for New England* (New Bedford, 1809), 107. Parents are recommended, *inter alia*, "to exercise themselves in reading the Holy Scriptures, and in observing the duties and precepts of holy living therein recommended; admonishing them to keep to that plainness and simplicity in apparel, speech, and behavior, which the spirit of truth led our forefathers into, and which becomes the humble, self-denying followers of the holy Jesus."

5 Pickard, 34 n.; will of John Whittier, filed in Probate and Insolvency Courts of Essex County, at Salem.

6 Listed as one of Haverhill's numerous shoe manufacturers in 1837, and evidently an early one. Chase, *History of Haverhill*, 536.

7 Undated manuscript in Haverhill Public Library. The items credited to John Whittier are dated from June 14, 1826, to Dec. 15, 1828.
8 "Monadnoc," *Poems by Ralph Waldo Emerson*, Everyman's Library (London, 1914), 55.
9 Fields, 52–53.
10 Mordell, 249.
11 *Whittier at Close Range*, 41.
12 Underwood, 48; Mrs. S. T. Pickard, in *Amesbury Daily News*, Dec. 18, 1901.
13 *Prose Works*, I, 341.
14 In undated manuscript in Haverhill Public Library, Abel Page credits John Whittier for yarn and home-made cloth, in the period 1826–1828; Carpenter, 298; Pickard, 19. A manuscript account in HPL, dated June 1, 1836, credits Abigail Whittier in the amount of $8.35 for cheese and similar articles, and for farm products.
15 Higginson, 107; Mrs. S. T. Pickard, *loc. cit.;* "My First Day in Lowell," *Prose Works*, 1, 369: "There is somehow a close affinity between moral purity and clean linen. . . ."
16 C. C. Chase in Underwood, 48; William Batchelder Greene, quoted in Kennedy (1), 26.
17 Pickard, 30.
18 *Ibid.*, 30–31.
19 Underwood, 47.
20 Fields, 36–37; *Prose Works*, I, 323, 325.
21 Henry Mann, *Features of Society in Old and in New England* (Providence, 1885), 54.
22 Pickard, 26; undated paper read by W. H. Dewhurst before the Whittier Home Association, Amesbury, and now filed in the "Snow-Bound desk" there. Dewhurst as a boy was in the service of the Whittiers at their Amesbury home.
23 Kennedy (1), 302–303. See also Lloyd W. Griffin, "Matthew Franklin Whittier, 'Ethan Spike,' " *The New England Quarterly*, XIV, 646–663 (Dec., 1941).
24 Dewhurst, *op. cit.*
25 Pickard, 26, 28; Higginson, 107–108.
26 Sparhawk, 67; Pickard, 27.
27 Pickard, 480, 488–489. The poem was first published in the *Independent*, Feb. 9, 1865.

28 Quoted by Underwood, 36.
29 Pickard, 13.
30 "Snow-Bound," *Poetical Works*, II, 136, 140.
31 *Whittier-Land*, 20.
32 "Snow-Bound," *Poetical Works*, II, 155.
33 For the list of books it contained, see Appendix B.
34 Originally the roof sloped on the northern side down to the first story, in Stuart fashion, but it was raised in 1801 to correspond to the rest of the roof. Pickard, 17; *Whittier-Land*, 28.
35 *Whittier-Land*, 27.
36 Pickard, 22. Another story told by Pickard, *ibid.*, is evidently apocryphal. A circus and menagerie visited Haverhill on the same day as President Monroe. The nine-year-old boy was eager to see the Chief Executive, but was not permitted to go into town that day. On the next day he plodded the three miles to Haverhill, "determined to see at least some footsteps in the street that the great man had left behind him. He found at last an impression of an elephant's foot in the road, and supposing this to be Monroe's track, he followed it as far as he could distinguish it. Then he went home, satisfied he had seen the footsteps of the greatest man in the country." In *A Narrative of a Tour of Observation, Made during the Summer of 1817, by James Monroe, President of the United States, through the North-eastern and North-western Departments of the Union . . .* (Philadelphia, 1818), ch. VII, 129–143, Haverhill is not mentioned as having been included in the itinerary.
37 Underwood, 55; Haverhill Town Records, I, 335; "To My Old Schoolmaster," *Poetical Works*, IV, 74.
38 Rebecca I. Davis, *Gleanings from Merrimac Valley*, Sheaf Number Two (Haverhill, 1886), 27–31. The building of "In School-Days" was sold for $15, moved from the foundations, and left in the road when the conveyance upon which it was being transported broke down. The shack is said to have been burned there by boys of the neighborhood.
39 A clear picture of New England public schools of this period is given in George H. Martin, *The Evolution of the Massachusetts Public School System* (New York, 1894), and in Clifton Johnson, ed., *The District School as It Was . . .* (Boston, 1897).
40 Pickard, 36; Martin and Johnson, *op. cit.;* John Pierpont, *The American Preceptor*, 1st ed. (Boston, 1823).

41 Quoted in Charles A. and Mary R. Beard, *The Rise of American Civilization*, 1-vol. ed. (New York, 1930), 180; Pickard, 40.

42 George H. Martin, *op. cit.*, 107, 111; Pickard, 38. The two teachers Whittier referred to were Joshua Coffin, regarding whom see Appendix C, and George Haskell, a sketch of whom appears in Pickard, 32.

I have been unable to determine exactly the period of Whittier's attendance at his district school. Records which each district school committee was required to keep, from 1814 on, have evidently disappeared or been destroyed.

43 "In School-Days," *Poetical Works*, II, 162.

The poverty of the formal educational resources then at Whittier's service is further accentuated by the town's appropriations for its district schools. In 1814, Whittier's first year at school, the town was to raise $1200 for the support of the six school districts. In 1821 this budget remained the same for seven, but the town voted to raise $2500 for poor relief and contingencies. (Haverhill Town Records, I.)

Note here also a manuscript sheet, now owned by HPL, from the farm accounts of the Whittier homestead:

| | |
|---|---|
| Masters board at Mr Elas 7 weeks and 1 d at 15 cents | $ 8.05 |
| Youse of School room at Mr Elas 7 weeks at | 3.50 |
| 1 Cord of wood found Mr. Whittiers — at 3 dol — 90 cents | 3.90 |
| Masters board at Capt James Giles 5 weeks at 1 dol — 10 cents | 5.50 |
| 1 Cord of wood found by Mr. Greene at $4 | 4.00 |
| Maj Ayers for School house 5 weeks at | 2.50 |
| Masters wages for 12 weeks at 10 dols for 26 days is | 27.69 |
| | $55.14 |
| Our money is | 53.54 |
| if the school keepeth next week we shall owe him — $1.60 | 1.60 |

44 For biographical notes on Coffin, see Appendix C.

45 In a letter copied in the *Historical and Genealogical Register*, XX, 267–268, Professor Felton said: "Many years ago I was his pupil. I have

never forgotten his kind and genial manners, and his unwearied labors, in helping his classes forward in their studies. His pleasant countenance and good humor, united to a great simplicity of character, stamped themselves on my memory, and are among the most agreeable recollections of my childhood. . . ."

46 *William Lloyd Garrison: The Story of His Life, Told by His Children* (New York, 1885), I, 280. Cf. Whittier's "To My Old Schoolmaster," *Poetical Works*, IV, 73; *Historical and Genealogical Register*, XX, 268.

47 Pickard, 39–40. Note, however, Whittier's "Yankee Gypsies," *Prose Works*, I, 336. He says that "a 'pawky auld carle' of a wandering Scotchman" first introduced him to the songs of Burns. Calling at the homestead, this "gaberlunzie" sang, with novel charm, "Bonny Doon," "Highland Mary," and "Auld Lang Syne."

48 "Burns," *Poetical Works*, IV, 95.

49 *A New Year's Address to the Patrons of the Essex Gazette, 1828, With a Letter, Hitherto Unpublished, by John G. Whittier* (Boston: Charles E. Goodspeed, 1903). Cf. *Whittier-Land*, 50–51.

50 *Poetical Works*, I, 253.

51 *Whittier-Land*, 25. Cf. Higginson, 18.

52 Boston, 1874, vii–viii. Cf. Pickard, 593; Higginson, 159–160.

53 Pickard, 39; Chauncey J. Hawkins, *The Mind of Whittier*, 25.

54 "Snow-Bound," *Poetical Works*, II, 157; Claflin, 13. Cf. *Rules of Discipline of the Yearly Meeting* . . . , 10: "And it is earnestly recommended to all members of our religious society [of Friends], that they discourage and suppress the reading of plays, pernicious novels, and other bad books."

55 In "The Agency of Evil," *Prose Works*, III, 251, Whittier wrote (1843): "How hardly effaced are the impressions of childhood! Even at this day, at the mention of the evil angel, an image rises before me like that with which I used especially to horrify myself in an old copy of *Pilgrim's Progress*. Horned, hoofed, scaly, and fire-breathing, his caudal extremity twisted tight with rage, I remember him, illustrating the tremendous encounter of Christian in the valley where 'Apollyon straddled over the whole breadth of the way.' "

56 In the *Haverhill Gazette*, February 27, 1830, Whittier said, in an editorial, "The North and the South," that as a boy he read a sermon by a Byfield pastor which Senator Hayne had cited. Whittier recalled having strongly disapproved of it as not representing the sentiments of New England.

57 Mary Haldane Coleman, "Whittier on John Randolph of Roanoke," *New England Quarterly*, VIII, 551–554 (Dec., 1935).

58 *Rules of Discipline of the Yearly Meeting* . . . , 42: ". . . among all of us as a peculiar people, called and chosen out of the world, and the errors and corruptions thereof."

59 Pickard, 39 n.

60 *Rules of Discipline of the Yearly Meeting* . . . , 114: ". . . one of the first and great causes which engaged our ancient friends to the orderly establishment of our Christian discipline, was the care of the poor. . . ."

61 Fields, 48.

62 Full treatment of the oppression of early Friends in New England is given in Richard P. Hallowell, *The Quaker Invasion of Massachusetts* (Boston, 1883), and George E. Ellis, *The Puritan Age and Rule in the Colony of the Massachusetts Bay, 1629–1685* (Boston, 1888), ch. XII.

63 William Sewel, *The History of the Rise, Increase and Progress of the Christian People Called Quakers* . . . (New York, 1844, 2 vols. in 1), 204 and *passim*. (Pickard, *Whittier-Land*, 25, said that the Whittiers' copy was dated 1825; that currently at the homestead is dated 1774.) Whittier, *Poetical Works*, I, 381.

64 Cf. *Rules of Discipline of the Yearly Meeting* . . . , 144–145: ". . . our peaceable principle, which hath always been to confide in the protection and Providence of Almighty God, and not in weapons of war; which practice of theirs may be attended with injustice, barbarity and bloodshed."

65 In Clarkson (London ed. 1806), see e.g., II, 312–319; Rufus M. Jones, *The Later Periods of Quakerism* (London, 1921), I, 320–321; II, 560, 619; Sydney Howard Gay, in *Scribner's Popular History of the United States* (New York, 1896), III, 117, 175. Note *Rules of Discipline* . . . , 100 ff. Testimonies, of increasing vigor, were adopted in 1727, 1760, 1773, and 1780 against slavery. The last: "Agreed, that no friend import, or in any ways purchase, dispose of or hold mankind as slaves; but that all those who have been held in a state of slavery be discharged therefrom. . . ."

66 *Rules of Discipline*, 47: ". . . we pressingly exhort all parents, and heads of families, to procure such useful learning for their children as their abilities will admit; and to encourage them, as well by example as by precept, to the frequent reading of the Holy Scriptures; and that they begin, as early as possible, to instil into their tender minds

the principles of truth and virtue; and instruct them in the nature and necessity of being born from above, without which, our Lord declared, no man shall see the kingdom of God. . . ."

67 In Underwood, 57.

68 See, e.g., Rufus M. Jones, *op. cit.*, I, 230 ff.; Whittier, *Poetical Works*, IV, 88–90. William Forster (1784–1854), father of William E. Forster, British statesman, was probably in Haverhill some time in December, 1822 to January, 1823.

69 Note Pickard, 35: "Before the days of steam and electricity, the Eastern members of the Society, attending their Yearly Meeting at Newport, R.I., generally performed the journey in their own carriages, depending largely upon their friends for entertainment by the way, in which pleasant service the Whittiers had their full share, sometimes receiving under their roof from ten to fifteen guests."

It is noteworthy, too, that Quaker meetings were held at times in the Whittier kitchen. Pickard, 21–22, tells this humorous incident: "One summer day, on such an occasion, this ox [Old Butler] had the curiosity to put his head in at the open window and take a survey of the assembly. While a sweet-voiced woman was speaking, Old Butler paid strict attention, but when she sat down and there arose a loud-voiced brother, the ox withdrew his head from the window, lifted his tail in [the] air, and went off bellowing. This bovine criticism was greatly enjoyed by the younger members of the meeting."

70 *Rules of Discipline* . . . , 72, 76: "Advised that friends keep their children to a constant, seasonable and orderly frequenting, as well of week-day as of First-day meetings; . . ." "Persons confessing with us, who absent themselves from our religious meetings, either on First-day or other days of the week, and disregard the advice and repeated endeavors of friends to stir them up to this necessary duty, are to be dealt with by the monthly meeting to which they belong, even to disowning such, if the case require it."

71 "The Meeting," *Poetical Works*, II, 281; Carpenter, 298. The "still forms on either side" were the men and the women, who sat on opposite sides of the meeting house.

72 "My Summer with Dr. Singletary," *Prose Works*, I, 199. Cf. Whittier's letter written in 1875 to another old-time resident of East Haverhill: "Your note carries me back to my boyhood, to the time

when I used to know you at 'Rocks Village.' How well I remember the place and the people! Colonel Johnson and his tavern; Esquire Frost and his store; Esquire Ladd and his blacksmith shop; Ephraim B. Orne and his combs; Poyen and his cigars! How plainly rises before me the figure of Dr. Weld in his drab coat and breeches, — a true gentleman of the old school, — a skillful physician, and benefactor of the people! Colonel Poor, who used to search our woods for ship timber; widow Pettee, who used to make my homespun coats and trousers; old 'aunt Morse,' who was regarded by the average juvenile mind as a witch, — all these and many more are associated with my recollections of Rocks Village." Pickard, 35–36.

73 Cotton was first converted into cloth by a power-loom, all under one roof, at Waltham in 1814. In 1823 the Merrimac Manufacturing Company began production at the newly established city of Lowell. F. W. Taussig, *The Tariff History of the United States*, 6th ed. (New York, 1914), 29, 32.

74 The will of John Whittier listed, among other things, one "buffalo skin," and only six pairs of blankets. With obvious reminiscence, J. G. Whittier wrote in "Patucket Falls," *Prose Works*, I, 365: "Rocks and trees, rapids, cascades, and other water-works are doubtless all very well; but on the whole, considering our seven months of frost, are not cotton shirts and woollen coats still better?" This essay first appeared in the Lowell *Middlesex Standard* on Aug. 29, 1844.

75 *Whittier-Land*, 33; Pickard, 14–15.

76 Pickard, 19.

77 Mrs. Phebe Grantham says she never heard him mention that he swam. Kennedy (1), 45, says that Whittier used to fish on Lake Kenoza. In a manuscript letter of July 26, 1871, now owned by HPL, Whittier said to R. Stuart Chase, "I am very sorry that I am not able to attend the Pic Nic at Kenoza Lake, a place made very dear to me by the memories of boyhood."

78 *Whittier-Land*, 34; "The Fall," *American Manufacturer*, Feb. 26, 1829.

79 *Whittier-Land*, 15; Pickard, 23–24, 60.

80 *The Friend*, Philadelphia, LV, 126 (Nov. 26, 1881); Fields, 95.

81 "Paradise Regained," *The Student's Milton*, ed. Frank A. Patterson (New York, 1931), 368.

82 In *The Boyhood of Famous Authors* (New York, 1897?), 94, William Henry Rideing says: ". . . if his gift had been less than genius it could

never have triumphed over the many disadvantages it had to contend with."

83 Quoted in Bliss Perry, *John Greenleaf Whittier*, 16.

## CHAPTER III

1 "My Namesake," *Poetical Works*, II, 119.
2 Pickard, 43.
3 *Ibid.*, 44.
4 *Ibid.*, 46–47.
5 These are in the Henry E. Huntington Library, San Marino, Calif., and in vol. I of the Oak Knoll Collection, Essex Institute, Salem, Mass.
6 See Mordell, 10. Byron died in April, 1824.
7 Summer residents in Whittier's day included Louis Agassiz, Longfellow (whom Whittier visited), John Lothrop Motley, William Hickling Prescott, and Daniel Webster. Nahant was sufficiently celebrated to attract there Harriet Martineau, who gave an appreciative description of the place in *Retrospect of Western Travel* (London, 1838), III, 140–147.
8 "A Retrospect," *Whittier-Land*, 35.
9 See John J. Currier, *History of Newburyport, Mass., 1764–1905* (Newburyport, 1906), I, 512–513. In *Prose Works*, III, 189, Whittier wrote (1879): "My father was a subscriber to his first paper, the *Free Press*, and the humanitarian tone of his editorials awakened a deep interest in our little household, which was increased by a visit which he made us."
10 In a note on "Early and Uncollected Verses" published as an Appendix to *Poetical Works*, IV, 301, Whittier said: "I suppose they should have died a natural death long ago, but their feline tenacity of life seems to contradict the theory of the 'survival of the fittest.' I have consented, at my publishers' request, to take the poor vagrants home and give them a more presentable appearance, in the hope that they may at least be of some interest to those who are curious enough to note the weak beginnings of the graduate of a small country district school, sixty years ago. That they met with some degree of favor at that time may be accounted for by the fact that the makers of verse were then few in number, with little competition in their unprofitable

vocation, and that the standard of criticism was not discouragingly high."

11 It is printed in *Poetical Works*, IV, 301–302. The Quakers refrain from using the conventional names for the days and the months, on the ground that they have a pagan or a mythological basis unsanctioned by Scripture. Whittier habitually dated his letters in the Quaker style, as, e.g., that of "28th of 11th mo., 1828," to A. W. Thayer. See Pickard, 67.

12 Pickard, 47–48, tells how Whittier received the news of his first appearance in print: "The paper came to him when he was with his father mending a stone wall by the roadside, picking up and placing the stones in position. As they were thus engaged, the postman passed them on horseback, and tossed the paper to the young man. His heart stood still a moment when he saw his own verses. Such delight as his comes only once in the lifetime of any aspirant to literary fame. His father at last called to him to put up the paper, and keep at work. But he could not resist the temptation to take the paper again and again from his pocket to stare at his lines in print. He has said he was sure that he did not read a word of the poem all the time he looked at it."

13 At that time Whittier was in his nineteenth year.

14 Cf. Pickard, 48.

15 The full story of Garrison's visit is told in Pickard, 48–49, and in *Whittier-Land*, 36–37.

16 Cf. *William Lloyd Garrison: The Story of His Life, Told by His Children* (New York, 1885), I, 67–68; Pickard, 1894 ed., I, 52.

17 *Ibid.*

18 *Newburyport Free Press*, Dec. 2, Aug. 3, Nov. 18, July 27, 1826.

19 *Ibid.*, Sept. 7, 1826.

20 *Ibid.*, Aug. 10, July 13, and Nov. 18, 1826.

21 *Ibid.*, Aug. 31, 1826.

22 *Ibid.*, Dec. 2, 1826.

23 Whittier was sensitive upon this score. In a letter from Amesbury dated Feb. 28, 1871, a photostat of which is in the Essex Institute, he said, ". . . I did not work at shoe-making except [for] some few experiments in the winter between 16 & 18." But the evidence is conclusive that he did make women's slippers, in a typical small shoeshop on the farm. Pickard mentioned the circumstances of that

work (p. 51), as did the earliest biographer, W. S. Kennedy (1), 49. Kennedy's authority was Moses Emerson, one of Whittier's former teachers in the district school. F. H. Underwood, whose biography was written with Whittier's approval, also spoke (p. 68) of his shoemaking. Likewise, Rebecca I. Davis, in *Gleanings from Merrimac Valley*, Sheaf Number Two (Haverhill, 1886), 15–16, reported these remarks of her uncle, who was foreman of the shop for which Whittier did piecework: "Upon his first entrance I was strongly attracted by his honest, open countenance and manly bearing, and as the employer was somewhat loth to give out work to beginners, I took special pains to make every suggestion of improvement in my power, and he obtained employment as long as he wished."

24 *Rules of Discipline of the Yearly Meeting, Held on Rhode Island, for New England*, 127: "It is the renewed concern of this meeting, to recommend a care for the offspring of parents, whose earnings or income are so small, as to render them incapable of giving their children a suitable and guarded education. . . ."

25 In 1826 two maiden ladies of the town gave a half acre of land on the north side of what is now Winter Street as the site for an academy. Other interested citizens provided the money for the erection of the building. Chase, *History of Haverhill*, 496; *Haverhill Gazette*, Jan. 6, 1827.

26 See Appendix C.

27 The *Haverhill Gazette* was first issued on Jan. 6, 1821. On Feb. 1, 1823, it absorbed the old Democratic *Essex Patriot*, which had been started by Nathaniel Greene. He was later postmaster of Boston and he founded the *American* (Boston) *Statesman*, forerunner of the present-day *Boston Post*. After several changes of title, the *Haverhill Gazette* resumed that title on Jan. 7, 1837, and retains it today. I have used the name uniformly in this book.

28 Pickard, 50.

29 Albert L. Bartlett, *Some Memories of Old Haverhill* (Haverhill, 1915), 88–89; *Haverhill Gazette*, May 5, 1827; *Whittier-Land*, 7. In a letter of March 17, 1890, addressed to Mr. Bartlett and now in the possession of HPL, Whittier said: "I do not know where a copy of the Ode referred to can be found, and I feel very sure it would poorly repay any effort to recover it. My impression is that it would not add to the honorable record of the Academy."

The dedicatory address at the exercises was made by the Honorable Leverett Saltonstall (Harvard 1802), of Salem, a lawyer and a member of Congress.

30 See Appendix C.

31 From a broadside *Catalogue of the Officers and Students of Haverhill Academy* (Haverhill, 1827), now owned by HPL.

32 Pickard, 50, 54–55.

33 Kennedy (2), 52–53; Underwood, 73–74.

34 Whittier, *Poetical Works*, II, 105. The first line correctly should read, "Where deed or word hath rendered less."

35 Quoted in Underwood, 75–78.

36 *Catalogue of Officers & Students of Haverhill Academy;* Pickard, 51.

37 Underwood, 73; Kennedy (2), 50 ff.

38 "A Retrospect," *Whittier-Land*, 35.

39 In a letter of Nov. 10, 1875, now in the possession of the HPL, addressed to Mayor Alpheus Currier of Haverhill on the occasion of the dedication of the HPL.

40 Quoted in Pickard, 57–58.

41 *Whittier-Land*, 66.

42 *Poetical Works*, II, 95–98.

43 The Connecticut Historical Society has a letter from Whittier to Lydia H. Sigourney dated Jan. (11?) 1833, in which he says: "I have warm & deep & kind feelings. I believe there is not a particle of mysanthropy in my disposition: and I am more at peace with the whole world than myself, not that *I & myself* are much in the habit of quarrelling. But, I believe in the holy realities of friendship — pure — lofty — intellectual, — a communion of kindred affinities — of mental similitudes, — a redemption from the miserable fetters of human selfishness — a practical obedience to the beautiful injunction of our Common Friend — '*Love thy neighbor as thyself*.' I believe too, that the pure love which we feel for our friends, is a part & portion of that love which we owe & offer to our Creator, and is acceptable to him, inasmuch as it is offered not to the decaying elements of humanity, but to those brighter & holier attributes, which are of themselves the emanations of the Divinity, — to those pure emotions of the heart & those high capacities of the soul in which that Divinity is most clearly manifested; — and that, in proportion as we draw men to each other in the holy communion & unforbidden

love of earthly friendship, we lessen the distance between our spirits and their Original Source, — just as the radii of a circle in approaching each other approach also their common centre."

44 *Whittier-Land*, 66.

45 See Appendix C.

46 *Rules of Discipline of the Yearly Meeting, Held on Rhode Island, for New England*, 65: "This meeting having deliberately considered the great exercise brought upon our society, by divers in profession with us, who are joined in marriage contrary to our known principles, and the wholesome discipline established among us, with persons either of our own or other persuasions, doth earnestly advise that all friends use their utmost endeavors to prevent such marriages, whensoever the parties' inclinations may come to their knowledge.

"And it is the sense and judgment of this meeting, that where any do marry, contrary to the established rules of the society, they should be dealt with in a spirit of Christian love and tenderness, agreeably to our known discipline."

47 *Whittier-Land*, 69.

48 *Poetical Works*, II, 69.

49 Oak Knoll Collection, V, 25.

50 *Whittier-Land*, 70–71.

51 Despite Governor Lincoln, the Association came into being, and took rank with the Handel and Haydn Society, which dated from 1815 in Boston. *Grove's Dictionary of Music and Musicians* (London, 3rd ed., 1927), I, 425.

52 *Haverhill Gazette*, March 17.

53 *Ibid.*, April 28, and May 5.

54 *Ibid.*, May 12, 1827.

55 *Poetical Works*, I, 11.

56 *Haverhill Gazette*, May 19, 1827.

57 *Ibid.*, July 28 and Sept. 29, 1827.

58 Ulrich Bonnell Phillips, *American Negro Slavery* (New York, 1918), 118–121.

59 *Haverhill Gazette*, July 7 and Aug. 4, 1827.

60 Fields, 24–29, and *Harper's New Monthly Magazine*, LXXXVI, 344 ff. (Feb. 1893).

61 *Oldtown Folks*, p. 321: "In the eyes of the New England people, it [Boston] was always a sort of mother-town, — a sacred city, the shrine

of that religious enthusiasm which founded the States of New England. There were the graves of her prophets and her martyrs, — those who had given their lives through the hardships of that enterprise in so ungenial a climate."

62 *Rules of Discipline of the Yearly Meeting, Held on Rhode Island . . .*, 52: ". . . it is advised that a watchful care be exercised over our youth, to prevent their going to stage-plays, horse-races, entertainments of music and dancing, or any such vain sports and pastimes. . . ."

63 Fields, 26.

64 Pickard, 41–42.

65 Manuscript records of the Committee of School District No. 5, West Amesbury. The school over which Whittier presided was accommodated in a house on Birch Meadow Road. Remodeled, the house is now occupied by Mr. Willard T. Kelly.

66 Aug. 23, 1830.

67 Manuscript records of the Committee of School District No. 5.

68 It was republished in *A New Year's Address to the Patrons of the Essex Gazette, 1828, With a Letter Hitherto Unpublished, by John G. Whittier* (Boston, 1903).

69 Chase, *History of Haverhill*, 634–635.

70 *Ibid.*, 498–499.

71 Whether or not he attended was not reported at the time.

72 Pickard, 92.

73 Mordell's statement that Whittier edited Dinsmoor's poems and wrote the preface to the book is open to doubt. The matter is covered in detail in J. A. Pollard, *Whittier's Early Years, 1807–1836* (Yale Ph.D. dissertation, 1937), 119–120.

74 *Boston Statesman*, May 1 and 3, June 14, 1828.

75 *Haverhill Gazette*, July 12 and Feb. 9, 1828.

76 *Ibid.*, Aug. 30, 1828.

77 *Ibid.*, Oct. 4 and 11, 1828.

78 Pickard, 64.

79 *Ibid.*, 67–68

80 Oak Knoll Collection, IV, 74. The letter is dated "28th Sept." from Danvers, and so is obviously of the year 1876 or later. It is addressed simply to "My friend."

81 Pickard, 506.

82 *Prose Works*, I, 348.

83 Pickard, 67.
84 See 41.
85 Carpenter, 300. Garrison, who was soon responsible for Whittier's entering anti-slavery work, was himself brought into it by the Quaker editor, Benjamin Lundy. See Garrison's editorial, Dec. 12, 1828, in the Bennington *Journal of the Times*.

## CHAPTER IV

1 Pickard, 67–68.
2 See Currier, 443. Thayer in the *Haverhill Gazette* of Jan. 3, 1829, wished Whittier success as joint editor of the *Philanthropist* and the *Manufacturer*. Two weeks later he printed a correction.
3 In its first issue, Aug. 29, 1828, the *Manufacturer* carried this editorial announcement: "This Paper will be devoted to the interests of Domestic Manufactures, and will be adapted to the wants of those residing in Manufacturing towns and villages. It will contain a great variety of Political, Religious, Moral, Literary and Practical information, with a copious summary of Intelligence, Foreign and Domestic. . . . Upon political questions the MANUFACTURER will always act with the friends of the American System. * * *"
4 Frank W. Taussig, *The Tariff History of the United States* (New York and London, 6th ed., 1914), 35.
5 *Ibid.*, 72. In 1824 Daniel Webster opposed passage of the tariff bill; in 1828 he adopted the protective theory. He defended his conversion as "a change of position to meet new circumstances." Claude Moore Fuess, *Daniel Webster* (Boston, 1930), I, 352–354, 377.
6 Vernon Louis Parrington, *The Romantic Revolution in America, 1800–1860* (New York, 1927), 242.
7 Pickard, 114.
8 *The Boston Directory* . . . (Boston: Charles Stimpson, Jr., 1829), 71, 331; Pickard, 73.
9 James Melvin Lee, *History of American Journalism* (Boston and New York, 1923), 133, 154–155; *Dictionary of American Biography*, *passim.*
10 See note 2, *supra*. The contents of the two Collier papers were sometimes so interchangeable as to suggest one editorial head in command.
11 Aug. 9 and 30, 1828.
12 Jan. 1, Feb. 12, Jan. 8, and March 5.

13 See Pickard, 775–785.
14 *American Manufacturer*, March 12, 1829.
15 *Haverhill Gazette*, Feb. 3, 1827.
16 *New England Weekly Review*, March 16; *American Manufacturer*, March 26, 1829.
17 The set of Burke's *Works* (Boston, 6 vol., 1806) in the library of the Whittier home at Amesbury is the most heavily marked of all the books there. The passage here quoted (III, 174) is among the many in the *Reflections* which have been pencilled in Whittier's fine hand. When he could have acquired the set of Burke is conjectural. On the title page of vol. I is the signature of Richard L. Coxe.
In the passage quoted, *nactus* is possibly a misprint for *natus*.
18 Jan. 22 and 29, Feb. 19, 1829.
19 Jan. 22, 1829.
20 April 2, 1829.
21 *American Manufacturer*, May 14 and 21, June 4, 1829.
22 April 2, 9, 16, and 23, 1829.
23 C. R. Fish, *The Rise of the Common Man, 1830–1850*, 164.
24 *American Manufacturer*, June 25, 1829.
25 Charles A. and Mary R. Beard, *The Rise of American Civilization* (New York, 1-vol. ed., 1930), I, 641–642.
26 Paragraph two of "Mechanics," *American Manufacturer*, Feb. 19, 1829.
27 Lucia Gray Swett, *John Ruskin's Letters to Francesca and Memoirs of the Alexanders* (Boston, 1931), 417. Letter now in HUL (Houghton).
28 A few of these included "To a Cousin," July 16, and "To ——," July 23, 1829, in the *Manufacturer;* "To My Cousin" and "To Mary," *Boston Courier*, June 9 and 13, 1829; and "To S.E.M.," *New England Weekly Review*, Sept. 14, 1829.
29 Mentioned in *American Manufacturer*, May 14 and 21, 1829.
30 *American Monthly Magazine*, I, 360 (Aug., 1829).
31 Pickard, 78–79.
32 In an account book of Bartlett, Gage and Company, Haverhill merchants, now owned by the Haverhill Historical Society, Whittier is credited with the sum of $5.40 for shoe binding in the period ending Aug. 31, 1829. This sum was part of a total credit of $78.40 allowed him for "labor" between June 8 and Aug. 31. It is possible that this labor was performed by John Whittier, who in the past had done shoe binding; but in view of his reported ill health, and his

death on June 11, 1830, this seems doubtful. The fact that Bartlett and Gage carried the account in John G. Whittier's name suggests that he was probably now acting as head of the family. He was credited by Bartlett and Gage with $21.93 for "labor" between Sept. 7 and Oct. 20, and was several times debited for merchandise.

33 John Neal, *Wandering Recollections of a Somewhat Busy Life* (Boston, 1869), 337.

34 Oak Knoll Collection, V, 1.

35 Poems "The Raven," Oct. 15, and "To a Friend," Sept. 3, 1829.

36 *Haverhill Gazette*, Aug. 22 and 29, 1829.

37 In a signed editorial on Dec. 26, 1829, Thayer said: "I have conducted the editorial department of this Gazette nearly three years; and with this number, resign that charge for the present, to our townsman, John Greenleaf Whittier. And in doing this, I feel gratified in being able to announce to the public, that the Essex Gazette is placed under the direction of a gentleman so abundantly competent to render it interesting, without reference to its locality, as well to distant readers, as to those in our own vicinity. * * *"

38 *Haverhill Gazette*, Jan. 2, 1830. In the first line of the second stanza Whittier speaks of his last year as "the first of manhood's years." He became twenty-two on Dec. 17, 1829.

39 Whittier returned to this subject in the *New England Weekly Review* of Dec. 6, 1830. Under head of "Parties," he said, in sum: "We are tired of the eternal cant of old party names. The time has been when these names signified something. They were signs of things — the rallying words of *principles*. It is not so now. . . ."

40 *Haverhill Gazette*, Feb. 27, 1830.

41 Whittier had attentively read Burke's remarks on the French Revolution, as the carefully marked set of Burke in the library of the home at Amesbury attests.

Whittier had printed an editorial on Infidelity in the *American Manufacturer* of Feb. 19, 1829.

42 In a review of vol. 2 of Moore's life of Byron, Whittier, in the *New England Weekly Review* of Feb. 14, 1831, called the book "pernicious" in its tendency because it exposed with "the most unscrupulous fidelity" the licentiousness of Byron's correspondence. Yet Whittier restated his admiration, "almost worship, [of] the sublimity of Byron's genius." Whittier many times repeated these sentiments, as in "The

Nervous Man," *New England Magazine*, Aug., 1832, and in his memoir included in his edition of *The Literary Remains of John G. C. Brainard* (Hartford, 1832), 36.

43 In September, 1832, it reappeared, signed as Whittier's, in the *Boston Literary Magazine;* and it was also included, as by Whittier, in J. Prince's *A Wreath for St. Crispin* (Boston, 1848), 209–210.

44 Whittier republished the tale, which "we plead guilty to the charge of writing . . . ," in the *New England Weekly Review* of July 26, 1830, in order to correct typographical errors.

45 *Haverhill Gazette*, April 10, 17, and 24, May 1 and 15.

46 Oak Knoll Collection, vol. I.

## CHAPTER V

1 His will, on file at the Probate and Insolvency Courts of Essex County, Salem, listed 185 acres of real estate valued at $2273.50, and personal estate appraised at $624.25. Debts amounted to $1391.25. Under the provisions of the will, Abigail Whittier was in December, 1830, empowered by the Court to sell real estate to the value of $800 in order to make settlement.

2 In the *Haverhill Gazette* of Jan. 23, 1830, Whittier mentioned his kindly reception by fellow editors. On Jan. 18 and March 8, Prentice lauded him in the *New England Weekly Review*. Whittier was commended also by N. P. Willis in the February issue of the *American Monthly Magazine*, by the *New York Amulet* on April 17, and by the *Philadelphia Album* — an old admirer of his — on May 8.

3 The circumstances leading up to Whittier's appointment as editor of the *Review* are treated fully by T. Franklin Currier in "Whittier and the *New England Weekly Review*," the *New England Quarterly*, VI, 589–597 (Sept., 1933).

4 See Appendix C.

5 S. G. Goodrich, *Recollections of a Lifetime* (New York and Auburn, 1856), I, 436.

6 *The Memorial History of Hartford County, Connecticut, 1633–1884*, ed. J. Hammond Trumbull (Boston, 1886), I, 614–615.

7 See Appendix C.

8 Sarah Gertrude Pomeroy, "Whittier in Connecticut — Centenary of Birth of American Poet," *Connecticut Magazine*, XI, 571 (1907).

9 *Memorial History of Hartford County, Connecticut*, I, 614–615.
10 Oak Knoll Collection, V, 17.
11 Pomeroy, *op. cit.*, 571–572.
12 In an interview published in the *Boston Daily Advertiser*, Dec. 16, 1891, on the eve of his last birthday.
13 Pickard, 82.
14 *Ibid.*
15 Claude G. Bowers, *The Party Battles of the Jackson Period* (Boston: Houghton Mifflin Co., 1922), 31.
16 Whittier requested repeatedly that credit be given if his works were recopied. On Oct. 4, 1830, he wrote: "If our articles are worth copying they may as well be credited to us. The 'Quilting Party,' 'Gertrude,' &c. &c. are ours, let them be *editorialized* where they will."
17 It is a curiosity that in the *American Manufacturer* of April 9, 1829, the always abstemious Whittier editorialized on "Cultivation of the Vine." He recommended a Mr. Bernard's treatise on the cultivation of the grapevine, and suggested that this industry was a logical one for promotion in warm parts of the United States.
18 The succeeding four appeared on Aug. 9 and 16, Sept. 6 and 20, 1830.
19 In the letter of 1829 referred to on p. 93 *ante*, Whittier said, among other things: "I have become a notable fellow in gallantry of late; I mean old-fashioned gallantry, however. I have given my whiskers a more ferocious appearance, and take the liberty of frightening into good nature those who will not be complaisant of their own accord."

Pickard (p. 71 n.) says that Whittier's correspondent sent this letter to him more than thirty years after it was written, and received this reply, dated Amesbury, Jan. 2, 1860: "I was about as much surprised to read that old letter of my boyhood as if I had seen the ghost of my former self. It was a very absurd and ridiculous epistle, — and the utter folly of it is more striking from the fact that at that very time I was in reality a shy, timid recluse, afraid of a shadow, especially the shadow of a woman. There is a period in life — a sort of tadpole state, between the boy and the man — when any sort of pretense, egotism, and self-conceit may be expected."
20 In the *Review* Whittier frequently championed Clay and the American System, as on Sept. 6 and Oct. 25, 1830, and on March 14 and 28, 1831. The last-dated editorial, "To the Friends of the American System in Connecticut," was one page long, in three wide columns.

On Aug. 16, 1830, Whittier defended himself against the charge by the *Catskill Recorder* — his one *bête noire* — of insincerity in advocating Clay.

21 In a letter written from Haverhill on March 5, 1831, and published in the *New England Weekly Review* of March 14, Whittier said, in part: "Mr. Cushing is the most popular candidate for Congress and I trust he will be elected at the next trial. The Editor of the Essex Gazette — an old and tried friend of mine — is opposed to Mr. C. — and, as you doubtless recollect, took me to task somewhat sharply for speaking in his favor. He calls my remarks 'pretty' and 'poetical.' — Thank him. I value his opinion upon such subjects as highly as I should that of a Block Islander in favor of my gentility."

22 This argument was a collision of immovable forces. Whittier had perhaps acquired some of Thayer's habit of firm opinions, which both men, as reformers, had. In the *Haverhill Gazette* of April 9, 1831, Thayer spoke of ". . . the political delinquency, the constitutional selfishness and meanness, and above all, the surpassing depravity" of Cushing. On June 25 he called Cushing "a *talking* man," and compared him to Aaron Burr.

23 "John C. Calhoun," *New England Weekly Review*, Feb. 14, 1831.

24 Oct. 25, 1830.

25 As, e.g., in *New England Weekly Review* of Nov. 14, 1831.

26 Jan. 24 and 31, Feb. 7, 1831.

27 Aug. 23 and Dec. 6, 1830.

28 *Whittier-Land*, 77.

29 Pickard (p. 89) assigns pp. 102–116, 254–261, and probably the first note in the Appendix to Whittier. Currier (pp. 12–16), surmises that Whittier probably wrote about forty pages in all.

30 Pickard, 87. The three-day-a-week service of the *Hudson* was advertised in the *New York Evening Post*, Jan. 3, 1831. Whittier reported the trip in "A Night in Long Island Sound," *New England Weekly Review*, Jan. 31, 1831.

31 HUL (Houghton).

32 HUL (Houghton).

33 Pickard, 92.

34 Rourke, *American Humor: A Study of the National Character* (New York: Harcourt, Brace & Co., 1931), 227.

35 March 19, 1831.

36 Another with this title appeared in the *New England Weekly Review* on Aug. 29, 1831.
37 C. R. Fish, *The Rise of the Common Man*, 281 ff.
38 *Whittier-Land*, 43–44.
39 Pp. 33–34; *New England Weekly Review*, Jan. 10, 1831.
40 Feb. 7, 1831.
41 *New England Weekly Review*, March 21, 1831. This letter was written in Haverhill, where Whittier was resting for his health. Barnard served as temporary editor of the *Review*. John Fulton, *Memoirs of Frederick A. P. Barnard* (New York, 1896), 50–51.
42 Seven years younger than Whittier, she lived from 1814 to 1842.
43 Whittier at this time was considering the offer of an editorship in Cincinnati, Ohio.
44 Letter now in possession of Connecticut Historical Society.
45 Whittier sent Dr. Crane back to Hartford with this note, dated Oct. 27, 1831, to Jonathan Law: "You have got Dr. Crane — but for me, I am off to Salem — notwithstanding the doctor's pledge to return with me 'hale and breathing' or with my bones neatly done up in his traveling trunk — I shall probably see Hartford in the course of a week or ten days." HUL (Houghton).
46 Oak Knoll Collection, III, 1.
47 Cf. *Prose Works*, I, 202–203: "In the midst of duties and responsibilities which I clearly comprehended, I found myself yielding to the absorbing egotism of sickness."
48 He said, in part: "I have endeavored to make the NEW ENGLAND REVIEW the vehicle of correct and honorable principles. I have indeed entered into the political discussions of the day with zeal and sincerity. . . . I have been accused of undue severity of remark — a want of political charity. I have certainly spoken plainly."
49 HUL (Houghton).
50 Concluding lines of Whittier's poem printed in *Haverhill Gazette*, Aug. 25, 1827. "Mine" originally read "thine."
51 Lines unidentified in Fitz-Greene Halleck's *Poetical Works*, eds. of 1847, 1854, 1865, or 1869.
52 Manuscript letter in Connecticut Historical Society, Hartford. Letter of Feb. 4 is in HUL (Houghton).
53 In an article, "Treason in the Camp."
54 Oak Knoll Collection, V, 4.

55 *Boston Daily Advertiser*, Dec. 16, 1891. Judge Cate occupied the Whittier home in Amesbury while the poet, much of the time from 1876 onward, lived with his Johnson cousins at Oak Knoll, Danvers.

56 First brought out on Oct. 22, 1831, by Whittier's friend Edwin Harriman. In its politics it was National Republican.

57 W. C. Bryant, *Prose Writings of William Cullen Bryant*, Parke Godwin, ed. (New York, 1884), II, 410.

58 In a letter written late in 1831 to Harriman, Whittier said: "Did you ever read Burke's speeches and writings? If not, read them attentively. They will prove valuable to you, as they have to me." Pickard, 163.

59 The dates were Sept. 8, 15, 29, and Oct. 6. Whittier mentioned the series in a letter to M. E. Smith (HUL — Houghton). In the *Gazette* of Oct. 6, Thayer identified Whittier in name by printing his name at the head of "the following just tribute to our worthy and distinguished townsman," from the Hartford *American Mercury*. The *Mercury* said that "few editors have been more extensively quoted than Mr. Whittier."

60 At the heart of Whittier's many strictures upon Jacksonism lay this passage marked by him in Burke's *Appeal*, III, 418–419: "Great discontents frequently arise in the best-constituted governments, from causes which no human wisdom can foresee, and no human power can prevent. . . . The indecision of those who happen to rule at the critical time, their supine neglect, or their precipitate and ill-judged attention, may aggravate the publick misfortunes. In such a state of things, the principles, now only sown, will shoot out and vegetate in full luxuriance. In such circumstances the minds of the people become sore and ulcerated. They are put out of humor with all publick men, and all publick parties; they are fatigued with their dissensions; they are irritated at their coalitions; they are made easily to believe (what much pains are taken to make them believe) that all oppositions are factious, and all courtiers base and servile. From their disgust at men, they are soon led to quarrel with their frame of government, which they presume gives nourishment to the vices, real or supposed, of those who administer it. Mistaking malignity for sagacity, they are soon led to cast off all hope from a good administration of affairs, and come to think that all reformation depends, not on the change of actors, but upon an alteration in the machinery."

61 Note a passage in Burke's *Appeal*, III, 427, marked by Whittier: "Such admirers were our fathers, to whom we owe this splendid inheritance. Let us improve it with zeal, but with fear. Let us follow our ancestors, men not without a rational, though without an exclusive confidence in themselves; who, by respecting the reason of others, who, by looking backward as well as forward, by the modesty as well as by the energy of their minds, went on, insensibly drawing this constitution nearer and nearer to its perfection, by never departing from its fundamental principles, nor introducing any amendment which had not a subsisting root in the laws, constitution, and usages of the kingdom."

62 Note a marked passage in Burke's *Reflections on the Revolution in France*, III, 186: "The true lawgiver ought to have a heart full of sensibility. He ought to love and respect his kind, and to fear himself. It may be allowed to his temperament to catch his ultimate object with an intuitive glance; but his movements toward it ought to be deliberate. Political arrangement, as it is a work for social ends, is to be only wrought by social means. There mind must conspire with mind. Time is required to produce that union of minds which alone can produce all the good we aim at. Our patience will produce more than our force."

63 This was merely the common party of all elements opposed to Jackson.

64 Printed in *Journal of the Proceedings of the National Republican Convention . . ., October 11, 1832* (Boston, 1832), 35–40, 9–43 [pagination imperfect].

65 Claude M. Fuess, *The Life of Caleb Cushing* (New York, 1923), I, 128–129.

66 Dr. Joseph Kittredge, of Andover, was one of the various candidates who at one time or another opposed Cushing.

67 John Merrill, of Newbury.

68 Edward C. Purdy, editor of the *Lowell Journal* in 1832–1833.

69 Probably the *Gloucester Telegraph*, published by William E. P. Rogers.

70 Published in Salem by Warwick Palfray, Jr.

71 Pickard, 168–169.

72 Cf. Higginson, 43.

73 "The Missionary," *Poetical Works*, IV, 354.

74 His friend Allen W. Dodge seems to have interviewed New York

publishers in his behalf. Dodge reported to Whittier by letter dated Feb. 18, 1832. Oak Knoll Collection, V, 3.

75 In an article, "Matrimony," in the *New England Weekly Review* of Aug. 22, 1831, Whittier said: "And what is marriage after all! — A leap in the dark — a launching out upon an untried ocean. . . . Marriage too often takes place before the parties have been able fully to understand each other. Call money if you please 'the root of all evil.' In the present state of society, it is the very mainspring of existence. . . . Love, without it, is but a beautiful delusion. . . . It is an old, but we fear a true saying, 'When Poverty comes in at the door Love goes out at the window.' "

76 The facts are set forth in a manuscript letter written by Whittier on December 21, 1887, now in Sterling Memorial Library, Yale University; another letter by Whittier, now in Haverhill Public Library written to Albert L. Bartlett, of Haverhill, March 17, 1890; and a fragment of an undated letter, possibly written by S. T. Pickard, also in Haverhill Public Library. Cf. Currier, 18–20.

77 Carpenter, 84; Currier, 19–20.

78 Whittier was familiar with the Moll Pitcher story as contained in Alonzo Lewis, *History of Lynn* (Boston, 1829), 207–208, whence he probably derived it. Cf. Mordell, 35.

79 Oct. 18, 1830. The poem is reprinted in *Whittier-Land*, 131–133.

80 Letter of May 7, 1832, from Whittier to Samuel Hanmer, Jr. Original now in Huntington Library; photostatic copy in Essex Institute.

81 Two other letters, from the publishers to Whittier, regarding it are in the Oak Knoll Collection, V, 6, 7.

82 HUL (Houghton).

83 *Literary Remains of John G. C. Brainard*, 35–36.

84 Manuscript letter from Whittier to Samuel Hanmer, Jr., and P. B. Goodsell, dated Haverhill, Oct. 11, 1832. Now in Connecticut Historical Society.

85 Published unsigned in the *Iris*. Comment by Pickard, 105–109.

86 See Whittier's sketch, "William Leggett," *Prose Works*, II, 184–215.

## CHAPTER VI

1 Channing, *Memoir*, III, 244.

2 Fish, *The Rise of the Common Man, 1830–1850*, 257, 258, 262.

3 *Ibid.*, 275.
4 *Carpenter*, 300.
5 *William Lloyd Garrison: The Story of His Life*, II, 215.
6 See A. B. Hart, *Slavery and Abolition, 1831–1841*, chs. 12 and 17; and G. H. Barnes, *The Antislavery Impulse, 1830–1844*, chs. 5, 8, and 9.
7 Barnes, chs. 6 and 7, pp. 57–58, 81, 85–86, 98, 99, and 13. Barnes rejects the accepted notion that Garrison was the real leader of the movement, as well as statements that the clergy in general opposed it. Barnes sees Abolition as merely one aspect of the Great Revival and the humanitarian impulse of the 1830's.
8 *Prose Works*, I, 92.
9 HUL (Houghton).
10 Connecticut Historical Society. Part of this letter is quoted on p. 100.
11 Whittier, on his part, had been attentive to Garrison. On April 17, 1830, Garrison was imprisoned in Baltimore for libelous remarks, in the *Genius of Universal Emancipation*, about a Newburyport shipmaster who had carried a cargo of slaves. Garrison was unable to pay the amount of the judgment against him, and he lay seven weeks in prison. Whittier, as he explained in a letter of March 14, 1864, to the editor of the *Boston Transcript*, wrote to Henry Clay requesting his help in liberating Garrison. Clay replied that he had learned through his friend Hezekiah Niles, of Baltimore, that Garrison had already been set free. Clay's intended help had been anticipated by Arthur Tappan, the wealthy New York humanitarian, who had authorized Benjamin Lundy to draw upon him to the extent of $100 to effect Garrison's release. See *Life* of Garrison, I, 171, 189–190; Underwood, 107–108. In the *Haverhill Gazette* of May 29, 1830, Whittier published an editorial deploring Garrison's imprisonment.

In the *American Manufacturer* of April 2, 1829, Whittier praised Garrison's work as editor of the Bennington *Journal of the Times*, and his course in resigning that charge to "devote his services to the cause of universal liberty. . . . A bolder pen never portrayed the evils of slavery, and a better or a kinder heart never throbbed with sympathy for the sufferings of humanity."
12 *Life* of Garrison, I, 331, 332; quotation in Rufus M. Jones, *The Later Periods of Quakerism*, II, 651; report, apparently by A. W. Thayer, in *Haverhill Gazette*, April 6, 1833.

13 Letter of May 2, 1870, to Lewis Tappan, now in Library of Congress.
14 *Prose Works*, III, 31.
15 *Ibid.*, III, 11 ff.
16 See Appendix D. Whittier perhaps derived his argument against colonization, in *Justice and Expediency*, from Benjamin Lundy. *Life* of Garrison, I, 97. Underwood (p. 112) says that the final words in the pamphlet originated with William Penn.
17 It was reviewed in the *Newburyport Herald* on May 27, 1833; in the *Lynn Record* (notice copied in *Haverhill Gazette* on June 1); in the *Liberator* on June 22; and in the *Haverhill Gazette* on July 6. In *Prose Works*, II, 219, Whittier wrote that N. P. Rogers, New Hampshire editor and Abolitionist, was one of the few people who voiced encouragement and sympathy to him upon the appearance of *Justice and Expediency*.
18 Whittier's letter of May 2, 1870, to Lewis Tappan, now in Library of Congress.
19 Pickard, 124; Underwood, 112. Whittier was acquainted with Moses Brown, and later in life told of having read to him the speech of the British Prime Minister concerning the passage of the Emancipation Act for the British possessions. Rayner W. Kelsey, *Centennial History of Moses Brown School, 1819–1919* (Providence, 1919), 32.
The most telling of the anti-slavery tracts, after Mrs. Stowe's *Uncle Tom's Cabin*, is said to have been Theodore Dwight Weld's *Slavery As It Is*. See G. H. Barnes, 139 and note.
20 Cf. Whittier, *Prose Works*, III, 58. No copies of this issue appear to exist.
21 *Prose Works*, III, 58–86.
22 *Haverhill Gazette*, July 6, 1833; A. B. Hart, 245.
23 Quoted by Pickard, 132.
24 The farm was now slightly smaller than John Whittier had left it. On Dec. 15, 1832, seven of the 185 acres were sold to Jacob Caldwell, who in 1828 had married Whittier's sister Mary. The deed of this sale, which brought $330, is now in possession of Haverhill Historical Society.
25 Pickard, 131.
26 In the *New England Magazine* of June 1, 1835, p. 492, the editors apologized for the low rate of pay to contributing authors: one dollar a page for prose, two dollars a page for verse.

27 *Poetical Works*, III, 11.
28 *Ibid.*, I, 17.
29 *Ibid.*, IV, 11. Storrs, president of old Western Reserve College at Hudson, Ohio, had been one of the anti-slavery leaders in the West.
30 An interesting critical notice of Whittier's poetry appeared in the *Shrine*, of Amherst College, in July, 1833. The writer, "M. M.," evidently an undergraduate with a rather mature attitude toward poetry, found in Whittier's work vigorous versification, an occupation with the emotions and passions of the mind, correct and fresh language, and an understanding of nature. The critic regretted, however, Whittier's tendency to delineate "the darker feelings of the human heart." He ended with this paragraph: "It is to Whittier, in our opinion, that the American public ought to look for a long and elaborate poem, which may redeem the poetical profligacy of our poets; and we trust that he will be induced to commence one, for we believe that there is no one — and we except not the poets of high name among us — who would succeed so well."
31 *Haverhill Gazette*, Sept. 14, Oct. 4, 1833.
32 *Ibid.*, Nov. 16, 1833. It was reported that the Administration candidates received votes ranging between 226 and 256, as against 178 to 198 for the men on the National Republican ticket. In a letter of Nov. 12 (now in Boston Public Library), Whittier told Garrison that "at the late Convention for the nomination of Senators for Essex, my nomination was lost by one vote."
33 The convention is described in G. H. Barnes, 53–56 and *passim;* Pickard, 132–136; Garrison, *Life*, I, 394–399; and Whittier, *Prose Works*, III, 171–186.
34 Boston Public Library.
35 Whittier, *Prose Works*, III, 180–184.
36 The British compensated their slaveholders for the emancipation decreed by Parliament in 1833.
37 *Declaration of the National Anti-Slavery Convention*, signed in Adelphi Hall, in the City of Philadelphia, on the sixth day of December, A.D., 1833.
38 *Prose Works*, III, 147.
39 Reported in the *Liberator*, Dec. 21, 1833.
40 On Jan. 4, 1834, Garrison started printing in the *Liberator* a column entitled "Refuge of Oppression." In this were republished deroga-

tory articles from journals north and south, such as the *New York Commercial Advertiser*, the *New York Courier & Enquirer*, the *New York Standard*, the *Boston Commercial Gazette*, the *Philadelphia Commercial Intelligencer*, the Washington *National Intelligencer*, the *New Bedford Gazette*, the *Worcester Aegis & Yeoman*, the *Portsmouth* (N.H.) *Journal*, the *Saco* (Me.) *Democrat*, and others.

41 *Whittier as a Politician*, ed. Pickard, 47.

42 *Prose Works*, III, 87.

43 *Address before the Anti-Slavery Society of Salem and the Vicinity*, Feb. 24, 1834, by Cyrus Pitt Grosvenor (Salem, 1834), 42–43. Whittier's writing of this letter is clearly established by internal evidence.

44 Published in the *Liberator*, Oct. 11, 1834.

45 Whittier possibly invaded even the columns of the *Newburyport Herald*, despite the anti-Abolition attitude of its editors. On May 6, 10, and 16, 1834, the *Herald* published a series of articles by "A Member of the Haverhill Anti-Slavery Society." In them the point of view, style of argumentation, and citations are much the same as in the anti-slavery arguments which Whittier was contributing to the *Haverhill Gazette*.

46 *Whittier as a Politician*, 47–51. Quoted by permission of Charles E. Goodspeed.

47 *The Anti-Slavery Impulse, 1830–1844*, 63.

48 *Haverhill Gazette*, March 1, 1834. Bacon (1802–1881), minister of First Church, New Haven, was one of the leading Congregational clergymen of Connecticut. Whittier was unduly severe upon him, for since 1823 Bacon had written and spoken forcefully against slavery. *Dictionary of American Biography* (New York, 1928), I, 481.

49 Letter in Pickard, 137–138. Cf. Mordell, 73. In Channing's *Memoir*, ch. IV, he tells of his gradual approach to Abolitionism, makes no mention of Whittier or his letter.

50 *Dictionary of American Biography* (New York, 1930), IV, 4–7.

51 *Prose Works*, II, 321–347.

52 On April 26, 1834, the *Liberator* published a one-column letter written by a member of the New England Yearly Meeting of the Society of Friends, urging this group against the support of colonization, and advocating its active support of Abolition. Whittier's hand is plain in the letter. On April 16 he wrote a similar appeal to the Friends; it appeared in the *American Anti-Slavery Reporter*, New York, Aug. 1834.

53 Pickard, 173.
54 Fuess, *The Life of Caleb Cushing*, I, 156–157; Pickard, 173–174.
55 Carpenter, 202–203.
56 *Ibid.*
57 *Poetical Works*, III, 24.
58 *Ibid.*, III, 19.
59 This and other gift books are described by Ralph Thompson, "The *Liberty Bell* and Other Anti-Slavery Gift-Books," the *New England Quarterly*, VII, 154–168 (March, 1934).
60 *Poetical Works*, IV, 9.
61 *Haverhill Gazette*, April 5, 1834.
62 The *Liberator*, April 19, 1834.
63 *Address to the People of the United States, by a Committee of the New-England Anti-Slavery Convention, Held in Boston on the 27th, 28th and 29th of May, 1834.* 16 pp. (Boston, 1834).
64 The *Liberator*, June 14, 1834.
65 *Ibid.*, June 21. After this meeting the tireless Whittier wrote a report which was published over the signature "W." in the *Haverhill Gazette* on June 21 and in the *Liberator* on July 5.
66 *The Anti-Slavery Impulse, 1830–1844*, 110.

## CHAPTER VII

1 The *Salem Landmark*, e.g., on Sept. 12, 1835, published a letter protesting against the Abolitionists and their activities.
2 *Haverhill Gazette*, Nov. 15, 1834. A. W. Thayer rejoiced over the first local success of the Whigs in five or six years, even over Caleb Cushing's election to Congress. At this time Robert Rantoul, with whom Whittier was to live in Boston, was chosen a State Representative from Gloucester.
3 *Boston Daily Advertiser*, Dec. 16, 1891.
4 C. R. Fish, 286.
5 State of Massachusetts, Archives Division. *Journal of the House of Representatives.* Sept. 2 to Nov. 4, 1835.
6 *Journal of the House . . .*, Jan. 7, 1835.
7 *Essex Institute Historical Collections*, XXXVII, 132–133 (April, 1901).
8 Oak Knoll Collection, vol. I.
9 The *Liberator*, Jan. 31, May 30, 1835; Feb. 7, 21, and 28.

10 *Poetical Works*, III, 30.
11 February, 1835.
12 *Poetical Works*, III, 35.
13 *The Romantic Revolution in America* . . . , 340, 350.
14 Garrison, *Life*, I, 441–442.
15 *Dictionary of American Biography*, VI, 491.
16 The *New York Commercial Advertiser*, e.g. (reported in *Haverhill Gazette*, Oct. 24, 1835), charged that Thompson had been dismissed by London employers for embezzlement, and from a scientific expedition to Botany Bay. G. H. Barnes, 63 and notes.
17 *Haverhill Gazette*, Jan. 17, June 13, 1835.
18 Manuscript diary of Elizabeth Whittier, in Whittier home at Amesbury. Cf. Pickard, 144.
19 Pickard, 145.
20 She was an Abolitionist. On June 6, 1835, the *Haverhill Gazette* reported her election as secretary of the Haverhill Female Anti-Slavery Society. She also wrote Abolitionist verses, such as "The Slave Trader" and "Our Countrymen," which appeared in the *Gazette* on March 21 and Aug. 22, 1835, respectively, and "To George Thompson," which the *Liberator* published on Oct. 8, 1836.
21 Fields, 44.
22 Cf. Pickard, 147–148; Albert L. Bartlett, *Some Memories of Old Haverhill* (Haverhill, 1915), 18–19.
23 Two of Daniel Webster's nieces were said to be at the Kent house at this time. Underwood, 117.
24 Pickard, 150 n.
25 Deacon Amos Giles was a prominent distiller of Salem, Mass.
26 Milton, Sonnet XII, lines 3–4. The third line reads, correctly: "When strait a barbarous noise environs me."
27 *Poetical Works*, III, 110.
28 Pickard, 191.
29 *Ibid.*, 153. Regarding the Concord riot, cf. Pickard, 151–152, and Underwood, 117–118.
30 *The Correspondence of Thomas Carlyle and Ralph Waldo Emerson, 1834–1872* (Boston, 1883), I, 84–85.
31 Copy of 9″ × 12″ handbill tipped in front of vol. V of the *Liberator* at the Massachusetts Historical Society.
32 Garrison, *Life*, II, 11, 34.

33 Whittier, *Prose Works*, III, 191.

34 The full story of this riot is given in Garrison, *Life*, II, 11 ff., and in Underwood, 121–122.

35 *Poetical Works*, IV, 325.

36 George Folsom, *The History of Saco and Biddeford* . . . (Saco, 1830), and William D. Williamson, *The History of the State of Maine* . . . (Hallowell, 1832). Cf. Pickard, 204.

37 A highly favorable review also appeared in the *Boston Atlas* on April 11, 1835.

38 *Poetical Works*, IV, 325. There is also a manuscript letter in the Yale University Library (Aldis Collection) which Whittier wrote from Amesbury on Oct. 24, 1877. He said, in part: "I quite agree with thee as regards 'Mogg Megone.' But the mischief is after you have made a thing, it persists in living & following you like Mrs. Shelley's Frankenstein."

39 *Poetical Works*, III, 321.

40 This was one of the last favors done for Whittier by Thayer as editor of the *Gazette*. On June 27, 1835, he relinquished control of the weekly and went to Philadelphia to edit the daily *Commercial Herald*.

41 Whittier's course was probably decided in part on financial grounds. In 1835, as provided by the Constitution of Massachusetts, legislators received no salary, only traveling expenses. Whittier was then in no position to serve his townsmen gratuitously in the legislature.

42 In the Oak Knoll Collection, V, 14, there are two letters, dated Oct. 31 and Nov. 19, 1835, from George Ropes, of Portland, urging Whittier to assume editorial charge of a newspaper which the Maine Anti-Slavery Society proposed to establish. Cf. Pickard, 157.

43 This letter was called "masterly" by Whittier's friend Isaac Pray in a letter dated Boston, Feb. 27, 1836 (Oak Knoll Collection, V, 16), but it was strongly condemned by the *Salem Gazette* on March 4, and by other newspapers.

44 John Davis, Everett's predecessor as Governor of Massachusetts, held the office in 1834–35. In 1836 he was United States Senator. Whittier's letter of March 2, with the mere salutation of "Dear friend," is in the Massachusetts Historical Society.

45 Comstock was a versifier of Boston, and in 1836 contributed prose articles to the *Boston Pearl*.

46 The Chief Justice of the court was William Cranch, father of C. P.

Cranch, painter and Transcendentalist poet. Regarding the trial, in addition to Mordell, 82–83, see *The Trial of Reuben Crandall, M.D., Charged with Publishing and Circulating Seditious and Incendiary Papers, &c., in the District of Columbia, with the Intent of Exciting Servile Insurrection.* Carefully reported . . . by a Member of the Bar, Washington City, 1836. The "seditious and incendiary" passages from Whittier's work are quoted on p. 7 of the pamphlet. For the poem, see Pickard, I, 125, and Whittier's *Poetical Works*, III, 234.

47 Following Thayer's departure in 1835, Erastus Brooks conducted the *Gazette* until July 1, 1836, when Whittier's brother-in-law, Jacob Caldwell, purchased it.

48 On March 1, 1836, Whittier wrote a long letter to Cushing about politics and slavery. In part he said: "A firm and steady support of Daniel Webster, without playing into the hands of the White and Harrison parties, or volunteering attacks upon the Van Buren party, is, it appears to me, the safest course for yourselves, and the best for the true interests of the State." Pickard, 175.

49 In the *Haverhill Gazette* of July 30, 1836, Whittier published an article, "John Milton — an Immediatist."

50 See "A Summons," *Poetical Works*, III, 40.

51 *Ibid.*, III, 38.

52 *Ibid.*, III, 43; II, 9. "The Frost Spirit" first appeared in the *New England Weekly Review* on Dec. 6, 1830.

53 The poem was unsigned, but internal evidence strongly indicates Whittier's authorship of it. Here is a perfect statement of the Quaker creed: help the helpless. The stanzaic form is the ballad, which Whittier used often. The thought, atmosphere, and characteristic phrasing are Whittier's. The defective rhymes are typical of him. Finally, such unsigned poems as appeared in newspapers edited by Whittier seem almost invariably to have been his own compositions.

54 On Jan. 10, 1836, Whittier wrote to A. W. Thayer: "The anti-slavery folks have circulated a petition to Cong. in the village, & it has been signed by about 120 legal voters. We shall plague Cushing with it — but he had as lief see the Old Enemy himself as see it. 'Tis nothing to the dose we shall fix for Congress next year. We'll haunt 'em and torment 'em till they behave better. * * *" HUL (Houghton). Copy of original.

55 In the Oak Knoll Collection, V, 18, there is a letter dated New York,

Oct. 16, 1836, in which William Green, Jr., authorized Whittier to draw on him at sight for this amount. Green added: "I will present your resignation to the Ex. Com. when they meet. We feel thankful for what influence you have exerted in the Cause of the oppressed."

56 C. R. Fish, 286–287.

57 The *Liberator*, Jan. 23 and May 28, 1836.

58 Pickard, 154–155, and others, following him, give the date erroneously as 1837. Whittier's report in the *Gazette* on June 4, 1836, may be taken as correct.

59 The *Liberator*, Oct. 1, 1836; *Haverhill Gazette*, July 16, 1836.

60 Pickard, 158.

61 De Poyen was a cousin of Count François de Vipart, with whom he came early in the nineteenth century to Rocks Village, East Haverhill, to make his home. Whittier's "The Countess" (*Poetical Works*, I, 253) was written in memory of Vipart's wife. Pickard, 453–454.

Like his brother, "Frank" Whittier had a literary flair. He lived for a number of years in Portland, Me., and contributed to the *Portland Transcript*, under the pen name of "Ethan Spike," a series of letters which had something of the humor and point of view of J. R. Lowell. See Lloyd W. Griffin, "Matthew Franklin Whittier, 'Ethan Spike,'" *The New England Quarterly*, XIV, 646–663 (Dec. 1941).

62 This cottage was enlarged and remodeled at various times, and it is now maintained as a museum by the Whittier Home Association. In 1851 the present Quaker meeting house was built, under Whittier's direction, on a site little more than one-eighth of a mile from his house. Pickard, 158–160.

63 Letter in Oak Knoll Collection, vol. I.

64 Pickard, 192.

65 Marcus Morton (1784–1864) was for sixteen successive years, 1828–1843, a candidate for Governor of Massachusetts, and was elected only in 1839 and 1842.

66 Oak Knoll Collection, vol. I. Cf. Pickard, 194.

67 Letter in possession of Haverhill Historical Society. Cf. Pickard, 195.

68 Letter in possession of Boston Public Library.

69 Bliss Perry, *John Greenleaf Whittier*, 31.

## CHAPTER VIII

1 *Life* of Garrison, II, 128–129, 183.
2 Pickard, 177; see pp. 199–200.
3 *Proceedings of the Pennsylvania Convention, Assembled to Organize a State Anti-Slavery Society, at Harrisburg, on the 31st of January and 1st, 2d and 3d of February 1837* (Philadelphia: Merrihew and Gunn, 1837), 9, 76–77. Cf. Pickard, 219.
4 *Poetical Works*, III, 47.
5 See 171; *Fourth Annual Report of the American Anti-Slavery Society* (New York: William S. Dorr, 1837).
6 *Life* of Garrison, II, 159.
7 *Proceedings of the Fourth New-England Anti-Slavery Convention, Held in Boston . . .* (Boston: Isaac Knapp, 1837).
8 See 145; Pickard, 206, 207.
9 Pickard, 206; *Life* of Garrison, II, 197.
10 *London and Westminster Review*, XXXII, 58 (Dec., 1838).
11 Pickard, 649.
12 *Ibid.*, 207.
13 Pickard, 214; Currier, 460.
14 Pickard, 205–206.
15 *Ibid.*, 1894 ed., I, 209. Del Floys is not listed in *Longworth's Almanac, New York-Register, and City Directory* during the period 1837–40.
16 Pickard, 210.
17 *Ibid.*, 214.
18 Currier, 30. See also letter from Whittier to Lucy Hooper, dated Aug. 17, 1837: "I send thee a copy of a book published in Boston, without my knowledge or consent, full of errors and ridiculously printed, merely for abolition purposes." Thomas Collection, Yale University Library.
19 Pickard, 239. On Jan. 10, 1836, Whittier by letter declined A. W. Thayer's offer of a non-Abolition editorial job in Philadelphia, saying, in part: "I feel, besides, too deep an interest in the struggle now going on between Slavery & Freedom, especially, as I have been somewhat active heretofore in the cause of Emancipation and as my *apparent* withdrawal from it might be construed very unfavorably to the cause as well as myself. I have I hope no fanaticism about me — *cant* of all kinds, religious, political, or moral, I abhor. But I regard the

contest now going on as of vital interest to the welfare of mankind, not in our country alone — but in all the world. It is a struggle for the rights of men everywhere. — In such a cause I must not *seem* to yield — especially at a time like this when its advocacy is so unpopular that its abandonment would subject me to the charge of cowardice and insincerity. * * *" HUL (Houghton); copy of original letter.

20 "Pennsylvania Hall," *Poetical Works*, III, 58.
21 *History of Pennsylvania Hall, Which Was Destroyed by a Mob, on the 17th of May, 1838* (Philadelphia: Merrihew and Gunn, 1838), 59–62, 145–156; Currier, 611.
22 Pickard, 234.
23 *History of Pennsylvania Hall*, 167–171.
24 See 186–187.
25 See 195. Cf. Pickard, 245–247.
26 See 195.
27 Pickard, 246.
28 *Ibid.*, 249–253.
29 *Ibid.*, 253.
30 See "My Namesake," *Poetical Works*, II, 116.
31 Pickard, 241.
32 Quoted in T. F. Currier, "Whittier's Philadelphia Friends in 1838," *Bulletin of Friends' Historical Association*, XXVII, 70 (1938).
33 As early as May, 1838, according to Pickard, 225.
34 Currier, *op. cit.*, 71–72.

## CHAPTER IX

1 *The Works of Lord Byron: Letters and Journals*, rev. ed., 6 vols. (London, 1922), III, 405.
2 *The Complete Works of Percy Bysshe Shelley*, ed. Roger Ingpen and Walter E. Peck, Julian Editions, 10 vols. (London, 1926–1930), X, 21.
3 Passage marked by Whittier in "A Letter from Mr. Burke, To a Member of the National Assembly; in Answer to Some Objections to His Book on French Affairs. 1791," in his set of Burke's *Works* (Boston, 6-vol. ed., 1806).
4 From other passages in Burke's *Works*, marked by Whittier.
5 Letter addressed to Samuel E. Sewall, Whittier's *Prose Works*, III, 88–89.

6 *Fourth Annual Report of the American Anti-Slavery Society*, New York, May 9, 1837 (New York, 1837).
7 Whittier, *Prose Works*, III, 190; Pickard, 207–208; Underwood, 125–128.
8 Pickard, 186; *Life* of Garrison, II, 310.
9 *Life* of Garrison, II, 326.
10 Letter in Clay Collection, Library of Congress.
11 Pickard, 269.
12 *Ibid.*, 175.
13 See, e.g., the editorial, "Political Abuses," *American Manufacturer*, April 2, 1829, which obviously refers to Adams.
14 *Life* of Garrison, III, 98.
15 Pickard, 209.
16 *Letters from John Quincy Adams to His Constituents of the Twelfth Congressional District in Massachusetts* . . . (Boston: Isaac Knapp, 1837). See also Whittier, *Prose Works*, III, 93.
17 Pickard, 195–196, 253–254.
18 *Ibid.*, 269.
19 *Ibid.*, 179–180.
20 Adams merely tantalized his opponents with one petition which he did not present. This cut at the objection that most of the petitioners were women, allegedly incompetent in public affairs. The petition implored Congress to memorialize the British government to dethrone Victoria, on the ground that women were beyond their ken when they assumed the management of public affairs. Pickard, 180–181.
21 *Ibid.*, 328–329.
22 Claude M. Fuess, *The Life of Caleb Cushing* (New York, 1923), I, 254.
23 Pickard, 126–127; letter of May, 1833, from Whittier to Cushing in regard to Whittier's forthcoming *Justice and Expediency* and a Boston speech of Cushing's on colonization.
24 Much of it given in Pickard and in Fuess; see also Carpenter, 202.
25 Pickard, 175–176.
26 *Ibid.*, 178–179.
27 *Ibid.*, 200.
28 Oak Knoll Collection, vol. I.
29 Pickard, 199, 201–202.
30 *Life* of Garrison, II, 260, 197.
31 *Ibid.*, II, 309.
32 Whittier, *Prose Works*, III, 100.

## CHAPTER X

1 Pickard, 255, 260.

2 *Ibid.*, 256. The Essex Institute has a copy of a letter (original in Cornell University Library), dated April 6, 1840, from Whittier to J. Miller McKim acknowledging receipt of the executive committee's resolutions. Whittier then indicated that he could not himself afford the expenses of the proposed trip, and assumed that the Anti-Slavery Society could not divide equally with him the $500 to $600 which the journey would cost.

3 See 30–31.

4 "Daniel Wheeler," *Poetical Works*, IV, 48. Gurney's relation to Whittier's state of mind was further shown in a letter which Whittier wrote his cousin Ann E. Wendell on July 13, 1840 (Pickard, 261–262).

5 Whittier referred to the anti-Constitution and anti-church stand of the Garrison group of Abolitionists. He referred to them further in a letter of Nov. 1840, addressed to Ann Wendell (Pickard, 266–267).

6 Pickard, 259–260.

7 *Ibid.*, 267.

8 See 187.

9 See 148.

10 Pickard, 272; *Elizabeth Lloyd and the Whittiers*, ed. T. F. Currier, 76.

11 An incident of the next year illustrated the personal difference between Garrison and Whittier, for example. Whittier was reported to have called at the A.A.-S.S. office in Boston, and this conversation followed. WHITTIER: "Why could we not all go on together?" GARRISON: "Why not, indeed? *We* stand just where we did. I see no reason why you cannot coöperate with the American Society." WHITTIER: "Oh, but the American Society is not what it once was. It has the hat, and the coat, and the waistcoat of the Old Society, but the life has passed out of it." GARRISON: "Are you not ashamed to come here wondering why we cannot go on together! No wonder you can't coöperate with a suit of old clothes!" *Life* of Garrison, III, 35.

12 Letters from Sturge and Tappan are located as follows: July 30, 1841, and April 21, 1847 (HUL [Houghton]); Dec. 22, 1848, Feb. 27, 1852, April 23, 1857, and Sept. 14, 1858 (Oak Knoll Collection). Manuscript letters, now in the Library of Congress, dated New York, Oct.

14 and Dec. 9, 1843, show that Tappan as directed paid Whittier $229.57 of Sturge's funds then remaining on hand.

13 Included in Whittier's *Poetical Works*, IV, 288. The record of the Sturge-Whittier trip is given by Sturge in his *A Visit to the United States in 1841* (London, 1842). Cf. Pickard, 267–273.

14 Currier, 467–469.

15 "Ego," *Poetical Works*, II, 102.

16 See 475–476.

17 Pickard, 281.

18 From copy, in Essex Institute, of original letter in possession of Frank Tracy Swett, Berkeley, Calif.

19 Two of the others were Moses A. Cartland, Whittier's cousin, and Joseph Healy.

20 Birney's letter, dated May 29, in Boston, was published in the *Haverhill Gazette* on June 27, 1835, and copied in the *Liberator* on July 4.

21 Pickard, 274.

22 *Ibid.*, 277.

23 *Ibid.*, 284–288. Whittier had tried to persuade the Reverend John Pierpont, of Hollis Street Church, to be a Liberty candidate for Congress, from Boston. Pierpont, sympathetic, said he must postpone his work for the slave until a clergyman became a free man.

24 Pickard, 292, 194. In a letter of Nov. 6, 1837, now in the Oak Knoll Collection, Morton, on the eve of another election, dodged Whittier's request of Oct. 30 for his opinion "upon several subjects connected with slavery." Morton said that after the election, given a favorable opportunity, he intended to express his views fully and frankly. In the *Dictionary of American Biography* he is said to have been all his life opposed to slavery.

25 See 193.

26 See 182.

27 See 181–182. Of interest is a letter, now in the Oak Knoll Collection, from H. I. Bowditch, dated Boston, Nov. 11 [1842]: "Friend Whittier. I have long known you, for though your face I have never seen — I have been warmed by your poetry — I write now to ask you for some few lines for poor Latimer — who is in Leverett St- jail — Think too of poor Massachusetts — who lies low, her constitution, laws & lawyers all being prostituted for the support of slavery — Give us, I pray you some loud trumpet peal in behalf of

New England's rights — You will excuse, I know, any impertinence you may perceive in thus warmly addressing one who is personally a stranger — If your Muse proves favorable to you — we want the result for the columns of the 'Latimer Journal and North Star' which will be published on Monday Wednesday & Friday until after Latimer's trial is concluded."

28 Pickard, 292; Whittier, *Poetical Works*, III, 80.
29 *Poetical Works*, III, 275, 282.
30 Pickard, 291–292.
31 Currier, 48.
32 Pickard, 293.
33 Currier, 48.

## CHAPTER XI

1 HUL (Houghton).
2 Information supplied by Thelma M. Smith and Leon Howard.
3 Pickard, 297–298.
4 Letter, in HUL, printed in Pickard, 300–301.
5 Parrington, *The Romantic Revolution in America, 1800–1860*, 464.
6 *Elizabeth Lloyd and the Whittiers*, 22.
7 Letter in Longfellow House, Cambridge.
8 Copy, in Longfellow House, of original letter.
9 *The Letters of Ralph Waldo Emerson*, ed. Ralph L. Rusk (New York, 1939), III, 306–307.
10 *The Heart of Emerson's Journals*, ed. Bliss Perry (Boston, 1926), 221.
11 Parrington, *op. cit.*, 399.
12 *Poetical Works*, III, 117. Of this 136-line satire, Frank B. Sanborn wrote (*Boston Evening Transcript*, July 24, 1902) that it "sounded the loud timbrel of derision over the defeat of Franklin Pierce and my mother's cousins, Moses Norris and Reuben Leavitt of Pittsfield, N.H., in the New Hampshire election of 1846, which sent John Parker Hale to the Senate, and broke down the long domination of pro-slavery Democracy in my native state. . . . The lament is put into the mouth of the elegant, imperious Frank Pierce, who had retired from the Senate to be the head of the 'Concord Clique' that ruled New Hampshire then. . . ."
13 *Dictionary of American Biography*, VIII, 105.

14 Pickard, 311–312.
15 Bearing upon the 1847 nomination, which he considered premature, Whittier wrote Hale letters of clear-headed advice on July 30, Oct. 2, and Nov. 8, 1847. See Pickard, 319–324, who incorrectly dated the last letter Aug. 11, inverting the digits in Whittier's Quaker-style date, "11th mo 8th."
16 HUL (Houghton).
17 Edward L. Pierce, *Memoir and Letters of Charles Sumner* (Boston: Roberts Brothers, 1893), III, 128.
18 *Poetical Works,* IV, 91–92.
19 This Sumner-Whittier material is from Pickard, 351–356.
20 *Poetical Works,* IV, 35.
21 Pickard, 288.
22 *Poetical Works,* III, 106.
23 Letter in Harvard College Library, quoted by Currier, 473.
24 Pickard, 364–366.
25 Harvard College Library.
26 Kennedy (2), 128.
27 Pickard, 374.
28 *Ibid.*, 383.
29 *Ibid.*, 386.
30 Other poems which Whittier wrote bearing on the 1856 campaign included "We're Free," "The Pass of the Sierra," "To Pennsylvania," "A Frémont Campaign Song," and "A Song Inscribed to the Frémont Clubs." Pickard, 388–389, quotes from a letter which Mrs. Jessie Benton Frémont wrote to Whittier from Pocaho, N.Y., on March 5, 1868, this passage relating to "The Pass of the Sierra": "The General had a case before the Supreme Court which has kept him some weeks in Washington, and yesterday, when he made time for a day at home with us, among other things he had to tell us was that a young lady has been introduced to him who had been on quite a tour in the California mountains, — to the Yo Semite, and into the Sierra Nevada. The point of it to us was that she told the General that on the first night they camped out in the Yo Semite mountains she could not sleep for the wildness and beauty made by the 'camp-fire's wall of dark.' When we lived two dreary years of enforced patience, waiting for the law's delay, in that same mountain country, I cut out and pasted to the wall, by the General's dressing-glass, where

he had to see it daily, those lines of yours. Many and many a time when the troubles of business depressed him, these words with their grand ideas, and the memories of a nobler life, put fresh heart into him. The young lady's quotation [from "The Pass of the Sierra"] reminded us of those times, and we talked them over, sitting again by a country home fireside — the wood fire, the dogs lying on the hearth, the pines loaded with snow, all as it used to be in the mountains, but within — health and peace and rest."

31 *Poetical Works*, III, 191–192.

32 Pickard, 425 n.

33 Amesbury *Villager*, June 5, 1856; cf. Pickard, 382–383.

34 Pickard, 435. Whittier, in a letter to W. S. Thayer dated Feb. 1, 1861, prayed for these attributes in Senator Seward, then supposed to be outlining in two speeches the policy of the incoming administration.

35 *Ibid.*, 432.

36 Whittier's relation to labor is treated fully in Chapter XVII.

37 *Poetical Works*, III, 290.

38 Pickard, 351.

39 *Poetical Works*, III, 317.

40 Letter of July 2, 1848, from Coffin to Whittier, in Oak Knoll Collection.

41 In regard to Whittier and his cousin, see Chapter XXIII.

42 Lowell, *The Function of the Poet, and Other Essays*, collected and edited by Albert Mordell (Boston, 1920), 136.

43 Whittier's religious position is fully treated in Chapter XXVII.

44 *Poetical Works*, II, 242.

45 *Life of Henry Wadsworth Longfellow, with extracts from his journals and correspondence*, ed. Samuel Longfellow (Boston, 1891), II, 348.

46 *Poetical Works*, III, 328.

47 *Ibid.*, IV, 76.

48 *Ibid.*, IV, 84.

49 Pickard, 420–421, says: " 'The Red River Voyageur' was suggested by reading a work on Manitoba, by J. W. Bond, who was the historiographer of the expedition of Governor Ramsey to Pembina in 1851. This passage, referring to the vesper bell of St. Boniface, must have been the kernel from which the poem grew: 'As I pass slowly along the lonely road that leads me from thee, Selkirk, mine eyes do

turn continually to gaze upon thy smiling, golden fields, and the lofty towers of St. Boniface, now burnished with the rays of the departing sun, while the sweet vesper bell reverberates afar and strikes so mournfully pleasant upon mine ear. I feel satisfied that, though absent thousands of weary miles, my thoughts will always dwell on thee with rapturous emotions.' This church was burned in 1860. The bells fell and were broken. Their fragments were collected from the ruins, sent to London and recast by their original founder, and, recrossing the Atlantic, took their place in the tower of the new cathedral of St. Boniface, where their chimes may be heard to-day, on memorable state occasions, very rarely in honor of American personages or events. They greeted General Sherman in 1880, and in 1882, when the Misses Banning of St. Paul, elocutionists, gave an effective rendering of Whittier's poem, the bells were again rung, in their honor, by order of the archbishop."

50 *Poetical Works*, IV, 269.

51 *Ibid.*, II, 22–23.

52 Pickard, 404–405.

## CHAPTER XII

1 See 145–146.

2 See 226–227.

3 Higginson, 78–79. See also Appendix E.

4 Frank Moore, *Anecdotes and Incidents of the War: North and South. 1860–1865* (New York, 1867), 215.

5 *Elizabeth Lloyd and the Whittiers*, 139–140.

6 *Poetical Works*, III, 218.

7 Pickard, 435. Pickard also prints, p. 436, a letter written during February, 1861, to F. H. Underwood in which Whittier elaborates these and other sentiments which he held respecting the situation.

8 Pickard, 432–433.

9 *Ibid.*, 433–434. Pickard incorrectly transcribed "*anything* short of."

10 Letter in Massachusetts Historical Society.

11 Pickard, 434.

12 HUL (Houghton).

13 *Poetical Works*, III, 220.

14 Pickard, 467–468; Carl Sandburg, *Abraham Lincoln: The War Years* (New York: Harcourt, Brace & Co., 1939), I, 561.

15 Pickard, 441.
16 Letter in HUL (Houghton), dated April 12, 1893, from G. W. Hanson to S. T. Pickard.
17 Sparhawk, 32–33. In the Oak Knoll Collection (VI, 87) is a letter of May 23, 1864, to Whittier from Gardiner Tufts, of the Massachusetts State Military Agency, Washington, acknowledging "your valued favor with its words of cheer. . . . If we, who are dispensers of the gifts, only carry out the designs and wishes of the donors many pangs of cruel war will be assuaged."
18 Pickard, 476–477.
19 *Ibid.*, 476.
20 HUL (Houghton).
21 *Poetical Works*, III, 223. The gratitude of the Frémont family to Whittier for these lines is described in a letter from Mrs. Frémont to S. T. Pickard, dated April, 1893. In September, 1863, while vacationing at Nahant, Mrs. Frémont, accompanied by her daughter Lilly and escorted by Zagonyi (Kossuth's friend who had fought with him for freedom in Hungary, and then by adoption for the United States in the Civil War), called on Whittier in Amesbury. Mrs. Frémont's long letter, and one written to her by Whittier on Oct. 24, 1863, appear in Pickard, 460–466.
22 Pickard, 444.
23 HUL (Houghton); cf. Pickard, 449–450.
24 *Atlantic Monthly*, Feb. 1863; *Poetical Works*, III, 240.
25 *Prose Works*, III, 146–147; *Proceedings of the American Anti-Slavery Society, at its third decade, held in the City of Philadelphia, Dec. 3d and 4th, 1863* (New York: American Anti-Slavery Society, 1864), 6–8. See 123.
26 The Loyal National League, *Opinions of Prominent Men Concerning the Great Questions of the Times* (New York: C. S. Westcott & Co., 1863).
27 "The Prisoner of Naples," 1851, *Poetical Works*, III, 336.
28 HUL (Houghton).
29 Pickard, 488–489; Sparhawk, 127.
30 From photostatic copy in Oak Knoll Collection, vol. II.
31 Mordell, 214, quoted from same letter.
32 *Prose Works*, III, 148–154.
33 Pickard, 451, gives the date as Jan. 24, 1863; the Amesbury *Villager* as Jan. 20.
34 Pickard, 451–452.

35 *Ibid.*, 454–459. The scope of the controversy over "Barbara Frietchie" is suggested by the bibliography of the subject, listed in Currier, 211–213.
36 Pickard, 475–476.
37 Mrs. Hawley's letter and Gen. Rice's of April 4, 1864, acknowledging Whittier's declination, are in the Oak Knoll Collection, VI, 84 and 85 respectively. Part of Gen. Rice's letter of invitation is given in Pickard, 476. Joseph R. Hawley was before the war a Hartford lawyer and, from 1857, editor of the *Press.* He entered the Civil War a captain and was retired as a major-general in January, 1866. Then he became editor of the *Hartford Courant* when the *Press* was merged with it. He was a leader in establishing the Republican Party in Connecticut, and drew Gideon Welles into it.
38 Pickard, 622–623.
39 Oak Knoll Collection, VI, 88.
40 Pickard, 487.
41 Huntington Library; copy in Essex Institute.
42 *Prose Works*, II, 274.
43 Pickard, 491–492; Currier, 618.
44 *Poetical Works*, III, 259, 261.
45 Letter in Massachusetts Historical Society.
46 HUL (Houghton).
47 Pickard, 485.
48 See 26.
49 Oak Knoll Collection, VI, 80.
50 *Poetical Works*, I, 253.
51 Pickard, 375–376.
52 See 258; *Poetical Works*, IV, 186.
53 HUL (Houghton).
54 The Oak Knoll Collection, VI, 17, has, for instance, a letter of May 20, 1857, in which Daniel Neall of Philadelphia sends a draft for $50 to add to the fund Whittier is raising for Coffin. See also Pickard, 395.
55 Pickard, 477–479.
56 *Ibid.*, 480.
57 *Ibid.*, 481.
58 Sarah Gertrude Pomeroy, *Little-Known Sisters of Well-Known Men* (Boston, 1912), 137.
59 Oak Knoll Collection, VI, 98.

## CHAPTER XIII

1 Pickard, 692.
2 *Poetical Works*, II, 142.
3 Pickard, 494.
4 See 42.
5 Letters to J. T. Fields and Lucy Larcom, Pickard, 497–498; "The Tent on the Beach," *Poetical Works*, IV, 227.
6 CII, 631–632.
7 See, e.g., *The London Quarterly Review*, No. CLVIII, n.s., No. 38, p. 241 (Jan., 1893).
8 Canby statement made in lecture at Yale University, Feb. 5, 1926.
9 Currier, 98–99; Oak Knoll Collection, VII, 35.
10 Pickard, 504, 501.
11 *Ibid.*, 504–505.
12 Editorial, "American Literature," *American Manufacturer*, July 16, 1829.
13 Pickard, 636.
14 Oak Knoll Collection, VII, 35; Currier, 102.
15 *Poetical Works*, IV, 227.
16 Pickard, 505. Pickard devotes 505–515 to the "Tent."
17 *Ibid.*, 507.
18 Letters in Yale University Library.
19 Pickard, 512. The immediate demand for a second edition gave Whittier his opportunity to make the "corrections and emendations." It took him three revisions to eliminate to his satisfaction "the self-praise and egotism which vexed me" — on pp. 45–46. See Currier, 102–104.
20 Pickard, 512.
21 Whittier's religious position is treated fully in Chapter XXVII.
22 *John Greenleaf Whittier*, English Men of Letters (New York: The Macmillan Co., 1902), 151.
23 Pickard, 514.
24 See 25.
25 Dean Farrar of Canterbury Cathedral wrote ("My American Friends," *The Independent*, XLIX, 1–2): "He asked Emerson how he treated requests for his autograph. Emerson said that he, at one time, always sent his autograph to any one who wrote to ask for it.

But when the applications came to be counted by hundreds, he had ceased to do so. 'But what do you do,' asked Whittier, 'when they inclose stamps?' 'Oh,' said Emerson, '*the stamps come in handy.*' This, however, was a bolder impropriation than the conscience of the Quaker poet could permit, and whenever a stamped envelop came he inclosed his signature in it."

26 See 451.
27 Pickard, 612.
28 *Bibliography*, 132.
29 Pickard, 613.
30 See 185.
31 *Poetical Works*, IV, 64–65.
32 Pickard, 667–668.
33 Oak Knoll Collection, VII, 37.
34 *Poetical Works*, II, 333.
35 Farrar, *Men I Have Known* (New York: Crowell, *c.* 1897), 162–163.
36 Pickard, 641.
37 Fields, 64.

## CHAPTER XIV

1 Pickard, 171.
2 See 79.
3 See *Prose Works*, III, 58.
4 *Poetical Works*, III, 334.
5 *Prose Works*, III, 59.
6 *The Rise of the Common Man, 1830–1850*, 23.
7 *Ibid.*, 75.
8 *Haverhill Gazette*, April 12, 1828.
9 *Ibid.*, Aug. 20, 1836.
10 Fish, *op. cit.*, 86.
11 Jan. 4, 1831.
12 *Haverhill Gazette*, May 12, 1827.
13 Chase, *History of Haverhill*, 501.
14 *Haverhill Gazette*, April 19, 1828.
15 See 102, and Pickard, 100, 307.
16 Pickard, 243.
17 *Poetical Works*, II, 43.

18 *Ibid.*, stanza XX.
19 Letter in New Hampshire Historical Society; copy in Essex Institute.
20 Pickard, 567.
21 *Ibid.*, 737–738. The first three sentences in this letter are quoted, 6.
22 See 201. The garden room and other parts of the Whittier home in Amesbury are described in detail by Pickard in *Whittier-Land*, 60–76, and by Sparhawk, 15–16, 23, and *passim*.
23 *Whittier-Land*, 80–81.
24 *Ibid.*, 96.
25 Fields, 55.
26 *Ibid.*, 74–75.
27 Emily Binney Smith, *Whittier* (Amesbury, 1935), 35.
28 *Whittier-Land*, 98–99.
29 Pickard, 606, 614. The three cousins were sisters, granddaughters of Whittier's uncle, Obadiah Whittier, an older brother of his father, John Whittier.

## CHAPTER XV

1 *Journals of Ralph Waldo Emerson*, ed. Edward Waldo Emerson and Waldo Emerson Forbes (Boston: Houghton Mifflin Co., 1910), II, 454.
2 *Ibid.*, III, 340.
3 *The Heart of Thoreau's Journals*, ed. Odell Shepard (Boston: Houghton Mifflin Co., 1927), 115.
4 See 196.
5 Huntington Library; photostatic copy in Essex Institute.
6 See 160–162.
7 Pickard, 565.
8 The Oak Knoll Collection, III, 89, has a letter postmarked Portland, June 17, 1889, in which Whittier tells Phebe Grantham: "I came here on sixth day last. I have only been in one sitting of the meeting. I shall not do more than look in once or twice more; and shall return to A. as early as 5th day. * * * I am not very well, but about as when I left Danvers. * * *"
9 In the Oak Knoll Collection are many letters in which Whittier deplores New England's winter weather. In one (III, 2) dated Ames-

bury, May 10, 1871, and addressed to Mrs. F. A. P. Barnard, wife of the old Hartford friend who was now president of Columbia College, he said: "I like New England in almost all respects, but I am fain to own that we have six weeks of weather in spring for which little can be said. I wd like to spend this month in the city from which thy letter dates. But, I am a poor traveller, and dare not undertake it in my present state of health." In another (XIV, 97), dated Amesbury, Nov. 18, 1885, Whittier said to Mrs. Woodman: "Winter seems to delay its coming: though we have had some damp disagreeable days there has been but little frost & no snow. I hope it will hold off a month for I dread the long dark winter more & more as I am older. * * *"

10 Mrs. Stowe, in a letter of Jan. 23, 1874 (Oak Knoll Collection, IX, 94), extended an invitation.
11 Pickard, 722.
12 *Ibid.*, 429.
13 *Ibid.*, 325–326.
14 *Ibid.*, 360–361.
15 *Ibid.*, 366–367, 419.
16 *Poetical Works*, II, 42.
17 Pickard, 541.
18 *Ibid.*, 644, 645.
19 Correspondence in HUL (Houghton).
20 *Prose Works*, I, 209.
21 Pickard, 366.
22 *Ibid.*, 665.
23 Fields, 53–54.
24 *Poetical Works*, I, 143.

## CHAPTER XVI

1 See 50.
2 *Poetical Works*, IV, 319.
3 *Prose Works*, III, 40.
4 *Ibid.*, II, 324–325. This article, with few changes, was republished in the *Pennsylvania Freeman* on April 25, 1839, when Whittier was editor.
5 *Life and Letters*, 606–607.

6 *Ibid.*, 607–608. Pickard reproduces, 608–609, Whittier's letter of acknowledgment, dated Amesbury, Oct. 21, 1875; and also tells of the way in which M. Charbonnier's letter was transmitted to Whittier through a well-known English Friend, J. B. Braithwaite.

7 *Poetical Works*, III, 356.

8 *Ibid.*, III, 361.

9 Letters from Thomas Collection, Yale University Library.

10 Oak Knoll Collection, VII, 82.

11 Thomas Collection, Yale University Library.

12 *Ibid.*

13 HUL (Houghton).

14 *Prose Works*, III, 229.

15 *Encyclopaedia Britannica*, 14th ed., IV, 58–59.

16 Pickard, 620–621. HUL (Houghton) has a letter dated Cannes, France, in which the chamberlain to Dom Pedro, in his behalf, thanked Whittier for the copy of *At Sundown* just received.

17 Pickard, 450; Currier, 228. The latter writes that the birds are "now preserved in the rooms of the Boston Society of Natural History, together with the autograph copy of the translation sent by the emperor to the poet."

18 From Brussels, June 13, 1865, M. Lisboa acknowledged Whittier's note of thanks for the translation of "The Red River Voyageur." Oak Knoll Collection, VII, 9.

19 *Ibid.*, VII, 6. Currier, 344, notes that James Cooley Fletcher "was acting secretary of the U.S. Legation in Rio de Janeiro in 1852/1853 and was intimate with Dom Pedro; he lived in Newburyport from 1856 to 1862, and was later (from 1873 to 1890) engaged in volunteer missionary work in Italy with headquarters at Naples."

20 Higginson, 100.

21 Pickard, 621.

22 Mrs. John T. Sargent, *Sketches and Reminiscences of the Radical Club* (Boston, 1880), 301–303. See also Mary B. Claflin, 53–54, quoted by Pickard, 621–622. Mrs. Sargent gave the date as Wednesday, June 14.

23 Letter in Library of Congress; quoted in Mordell, 279.

24 *New England Magazine*, n.s., VII, 297 (Nov., 1892). This story in part is confirmed by Charlotte Grimké in the *New England Magazine*, n.s., VIII, 473 (June, 1893).

25 HUL (Houghton). Whittier maintained his interest in Dom Pedro to the end. When the emperor retired to Portugal, the United States Minister at Lisbon, George B. Loring, conveyed Whittier's greetings. On Dec. 22, 1889, Mr. Loring replied: "I was happy in being able to make the old emperor comfortable [in Loring's own apartments]. He looks very old, has no light or joy in his face, and dwells on the past with touching devotion. He talks of you and Longfellow and Agassiz, and Alexander Agassiz and Quincy Shaw, as if you had all been his brothers." Pickard, 743–744. Besides Pickard, Mary Wilhelmine Williams, in her *Dom Pedro the Magnanimous, Second Emperor of Brazil* (University of North Carolina Press, 1937), tells of the relations between Dom Pedro and Whittier, and in detail of the Abolitionist movement in Brazil.

26 *Poetical Works*, IV, 72.

27 See 137 ff.

28 Pickard, 363–364.

29 Letter in Henry E. Huntington Library.

30 *Prose Works*, III, 135–136.

## CHAPTER XVII

1 See 68–69.

2 In the issues of Feb. 19, April 16, 23, and 30, July 9 and 16, and April 9, respectively. Whittier returned to this subject later in editorials entitled "The Working men's Party" and "The Working Men," which appeared in the *New England Weekly Review* on Aug. 23 and Dec. 6, 1830, respectively. And in another editorial on "Aristocracy," which was published in the *Haverhill Gazette* on Sept. 17, 1836, Whittier stung economically privileged people who, he said, would substitute for our democratic institutions the "power and pomp of European Aristocracy." He berated them for upholding, as he alleged, the *rights of property* as against the *rights of man;* for upholding slavery and opposing Abolition.

3 J. R. Commons and others, *History of Labour in the United States* (New York: The Macmillan Co., 1918), I, 408–409.

4 William Cullen Bryant published a strong editorial on the same subject in the *New York Evening Post* on June 13, 1836.

5 "The City of a Day," *Prose Works*, I, 353 and *passim*.

6 *Prose Works*, I, 377 and *passim.*
7 *Poetical Works*, III, 304.
8 Letter in Yale University Library.
9 *A Succinct Account of the Late Difficulties on the Salisbury Corporation* (Salisbury: Currier & Gerrish, 1852).
10 Quoted in T. W. Higginson, 88.
11 *A Succinct Account of the Late Difficulties on the Salisbury Corporation.*
12 Fields, 88–89.
13 Emily Binney Smith, *Whittier*, 29.
14 Pickard, 589.
15 See 114.
16 Pickard, 721–722.
17 Commons, *op. cit.*, II, 185–191.
18 *Poetical Works*, III, 367.
19 Pickard, 640.
20 *Ibid.*, 645–646.
21 *Literary Friends and Acquaintance; a Personal Retrospect of American Authorship* (New York: Harper & Bros., 1900), 135–136.
22 See "The Abolitionists," *Prose Works*, III, 68.
23 Carl Sandburg, *Abraham Lincoln: The War Years* (New York: Harcourt, Brace & Co., 1939), I, 380.
24 Oak Knoll Collection, XII, 77.
25 *Dictionary of American Biography*, I, 231.
26 Letter in HUL (Houghton); cf. Pickard, 735–736.
27 Pickard, 736. Regarding the presidential election of 1872, Whittier wrote: "In the long struggle of well-nigh forty years, I can honestly say that no consideration of private interest, nor my natural love of peace and retirement and the good-will of others, have kept me silent when a word could be fitly spoken for human rights." *Prose Works*, III, 165.
28 *A Literary History of America* (New York: Charles Scribner's Sons, 1928), 359.
29 Pickard, 742–743.

## CHAPTER XVIII

1 Fields, 6.
2 *The Education of Henry Adams* (Boston: Houghton Mifflin Co., 1918), 211.

3 *New England Weekly Review*, Jan. 2, 1832.
4 See 14–15, 149, 181–182.
5 *Poetical Works*, II, 103.
6 *Prose Works*, II, 426–427.
7 Whittier was himself abstemious. About the only drink he appears to have taken in his life was a concession to seasickness on his trip from Hartford to New York at the end of December, 1830. In his letter of Dec. 31 to Jonathan Law, now in the Houghton Library at Harvard, he said: "The glass of brandy which I have just drank seems inclined to behave properly and keep its place." At the Boston dinners of *Atlantic* contributors which he attended, Whittier was said by T. W. Higginson (p. 89) to have been one of the few who took no wine.
8 In an editorial in the *Brooklyn Daily Times* on May 22, 1858, Whitman referred to the campaign of "some years ago" against capital punishment: "We recollect the meetings for discussing this Capital Punishment question, which used to be held in New York in a moderate sized room in Broadway, near Lispenard street. A visitor there would have found a remarkable collection of 'heads.' The *Democratic Review* writers were frequently quoted — some were present to speak for themselves, or as listeners. We allude to Bryant, Judge Edmonds, O'Sullivan, Whittier, Hawthorne, old Major D'Aveza, and others." See *The Uncollected Poetry and Prose of Walt Whitman*, coll. and ed. by Emory Holloway (Garden City: Doubleday, Page, 1921), II, 15.
9 *Prose Works*, III, 58.
10 Pickard, 506.
11 See 86, 136, 145–146, 149, 181–182.
12 *Life* of Garrison, III, 300.
13 On March 19 and 26 and July 16, respectively. Abstemious Friend though he was, Whittier wrote an editorial entitled "Cultivation of the Vine" for the *American Manufacturer* of April 9, 1829. In regard to a translation of Bernard's treatise on the cultivation of the grapevine, Whittier said: "We hope this book will be extensively read. * * * In all parts of this country the grape vine may be cultivated to considerable extent, although it would hardly become a source of profit in New England. * * *"
14 See 180.

15 See 184.
16 See 155.
17 Carl Sandburg, *Abraham Lincoln: The War Years* (New York: Harcourt, Brace & Co., 1939), I, 231.
18 Currier, 451, mentions "a total of about forty possibilities."
19 In the respective issues of Sept. 20, Nov. 22, Dec. 27, 1830, and Jan. 17, and Sept. 5, 1831.
20 Sept. 13, Dec. 6, 1830; Feb. 21, Oct. 24, 1831, respectively.
21 See 84, for his comment of Feb. 21, 1831, in the *New England Weekly Review.*
22 See 155.
23 *Ibid.*
24 Letter books of Lewis Tappan, Library of Congress.
25 *Poetical Works,* IV, 230.
26 Pickard, 513. Godkin's review appeared in the issue of March 7, 1867; Whittier's letter dated the 9th was published in *The Nation* of March 14.

## CHAPTER XIX

1 See 53.
2 Thomas H. Huxley, *Science and Education, Essays,* Author's edition (New York: D. Appleton & Co., n.d.), 174.
3 Whittier's interest in Goethe and other German writers is traced in Iola Kay Eastburn's dissertation, *Whittier's Relation to German Life and Thought.* Americana Germanica, no. 20 (Philadelphia: University of Pennsylvania, 1915), 80, and *passim.*
4 These appeared, respectively, in the: *Haverhill Gazette,* May 1, 1830; *Bouquet,* June 16, 1832; *American Manufacturer,* Dec. 25, 1828; *New England Weekly Review,* July 26 and Nov. 8, 1830.
5 *Democracy in America,* tr. by Henry Reeve, 3d ed. (London, 1838), II, 248–249.
6 "The Abolitionists," *Prose Works,* III, 67.
7 *Prose Works,* II, 35.
8 *Ibid.,* II, 71.
9 *Ibid.,* II, 57–58.
10 *Ibid.,* II, 89.
11 March 1, April 5, 1849; *Prose Works,* II, 348–367.

12 *Prose Works*, II, 350.
13 *Ibid.*, II, 69.
14 *Ibid.*, III, 207–208.
15 See 23, 27.
16 *Poetical Works*, I, 11.
17 Pickard, 553.
18 *Ibid.*, 626–627. Kingsley wrote to his wife, from Cambridge on Feb. 19, 1874: ". . . Yesterday, in Boston, dear old Whittier called on me and we had a most loving and like minded talk about the other world. He is an old saint." — *Charles Kingsley: His Letters and Memories of His Life*, ed. by his wife (London: Macmillan, 1891), II, 313.
19 James Stacy Stevens has explored this subject in *Whittier's Use of the Bible*. Orono, Me., *The Maine Bulletin*, Dec. 1930, vol. 33. (University of Maine Studies, 2d series, no. 16.)
20 *Prose Works*, I, 327; II, 200, and *passim*.
21 It is of passing interest that Whittier taught himself German, perhaps, like Carlyle, during illness. Whittier translated Goethe's "Erl-King" into English. On Nov. 8, 1848, he said in a letter (Yale University Library) to Thomas Tracy that he was studying German.
22 *Prose Works*, II, 217.
23 *The Letters of Ralph Waldo Emerson*, ed. Ralph L. Rusk (Columbia University Press, 1939), IV, 336.
24 Oak Knoll Collection, XIII, 7.
25 Oak Knoll, VIII, 40, 70.
26 Arthur Christy, "Orientalism in New England: Whittier," *American Literature*, I, 392, 372 (Jan., 1930).
27 Arthur Christy, "The Orientalism of Whittier," *American Literature*, V, 248–250 (Nov., 1933). Whittier liked the Chinese proverb: "You cannot prevent the birds of sadness from flying over your head, but you may prevent them from stopping to build their nests in your hair." Elizabeth Stuart Phelps, "Whittier's Sense of Humor," *McClure's Magazine*, VII, 116 (July, 1896).
28 Huntington Library: photostatic copy in Essex Institute.
29 *Poetical Works*, II, 294.
30 See 282.
31 *American Literature*, V, 249–250 (Nov., 1933); *The Villager*, Nov. 28, 1872.
32 In the Oak Knoll Collection (XII, 67) is a letter of Nov. 8, 1886, ad-

dressed to Whittier by William Gray, of Boston. Gray remarked his pleasure that Harvard had that day given Whittier the honorary LL.D. He enclosed a letter from President Eliot, which Gray sent on to Holmes, who in turn wrote to Eliot. Whittier was a trustee also of Brown University, from 1869 to 1892. In 1860 the faculty of Haverford College recommended that an honorary M.A. be conferred upon Whittier.

## CHAPTER XX

1 Pickard, 17, 22.
2 See 7.
3 Pickard, 19.
4 See 196 ff.
5 Pickard, 267.
6 *New England Weekly Review*, July 18, 1831.
7 *Prose Works*, I, 202–203.
8 Pickard, 552, n.
9 *Ibid.*, 302.
10 *Ibid.*, 553.
11 Corporation Records of Brown University, III, 408, June 30, 1870.
12 Records of the Overseers of Harvard University, vols. IX and X, consulted by permission.
13 Pickard, 255.
14 *Ibid.*, 336–337.
15 See 205; Vincent Y. Bowditch, *Life and Correspondence of Henry Ingersoll Bowditch* (Boston: Houghton Mifflin Co., 1902), II, 321.
16 Bowditch, *op. cit.*, I, 140.
17 Pickard, 529.
18 Higginson, 171.
19 *Boston Daily Advertiser*, Dec. 16, 1891.
20 Pickard, 552–553, 511.
21 HUL (Houghton). Pickard, 555, wrote: "Dr. Jeffries, an authority in color-blindness, says that Whittier was a typical specimen of the infirmity. . . ." Obviously Dr. Jeffries frequently saw Whittier as a patient.
22 "The Ill Health of the Poet Whittier," *Cleveland Medical Journal*, Sept., 1903.

23 Huntington Library, from copy in Essex Institute.
24 Quoted in Lewis J. Moorman, *Tuberculosis and Genius,* University of Chicago Press, 29.

## CHAPTER XXI

1 Pickard, 600.
2 See Lloyd W. Griffin, "Matthew Franklin Whittier, 'Ethan Spike,' " *New England Quarterly,* XIV, 646–663 (Dec., 1941).
3 Rourke, *American Humor: A Study of the National Character* (New York: Harcourt, Brace & Co., 1931), 227.
4 *Poetical Works,* I, 263.
5 Pickard, 555–556. Underwood, 386, quotes Nora Perry to the same effect.
6 See 249–250.
7 In many prose articles, such as his first editorial in the *Pennsylvania Freeman* on March 15, 1838, he deplored wealthy Quakers' aligning themselves with "propitty" and against the slaves and the Abolitionists.
8 *Abraham Lincoln: The Prairie Years* (New York: Harcourt, Brace & Co., 1926), II, 298–299.
9 Conversation with G. W. Pickard at Seabrook Beach, N.H., autumn, 1935.
10 Pickard, 283. Whittier outgrew the old-school Quaker prejudice against music. He would probably have laughed at the experience of one Sarah Speakman. She came to love music, and would break out into unpremeditated song. At such times her grandmother, Phoebe Schofield, a widely traveled Quaker minister, would rebuke her by asking, "Art thou in pain?" [Wendell Phillips Garrison] *In Memoriam. Sarah A. McKim, 1813–1891* (New York: privately printed at DeVinne Press, 1891), 9.
11 Fields, 77.
12 *Whittier-Land,* 82.
13 HUL (Houghton).
14 Pp. 517–519.
15 *Ibid.,* 438.
16 P. 191.
17 See 139–142.

18 Pickard, 223.

19 *Ibid.*, 413–414.

20 Unluckily, I mis-filed my transcript of this letter, after showing it to a friend. Necessarily I here quote from memory. Sarah Orne Jewett visited Whittier at Amesbury soon after the degree-granting, and she wrote Mrs. Fields: "The LL.D. had evidently given pleasure, though he was quite shy about it." F. O. Matthiessen, *Sarah Orne Jewett* (Boston: Houghton Mifflin Co., 1929), 128.

21 Kennedy (1), 357.

22 Pickard, 191–192, 661.

23 For example: "Mourning," *Haverhill Gazette*, June 12, 1830; last paragraph of "The Bachelor's Dream," Oct. 4, 1830, and "Matrimony," Aug. 22, 1831, both in *New England Weekly Review.*

24 These letters are in Houghton Library, Harvard University.

25 Quoted by T. F. Currier in "Whittier's Philadelphia Friends in 1838," *Bulletin of Friends' Historical Association*, XXVII, 59, (1938).

26 Pickard, 348.

27 Houghton Library has a letter in Weld's longhand, signed also by Miss Grimké, requesting Whittier to attend their wedding at the home of a Mrs. Frost.

28 See 164–166.

29 *Whittier-Land*, 119–120.

30 Pickard, 522.

31 Caroline Ticknor, *Glimpses of Authors* (Boston: Houghton Mifflin Co., 1922), 82.

32 Pickard, 437.

33 HUL (Houghton).

34 Pickard, 701.

35 Oak Knoll Collection, IV, 83.

36 *Gail Hamilton's Life in Letters*, ed. H. Augusta Dodge (Boston: Lee & Shepard, 1901), 346.

37 Pickard, 515–516.

38 Letter in Morgan Library, New York; Pickard, 514–515.

39 *Poetical Works*, II, 271.

40 *Whittier-Land*, 118. Pickard in that brief book printed, 111 ff., some of the "foolish verses" referred to, including "How They Climbed Chocorua."

## CHAPTER XXII

1 Howells, *Literary Friends and Acquaintance: A Personal Retrospect of American Authorship*, 135; Ferris Greenslet, *The Life of Thomas Bailey Aldrich* (Boston: Houghton Mifflin Co., 1908), 176.
2 Stedman, *Poets of America* (Boston: Houghton, Mifflin & Co., 1885), 100.
3 See 35.
4 Pickard, 603.
5 *Prose Works*, I, 92.
6 Howells, *op. cit.*, 138.
7 Pickard, 732.
8 *Ibid.*, 595.
9 LVIII, 30–32.
10 Kennedy (1), 305, 306.
11 See 275.
12 Pickard, 696.
13 Fields, 76.
14 In July 1872 Emerson's house at Concord burned. Lowell and other friends raised $17,000 to build a new one, enable Emerson to travel for his health and a rest, and to relieve him from the burden of lecturing.
15 Pickard, 577. Whittier in 1858 was elected a member of this club, which dined on the last Saturday evening of every month at the old Parker's Hotel.
16 *Ibid.*, 590.
17 *Ibid.*, 405, 535; Fields, 66–67.
18 Carl Van Doren, in the *Dictionary of American Biography*, wrote that from 1871 "the decline in his powers was regular if not rapid," and added: "Outwardly calm and smiling, inwardly he grew blank; . . ."
19 Letter, in Essex Institute, from Rantoul to Dr. Maurice D. Clarke and Judge Ira A. Abbott, dated June 17, 1899.
20 Pickard, 721.
21 *Ibid.*, 677–678. The quotation is stanza six from Wordsworth's "Extempore Effusion upon the Death of James Hogg."
22 Pickard, 635 n.
23 *Ibid.*, 635–636.
24 *Poetical Works*, II, 168.

25 Underwood, 310. Among others who described the episode is Bernard DeVoto, *Mark Twain's America* (Boston: Little, Brown & Co., 1932), 196–205.

26 Pickard, 639.

27 *Ibid.*, 637–638.

28 *Ibid.*, 725–726. Pickard gives pp. 725–728 to the story of the whole celebration.

29 *Poetical Works*, IV, 113.

30 Pickard, 648.

31 Whittier in October, 1886, wrote to Harriet Minot Pitman: "I expect to go to Amesbury the first of next week to meet my niece Elizabeth Pickard, and to vote at election. I shall not vote for ——. He and the rest of the so-called Independents have gone over entirely to the Democratic party. I am a Republican still. If my party makes a bad nomination, I shall not vote it, but shall not stultify myself by going over to a party which has done its worst to destroy the Union and sustain slavery." *Ibid.*, 716.

32 See Max L. Griffin, "Whittier and Hayne: A Record of Friendship," *American Literature*, XIX, 41–58 (March, 1947).

33 Claflin, 84.

34 Oak Knoll Collection, X, 21.

35 Pickard, 572.

36 Pickard, 580.

37 Pickard, 583–588, gives the full story of Whittier's fight to get the resolutions of censure annulled, and parts of it are also given in Edward L. Pierce, *Memoir and Letters of Charles Sumner* (Boston: Roberts Brothers, 1877–1893), vol. 4. The lines to Sumner are in Whittier's *Poetical Works*, IV, 127. Whittier's letter of Feb. 17, 1874, is in HUL (Houghton).

38 Pickard, 580–581 (1907 ed.), gives both letters, but not the correct dates. The letter to Dr. Chapin was dated Dec. 2, 1872, and appeared in the *Springfield Republican* on Dec. 6.

39 Pickard, 613.

40 *Ibid.*, 628.

41 *Whittier's Life at Oak Knoll*, 20.

42 Letters in Massachusetts Historical Society Collections.

43 Pickard, 685; George F. Hoar, *Autobiography of Seventy Years* (New York: Scribner's, 1905), I, 289.

44 Pickard, 595.
45 Fields, 63.
46 See 291 ff.
47 Essex Institute; Pickard, 690.
48 But in the Oak Knoll Collection, XI, 38, there is a letter from his son J. A. Bright, dated Rochdale, April 8, 1880, which includes this comment: "I have a most pleasant recollection of the short visit I paid to Amesbury in 1872 and of your kind reception of me then."
49 Pickard, 739.
50 *Ibid.*, 705–708. See also Samuel T. Pickard, "Unpublished Correspondence between Whittier and John Bright," *The Independent*, LI: 7–9 (Jan. 5, 1899).
51 See 270.
52 *Letters of Matthew Arnold, 1848–1888*, coll. and arr. by George W. E. Russell (New York: Macmillan & Co., 1895), II, 273.
53 Fields, 64.
54 Pickard, 528–529.
55 *The Life of Charles Dickens* (London: Chapman and Hall, 1874), III, 357, 369.
56 Letter in Houghton Library, Harvard, the gift of Mrs. Roland Thaxter.
57 Fields, 61–62. The poem "To Lydia Maria Child" is in *Poetical Works*, IV, 120.
58 Pickard, 713.
59 Celebrating the fiftieth year of Victoria's reign.
60 Introduction to the second book of *The Reason of Church Government Urged against Prelaty*. "But if she [the Church] lift up her drooping head and prosper, among those that have something more than wished her welfare, I have my charter and freehold of rejoicing to me and my heirs."
61 Pickard, 728–730.

## CHAPTER XXIII

1 Pickard, 715.
2 Meredith, *An Essay on Comedy and of the Uses of the Comic Spirit*, ed. Lane Cooper (New York: Charles Scribner's Sons, 1918 ed.), 118.
3 Letter in Yale University Library.

4 *The Outlook*, CXXVII, 97 (Jan. 19, 1921).
5 T. F. Currier, "Whittier's Philadelphia Friends in 1838," *Bulletin of Friends' Historical Association*, XXVII, 61 (1938); Pickard, 283.
6 HUL (Houghton). Haverford College now owns the Bass Otis portrait of Whittier.
7 "A Visit to Whittier," *The Bookman*, New York, VIII, 459, 461 (Jan. 1899). Quoted by Pickard, *Whittier-Land*, 126.
8 HUL (Houghton).
9 *Whittier's Life at Oak Knoll*, 26.
10 HUL (Houghton).
11 See 364.
12 Pickard, 404, 408, 276–277.
13 Sparhawk, 78.
14 Huntington Library; photostatic copy in Essex Institute.
15 Pickard, 471–473.
16 Included in *Prose Works*, II, 286.
17 Fields, 16–17.
18 Pickard, 686.
19 *Whittier's Life at Oak Knoll*, 14.
20 Oak Knoll Collection, XII, 35.
21 See 398.
22 *Elizabeth Lloyd and the Whittiers* (Harvard University Press, 1939), 141.
23 Letter from Dillwyn Parrish, Philadelphia, April 12, 1859, in Oak Knoll Collection, VI, 39.
24 *Elizabeth Lloyd and the Whittiers*, 129.
25 *Ibid.*, 137, 141, 144.
26 *Ibid.*, 146.
27 *Poetical Works*, II, 57.
28 Oak Knoll Collection, XVI, 47.
29 New Hampshire Historical Society Collections, from copy in Essex Institute.
30 The Oak Knoll Collection and the New Hampshire Historical Society Collections have letters of acknowledgment from Whittier dated, e.g., April 26, 1878, Jan. 19, 1883, and Feb. 8, 1887.
31 Pp. 211–214, 274–275.
32 See 161–162.
33 *Poetical Works*, IV, 26.
34 *Elizabeth Lloyd and the Whittiers*, 80.

35 Pickard, 480–481.
36 Currier, 118.
37 Huntington Library; photostatic copy in Essex Institute.
38 *Ibid.*
39 Oak Knoll Collection, XVI, 50.
40 Pickard, 552.
41 Oak Knoll Collection, XVI, 46 a.
42 Daniel Dulaney Addison, *Lucy Larcom, Life, Letters and Diary* (Boston: Houghton, Mifflin & Co., 1895), 218. The diary entry is for Feb. 20, 1882. Miss Larcom had recently become an Episcopalian, under the inspiration of Phillips Brooks.
43 *Poetical Works*, IV, 122.
44 Oak Knoll Collection, XIII, 60. Higginson, 108–109, gives Whittier's letter dated Amesbury, June 21, 1850, and addressed to R. W. Griswold, which opened the door to the Cary sisters.
45 Houghton Library at Harvard has a copy of a letter of May 2, 1878, in which Whittier tells Gail Hamilton how much he regrets the death of Allen Dodge — "a true & genuine friend, warm-hearted, genial, & appreciative of all that was best in us." Whittier added that he was groomsman at his wedding with "the charming Miss [Eliza] Tileston" — before M. A. Dodge was born. The date was Nov., 1832.
46 Letter from Gail Hamilton to Whittier dated Dec. 18, 1868, in Oak Knoll Collection, XV, 80.
47 H. Augusta Dodge, ed., *Gail Hamilton's Life in Letters* (Boston: Lee & Shepard, 1901), v.
48 *Ibid.*, 345.
49 *Ibid.*, 579.
50 *Ibid.*, 387.
51 Pickard, 577–578.
52 Oak Knoll Collection, XV, 78.
53 Copy of letter in HUL (Houghton).
54 Pickard, 520. Of the three sons born to the Thaxters, the oldest was a mental defective, and was his mother's care as long as she lived.
55 Letter in Haverhill Public Library.
56 HUL (Houghton).
57 *Ibid.*
58 *Whittier: Notes of His Life and of His Friendships*, 73.

59 Ticknor-Fields Correspondence, Huntington Library; photostatic copy in Essex Institute.
60 Pickard, 654.
61 *Ibid.*, 676.
62 Oak Knoll Collection, XVI, 34.
63 Pickard, 681.
64 *Ibid.*, 759.
65 In the poem "To Roy," *Haverhill Gazette*, Aug. 11. Whittier dedicated his "Among the Hills," when first published in the *Atlantic*, to Mrs. Fields "in grateful acknowledgment of the strength and inspiration I have found in her friendship and sympathy."
66 *Poetical Works*, III, 50.
67 Pickard, 589.
68 *Ibid.*, 535.
69 *Prose Works*, III, 227, 247.
70 *Ibid.*, III, 227–228.
71 Pickard, 673–674; Anne Tillinghast Weeden, *The Women's College in Brown University: Its Origin and Development* (Providence, 1912), 8, 13.
72 Oak Knoll Collection, VII, 87.
73 Pickard, 754.
74 *Poetical Works*, IV, 222.
75 Oak Knoll Collection, XI, 68.

## CHAPTER XXIV

1 *The Letters of Robert Burns*, ed. J. DeLancey Ferguson (Oxford: Clarendon Press, 1931), II, 200–201.
2 Pickard, 454.
3 *Ibid.*, 700–701.
4 Whittier was unable to discriminate between red and green, a fact his mother discovered when he was a boy. He could not tell the leaf from the fruit of wild strawberries. As a balance, he appreciated yellows unusually well, and on this account preferred the goldenrod as the national flower. He said with amusement, "I have always thought the rainbow *beautiful*, but they tell me I have never seen it. Its only color to me is yellow." Pickard, 554–555.
5 *Ibid.*, 507, 546.
6 Letter in Carroll A. Wilson collection.

7 Sparhawk, 126.
8 Pickard, 305.
9 "Whittier's Literary Methods," *The Independent*, LI, 1258–1259 (Sept. 30, 1897).
10 *Whittier's Life at Oak Knoll*, 21.
11 *Ibid.*, 19–20. This account is drawn both from Mrs. Woodman's version and Whittier's, erroneous in several respects, given in the headnote to the poem in *Poetical Works*, III, 191.
12 See 253.
13 Pickard, 488, 662–663.
14 Laura Stedman and George M. Gould, *Life and Letters of Edmund Clarence Stedman* (New York: Moffat, Yard & Co., 1910), II, 449.
15 Pickard, 318–319.
16 Letter in Historical Society of Pennsylvania.
17 Oak Knoll Collection, VII, 73.
18 Pickard, 547–548.
19 See 242.
20 Pickard, 342–343.
21 *Ibid.*, 341–342.
22 *Ibid.*, 549.
23 *Ibid.*, 406 ff.
24 *Ibid.*, 413, *passim.*
25 *Ibid.*, 416.
26 Underwood, 218.
27 Pickard, 443–444; *Poetical Works*, II, 56.
28 Pickard, 448–449.
29 *Ibid.*, 450.
30 *Ibid.*, 494.
31 *Ibid.*, 495–497.
32 *Ibid.*, 497.
33 *Bibliography of John Greenleaf Whittier*, 99–100.
34 Pickard, "Whittier's Literary Methods," *The Independent*, XLIX, 1258–1259 (Sept. 30, 1897).
35 HUL (Houghton).
36 Currier, 123–126.
37 *Ibid.*, 587–588.
38 *Ibid.*, 588.
39 These letters, printed in Currier, 377–378, are in the American Antiquarian Society.

40 Pickard, 509–510.

41 Kathryn Anderson McEuen, "Whittier's Rhymes," *American Speech*, XX, 51–57 (Feb. 1945).

42 *Yale Review*, II, 280 (1913).

43 Letter in Carroll A. Wilson Collection.

## CHAPTER XXV

1 *Poetical Works*, II, 19.

2 Fields, 90.

3 "Hampton Beach," "The Lakeside," *Poetical Works*, II, 14, 18.

4 HUL (Houghton). The quotation is from Emerson's "Ode Sung in the Town Hall, Concord, July 4, 1857."

5 *Ibid.*

6 See 373.

7 Fields, 74–76.

8 Poole, *The Great White Hills of New Hampshire* (Garden City: Doubleday & Co., 1946), 327.

9 Pickard, 378.

10 Fields, 31; see 425.

11 *Poetical Works*, II, 56.

12 Pickard, 604.

13 Poole, *op. cit.*, 328. J. Warren Thyng, "Reminiscences of Whittier," *Granite State Magazine*, III, 91 (March–April, 1907), confirms that Inness and Starr King were among other people attracted to the area.

14 *Poetical Works*, I, 261.

15 Pickard, 336.

16 American Guide Series. *New Hampshire: A Guide to the Granite State* (Boston: Houghton Mifflin Co., 1938), 277.

17 *Poetical Works*, I, 260.

18 *Ibid.*, II, 181.

19 *Ibid.*, II, 86.

20 *Ibid.*, II, 28.

21 Pickard, 534.

22 *Poetical Works*, II, 30.

23 Maria S. Porter, *Recollections of Louisa May Alcott, John Greenleaf Whittier, and Robert Browning* (Boston, 1893), 31.

24 *Poetical Works*, II, 74.

25 *Ibid.*, II, 29–30.
26 *Ibid.*, II, 76, 78.
27 *Ibid.*, II, 85.
28 *Ibid.*, II, 66.
29 *Ibid.*, I, 265.
30 *Whittier-Land*, 109–118; see 368.
31 Pickard, 669.
32 *Ibid.*
33 *Ibid.*, 681–682.
34 *Poetical Works*, II, 28–29.
35 *Ibid.*, II, 84.
36 *Ibid.*, II, 88–89.
37 Pickard, 716.

## CHAPTER XXVI

1 Pickard, 567–568.
2 *Ibid.*, 648–649.
3 *Poetical Works*, II, 169.
4 Pickard, 122.
5 Letter, dated Nov. 22, 1886, in Massachusetts Historical Society.
6 Oak Knoll Collection has copy of Whittier's letter, dated Aug. 27, and Holmes's original (XII, 55).
7 Pickard, 555: "After he had passed middle life, his right ear lost its sensitiveness, and he became partially deaf. A severe cold would occasionally make it difficult for him to understand what was said by voices which were not familiar to him. But a familiar voice did not need to be much raised above its natural pitch in conversation. This dullness of hearing was not considered by him an unmixed evil, as in many ways it shielded him from annoyance."
8 Pickard, 712–713.
9 *Ibid.*, 741–742.
10 *Ibid.*, 734.
11 *Ibid.*, 743.
12 *Ibid.*, 744–745.
13 Letter in Haverhill Public Library from Bell K. Hartley, Salem, Iowa, June 20, 1936.
14 See 285.

15 *New England Weekly Review*, Aug. 29, 1831.
16 Letters in Oak Knoll Collection, XII, 13 and 18, and V, 70.
17 Letter in Oak Knoll Collection, XII, 78.
18 Letter in HUL (Houghton).
19 Essay, Series II, on "Character."
20 Oak Knoll Collection, VIII, 19; Pickard, 531. Of Whittier's ability to read verse, Pickard wrote, 710–711: "Mr. Whittier's voice in reading poetry, whether his own or others', was fuller and stronger than in ordinary conversation or in reading prose. There was a depth and sonorousness in it that would surprise any one who, accustomed only to his conversation, heard him read verse for the first time. If he could have read in public with the same voice he used in a small company of friends, an audience of thousands would have been delighted with his rendering of a poem. . . ."
21 Letters in Oak Knoll Collection.
22 Pickard, 602.
23 Letters in Oak Knoll Collection, Harvard College Library, and *Danvers Mirror*, July 14, 1883.
24 New Hampshire Historical Society Collections; copy in Essex Institute.
25 Oak Knoll Collection, XVI, 45a, and HUL (Houghton).
26 Oak Knoll, X, 43.
27 *Ibid.*, XIII, 23.
28 Pickard, 392–393.
29 Caroline Ticknor, *Glimpses of Authors* (Boston: Houghton Mifflin Co., 1922), 76.
30 Currier, 172.
31 Letters in HUL (Houghton) and in Oak Knoll Collection, XI, 31; XVI, 3.
32 Pickard, 304–305.
33 See 282, 348–349.
34 Pickard, 558–559.
35 *Ibid.*, 557–558.
36 *Ibid.*, 559–560.
37 Oak Knoll Collection, XIV, 54; XV, 14.
38 Pickard, 560.
39 Letters in possession of Mrs. Fred M. West, Detroit, Mich., and used by her permission.

40 Oak Knoll Collection, XIV, 55 ff.
41 Pickard, 653–654.
42 Oak Knoll Collection, XIV, 62.
43 Dr. Maria Dowdell-Wilson, long a neighbor and always an intimate friend, said: "That fire was a perpetual source of pleasure and annoyance to us all. It was an old-fashioned Franklin stove, that smoked on the slightest provocation, and scattered the ashes over the hearth. At the same time it had a habit of throwing out the most charming gleams and shadows, especially if driftwood was being burned. Mr. Whittier was very jealous of any one else tending or poking the fire. Often I have unconsciously taken the tongs to touch up a brand, when his hand would stay mine, and he would say, 'Thee must not touch that, it is just right,' and perhaps the next minute he would have the tongs and do just what I had attempted. I have frequently gone in at twilight and found him lying on the lounge, watching the flitting shadows, and repeating aloud from some favorite author, generally Scott or Burns. His mood and conversation at such times were particularly delightful. The beautiful poem 'Burning Drift-Wood' was doubtless inspired by such experiences." And Mrs. Pitman wrote to him in 1885: "You were a veritable fire-worshiper. I see you coming from the closet, bringing wood. Now I see you by the stove, *sitting on nothing*. You had a firm backbone, as was suitable to a Quaker and an old abolitionist." Pickard, 745–746.
44 *Literary World*, Dec. 1, 1877, p. 122.
45 Fields, 48.
46 Letter in New Hampshire Historical Society Collections.
47 Pickard, 581–582.
48 *Ibid.*, 622.
49 *Ibid.*, 532–533.
50 *Whittier and His Schoolmates, 1827–1885: Re-union of the Schoolmates of John Greenleaf Whittier at St. John's Rectory, Haverhill, Mass., September 10, 1885* (Haverhill, 1886), 17.
51 Pickard, 614–615, and Oak Knoll Collection.
52 Pickard, 661.
53 *Ibid.*, 572.
54 Oak Knoll Collection, vol. II.
55 Oak Knoll Collection, and HUL (Houghton).
56 Copy in Oak Knoll Collection, vol. III.

57 Leaflet, "Visit of the Jubilee Singers to the Poet John G. Whittier" (Boston, Nov. 7, 1879).
58 Oak Knoll Collection, IV, XV, 28, and HPL.
59 Oak Knoll Collection, XIV, 53. There was a yellow-fever epidemic in the Southwest.
60 Letter quoted by permission of owner, Alfred Calvin Gaunt.
61 Pickard, 746–747.
62 *Ibid.*, 677.
63 Aaron M. Powell, *Personal Reminiscences of the Anti-Slavery and Other Reforms and Reformers* (pub. Anne Rice Powell, New York: Caulon Press, 1899), 187–188.
64 Pickard, 719–720. Emerson's idea is developed in "Threnody" and elsewhere in his writings.
65 Paul M. Angle, *The Lincoln Reader* (Rutgers University Press, 1947), 437.
66 Pickard, 683–684.
67 *Ibid.*, 720. Pickard erroneously gives the year as 1887.
68 *Ibid.*, 644.
69 In a letter of March 6, 1881, to Whittier (Pickard, 667–668), Holmes mentions his article, which is in CXXXII, 137–138 of the *Review*.
70 Pickard, 704.
71 *Ibid.*, 705.
72 See 271.
73 Mary Negreponte, "John Greenleaf Whittier," *The Westminster Review*, CXXXIX, 7–11 (Jan., 1893).
74 Henry Wilder Foote, *Three Centuries of American Hymnody* (Harvard University Press, 1940), 255–257, 261.
75 John Julian, *A Dictionary of Hymnology*, revised ed. (London: John Murray, 1907), 1278.
76 Foote, *op. cit.*, 256.
77 *Ibid.*, 237, 259, 262.
78 *Ibid.*, 261.
79 Edward S. Ninde, *The Story of the American Hymn* (New York: The Abingdon Press, 1921), 234.
80 New Series, XIX, 244.

## CHAPTER XXVII

1 Pickard, 639.
2 *Ibid.*, 262–263.
3 "Trust," *Poetical Works*, II, 243.
4 *Poetical Works*, II, 252.
5 Pickard, 413, 480.
6 *Poetical Works*, II, 269.
7 Pickard, 485.
8 *Ibid.*, 625.
9 "What the Voice Said" (1847), *Poetical Works*, II, 215; "At Washington" (1845), *ibid.*, III, 110.
10 "The Over-Heart," *ibid.*, II, 250.
11 Pickard, 633; "Revelation," *Poetical Works*, II, 343.
12 For a brilliant exposition, see Arthur O. Lovejoy, *The Great Chain of Being* (Cambridge: Harvard University Press, 1936).
13 Pierpont Morgan Library.
14 *Poetical Works*, II, 272.
15 "Trinitas" (1858), *ibid.*, II, 243. Beecher said: "I accept without analysis the tri-personality of God. I accept the Trinity; perhaps because I was educated to it. No matter why, I accept it." (Lyman Abbott, *Henry Ward Beecher*, 1903, p. 432.) Bushnell argued that we experience one God under three different expressions. Beyond that fact, he held, all relating to it was a mystery which the human mind could not penetrate. (*Dictionary of American Biography*, III, 352). "The Proselytes, a Sketch," published in the *New England Magazine* for Sept. 1833, shows that Whittier already had read the Church Fathers.
16 Pickard, 631.
17 *The History of the Rise, Increase and Progress of the Christian People Called Quakers* . . . (New York, 1844 ed.), II, 405.
18 *Poetical Works*, II, 326.
19 Pickard, 210. *Ibid.*, 262–263, for letter of Nov., 1840, to Richard Mott.
20 "Raphael," *Poetical Works*, II, 100.
21 *Prose Works*, III, 262.
22 Included in *Poetical Works*, II, 233. Sumner wrote to Whittier on Dec. 6, 1848: "Your poem in the last 'Era' has touched my heart.

May God preserve you in strength and courage for all good works! . . . The literature of the world is turning against slavery. We shall have it soon in a state of moral blockade. I admire Bailey as an editor very much. His articles show infinite sagacity and tact. . . . But I took my pen merely to inquire after your health. There are few to whom I would allot a larger measure of the world's blessings than to yourself had I any control, for there are few who deserve them more." Edward L. Pierce, *Memoir and Letters of Charles Sumner* (Boston: Roberts Brothers, 1893), III, 185.

23 "The Last Walk in Autumn," *Poetical Works*, II, 43.
24 "At Last," *ibid.*, II, 334.
25 "Hampton Beach," *ibid.*, II, 15.
26 *Prose Works*, III, 272.
27 *Poetical Works*, II, 74–75; *ante*, 556.
28 Pickard, 470.
29 *Poetical Works*, I, 40.
30 *Ibid.*, II, 265; Pickard, 265.
31 Pickard, 606.
32 *Ibid.*, 677, 709–710.
33 *Ibid.*, 651–652.
34 *Ibid.*, 478–479.
35 *Ibid.*, 628, 723, 690.
36 *Poetical Works*, II, 334.
37 See *Prose Works*, III, 313, 362.
38 In an editorial entitled "Catholics," *American Manufacturer*, April 30, 1829, Whittier said: "We rejoice in common with all liberal minded men, that the prospect of Catholic Emancipation is brightening in England. * * * This oppression of the Catholics is not only barbarous in the extreme, but it has not even that common excuse for tyranny, viz: — that it is necessary for the support of the government. — It is idle to talk of danger from the influence of popery in this enlightened age." See also *Prose Works*, III, 306; Pickard, 281.
39 *Poetical Works*, II, 229.
40 Pickard, 280.
41 *Prose Works*, III, 309.
42 *Ibid.*, III, 306.
43 *Ibid.*, III, 313.
44 *The Rise of the Common Man, 1830–1850* (New York, 1927), 25.

45 Rufus M. Jones, *The Later Periods of Quakerism* (London, 1921), 665, 647.

## CHAPTER XXVIII

1 Fields, 100.
2 Sparhawk, 166–167.
3 Oak Knoll Collection, III, 100.
4 Pickard, 748–750, prints the two December letters.
5 Helen Keller, *The Story of My Life* (New York: Doubleday, Page & Co., 1903), 136.
6 From letters in Oak Knoll Collection.
7 HUL (Houghton).
8 Oak Knoll Collection, IV, 26; XV, 45.
9 Pickard, 757.
10 *Ibid.*, 751–752.
11 *Ibid.*, 753.
12 *Ibid.*, 751.
13 *Ibid.*
14 *Ibid.*, 754.
15 *Ibid.*, 755–756.
16 *Ibid.*, 758. Miss Johnson's telegram is on p. 756.
17 *Ibid.*, 760.
18 *Ibid.*
19 *Ibid.* Pickard's full account of Whittier's last days, in Hampton Falls, occupies pp. 760–773.
20 Oak Knoll Collection, IV, 53.
21 Pickard, 764. The Gove and Whittier families, both Quaker, had been well acquainted. When Miss Gove's mother died, Whittier wrote "The Friend's Burial," published in the *Atlantic* for July, 1873. Miss Gove sold "Elmfield" in 1937, and died in Bradford, Mass., on Nov. 11, 1942, at the age of 85.
22 Ferris Greenslet, *The Life of Thomas Bailey Aldrich* (Boston: Houghton Mifflin Co., 1908), 258.
23 Pickard, 765 ff.

## *BIBLIOGRAPHY*

OF THE GREAT NUMBER of books and other sources which have been sifted for material for this book, the following are of main importance:

### MANUSCRIPT COLLECTIONS, RECORDS, AND FILES

John Quincy Adams Letters and Speeches, Library of Congress, Washington, D.C.
Aldis Collection, Yale University, New Haven, Connecticut.
American Antiquarian Society, Worcester, Massachusetts.
Boston Public Library.
Brown University (Providence, Rhode Island), Corporation Records.
Henry Clay Correspondence, Library of Congress.
Commonwealth of Massachusetts, Archives Division, Boston.
Connecticut Historical Society, Hartford.
Essex County Probate and Insolvency Courts, Salem, Massachusetts.
Essex Institute (Salem), Oak Knoll Collection.
Private collection of Alfred Calvin Gaunt, Methuen, Massachusetts.
Harvard University (Cambridge, Massachusetts), Records of the Overseers.
Haverhill (Massachusetts) Historical Society.
Haverhill Public Library.
Haverhill Town Records.
Historical Society of Pennsylvania, Philadelphia.
Longfellow-Whittier Letters, Longfellow House, Cambridge.
Lowell (Massachusetts) Historical Society.
Massachusetts Historical Society, Boston.
Pierpont Morgan Library, New York City.
Louise Chandler Moulton Papers, Library of Congress.
New Hampshire Historical Society, Concord.
New York Public Library.
Pickard-Whittier Papers, Harvard College Library.

Society of Friends, Central Office, London.

Charles Sumner Letterbooks, Harvard College Library.

Benjamin and Lewis Tappan Papers, Library of Congress.

Thaxter-Whittier Correspondence, Harvard College Library.

Thomas Collection, Yale University Library.

Ticknor & Fields-Whittier Letters, Henry E. Huntington Library, San Marino, California.

West Amesbury (Massachusetts), Records of Committee of School District No. 5.

Private collection of Mrs. Fred M. West, Detroit, Michigan.

Private collection of Earle O. Whittier, Washington.

Whittier Home Association, Amesbury, Massachusetts.

Private collection of the late Carroll A. Wilson, New York City.

## WORKS ABOUT WHITTIER

### BOOKS

Albree, John, *Whittier Correspondence from the Oak Knoll Collections* (Salem: Essex Book and Print Club, 1911).

Bennett, Whitman, *Whittier, Bard of Freedom* (University of North Carolina Press, 1941).

Burton, Richard, *John Greenleaf Whittier*, The Beacon Biographies (Boston: Small, Maynard, 1901).

Carpenter, George Rice, *John Greenleaf Whittier*, American Men of Letters (Boston: Houghton Mifflin Co., 1903).

Claflin, Mrs. Mary B., *Personal Recollections of John G. Whittier* (New York: Thomas Y. Crowell & Co., 1893).

Currier, Thomas Franklin, *A Bibliography of John Greenleaf Whittier* (Harvard University Press, 1937).

Currier, Thomas Franklin, ed., *Elizabeth Lloyd and the Whittiers. A Budget of Letters* (Harvard University Press, 1939).

Denervaud, Marie V., *Whittier's Unknown Romance; Letters to Elizabeth Lloyd* (Boston: Houghton Mifflin Co., 1922).

Eastburn, Iola Kay, *Whittier's Relation to German Life and Thought*. Americana Germanica, no. 20 (Philadelphia: University of Pennsylvania, 1915).

Fields, Mrs. James T., *Whittier, Notes of His Life and Friendships* (New York: Harper & Bros., 1893).

Flower, B. O., *Whittier: Prophet, Seer and Man* (Boston: Arena Publishing Co., 1896).

Hawkins, Chauncey J., *The Mind of Whittier: a Study of Whittier's Fundamental Religious Ideas* (New York: Thomas Whittaker, 1904).

Higginson, Thomas Wentworth, *John Greenleaf Whittier*, English Men of Letters (New York: The Macmillan Co., 1902).

Kennedy, William Sloane, *John Greenleaf Whittier; His Life, Genius and Writings* (Boston: S. E. Cassino, 1882; Chicago: The Werner Co., 1895).

Kennedy, William Sloane, *John G. Whittier, The Poet of Freedom* (New York: Funk & Wagnalls Co., 1892).

Linton, William James, *Life of John Greenleaf Whittier*, Great Writers (London: Walter Scott, 1893).

Mordell, Albert, *Quaker Militant: John Greenleaf Whittier* (Boston: Houghton Mifflin Co., 1933).

Perry, Bliss, *John Greenleaf Whittier; a Sketch of His Life, with Selected Poems* (Boston: Houghton Mifflin Co., 1907).

Pickard, Samuel T., *Life and Letters of John Greenleaf Whittier*. [The authorized biography] (Boston: Houghton Mifflin Co., 2 vols., 1894. Rev. ed., 1 vol., 1907).

Pickard, Samuel T., ed., *Whittier as a Politician. Illustrated by His Letters to Professor Elizur Wright, Jr. . . .* (Boston: Charles E. Goodspeed, 1900).

Pickard, Samuel T., *Whittier-Land. A Handbook of North Essex . . .* (Boston: Houghton Mifflin Co., 1904).

Smith, Emily Binney, *Whittier* [anecdotes] (Amesbury: The Whittier Press, 1935).

Sparhawk, Frances Campbell, *Whittier at Close Range* (Boston: The Riverdale Press, 1925).

Underwood, Francis H., *John Greenleaf Whittier; a Biography* (Boston: James R. Osgood & Co., 1884).

*Whittier and His Schoolmates, 1827–1885: Re-union of the Schoolmates of John Greenleaf Whittier at St. John's Rectory, Haverhill, Mass., September 10, 1885* (Haverhill, 1886).

Woodman, Mrs. Abby J., *Reminiscences of John Greenleaf Whittier's Life at Oak Knoll, Danvers, Mass.* (Salem: Essex Institute, 1908).

ARTICLES

Abbott, Lyman, "Snap-shots of My Contemporaries. John G. Whittier, Mystic," *The Outlook*, CXXVII, 96–98 (Jan. 19, 1921).

Christy, Arthur, "Orientalism in New England: Whittier," *American Literature*, I, 372–392 (Jan., 1930).

Christy, Arthur, "The Orientalism of Whittier," *American Literature*, V, 247–257 (Nov., 1933).

Coleman, Mary Haldane, "Whittier on John Randolph of Roanoke," *New England Quarterly*, VIII, 551–554 (Dec., 1935).

Currier, T. Franklin, "Whittier and the *New England Weekly Review*," *New England Quarterly*, VI, 589–597 (Sept., 1933).

Currier, Thomas Franklin, "Whittier's Philadelphia Friends in 1838," *Bulletin of Friends' Historical Association*, XXVII, 58–72 (1938).

French, Elizabeth, transcriber, "English Ancestry of the Whittier and Rolfe Families," *New England Historical and Genealogical Register*, LXVI, 244–257 (July, 1912).

Gosse, Edmund, "A Visit to Whittier," *The Bookman*, New York, VIII, 459–462 (Jan., 1899). Included in his *Portraits and Sketches* (London: William Heinemann, 1912), 135–147.

Gould, George M., "The Ill Health of the Poet Whittier," *Cleveland Medical Journal* (Sept., 1903).

Griffin, Lloyd W., "Matthew Franklin Whittier, 'Ethan Spike,' " *New England Quarterly*, XIV, 646–663 (Dec., 1941).

Griffin, Max L., "Whittier and Hayne: A Record of Friendship," *American Literature*, XIX, 41–58 (March, 1947).

Grimké, Charlotte Forten, "Personal Recollections of Whittier," *New England Magazine*, n.s., VII, 468–476 (June, 1893).

"John Greenleaf Whittier," *London Quarterly Review*, n.s., XIX, 224–244 (Jan., 1893).

McEuen, Kathryn Anderson, "Whittier's Rhymes," *American Speech*, XX, 51–57 (Feb., 1945).

Negreponte, Mary, "John Greenleaf Whittier," *Westminster Review*, CXXXIX, 7–11 (Jan., 1893).

Pickard, Samuel T., "Unpublished Correspondence between Whittier and John Bright," *The Independent*, LI, 7–9 (Jan. 5, 1899).

Pickard, Samuel T., "Whittier's Literary Methods," *The Independent*, XLIX, 1258–1259 (Sept. 30, 1897).

Pomeroy, Sarah Gertrude, "Whittier in Connecticut — Centenary of Birth of American Poet," *Connecticut Magazine*, XI, 571 (1907).

Rantoul, Robert S., "Some Personal Reminiscences of the Poet Whittier," *Essex Institute Historical Collections*, XXXVII, 129–144 (April, 1901).

Richardson, C. F., "The Morals of the Rhyming Dictionary," *Yale Review* II, 269–281 (Jan., 1913).

Sparhawk, Frances Campbell, "Whittier, the Poet and the Man," *New England Magazine*, n. s., VII, 293–298 (Nov., 1892).

Stevens, James Stacy, "Whittier's Use of the Bible," *The Maine Bulletin*, XXXIII (Orono: University of Maine Studies, 2d series, No. 16, Dec., 1930).

Thompson, Ralph, "The *Liberty Bell* and Other Anti-Slavery Gift-Books," *New England Quarterly*, VII, 154–168 (March, 1934).

Ward, Elizabeth Stuart Phelps, "Whittier's Sense of Humor," *McClure's Magazine*, VII, 114–121 (July, 1896).

Woodwell, Roland H., "The Hussey Ancestry of the Poet Whittier," *Essex Institute Historical Collections*, LXX, 58–68 (Jan., 1934).

## LEAFLETS AND PAMPHLETS

*Address to the People of the United States, by a Committee of the New-England Anti-Slavery Convention, Held in Boston on the 27th, 28th and 29th of May, 1834* (Boston, 1834).

*Catalogue of Officers & Students of Haverhill Academy. Haverhill, Massachusetts.* July, 1828. (Haverhill, 1828). Also 1827 issue.

*Declaration of the National Anti-Slavery Convention, Signed in Adelphi Hall, in the City of Philadelphia, on the sixth day of December, 1833.*

*Fourth Annual Report of the American Anti-Slavery Society* (New York: William S. Dorr, 1837).

*General Catalogue of the Theological Seminary, Andover, Massachusetts, 1808–1908* (Boston [1909]).

Grosvenor, Cyrus Pitt, *Address before the Anti-Slavery Society of Salem and the Vicinity, February 24, 1834* (Salem, 1834).

*History of Pennsylvania Hall, Which Was Destroyed by a Mob, on the 17th of May, 1838* (Philadelphia: Merrihew and Gunn, 1838).

*Journal of the Proceedings of the National Republican Convention, held at Worcester, October 11, 1832* (Boston, 1832).

*List of Freemen, Massachusetts Bay Colony, from 1630 to 1691* . . . , arr. by H. F. Andrews (Exira, Iowa, 1906).

McKim, J. Miller, *Proceedings of the American Anti-Slavery Society at Its Third Decade, Held in the City of Philadelphia, Dec. 3d and 4th, 1863* (New York: American Anti-Slavery Society, 1864).

*A New Year's Address to the Patrons of the Essex Gazette, 1828, With a Letter, Hitherto Unpublished, by John G. Whittier* (Boston: Charles E. Goodspeed, 1903).

*Proceedings of the Fourth New-England Anti-Slavery Convention, Held in Boston* . . . (Boston: Isaac Knapp, 1837).

*Proceedings of the New-England Anti-Slavery Convention, Held in Boston on the 27th, 28th and 29th of May, 1834* (Boston, 1834).

*Proceedings of the Pennsylvania Convention, Assembled to Organize a State Anti-Slavery Society, at Harrisburg, on the 31st of January and 1st, 2d and 3d of February 1837* (Philadelphia: Merrihew and Gunn, 1837).

*A Succinct Account of the Late Difficulties on the Salisbury Corporation* (Salisbury: Currier & Gerrish, 1852).

*The Trial of Reuben Crandall, M.D., Charged with Publishing and Circulating Seditious and Incendiary Papers, &c., in the District of Columbia, with the Intent of Exciting Servile Insurrection.* Carefully reported . . . by a Member of the Bar (Washington City, 1836).

*Visit of the Jubilee Singers to the Poet John G. Whittier* (Boston, Nov. 7, 1879).

Weeden, Anne Tillinghast, *The Women's College in Brown University: Its Origin and Development* (Providence, 1912).

SECONDARY BOOKS

Adams, J. Q., *Letters from John Quincy Adams to His Constituents of the Twelfth Congressional District in Massachusetts* . . . (Boston: Isaac Knapp, 1837).

Addison, Daniel Dulaney, *Lucy Larcom, Life, Letters and Diary* (Boston: Houghton Mifflin Co., 1895).

Banks, Charles Edward, *The Planters of the Commonwealth* (Boston: Houghton Mifflin Co., 1930).

Barnes, Gilbert Hobbs, *The Antislavery Impulse, 1830–1844* (New York: D. Appleton-Century Co., ©1933).

Bartlett, Albert L., *The Haverhill Academy and the Haverhill High School, 1827–1890* (Haverhill, 1890).

Bartlett, Albert L., *Some Memories of Old Haverhill* (Haverhill, 1915).

Beard, Charles A. and Mary R., *The Rise of American Civilization*, 1-vol. ed. (New York: The Macmillan Co., 1930).

Bingham, Caleb, *The American Preceptor*, 2d ed. (Hartford, 1810).

*The Boston Directory*, 1829.

Bowditch, Vincent Y., *Life and Correspondence of Henry Ingersoll Bowditch* (Boston: Houghton Mifflin Co., 1902).

Bowers, Claude G., *The Party Battles of the Jackson Period* (Boston: Houghton Mifflin Co., 1922).

Bryant, William Cullen, *Prose Writings*, ed. Parke Godwin (New York: D. Appleton & Co., 1884).

Burke, Edmund, *Works* (Boston: John West and O. C. Greenleaf, 1806).

Channing, William Ellery, *Memoir*, 5th ed. (Boston: W. Crosby and H. P. Nichols, 1851).

Channing, William Ellery, *Works*, 8th complete ed. (Boston: J. Munroe and Co., 1848).

Chase, George Wingate, *The History of Haverhill from Its First Settlement, in 1640, to the Year 1860* (Haverhill, 1861).

Clarkson, Thomas, *A Portraiture of Quakerism* (London: Longman, Hurst, Rees, and Orme, 1806).

Commons, J. R., and others, *History of Labour in the United States* (New York: The Macmillan Co., 1918).

Currier, John J., *History of Newburyport, Mass., 1764–1905* (Newburyport, 1906).

Davis, Rebecca I., *Gleanings from Merrimac Valley*, Sheaf Number Two (Haverhill, 1886).

*The Descendants of Thomas Whittier and Ruth Green of Salisbury & Haverhill, Massachusetts.* Compiled by Charles Collyer Whittier. Edited and supplemented by Earle O. Whittier (Rutland, Vt.: The Tuttle Publishing Co., 1937).

*Dictionary of American Biography.*

*Dictionary of American History.*

*Dictionary of National Biography.*

Ellis, George E., *The Puritan Age and Rule in the Colony of the Massachusetts Bay, 1629–1685* (Boston: Houghton Mifflin Co., 1888).

Emerson, R. W., *The Heart of Emerson's Journals*, ed. Bliss Perry (Boston: Houghton Mifflin Co., 1926).

Emerson, R. W., *Journals of Ralph Waldo Emerson*, ed. Edward Waldo Emerson and Waldo Emerson Forbes (Boston: Houghton Mifflin Co., 1910).

Emerson, R. W., *The Letters of Ralph Waldo Emerson*, ed. Ralph L. Rusk (Columbia University Press, 1939).

*Encyclopaedia Britannica.*

*Encyclopaedia of the Social Sciences.*

*The Farmer's Almanac* (Worcester, 1807).

Fish, Carl Russell, *The Rise of the Common Man, 1830–1850* (New York: The Macmillan Co., 1927).

Foote, Henry Wilder, *Three Centuries of American Hymnody* (Harvard University Press, 1940).

Fuess, Claude Moore, *The Life of Caleb Cushing* (New York: Harcourt, Brace & Co., 1923).

Fulton, John, *Memoirs of Frederick A. P. Barnard* (New York: The Macmillan Co., 1896).

*Garrison, William Lloyd: The Story of His Life, Told by his Children* (New York: The Century Co., 1885).

Greenleaf, James Edward, comp., *Genealogy of the Greenleaf Family* (Boston, 1896).

Greenslet, Ferris, *The Life of Thomas Bailey Aldrich* (Boston: Houghton Mifflin Co., 1908).

Hallowell, Richard P., *The Quaker Invasion of Massachusetts* (Boston: Houghton Mifflin Co., 1883).

Hamilton, Gail, *Gail Hamilton's Life in Letters*, ed. H. Augusta Dodge (Boston: Lee & Shepard, 1901).

Hamilton, Thomas, *Men and Manners in America* (Edinburgh: W. Blackwood & Sons, 1843).

Hart, Albert Bushnell, ed., *Commonwealth History of Massachusetts* (New York: The States History Co., 1927).

Hart, Albert Bushnell, *Slavery and Abolition, 1831–1841* (New York: Harper & Bros., 1906).

*History of Essex County, Massachusetts*, D. Hamilton Hurd, compiler (Philadelphia: J. W. Lewis & Co., 1880).

Hoar, George F., *Autobiography of Seventy Years* (New York: Charles Scribner's Sons, 1905).

Howells, William Dean, *Literary Friends and Acquaintance; a Personal Retrospect of American Authorship* (New York: Harper & Bros., 1900).

Johnson, Clifton, ed., *The District School as It Was; by One Who Went to It* (Boston: Lee & Shepard, 1897).

Johnson, Clifton, *The Farmer's Boy* (New York: T. Y. Crowell & Co., 1907).

Jones, Rufus M., *The Later Periods of Quakerism* (London: Macmillan & Co., Ltd., 1921).

Jones, Rufus M., *The Quakers in the American Colonies* (London: Macmillan & Co., Ltd., 1911).

Kimball, E. A., *The Peaslees and Others of Haverhill and Vicinity* (Haverhill, 1899).

Kingsley, Charles, *Charles Kingsley: His Letters and Memories of His Life*, ed. by his wife (London: Macmillan & Co., Ltd., 1891).

Lee, James Melvin, *History of American Journalism*, rev. ed. (Boston: Houghton Mifflin Co., 1923).

Leonard, William Ellery, *Byron and Byronism in America* (Boston, 1905).

Longfellow, H. W., *Life of Henry Wadsworth Longfellow*, with extracts from his journals and correspondence, ed. Samuel Longfellow (Boston: Houghton Mifflin Co., c 1891).

Lovejoy, Arthur O., *The Great Chain of Being* (Harvard University Press, 1936).

Loyal National League, *Opinions of Prominent Men Concerning the Great Questions of the Times* (New York: C. S. Westcott & Co., 1863).

Mann, Henry, *Features of Society in Old and in New England* (Providence, 1885).

Martin, George H., *The Evolution of the Massachusetts Public School System* (New York: D. Appleton & Co., 1894).

Martineau, Harriet, *Retrospect of Western Travel* (London: Saunders & Otley, 1838).

*Massachusetts Soldiers and Sailors of the Revolutionary War* (Boston: Wright & Potter Printing Co., 1908).

*The Memorial History of Hartford County, Connecticut, 1633–1884*, ed. J. Hammond Trumbull (Boston: E. L. Osgood, 1886).

Merrill, Joseph, *History of Amesbury, 1637–1880* (Haverhill, 1880).

Milton, John, *The Student's Milton*, ed. Frank Allen Patterson (New York: F. S. Crofts & Co., 1931).

Moore, Frank, *Anecdotes, Poetry, and Incidents of the War: North and South, 1860–1865* (New York: Bible House, 1867).

Mott, Frank Luther, *A History of American Magazines, 1741–1850* (New York: D. Appleton & Co., 1930).

*Municipal History of Essex County in Massachusetts*, Benjamin F. Arrington, editor-in-chief (New York: Lewis Historical Publishing Co., 1922).

Murray, Lindley, *The English Reader*, 5th ed. (York, 1805).

*National Cyclopaedia of American Biography.*

Neal, John, *Wandering Recollections of a Somewhat Busy Life* (Boston: Roberts Brothers, 1869).

Ninde, Edward S., *The Story of the American Hymn* (New York:The Abingdon Press, 1921).

Parrington, Vernon Louis, *The Romantic Revolution in America, 1800–1860* (New York: Harcourt, Brace & Co., 1927).
Phillips, Ulrich Bonnell, *American Negro Slavery* (New York: D. Appleton & Co., 1918).
Pierce, Edward L., *Memoir and Letters of Charles Sumner* (Boston: Roberts Bros., 1877–1893).
Pope, Charles Henry, *The Pioneers of Massachusetts* (Boston: C. H. Pope, 1900).
Porter, Maria S., *Recollections of Louisa May Alcott, John Greenleaf Whittier, and Robert Browning* (Boston: New England Magazine Corp., 1893).
Prince, J., *A Wreath for St. Crispin* (Boston: Bela Marsh, 1848).
*Records and Files of the Quarterly Courts of Essex County, Massachusetts* (Salem: The Essex Institute, 1911).
*Records of the Governor and Company of the Massachusetts Bay in New England*, ed. N. B. Shurtleff (Boston: W. White, Printer to the Commonwealth, 1853).
Rourke, Constance, *American Humor. A Study of the National Character* (New York: Harcourt, Brace & Co., 1931).
*Rules of Discipline of the Yearly Meeting Held on Rhode Island, for New England* (New Bedford, 1809).
Sandburg, Carl, *Abraham Lincoln: The Prairie Years* (New York: Harcourt, Brace & Co., 1926); *The War Years*, 1939.
Sargent, Mrs. John T., *Sketches and Reminiscences of the Radical Club* (Boston: J. R. Osgood & Co., 1880).
Sewel, William, *The History of the Rise, Increase and Progress of the Christian People Called Quakers* . . . (New York, 1844).
Small, Walter Herbert, *Early New England Schools* (Boston: Ginn & Co., 1914).
Stedman, Edmund Clarence, *Poets of America* (Boston: Houghton Mifflin Co., 1885).
Stowe, Harriet Beecher, *Oldtown Folks* (Boston: Houghton Mifflin Co., 1881).
Sturge, Joseph, *A Visit to the United States in 1841* (London, 1842).
Taussig, Frank W., *The Tariff History of the United States*, 6th ed. (New York: G. P. Putnam's Sons, 1914).
Thoreau, H. D., *The Heart of Thoreau's Journals*, ed. Odell Shepard (Boston: Houghton Mifflin Co., 1927).
Ticknor, Caroline, *Glimpses of Authors* (Boston: Houghton Mifflin Co., 1922).

United States Census.

*Vital Records of Haverhill, Mass., to the End of the Year 1849* (Topsfield, Mass., 1911).

Whitman, Walt, *The Uncollected Poetry and Prose of Walt Whitman*, coll. and ed. by Emory Holloway (Garden City: Doubleday, Page & Co., 1921).

Williams, Mary Wilhelmine, *Dom Pedro the Magnanimous, Second Emperor of Brazil* (University of North Carolina Press, 1937).

MAGAZINES

*American Literature.*
*American Monthly Magazine.*
*American Monthly Review.*
*American Quarterly Review.*
*American Speech.*
*Athenaeum; or Spirit of the English Magazines.*
*Atlantic Monthly.*
*Bookman* (New York).
*Boston Literary Magazine.*
*Bouquet* (Boston).
*Bulletin of Friends' Historical Association.*
*Casket; or Flowers of Literature, Wit, and Sentiment.*
*Columbian Star* (Philadelphia).
*Connecticut Magazine.*
*Democratic Review* (*United States Magazine and*).
*Essex Institute Historical Collections.*
*Friend* (Philadelphia).
*Godey's Lady's Book.*
*Granite State Magazine.*
*Independent* (New York).
*Knickerbocker.*
*Ladies' Magazine and Literary Gazette.*
*Ladies' Miscellany.*
*Literary World* (Boston).
*London Quarterly Review.*
*Nation* (New York).
*New England Historical and Genealogical Register.*
*New England Magazine.*
*New England Quarterly.*
*New Monthly Magazine.*
*New York Amulet and Ladies' Chronicle.*
*New York Mirror.*
*North American Review.*
*Pearl* (Hartford, Boston).
*Philadelphia Album.*
*Westminster Review* (London).
*Yale Review.*
*Yankee; or, Yankee and Boston Literary Gazette.*

NEWSPAPERS

*American Anti-Slavery Reporter.*
*American Manufacturer.*
*American Traveller* (Boston).
*Amesbury Daily News.*
*Bennington Journal of the Times.*
*Boston Atlas.*

*Boston Courier.*
*Boston Daily Advertiser.*
*Boston Recorder and Telegraph.*
*Columbian Daily Centinel* (Boston).
*Connecticut Mirror.*
*Essex Register* (Salem).
*Essex Transcript* (Amesbury).
*Haverhill Gazette.*
*Haverhill Iris.*
*Liberator* (Boston).
*Middlesex Standard* (Lowell).
*National Era* (Washington).
*National Philanthropist* (Boston).
*Newburyport Free Press.*
*Newburyport Herald.*
*New England Weekly Review.*
*New York Evening Post.*
*Pennsylvania Freeman.*
*Salem Gazette.*
*Salem Landmark.*
*Salem Observer.*
*Villager* (Amesbury and Salisbury).

# *Appendix A*

## GENEALOGY

### *First Generation*

### THOMAS WHITTIER (*c.* 1620–1696) and RUTH GREEN

ADDITIONAL FACTS regarding the presumed Huguenot strain in Thomas Whittier are: (1) in the church warden's accounts of St. Edmund's Church, Salisbury, England, which go as far back as 1510, it is recorded that twelve pence was then received for the hire of the best cross and candle for the burial of Anceline Whithier; (2) in 1556 Robert Wythyer was a warden of St. Edmund's; (3) other entries in the register show the family name spelled also variously as Withieres and Wythere — perhaps suggesting Norman influence. The most likely derivation of the name *Whittier* seems to be from *white tawyer* (one who prepares white leather); this suggestion finds support in the Whittier coat of arms. But there appears no sign that *white tawyer* was translated from a Norman equivalent. (Manuscript material in possession of Earle O. Whittier, Washington.)

Thomas Whittier in 1638 accompanied to New England his uncle and aunt, John and Mrs. Anne Rolfe. He appeared in the ship's register as "Thomas Whittle, 18, servant," and his name was linked directly with theirs. There is no record among the other 109 passengers of the second uncle, Henry Rolfe, or of the Rolfes' alleged relative, Ruth Green, who became Whittier's wife in 1646, the year before he settled at Haverhill. (See Charles Edward Banks, *The Planters of the Commonwealth* [Boston, 1930], 195–198.) No student of Whittier has clearly accounted for Ruth Green on that voyage, and nothing is known of her family. (*Descendants of Thomas Whittier and Ruth Green*, 15.)

Although the majority of the Bay Colony settlers came from Puritan East Anglia (Suffolk, Essex, Norfolk, and eastern Hertfordshire), the majority of the settlers of Amesbury, Andover, Haverhill, Newbury, and

Salisbury were men from Berkshire, Hampshire, and Wiltshire, especially from around Newbury in Berkshire, Andover in Hampshire, and Marlborough and Salisbury in Wiltshire. Albert Bushnell Hart, ed., *Commonwealth History of Massachusetts* (New York, 1927), I, 56–57.

Thomas Whittier was not granted the rights of a freeman until 1666, but he was qualified to hold office under the terms of a General Court ruling in 1647. Henceforth non-freemen were permitted to take the oath of fidelity, which qualified them to serve as jurymen, and to vote for Selectmen and on matters concerning roads, schools, and distribution of lands. Manuscript material in possession of Earle O. Whittier; and *Commonwealth History . . .*, I, 122, 171.

Whittier took the oath of fidelity in Haverhill on May 7, 1650. *Records and Files of the Quarterly Courts of Essex County, Massachusetts* (Salem: The Essex Institute, 1911), I, 203.

In 1648 his property was valued in the Court Records at £80, and at least six times he shared in a division of the available lands. (Chase, *History of Haverhill*, 72, and manuscript material in possession of Earle O. Whittier.) Thomas was seven times a Selectman, at various times between 1656 and 1687, and he thus set an example of service followed by his great-grandson, John G. Whittier's father. Seven times also Thomas was Moderator, between 1668 and 1688, and in 1669 he served as Constable. In religious matters, which were then virtually synonymous with civil, Thomas in 1681 was appointed to a two-man committee to repair the meeting house and to make room in it for women worshipers. (Manuscript material in possession of Earle O. Whittier.) For Thomas Whittier's other services, see Chase, *op. cit.*, 74, 134, 145.

Much more significant, in the family history of John G. Whittier, was the religious service which Thomas Whittier performed in 1652. Joseph Peasley and Thomas Macy, of Haverhill and Salisbury, respectively, who soon became Quakers, were already touched by Quaker doctrines. Upon occasion they were self-appointed preachers. This Gospel-ministry ran counter to the custom of the iron theocracy which then ruled the colony, and the General Court forbade the pair to exhort the people on the Sabbath, in the absence of a minister. Whereupon Lieutenant Robert Pike declared, ". . . such persons as did act in making that law, did break their oath to the country, for it is against the liberty of the country, both civil and ecclesiastical." For his impudence Pike was heavily fined. A petition for his pardon was then sent to the General Court by Essex County people, who in turn were commanded to withdraw it or also be penalized. Only sixteen had the courage to refuse. One of them was Thomas Whittier. He thereby delayed until May 23, 1666, his acquisition of the rights of a freeman. On February 14, 1668, Whittier took the freeman's oath and was granted the franchise. Chase, *op. cit.*, p. 80; *Records and Files of the Quarterly Courts of Essex County, Massachusetts*, I, 366–368; IV, 24; Charles Henry Pope, *The Pioneers of Massachusetts* (Boston, 1900), 495; H. F. Andrews, arr., *List of Freemen, Massachusetts Bay Colony, from 1630 to 1691* . . . (Exira, Iowa, 1906).

### *Second Generation*

### JOSEPH WHITTIER (1669–1739 or 1740) and MARY PEASLEY

The Peasleys had the same regard for civic duties as the Whittiers. The first Joseph Peasley was in Haverhill in 1645, and was a freeman from 1646. As a lay preacher he is known to have supplied the place of a minister in Amesbury. Church records praised him as a "gifted brother," but the General Court restrained him. Undaunted, his Quaker son, Joseph, Jr., in 1699 petitioned with others for the right to hold meetings of the Society of Friends in the town's new meeting house. This petition the authorities denied.

Like the Whittiers, the Peasleys shared periodically in the division of lands, one time apparently with too much enthusiasm. In 1686, Joseph, Jr., among others, was reported for trespassing on the town's ways and common lands. Yet in 1705 he was a member of a committee to consider the claims of people to the town's undivided lands. He, father of Mary Peasley Whittier, was both a physician and a licensed operator of a sawmill. Between 1669 and 1675 he built, with bricks brought from England, the "Old Garrison House," which still stands at Rocks Village, East Haverhill. Here he held the first Quaker meetings on record in this area. This house was considered one of Haverhill's strongest places of refuge in the time of King Philip's War. Chase, *op. cit.*, 60, 72, 176, 644, 143, 164, 215. *Whittier-Land*, 47. E. A. Kimball, *The Peaslees and Others of Haverhill* (Haverhill, 1899), 13.

### *Third Generation*

### Joseph Whittier, Jr. (1716–1796) and Sarah Greenleaf

The Greenleafs are believed to have been French Huguenot refugees, by name Feuillevert (see Whittier's poem, "A Name," *Poetical Works*, II, 176), who went to England in the sixteenth century and settled at Ipswich, Suffolk. Here Edmund Greenleaf, born about 1590, in about the year 1612 married Sarah Dole, probably herself of French origin, and came to Newbury in 1635. He was admitted a freeman on March 13, 1639, and on May 22 of that year was given permission "to keep a house of entertainment" — i.e., a tavern. He also rendered civil and military service. In 1639 he was appointed ensign of the company at Newbury, and in 1642 a lieutenant.

Tristram and Nathaniel, the men in the third and fourth generations in the direct line of descent to Sarah Greenleaf, also saw military service. Stephen, of the second generation, was a religious man, a representative to the General Court (1676–1686), and a member of the Council of Safety (1689). His son, Stephen, Jr. (1652–1743), on the contrary, was known as the "great Indian fighter." He was commissioned ensign in 1670 and captain of militia in 1686.

Numerous Whittiers — whether or not descended directly in the line of youngest sons from Thomas Whittier — bore arms during the eighteenth century. During the War of the Revolution there was a scattering of Whittiers as well as of Greenleafs among the Haverhill muster rolls. James Edward Greenleaf, compiler, *Genealogy of the Greenleaf Family* (Boston, 1896), 71–72; *Massachusetts Soldiers and Sailors of the Revolutionary War* (Boston, 1908), VI, 848–854; XVII, 276–279; Chase, *op. cit.*, 347, 388–389, 393, and 395, n.; B. B. Whittier, *The Ancestry and Descendants of Edmund Whittier* (East Lansing, Mich., 1917), Nos. 23, 56, 86, 127, and 137.

### *Fourth Generation*

### John Whittier (1762–1830) and Abigail Hussey

In the first three generations of this Whittier branch there were ten, nine, and eleven children, respectively. The poet's parents had four children, he himself never married, and one brother, Matthew Franklin, had only two male descendants, neither of whom left children. (One died just under a year after birth, and the other, Charles Franklin Whittier, first child of M. F. Whittier's third marriage and brother of the poet's favorite niece, Elizabeth Hussey Whittier, lived from 1843 to about 1909, but left no issue.) Hence this branch of the Whittier family, which was descended from the pioneer American ancestor to the fifth generation by three young sons in succession, ended with the sixth generation. By some unexplained genetic mystery, the male branch died when it had reached its finest culture and when it seemed fittest to survive.

There has been considerable speculation concerning genetic phenomena in Whittier, chiefly on two points: (1) as in Pickard, I, 9–10 (1894 ed.), that "the delicacy of his physical frame and the unusual development of intellectual and spiritual force may be taken as confirmation of the theory that the older children of a family inherit a large share of physical strength, while the younger ones come into possession of a corresponding share of nerve and brain power"; (2) as in Mordell, *Quaker Militant: John Greenleaf Whittier*, chiefly chapter XXII, that Whittier's celibacy and the exhaustion of the male line in the sixth generation of his branch of the family, indicated sterility in him.

Dr. Milislav Demerec, of the Carnegie Institution of Washington, Department of Genetics, Cold Spring Harbor, N.Y., states that there is no genetic principle involved under (1), and that there is no ground for such assumptions as in (2). Under (1) it is to be noted merely that, on the biological principle of variation, the quality of children in a family usually varies.

Dr. Demerec declares that Whittier's inheritance could be explained only by studying it carefully through several generations. So far, nothing sufficiently definite is known concerning the inheritance of Whittier's direct ancestors, whose characters are thought to be of a complicated type, to make possible such an explanation. Dr. Demerec says that the inheritance of only a few simple types of human characters is known; that, for want of the knowledge of complicated types, it is thus impossible to explain the poet's inheritance by reference to completed studies of types of people similar to the Whittiers.

On the subject of John Whittier's position in Haverhill, these facts are of interest. From 1805, the year after his marriage, through 1816 he was nine times a Selectman of the town. (Haverhill Town Records, I, 200, 214, 228, 243, 298, 309, 326, 327, 339, 346, 361, 372.) He likewise served in other capacities, as Thomas Whittier had done. In 1803–1804 he was Assessor (*ibid.*, I, 158, 173, 181, 193), and in 1811 he was a member of the budget committee (*ibid.*, I, 203). His service was further diversified, for in 1818 he was on the committee to inspect the several bridges needing repair (*ibid.*, I, 402). That his later lack of sympathy with the proposal of a classical education for Greenleaf was probably due rather to lack of funds than to lack of interest in education, is suggested by his service for fourteen years, between 1803 and 1825, on the Third District School Committee (*ibid.*, I, 167, 259, 271, 309, 320, 335, 417, 445; II, 6, 22, 37, 42, 66). Likewise, as his son has recorded, he "was often called upon to act as arbitrator in matters at issue between neighbors" (Carpenter, 297).

It is of interest that, in his time, Benjamin Franklin's father, in Boston, was sought out for the kind of services and qualities which brought Haverhill people to John Whittier. Josiah Franklin's "great excellence lay in a sound understanding and solid judgment in prudential matters, both in private and public affairs." *Autobiography of Benjamin Franklin*, The Century Classics (New York, 1910), 15.

The tie between the town of Haverhill and the boy Whittier on the farm was further strengthened by his Uncle Moses' participation in town affairs. In 1803 and 1811 he was a Surveyor of Highways for District Thirteen, and four times between 1806 and 1818 he served on the Third District School Committee. Haverhill Town Records, I, 160, 285; II, 216, 320, 335, 402.

One curious family feature, probably with an influence on the poet, was the comparatively late age at which each of his direct ancestors became a father for the last time: forty-nine, forty-eight, and forty-three. John Whittier was forty-seven when his *first* son, the poet, was born. Moreover, all three wives of the Whittiers previous to the poet's own mother — who was nearly twenty-six years old at the time of his birth — had their last children comparatively late in life: Ruth Green Whittier and Mary Peasley Whittier at approximately forty-three, and Sarah Greenleaf Whittier at about thirty-nine. Parents who had thus passed their first youth might have been expected to raise their children, as J. G. Whittier was indeed raised, in an atmosphere of sober and purposeful stability. (The date of Ruth Green's birth is unknown, but it may be assumed that she was twenty or above when she married Thomas Whittier in 1646. Joseph Whittier was born on May 8, 1669.)

# Appendix B

## THE LIBRARY OF JOHN WHITTIER (*c.* 1822)

THE COMPOSITION of the library at the homestead during John Greenleaf Whittier's boyhood is determined by:

1. The rhymed list of his father's books which Whittier wrote, about 1823–24, and which is printed in *Whittier-Land*, 24–25.
2. *Snow-Bound.*
3. Whittier's preface to *Child Life in Prose* (Boston, 1874).

The dates given are in all possible instances those of the first editions. Otherwise, the date for each book is taken from the catalogue card in the Sterling Memorial Library, Yale University.

Agrippa von Nettesheim, Heinrich Cornelius (1486?–1535)
*De Occulta Philosophia* (Antwerp, 1531). The fourth book was published in London by J. Harrison in 1655, as translated into English by Robert Turner.

Barclay, Robert (1648–1690)
*An Apology for the True Christian Divinity, as the Same Is Held Forth, and Preached by the People, Called, in Scorn, Quakers* . . . (London, 1st ed., 1678).

Baxter, Richard (1615–1691)
*A Call to the Unconverted to Turn and Live, and Accept of Mercy, While Mercy May Be Had, As Ever They Will Find Mercy in the Day of Their Extremity from the Living God* (Glasgow, 1792; Northampton, 1806).

*Bible, The.*

Bingham, Caleb (1757–1817)
*The American Preceptor: Being a New Selection of Lessons for Reading and Speaking. Designed for the Use of Schools* (Boston, 1st ed., 1794). The edition owned by the Whittiers must have contained Cowper's poem, "On the Loss of the Royal George."

Bruce, James (1730–1794)

*An Interesting Narrative of Travels into Abyssinia, to Discover the Source of the Nile* (Boston, 2d American ed., 1798).

Bunyan, John (1628–1688)

*The Christian Pilgrim [Pilgrim's Progress]: Containing an Account of the Wonderful Adventures and Miraculous Escapes of a Christian in His Travels from the Land of Destruction to the New Jerusalem* (Worcester: Isaiah Thomas Jr., 1st American ed., October 1798).

Chalkley, Thomas (1675–1741)

*A Journal or Historical Account of His Life, Travels, and Christian Experiences* (London, 3d ed., 1751). Note also *A Collection of the Works of Thomas Chalkley* [inc. the *Journal*] (Philadelphia: Benjamin Franklin and David Hall, 1st ed., 1749).

Clarkson, Thomas (1760–1846)

*A Portraiture of Quakerism, as Taken from a View of the Moral Education, Discipline, Peculiar Customs, Religious Principles, Political and Civil Oeconomy, and Character of the Society of Friends* (London, 1st ed., 1806).

Dyer, Mary Marshall (1780–?)

*A Portraiture of Shakerism, Exhibiting a General View of Their Character and Conduct, from the First Appearance of Ann Lee in New-England* (Concord, N.H., 1822).

Ellwood, Thomas (1639–1713)

*Davideis: A Sacred Poem in Five Books*, 1712. Note also *A Collection of Poems on Various Subjects*, n.d.

*Farmer's Almanack, The*, ed. Robert Bailey Thomas.

Foss, Daniel (?)

*A Journal of the Shipwreck and Sufferings of Daniel Foss, (a Native of Elkton, Maryland) Who Was the Only Person Saved from on Board the Brig Negociator, of Philadelphia, Which Foundered in the Pacific Ocean, on the 26th Nov. 1809 — and Who Lived Five Years on a Small Barren Island — During Which Time He Subsisted on Seals, and Never Saw the Face of Any Human Creature . . .* (Boston, 1816).

Malcolm of Salem

In the rhymed book-list of 1823–24, the lines "Malcolm of Salem's narrative beside, /Who lost his ship's crew, unless belied" may possibly refer to Alexander Malcom, of Marblehead, a seaman on the schooner *Boys.* This ship of Marblehead registry sailed from Charlestown early in 1821 and was never heard from again. Malcom's fate was recorded in *Vital Records of Marblehead, Massachusetts . . .* (Salem, 1904), II, 608.

Murray, Lindley (1745–1826)

*The English Reader; or, Pieces in Prose and Poetry, Selected from the Best Writers. . . . With a Few Preliminary Observations on the Principles of Good Reading* ([York?] 1799). The Whittiers' copy must have contained Gray's "Elegy Written in a Country Churchyard."

Penn, William (1644–1718)

Collected or selected *Works* were published in 1726, 1771, 1782, and 1825. Penn's *Essay towards the Present and Future Peace of Europe, by the Establishment of an European Dyet, Parliament, or Estates*, was written in 1693.

Riley, James (1777–1840)

*An Authentic Narrative of the Loss of the American Brig Commerce, Wrecked on the Western Coast of Africa, in the Month of August, 1815. With an Account of the Sufferings of Her Surviving Officers and Crew, Who Were Enslaved by the Wandering Arabs on the Great African Desart, or Zahahrah* . . . (Hartford, 1817).

Rollin, Charles (1661–1741)

*The Ancient History of the Egyptians, Carthaginians, Assyrians, Babylonians, Medes and Persians, Macedonians, and Grecians*, translated from the French (London, 5th ed., 7 vol., 1768; 10th ed., 8 vol., 1804).

Scott, Sir Walter (1771–1832)

*The Pirate* (Edinburgh, 1st ed., 1822; Albany, 1822; Hartford, 1822).

Sewel, William (1654–1720)

*History of the Rise, Increase, and Progress of the Christian People Called Quakers*, translated from the Dutch by himself (1st ed., 1722; 2d ed., London, 1725; 1st American ed., 1728).

Smith, Elias (1769–1846)

Whittier's "Elias Smith's 'Universalism' " perhaps refers to *The Life, Conversion, Preaching, Travels and Sufferings of Elias Smith*, published 1816. (But Smith was a Universalist only in 1818–1823.)

Weld, Isaac, Jr. (1774–1856)

*Illustrations of the Scenery of Killarney and the Surrounding Country* . . . (London, 1807). Or *Travels through the States of North America, and the Provinces of Upper and Lower Canada, during the Years 1795, 1796, and 1797* (London, 3d ed., 2 vol., 1800).

BIOGRAPHIES

(Authors unknown)

| | |
|---|---|
| Addison, Joseph | Gay, John |
| Akenside, Mark | Gray, Thomas |
| Armstrong, John | Milton, John |
| Burroughs, Stephen | Penn, William |
| Doddridge, Philip | Pope, Alexander |
| Dyer, John | Prior, Matthew |
| Fenelon, François de | Scott, Sir Walter |
| Fox, George | Tufts, Henry |
| Franklin, Benjamin | Young, Edward |

# *Appendix C*

## BIOGRAPHICAL SKETCHES

EVELINA BRAY

She was born at Marblehead, Massachusetts, on October 14, 1810. She attended Marblehead Academy, Haverhill Academy, and finally Ipswich Seminary for Female Teachers, from which she was graduated in 1832. Her diploma was signed by Mary Lyon, founder of Mt. Holyoke College. Miss Bray taught in many Southern and Middle Western cities, usually in schools conducted under Episcopal auspices.

Her life with the Reverend Mr. Downey is said to have been unhappy. He was completely deaf, and seems to have been an eccentric man of quixotic temperament. In large cities of the country he preached against Catholicism, and for such utterances in New York City he was nearly stoned to death. He died in 1889. Mrs. Downey continued to live for a time thereafter in New York City, and then resided successively in Marblehead and in West Newbury, Massachusetts. She died there on January 17, 1895, and was buried in New York City.

A few facts in this sketch are from a paper, now in the possession of the Haverhill Historical Society, which S. T. Pickard read before the Haverhill Whittier Club on June 20, 1903. Most of the foregoing information, however, has been supplied by Mrs. Downey's nephew, the Reverend Henry E. Bray, of Framingham, Massachusetts. He says that it has been a legend in his family that Whittier sought his aunt's hand, but that proof of this is wanting. Yet when the Reverend Mr. Bray questioned her closely about the legend, she did not deny the truth of it. At any rate, she was a lively and pleasure-loving girl, and would hardly, in her nephew's opinion, have married a quiet Quaker.

OLIVER CARLTON

Carlton was graduated in 1824, and, like Joshua Coffin, he had an M.A. degree from Dartmouth. He was a tutor there in 1825–1826. He taught also at Windsor, Vermont, in 1827; at Haverhill, 1827–1830; at Marblehead, 1830–1832; at Portsmouth, 1856–1860; and at Salem, 1832–1856 and 1860–1862. See G. T. Chapman, *Sketches of the Alumni of Dartmouth College* (Cambridge, 1867), 221, and the Salem *Essex Register*, July 29, 1833.

JOSHUA COFFIN

Coffin was born in Newbury, Massachusetts, on October 12, 1792, and died there on June 24, 1864. At Dartmouth he had high rank as a student, but a cataract forming on one eye interrupted his course. He was graduated A.B. in 1823, as of the Class of 1817, and in 1826 he received the degree of A.M., which was then granted to graduates of good standing on payment of a fee. He taught at Newbury, Haverhill, Rowley, Ipswich, and Tyngsboro, Massachusetts, at Hampton, New Hampshire, in Vermont, and in Philadelphia from 1833 to 1843. For a time he was also connected with the postoffice in Philadelphia, but was dismissed for his Abolitionism during the administration of President Tyler. In December 1838 Coffin had been sent on a perilous mission to rescue two free Negroes who had been kidnapped and who were then in bondage in the South. He succeeded in locating one of them, and returned him north by steamer. Coffin remarked, "I have in fact kidnapped him into freedom." Coffin was a devoted antiquarian, and he published in 1845 *A Sketch of the History of Newbury, Newburyport, and West Newbury, from 1635 to 1845*, the genealogies of the Woodman and Tappan families, and numerous articles in periodicals.

These facts were obtained from the Office of Alumni Records, Dartmouth College, and from the *Historical and Genealogical Register* (Boston, 1866), XX, 267–270.

ISAAC E. CRARY

Crary's dates were 1804–1854. He assisted Prentice with the *New England Weekly Review*. In 1832 he went to southern Michigan, five years before the territory was admitted to the Union as a State. He became nominally a brigadier-general in the territorial militia organization, and in October, 1835, he was elected a delegate to Congress. In 1837 he became Michigan's first Representative to Congress, and served until 1841. He was one of the founders of the University of Michigan. In the constituent convention of 1835 he was chairman of the Committee on Education, and he prepared the article on education adopted by the convention. See *Dictionary of American Biography* (New York, 1930), IV, 514–515.

GEORGE D. PRENTICE

Prentice, born in Connecticut, lived from December 18, 1802, to January 22, 1870. He helped to pay his own expenses at Brown University, from which he was graduated in 1823. He practiced law briefly, and then in 1827 was a newspaper editor in New London. He was first editor of the *New England Weekly Review* when it was established in 1828. His biography of Clay appeared in 1831. Prentice was invited to become editor of the *Louisville Daily Journal*, which first appeared on November 24, 1830. He soon won a reputation for fearlessness and ability; more than once he was forced to physical combat to defend published statements. He made the *Journal* the most influential Whig publication in the South and West. He was not an Abolitionist, but was a Unionist. He upheld Lincoln's administration so vigorously as to be largely responsible for Kentucky's refusal to secede from the Union. However, Prentice's two sons entered the Confederate army, and one of them was killed in battle. Prentice's ardor was cooled by the Emancipation Proclamation, but he adhered to his belief in the Union. On November 8, 1868, after he had withdrawn from the management of the *Journal*, it was merged in the *Louisville Courier-Journal*. As such the newspaper became nationally famous under Henry Watterson. See *Dictionary of American Biography* (New York, 1935) XV, 186–187.

ABIJAH WYMAN THAYER

Thayer was born at Peterborough, New Hampshire, on January 5, 1796. In 1810 he was sent to Boston to learn printing with Lincoln and Edmunds. Except for a time in 1812 when he was drafted as a guard at Fort Independence, Boston Harbor, he remained with that firm, in Cornhill, until 1817. After two years with an Andover book-printing house he took editorial charge in 1819, for one year, of the *Concord* (New Hampshire) *Gazette*. In 1821 he became editor of the *Portland* (Maine) *Independent Statesman*, which published many of Longfellow's early poems, and which was the only large newspaper in Maine to advocate the election of

John Quincy Adams as President. Thayer became editor of the *Haverhill Gazette* on February 10, 1827, and left it on June 27, 1835, to become editor of the daily *Philadelphia Commercial Herald*. He died at Northampton, Mass., where he was also an editor, on April 24, 1864.

Thayer's elder son, William Sidney Thayer (Harvard 1850), was an associate editor of the *New York Evening Post*, and also, from 1861, United States Consul General to Egypt, where he died on April 10, 1864. The younger son, James B. Thayer, was a distinguished professor at the Harvard Law School from 1873 to his death in 1902. In 1901 he received the honorary degree of LL.D. from Yale.

Most of these facts are from the *Haverhill Gazette*, December 17, 1898, and from the *New England Historical and Genealogical Register*, XVIII, 300–301.

ELIAS WELD

Dr. Weld was born in Braintree, Massachusetts, on March 11, 1772, the son of the Reverend Ezra Weld (Yale 1759) and Anna Weld. He was a member of the Massachusetts Medical Society as early as 1811. He practiced for some years in Haverhill, and must have gone before 1820 to Hallowell, Maine. He apparently left Hallowell before 1849, for on May 2 of that year his wife, Abigail, died in Belleville, New Jersey. (*Vital Records of Hallowell*, VI, 67.) On June 25, 1850, he married Mrs. Isabel Blish, of Richmond, Maine. (*Ibid.*, II, 42.) He died in Hudson, Ohio, on May 4, 1863.

These facts are from Dr. James A. Spalding, *Maine Physicians of 1820* (Lewiston, 1928), 176–177; Emma H. Nason, *Old Hallowell on the Kennebec* (Augusta, Maine, 1909), 305; *Records of the Town of Braintree, 1640 to 1793* (Randolph, Mass., 1886), 835; F. B. Dexter, *Biographical Sketches of the Graduates of Yale College . . .* (New York, 1896), II, 631–633; *Whittier-Land*, 50; and from various individuals through correspondence.

# *Appendix D*

## DEBT TO BURKE AND MILTON

WHITTIER'S CLOSE KNOWLEDGE of Burke's writings is explained on pages 65–65, and pertinent note.

In the *Haverhill Gazette* of May 24, 1828, was published an article by Whittier entitled "The Prose Works of Milton." Even before 1820, through Dr. Weld's library, he must have become acquainted with these writings. In the two-volume edition of Milton's prose works which he seems to have acquired in 1836 and which is still in the Whittier home at Amesbury, he marked many passages, including this in *Of the Reformation in England, and the Causes That Hitherto Have Hindered It* (I, 54–55):

MILTON

"Go on both hand in hand, O Nations, never to be disunited; to be the praise and the heroic song of all posterity; merit this, but seek only virtue, not to extend your limits, . . . but to settle the pure worship of God in his church, and justice in the state. Then shall the hardest difficulties smooth out themselves before ye; envy shall sink to hell, craft and malice be confounded, whether it be homebred mischief or outlandish cunning; yea, other nations will then covet to serve ye, for lordship and victory are but the pages of justice and virtue. Commit securely to true wisdom the vanquishing and un-

WHITTIER ("Justice and Expediency," *Prose Works*, III, 12)

"So long as we take counsel of the world's policy instead of the justice of heaven, so long as we follow a mistaken political expediency in opposition to the express commands of God, so long will the wrongs of the slaves rise like a cloud of witnesses against us at the inevitable bar."

casing of craft and subtilty, which are but her two runagates. Join your invincible might to do worthy and godlike deeds; and then he that seeks to break your union, a cleaving curse be his inheritance to all generations."

BURKE (*Reflections on the Revolution in France*, III, 178)
"It is with the greatest difficulty that I am able to separate policy from justice. Justice is itself the great standing policy of civil society; and any eminent departure from it, under any circumstances, lies under the suspicion of being no policy at all."

MILTON (*loc. cit.*, I, 34)
"To make men governable in this manner, their precepts mainly tend to break a national spirit and courage, by countenancing open riot, luxury, and ignorance, till having thus disfigured and made men beneath men, . . . they deliver up the poor transformed heifer of the commonwealth to be stung and vexed with the breese and goad of oppression, under the custody of some Argus with a hundred eyes of jealousy. To be plainer, sir, how to solder, how to stop a leak, how to keep up the floating carcase of a crazy and diseased monarchy or state, betwixt wind and water, swimming still

WHITTIER (*loc. cit.*, III, 42)
[The wasteful and blighting influences of slave labor] "seem the evidence of the displeasure of Him who created man after His own image, at the unnatural attempt to govern the bones and sinews, the bodies and souls, of one portion of His children by the caprice, the avarice, the lusts of another; at that utter violation of the design of His merciful Providence, whereby the entire dependence of millions of His rational creatures is made to centre upon the will, the existence, the ability, of their fellow-mortals, instead of resting under the shadow of His own Infinite Power and exceeding love."

upon her own dead lees, that now is the deep design of a politician. Alas, sir! a commonwealth ought to be but as one huge christian personage, one mighty growth and stature of an honest man, as big and compact in virtue as in body; for look what the grounds and causes are of single happiness to one man; the same ye shall find them to a whole state. . . ."

BURKE (*Appeal from the New to the Old Whigs*, III, 427)
"Such admirers were our fathers, to whom we owe this splendid inheritance [the Constitution]. Let us improve it with zeal, but with fear. Let us follow our ancestors, men not without a rational, though without an exclusive confidence in themselves; who, by respecting the reason of others, who, by looking backward as well as forward, by the modesty as well as by the energy of their minds, went on, insensibly drawing this constitution nearer and nearer to its perfection, by never departing from its fundamental principles, nor introducing any amendment which had not a subsisting root in the laws, constitution, and usages of the kingdom."

WHITTIER (*loc. cit.*, III, 28)
"A sacred regard to free principles originated our independence, not the paltry amount of practical evil complained of. And although our fathers left their great work unfinished, it is our duty to follow out their principles. Short of liberty and equality we cannot stop without doing injustice to their memories. If our fathers intended that slavery should be perpetual, that our practice should forever give the lie to our professions, why is the great constitutional compact so guardedly silent on the subject of human servitude?"

# *Appendix E*

THIS ARTICLE, unusually significant of Whittier's political and social views, was published in the *Essex Transcript*, of Amesbury and Salisbury Mills, on November 17, 1859.

## THE LESSON OF THE DAY

The painful intelligence of the tragic events at Harper's Ferry has affected us, in common with every right-minded man, with profound sorrow and regret. With our natural loathing of violence and bloodshed, and with the stern and emphatic condemnation which we are compelled to pronounce upon this and all similar attempts to promote the good of freedom by the evil of servile strife and civil war, — is mingled a deep pity for the misguided actors in this outbreak. In condemning the mad scheme we cannot forget the wrongs and outrages which caused it. Our abhorrence of human slavery is only deepened and intensified by it.

For ourselves, from the very outset of the anti-slavery movement, we have relied upon no other instrumentalities than moral and political action — the one in accordance with the peaceful precepts of Christianity, the other in conformity with the Constitution of the United States. With Dr. Franklin we have been prepared to go to "the very verge of our constitutional power" to discountenance and limit the great evil of our land; but with slavery in the States we have never intermeddled ourselves, nor countenanced others in so doing. Our arguments and appeals have been addressed to the white man and not to his slaves. Holding as we do that the destruction of one human life would be too great a price to pay for any social or political change, we regard with horror all attempts to promote a servile insurrection. Nor would we, under any circumstances, encourage forcible resistance even to a law as unjust and cruel as we regard the Fugitive Slave Law. Where duty to God and man required us to refuse active obedience to such enactments, we would submit, as good citizens, to the penalty incurred.

We are well aware that our sentiments on the subject of non-resistance are not shared by the great majority of professing Christians. We know that it is the popular doctrine that bloodshed is justifiable in defence of life and property, or in the assertion of liberty. This doctrine lies, indeed, at the foundation of our government. Our Fourth of July orations — our monuments, our literature — are all revolutionary. The right of revolution on the part of an oppressed people is taught in the school-room and the pulpit. Virginia flaunts in the eyes of her slaves, the incendiary picture on her official seal, of Liberty, armed to the teeth, trampling on the decapitated body of a tyrant, with its motto, "*So always to tyrants.*" In this view of the matter, the wonder is, not that occasionally an insurrection or outbreak like that at Harper's Ferry occurs, but that revolt, in one form or another, is not the normal condition of States embracing within themselves the extremes of liberty and slavery. None saw more clearly than Jefferson and Madison, the dangerous character of the institution of domestic slavery. "The hour of emancipation," said the former, and his words have now a striking significance, "is advancing in the march of time. It must come, if not brought on by the generous energies of our own minds, it must come by the bloody process of St. Domingo." In all ages of the world, the deprivation of personal freedom has been regarded as a sufficient excuse for bloody resistance. All history is monumental as a grave-yard with warnings of this inevitable tendency of oppression. The serfs of Europe have often signalized their manhood by rebellions. Ten years ago there occurred a servile insurrection and massacre in Poland. Every island of the Antilles has been burned over by the fiery track of revolt. A violation of Natural Law and Divine order, slavery contains within itself the elements of perpetual unrest.

The slave needs no incentive from without. It is a noteworthy and very suggestive fact, that the only really formidable insurrections at the South — those of South Carolina and Virginia — originated among the slaves themselves, and took place previous to the present anti-slavery movement. Interference from without has proved a signal failure; and the folly and madness of the Harper's Ferry experiment will not be likely to be repeated in the present century. If the slaves are ever to be freed by violence — (which we do not believe) — it must be done by themselves, and not by white sympathizers, however brave or self-sacrificing. The prayer of every friend of humanity should be that Peace and Freedom may go hand in hand together; that patience, forbearance, and kindness, may keep pace with fidelity to free principles; that no unjustifiable and illegal act may be permitted to embarrass and retard a movement which looks to the welfare and happiness, not of the slave alone, but the master also. Wrong and violence, fraud and conspiracy, are the expedients of conscious weakness and error, not of truth and justice. The North owes it to herself to see to it that the South has no good reason to complain of secret and illegal conspiracies. What she does should be open as the day — frank, honest and aboveboard, without concealment and without compromise.

The lesson of this event should not be lost upon our Southern neighbors. It adds another to the many proofs afforded in history of the dangerous nature of slavery — of the insecurity and peril of every community which admits it. It shows that it is not safe for slaveholders, in behalf of their institution, to experiment too far upon the forbearance and patience of those who abhor it. The aggressions of the Slave Power upon Northern rights have a tendency to provoke a retaliation upon slavery. In fact, the moving cause of this miserable outbreak may be distinctly traced to the attempts to extend slavery, which have for years agitated the country. The invasion of Texas, Cuba and Nicaragua by armed hordes from the slave States, for the purpose of acquiring new slave territory, furnished the hint and excuse for the filibustering of Brown at Harper's Ferry. The Repeal of the Missouri Compromise, and the armed invasion of Kansas by Missouri slave-holders with the avowed purpose of introducing slavery by force of arms into a free territory, was a dangerous example to such men as Brown and his followers. The Fugitive slave Law, wherever its cruel and unconstitutional provisions have been enforced, has awakened indignation and pity. The Dred Scott decision, by virtually outlawing the free people of color and declaring that they have "no rights which the white man is bound to respect," has converted half a million of men into deadly enemies of a government which demands allegiance while it denies protection. The time is near at hand, we feel safe in predicting, when the intelligent slaveholder will regard the Repeal of the Missouri Compromise, the Fugitive Slave Law, and the Dred Scott decision, as measures suicidal to their professed object; and falling back upon the doctrine of the Fathers of the Republic, will repudiate the new maxims and measures of his party leaders.

The slave States, under the most favorable circumstances, cannot look for the quiet and security of free and well-ordered Commonwealths. The Eternal Laws cannot be violated with safety. A working population driven by bruit force to unpaid toil, must be necessarily unstable, unreliable, and dangerous. But they have it in their power to secure an immunity from outward interference. To do this, they must abandon all attempts to extend slavery. They must not repeat the atrocity of seeking, as in Kansas, to force with bayonet and bowie knife the detestable wrong upon a free community. They must put a check upon their filibusters. They must cease to encourage pirates to open anew the slave trade. They must respect the laws and institutions of the free States, if they would have their own respected. They must not threaten disunion and civil war if they cannot place their favorite partizans in office. They must beware how, in reclaiming their fugitives, they trample on the rights and liberties of the free States. They must not outrage the moral sensibilities of the world by cruelties which the sun of the nineteenth century cannot look upon — the hunting of men and women with dogs and guns — the deliberate roasting to death of criminals over a slow fire! In a word, if they would be left unmolested in the enjoyment or endurance of their peculiar institution, they must learn to keep it entirely to themselves. Christianity and civilization have placed it in a moral quarantine from which it can only stray at its peril.

The South has no good reason to complain of the Anti-Slavery North on the score of liberality and magnanimity. We forbear to dwell upon the unworthy compromises of right and principle by Northern politicians and churches, dishonorable alike to the conceders and the exactors. But when did ever William H. Seward and his colleagues refuse their support to a measure because it was introduced by slave-holders, or their vote because it was for the benefit of a Southern locality? Was Speaker Banks less liberal to the South in the arrangement of Committees than Speaker Orr has been to the North? Did Boston, New York and Philadelphia hesitate to aid fever smitten Norfolk because its inhabitants held slaves? Did the appeal of a Virginia woman for the purchase of Mt. Vernon, find a warmer response in South Carolina than in Massachusetts, although the citizens of the latter State can only visit that shrine of patriotism with padlocked lips, and by sufferance of Vigilance committees[?]. What southern statesman has been insulted or maltreated for the free expression of his pro-slavery sentiments? And who can doubt, in the event of a disposition on the part of the slave States to relieve themselves of the great evil, that the free States would cheerfully bear their full proportion of the pecuniary sacrifice?

Everything now indicates that at the next Presidential election the Republican party will be successful. The moral and political influence of that party will, of course, be exerted to place the government where it was left by the Fathers of the Revolution. There is not a plank in its platform which has not been hewn and squared by Washington, Jefferson, Pinckney and Wythe. While it will repress all interference with slavery in the States where it exists, it will at the same time forbid its further extension, and secure the free States and territories from its aggressions. It will interpret the Constitution in the light shed upon it by the Declaration of Independence, the Ordinance of 1787, and the words of the Preamble affixed to the instrument itself, wherein its framers defined its object to be the promotion of "domestic tranquility and the security of the blessings of Liberty to themselves and their posterity." And with whatever unfounded apprehensions they may now look forward to the inauguration of a Republican Administration, no part of the country will have greater reason for thanksgiving in that event, than the slave States themselves.

# INDEX

# Index

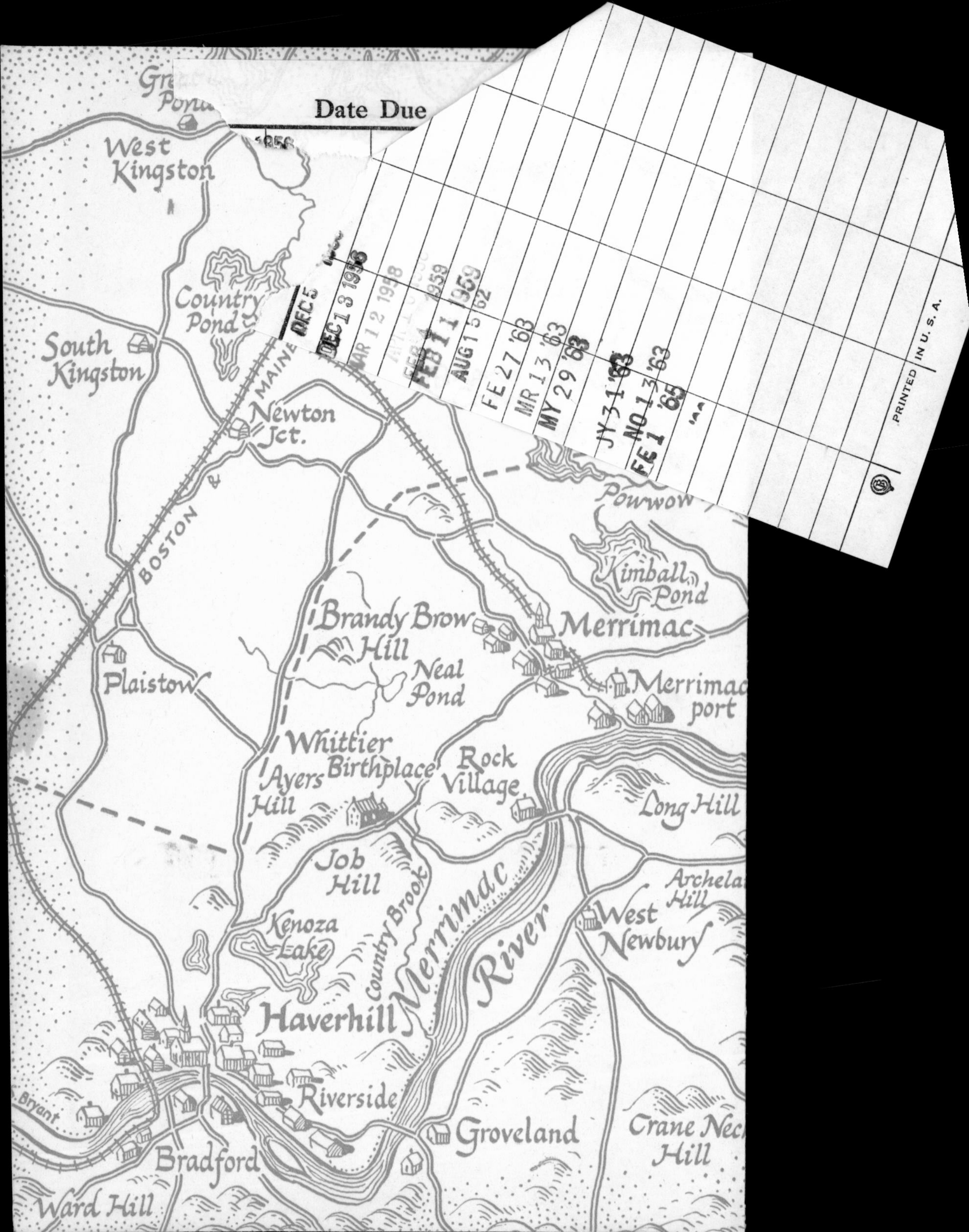

West Kingston
Country Pond
South Kingston
Newton Jct.
Boston & Maine
Plaistow
Brandy Brow Hill
Neal Pond
Merrimac
Merrimac port
Kimball Pond
Powwow
Whittier Birthplace
Ayers Hill
Rock Village
Long Hill
Job Hill
Country Brook
Kenoza Lake
Merrimac River
Haverhill
Archela Hill
West Newbury
Riverside
Groveland
Crane Nec Hill
Bradford
Bryant
Ward Hill
Date Due
MAR 12 1958
FEB 11 1959
FE 27 '63
MR 13 '63
MY 29 '63
NO 13 '63
FE 1 '65
PRINTED IN U. S. A.